BUTTERWORTHS STUDENT STATUTES

COMPANY LAW

BUTTERWORTHS STUDENT STATUTES

Company Law

Fourth edition

PROFESSOR CHRISTOPHER RYAN, LLB (Hons), LLM

Barrister and Solicitor of the High Court (NZ)

City University

Butterworths
LexisNexis™

Members of the LexisNexis Group worldwide

United Kingdom	LexisNexis Butterworths Tolley, a Division of Reed Elsevier (UK) Ltd, Halsbury House, 35 Chancery Lane, LONDON WC2A 1EL and 4 Hill Street, EDINBURGH EH2 3JZ
Argentina	LexisNexis Argentina, BUENOS AIRES
Australia	LexisNexis Butterworths, CHATSWOOD, New South Wales.
Austria	LexisNexis Verlag ARD Orac GmbH & Co KG, VIENNA
Canada	LexisNexis Butterworths MARKHAM, Ontario
Chile	LexisNexis Chile Ltda, SANTIAGO DE CHILE
Czech Republic	Nakladatelství Orac sro, PRAGUE
France	Editions du Juris-Classeur SA, PARIS
Hong Kong	LexisNexis Butterworths, HONG KONG
Hungary	HVG-Orac, BUDAPEST
India	LexisNexis Butterworths, NEW DELHI
Ireland	Butterworths (Ireland) Ltd, DUBLIN
Italy	Giuffrè Editore, MILAN
Malaysia	Malayan Law Journal Sdn Bhd, KUALA LUMPUR
New Zealand	LexisNexis Butterworths, WELLINGTON
Poland	Wydawnictwo Prawnicze LexisNexis, WARSAW
Singapore	LexisNexis Butterworths, SINGAPORE
South Africa	Butterworths SA, DURBAN
Switzerland	Stämpfli Verlag AG, BERNE
USA	LexisNexis, DAYTON, OHIO

© Reed Elsevier (UK) Ltd 2002

A CIP Catalogue record for this book is available from the British Library.

ISBN 0 406 95943 9

Typeset by Kerrypress Ltd, Luton, Bedfordshire

Printed in England by Clays Ltd, St Ives plc

Visit Butterworths LexisNexis *direct* at www.butterworths.com

Preface

In recent years many areas of company law have been increasingly dominated by statutory provisions. This has posed the problem of how to make such legislation available to the large student body now taking company law and related subjects, a group which includes law, accountancy, banking, management and business students.

In the past many courses have relied on *Butterworths Company Law Handbook*. Students cannot be expected, however, to purchase such a large volume when their courses necessarily focus on only a fraction of that material.

It is intended that this shorter, more selective, collection of statutory materials, offered at a modest price, will solve the problem. In addition, the unannotated format means that this volume is suitable for use in examinations.

Any selection of legislation will inevitably omit material that some readers would have found useful but all the main legislation, and particularly that which is common to the majority of student courses, has been included. In order to keep the book to a manageable size, sections are not always reproduced in full.

In the previous edition only the Companies (Tables A-F) Regulations 1985, and the Public Offers of Securities Regulations 1995 were included. Six additional, relevant Statutory Instruments are included in this new edition. The previous edition did contain the Partnership Act 1890 and the Limited Partnership Act 1907, because many courses teaching company law make comparisons between the company and the partnership as methods or vehicles for carrying on business. Added to those Acts in this edition are the Limited Liability Partnership Act 2000 and the Limited Liability Partnership Regulations 2001. The Business Names Act 1985 reappears because of its relevance to all the recognised methods of carrying on business. The provisions of the Insolvency Act 1986, the Company Directors Disqualification Act 1986 and the Criminal Justice Act 1993, together with the new addition of related statutory instruments, primarily are included with an eye to being as comprehensive as possible of provisions affecting the liability of company directors.

New to this edition is the inclusion of the legislation outside the Companies Act 1985 which relates to the transfer of shares namely the Forged Transfers Act 1891, the Forged Transfers Act 1892 and the Stock Transfer Act 1963. Also included are the provisions relevant to companies and company law from the Financial Services and Markets Act 2000, which Act replaced the Financial Services Act 1986.

Finally, sincere thanks are due to Butterworths editorial staff for their assistance in compiling this volume.

CL Ryan

City University, London
September 2002

Contents

Contents

PART I

COMPANIES STATUTES

Forged Transfers Act 1891

An Act for preserving Purchasers of Stock from Losses by Forged Transfers

[5th August 1891]

1 Power to make compensation for losses from forged transfer

(1) Where a company or local authority issue or have issued shares, stock, or securities transferable by an instrument in writing [or by an exempt transfer, within the meaning of the Stock Transfer Act 1982] or by an entry, in any books or register kept by or on behalf of the company or local authority, they shall have power to make compensation by a cash payment out of their funds for any loss arising from a transfer of any such shares, stock, or securities, in pursuance of a [forged instrument] or of a transfer under a forged power of attorney, [whether such loss arises, and whether the [instrument or power] of attorney was forged before or after the passing of this Act, and whether the person receiving such compensation, or any person through whom he claims, has or has not paid any fee or otherwise contributed to any fund out of which the compensation is paid].

[(1A) In subsection (1) above "instrument" has the same meaning as in Part I of the Forgery and Counterfeiting Act 1981.]

(2) Any company or local authority may, if they think fit, provide, either by fees not exceeding the rate of [5p] on every one hundred pounds transferred [with a minimum charge equal to that for twenty-five pounds] to be paid by the transferee upon the entry of the transfer in the books of the company or local authority, or by insurance, reservation of capital, accumulation of income, or in any other manner which they may resolve upon, a fund to meet claims for such compensation.

(3) For the purpose of providing such compensation any company may borrow on the security of their property, and any local authority may borrow with the like consent and on the like security and subject to the like conditions as to repayment by means of instalments or the provision of a sinking fund and otherwise as in the case of the securities in respect of which compensation is to be provided, but any money so borrowed by a local authority shall be repaid within a term not longer than five years. Any expenses incurred by a local authority in making compensation, or in the repayment of, or the payment of interest on, or otherwise in connexion with, any loan raised as aforesaid, shall, except so far as they may be met by such fees as aforesaid, be paid out of the [revenues] on which the security in respect of which compensation is to be made is charged.

(4) Any such company or local authority may impose such reasonable restrictions on the transfer of their shares, stock, or securities, or with respect to powers of

attorney for the transfer thereof, as they may consider requisite for guarding against losses arising from forgery.

(5)   Where a company or local authority compensate a person under this Act for any loss arising from forgery, the company or local authority shall, without prejudice to any other rights or remedies, have the same rights and remedies against the person liable for the loss as the person compensated would have had.

NOTES

Sub-s (1): first words in square brackets inserted, and second words in square brackets substituted, by the Stock Transfer Act 1982, s 3, Sch 2; third words in square brackets inserted by the Forged Transfers Act 1892, ss 2, 3, words in square brackets therein substituted by the Stock Transfer Act 1982, s 3, Sch 2.

Sub-s (1A): inserted by the Stock Transfer Act 1982, s 3, Sch 2.

Sub-s (2): reference to "5p" substituted by virtue of the Decimal Currency Act 1969, s 10(1); final words in square brackets inserted by the Forged Transfers Act 1892, ss 2, 3.

Sub-s (3): word in square brackets substituted by SI 1990/1285, art 2, Schedule, Part I, para 1.

2 Definitions

For the purposes of this Act—

The expression "company" shall mean any company incorporated by or in pursuance of any Act of Parliament, or by royal charter.

[The expression "local authority" shall mean—
- [(a) a billing authority or a precepting authority, as defined in section 69 of the Local Government Finance Act 1992;
- [(aa)a council constituted under section 2 of the Local Government etc (Scotland) Act 1994;]
- (ab) . . . a combined fire authority, as defined in section 144 of the Local Government Finance Act 1988;]
- (b) a levying body within the meaning of section 74 of that Act; and
- (c) a body as regards which section 75 of that Act applies.]

NOTES

Definition "local authority" substituted by SI 1990/1285, art 2, Schedule, Pt I, para 2, paras (a), (aa), (ab) thereof substituted for original para (a) by the Local Government Finance Act 1992, s 117(1), Sch 13, para 1, para (aa) further substituted by SI 1996/974, art 2(1), Sch 1, Pt I, para 1, in para (ab) words omitted repealed by the Police and Magistrates' Courts Act 1994, s 93, Sch 9, Pt I.

Forged Transfers Act 1892

1892 CHAPTER 36

Section
1 Short title
4 Provision where one company takes over shares, etc, of another company

An Act to remove doubts as to the meaning of the Forged Transfers Act 1891

[27th June 1892]

1 Short title

This Act may be cited as the Forged Transfers Act 1892 and this Act and the Forged Transfers Act 1891 may be cited together as the Forged Transfers Acts 1891 and 1892.

4 Provision where one company takes over shares, etc, of another company

Where the shares, stock, or securities of a company or local authority have by amalgamation or otherwise become the shares, stock, or securities of another company or local authority, the last-mentioned company and authority shall have the same power under the Forged Transfers Act 1891 and this Act, as the original company or authority would have had if it had continued.

Stock Transfer Act 1963

1963 CHAPTER 18

Section
1 Simplified transfer of securities
2 Supplementary provisions as to simplified transfer
3 Additional provisions as to transfer forms
4 Interpretation
6 Short title and commencement

An Act to amend the law with respect to the transfer of securities

[10th July 1963]

1 Simplified transfer of securities

(1) Registered securities to which this section applies may be transferred by means of an instrument under hand in the form set out in Schedule 1 to this Act (in this Act referred to as a stock transfer), executed by the transferor only and specifying (in addition to the particulars of the consideration, of the description and number or amount of the securities, and of the person by whom the transfer is made) the full name and address of the transferee.

(2)   The execution of a stock transfer need not be attested; and where such a transfer has been executed for the purpose of a stock exchange transaction, the particulars of the consideration and of the transferee may either be inserted in that transfer or, as the case may require, supplied by means of separate instruments in the form set out in Schedule 2 to this Act (in this Act referred to as brokers transfers), identifying the stock transfer and specifying the securities to which each such instrument relates and the consideration paid for those securities.

(3)   Nothing in this section shall be construed as affecting the validity of any instrument which would be effective to transfer securities apart from this section; and any instrument purporting to be made in any form which was common or usual before the commencement of this Act, or in any other form authorised or required for that purpose apart from this section, shall be sufficient, whether or not it is completed in accordance with the form, if it complies with the requirements as to execution and contents which apply to a stock transfer.

(4)   This section applies to fully paid up registered securities of any description, being—
   (a)   securities issued by any company within the meaning of the [Companies Act 1985] except a company limited by guarantee or an unlimited company;
   (b)   securities issued by any body (other than a company within the meaning of the said Act) incorporated in Great Britain by or under any enactment or by Royal Charter except a building society within the meaning of the Building Societies Act [1986] or a society registered under the Industrial and Provident Societies Act 1893;
   (c)   securities issued by the Government of the United Kingdom, except stock or bonds in [the National Savings Stock Register] . . . , and except national savings certificates;
   (d)   securities issued by any local authority;
   [(e)   units of an authorised unit trust scheme or a recognised scheme within the meaning of [Part 17 of the Financial Services and Markets Act 2000]];
   [(f)   shares issued by an open-ended investment company within the meaning of the Open-Ended Investment Companies Regulations 2001].

NOTES

Sub-s (4): in para (a) words "Companies Act 1985" in square brackets substituted by the Companies Consolidation (Consequential Provisions) Act 1985, s 30, Sch 2.

Sub-s (4): in para (b) year "1986" in square brackets substituted by the Building Societies Act 1986, s 120, Sch 18, Part I, para 5.

Sub-s (4): in para (c) words "the National Savings Stock Register" in square brackets substituted by the Post Office Act 1969, s 108(1)(f).

Sub-s (4): in para (c) words omitted repealed by the Finance Act 1964, ss 24, 26(7), Sch 8, para 10, Sch 9.

Sub-s (4): para (e) substituted by the Financial Services Act 1986, s 212(2), Sch 16, para 4.

Sub-s (4): in para (e) words "Part 17 of the Financial Services and Markets Act 2000" in square brackets substituted by SI 2001/3649, art 270.

Date in force: 1 December 2001: see SI 2001/3649, art 1.

Sub-s (4): para (f) inserted by SI 1996/2827, reg 75, Sch 8, para 2.

Sub-s (4): para (f) substituted by SI 2001/1228, reg 84, Sch 7, Pt I, para 2.

Date in force: 1 December 2001 (being the date on which the Financial Services and Markets Act 2000, s 19, came into force): see SI 2001/3538, art 2(1) and SI 2001/1228, reg 1(2)(c).

2 Supplementary provisions as to simplified transfer

(1) Section 1 of this Act shall have effect in relation to the transfer of any securities to which that section applies notwithstanding anything to the contrary in any enactment or instrument relating to the transfer of those securities; but nothing in that section affects—

  (a) any right to refuse to register a person as the holder of any securities on any ground other than the form in which those securities purport to be transferred to him: or

  (b) any enactment or rule of law regulating the execution of documents by companies or other bodies corporate, or any articles of association or other instrument regulating the execution of documents by any particular company or body corporate.

(2) Subject to the provisions of this section, any enactment or instrument relating to the transfer of securities to which section 1 of this Act applies shall, with any necessary modifications, apply in relation to an instrument of transfer authorised by that section as it applies in relation to an instrument of transfer to which it applies apart from this subsection; and without prejudice to the generality of the foregoing provision, the reference in [section 184 of the Companies Act 1985] (certification of transfers) to any instrument of transfer shall be construed as including a reference to a brokers transfer.

(3) In relation to the transfer of securities by means of a stock transfer and a brokers transfer—

  (a) any reference in any enactment or instrument (including in particular [section 183(1) and (2) of the Companies Act 1985] . . .) to the delivery or lodging of an instrument (or proper instrument) of transfer shall be construed as a reference to the delivery or lodging of the stock transfer and the brokers transfer;

  (b) any such reference to the date on which an instrument of transfer is delivered or lodged shall be construed as a reference to the data by which the later of those transfers to be delivered or lodged has been delivered or lodged; *and*

  (c) *subject to the foregoing provisions of this subsection, the brokers transfer (and not the stock transfer) shall be deemed to be the conveyance or transfer for the purposes of the enactments relating to stamp duty.*

(4) . . .

NOTES

Sub-s (2): words in square brackets substituted by the Companies Consolidation (Consequential Provisions) Act 1985, s 30, Sch 2.

Sub-s (3): words in square brackets substituted by the Companies Consolidation (Consequential Provisions) Act 1985, s 30, Sch 2.

Sub-s (3): in para (a) words omitted repealed by the Finance Act 1999, s 139, Sch 20, Pt V(5).

Date in force: this repeal has effect in relation to instruments executed on or after 6 February 2000: see the Finance Act 1999, Sch 20, Pt V(5).

Sub-s (3): para (c) prospectively repealed by the Finance Act 1990, s 132, Sch 19, Part VI, as to the effect of this repeal see the notes to Sch 19, Part VI.

Sub-s (4): repealed by the Requirements of Writing (Scotland) Act 1995, s 14(2), Sch 5.

3 Additional provisions as to transfer forms

(1) References in this Act to the forms set out in Schedule 1 and Schedule 2 include references to forms substantially corresponding to those forms respectively.

(2) The Treasury may by order amend the said Schedules either by altering the forms set out therein or by substituting different forms for those forms or by the addition of forms for use as alternatives to those forms; and references in this Act to the forms set out in those Schedules (including references in this section) shall be construed accordingly.

(3) Any order under subsection (2) of this section which substitutes a different form for a form set out in Schedule 1 to this Act may direct that subsection (3) of section 1 of this Act shall apply, with any necessary modifications, in relation to the form for which that form is substituted as it applies to any form which was common or usual before the commencement of this Act.

(4) Any order of the Treasury under this section shall be made by statutory instrument, and may be varied or revoked by a subsequent order; and any statutory instrument made by virtue of this section shall be subject to annulment in pursuance of a resolution of either House of Parliament.

[(5) An order under subsection (2) of this section may—
  (a) provide for forms on which some of the particulars mentioned in subsection (1) of section 1 of this Act are not required to be specified;
  (b) provide for that section to have effect, in relation to such forms as are mentioned in the preceding paragraph or other forms specified in the order, subject to such amendments as are so specified (which may include an amendment of the reference in subsection (1) of that section to an instrument under hand);
  (c) provide for all or any of the provisions of the order to have effect in such cases only as are specified in the order.]

NOTES

Sub-s (5): inserted by the Stock Exchange (Completion of Bargains) Act 1976, s 6.

4 Interpretation

(1) In this Act the following expressions have the meanings hereby respectively assigned to them, that is to say—
  "local authority" means, in relation to England and Wales,
      [[(a) a billing authority or a precepting authority, as defined in section 69 of the Local Government Finance Act 1992;
      (aa) . . . a combined fire authority, as defined in section 144 of the Local Government Finance Act 1988;]

(b) a levying body within the meaning of section 74 of that Act; and

(c) a body as regards which section 75 of that Act applies,]

and, in relation to Scotland, a county council, a town council and any statutory authority, commissioners or trustees to whom section 270 of the Local Government (Scotland) Act 1947 applies;

"registered securities" means transferable securities the holders of which are entered in a register (whether maintained in Great Britain or not);

"securities" means shares, stock, debentures, debenture stock, loan stock, bonds, units of a [collective investment scheme within the meaning of the [Financial Services and Markets Act 2000]], and other securities of any description;

"stock exchange transaction" means a sale and purchase of securities in which each of the parties is a member of a stock exchange acting in the ordinary course of his business as such or is acting through the agency of such a member;

"stock exchange" means the Stock Exchange, London, and any other stock exchange (whether in Great Britain or not) which is declared by order of the Treasury to be a recognised stock exchange for the purposes of this Act.

(2) Any order of the Treasury under this section shall be made by statutory instrument, and may be varied or revoked by a subsequent order.

NOTES

Sub-s (1): in definition "local authority" paras (a)–(c) substituted by SI 1990/776, art 8, Sch 3, para 8.

Sub-s (1): in definition "local authority" paras (a), (aa) further substituted for para (a), by the Local Government Finance Act 1992, s 117(1), Sch 13, para 12.

Sub-s (1): in definition "local authority" in para (aa) words omitted repealed by the Police and Magistrates' Courts Act 1994, s 93, Sch 9, Pt I.

Sub-s (1): in definition "securities" words in square brackets beginning with the words "collective investment scheme" substituted by the Financial Services Act 1986, s 212(2), Sch 16, para 4.

Sub-s (1): in definition "securities" words "Financial Services and Markets Act 2000" in square brackets substituted by SI 2001/3649, art 271.

Date in force: 1 December 2001: see SI 2001/3649, art 1.

6 Short title and commencement

(1) This Act may be cited as the Stock Transfer Act 1963.

(2) Subsection (3) of section 5 of this Act shall come into force on the passing of this Act, and the remaining provisions of this Act shall come into force on such date as the Treasury may by order made by statutory instrument direct.

Companies Act 1985

1985 CHAPTER 6

ARRANGEMENT OF SECTIONS

PART I
FORMATION AND REGISTRATION OF COMPANIES; JURIDICAL STATUS AND MEMBERSHIP

CHAPTER I
COMPANY FORMATION

CHAPTER II
COMPANY NAMES

PART V
SHARE CAPITAL, ITS INCREASE, MAINTENANCE AND REDUCTION

CHAPTER I
GENERAL PROVISIONS ABOUT SHARE CAPITAL

CHAPTER II
CLASS RIGHTS

CHAPTER III
SHARE PREMIUMS

CHAPTER IV
REDUCTION OF SHARE CAPITAL

CHAPTER VIII
MISCELLANEOUS PROVISIONS ABOUT SHARES AND DEBENTURES

PART VII
ACCOUNTS AND AUDIT

CHAPTER I
PROVISIONS APPLYING TO COMPANIES GENERALLY

PART XI
COMPANY ADMINISTRATION AND PROCEDURE

CHAPTER I
COMPANY IDENTIFICATION

CHAPTER II
REGISTER OF MEMBERS

CHAPTER V
AUDITORS

PART XII
REGISTRATION OF CHARGES

CHAPTER I
REGISTRATION OF CHARGES (ENGLAND AND WALES)

PART XIII
ARRANGEMENTS AND RECONSTUCTIONS

An Act to consolidate the greater part of the Companies Acts

[11th March 1985]

PART I
FORMATION AND REGISTRATION OF COMPANIES;
JURIDICAL STATUS AND MEMBERSHIP

Chapter I
Company Formation

Memorandum of association

1 Mode of forming incorporated company

(1)   Any two or more persons associated for a lawful purpose may, by subscribing their names to a memorandum of association and otherwise complying with the requirements of this Act in respect of registration, form an incorporated company, with or without limited liability.

(2)   A company so formed may be either—
  (a)   a company having the liability of its members limited by the memorandum to the amount, if any, unpaid on the shares respectively held by them ("a company limited by shares");
  (b)   a company having the liability of its members limited by the memorandum to such amount as the members may respectively thereby undertake to contribute to the assets of the company in the event of its being wound up ("a company limited by guarantee"); or
  (c)   a company not having any limit on the liability of its members ("an unlimited company").

(3)   A "public company" is a company limited by shares or limited by guarantee and having a share capital, being a company—
  (a)   the memorandum of which states that it is to be a public company, and
  (b)   in relation to which the provisions of this Act or the former Companies Acts as to the registration or re-registration of a company as a public company have been complied with on or after 22nd December 1980;

and a "private company" is a company that is not a public company.

[(3A)   Notwithstanding subsection (1), one person may, for a lawful purpose, by subscribing his name to a memorandum of association and otherwise complying with the requirements of this Act in respect of registration, form an incorporated company being a private company limited by shares or by guarantee.]

(4)   With effect from 22nd December 1980, a company cannot be formed as, or become, a company limited by guarantee with a share capital.

NOTES
Sub-s (3A): inserted by SI 1992/1699, reg 2(b), Schedule, para 1.

2 Requirements with respect to memorandum

(1)   The memorandum of every company must state—
  (a)   the name of the company;
  (b)   whether the registered office of the company is to be situated in England and Wales, or in Scotland;
  (c)   the objects of the company.

(2)   Alternatively to subsection (1)(b), the memorandum may contain a statement that the company's registered office is to be situated in Wales; and a company whose registered office is situated in Wales may by special resolution alter its memorandum so as to provide that its registered office is to be so situated.

(3)   The memorandum of a company limited by shares or by guarantee must also state that the liability of its members is limited.

(4)   The memorandum of a company limited by guarantee must also state that each member undertakes to contribute to the assets of the company if it should be wound up while he is a member, or within one year after he ceases to be a member, for payment of the debts and liabilities of the company contracted before he ceases to be a member, and of the costs, charges and expenses of winding up, and for adjustment of the rights of the contributories among themselves, such amount as may be required, not exceeding a specified amount.

(5)   In the case of a company having a share capital—
  (a)   the memorandum must also (unless it is an unlimited company) state the amount of the share capital with which the company proposes to be registered and the division of the share capital into shares of a fixed amount;
  (b)   no subscriber of the memorandum may take less than one share; and
  (c)   there must be shown in the memorandum against the name of each subscriber the number of shares he takes.

(6)   [Subject to subsection (6A), the memorandum] must be signed by each subscriber in the presence of at least one witness, who must attest the signature; *and that attestation is sufficient in Scotland as well as in England and Wales.*

[(6A)   Where the memorandum is delivered to the registrar otherwise than in legible form and is authenticated by each subscriber in such manner as is directed by the registrar, the requirements in subsection (6) for signature in the presence of at least one witness and for attestation of the signature do not apply.]

(7)   A company may not alter the conditions contained in its memorandum except in the cases, in the mode and to the extent, for which express provision is made by this Act.

NOTES
Sub-s (6): words "Subject to subsection (6A), the memorandum" in square brackets substituted by SI 2000/3373, art 2(1), (2).
Date in force: 22 December 2000: see SI 2000/3373, art 1(1).

Sub-s (6): words "and that attestation is sufficient in Scotland as well as in England and Wales" in italics repealed, in relation to Scotland, by the Requirements of Writing (Scotland) Act 1995, s 14(2), Sch 5.

Sub-s (6A): inserted by SI 2000/3373, art 2(1), (3).

Date in force: 22 December 2000: see SI 2000/3373, art 1(1).

3 Forms of memorandum

(1) Subject to the provisions of sections 1 and 2, the form of the memorandum of association of—

(a) a public company, being a company limited by shares,

(b) a public company, being a company limited by guarantee and having a share capital,

(c) a private company limited by shares,

(d) a private company limited by guarantee and not having a share capital,

(e) a private company limited by guarantee and having a share capital, and

(f) an unlimited company having a share capital,

shall be as specified respectively for such companies by regulations made by the Secretary of State, or as near to that form as circumstances admit.

(2) Regulations under this section shall be made by statutory instrument subject to annulment in pursuance of a resolution of either House of Parliament.

[3A Statement of company's objects: general commercial company]

[Where the company's memorandum states that the object of the company is to carry on business as a general commercial company—

(a) the object of the company is to carry on any trade or business whatsoever, and

(b) the company has power to do all such things as are incidental or conducive to the carrying on of any trade or business by it.]

NOTES

Inserted by the Companies Act 1989, s 110(1).

[4 Resolution to alter objects]

[(1) A company may by special resolution alter its memorandum with respect to the statement of the company's objects.

(2) If an application is made under the following section, an alteration does not have effect except in so far as it is confirmed by the court.]

NOTES

Substituted by the Companies Act 1989, s 110(2).

5 Procedure for objecting to alteration

(1) Where a company's memorandum has been altered by special resolution under section 4, application may be made to the court for the alteration to be cancelled.

(2)   Such an application may be made—
   (a)   by the holders of not less in the aggregate than 15 per cent in nominal value of the company's issued share capital or any class of it or, if the company is not limited by shares, not less than 15 per cent of the company's members; or
   (b)   by the holders of not less than 15 per cent of the company's debentures entitling the holders to object to an alteration of its objects;

but an application shall not be made by any person who has consented to or voted in favour of the alteration.

(3)   The application must be made within 21 days after the date on which the resolution altering the company's objects was passed, and may be made on behalf of the persons entitled to make the application by such one or more of their number as they may appoint in writing for the purpose.

(4)   The court may on such an application make an order confirming the alteration either wholly or in part and on such terms and conditions as it thinks fit, and may—
   (a)   if it thinks fit, adjourn the proceedings in order that an arrangement may be made to its satisfaction for the purchase of the interests of dissentient members, and
   (b)   give such directions and make such orders as it thinks expedient for facilitating or carrying into effect any such arrangement.

(5)   The court's order may (if the court thinks fit) provide for the purchase by the company of the shares of any members of the company, and for the reduction accordingly of its capital, and may make such alterations in the company's memorandum and articles as may be required in consequence of that provision.

(6)   If the court's order requires the company not to make any, or any specified, alteration in its memorandum or articles, the company does not then have power without the leave of the court to make any such alteration in breach of that requirement.

(7)   An alteration in the memorandum or articles of a company made by virtue of an order under this section, other than one made by resolution of the company, is of the same effect as if duly made by resolution; and this Act applies accordingly to the memorandum or articles as so altered.

(8)   The debentures entitling the holders to object to an alteration of a company's objects are any debentures secured by a floating charge which were issued or first issued before 1st December 1947 or form part of the same series as any debentures so issued; and a special resolution altering a company's objects requires the same notice to the holders of any such debentures as to members of the company.

   In the absence of provisions regulating the giving of notice to any such debenture holders, the provisions of the company's articles regulating the giving of notice to members apply.

6 Provisions supplementing ss 4, 5

(1)   Where a company passes a resolution altering its objects, then—
  (a)   if with respect to the resolution no application is made under section 5, the company shall within 15 days from the end of the period for making such an application deliver to the registrar of companies a printed copy of its memorandum as altered; and
  (b)   if such an application is made, the company shall—
    (i)   forthwith give notice (in the prescribed form) of that fact to the registrar, and
    (ii)   within 15 days from the date of any order cancelling or confirming the alteration, deliver to the registrar an office copy of the order and, in the case of an order confirming the alteration, a printed copy of the memorandum as altered.

(2)   The court may by order at any time extend the time for the delivery of documents to the registrar under subsection (1)(b) for such period as the court may think proper.

(3)   If a company makes default in giving notice or delivering any document to the registrar of companies as required by subsection (1), the company and every officer of it who is in default is liable to a fine and, for continued contravention, to a daily default fine.

(4)   The validity of an alteration of a company's memorandum with respect to the objects of the company shall not be questioned on the ground that it was not authorised by section 4, except in proceedings taken for the purpose (whether under section 5 or otherwise) before the expiration of 21 days after the date of the resolution in that behalf.

(5)   Where such proceedings are taken otherwise than under section 5, subsections (1) to (3) above apply in relation to the proceedings as if they had been taken under that section, and as if an order declaring the alteration invalid were an order cancelling it, and as if an order dismissing the proceedings were an order confirming the alteration.

Articles of association

7 Articles prescribing regulations for companies

(1)   There may in the case of a company limited by shares, and there shall in the case of a company limited by guarantee or unlimited, be registered with the memorandum articles of association signed by the subscribers to the memorandum and prescribing regulations for the company.

(2)   In the case of an unlimited company having a share capital, the articles must state the amount of share capital with which the company proposes to be registered.

(3)   Articles must—
  (a)   be printed,
  (b)   be divided into paragraphs numbered consecutively, and

(c)   [subject to subsection (3A),] be signed by each subscriber of the memorandum in the presence of at least one witness who must attest the signature *(which attestation is sufficient in Scotland as well as in England and Wales).*

[(3A)   Where the articles are delivered to the registrar otherwise than in legible form and are authenticated by each subscriber to the memorandum in such manner as is directed by the registrar, the requirements in subsection (3)(c) for signature in the presence of at least one witness and for attestation of the signature do not apply.]

NOTES

Sub-s (3): in para (c) words "subject to subsection (3A)," in square brackets inserted by SI 2000/3373, art 3(1), (2).

Date in force: 22 December 2000: see SI 2000/3373, art 1(1).

Sub-s (3): in para (c) words "(which attestation is sufficient in Scotland as well as in England and Wales)" in italics repealed, in relation to Scotland, by the Requirements of Writing (Scotland) Act 1995, s 14(2), Sch 5.

Sub-s (3A): inserted by SI 2000/3373, art 3(1), (3).

Date in force: 22 December 2000: see SI 2000/3373, art 1(1).

8 Tables A, C, D and E

(1)   Table A is as prescribed by regulations made by the Secretary of State; and a company may for its articles adopt the whole or any part of that Table.

(2)   In the case of a company limited by shares, if articles are not registered or, if articles are registered, in so far as they do not exclude or modify Table A, that Table (so far as applicable, and as in force at the date of the company's registration) constitutes the company's articles, in the same manner and to the same extent as if articles in the form of that Table had been duly registered.

(3)   If in consequence of regulations under this section Table A is altered, the alteration does not affect a company registered before the alteration takes effect, or repeal as respects that company any portion of the Table.

(4)   The form of the articles of association of—
   (a)   a company limited by guarantee and not having a share capital,
   (b)   a company limited by guarantee and having a share capital, and
   (c)   an unlimited company having a share capital,

shall be respectively in accordance with Table C, D or E prescribed by regulations made by the Secretary of State, or as near to that form as circumstances admit.

(5)   Regulations under this section shall be made by statutory instrument subject to annulment in pursuance of a resolution of either House of Parliament.

[8A Table G]

[(1)   The Secretary of State may by regulations prescribe a Table G containing articles of association appropriate for a partnership company, that is, a company limited by shares whose shares are intended to be held to a substantial extent by or on behalf of its employees.

(2)   A company limited by shares may for its articles adopt the whole or any part of that Table.

(3)   If in consequence of regulations under this section Table G is altered, the alteration does not affect a company registered before the alteration takes effect, or repeal as respects that company any portion of the Table.

(4)   Regulations under this section shall be made by statutory instrument which shall be subject to annulment in pursuance of a resolution of either House of Parliament.]

NOTES

Inserted by the Companies Act 1989, s 128.
Date in force: to be appointed: see Companies Act 1989, s 215(2).

9 Alteration of articles by special resolution

(1)   Subject to the provisions of this Act and to the conditions contained in its memorandum, a company may by special resolution alter its articles.

(2)   Alterations so made in the articles are (subject to this Act) as valid as if originally contained in them, and are subject in like manner to alteration by special resolution.

Registration and its consequences

10 Documents to be sent to registrar

(1)   The company's memorandum and articles (if any) shall be delivered—
   (a)   to the registrar of companies for England and Wales, if the memorandum states that the registered office of the company is to be situated in England and Wales, or that it is to be situated in Wales; and
   (b)   to the registrar of companies for Scotland, if the memorandum states that the registered office of the company is to be situated in Scotland.

(2)   With the memorandum there shall be delivered a statement in the prescribed form containing the names and requisite particulars of—
   (a)   the person who is, or the persons who are, to be the first director or directors of the company; and
   (b)   the person who is, or the persons who are, to be the first secretary or joint secretaries of the company;

and the requisite particulars in each case are those set out in Schedule 1.

[(2A)   Where any statement delivered under subsection (2) includes an address specified in reliance on paragraph 5 of Schedule 1 there shall be delivered with the statement, a statement in the prescribed form containing particulars of the usual residential address of the director or secretary whose address is so specified.]

(3)   The statement [under subsection (2)] shall be signed by or on behalf of the subscribers of the memorandum and shall contain a consent signed by each of the persons named in it as a director, as secretary or as one of joint secretaries, to act in the relevant capacity.

(4)   Where a memorandum is delivered by a person as agent for the subscribers, the statement shall specify that fact and the person's name and address.

(5)   An appointment by any articles delivered with the memorandum of a person as director or secretary of the company is void unless he is named as a director or secretary in the statement.

(6)   There shall in the statement be specified the intended situation of the company's registered office on incorporation.

NOTES

Sub-s (2A): inserted by SI 2002/912, reg 16, Sch 2, para 1(1), (2).
Date in force: 2 April 2002: see SI 2002/912, reg 1(2).
Sub-s (3): words "under subsection (2)" in square brackets inserted by SI 2002/912, reg 16, Sch 2, para 1(1), (3).
Date in force: 2 April 2002: see SI 2002/912, reg 1(2).

11 Minimum authorised capital (public companies)

When a memorandum delivered to the registrar of companies under section 10 states that the association to be registered is to be a public company, the amount of the share capital stated in the memorandum to be that with which the company proposes to be registered must not be less than the authorised minimum (defined in section 118).

12 Duty of registrar

(1)   The registrar of companies shall not register a company's memorandum delivered under section 10 unless he is satisfied that all the requirements of this Act in respect of registration and of matters precedent and incidental to it have been complied with.

(2)   Subject to this, the registrar shall retain and register the memorandum and articles (if any) delivered to him under that section.

(3)   [Subject to subsection (3A), a statutory declaration] in the prescribed form by—

 (a)   a solicitor engaged in the formation of a company, or
 (b)   a person named as a director or secretary of the company in the statement delivered under section 10(2),

that those requirements have been complied with shall be delivered to the registrar of companies, and the registrar may accept such a declaration as sufficient evidence of compliance.

[(3A)   In place of the statutory declaration referred to in subsection (3), there may be delivered to the registrar of companies using electronic communications a statement made by a person mentioned in paragraph (a) or (b) of subsection (3) that the requirements mentioned in subsection (1) have been complied with; and the registrar may accept such a statement as sufficient evidence of compliance.

(3B)   Any person who makes a false statement under subsection (3A) which he knows to be false or does not believe to be true is liable to imprisonment or a fine, or both.]

NOTES

Sub-s (3): words "Subject to subsection (3A), a statutory declaration" in square brackets substituted by SI 2000/3373, art 4(1), (2).

Date in force: 22 December 2000: see SI 2000/3373, art 1(1).

Sub-ss (3A), (3B): inserted by SI 2000/3373, art 4(1), (3).

Date in force: 22 December 2000: see SI 2000/3373, art 1(1).

13 Effect of registration

(1)   On the registration of a company's memorandum, the registrar of companies shall give a certificate that the company is incorporated and, in the case of a limited company, that it is limited.

(2)   The certificate may be signed by the registrar, or authenticated by his official seal.

(3)   From the date of incorporation mentioned in the certificate, the subscribers of the memorandum, together with such other persons as may from time to time become members of the company, shall be a body corporate by the name contained in the memorandum.

(4)   That body corporate is then capable forthwith of exercising all the functions of an incorporated company, but with such liability on the part of its members to contribute to its assets in the event of its being wound up as is provided by this Act [and the Insolvency Act].

This is subject, in the case of a public company, to section 117 (additional certificate as to amount of allotted share capital).

(5)   The persons named in the statement under section 10 as directors, secretary or joint secretaries are, on the company's incorporation, deemed to have been respectively appointed as its first directors, secretary or joint secretaries.

(6)   Where the registrar registers an association's memorandum which states that the association is to be a public company, the certificate of incorporation shall contain a statement that the company is a public company.

(7)   A certificate of incorporation given in respect of an association is conclusive evidence—

    (a)   that the requirements of this Act in respect of registration and of matters precedent and incidental to it have been complied with, and that the association is a company authorised to be registered, and is duly registered, under this Act, and

    (b)   if the certificate contains a statement that the company is a public company, that the company is such a company.

NOTES

Sub-s (4): words in square brackets inserted by the Insolvency Act 1986, s 439(1), Sch 13, Part I.

14 Effect of memorandum and articles

(1) Subject to the provisions of this Act, the memorandum and articles, when registered, bind the company and its members to the same extent as if they respectively had been signed and sealed by each member, and contained covenants on the part of each member to observe all the provisions of the memorandum and of the articles.

(2) Money payable by a member to the company under the memorandum or articles is a debt due from him to the company, and in England and Wales is of the nature of a specialty debt.

16 Effect of alteration on company's members

(1) A member of a company is not bound by an alteration made in the memorandum or articles after the date on which he became a member, if and so far as the alteration—

(a) requires him to take or subscribe for more shares than the number held by him at the date on which the alteration is made; or

(b) in any way increases his liability as at that date to contribute to the company's share capital or otherwise to pay money to the company.

(2) Subsection (1) operates notwithstanding anything in the memorandum or articles; but it does not apply in a case where the member agrees in writing, either before or after the alteration is made, to be bound by the alteration.

17 Conditions in memorandum which could have been in articles

(1) A condition contained in a company's memorandum which could lawfully have been contained in articles of association instead of in the memorandum may be altered by the company by special resolution; but if an application is made to the court for the alteration to be cancelled, the alteration does not have effect except in so far as it is confirmed by the court.

(2) This section—

(a) is subject to section 16, and also to Part XVII (court order protecting minority), and

(b) does not apply where the memorandum itself provides for or prohibits the alteration of all or any of the conditions above referred to, and does not authorise any variation or abrogation of the special rights of any class of members.

(3) Section 5 (except subsections (2)(b) and (8)) and section 6(1) to (3) apply in relation to any alteration and to any application made under this section as they apply in relation to alterations and applications under sections 4 to 6.

A company's membership

22 Definition of "member"

(1)   The subscribers of a company's memorandum are deemed to have agreed to become members of the company, and on its registration shall be entered as such in its register of members.

(2)   Every other person who agrees to become a member of a company, and whose name is entered in its register of members, is a member of the company.

[23 Membership of holding company]

[(1)   Except as mentioned in this section, a body corporate cannot be a member of a company which is its holding company and any allotment or transfer of shares in a company to its subsidiary is void.

(2)   The prohibition does not apply where the subsidiary is concerned only as personal representative or trustee unless, in the latter case, the holding company or a subsidiary of it is beneficially interested under the trust.

For the purpose of ascertaining whether the holding company or a subsidiary is so interested, there shall be disregarded—
  (a)   any interest held only by way of security for the purposes of a transaction entered into by the holding company or subsidiary in the ordinary course of a business which includes the lending of money;
  (b)   any such interest as is mentioned in Part I of Schedule 2.

[(3)   The prohibition does not apply where shares in the holding company are held by the subsidiary in the ordinary course of its business as an intermediary.

For this purpose a person is an intermediary if that person—
  (a)   carries on a bona fide business of dealing in securities;
  (b)   is a member of an EEA exchange (and satisfies any requirements for recognition as a dealer in securities laid down by that exchange) or is otherwise approved or supervised as a dealer in securities under the laws of an EEA State; and
  (c)   does not carry on an excluded business.

(3A)   The excluded businesses are the following—
  (a)   any business which consists wholly or mainly in the making or managing of investments;
  (b)   any business which consists wholly or mainly in, or is carried on wholly or mainly for the purpose of, providing services to persons who are connected with the person carrying on the business;
  (c)   any business which consists in insurance business;
  (d)   any business which consists in managing or acting as trustee in relation to a pension scheme or which is carried on by the manager or trustee of such a scheme in connection with or for the purposes of the scheme;
  (e)   any business which consists in operating or acting as trustee in relation to a collective investment scheme or is carried on by the operator or trustee of such a scheme in connection with or for the purposes of the scheme.

(3B)   For the purposes of subsections (3) and (3A)—
   (a)   the question whether a person is connected with another shall be determined in accordance with the provisions of section 839 of the Income and Corporation Taxes Act 1988;
   (b)   "collective investment scheme" has the meaning given in [section 236 of the Financial Services and Markets Act 2000];
   (c)   "EEA exchange" means a market which appears on the list drawn up by an EEA State pursuant to Article 16 of Council Directive 93/22/EEC on investment services in the securities field;
   [(d)   "insurance business" means business which consists of the effecting or carrying out of contracts of insurance;
   (e)   "securities" includes—
      (i)   options,
      (ii)   futures, and
      (iii)   contracts for differences,
      and rights or interests in those investments;]
   (f)   "trustee" and "the operator" shall, in relation to a collective investment scheme, be construed in accordance with [section 237(2) of the Financial Services and Markets Act 2000].

[(3BA)   Subsection (3B) must be read with—
   (a)   section 22 of the Financial Services and Markets Act 2000;
   (b)   any relevant order under that section; and
   (c)   Schedule 2 to that Act.]

(3C)   Where—
   (a)   a subsidiary which is a dealer in securities has purportedly acquired shares in its holding company in contravention of the prohibition in subsection (1); and
   (b)   a person acting in good faith has agreed, for value and without notice of that contravention, to acquire shares in the holding company from the subsidiary or from someone who has purportedly acquired the shares after their disposal by the subsidiary,

any transfer to that person of the shares mentioned in paragraph (a) shall have the same effect as it would have had if their original acquisition by the subsidiary had not been in contravention of the prohibition.]

(4)   Where a body corporate became a holder of shares in a company—
   (a)   before 1st July 1948, or
   (b)   on or after that date and before [20th October 1997], in circumstances in which this section as it then had effect did not apply,

but at any time [on or after [20th October 1997]] falls within the prohibition in subsection (1) above in respect of those shares, it may continue to be a member of that company; but for so long as that prohibition would apply, apart from this subsection, it has no right to vote in respect of those shares at meetings of the company or of any class of its members.

(5)   Where a body corporate becomes a holder of shares in a company [on or after [20th October 1997]] in circumstances in which the prohibition in subsection (1)

does not apply, but subsequently falls within that prohibition in respect of those shares, it may continue to be a member of that company; but for so long as that prohibition would apply, apart from this subsection, it has no right to vote in respect of those shares at meetings of the company or of any class of its members.

(6)   Where a body corporate is permitted to continue as a member of a company by virtue of subsection (4) or (5), an allotment to it of fully paid shares in the company may be validly made by way of capitalisation of reserves of the company; but for so long as the prohibition in subsection (1) would apply, apart from subsection (4) or (5), it has no right to vote in respect of those shares at meetings of the company or of any class of its members.

(7)   The provisions of this section apply to a nominee acting on behalf of a subsidiary as to the subsidiary itself.

(8)   In relation to a company other than a company limited by shares, the references in this section to shares shall be construed as references to the interest of its members as such, whatever the form of that interest.]

NOTES

Substituted by the Companies Act 1989, s 129(1).

Sub-ss (3), (3A), (3B), (3C): substituted, for sub-s (3) as originally enacted, by SI 1997/2306, reg 2.

Sub-s (3B): in para (b) words "section 236 of the Financial Services and Markets Act 2000" in square brackets substituted by SI 2001/3649, art 4(1), (2).

Date in force: 1 December 2001: see SI 2001/3649, art 1.

Sub-s (3B): paras (d), (e) substituted by SI 2001/3649, art 4(1), (3).

Date in force: 1 December 2001: see SI 2001/3649, art 1.

Sub-s (3B): in para (f) words "section 237(2) of the Financial Services and Markets Act 2000" in square brackets substituted by SI 2001/3649, art 4(1), (4).

Date in force: 1 December 2001: see SI 2001/3649, art 1.

Sub-s (3BA): inserted by SI 2001/3649, art 4(1), (5).

Date in force: 1 December 2001: see SI 2001/3649, art 1.

Sub-s (4): first words in square brackets substituted by SI 1997/2306, reg 3; second words in square brackets substituted by SI 1990/1707, art 8, as amended by SI 1990/1707, art 8(2), words in square brackets therein substituted by SI 1997/2306, reg 3.

Sub-s (5): first words in square brackets substituted by SI 1990/1392, art 8, as amended by SI 1990/1707, art 8(2), words in square brackets therein substituted by SI 1997/2306, reg 3.

24 Minimum membership for carrying on business

If a company[, other than a private company limited by shares or by guarantee,] carries on business without having at least two members and does so for more than 6 months, a person who, for the whole or any part of the period that it so carries on business after those 6 months—

(a)   is a member of the company, and

(b)   knows that it is carrying on business with only one member,

is liable (jointly and severally with the company) for the payment of the company's debts contracted during the period or, as the case may be, that part of it.

NOTES
Words in square brackets inserted by SI 1992/1699, reg 2(b), Schedule, para 2.

Chapter II
Company Names

25 Name as stated in memorandum

(1) The name of a public company must end with the words "public limited company" or, if the memorandum states that the company's registered office is to be situated in Wales, those words or their equivalent in Welsh ("cwmni cyfyngedig cyhoeddus"); and those words or that equivalent may not be preceded by the word "limited" or its equivalent in Welsh ("cyfyngedig").

(2) In the case of a company limited by shares or by guarantee (not being a public company), the name must have "limited" as its last word, except that—
(a) this is subject to section 30 (exempting, in certain circumstances, a company from the requirement to have "limited" as part of the name), and
(b) if the company is to be registered with a memorandum stating that its registered office is to be situated in Wales, the name may have "cyfyngedig" as its last word.

26 Prohibition on registration of certain names

(1) A company shall not be registered under this Act by a name—
(a) which includes, otherwise than at the end of the name, any of the following words or expressions, that is to say, "limited", "unlimited" or "public limited company" or their Welsh equivalents ("cyfyngedig", "anghyfynge-dig" and "cwmni cyfyngedig cyhoeddus" respectively);
(b) which includes, otherwise than at the end of the name, an abbreviation of any of those words or expressions;
[(bb) which includes, at any place in the name, the expressions "investment company with variable capital" or "open-ended investment company" or their Welsh equivalents ("cwmni buddsoddi â chyfalaf newidiol" and "cwmni buddsoddiant penagored" respectively);]
[(bbb) which includes, at any place in the name, the expression "limited liability partnership" or its Welsh equivalent ("partneriaeth atebolrwydd cyfynge-dig");]
(c) which is the same as a name appearing in the registrar's index of company names;
(d) the use of which by the company would in the opinion of the Secretary of State constitute a criminal offence; or
(e) which in the opinion of the Secretary of State is offensive.

(2) Except with the approval of the Secretary of State, a company shall not be registered under this Act by a name which—
(a) in the opinion of the Secretary of State would be likely to give the impression that the company is connected in any way with Her Majesty's Government or with any local authority; or

(b) includes any word or expression for the time being specified in regulations under section 29.

"Local authority" means any local authority within the meaning of the Local Government Act 1972 or the Local Government (Scotland) Act 1973, the Common Council of the City of London or the Council of the Isles of Scilly.

(3) In determining for purposes of subsection (1)(c) whether one name is the same as another, there are to be disregarded—
(a) the definite article, where it is the first word of the name;
(b) the following words and expressions where they appear at the end of the name, that is to say—

"company" or its Welsh equivalent ("cwmni"),
"and company" or its Welsh equivalent ("a'r cwmni"),
"company limited" or its Welsh equivalent ("cwmni cyfyngedig"),
"and company limited" or its Welsh equivalent ("a'r cwmni cyfyngedig"),
"limited" or its Welsh equivalent ("cyfyngedig"),
"unlimited" or its Welsh equivalent ("anghyfyngedig"), . . .
"public limited company" or its Welsh equivalent ("cwmni cyfyngedig cyhoeddus"); [. . .
"investment company with variable capital" or its Welsh equivalent ("cwmni buddsoddi a chyfalaf newidiol");] [and
"open-ended investment company" or its Welsh equivalent ("cwmni buddsoddiant penagored");]

(c) abbreviations of any of those words or expressions where they appear at the end of the name; and
(d) type and case of letters, accents, spaces between letters and punctuation marks;

and "and" and "&" are to be taken as the same.

NOTES

Sub-s (1): para (bb) inserted by SI 1996/2827, reg 75, Sch 8, para 4(a).
Sub-s (1): para (bb) substituted by SI 2001/1228, reg 84, Sch 7, Pt I, para 3(1), (2).
Date in force: 1 December 2001 (being the date on which the Financial Services and Markets Act 2000, s 19, came into force): see SI 2001/3538, art 2(1) and SI 2001/1228, reg 1(2)(c).
Sub-s (1): para (bbb) inserted by SI 2001/1090, reg 9(1), Sch 5, para 9.
Date in force: 6 April 2001: see SI 2001/1090, reg 1.
Sub-s (3): in para (b) in entry relating to "unlimited" word omitted repealed by SI 1996/2827, reg 75, Sch 8, para 4(b).
Sub-s (3): in para (b) entry relating to "investment company with variable capital" and word omitted immediately preceding it inserted by SI 1996/2827, reg 75, Sch 8, para 4(b).
Sub-s (3): in para (b) word omitted immediately following "public limited company" repealed by SI 2001/1228, reg 84, Sch 7, Pt I, para 3(1), (3).
Date in force: 1 December 2001 (being the date on which the Financial Services and Markets Act 2000, s 19, came into force): see SI 2001/3538, art 2(1) and SI 2001/1228, reg 1(2)(c).
Sub-s (3): in para (b) entry relating to "open-ended investment company" and word "and" immediately preceding it inserted by SI 2001/1228, reg 84, Sch 7, Pt I, para 3(1), (3).

Date in force: 1 December 2001 (being the date on which the Financial Services and Markets Act 2000, s 19, came into force): see SI 2001/3538, art 2(1) and SI 2001/1228, reg 1(2)(c).

28 Change of name

(1)   A company may by special resolution change its name (but subject to section 31 in the case of a company which has received a direction under subsection (2) of that section from the Secretary of State).

(2)   Where a company has been registered by a name which—
    (a)   is the same as or, in the opinion of the Secretary of State, too like a name appearing at the time of the registration in the registrar's index of company names, or
    (b)   is the same as or, in the opinion of the Secretary of State, too like a name which should have appeared in that index at that time,

the Secretary of State may within 12 months of that time, in writing, direct the company to change its name within such period as he may specify.

Section 26(3) applies in determining under this subsection whether a name is the same as or too like another.

(3)   If it appears to the Secretary of State that misleading information has been given for the purpose of a company's registration with a particular name, or that undertakings or assurances have been given for that purpose and have not been fulfilled, he may within 5 years of the date of its registration with that name in writing direct the company to change its name within such period as he may specify.

(4)   Where a direction has been given under subsection (2) or (3), the Secretary of State may by a further direction in writing extend the period within which the company is to change its name, at any time before the end of that period.

(5)   A company which fails to comply with a direction under this section, and any officer of it who is in default, is liable to a fine and, for continued contravention, to a daily default fine.

(6)   Where a company changes its name under this section, the registrar of companies shall (subject to section 26) enter the new name on the register in place of the former name, and shall issue a certificate of incorporation altered to meet the circumstances of the case; and the change of name has effect from the date on which the altered certificate is issued.

(7)   A change of name by a company under this section does not affect any rights or obligations of the company or render defective any legal proceedings by or against it; and any legal proceedings that might have been continued or commenced against it by its former name may be continued or commenced against it by its new name.

32 Power to require company to abandon misleading name

(1) If in the Secretary of State's opinion the name by which a company is registered gives so misleading an indication of the nature of its activities as to be likely to cause harm to the public, he may direct it to change its name.

(2) The direction must, if not duly made the subject of an application to the court under the following subsection, be complied with within a period of 6 weeks from the date of the direction or such longer period as the Secretary of State may think fit to allow.

(3) The company may, within a period of 3 weeks from the date of the direction, apply to the court to set it aside; and the court may set the direction aside or confirm it and, if it confirms the direction, shall specify a period within which it must be complied with.

(4) If a company makes default in complying with a direction under this section, it is liable to a fine and, for continued contravention, to a daily default fine.

(5) Where a company changes its name under this section, the registrar shall (subject to section 26) enter the new name on the register in place of the former name, and shall issue a certificate of incorporation altered to meet the circumstances of the case; and the change of name has effect from the date on which the altered certificate is issued.

(6) A change of name by a company under this section does not affect any of the rights or obligations of the company, or render defective any legal proceedings by or against it; and any legal proceedings that might have been continued or commenced against it by its former name may be continued or commenced against it by its new name.

33 Prohibition on trading under misleading name

(1) A person who is not a public company is guilty of an offence if he carries on any trade, profession or business under a name which includes, as its last part, the words "public limited company" or their equivalent in Welsh ("cwmni cyfyngedig cyhoeddus").

(2) A public company is guilty of an offence if, in circumstances in which the fact that it is a public company is likely to be material to any person, it uses a name which may reasonably be expected to give the impression that it is a private company.

(3) A person guilty of an offence under subsection (1) or (2) and, if that person is a company, any officer of the company who is in default, is liable to a fine and, for continued contravention, to a daily default fine.

Chapter III
A Company's Capacity; Formalities of Carrying on Business

[35 A company's capacity not limited by its memorandum]

[(1)   The validity of an act done by a company shall not be called into question on the ground of lack of capacity by reason of anything in the company's memorandum.

(2)   A member of a company may bring proceedings to restrain the doing of an act which but for subsection (1) would be beyond the company's capacity; but no such proceedings shall lie in respect of an act to be done in fulfilment of a legal obligation arising from a previous act of the company.

(3)   It remains the duty of the directors to observe any limitations on their powers flowing from the company's memorandum; and action by the directors which but for subsection (1) would be beyond the company's capacity may only be ratified by the company by special resolution.

A resolution ratifying such action shall not affect any liability incurred by the directors or any other person; relief from any such liability must be agreed to separately by special resolution.

(4)   The operation of this section is restricted by [section 65(1) of the Charities Act 1993] and section 112(3) of the Companies Act 1989 in relation to companies which are charities; and section 322A below (invalidity of certain transactions to which directors or their associates are parties) has effect notwithstanding this section.]

NOTES

Substituted, together with ss 35A, 35B, for s 35 as originally enacted, by the Companies Act 1989, s 108(1).

Sub-s (4): words in square brackets substituted by the Charities Act 1993, s 98(1), Sch 6, para 20(2).

[35A Power of directors to bind the company]

[(1)   In favour of a person dealing with a company in good faith, the power of the board of directors to bind the company, or authorise others to do so, shall be deemed to be free of any limitation under the company's constitution.

(2)   For this purpose—
    (a)   a person "deals with" a company if he is a party to any transaction or other act to which the company is a party;
    (b)   a person shall not be regarded as acting in bad faith by reason only of his knowing that an act is beyond the powers of the directors under the company's constitution; and
    (c)   a person shall be presumed to have acted in good faith unless the contrary is proved.

(3)   The references above to limitations on the directors' powers under the company's constitution include limitations deriving—

   (a) from a resolution of the company in general meeting or a meeting of any class of shareholders, or

   (b) from any agreement between the members of the company or of any class of shareholders.

(4)   Subsection (1) does not affect any right of a member of the company to bring proceedings to restrain the doing of an act which is beyond the powers of the directors; but no such proceedings shall lie in respect of an act to be done in fulfilment of a legal obligation arising from a previous act of the company.

(5)   Nor does that subsection affect any liability incurred by the directors, or any other person, by reason of the directors' exceeding their powers.

(6)   The operation of this section is restricted by [section 65(1) of the Charities Act 1993] and section 112(3) of the Companies Act 1989 in relation to companies which are charities; and section 322A below (invalidity of certain transactions to which directors or their associates are parties) has effect notwithstanding this section.]

NOTES

Substituted, together with new ss 35, 35B, for s 35 as originally enacted, by the Companies Act 1989, s 108.

Sub-s (6): words in square brackets substituted by the Charities Act 1993, s 98(1), Sch 6, para 20(2).

[35B No duty to enquire as to capacity of company or authority of directors]

[A party to a transaction with a company is not bound to enquire as to whether it is permitted by the company's memorandum or as to any limitation on the powers of the board of directors to bind the company or authorise others to do so.]

NOTES

Substituted, together with new ss 35, 35A, for s 35 as originally enacted, by the Companies Act 1989, s 108.

[36 Company contracts: England and Wales]

[Under the law of England and Wales a contract may be made—
   (a) by a company, by writing under its common seal, or
   (b) on behalf of a company, by any person acting under its authority, express or implied;

and any formalities required by law in the case of a contract made by an individual also apply, unless a contrary intention appears, to a contract made by or on behalf of a company.]

NOTES

Substituted by the Companies Act 1989, s 130(1).

[36A Execution of documents: England and Wales]

[(1)   Under the law of England and Wales the following provisions have effect with respect to the execution of documents by a company.

(2)   A document is executed by a company by the affixing of its common seal.

(3)   A company need not have a common seal, however, and the following subsections apply whether it does or not.

(4)   A document signed by a director and the secretary of a company, or by two directors of a company, and expressed (in whatever form of words) to be executed by the company has the same effect as if executed under the common seal of the company.

(5)   A document executed by a company which makes it clear on its face that it is intended by the person or persons making it to be a deed has effect, upon delivery, as a deed; and it shall be presumed, unless a contrary intention is proved, to be delivered upon its being so executed.

(6)   In favour of a purchaser a document shall be deemed to have been duly executed by a company if it purports to be signed by a director and the secretary of the company, or by two directors of the company, and, where it makes it clear on its face that it is intended by the person or persons making it to be a deed, to have been delivered upon its being executed.

   A "purchaser" means a purchaser in good faith for valuable consideration and includes a lessee, mortgagee or other person who for valuable consideration acquires an interest in property.]

NOTES

Inserted by the Companies Act 1989, s 130(2).

[36B Execution of documents by companies]

[(1)   Notwithstanding the provisions of any enactment, a company need not have a company seal.

(2)   For the purposes of any enactment—
   (a)   providing for a document to be executed by a company by affixing its common seal; or
   (b)   referring (in whatever terms) to a document so executed,

a document signed or subscribed by or on behalf of the company in accordance with the provisions of the Requirements of Writing (Scotland) Act 1995 shall have effect as if so executed.

(3)   In this section "enactment" includes an enactment contained in a statutory instrument.]

NOTES

Inserted by the Companies Act 1989, s 130(3).
Substituted by the Requirements of Writing (Scotland) Act 1995, s 14(1), Sch 4, para 51.

[36C Pre-incorporation contracts, deeds and obligations]

[(1)   A contract which purports to be made by or on behalf of a company at a time when the company has not been formed has effect, subject to any agreement to the contrary, as one made with the person purporting to act for the company or as agent for it, and he is personally liable on the contract accordingly.

(2)   Subsection (1) applies—
  (a)   to the making of a deed under the law of England and Wales, and
  (b)   to the undertaking of an obligation under the law of Scotland,

as it applies to the making of a contract.]

NOTES
Inserted by the Companies Act 1989, s 130(4).

42 Events affecting a company's status

(1)   A company is not entitled to rely against other persons on the happening of any of the following events—
  (a)   the making of a winding-up order in respect of the company, or the appointment of a liquidator in a voluntary winding up of the company, or
  (b)   any alteration of the company's memorandum or articles, or
  (c)   any change among the company's directors, or
  (d)   (as regards service of any document on the company) any change in the situation of the company's registered office,

if the event had not been officially notified at the material time and is not shown by the company to have been known at that time to the person concerned, or if the material time fell on or before the 15th day after the date of official notification (or, where the 15th day was a non-business day, on or before the next day that was not) and it is shown that the person concerned was unavoidably prevented from knowing of the event at that time.

(2)   In subsection (1)—
  (a)   "official notification" and "officially notified" have the meanings given by section 711(2) (registrar of companies to give public notice of the issue or receipt by him of certain documents), and
  (b)   "non-business day" means a Saturday or Sunday, Christmas Day, Good Friday and any other day which is a bank holiday in the part of Great Britain where the company is registered.

PART III

CAPITAL ISSUES

NOTES
Repealed for certain purposes by the Financial Services Act 1986, s 212(3), Sch 17, Pt I (see SI 1986/2246, SI 1988/740, SI 1988/1960, SI 1988/2285 and SI 1995/1538), and prospectively repealed for remaining purposes by the Financial Services Act 1986, s 212(3), Sch 17, Pt I, as from a day to be appointed.

Chapter I
Issues by Companies Registered, or to be Registered, in Great Britain

NOTES

Repealed for certain purposes by the Financial Services Act 1986, s 212(3), Sch 17, Pt I (see SI 1986/2246, SI 1988/740, SI 1988/1960, SI 1988/2285 and SI 1995/1538), and prospectively repealed for remaining purposes by the Financial Services Act 1986, s 212(3), Sch 17, Pt I, as from a day to be appointed.

The prospectus

NOTES

Repealed for certain purposes by the Financial Services Act 1986, s 212(3), Sch 17, Pt I (see SI 1986/2246, SI 1988/740, SI 1988/1960, SI 1988/2285 and SI 1995/1538), and prospectively repealed for remaining purposes by the Financial Services Act 1986, s 212(3), Sch 17, Pt I, as from a day to be appointed.

58 Document offering shares etc for sale deemed a prospectus

(1) If a company allots or agrees to allot its shares or debentures with a view to all or any of them being offered for sale to the public, any document by which the offer for sale to the public is made is deemed for all purposes a prospectus issued by the company.

(2) All enactments and rules of law as to the contents of prospectuses, and to liability in respect of statements in and omissions from prospectuses, or otherwise relating to prospectuses, apply and have effect accordingly, as if the shares or debentures had been offered to the public for subscription and as if persons accepting the offer in respect of any shares or debentures were subscribers for those shares or debentures.

This is without prejudice to the liability (if any) of the persons by whom the offer is made, in respect of mis-statements in the document or otherwise in respect of it.

(3) For purposes of this Act it is evidence (unless the contrary is proved) that an allotment of, or an agreement to allot, shares or debentures was made with a view to their being offered for sale to the public if it is shown—

(a) that an offer of the shares or debentures (or of any of them) for sale to the public was made within 6 months after the allotment or agreement to allot, or

(b) that at the date when the offer was made the whole consideration to be received by the company in respect of the shares or debentures had not been so received.

(4) Section 56 as applied by this section has effect as if it required a prospectus to state, in addition to the matters required by that section—

(a) the net amount of the consideration received or to be received by the company in respect of the shares or debentures to which the offer relates, and

(b) the place and time at which the contract under which those shares or debentures have been or are to be allotted may be inspected.

NOTES
Repealed for certain purposes by the Financial Services Act 1986, s 212(3), Sch 17, Pt I (see SI 1986/2246, SI 1988/740, SI 1988/1960, SI 1988/2285 and SI 1995/1538), and prospectively repealed for remaining purposes by the Financial Services Act 1986, s 212(3), Sch 17, Pt I, as from a day to be appointed.

59 Rule governing what is an "offer to the public"

(1) Subject to the next section, any reference in this Act to offering shares or debentures to the public is to be read (subject to any provision to the contrary) as including a reference to offering them to any section of the public, whether selected as members or debenture holders of the company concerned, or as clients of the person issuing the prospectus, or in any other manner.

(2) The same applies to any reference in this Act, or in a company's articles, to an invitation to the public to subscribe for shares or debentures.

NOTES
Repealed for certain purposes by the Financial Services Act 1986, s 212(3), Sch 17, Pt I (see SI 1986/2246, SI 1988/740, SI 1988/1960, SI 1988/2285 and SI 1995/1538) and for remaining purposes by SI 2001/3649, art 5.
Date in force (in so far as relating to the remaining purposes): 1 December 2001: see SI 2001/3649, art 1.

60 Exceptions from rule in s 59

(1) Section 59 does not require an offer or invitation to be treated as made to the public if it can properly be regarded, in all the circumstances, as not being calculated to result, directly or indirectly, in the shares or debentures becoming available for subscription or purchase by persons other than those receiving the offer or invitation, or otherwise as being a domestic concern of the persons receiving and making it.

(2) In particular, a provision in a company's articles prohibiting invitations to the public to subscribe for shares or debentures is not to be taken as prohibiting the making to members or debenture holders of an invitation which can properly be regarded as falling within the preceding subsection.

(3) For purposes of that subsection, an offer of shares in or debentures of a private company, or an invitation to subscribe for such shares or debentures, is to be regarded (unless the contrary is proved) as being a domestic concern of the persons making and receiving the offer or invitation if it falls within any of the following descriptions.

(4) It is to be so regarded if it is made to—
  (a) an existing member of the company making the offer or invitation,
  (b) an existing employee of that company,
  (c) a member of the family of such a member or employee, or
  (d) an existing debenture holder.

(5) For purposes of subsection (4)(c), the members of a person's family are—

(a) the person's husband or wife, widow or widower and children (including stepchildren) and their descendants, and

(b) any trustee (acting in his capacity as such) of a trust the principal beneficiary of which is the person him or herself, or any of those relatives.

(6) The offer or invitation is also to be so regarded if it is to subscribe for shares or debentures to be held under an employees' share scheme.

(7) The offer or invitation is also to be so regarded if it falls within subsection (4) or (6) and it is made on terms which permit the person to whom it is made to renounce his right to the allotment of shares or issue of debentures, but only in favour—

(a) of such a person as is mentioned in any of the paragraphs of subsection (4), or

(b) where there is an employees' share scheme, of a person entitled to hold shares or debentures under the scheme.

(8) Where application has been made to [the competent authority for the purposes of Part IV of the Financial Services Act 1986] for admission of any securities to the Official List of the Stock Exchange, then an offer of those securities for subscription or sale to a person whose ordinary business it is to buy or sell shares or debentures (whether as principal or agent) is not deemed an offer to the public for purposes of this Part.

NOTES

Repealed for certain purposes by the Financial Services Act 1986, s 212(3), Sch 17, Pt I (see SI 1986/2246, SI 1988/740, SI 1988/1960, SI 1988/2285 and SI 1995/1538) and for remaining purposes by SI 2001/3649, art 5.

Date in force (in so far as relating to the remaining purposes): 1 December 2001: see SI 2001/3649, art 1.

62 Meaning of "expert"

The expression "expert", in both Chapters of this Part, includes engineer, valuer, accountant and any other person whose profession gives authority to a statement made by him.

NOTES

Repealed for certain purposes by the Financial Services Act 1986, s 212(3), Sch 17, Pt I (see SI 1986/2246, SI 1988/740, SI 1988/1960, SI 1988/2285 and SI 1995/1538), and prospectively repealed for remaining purposes by the Financial Services Act 1986, s 212(3), Sch 17, Pt I, as from a day to be appointed.

PART IV
ALLOTMENT OF SHARES AND DEBENTURES

General provisions as to allotment

80 Authority of company required for certain allotments

(1)   The directors of a company shall not exercise any power of the company to allot relevant securities, unless they are, in accordance with this section [or section 80A], authorised to do so by—
   (a)   the company in general meeting; or
   (b)   the company's articles.

(2)   In this section "relevant securities" means—
   (a)   shares in the company other than shares shown in the memorandum to have been taken by the subscribers to it or shares allotted in pursuance of an employees' share scheme, and
   (b)   any right to subscribe for, or to convert any security into, shares in the company (other than shares so allotted);

and a reference to the allotment of relevant securities includes the grant of such a right but (subject to subsection (6) below), not the allotment of shares pursuant to such a right.

(3)   Authority under this section may be given for a particular exercise of the power or for its exercise generally, and may be unconditional or subject to conditions.

(4)   The authority must state the maximum amount of relevant securities that may be allotted under it and the date on which it will expire, which must be not more than 5 years from whichever is relevant of the following dates—
   (a)   in the case of an authority contained in the company's articles at the time of its original incorporation, the date of that incorporation; and
   (b)   in any other case, the date on which the resolution is passed by virtue of which the authority is given;

but such an authority (including an authority contained in the articles) may be previously revoked or varied by the company in general meeting.

(5)   The authority may be renewed or further renewed by the company in general meeting for a further period not exceeding 5 years; but the resolution must state (or restate) the amount of relevant securities which may be allotted under the authority or, as the case may be, the amount remaining to be allotted under it, and must specify the date on which the renewed authority will expire.

(6)   In relation to authority under this section for the grant of such rights as are mentioned in subsection (2)(b), the reference in subsection (4) (as also the corresponding reference in subsection (5)) to the maximum amount of relevant securities that may be allotted under the authority is to the maximum amount of shares which may be allotted pursuant to the rights.

(7)   The directors may allot relevant securities, notwithstanding that authority under this section has expired, if they are allotted in pursuance of an offer or agreement made by the company before the authority expired and the authority allowed it to make an offer or agreement which would or might require relevant securities to be allotted after the authority expired.

(8)   A resolution of a company to give, vary, revoke or renew such an authority may, notwithstanding that it alters the company's articles, be an ordinary resolution; but it is in any case subject to section 380 of this Act (copy to be forwarded to registrar within 15 days).

(9)   A director who knowingly and wilfully contravenes, or permits or authorises a contravention of, this section is liable to a fine.

(10)   Nothing in this section affects the validity of any allotment.

(11)   This section does not apply to any allotment of relevant securities by a company, other than a public company registered as such on its original incorporation, if it is made in pursuance of an offer or agreement made before the earlier of the following two dates—
  (a)   the date of the holding of the first general meeting of the company after its registration or re-registration as a public company, and
  (b)   22nd June 1982;

but any resolution to give, vary or revoke an authority for the purposes of section 14 of the Companies Act 1980 or this section has effect for those purposes if passed at any time after the end of April 1980.

NOTES
Sub-s (1): words in square brackets inserted by the Companies Act 1989, s 115(1).

[80A Election by private company as to duration of authority]

[(1)   A private company may elect (by elective resolution in accordance with section 379A) that the provisions of this section shall apply, instead of the provisions of section 80(4) and (5), in relation to the giving or renewal, after the election, of an authority under that section.

(2)   The authority must state the maximum amount of relevant securities that may be allotted under it and may be given—
  (a)   for an indefinite period, or
  (b)   for a fixed period, in which case it must state the date on which it will expire.

(3)   In either case an authority (including an authority contained in the articles) may be revoked or varied by the company in general meeting.

(4)   An authority given for a fixed period may be renewed or further renewed by the company in general meeting.

(5)   A resolution renewing an authority—

(a) must state, or re-state, the amount of relevant securities which may be allotted under the authority or, as the case may be, the amount remaining to be allotted under it, and

(b) must state whether the authority is renewed for an indefinite period or for a fixed period, in which case it must state the date on which the renewed authority will expire.

(6) The references in this section to the maximum amount of relevant securities that may be allotted shall be construed in accordance with section 80(6).

(7) If an election under this section ceases to have effect, an authority then in force which was given for an indefinite period or for a fixed period of more than five years—

(a) if given five years or more before the election ceases to have effect, shall expire forthwith, and

(b) otherwise, shall have effect as if it had been given for a fixed period of five years.]

NOTES
Inserted by the Companies Act 1989, s 115(1).

81 Restriction on public offers by private company

(1) A private limited company (other than a company limited by guarantee and not having a share capital) commits an offence if it—

(a) offers to the public (whether for cash or otherwise) any shares in or debentures of the company; or

(b) allots or agrees to allot (whether for cash or otherwise) any shares in or debentures of the company with a view to all or any of those shares or debentures being offered for sale to the public (within the meaning given to that expression by sections 58 to 60).

(2) A company guilty of an offence under this section, and any officer of it who is in default, is liable to a fine.

(3) Nothing in this section affects the validity of any allotment or sale of shares or debentures, or of any agreement to allot or sell shares or debentures.

NOTES
Repealed for certain purposes by the Financial Services Act 1986, s 212(3), Sch 17, Part I (see SI 1986/2246 and SI 1988/740).

82 Application for, and allotment of, shares and debentures

(1) No allotment shall be made of a company's shares or debentures in pursuance of a prospectus issued generally, and no proceedings shall be taken on applications made in pursuance of a prospectus so issued, until the beginning of the third day after that on which the prospectus is first so issued or such later time (if any) as may be specified in the prospectus.

(2) The beginning of that third day, or that later time, is "the time of the opening of the subscription lists".

(3) In subsection (1), the reference to the day on which the prospectus is first issued generally is to the day when it is first so issued as a newspaper advertisement'; and if it is not so issued as a newspaper advertisement before the third day after that on which it is first so issued in any other manner, the reference is to the day on which it is first so issued in any manner.

(4) In reckoning for this purpose the third day after another day—
  (a) any intervening day which is a Saturday or Sunday, or is a bank holiday in any part of Great Britain, is to be disregarded; and
  (b) if the third day (as so reckoned) is itself a Saturday or Sunday, or a bank holiday, there is to be substituted the first day after that which is none of them.

(5) The validity of an allotment is not affected by any contravention of subsections (1) to (4); but in the event of contravention, the company and every officer of it who is in default is liable to a fine.

(6) As applying to a prospectus offering shares or debentures for sale, the above provisions are modified as follows—
  (a) for references to allotment, substitute references to sale; and
  (b) for the reference to the company and every officer of it who is in default, substitute a reference to any person by or through whom the offer is made and who knowingly and wilfully authorised or permits the contravention.

(7) An application for shares in or debentures of a company which is made in pursuance of a prospectus issued generally is not recoverable until after the expiration of the third day after the time of the opening of the subscription lists, or the giving before the expiration of that day of the appropriate public notice; and that notice is one given by some person responsible under section 67 to 69 for the prospectus and having the effect under those sections of excluding or limiting the responsibility of the giver.

NOTES

Repealed by the Financial Services Act 1986, s 212(3), Sch 17, Pt I.

Date in force (for certain purposes): 12 January 1987: see SI 1986/2246, art 5, Sch 4.

Date in force (for certain purposes): 16 February 1987: see SI 1986/2246, art 5, Sch 4.

Date in force (for certain purposes): 29 April 1988: see SI 1988/740, art 2, Schedule.

Date in force (for certain purposes): 10 May 1999: see SI 1999/727, art 2(a).

Date in force (for remaining purposes): to be appointed: see the Financial Services Act 1986, s 211(1).

83 No allotment unless minimum subscription received

(1) No allotment shall be made of any share capital of a company offered to the public for subscription unless—
  (a) there has been subscribed the amount stated in the prospectus as the minimum amount which, in the opinion of the directors, must be raised by the issue of share capital in order to provide for the matters specified in paragraph 2 of Schedule 3 (preliminary expenses, purchase of property, working capital, etc); and

(b) the sum payable on application for the amount so stated has been paid to and received by the company.

(2) For purposes of subsection (1)(b), a sum is deemed paid to the company, and received by it, if a cheque for that sum has been received in good faith by the company and the directors have no reason for suspecting that the cheque will not be paid.

(3) The amount so stated in the prospectus is to be reckoned exclusively of any amount payable otherwise than in cash and is known as "the minimum subscription".

(4) If the above conditions have not been complied with on the expiration of 40 days after the first issue of the prospectus, all money received from applicants for shares shall be forthwith repaid to them without interest.

(5) If any of the money is not repaid within 48 days after the issue of the prospectus, the directors of the company are jointly and severally liable to repay it with interest at the rate of 5 per cent per annum from the expiration of the 48th day; except that a director is not so liable if he proves that the default in the repayment of the money was not due to any misconduct or negligence on his part.

(6) Any condition requiring or binding an applicant for shares to waive compliance with any requirement of this section is void.

(7) This section does not apply to an allotment of shares subsequent to the first allotment of shares offered to the public for subscription.

NOTES

Repealed by the Financial Services Act 1986, s 212(3), Sch 17, Pt I.
Date in force (for certain purposes): 12 January 1987: see SI 1986/2246, art 5, Sch 4.
Date in force (for certain purposes): 16 February 1987: see SI 1986/2246, art 5, Sch 4.
Date in force (for certain purposes): 29 April 1988: see SI 1988/740, art 2, Schedule.
Date in force (for certain purposes): 10 May 1999: see SI 1999/727, art 2(a).
Date in force (for remaining purposes): to be appointed: see the Financial Services Act 1986, s 211(1).

84 Allotment where issue not fully subscribed

(1) No allotment shall be made of any share capital of a public company offered for subscription unless—
   (a) that capital is subscribed for in full; or
   (b) the offer states that, even if the capital is not subscribed for in full, the amount of that capital subscribed for may be allotted in any event or in the event of the conditions specified in the offer being satisfied;

and, where conditions are so specified, no allotment of the capital shall be made by virtue of paragraph (b) unless those conditions are satisfied.

This is without prejudice to section 83.

(2) If shares are prohibited from being allotted by subsection (1) and 40 days have elapsed after the first issue of the prospectus, all money received from applicants for shares shall be forthwith repaid to them without interest.

(3) If any of the money is not repaid within 48 days after the issue of the prospectus, the directors of the company are jointly and severally liable to repay it with interest at the rate of 5 per cent per annum from the expiration of the 48th day; except that a director is not so liable if he proves that the default in repayment was not due to any misconduct or negligence on his part.

(4) This section applies in the case of shares offered as wholly or partly payable otherwise than in cash as it applies in the case of shares offered for subscription (the word "subscribed" in subsection (1) being construed accordingly).

(5) In subsections (2) and (3) as they apply to the case of shares offered as wholly or partly payable otherwise than in cash, references to the repayment of money received from applicants for shares include—

(a) the return of any other consideration so received (including, if the case so requires, the release of the applicant from any undertaking), or

(b) if it is not reasonably practicable to return the consideration, the payment of money equal to its value at the time it was so received,

and references to interest apply accordingly.

(6) Any condition requiring or binding an applicant for shares to waive compliance with any requirement of this section is void.

NOTES

Sub-s (1): words in italics repealed for certain purposes by the Financial Services Act 1986, s 212(3), Sch 17, Part I (see SI 1986/2246 and SI 1988/740), and prospectively repealed for remaining purposes by the Financial Services Act 1986, s 212(3), Sch 17, Part I, as from a day to be appointed.

85 Effect of irregular allotment

(1) An allotment made by a company to an applicant in contravention of section *83 or* 84 is voidable at the instance of the applicant within one month after the date of the allotment, and not later, and is so voidable notwithstanding that the company is in the course of being wound up.

(2) If a director of a company knowingly contravenes, or permits or authorises the contravention of, any provision of either of those sections with respect to allotment, he is liable to compensate the company and the allottee respectively for any loss, damages or costs which the company or the allottee may have sustained or incurred by the contravention.

(3) But proceedings to recover any such loss, damages or costs shall not be commenced after the expiration of 2 years from the date of the allotment.

NOTES

Sub-s (1): words in italics repealed for certain purposes by the Financial Services Act 1986, s 212(3), Sch 17, Part I (see SI 1986/2246 and SI 1988/740), and prospectively repealed for remaining purposes by the Financial Services Act 1986, s 212(3), Sch 17, Part I, as from a day to be appointed.

89 Offers to shareholders to be on pre-emptive basis

(1) Subject to the provisions of this section and the seven sections next following, a company proposing to allot equity securities (defined in section 94)—

(a) shall not allot any of them on any terms to a person unless it has made an offer to each person who holds relevant shares or relevant employee shares to allot to him on the same or more favourable terms a proportion of those securities which is as nearly as practicable equal to the proportion in nominal value held by him of the aggregate of relevant shares and relevant employee shares, and

(b) shall not allot any of those securities to a person unless the period during which any such offer may be accepted has expired or the company has received notice of the acceptance or refusal of every offer so made.

(2) Subsection (3) below applies to any provision of a company's memorandum or articles which requires the company, when proposing to allot equity securities consisting of relevant shares of any particular class, not to allot those securities on any terms unless it has complied with the condition that it makes such an offer as is described in subsection (1) to each person who holds relevant shares or relevant employee shares of that class.

(3) If in accordance with a provision to which this subsection applies—

(a) a company makes an offer to allot securities to such a holder, and

(b) he or anyone in whose favour he has renounced his right to their allotment accepts the offer,

subsection (1) does not apply to the allotment of those securities, and the company may allot them accordingly; but this is without prejudice to the application of subsection (1) in any other case.

(4) Subsection (1) does not apply to a particular allotment of equity securities if these are, or are to be, wholly or partly paid up otherwise than in cash; and securities which a company has offered to allot to a holder of relevant shares or relevant employee shares may be allotted to him, or anyone in whose favour he has renounced his right to their allotment, without contravening subsection (1)(b).

(5) Subsection (1) does not apply to the allotment of securities which would, apart from a renunciation or assignment of the right to their allotment, be held under an employees' share scheme.

91 Exclusion of ss 89, 90 by private company

(1) Section 89(1), section 90(1) to (5) or section 90(6) may, as applying to allotments by a private company of equity securities or to such allotments of a particular description, be excluded by a provision contained in the memorandum or articles of that company.

(2) A requirement or authority contained in the memorandum or articles of a private company, if it is inconsistent with any of those subsections, has effect as a provision excluding that subsection; but a provision to which section 89(3) applies is not to be treated as inconsistent with section 89(1).

92 Consequences of contravening ss 89, 90

(1)   If there is a contravention of section 89(1), or of section 90(1) to (5) or section 90(6), or of a provision to which section 89(3) applies, the company, and every officer of it who knowingly authorised or permitted the contravention, are jointly and severally liable to compensate any person to whom an offer should have been made under the subsection or provision contravened for any loss, damage, costs or expenses which the person has sustained or incurred by reason of the contravention.

(2)   However, no proceedings to recover any such loss, damage, costs or expenses shall be commenced after the expiration of 2 years from the delivery to the registrar of companies of the return of allotments in question or, where equity securities other than shares are granted, from the date of the grant.

93 Saving for other restrictions as to offers

(1)   Sections 89 to 92 are without prejudice to any enactment by virtue of which a company is prohibited (whether generally or in specified circumstances) from offering or allotting equity securities to any person.

(2)   Where a company cannot by virtue of such an enactment offer or allot equity securities to a holder of relevant shares or relevant employee shares, those sections have effect as if the shares held by that holder were not relevant shares or relevant employee shares.

94 Definitions for ss 89–96

(1)   The following subsections apply for the interpretation of sections 89 to 96.

(2)   "Equity security", in relation to a company, means a relevant share in the company (other than a share shown in the memorandum to have been taken by a subscriber to the memorandum or a bonus share), or a right to subscribe for, or to convert securities into, relevant shares in the company.

(3)   A reference to the allotment of equity securities or of equity securities consisting of relevant shares of a particular class includes the grant of a right to subscribe for, or to convert any securities into, relevant shares in the company or (as the case may be) relevant shares of a particular class; but such a reference does not include the allotment of any relevant shares pursuant to such a right.

(4)   "Relevant employee shares", in relation to a company, means shares of the company which would be relevant in it but for the fact that they are held by a person who acquired them in pursuance of an employees' share scheme.

(5)   "Relevant shares", in relation to a company, means shares in the company other than—
   (a)   shares which as respects dividends and capital carry a right to participate only up to a specified amount in a distribution, and
   (b)   shares which are held by a person who acquired them in pursuance of an employees' share scheme or, in the case of shares which have not been allotted, are to be allotted in pursuance of such a scheme.

(6)   A reference to a class of shares is to shares to which the same rights are attached as to voting and as to participation, both as respects dividends and as respects capital, in a distribution.

(7)   In relation to an offer to allot securities required by section 89(1) or by any provision to which section 89(3) applies, a reference in sections 89 to 94 (however expressed) to the holder of shares of any description is to whoever was at the close of business on a date, to be specified in the offer and to fall in the period of 28 days immediately before the date of the offer, the holder of shares of that description.

95 Disapplication of pre-emption rights

(1)   Where the directors of a company are generally authorised for purposes of section 80, they may be given power by the articles, or by a special resolution of the company, to allot equity securities pursuant to that authority as if—
   (a)   section 89(1) did not apply to the allotment, or
   (b)   that subsection applied to the allotment with such modifications as the directors may determine;

and where the directors make an allotment under this subsection, sections 89 to 94 have effect accordingly.

(2)   Where the directors of a company are authorised for purposes of section 80 (whether generally or otherwise), the company may by special resolution resolve either—
   (a)   that section 89(1) shall not apply to a specified allotment of equity securities to be made pursuant to that authority, or
   (b)   that that subsection shall apply to the allotment with such modifications as may be specified in the resolution;

and where such a resolution is passed, sections 89 to 94 have effect accordingly.

(3)   The power conferred by subsection (1) or a special resolution under subsection (2) ceases to have effect when the authority to which it relates is revoked or would (if not renewed) expire; but if the authority is renewed, the power or (as the case may be) the resolution may also be renewed, for a period not longer than that for which the authority is renewed, by a special resolution of the company.

(4)   Notwithstanding that any such power or resolution has expired, the directors may allot equity securities in pursuance of an offer or agreement previously made by the company, if the power or resolution enabled the company to make an offer or agreement which would or might require equity securities to be allotted after it expired.

(5)   A special resolution under subsection (2), or a special resolution to renew such a resolution, shall not be proposed unless it is recommended by the directors and there has been circulated, with the notice of the meeting at which the resolution is proposed, to the members entitled to have that notice a written statement by the directors setting out—
   (a)   their reasons for making the recommendation,
   (b)   the amount to be paid to the company in respect of the equity securities to be allotted, and

(c) the directors' justification of that amount.

(6) A person who knowingly or recklessly authorises or permits the inclusion in a statement circulated under subsection (5) of any matter which is misleading, false or deceptive in a material particular is liable to imprisonment or a fine, or both.

Amount to be paid for shares; the means of payment

99 General rules as to payment for shares on allotment

(1) Subject to the following provisions of this Part, shares allotted by a company, and any premium on them, may be paid up in money or money's worth (including goodwill and know-how).

(2) A public company shall not accept at any time, in payment up of its shares or any premium on them, an undertaking given by any person that he or another should do work or perform services for the company or any other person.

(3) If a public company accepts such an undertaking in payment up of its shares or any premium on them, the holder of the shares when they or the premium are treated as paid up (in whole or in part) by the undertaking is liable—

(a) to pay the company in respect of those shares an amount equal to their nominal value, together with the whole of any premium or, if the case so requires, such proportion of that amount as is treated as paid up by the undertaking; and

(b) to pay interest at the appropriate rate on the amount payable under paragraph (a) above.

(4) This section does not prevent a company from allotting bonus shares to its members or from paying up, with sums available for the purpose, any amounts for the time being unpaid on any of its shares (whether on account of the nominal value of the shares or by way of premium).

(5) The reference in subsection (3) to the holder of shares includes any person who has an unconditional right to be included in the company's register of members in respect of those shares or to have an instrument of transfer of them executed in his favour.

100 Prohibition on allotment of shares at a discount

(1) A company's shares shall not be allotted at a discount.

(2) If shares are allotted in contravention of this section, the allottee is liable to pay the company an amount equal to the amount of the discount, with interest at the appropriate rate.

101 Shares to be allotted as at least one-quarter paid-up

(1) A public company shall not allot a share except as paid up at least as to one-quarter of its nominal value and the whole of any premium on it.

(2) Subsection (1) does not apply to shares allotted in pursuance of an employees' share scheme.

(3)   If a company allots a share in contravention of subsection (1), the share is to be treated as if one-quarter of its nominal value, together with the whole of any premium on it, had been received.

(4)   But the allottee is liable to pay the company the minimum amount which should have been received in respect of the share under subsection (1) (less the value of any consideration actually applied in payment up, to any extent, of the share and any premium on it), with interest at the appropriate rate.

(5)   Subsections (3) and (4) do not apply to the allotment of bonus shares, unless the allottee knew or ought to have known the shares were allotted in contravention of subsection (1).

102 Restriction on payment by long-term undertaking

(1)   A public company shall not allot shares as fully or partly paid up (as to their nominal value or any premium on them) otherwise than in cash if the consideration for the allotment is or includes an undertaking which is to be, or may be, performed more than 5 years after the date of the allotment.

(2)   If a company allots shares in contravention of subsection (1), the allottee is liable to pay the company an amount equal to the aggregate of their nominal value and the whole of any premium (or, if the case so requires, so much of that aggregate as is treated as paid up by the undertaking), with interest at the appropriate rate.

(3)   Where a contract for the allotment of shares does not contravene subsection (1), any variation of the contract which has the effect that the contract would have contravened the subsection, if the terms of the contract as varied had been its original terms, is void.

(4)   Subsection (3) applies also to the variation by a public company of the terms of a contract entered into before the company was re-registered as a public company.

(5)   The following subsection applies where a public company allots shares for a consideration which consists of or includes (in accordance with subsection (1)) an undertaking which is to be performed within 5 years of the allotment, but the undertaking is not performed within the period allowed by the contract for the allotment of the shares.

(6)   The allottee is then liable to pay the company, at the end of the period so allowed, an amount equal to the aggregate of the nominal value of the shares and the whole of any premium (or, if the case so requires, so much of that aggregate as is treated as paid up by the undertaking), with interest at the appropriate rate.

(7)   A reference in this section to a contract for the allotment of shares includes an ancillary contract relating to payment in respect of them.

103 Non-cash consideration to be valued before allotment

(1)   A public company shall not allot shares as fully or partly paid up (as to their nominal value or any premium on them) otherwise than in cash unless—
  (a)   the consideration for the allotment has been independently valued under section 108; and

    (b)   a report with respect to its value has been made to the company by a person appointed by the company (in accordance with that section) during the 6 months immediately preceding the allotment of the shares; and

    (c)   a copy of the report has been sent to the proposed allottee.

(2)   Where an amount standing to the credit of any of a company's reserve accounts, or of its profit and loss account, is applied in paying up (to any extent) any shares allotted to members of the company or any premiums on shares so allotted, the amount applied does not count as consideration for the allotment, and accordingly subsection (1) does not apply in that case.

(3)   Subsection (1) does not apply to the allotment of shares by a company in connection with an arrangement providing for the allotment of shares in that company on terms that the whole or part of the consideration for the shares allotted is to be provided by the transfer to that company (or the cancellation) of all or some of the shares, or of all or some of the shares of a particular class, in another company (with or without the issue to that company of shares, or of shares of any particular class, in that other company).

(4)   But subsection (3) does not exclude the application of subsection (1) unless under the arrangement it is open to all the holders of the shares in the other company in question (or, where the arrangement applies only to shares of a particular class, to all the holders of shares in that other company, being holders of shares of that class) to take part in the arrangement.

In determining whether that is the case, shares held by or by a nominee of the company proposing to allot the shares in connection with the arrangement, or by or by a nominee of a company which is that company's holding company or subsidiary or a company which is a subsidiary of its holding company, shall be disregarded.

(5)   Subsection (1) also does not apply to the allotment of shares by a company in connection with its proposed merger with another company; that is, where one of the companies proposes to acquire all the assets and liabilities of the other in exchange for the issue of shares or other securities of that one to shareholders of the other, with or without any cash payment to shareholders.

(6)   If a company allots shares in contravention of subsection (1) and either—

    (a)   the allottee has not received the valuer's report required by that subsection to be sent to him; or

    (b)   there has been some other contravention of this section or section 108 which the allottee knew or ought to have known amounted to a contravention,

the allottee is liable to pay the company an amount equal to the aggregate of the nominal value of the shares and the whole of any premium (or, if the case so requires, so much of that aggregate as is treated as paid up by the consideration), with interest at the appropriate rate.

(7)   In this section—

    (a)   "arrangement" means any agreement, scheme or arrangement (including an arrangement sanctioned in accordance with section 425 (company compromise with creditors and members) or [section 110 of the Insolvency Act] (liquidator in winding up accepting shares as consideration for sale of company property)), and

(b) any reference to a company, except where it is or is to be construed as a reference to a public company, includes any body corporate and any body to which letters patent have been issued under the Chartered Companies Act 1837.

NOTES
Sub-s (7): words in square brackets substituted, subject to transitional provisions, by the Insolvency Act 1986, ss 437, 439(1), Sch 11, Sch 13, Part I.

104 Transfer to public company of non-cash asset in initial period

(1) A public company formed as such shall not, unless the conditions of this section have been complied with, enter into an agreement with a person for the transfer by him during the initial period of one or more non-cash assets to the company or another, if—

(a) that person is a subscriber to the company's memorandum, and

(b) the consideration for the transfer to be given by the company is equal in value at the time of the agreement to one-tenth or more of the company's nominal share capital issued at that time.

(2) The "initial period" for this purpose is 2 years beginning with the date of the company being issued with a certificate under section 117 (or the previous corresponding provision) that it was entitled to do business.

(3) This section applies also to a company re-registered as a public company (except one re-registered under section 8 of the Companies Act 1980 or section 2 of the Consequential Provisions Act), or registered under section 685 (joint stock company) or the previous corresponding provision; but in that case—

(a) there is substituted a reference in subsection (1)(a) to a person who is a member of the company on the date of registration or re-registration, and

(b) the initial period is then 2 years beginning with that date.

In this subsection the reference to a company re-registered as a public company includes a private company so re-registered which was a public company before it was a private company.

(4) The conditions of this section are as follows—

(a) the consideration to be received by the company, and any consideration other than cash to be given by the company, must have been independently valued under section 109;

(b) a report with respect to the consideration to be so received and given must have been made to the company in accordance with that section during the 6 months immediately preceding the date of the agreement;

(c) the terms of the agreement must have been approved by an ordinary resolution of the company; and

(d) not later than the giving of the notice of the meeting at which the resolution is proposed, copies of the resolution and report must have been circulated to the members of the company entitled to receive the notice and, if the person with whom the agreement in question is proposed to be made is not then a member of the company so entitled, to that person.

(5)　In subsection (4)(a)—
  (a)　the reference to the consideration to be received by the company is to the asset to be transferred to it or the advantage to the company of the asset's transfer to another person; and
  (b)　the specified condition is without prejudice to any requirement to value any consideration for purposes of section 103.

(6)　In the case of the following agreements, this section does not apply—
  (a)　where it is part of the company's ordinary business to acquire, or arrange for other persons to acquire, assets of a particular description, an agreement entered into by the company in the ordinary course of its business for the transfer of an asset of that description to it or to such a person, as the case may be;
  (b)　an agreement entered into by the company under the supervision of the court, or of an officer authorised by the court for the purpose, for the transfer of an asset to the company or to another.

105 Agreements contravening s 104

(1)　The following subsection applies if a public company enters into an agreement contravening section 104, the agreement being made with the person referred to in subsection (1)(a) or (as the case may be) subsection (3) of that section, and either—
  (a)　that person has not received the valuer's report required for compliance with the conditions of the section, or
  (b)　there has been some other contravention of the section or of section 108(1), (2) or (5) or section 109, which he knew or ought to have known amounted to a contravention.

(2)　The company is then entitled to recover from that person any consideration given by it under the agreement, or an amount equal to the value of the consideration at the time of the agreement; and the agreement, so far as not carried out, is void.

(3)　However, if the agreement is or includes an agreement for the allotment of shares in the company, then—
  (a)　whether or not the agreement also contravenes section 103, subsection (2) above does not apply to it in so far as it is for the allotment of shares; and
  (b)　the allottee is liable to pay the company an amount equal to the aggregate of the nominal value of the shares and the whole of any premium (or, if the case so requires, so much of that aggregate as is treated as paid up by the consideration), with interest at the appropriate rate.

106 Shares issued to subscribers of memorandum

Shares taken by a subscriber to the memorandum of a public company in pursuance of an undertaking of his in the memorandum, and any premium on the shares, shall be paid up in cash.

Valuation provisions

108 Valuation and report (s 103)

(1)   The valuation and report required by section 103 (or, where applicable, section 44) shall be made by an independent person, that is to say a person qualified at the time of the report to be appointed, or continue to be, an auditor of the company.

(2)   However, where it appears to the independent person (from here on referred to as "the valuer") to be reasonable for the valuation of the consideration, or part of it, to be made (or for him to accept such a valuation) by another person who—
  (a)   appears to him to have the requisite knowledge and experience to value the consideration or that part of it; and
  (b)   is not an officer or servant of the company or any other body corporate which is that company's subsidiary or holding company or a subsidiary of that company's holding company or a partner or employee of such an officer or servant,

he may arrange for or accept such a valuation, together with a report which will enable him to make his own report under this section and provide the note required by subsection (6) below.

(3)   The reference in subsection (2)(b) to an officer or servant does not include an auditor.

(4)   The valuer's report shall state—
  (a)   the nominal value of the shares to be wholly or partly paid for by the consideration in question;
  (b)   the amount of any premium payable on the shares;
  (c)   the description of the consideration and, as respects so much of the consideration as he himself has valued, a description of that part of the consideration, the method used to value it and the date of the valuation;
  (d)   the extent to which the nominal value of the shares and any premium are to be treated as paid up—
    (i)   by the consideration;
    (ii)   in cash.

(5)   Where the consideration or part of it is valued by a person other than the valuer himself, the latter's report shall state that fact and shall also—
  (a)   state the former's name and what knowledge and experience he has to carry out the valuation, and
  (b)   describe so much of the consideration as was valued by the other person, and the method used to value it, and specify the date of the valuation.

(6)   The valuer's report shall contain or be accompanied by a note by him—
  (a)   in the case of a valuation made by a person other than himself, that it appeared to himself reasonable to arrange for it to be so made or to accept a valuation so made;
  (b)   whoever made the valuation, that the method of valuation was reasonable in all the circumstances;
  (c)   that it appears to the valuer that there has been no material change in the value of the consideration in question since the valuation; and

(d) that on the basis of the valuation the value of the consideration, together with any cash by which the nominal value of the shares or any premium payable on them is to be paid up, is not less than so much of the aggregate of the nominal value and the whole of any such premium as is treated as paid up by the consideration and any such cash.

(7) Where the consideration to be valued is accepted partly in payment up of the nominal value of the shares and any premium and partly for some other consideration given by the company, section 103 (and, where applicable, section 44) and the foregoing provisions of this section apply as if references to the consideration accepted by the company included the proportion of that consideration which is properly attributable to the payment up of that value and any premium; and—

(a) the valuer shall carry out, or arrange for, such other valuations as will enable him to determine that proportion; and

(b) his report shall state what valuations have been made under this subsection and also the reason for, and method and date of, any such valuation and any other matters which may be relevant to that determination.

109 Valuation and report (s 104)

(1) Subsections (1) to (3) and (5) of section 108 apply also as respects the valuation and report for the purposes of section 104.

(2) The valuer's report for those purposes shall—

(a) state the consideration to be received by the company, describing the asset in question (specifying the amount to be received in cash) and the consideration to be given by the company (specifying the amount to be given in cash);

(b) state the method and date of valuation;

(c) contain or be accompanied by a note as to the matters mentioned in section 108(6)(a) to (c); and

(d) contain or be accompanied by a note that on the basis of the valuation the value of the consideration to be received by the company is not less than the value of the consideration to be given by it.

(3) A reference in section 104 or this section to consideration given for the transfer of an asset includes consideration given partly for its transfer; but—

(a) the value of any consideration partly so given is to be taken as the proportion of the consideration properly attributable to its transfer;

(b) the valuer shall carry out or arrange for such valuations of anything else as will enable him to determine that proportion; and

(c) his report for purposes of section 104 shall state what valuation has been made under this subsection and also the reason for and method and date of any such valuation and any other matters which may be relevant to that determination.

110 Entitlement of valuer to full disclosure

(1) A person carrying out a valuation or making a report under section 103 or 104, with respect to any consideration proposed to be accepted or given by a company, is

entitled to require from the officers of the company such information and explanation as he thinks necessary to enable him to carry out the valuation or make the report and provide a note under section 108(6) or (as the case may be) section 109(2)(c).

(2) A person who knowingly or recklessly makes a statement which—
 (a) is misleading, false or deceptive in a material particular, and
 (b) is a statement to which this subsection applies,

is guilty of an offence and liable to imprisonment or a fine, or both.

(3) Subsection (2) applies to any statement made (whether orally or in writing) to a person carrying out a valuation or making a report under section 108 or 109, being a statement which conveys or purports to convey any information or explanation which that person requires, or is entitled to require, under subsection (1) of this section.

111 Matters to be communicated to registrar

(1) A company to which a report is made under section 108 as to the value of any consideration for which, or partly for which, it proposes to allot shares shall deliver a copy of the report to the registrar of companies for registration at the same time that it files the return of the allotments of those shares under section 88.

(2) A company which has passed a resolution under section 104 with respect to the transfer of an asset shall, within 15 days of so doing, deliver to the registrar of companies a copy of the resolution together with the valuer's report required by that section.

(3) If default is made in complying with subsection (1), every officer of the company who is in default is liable to a fine and, for continued contravention, to a daily default fine; but this is subject to the same exception as is made by section 88(6) (relief on application to the court) in the case of default in complying with that section.

(4) If a company fails to comply with subsection (2), it and every officer of it who is in default is liable to a fine and, for continued contravention, to a daily default fine.

Other matters arising out of allotment, &c

[111A Right to damages, &c not affected]

[A person is not debarred from obtaining damages or other compensation from a company by reason only of his holding or having held shares in the company or any right to apply or subscribe for shares or to be included in the company's register in respect of shares.]

NOTES

Inserted by the Companies Act 1989, s 131(1).

112 Liability of subsequent holders of shares allotted

(1)   If a person becomes a holder of shares in respect of which—
  (a)   there has been a contravention of section 99, 100, 101 or 103; and
  (b)   by virtue of that contravention, another is liable to pay any amount under the section contravened,

that person is also liable to pay that amount (jointly and severally with any other person so liable), unless he is exempted from liability by subsection (3) below.

(2)   If a company enters into an agreement in contravention of section 104 and—
  (a)   the agreement is or includes an agreement for the allotment of shares in the company; and
  (b)   a person becomes a holder of shares allotted under the agreement; and
  (c)   by virtue of the agreement and allotment under it, another person is liable to pay any amount under section 105,

the person who becomes the holder of the shares is also liable to pay that amount (jointly and severally with any other person so liable), unless he is exempted from liability by the following subsection; and this applies whether or not the agreement also contravenes section 103.

(3)   A person otherwise liable under subsection (1) or (2) is exempted from that liability if either—
  (a)   he is a purchaser for value and, at the time of the purchase, he did not have actual notice of the contravention concerned; or
  (b)   he derived title to the shares (directly or indirectly) from a person who became a holder of them after the contravention and was not liable under subsection (1) or (as the case may be) subsection (2).

(4)   References in this section to a holder, in relation to shares in a company, include any person who has an unconditional right to be included in the company's register of members in respect of those shares or to have an instrument of transfer of the shares executed in his favour.

(5)   As subsections (1) and (3) apply in relation to the contraventions there mentioned, they also apply—
  (a)   to a contravention of section 102; and
  (b)   to a failure to carry out a term of a contract as mentioned in subsections (5) and (6) of that section.

113 Relief in respect of certain liabilities under ss 99 ff

(1)   Where a person is liable to a company under—
  (a)   section 99, 102, 103 or 105;
  (b)   section 112(1) by reference to a contravention of section 99 or 103; or
  (c)   section 112(2) or (5),

in relation to payment in respect of any shares in the company, or is liable by virtue of an undertaking given to it in, or in connection with, payment for any such shares, the person so liable may make an application to the court to be exempted in whole or in part from the liability.

(2) If the liability mentioned in subsection (1) arises in relation to payment in respect of any shares, the court may, on an application under that subsection, exempt the applicant from the liability only—

    (a) if and to the extent that it appears to the court just and equitable to do so having regard to the matters mentioned in the following subsection,

    (b) if and to the extent that it appears to the court just and equitable to do so in respect of any interest which he is liable to pay the company under any of the relevant sections.

(3) The matters to be taken into account by the court under subsection (2)(a) are—

    (a) whether the applicant has paid, or is liable to pay, any amount in respect of any other liability arising in relation to those shares under any of the relevant sections, or of any liability arising by virtue of any undertaking given in or in connection with payment for those shares;

    (b) whether any person other than the applicant has paid or is likely to pay (whether in pursuance of an order of the court or otherwise) any such amount; and

    (c) whether the applicant or any other person has performed in whole or in part, or is likely so to perform, any such undertaking, or has done or is likely to do any other thing in payment or part payment for the shares.

(4) Where the liability arises by virtue of an undertaking given to the company in, or in connection with, payment for shares in it, the court may, on an application under subsection (1), exempt the applicant from the liability only if and to the extent that it appears to the court just and equitable to do so having regard to—

    (a) whether the applicant has paid or is liable to pay any amount in respect of liability arising in relation to the shares under any of the provisions mentioned in that subsection; and

    (b) whether any person other than the applicant has paid or is likely to pay (whether in pursuance of an order of the court or otherwise) any such amount.

(5) In determining whether it should exempt the applicant in whole or in part from any liability, the court shall have regard to the following overriding principles, namely—

    (a) that a company which has allotted shares should receive money or money's worth at least equal in value to the aggregate of the nominal value of those shares and the whole of any premium or, if the case so requires, so much of that aggregate as is treated as paid up; and

    (b) subject to this, that where such a company would, if the court did not grant the exemption, have more than one remedy against a particular person, it should be for the company to decide which remedy it should remain entitled to pursue.

(6) If a person brings proceedings against another ("the contributor") for a contribution in respect of liability to a company arising under any of sections 99 to 105 or 112, and it appears to the court that the contributor is liable to make such a contribution, the court may exercise the powers of the following subsection.

(7)   The court may, if and to the extent that it appears to it, having regard to the respective culpability (in respect of the liability to the company) of the contributor and the person bringing the proceedings, that it is just and equitable to do so—

  (a)   exempt the contributor in whole or in part from his liability to make such a contribution; or

  (b)   order the contributor to make a larger contribution than, but for this subsection, he would be liable to make.

(8)   Where a person is liable to a company under section 105(2), the court may, on application, exempt him in whole or in part from that liability if and to the extent that it appears to the court just and equitable to do so having regard to any benefit accruing to the company by virtue of anything done by him towards the carrying out of the agreement mentioned in that subsection.

114 Penalty for contravention

If a company contravenes any of the provisions of sections 99 to 104 and 106 the company and any officer of it who is in default is liable to a fine.

115 Undertakings to do work, etc

(1)   Subject to section 113, an undertaking given by any person, in or in connection with payment for shares in a company, to do work or perform services or to do any other thing, if it is enforceable by the company apart from this Act, is so enforceable notwithstanding that there has been a contravention in relation to it of section 99, 102 or 103.

(2)   Where such an undertaking is given in contravention of section 104 in respect of the allotment of shares, it is so enforceable notwithstanding the contravention.

PART V

SHARE CAPITAL, ITS INCREASE, MAINTENANCE AND REDUCTION

Chapter I
General Provisions about Share Capital

117 Public company share capital requirements

(1)   A company registered as a public company on its original incorporation shall not do business or exercise any borrowing powers unless the registrar of companies has issued it with a certificate under this section or the company is re-registered as a private company.

(2)   The registrar shall issue a company with such a certificate if, on an application made to him by the company in the prescribed form, he is satisfied that the nominal value of the company's allotted share capital is not less than the authorised minimum, and there is delivered to him a statutory declaration complying with the following subsection. [This subsection is subject to subsection (3A).]

(3)   The statutory declaration must be in the prescribed form and be signed by a director or secretary of the company; and it must—

(a) state that the nominal value of the company's allotted share capital is not less than the authorised minimum;

(b) specify the amount paid up, at the time of the application, on the allotted share capital of the company;

(c) specify the amount, or estimated amount, of the company's preliminary expenses and the persons by whom any of those expenses have been paid or are payable; and

(d) specify any amount or benefit paid or given, or intended to be paid or given, to any promoter of the company, and the consideration for the payment or benefit.

[(3A) In place of the statutory declaration referred to in subsection (2), there may be delivered to the registrar of companies using electronic communications a statement made by a director or secretary of the company complying with the requirements of subsection (3)(a) to (d).]

(4) For the purposes of subsection (2), a share allotted in pursuance of an employees' share scheme may not be taken into account in determining the nominal value of the company's allotted share capital unless it is paid up at least as to one-quarter of the nominal value of the share and the whole of any premium on the share.

(5) The registrar may accept a statutory declaration [or statement] delivered to him under this section as sufficient evidence of the matters stated in it.

(6) A certificate under this section in respect of a company is conclusive evidence that the company is entitled to do business and exercise any borrowing powers.

(7) If a company does business or exercises borrowing powers in contravention of this section, the company and any officer of it who is in default is liable to a fine.

[(7A) Any person who makes a false statement under subsection (3A) which he knows to be false or does not believe to be true is liable to imprisonment or a fine, or both.]

(8) Nothing in this section affects the validity of any transaction entered into by a company; but, if a company enters into a transaction in contravention of this section and fails to comply with its obligations in that connection within 21 days from being called upon to do so, the directors of the company are jointly and severally liable to indemnify the other party to the transaction in respect of any loss or damage suffered by him by reason of the company's failure to comply with those obligations.

NOTES

Sub-s (2): words "This subsection is subject to subsection (3A)." in square brackets inserted by SI 2000/3373, art 9(1), (2).
Date in force: 22 December 2000: see SI 2000/3373, art 1(1).
Sub-s (3A): inserted by SI 2000/3373, art 9(1), (3).
Date in force: 22 December 2000: see SI 2000/3373, art 1(1).
Sub-s (5): words "or statement" in square brackets inserted by SI 2000/3373, art 9(1), (4).
Date in force: 22 December 2000: see SI 2000/3373, art 1(1).
Sub-s (7A): inserted by SI 2000/3373, art 9(1), (5).
Date in force: 22 December 2000: see SI 2000/3373, art 1(1).

118 The authorised minimum

(1)   In this Act, "the authorised minimum" means £50,000, or such other sum as the Secretary of State may by order made by statutory instrument specify instead.

(2)   An order under this section which increases the authorised minimum may—

(a)   require any public company having an allotted share capital of which the nominal value is less than the amount specified in the order as the authorised minimum to increase that value to not less than that amount or make application to be re-registered as a private company;

(b)   make, in connection with any such requirement, provision for any of the matters from which provision is made by this Act relating to a company's registration, re-registration or change of name, to payment for any share comprised in a company's capital and to offers of shares in or debentures of a company to the public, including provision as to the consequences (whether in criminal law or otherwise) of a failure to comply with any requirement of the order; and

(c)   contain such supplemental and transitional provisions as the Secretary of State thinks appropriate, make different provision for different cases and, in particular, provide for any provision of the order to come into operation on different days for different purposes.

(3)   An order shall not be made under this section unless a draft of it has been laid before Parliament and approved by resolution of each House.

121 Alteration of share capital (limited companies)

(1)   A company limited by shares or a company limited by guarantee and having a share capital, if so authorised by its articles, may alter the conditions of its memorandum in any of the following ways.

(2)   The company may—

(a)   increase its share capital by new shares of such amount as it thinks expedient;

(b)   consolidate and divide all or any of its share capital into shares of larger amount than its existing shares;

(c)   convert all or any of its paid-up shares into stock, and re-convert that stock into paid-up shares of any denomination;

(d)   sub-divide its shares, or any of them, into shares of smaller amount than is fixed by the memorandum (but subject to the following subsection);

(e)   cancel shares which, at the date of the passing of the resolution to cancel them, have not been taken or agreed to be taken by any person, and diminish the amount of the company's share capital by the amount of the shares so cancelled.

(3)   In any sub-division under subsection (2)(d) the proportion between the amount paid and the amount, if any, unpaid on each reduced share must be the same as it was in the case of the share from which the reduced share is derived.

(4)   The powers conferred by this section must be exercised by the company in general meeting.

(5)   A cancellation of shares under this section does not for purposes of this Act constitute a reduction of share capital.

122 Notice to registrar of alteration

(1)   If a company having a share capital has—
  (a)   consolidated and divided its share capital into shares of larger amount than its existing shares; or
  (b)   converted any shares into stock; or
  (c)   re-converted stock into shares; or
  (d)   sub-divided its shares or any of them; or
  (e)   redeemed any redeemable shares; or
  (f)   cancelled any shares (otherwise than in connection with a reduction of share capital under section 135),

it shall within one month after so doing give notice in the prescribed form to the registrar of companies, specifying (as the case may be) the shares consolidated, divided, converted, sub-divided, redeemed or cancelled, or the stock re-converted.

(2)   If default is made in complying with this section, the company and every officer of it who is in default is liable to a fine and, for continued contravention, to a daily default fine.

123 Notice to registrar of increased share capital

(1)   If a company having a share capital (whether or not its shares have been converted into stock) increases its share capital beyond the registered capital, it shall within 15 days after the passing of the resolution authorising the increase, give to the registrar of companies notice of the increase, and the registrar shall record the increase.

(2)   The notice must include such particulars as may be prescribed with respect to the classes of shares affected and the conditions subject to which the new shares have been or are to be issued.

(3)   There shall be forwarded to the registrar together with the notice a printed copy of the resolution authorising the increase, or a copy of the resolution in some other form approved by the registrar.

(4)   If default is made in complying with this section, the company and every officer of it who is in default is liable to a fine and, for continued contravention, to a daily default fine.

Chapter II
Class Rights

125 Variation of class rights

(1)   This section is concerned with the variation of the rights attached to any class of shares in a company whose share capital is divided into shares of different classes.

(2)   Where the rights are attached to a class of shares otherwise than by the company's memorandum, and the company's articles do not contain provision with respect to the variation of the rights, those rights may be varied if, but only if—

(a)   the holders of three-quarters in nominal value of the issued shares of that class consent in writing to the variation; or

(b)   an extraordinary resolution passed at a separate general meeting of the holders of that class sanctions the variation;

and any requirement (howsoever imposed) in relation to the variation of those rights is complied with to the extent that it is not comprised in paragraphs (a) and (b) above.

(3)   Where—

(a)   the rights are attached to a class of shares by the memorandum or otherwise;

(b)   the memorandum or articles contain provision for the variation of those rights; and

(c)   the variation of those rights is connected with the giving, variation, revocation or renewal of an authority for allotment under section 80 or with a reduction of the company's share capital under section 135;

those rights shall not be varied unless—

(i)   the condition mentioned in subsection (2)(a) or (b) above is satisfied; and

(ii)   any requirement of the memorandum or articles in relation to the variation of rights of that class is complied with to the extent that it is not comprised in that condition.

(4)   If the rights are attached to a class of shares in the company by the memorandum or otherwise and—

(a)   where they are so attached by the memorandum, the articles contain provision with respect to their variation which had been included in the articles at the time of the company's original incorporation; or

(b)   where they are so attached otherwise, the articles contain such provision (whenever first so included),

and in either case the variation is not connected as mentioned in subsection (3)(c), those rights may only be varied in accordance with that provision of the articles.

(5)   If the rights are attached to a class of shares by the memorandum, and the memorandum and articles do not contain provision with respect to the variation of those rights, those rights may be varied if all the members of the company agree to the variation.

(6)   The provisions of section 369 (length of notice for calling company meetings), section 370 (general provisions as to meetings and votes), and sections 376 and 377 (circulation of members' resolutions) and the provisions of the articles relating to general meetings shall, so far as applicable, apply in relation to any meeting of shareholders required by this section or otherwise to take place in connection with the variation of the rights attached to a class of shares, and shall so apply with the necessary modifications and subject to the following provisions, namely—

(a)   the necessary quorum at any such meeting other than an adjourned meeting shall be two persons holding or representing by proxy at least one-third in nominal value of the issued shares of the class in question and at an adjourned meeting one person holding shares of the class in question or his proxy;

(b) any holder of shares of the class in question present in person or by proxy may demand a poll.

(7) Any alteration of a provision contained in a company's articles for the variation of the rights attached to a class of shares, or the insertion of any such provision into the articles, is itself to be treated as a variation of those rights.

(8) In this section and (except where the context otherwise requires) in any provision for the variation of the rights attached to a class of shares contained in a company's memorandum or articles, references to the variation of those rights are to be read as including references to their abrogation.

126 Saving for court's powers under other provisions

Nothing in subsections (2) to (5) of section 125 derogates from the powers of the court under the following sections of this Act, namely—

sections 4 to 6 (company resolution to alter objects),

section 54 (litigated objection to public company becoming private by re-registration),

section 425 (court control of company compromising with members and creditors),

section 427 (company reconstruction or amalgamation),

sections 459 to 461 (protection of minorities).

127 Shareholders' right to object to variation

(1) This section applies if, in the case of a company whose share capital is divided into different classes of shares—

(a) provision is made by the memorandum or articles for authorising the variation of the rights attached to any class of shares in the company, subject to—

(i) the consent of any specified proportion of the holders of the issued shares of that class, or

(ii) the sanction of a resolution passed at a separate meeting of the holders of those shares,

and in pursuance of that provision the rights attached to any such class of shares are at any time varied; or

(b) the rights attached to any class of shares in the company are varied under section 125(2).

(2) The holders of not less in the aggregate than 15 per cent of the issued shares of the class in question (being persons who did not consent to or vote in favour of the resolution for the variation), may apply to the court to have the variation cancelled; and if such an application is made, the variation has no effect unless and until it is confirmed by the court.

(3) Application to the court must be made within 21 days after the date on which the consent was given or the resolution was passed (as the case may be), and may

be made on behalf of the shareholders entitled to make the application by such one or more of their number as they may appoint in writing for the purpose.

(4)   The court, after hearing the applicant and any other persons who apply to the court to be heard and appear to the court to be interested in the application, may, if satisfied having regard to all the circumstances of the case, that the variation would unfairly prejudice the shareholders of the class represented by the applicant, disallow the variation and shall, if not satisfied, confirm it.

The decision of the court on any such application is final.

(5)   The company shall within 15 days after the making of an order by the court on such an application forward a copy of the order to the registrar of companies; and, if default is made in complying with this provision, the company and every officer of it who is in default is liable to a fine and, for continued contravention, to a daily default fine.

(6)   "Variation", in this section, includes abrogation; and "varied" is to be construed accordingly.

128 Registration of particulars of special rights

(1)   If a company allots shares with rights which are not stated in its memorandum or articles, or in any resolution or agreement which is required by section 380 to be sent to the registrar of companies, the company shall deliver to the registrar of companies, within one month from allotting the shares, a statement in the prescribed form containing particulars of those rights.

(2)   This does not apply if the shares are in all respects uniform with shares previously allotted; and shares are not for this purpose to be treated as different from shares previously allotted by reason only that the former do not carry the same rights to dividends as the latter during the 12 months immediately following the former's allotment.

(3)   Where the rights attached to any shares of a company are varied otherwise than by an amendment of the company's memorandum or articles or by a resolution or agreement subject to section 380, the company shall within one month from the date on which the variation is made deliver to the registrar of companies a statement in the prescribed form containing particulars of the variation.

(4)   Where a company (otherwise than by any such amendment, resolution or agreement as is mentioned above) assigns a name or other designation, or a new name or other designation, to any class of its shares, it shall within one month from doing so deliver to the registrar of companies a notice in the prescribed form giving particulars of the name or designation so assigned.

(5)   If a company fails to comply with this section, the company and every officer of it who is in default is liable to a fine and, for continued contravention, to a daily default fine.

Chapter III
Share Premiums

130 Application of share premiums

(1)   If a company issues shares at a premium, whether for cash or otherwise, a sum equal to the aggregate amount or value of the premiums on those shares shall be transferred to an account called "the share premium account".

(2)   The share premium account may be applied by the company in paying up unissued shares to be allotted to members as fully paid bonus shares, or in writing off—
  (a)   the company's preliminary expenses; or
  (b)   the expenses of, or the commission paid or discount allowed on, any issue of shares or debentures of the company,

or in providing for the premium payable on redemption of debentures of the company.

(3)   Subject to this, the provisions of this Act relating to the reduction of a company's share capital apply as if the share premium account were part of its paid up share capital.

(4)   Sections 131 and 132 below give relief from the requirements of this section, and in those sections references to the issuing company are to the company issuing shares as above mentioned.

Chapter IV
Reduction of Share Capital

135 Special resolution for reduction of share capital

(1)   Subject to confirmation by the court, a company limited by shares or a company limited by guarantee and having a share capital may, if so authorised by its articles, by special resolution reduce its share capital in any way.

(2)   In particular, and without prejudice to subsection (1), the company may—
  (a)   extinguish or reduce the liability on any of its shares in respect of share capital not paid up; or
  (b)   either with or without extinguishing or reducing liability on any of its shares, cancel any paid-up share capital which is lost or unrepresented by available assets; or
  (c)   either with or without extinguishing or reducing liability on any of its shares, pay off any paid-up share capital which is in excess of the company's wants;

and the company may, if and so far as is necessary, alter its memorandum by reducing the amount of its share capital and of its shares accordingly.

(3)   A special resolution under this section is in this Act referred to as "a resolution for reducing share capital".

136 Application to court for order of confirmation

(1)   Where a company has passed a resolution for reducing share capital, it may apply to the court for an order confirming the reduction.

(2)   If the proposed reduction of share capital involves either—
   (a)   diminution of liability in respect of unpaid share capital; or
   (b)   the payment to a shareholder of any paid-up share capital,

and in any other case if the court so directs, the next three subsections have effect, but subject throughout to subsection (6).

(3)   Every creditor of the company who at the date fixed by the court is entitled to any debt or claim which, if that date were the commencement of the winding up of the company, would be admissible in proof against the company is entitled to object to the reduction of capital.

(4)   The court shall settle a list of creditors entitled to object, and for that purpose—
   (a)   shall ascertain, as far as possible without requiring an application from any creditor, the names of those creditors and the nature and amount of their debts or claims; and
   (b)   may publish notices fixing a day or days within which creditors not entered on the list are to claim to be so entered or are to be excluded from the right of objecting to the reduction of capital.

(5)   If a creditor entered on the list whose debt or claim is not discharged or has not determined does not consent to the reduction, the court may, if it thinks fit, dispense with the consent of that creditor, on the company securing payment of his debt or claim by appropriating (as the court may direct) the following amount—
   (a)   if the company admits the full amount of the debt or claim or, though not admitting it, is willing to provide for it, then the full amount of the debt or claim;
   (b)   if the company does not admit, and is not willing to provide for, the full amount of the debt or claim, or if the amount is contingent or not ascertained, then an amount fixed by the court after the like enquiry and adjudication as if the company were being wound up by the court.

(6)   If a proposed reduction of share capital involves either the diminution of any liability in respect of unpaid share capital or the payment to any shareholder of any paid-up share capital, the court may, if having regard to any special circumstances of the case it thinks proper to do so, direct that subsections (3) to (5) of this section shall not apply as regards any class or any classes of creditors.

137 Court order confirming reduction

(1)   The court, if satisfied with respect to every creditor of the company who under section 136 is entitled to object to the reduction of capital that either—
   (a)   his consent to the reduction has been obtained; or
   (b)   his debt or claim has been discharged or has determined, or has been secured,

may make an order confirming the reduction on such terms and conditions as it thinks fit.

(2)   Where the court so orders, it may also—

(a)   if for any special reason it thinks proper to do so, make an order directing that the company shall, during such period (commencing on or at any time after the date of the order) as is specified in the order, add to its name as its last words the words "and reduced"; and

(b)   make an order requiring the company to publish (as the court directs) the reasons for reduction of capital or such other information in regard to it as the court thinks expedient with a view to giving proper information to the public and (if the court thinks fit) the causes which led to the reduction.

(3)   Where a company is ordered to add to its name the words "and reduced", those words are, until the expiration of the period specified in the order, deemed to be part of the company's name.

139 Public company reducing capital below authorised minimum

(1)   This section applies where the court makes an order confirming a reduction of a public company's capital which has the effect of bringing the nominal value of its allotted share capital below the authorised minimum.

(2)   The registrar of companies shall not register the order under section 138 unless the court otherwise directs, or the company is first re-registered as a private company.

(3)   The court may authorise the company to be so re-registered without its having passed the special resolution required by section 53; and where that authority is given, the court shall specify in the order the alterations in the company's memorandum and articles to be made in connection with that re-registration.

(4)   The company may then be re-registered as a private company, if an application in the prescribed form and signed by a director or secretary of the company is delivered to the registrar, together with a printed copy of the memorandum and articles as altered by the court's order.

(5)   On receipt of such an application, the registrar shall retain it and the other documents delivered with it and issue the company with a certificate of incorporation appropriate to a company that is not a public company; and—

(a)   the company by virtue of the issue of the certificate becomes a private company, and the alterations in the memorandum and articles set out in the court's order take effect; and

(b)   the certificate is conclusive evidence that the requirements of this section in respect of re-registration and of matters precedent and incidental thereto have been complied with, and that the company is a private company.

Chapter V
Maintenance of Capital

142 Duty of directors on serious loss of capital

(1)   Where the net assets of a public company are half or less of its called-up share capital, the directors shall, not later than 28 days from the earliest day on which that fact is known to a director of the company, duly convene an extraordinary general meeting of the company for a date not later than 56 days from that day for the purpose of considering whether any, and if so what, steps should be taken to deal with the situation.

(2)   If there is a failure to convene an extraordinary general meeting as required by subsection (1), each of the directors of the company who—
   (a)   knowingly and wilfully authorises or permits the failure, or
   (b)   after the expiry of the period during which that meeting should have been convened, knowingly and wilfully authorises or permits the failure to continue,

is liable to a fine.

(3)   Nothing in this section authorises the consideration, at a meeting convened in pursuance of subsection (1), of any matter which could not have been considered at that meeting apart from this section.

143 General rule against company acquiring own shares

(1)   Subject to the following provisions, a company limited by shares or limited by guarantee and having a share capital shall not acquire its own shares, whether by purchase, subscription or otherwise.

(2)   If a company purports to act in contravention of this section, the company is liable to a fine, and every officer of the company who is in default is liable to imprisonment or a fine, or both; and the purported acquisition is void.

(3)   A company limited by shares may acquire any of its own fully paid shares otherwise than for valuable consideration; and subsection (1) does not apply in relation to—
   (a)   the redemption or purchase of shares in accordance with Chapter VII of this Part,
   (b)   the acquisition of shares in a reduction of capital duly made,
   (c)   the purchase of shares in pursuance of an order of the court under section 5 (alteration of objects), section 54 (litigated objection to resolution for company to be re-registered as private) or Part XVII (relief to members unfairly prejudiced), or
   (d)   the forfeiture of shares, or the acceptance of shares surrendered in lieu, in pursuance of the articles, for failure to pay any sum payable in respect of the shares.

146 Treatment of shares held by or for public company

(1) Except as provided by section 148, the following applies to a public company—

    (a) where shares in the company are forfeited, or surrendered to the company in lieu, in pursuance of the articles, for failure to pay any sum payable in respect of the shares;

    [(aa) where shares in the company are surrendered to the company in pursuance of section 102C(1)(b) of the Building Societies Act 1986;]

    (b) where shares in the company are acquired by it (otherwise than by any of the methods mentioned in section 143(3)(a) to (d)) and the company has a beneficial interest in the shares;

    (c) where the nominee of the company acquires shares in the company from a third person without financial assistance being given directly or indirectly by the company and the company has a beneficial interest in the shares; or

    (d) where a person acquires shares in the company with financial assistance given to him directly or indirectly by the company for the purpose of or in connection with the acquisition, and the company has a beneficial interest in the shares.

Schedule 2 to this Act has effect for the interpretation of references in this subsection to the company having a beneficial interest in shares.

(2) Unless the shares or any interest of the company in them are previously disposed of, the company must, not later than the end of the relevant period from their forfeiture or surrender or, in a case within subsection (1)(b), (c) or (d), their acquisition—

    (a) cancel them and diminish the amount of the share capital by the nominal value of the shares cancelled, and

    (b) where the effect of cancelling the shares will be that the nominal value of the company's allotted share capital is brought below the authorised minimum, apply for re-registration as a private company, stating the effect of the cancellation.

(3) For this purpose "the relevant period" is—

    (a) 3 years in the case of shares forfeited or surrendered to the company in lieu of forfeiture, or acquired as mentioned in subsection (1)(b) or (c);

    (b) one year in the case of shares acquired as mentioned in subsection (1)(d).

(4) The company and, in a case within subsection (1)(c) or (d), the company's nominee or (as the case may be) the other shareholder must not exercise any voting rights in respect of the shares; and any purported exercise of those rights is void.

NOTES

Sub-s (1): para (aa) inserted, in relation to relation to a transfer of business of a building society in any case where the decision of the board of directors of the society to enter into the transfer in question is made public after 22 January 1997, by the Building Societies Act 1986, s 102C(5).

147 Matters arising out of compliance with s 146(2)

(1)   The directors may take such steps as are requisite to enable the company to carry out its obligations under section 146(2) without complying with sections 135 and 136 (resolution to reduce share capital; application to court for approval).

(2)   The steps taken may include the passing of a resolution to alter the company's memorandum so that it no longer states that the company is to be a public company; and the resolution may make such other alterations in the memorandum as are requisite in the circumstances.

Such a resolution is subject to section 380 (copy to be forwarded to registrar within 15 days).

(3)   The application for re-registration required by section 146(2)(b) must be in the prescribed form and be signed by a director or secretary of the company, and must be delivered to the registrar of companies together with a printed copy of the memorandum and articles of the company as altered by the resolution.

(4)   If the registrar is satisfied that the company may be re-registered under section 146, he shall retain the application and other documents delivered with it and issue the company with a certificate of incorporation appropriate to a company that is not a public company; and—
  (a)   the company by virtue of the issue of the certificate becomes a private company, and the alterations in the memorandum and articles set out in the resolution take effect accordingly, and
  (b)   the certificate is conclusive evidence that the requirements of sections 146 to 148 in respect of re-registration and of matters precedent and incidental to it have been complied with, and that the company is a private company.

150 Charges of public companies on own shares

(1)   A lien or other charge of a public company on its own shares (whether taken expressly or otherwise), except a charge permitted by any of the following subsections, is void.

This is subject to section 6 of the Consequential Provisions Act (saving for charges of old public companies on their own shares).

(2)   In the case of any description of company, a charge on its own shares is permitted if the shares are not fully paid and the charge is for any amount payable in respect of the shares.

(3)   In the case of a company whose ordinary business—
  (a)   includes the lending of money, or
  (b)   consists of the provision of credit or the bailment (in Scotland, hiring) of goods under a hire purchase agreement, or both,

a charge of the company on its own shares is permitted (whether the shares are fully paid or not) if it arises in connection with a transaction entered into by the company in the ordinary course of its business.

(4)   In the case of a company which is re-registered or is registered under section 680 as a public company, a charge on its own shares is permitted if the charge was

in existence immediately before the company's application for re-registration or (as the case may be) registration.

This subsection does not apply in the case of such a company as is referred to in section 6(3) of the Consequential Provisions Act (old public company remaining such after 22nd March 1982, not having applied to be re-registered as public company).

Chapter VI

Financial Assistance by a Company for Acquisition of its Own Shares

Provisions applying to both public and private companies

151 Financial assistance generally prohibited

(1)   Subject to the following provisions of this Chapter, where a person is acquiring or is proposing to acquire shares in a company, it is not lawful for the company or any of its subsidiaries to give financial assistance directly or indirectly for the purpose of that acquisition before or at the same time as the acquisition takes place.

(2)   Subject to those provisions, where a person has acquired shares in a company and any liability has been incurred (by that or any other person), for the purpose of that acquisition, it is not lawful for the company or any of its subsidiaries to give financial assistance directly or indirectly for the purpose of reducing or discharging the liability so incurred.

(3)   If a company acts in contravention of this section, it is liable to a fine, and every officer of it who is in default is liable to imprisonment or a fine, or both.

152 Definitions for this Chapter

(1)   In this Chapter—
  (a)   "financial assistance" means—
      (i)   financial assistance given by way of gift,
      (ii) financial assistance given by way of guarantee, security or indemnity, other than an indemnity in respect of the indemnifier's own neglect or default, or by way of release or waiver,
      (iii) financial assistance given by way of a loan or any other agreement under which any of the obligations of the person giving the assistance are to be fulfilled at a time when in accordance with the agreement any obligation of another party to the agreement remains unfulfilled, or by way of the novation of, or the assignment of rights arising under, a loan or such other agreement, or
      (iv) any other financial assistance given by a company the net assets of which are thereby reduced to a material extent or which has no net assets;
  (b)   "distributable profits", in relation to the giving of any financial assistance—
      (i)   means those profits out of which the company could lawfully make a distribution equal in value to that assistance, and

      (ii) includes, in a case where the financial assistance is or includes a non-cash asset, any profit which, if the company were to make a distribution of that asset, would under section 276 (distributions in kind) be available for that purpose,

    and

  (c) "distribution" has the meaning given by section 263(2).

(2) In subsection (1)(a)(iv), "net assets" means the aggregate of the company's assets, less the aggregate of its liabilities ("liabilities" to include any provision for liabilities or charges within paragraph 89 of Schedule 4).

(3) In this Chapter—

  (a) a reference to a person incurring a liability includes his changing his financial position by making an agreement or arrangement (whether enforceable or unenforceable, and whether made on his own account or with any other person) or by any other means, and

  (b) a reference to a company giving financial assistance for the purpose of reducing or discharging a liability incurred by a person for the purpose of the acquisition of shares includes its giving such assistance for the purpose of wholly or partly restoring his financial position to what it was before the acquisition took place.

153 Transactions not prohibited by s 151

(1) Section 151(1) does not prohibit a company from giving financial assistance for the purpose of an acquisition of shares in it or its holding company if—

  (a) the company's principal purpose in giving that assistance is not to give it for the purpose of any such acquisition, or the giving of the assistance for that purpose is but an incidental part of some larger purpose of the company, and

  (b) the assistance is given in good faith in the interests of the company.

(2) Section 151(2) does not prohibit a company from giving financial assistance if—

  (a) the company's principal purpose in giving the assistance is not to reduce or discharge any liability incurred by a person for the purpose of the acquisition of shares in the company or its holding company, or the reduction or discharge of any such liability is but an incidental part of some larger purpose of the company, and

  (b) the assistance is given in good faith in the interests of the company.

(3) Section 151 does not prohibit—

  (a) a distribution of a company's assets by way of dividend lawfully made or a distribution made in the course of the company's winding up,

  (b) the allotment of bonus shares,

  (c) a reduction of capital confirmed by order of the court under section 137,

  (d) a redemption or purchase of shares made in accordance with Chapter VII of this Part,

  (e) anything done in pursuance of an order of the court under section 425 (compromises and arrangements with creditors and members),

(f)   anything done under an arrangement made in pursuance of [section 110 of the Insolvency Act] (acceptance of shares by liquidator in winding up as consideration for sale of property), or

(g)   anything done under an arrangement made between a company and its creditors which is binding on the creditors by virtue of [Part I of the Insolvency Act].

(4)   Section 151 does not prohibit—

(a)   where the lending of money is part of the ordinary business of the company, the lending of money by the company in the ordinary course of its business,

[(b)   the provision by a company, in good faith in the interests of the company, of financial assistance for the purposes of an employees' share scheme,]

[(bb) without prejudice to paragraph (b), the provision of financial assistance by a company or any of its subsidiaries for the purposes of or in connection with anything done by the company (or [a company in the same group]) for the purpose of enabling or facilitating transactions in shares in the first-mentioned company between, and involving the acquisition of beneficial ownership of those shares by, any of the following persons—

(i)   the bona fide employees or former employees of that company or of another company in the same group; or

(ii)   the wives, husbands, widows, widowers, children or step-children under the age of eighteen of any such employees or former employees,]

(c)   the making by a company of loans to persons (other than directors) employed in good faith by the company with a view to enabling those persons to acquire fully paid shares in the company or its holding company to be held by them by way of beneficial ownership.

[(5)   For the purposes of subsection (4)(bb) a company is in the same group as another company if it is a holding company or subsidiary of that company, or a subsidiary of a holding company of that company.]

NOTES

Sub-s (3): in paras (f), (g) words in square brackets substituted, subject to transitional provisions, by the Insolvency Act 1986, ss 437, 439(1), Sch 11, Sch 13, Part I.

Sub-s (4): para (b) substituted by the Companies Act 1989, s 132; para (bb) inserted by the Financial Services Act 1986, s 196, words in square brackets therein substituted by the Companies Act 1989, s 144(4), Sch 18, para 33(2).

Sub-s (5): inserted by the Financial Services Act 1986, s 196; substituted by the Companies Act 1989, s 144(4), Sch 18, para 33(3).

154 Special restriction for public companies

(1)   In the case of a public company, section 153(4) authorises the giving of financial assistance only if the company has net assets which are not thereby reduced or, to the extent that those assets are thereby reduced, if the assistance is provided out of distributable profits.

(2)   For this purpose the following definitions apply—

(a)   "net assets" means the amount by which the aggregate of the company's assets exceeds the aggregate of its liabilities (taking the amount of both assets and liabilities to be as stated in the company's accounting records immediately before the financial assistance is given);

(b) "liabilities" includes any amount retained as reasonably necessary for the purpose of providing for any liability or loss which is either likely to be incurred, or certain to be incurred but uncertain as to amount or as to the date on which it will arise.

Private companies

155 Relaxation of s 151 for private companies

(1) Section 151 does not prohibit a private company from giving financial assistance in a case where the acquisition of shares in question is or was an acquisition of shares in the company or, if it is a subsidiary of another private company, in that other company if the following provisions of this section, and sections 156 to 158, are complied with as respects the giving of that assistance.

(2) The financial assistance may only be given if the company has net assets which are not thereby reduced or, to the extent that they are reduced, if the assistance is provided out of distributable profits.

Section 154(2) applies for the interpretation of this subsection.

(3) This section does not permit financial assistance to be given by a subsidiary, in a case where the acquisition of shares in question is or was an acquisition of shares in its holding company, if it is also a subsidiary of a public company which is itself a subsidiary of that holding company.

(4) Unless the company proposing to give the financial assistance is a wholly-owned subsidiary, the giving of assistance under this section must be approved by special resolution of the company in general meeting.

(5) Where the financial assistance is to be given by the company in a case where the acquisition of shares in question is or was an acquisition of shares in its holding company, that holding company and any other company which is both the company's holding company and a subsidiary of that other holding company (except, in any case, a company which is a wholly-owned subsidiary) shall also approve by special resolution in general meeting the giving of the financial assistance.

(6) [Subject to subsection (6A), the directors of the company] proposing to give the financial assistance and, where the shares acquired or to be acquired are shares in its holding company, the directors of that company and of any other company which is both the company's holding company and a subsidiary of that other holding company shall before the financial assistance is given make a statutory declaration in the prescribed form complying with the section next following.

[(6A) In place of the statutory declaration referred to in subsection (6), there may be delivered to the registrar of companies under section 156(5) a statement made by the persons mentioned in subsection (6) above complying with the section next following.]

Sub-s (6): words "Subject to subsection (6A), the directors of the company" in square brackets substituted by SI 2000/3373, art 10(1), (2).

Date in force: 22 December 2000: see SI 2000/3373, art 1(1).

Sub-s (6A): inserted by SI 2000/3373, art 10(1), (3).

Date in force: 22 December 2000: see SI 2000/3373, art 1(1).

156 Statutory declaration under s 155

(1)   A statutory declaration made by a company's directors under section 155(6) shall contain such particulars of the financial assistance to be given, and of the business of the company of which they are directors, as may be prescribed, and shall identify the person to whom the assistance is to be given.

[(1A)   A statement made by a company's directors under section 155(6A) shall state—
- (a)   the names and addresses of all the directors of the company,
- (b)   whether the business of the company is that of a banking company or insurance company or some other business,
- (c)   that the company or (as the case may be) a company (naming such company) of which it is the holding company is proposing to give financial assistance in connection with the acquisition of shares in the company or (as the case may be) its holding company (naming that holding company),
- (d)   whether the assistance is for the purpose of that acquisition or for reducing or discharging a liability incurred for the purpose of that acquisition,
- (e)   the name and address of the person to whom the assistance is to be given (and in the case of a company its registered office),
- (f)   the name of the person who has acquired or will acquire the shares and the number and class of the shares acquired or to be acquired,
- (g)   the principal terms on which the assistance will be given,
- (h)   the form the financial assistance will take (stating the amount of cash or value of any asset to be transferred to the person assisted), and
- (i)   the date on which the assistance is to be given.]

(2)   The declaration [under section 155(6) or (as the case may be) statement under section 155(6A)] shall state that the directors have formed the opinion, as regards the company's initial situation immediately following the date on which the assistance is proposed to be given, that there will be no ground on which it could then be found to be unable to pay its debts; and either—
- (a)   if it is intended to commence the winding up of the company within 12 months of that date, that the company will be able to pay its debts in full within 12 months of the commencement of the winding up, or
- (b)   in any other case, that the company will be able to pay its debts as they fall due during the year immediately following that date.

(3)   In forming their opinion for purposes of subsection (2), the directors shall take into account the same liabilities (including contingent and prospective liabilities) as would be relevant under [section 122 of the Insolvency Act] (winding up by the court) to the question whether the company is unable to pay its debts.

(4) The directors' statutory declaration [or statement] shall have annexed to it a report addressed to them by their company's auditors stating that—

    (a) they have enquired into the state of affairs of the company, and

    (b) they are not aware of anything to indicate that the opinion expressed by the directors in the declaration [or statement] as to any of the matters mentioned in subsection (2) of this section is unreasonable in all the circumstances.

(5) The statutory declaration [or statement] and auditors' report shall be delivered to the registrar of companies—

    (a) together with a copy of any special resolution passed by the company under section 155 and delivered to the registrar in compliance with section 380, or

    (b) where no such resolution is required to be passed, within 15 days after the making of the declaration [or statement].

(6) If a company fails to comply with subsection (5), the company and every officer of it who is in default is liable to a fine and, for continued contravention, to a daily default fine.

(7) A director of a company who makes a statutory declaration [or statement] under section 155 without having reasonable grounds for the opinion expressed in it is liable to imprisonment or a fine, or both.

NOTES

Sub-s (1A): inserted by SI 2000/3373, art 11(1), (2).

Date in force: 22 December 2000: see SI 2000/3373, art 1(1).

Sub-s (2): words "under section 155(6) or (as the case may be) statement under section 155(6A)" in square brackets inserted by SI 2000/3373, art 11(1), (3).

Date in force: 22 December 2000: see SI 2000/3373, art 1(1).

Sub-s (3): words "section 122 of the Insolvency Act" in square brackets substituted, subject to transitional provisions, by the Insolvency Act 1986, ss 437, 439(1), Sch 11, Sch 13, Pt I.

Sub-s (4): words "or statement" in square brackets in both places they occur inserted by SI 2000/3373, art 11(1), (4).

Date in force: 22 December 2000: see SI 2000/3373, art 1(1).

Sub-s (5): words "or statement" in square brackets in both places they occur inserted by SI 2000/3373, art 11(1), (4).

Date in force: 22 December 2000: see SI 2000/3373, art 1(1).

Sub-s (7): words "or statement" in square brackets inserted by SI 2000/3373, art 11(1), (4).

Date in force: 22 December 2000: see SI 2000/3373, art 1(1).

157 Special resolution under s 155

(1) A special resolution required by section 155 to be passed by a company approving the giving of financial assistance must be passed on the date on which the directors of that company make the statutory declaration [or statement] required by that section in connection with the giving of that assistance, or within the week immediately following that date.

(2) Where such a resolution has been passed, an application may be made to the court for the cancellation of the resolution—

    (a) by the holders of not less in the aggregate than 10 per cent in nominal value of the company's issued share capital or any class of it, or

(b) if the company is not limited by shares, by not less than 10 per cent of the company's members;

but the application shall not be made by a person who has consented to or voted in favour of the resolution.

(3) Subsections (3) to (10) of section 54 (litigation to cancel resolution under section 53) apply to applications under this section as to applications under section 54.

(4) A special resolution passed by a company is not effective for purposes of section 155—

(a) unless the declaration [or statement] made in compliance with subsection (6) of that section by the directors of the company, together with the auditors' report annexed to it, is available for inspection by members of the company at the meeting at which the resolution is passed,

(b) if it is cancelled by the court on an application under this section.

NOTES

Sub-s (1): words "or statement" in square brackets inserted by SI 2000/3373, art 31(2).
Date in force: 22 December 2000: see SI 2000/3373, art 1(1).
Sub-s (4): in para (a) words "or statement" in square brackets inserted by SI 2000/3373, art 31(2).
Date in force: 22 December 2000: see SI 2000/3373, art 1(1).

158 Time for giving financial assistance under s 155

(1) This section applies as to the time before and after which financial assistance may not be given by a company in pursuance of section 155.

(2) Where a special resolution is required by that section to be passed approving the giving of the assistance, the assistance shall not be given before the expiry of the period of 4 weeks beginning with—

(a) the date on which the special resolution is passed, or

(b) where more than one such resolution is passed, the date on which the last of them is passed,

unless, as respects that resolution (or, if more than one, each of them), every member of the company which passed the resolution who is entitled to vote at general meetings of the company voted in favour of the resolution.

(3) If application for the cancellation of any such resolution is made under section 157, the financial assistance shall not be given before the final determination of the application unless the court otherwise orders.

(4) The assistance shall not be given after the expiry of the period of 8 weeks beginning with—

(a) the date on which the directors of the company proposing to give the assistance made their statutory declaration [or statement] under section 155, or

(b) where that company is a subsidiary and both its directors and the directors of any of its holding companies made such a declaration [or statement], the date on which the earliest of the declarations [or statements] is made, unless the court, on an application under section 157, otherwise orders.

NOTES

Sub-s (4): in paras (a), (b) words "or statement" in square brackets inserted by SI 2000/3373, art 31(2).

Date in force: 22 December 2000: see SI 2000/3373, art 1(1).

Sub-s (4): in para (b) words "or statements" in square brackets inserted by SI 2000/3373, art 31(2).

Date in force: 22 December 2000: see SI 2000/3373, art 1(1).

Chapter VII
Redeemable Shares; Purchase by a Company of its Own Shares

Redemption and purchase generally

159 Power to issue redeemable shares

(1) Subject to the provisions of this Chapter, a company limited by shares or limited by guarantee and having a share capital may, if authorised to do so by its articles, issue shares which are to be redeemed or are liable to be redeemed at the option of the company or the shareholder.

(2) No redeemable shares may be issued at a time when there are no issued shares of the company which are not redeemable.

(3) Redeemable shares may not be redeemed unless they are fully paid; and the terms of redemption must provide for payment on redemption.

[159A Terms and manner of redemption]

[(1) Redeemable shares may not be issued unless the following conditions are satisfied as regards the terms and manner of redemption.

(2) The date on or by which, or dates between which, the shares are to be or may be redeemed must be specified in the company's articles or, if the articles so provide, fixed by the directors, and in the latter case the date or dates must be fixed before the shares are issued.

(3) Any other circumstances in which the shares are to be or may be redeemed must be specified in the company's articles.

(4) The amount payable on redemption must be specified in, or determined in accordance with, the company's articles, and in the latter case the articles must not provide for the amount to be determined by reference to any person's discretion or opinion.

(5) Any other terms and conditions of redemption shall be specified in the company's articles.

(6) Nothing in this section shall be construed as requiring a company to provide in its articles for any matter for which provision is made by this Act.]

NOTES
Inserted by the Companies Act 1989, s 133(2).
Date in force: to be appointed: see Companies Act 1989, s 215(2).

160 Financing etc of redemption

(1) Subject to the next subsection and to sections 171 (private companies redeeming or purchasing own shares out of capital) and 178(4) (terms of redemption or purchase enforceable in a winding up)—

   (a) redeemable shares may only be redeemed out of distributable profits of the company or out of the proceeds of a fresh issue of shares made for the purposes of the redemption; and

   (b) any premium payable on redemption must be paid out of distributable profits of the company.

(2) If the redeemable shares were issued at a premium, any premium payable on their redemption may be paid out of the proceeds of a fresh issue of shares made for the purposes of the redemption, up to an amount equal to—

   (a) the aggregate of the premiums received by the company on the issue of the shares redeemed, or

   (b) the current amount of the company's share premium account (including any sum transferred to that account in respect of premiums on the new shares),

whichever is the less; and in that case the amount of the company's share premium account shall be reduced by a sum corresponding (or by sums in the aggregate corresponding) to the amount of any payment made by virtue of this subsection out of the proceeds of the issue of the new shares.

(3) Subject to the following provisions of this Chapter, redemption of shares may be effected on such terms and in such manner as may be provided by the company's articles.

(4) Shares *redeemed under this section* [redeemed under this Chapter] shall be treated as cancelled on redemption, and the amount of the company's issued share capital shall be diminished by the nominal value of those shares accordingly; but the redemption of shares by a company is not to be taken as reducing the amount of the company's authorised share capital.

(5) Without prejudice to subsection (4), where a company is about to redeem shares, it has power to issue shares up to the nominal value of the shares to be redeemed as if those shares had never been issued.

NOTES
Sub-s (3): prospectively repealed by the Companies Act 1989, ss 133(3), 212, Sch 24, as from a day to be appointed.
Sub-s (4): words in italics prospectively repealed and words in square brackets prospectively substituted by the Companies Act 1989, s 133(3), as from a day to be appointed.

162 Power of company to purchase own shares

(1) Subject to the following provisions of this Chapter, a company limited by shares or limited by guarantee and having a share capital may, if authorised to do so by its articles, purchase its own shares (including any redeemable shares).

(2) *Sections 159 to 161 apply to the purchase by a company under this section of its own shares as they apply to the redemption of redeemable shares, save that the terms and manner of purchase need not be determined by the articles as required by section 160(3).*

[(2) Sections 159, 160 and 161 apply to the purchase by a company under this section of its own shares as they apply to the redemption of redeemable shares.]

(3) A company may not under this section purchase its shares if as a result of the purchase there would no longer be any member of the company holding shares other than redeemable shares.

NOTES
Sub-s (2): prospectively substituted by the Companies Act 1989, s 133(4), as from a day to be appointed.

163 Definitions of "off-market" and "market" purchase

(1) A purchase by a company of its own shares is "off-market" if the shares either—
  (a) are purchased otherwise than on [a recognised investment exchange], or
  (b) are purchased on [a recognised investment exchange] but are not subject to a marketing arrangement on [that investment exchange].

(2) For this purpose, a company's shares are subject to a marketing arrangement on [a recognised investment exchange] if either—
  (a) they are listed [under [Part 6 of the Financial Services and Markets Act 2000]]; or
  (b) the company has been afforded facilities for dealings in those shares to take place on [that investment exchange] without prior permission for individual transactions from the authority governing [that investment exchange] and without limit as to the time during which those facilities are to be available.

(3) A purchase by a company of its own shares is a "market purchase" if it is a purchase made on [a recognised investment exchange], other than a purchase which is an off-market purchase by virtue of subsection (1)(b).

[(4) "Recognised investment exchange" means a recognised investment exchange other than an overseas investment exchange.

(5) Expressions used in the definition contained in subsection (4) have the same meaning as in Part 18 of the Financial Services and Markets Act 2000.]

NOTES
Sub-s (1): words "a recognised investment exchange" in square brackets in both places they occur and words "that investment exchange" in square brackets substituted by the Financial Services Act 1986, s 212(2), Sch 16, para 17.

Sub-s (2): words "a recognised investment exhange" in square brackets substituted by the Financial Services Act 1986, s 212(2), Sch 16, para 17.

Sub-s (2): in para (a) words in square brackets beginning with the word "under" substituted by the Financial Services Act 1986, s 212(2), Sch 16, para 17.

Sub-s (2): in para (a) words "Part 6 of the Financial Services and Markets Act 2000" in square brackets substituted by SI 2001/3649, art 6(1), (2).

Date in force: 1 December 2001: see SI 2001/3649, art 1.

Sub-s (2): in para (b) words "that investment exchange" in square brackets in both places they occur substituted by the Financial Services Act 1986, s 212(2), Sch 16, para 17.

Sub-s (3): words "a recognised investment exchange" in square brackets substituted by the Financial Services Act 1986, s 212(2), Sch 16, para 17.

Sub-ss (4), (5): substituted, for sub-s (4) (as inserted by the Financial Services Act 1986, s 212(2), Sch 16, para 17), by SI 2001/3649, art 6(1), (3).

Date in force: 1 December 2001: see SI 2001/3649, art 1.

164 Authority for off-market purchase

(1)   A company may only make an off-market purchase of its own shares in pursuance of a contract approved in advance in accordance with this section or under section 165 below.

(2)   The terms of the proposed contract must be authorised by a special resolution of the company before the contract is entered into; and the following subsections apply with respect to that authority and to resolutions conferring it.

(3)   Subject to the next subsection, the authority may be varied, revoked or from time to time renewed by special resolution of the company.

(4)   In the case of a public company, the authority conferred by the resolution must specify a date on which the authority is to expire; and in a resolution conferring or renewing authority that date must not be later than 18 months after that on which the resolution is passed.

(5)   A special resolution to confer, vary, revoke or renew authority is not effective if any member of the company holding shares to which the resolution relates exercises the voting rights carried by any of those shares in voting on the resolution and the resolution would not have been passed if he had not done so.

For this purpose—
(a)   a member who holds shares to which the resolution relates is regarded as exercising the voting rights carried by those shares not only if he votes in respect of them on a poll on the question whether the resolution shall be passed, but also if he votes on the resolution otherwise than on a poll;
(b)   notwithstanding anything in the company's articles, any member of the company may demand a poll on that question; and
(c)   a vote and a demand for a poll by a person as proxy for a member are the same respectively as a vote and a demand by the member.

(6)   Such a resolution is not effective for the purposes of this section unless (if the proposed contract is in writing) a copy of the contract or (if not) a written memorandum of its terms is available for inspection by members of the company both—

(a)   at the company's registered office for not less than 15 days ending with the date of the meeting at which the resolution is passed, and

(b)   at the meeting itself.

A memorandum of contract terms so made available must include the names of any members holding shares to which the contract relates; and a copy of the contract so made available must have annexed to it a written memorandum specifying any such names which do not appear in the contract itself.

(7)   A company may agree to a variation of an existing contract so approved, but only if the variation is authorised by a special resolution of the company before it is agreed to; and subsections (3) to (6) above apply to the authority for a proposed variation as they apply to the authority for a proposed contract, save that a copy of the original contract or (as the case may require) a memorandum of its terms, together with any variations previously made, must also be available for inspection in accordance with subsection (6).

165 Authority for contingent purchase contract

(1)   A contingent purchase contract is a contract entered into by a company and relating to any of its shares—

(a)   which does not amount to a contract to purchase those shares, but

(b)   under which the company may (subject to any conditions) become entitled or obliged to purchase those shares.

(2)   A company may only make a purchase of its own shares in pursuance of a contingent purchase contract if the contract is approved in advance by a special resolution of the company before the contract is entered into; and subsections (3) to (7) of section 164 apply to the contract and its terms.

166 Authority for market purchase

(1)   A company shall not make a market purchase of its own shares unless the purchase has first been authorised by the company in general meeting.

(2)   That authority—

(a)   may be general for that purpose, or limited to the purchase of shares of any particular class or description, and

(b)   may be unconditional or subject to conditions.

(3)   The authority must—

(a)   specify the maximum number of shares authorised to be acquired,

(b)   determine both the maximum and the minimum prices which may be paid for the shares, and

(c)   specify a date on which it is to expire.

(4)   The authority may be varied, revoked or from time to time renewed by the company in general meeting, but this is subject to subsection (3) above; and in a resolution to confer or renew authority, the date on which the authority is to expire must not be later than 18 months after that on which the resolution is passed.

(5)   A company may under this section make a purchase of its own shares after the expiry of the time limit imposed to comply with subsection (3)(c), if the contract of purchase was concluded before the authority expired and the terms of the authority permitted the company to make a contract of purchase which would or might be executed wholly or partly after its expiration.

(6)   A resolution to confer or vary authority under this section may determine either or both the maximum and minimum prices for purchase by—
    (a)   specifying a particular sum, or
    (b)   providing a basis or formula for calculating the amount of the price in question without reference to any person's discretion or opinion.

(7)   A resolution of a company conferring, varying, revoking or renewing authority under this section is subject to section 380 (resolution to be sent to registrar of companies within 15 days).

168 Payments apart from purchase price to be made out of distributable profits

(1)   A payment made by a company in consideration of—
    (a)   acquiring any right with respect to the purchase of its own shares in pursuance of a contract approved under section 165, or
    (b)   the variation of a contract approved under section 164 or 165, or
    (c)   the release of any of the company's obligations with respect to the purchase of any of its own shares under a contract approved under section 164 or 165 or under a contract for a purchase authorised under section 166,

must be made out of the company's distributable profits.

(2)   If the requirements of subsection (1) are not satisfied in relation to a contract—
    (a)   in a case within paragraph (a) of the subsection, no purchase by the company of its own shares in pursuance of that contract is lawful under this Chapter,
    (b)   in a case within paragraph (b), no such purchase following the variation is lawful under this Chapter, and
    (c)   in a case within paragraph (c), the purported release is void.

169 Disclosure by company of purchase of own shares

(1)   Within the period of 28 days beginning with the date on which any shares purchased by a company under this Chapter are delivered to it, the company shall deliver to the registrar of companies for registration a return in the prescribed form stating with respect to shares of each class purchased the number and nominal value of those shares and the date on which they were delivered to the company.

(2)   In the case of a public company, the return shall also state—
    (a)   the aggregate amount paid by the company for the shares; and
    (b)   the maximum and minimum prices paid in respect of shares of each class purchased.

(3)   Particulars of shares delivered to the company on different dates and under different contracts may be included in a single return to the registrar; and in such a

case the amount required to be stated under subsection (2)(a) is the aggregate amount paid by the company for all the shares to which the return relates.

(4)   Where a company enters into a contract approved under section 164 or 165, or a contract for a purchase authorised under section 166, the company shall keep at its registered office—

(a)   if the contract is in writing, a copy of it; and

(b)   if not, a memorandum of its terms,

from the conclusion of the contract until the end of the period of 10 years beginning with the date on which the purchase of all the shares in pursuance of the contract is completed or (as the case may be) the date on which the contract otherwise determines.

(5)   Every copy and memorandum so required to be kept shall . . . be open to inspection without charge—

(a)   by any member of the company, and

(b)   if it is a public company, by any other person.

(6)   If default is made in delivering to the registrar any return required by this section, every officer of the company who is in default is liable to a fine and, for continued contravention, to a daily default fine.

(7)   If default is made in complying with subsection (4), or if an inspection required under subsection (5) is refused, the company and every officer of it who is in default is liable to a fine and, for continued contravention, to a daily default fine.

(8)   In the case of a refusal of an inspection required under subsection (5) of a copy or memorandum, the court may by order compel an immediate inspection of it.

(9)   The obligation of a company under subsection (4) to keep a copy of any contract or (as the case may be) a memorandum of its terms applies to any variation of the contract so long as it applies to the contract.

NOTES

Sub-s (5): words omitted repealed by the Companies Act 1989, ss 143(2), 212, Sch 24.

170 The capital redemption reserve

(1)   Where under this Chapter shares of a company are redeemed or purchased wholly out of the company's profits, the amount by which the company's issued share capital is diminished in accordance with section 160(4) on cancellation of the shares redeemed or purchased shall be transferred to a reserve, called "the capital redemption reserve".

(2)   If the shares are redeemed or purchased wholly or partly out of the proceeds of a fresh issue and the aggregate amount of those proceeds is less than the aggregate nominal value of the shares redeemed or purchased, the amount of the difference shall be transferred to the capital redemption reserve.

(3)   But subsection (2) does not apply if the proceeds of the fresh issue are applied by the company in making a redemption or purchase of its own shares in addition to a payment out of capital under section 171.

(4)   The provisions of this Act relating to the reduction of a company's share capital apply as if the capital redemption reserve were paid-up share capital of the company, except that the reserve may be applied by the company in paying up its unissued shares to be allotted to members of the company as fully paid bonus shares.

Redemption or purchase of own shares out of capital (private companies only)

171   Power of private companies to redeem or purchase own shares out of capital

(1)   Subject to the following provisions of this Chapter, a private company limited by shares or limited by guarantee and having a share capital may, if so authorised by its articles, make a payment in respect of the redemption or purchase under section 160 or (as the case may be) section 162, of its own shares otherwise than out of its distributable profits or the proceeds of a fresh issue of shares.

(2)   References below in this Chapter to payment out of capital are (subject to subsection (6)) to any payment so made, whether or not it would be regarded apart from this section as a payment out of capital.

(3)   The payment which may (if authorised in accordance with the following provisions of this Chapter) be made by a company out of capital in respect of the redemption or purchase of its own shares is such an amount as, taken together with—
  (a)   any available profits of the company, and
  (b)   the proceeds of any fresh issue of shares made for the purposes of the redemption or purchase,

is equal to the price of redemption or purchase; and the payment permissible under this subsection is referred to below in this Chapter as the permissible capital payment for the shares.

(4)   Subject to subsection (6), if the permissible capital payment for shares redeemed or purchased is less than their nominal amount, the amount of the difference shall be transferred to the company's capital redemption reserve.

(5)   Subject to subsection (6), if the permissible capital payment is greater than the nominal amount of the shares redeemed or purchased—
  (a)   the amount of any capital redemption reserve, share premium account or fully paid share capital of the company, and
  (b)   any amount representing unrealised profits of the company for the time being standing to the credit of any reserve maintained by the company in accordance with paragraph 34 of Schedule 4 [or paragraph 34 of Schedule 8] (revaluation reserve),

may be reduced by a sum not exceeding (or by sums not in the aggregate exceeding) the amount by which the permissible capital payment exceeds the nominal amount of the shares.

(6)   Where the proceeds of a fresh issue are applied by a company in making any redemption or purchase of its own shares in addition to a payment out of capital

under this section, the references in subsections (4) and (5) to the permissible capital payment are to be read as referring to the aggregate of that payment and those proceeds.

NOTES

Sub-s (5): in para (b) words "or paragraph 34 of Schedule 8" in square brackets inserted by SI 1997/220, reg 7(1).

Date in force: this amendment applies to annual accounts approved by the board of directors on or after 1 March 1997, and to directors' and auditors' reports on such accounts: see SI 1997/220, reg 1(3); for transitional provision see reg 1(4) thereof.

172 Availability of profits for purposes of s 171

(1) The reference in section 171(3)(a) to available profits of the company is to the company's profits which are available for distribution (within the meaning of Part VIII); but the question whether a company has any profits so available and the amount of any such profits are to be determined for purposes of that section in accordance with the following subsections, instead of sections 270 to 275 in that Part.

(2) Subject to the next subsection, that question is to be determined by reference to—
  (a) profits, losses, assets and liabilities,
  (b) provisions of any of the kinds mentioned in paragraphs 88 and 89 of Schedule 4 (depreciation, diminution in value of assets, retentions to meet liabilities, etc), and
  (c) share capital and reserves (including undistributable reserves),

as stated in the relevant accounts for determining the permissible capital payment for shares.

(3) The relevant accounts for this purpose are such accounts, prepared as at any date within the period for determining the amount of the permissible capital payment, as are necessary to enable a reasonable judgment to be made as to the amounts of any of the items mentioned in subsection (2)(a) to (c) above.

(4) For purposes of determining the amount of the permissible capital payment for shares, the amount of the company's available profits (if any) determined in accordance with subsections (2) and (3) is treated as reduced by the amount of any distributions lawfully made by the company after the date of the relevant accounts and before the end of the period for determining the amount of that payment.

(5) The reference in subsection (4) to distributions lawfully made by the company includes—
  (a) financial assistance lawfully given out of distributable profits in a case falling within section 154 or 155,
  (b) any payment lawfully made by the company in respect of the purchase by it of any shares in the company (except a payment lawfully made otherwise than out of distributable profits), and
  (c) a payment of any description specified in section 168(1) lawfully made by the company.

(6)   References in this section to the period for determining the amount of the permissible capital payment for shares are to the period of 3 months ending with the date on which the statutory declaration of the directors purporting to specify the amount of that payment is made in accordance with subsection (3) of the section next following.

173 Conditions for payment out of capital

(1)   Subject to any order of the court under section 177, a payment out of capital by a private company for the redemption or purchase of its own shares is not lawful unless the requirements of this and the next two sections are satisfied.

(2)   The payment out of capital must be approved by a special resolution of the company.

(3)   The company's directors must make a statutory declaration specifying the amount of the permissible capital payment for the shares in question and stating that, having made full inquiry into the affairs and prospects of the company, they have formed the opinion—

(a)   as regards its initial situation immediately following the date on which the payment out of capital is proposed to be made, that there will be no grounds on which the company could then be found unable to pay its debts, and

(b)   as regards its prospects for the year immediately following that date, that, having regard to their intentions with respect to the management of the company's business during that year and to the amount and character of the financial resources which will in their view be available to the company during that year, the company will be able to continue to carry on business as a going concern (and will accordingly be able to pay its debts as they fall due) throughout that year.

(4)   In forming their opinion for purposes of subsection (3)(a), the directors shall take into account the same liabilities (including prospective and contingent liabilities) as would be relevant under [section 122 of the Insolvency Act] (winding up by the court) to the question whether a company is unable to pay its debts.

(5)   The directors' statutory declaration must be in the prescribed form and contain such information with respect to the nature of the company's business as may be prescribed, and must in addition have annexed to it a report addressed to the directors by the company's auditors stating that—

(a)   they have inquired into the company's state of affairs; and

(b)   the amount specified in the declaration as the permissible capital payment for the shares in question is in their view properly determined in accordance with sections 171 and 172; and

(c)   they are not aware of anything to indicate that the opinion expressed by the directors in the declaration as to any of the matters mentioned in subsection (3) is unreasonable in all the circumstances.

(6)   A director who makes a declaration under this section without having reasonable grounds for the opinion expressed in the declaration is liable to imprisonment or a fine, or both.

Sub-s (4): words in square brackets substituted, subject to transitional provisions, by the Insolvency Act 1986, ss 437, 439(1), Sch 11, Sch 13, Part I.

174 Procedure for special resolution under s 173

(1)   The resolution required by section 173 must be passed on, or within the week immediately following, the date on which the directors make the statutory declaration required by that section; and the payment out of capital must be made no earlier than 5 nor more than 7 weeks after the date of the resolution.

(2)   The resolution is ineffective if any member of the company holding shares to which the resolution relates exercises the voting rights carried by any of those shares in voting on the resolution and the resolution would not have been passed if he had not done so.

(3)   For purposes of subsection (2), a member who holds such shares is to be regarded as exercising the voting rights carried by them in voting on the resolution not only if he votes in respect of them on a poll on the question whether the resolution shall be passed, but also if he votes on the resolution otherwise than on a poll; and, notwithstanding anything in a company's articles, any member of the company may demand a poll on that question.

(4)   The resolution is ineffective unless the statutory declaration and auditors' report required by the section are available for inspection by members of the company at the meeting at which the resolution is passed.

(5)   For purposes of this section a vote and a demand for a poll by a person as proxy for a member are the same (respectively) as a vote and demand by the member.

175 Publicity for proposed payment out of capital

(1)   Within the week immediately following the date of the resolution for payment out of capital the company must cause to be published in the Gazette a notice—
  (a)   stating that the company has approved a payment out of capital for the purpose of acquiring its own shares by redemption or purchase or both (as the case may be);
  (b)   specifying the amount of the permissible capital payment for the shares in question and the date of the resolution under section 173;
  (c)   stating that the statutory declaration of the directors and the auditors' report required by that section are available for inspection at the company's registered office; and
  (d)   stating that any creditor of the company may at any time within the 5 weeks immediately following the date of the resolution for payment out of capital apply to the court under section 176 for an order prohibiting the payment.

(2)   Within the week immediately following the date of the resolution the company must also either cause a notice to the same effect as that required by subsection (1) to be published in an appropriate national newspaper or give notice in writing to that effect to each of its creditors.

(3) "An appropriate national newspaper" means a newspaper circulating through-out England and Wales (in the case of a company registered in England and Wales), and a newspaper circulating throughout Scotland (in the case of a company registered in Scotland).

(4) References below in this section to the first notice date are to the day on which the company first publishes the notice required by subsection (1) or first publishes or gives the notice required by subsection (2) (whichever is the earlier).

(5) Not later than the first notice date the company must deliver to the registrar of companies a copy of the statutory declaration of the directors and of the auditors' report required by section 173.

(6) The statutory declaration and auditors' report—
- (a) shall be kept at the company's registered office throughout the period beginning with the first notice date and ending 5 weeks after the date of the resolution for payment out of capital, and
- (b) shall . . . be open to the inspection of any member or creditor of the company without charge.

(7) If an inspection required under subsection (6) is refused, the company and every officer of it who is in default is liable to a fine and, for continued contravention, to a daily default fine.

(8) In the case of refusal of an inspection required under subsection (6) of a declaration or report, the court may by order compel an immediate inspection of that declaration or report.

NOTES

Sub-s (6): in para (b) words omitted repealed by the Companies Act 1989, ss 143(3), 212, Sch 24.

176 Objections by company's members or creditors

(1) Where a private company passes a special resolution approving for purposes of this Chapter any payment out of capital for the redemption or purchase of any of its shares—
- (a) any member of the company other than one who consented to or voted in favour of the resolution; and
- (b) any creditor of the company,

may within 5 weeks of the date on which the resolution was passed apply to the court for cancellation of the resolution.

(2) The application may be made on behalf of the persons entitled to make it by such one or more of their number as they may appoint in writing for the purpose.

(3) If an application is made, the company shall—
- (a) forthwith give notice in the prescribed form of that fact to the registrar of companies; and
- (b) within 15 days from the making of any order of the court on the hearing of the application, or such longer period as the court may by order direct, deliver an office copy of the order to the registrar.

(4)   A company which fails to comply with subsection (3), and any officer of it who is in default, is liable to a fine and for continued contravention, to a daily default fine.

177 Powers of court on application under s 176

(1)   On the hearing of an application under section 176 the court may, if it thinks fit, adjourn the proceedings in order that an arrangement may be made to the court's satisfaction for the purchase of the interests of dissentient members or for the protection of dissentient creditors (as the case may be); and the court may give such directions and make such orders as it thinks expedient for facilitating or carrying into effect any such arrangement.

(2)   Without prejudice to its powers under subsection (1), the court shall make an order on such terms and conditions as it thinks fit either confirming or cancelling the resolution; and, if the court confirms the resolution, it may in particular by order alter or extend any date or period of time specified in the resolution or in any provision in this Chapter which applies to the redemption or purchase of shares to which the resolution refers.

(3)   The court's order may, if the court thinks fit, provide for the purchase by the company of the shares of any of its members and for the reduction accordingly of the company's capital, and may make such alterations in the company's memorandum and articles as may be required in consequence of that provision.

(4)   If the court's order requires the company not to make any, or any specified, alteration in its memorandum or articles, the company has not then power without leave of the court to make any such alteration in breach of the requirement.

(5)   An alteration in the memorandum or articles made by virtue of an order under this section, if not made by resolution of the company, is of the same effect as if duly made by resolution; and this Act applies accordingly to the memorandum or articles as so altered.

Supplementary

178 Effect of company's failure to redeem or purchase

(1)   This section has effect where a company has, on or after 15th June 1982,—
   (a)   issued shares on terms that they are or are liable to be redeemed, or
   (b)   agreed to purchase any of its own shares.

(2)   The company is not liable in damages in respect of any failure on its part to redeem or purchase any of the shares.

(3)   Subsection (2) is without prejudice to any right of the holder of the shares other than his right to sue the company for damages in respect of its failure; but the court shall not grant an order for specific performance of the terms of redemption or purchase if the company shows that it is unable to meet the costs of redeeming or purchasing the shares in question out of distributable profits.

(4)   If the company is wound up and at the commencement of the winding up any of the shares have not been redeemed or purchased, the terms of redemption or purchase may be enforced against the company; and when shares are redeemed or purchased under this subsection, they are treated as cancelled.

(5)   However, subsection (4) does not apply if—
   (a)   the terms provided for the redemption or purchase to take place at a date later than that of the commencement of the winding up, or
   (b)   during the period beginning with the date on which the redemption or purchase was to have taken place and ending with the commencement of the winding up the company could not at any time have lawfully made a distribution equal in value to the price at which the shares were to have been redeemed or purchased.

(6)   There shall be paid in priority to any amount which the company is liable under subsection (4) to pay in respect of any shares—
   (a)   all other debts and liabilities of the company (other than any due to members in their character as such),
   (b)   if other shares carry rights (whether as to capital or as to income) which are preferred to the rights as to capital attaching to the first-mentioned shares, any amount due in satisfaction of those preferred rights;

but, subject to that, any such amount shall be paid in priority to any amounts due to members in satisfaction of their rights (whether as to capital or income) as members.

(7)   . . .

NOTES

Sub-s (7): repealed by the Insolvency Act 1985, s 235, Sch 10, Part II.

Chapter VIII
Miscellaneous Provisions about Shares and Debentures

Share and debenture certificates, transfers and warrants

182 Nature, transfer and numbering of shares

(1)   The shares or other interest of any member in a company—
   (a)   are personal estate or, in Scotland, moveable property and are not in the nature of real estate or heritage,
   (b)   are transferable in manner provided by the company's articles, but subject to the Stock Transfer Act 1963 (which enables securities of certain descriptions to be transferred by a simplified process) [and to regulations made under section 207 of the Companies Act 1989 (which enable title to securities to be evidenced and transferred without a written instrument)].

(2)   Each share in a company having a share capital shall be distinguished by its appropriate number; except that, if at any time all the issued shares in a company, or all the issued shares in it of a particular class, are fully paid up and rank pari passu for all purposes, none of those shares need thereafter have a distinguishing number

so long as it remains fully paid up and ranks pari passu for all purposes with all shares of the same class for the time being issued and fully paid up.

NOTES

Sub-s (1): in sub-para (b) words from "and to regulations" to "a written instrument)" in square brackets inserted by SI 2001/3755, reg 51, Sch 7, Pt 1, para 7.

Date in force: 26 November 2001: see SI 2001/3755, reg 1.

183 Transfer and registration

(1)   It is not lawful for a company to register a transfer of shares in or debentures of the company unless a proper instrument of transfer has been delivered to it, or the transfer is an exempt transfer within the Stock Transfer Act 1982 [or is in accordance with regulations made under section 207 of the Companies Act 1989].

This applies notwithstanding anything in the company's articles.

(2)   Subsection (1) does not prejudice any power of the company to register as shareholder or debenture holder a person to whom the right to any shares in or debentures of the company has been transmitted by operation of law.

(3)   A transfer of the share or other interest of a deceased member of a company made by his personal representative, although the personal representative is not himself a member of the company, is as valid as if he had been such a member at the time of the execution of the instrument of transfer.

(4)   On the application of the transferor of any share or interest in a company, the company shall enter in its register of members the name of the transferee in the same manner and subject to the same conditions as if the application for the entry were made by the transferee.

(5)   If a company refuses to register a transfer of shares or debentures, the company shall, within 2 months after the date on which the transfer was lodged with it, send to the transferee notice of the refusal.

(6)   If default is made in complying with subsection (5), the company and every officer of it who is in default is liable to a fine and, for continued contravention, to a daily default fine.

NOTES

Sub-s (1): words "or is in accordance with regulations made under section 207 of the Companies Act 1989" in square brackets inserted by SI 2001/3755, reg 51, Sch 7, Pt 1, para 8.

Date in force: 26 November 2001: see SI 2001/3755, reg 1.

184 Certification of transfers

(1)   The certification by a company of any instrument of transfer of any shares in, or debentures of, the company is to be taken as a representation by the company to any person acting on the faith of the certification that there have been produced to the company such documents as on their face show a prima facie title to the shares or debentures in the transferor named in the instrument.

However, the certification is not to be taken as a representation that the transferor has any title to the shares or debentures.

(2)   Where a person acts on the faith of a false certification by a company made negligently, the company is under the same liability to him as if the certification had been made fraudulently.

(3)   For purposes of this section—
   (a)   an instrument of transfer is deemed certificated if it bears the words "certificate lodged" (or words to the like effect);
   (b)   the certification of an instrument of transfer is deemed made by a company if—
      (i)   the person issuing the instrument is a person authorised to issue certificated instruments of transfer on the company's behalf, and
      (ii)   the certification is signed by a person authorised to certificate transfers on the company's behalf or by an officer or servant either of the company or of a body corporate so authorised;
   (c)   a certification is deemed signed by a person if—
      (i)   it purports to be authenticated by his signature or initials (whether handwritten or not), and
      (ii)   it is not shown that the signature or initials was or were placed there neither by himself nor by a person authorised to use the signature or initials for the purpose of certificating transfers on the company's behalf.

185 Duty of company as to issue of certificates

(1)   Subject to the following provisions, every company shall—
   (a)   within 2 months after the allotment of any of its shares, debentures or debenture stock, and
   (b)   within 2 months after the date on which a transfer of any such shares, debentures or debenture stock is lodged with the company,

complete and have ready for delivery the certificates of all shares, the debentures and the certificates of all debenture stock allotted or transferred (unless the conditions of issue of the shares, debentures or debenture stock otherwise provide).

(2)   For this purpose, "transfer" means a transfer duly stamped and otherwise valid, or an exempt transfer within the Stock Transfer Act 1982, and does not include such a transfer as the company is for any reason entitled to refuse to register and does not register.

(3)   Subsection (1) does not apply in the case of a transfer to any person where, by virtue of regulations under section 3 of the Stock Transfer Act 1982, he is not entitled to a certificate or other document of or evidencing title in respect of the securities transferred; but if in such a case the transferee—
   (a)   subsequently becomes entitled to such a certificate or other document by virtue of any provision of those regulations, and
   (b)   gives notice in writing of that fact to the company,

this section has effect as if the reference in subsection (1)(b) to the date of the lodging of the transfer were a reference to the date of the notice.

[(4) Subsection (4A) applies in relation to a company—
   (a) of which shares or debentures are allotted to a financial institution,
   (b) of which debenture stock is allotted to a financial institution, or
   (c) with which a transfer for transferring shares, debentures or debenture stock to a financial institution is lodged.

(4A) The company is not required, in consequence of that allotment or transfer, to comply with subsection (1).

(4B) "Financial institution" means—
   (a) a recognised clearing house acting in relation to a recognised investment exchange; or
   (b) a nominee of—
      (i) a recognised clearing house acting in that way; or
      (ii) a recognised investment exchange.

(4C) No person may be a nominee for the purposes of this section unless he is a person designated for those purposes in the rules of the recognised investment exchange in question.

(4D) Expressions used in subsections (4B) and (4C) have the same meaning as in Part 18 of the Financial Services and Markets Act 2000.]

(5) If default is made in complying with subsection (1), the company and every officer of it who is in default is liable to a fine and, for continued contravention, to a daily default fine.

(6) If a company on which a notice has been served requiring it to make good any default in complying with subsection (1) fails to make good the default within 10 days after service of the notice, the court may, on the application of the person entitled to have the certificates or the debentures delivered to him, exercise the power of the following subsection.

(7) The court may make an order directing the company and any officer of it to make good the default within such time as may be specified in the order; and the order may provide that all costs of and incidental to the application shall be borne by the company or by an officer of it responsible for the default.

NOTES

Sub-ss (4), (4A)–(4D): substituted, for sub-s (4) as originally enacted, by SI 2001/3649, art 7(1).

Date in force: 1 December 2001: see SI 2001/3649, art 1.

[186 Certificate to be evidence of title]

[[(1)] A certificate under the common seal of the company . . . specifying any shares held by a member is—
   (a) in England and Wales, prima facie evidence, and
   (b) in Scotland, sufficient evidence unless the contrary is shown,

of his title to the shares.

[(2) Without prejudice to subsection (1), as respects Scotland a certificate specifying any shares held by a member and subscribed by the company in accordance with the Requirements of Writing (Scotland) Act 1995 is, unless the contrary is shown, sufficient evidence of his title to the shares.]]

NOTES

Substituted by the Companies Act 1989, s 130(7), Sch 17, para 5.

Sub-s (1): numbered as such by the Requirements of Writing (Scotland) Act 1995, s 14(1), Sch 4, para 55; words omitted repealed by the Law Reform (Miscellaneous Provisions) (Scotland) Act 1990, s 74, Sch 8, Part II, para 33, Sch 9.

Sub-s (2): inserted, in relation to Scotland only, by the Requirements of Writing (Scotland) Act 1995, s 14(1), Sch 4, para 55.

Debentures

190 Register of debenture holders

(1)   A company registered in England and Wales shall not keep in Scotland any register of holders of debentures of the company or any duplicate of any such register or part of any such register which is kept outside Great Britain.

(2)   A company registered in Scotland shall not keep in England and Wales any such register or duplicate as above-mentioned.

(3)   Neither a register of holders of debentures of a company nor a duplicate of any such register or part of any such register which is kept outside Great Britain shall be kept in England and Wales (in the case of a company registered in England and Wales) or in Scotland (in the case of a company registered in Scotland) elsewhere than—

(a)   at the company's registered office; or

(b)   at any office of the company at which the work of making it up is done; or

(c)   if the company arranges with some other person for the making up of the register or duplicate to be undertaken on its behalf by that other person, at the office of that other person at which the work is done.

(4)   Where a company keeps (in England and Wales or in Scotland, as the case may be) both such a register and such a duplicate, it shall keep them at the same place.

(5)   Every company which keeps any such register or duplicate in England and Wales or Scotland shall send to the registrar of companies notice (in the prescribed form) of the place where the register or duplicate is kept and of any change in that place.

(6)   But a company is not bound to send notice under subsection (5) where the register or duplicate has, at all times since it came into existence, been kept at the company's registered office.

191 Right to inspect register

(1)   Every register of holders of debentures of a company shall, except when duly closed . . ., be open to the inspection—

(a)   of the registered holder of any such debentures or any holder of shares in the company without fee; and

(b)   of any other person on payment of [such fee as may be prescribed].

(2)   Any such registered holder of debentures or holder of shares, or any other person, may require a copy of the register of the holders of debentures of the company or any part of it, on payment of [such fee as may be prescribed].

(3)   A copy of any trust deed for securing an issue of debentures shall be forwarded to every holder of any such debentures at his request on payment [of such fee as may be prescribed]
(a), (b). .

(4)   If inspection is refused, or a copy is refused or not forwarded, the company and every officer of it who is in default is liable to a fine and, for continued contravention, to a daily default fine.

(5)   Where a company is in default as above-mentioned, the court may by order compel an immediate inspection of the register or direct that the copies required be sent to the person requiring them.

(6)   For purposes of this section, a register is deemed to be duly closed if closed in accordance with provisions contained in the articles or in the debentures or, in the case of debenture stock, in the stock certificates, or in the trust deed or other document securing the debentures or debenture stock, during such period or periods not exceeding in the whole 30 days in any year, as may be therein specified.

(7)   Liability incurred by a company from the making or deletion of an entry in its register of debenture holders, or from a failure to make or delete any such entry, is not enforceable more than 20 years after the date on which the entry was made or deleted or, in the case of any such failure, the failure first occurred.

This is without prejudice to any lesser period of limitation.

NOTES

Sub-s (1): words omitted repealed, and words in square brackets substituted, by the Companies Act 1989, ss 143(4)(a), 212, Sch 24.

Sub-s (2): words in square brackets substituted by the Companies Act 1989, s 143(4)(b).

Sub-s (3): words in square brackets inserted, and words omitted repealed, by the Companies Act 1989, ss 143(4)(c), 212, Sch 24.

193 Perpetual debentures

A condition contained in debentures, or in a deed for securing debentures, is not invalid by reason only that the debentures are thereby made irredeemable or redeemable only on the happening of a contingency (however remote), or on the expiration of a period (however long), any rule of equity to the contrary notwithstanding.

This applies to debentures whenever issued, and to deeds whenever executed.

194 Power to re-issue redeemed debentures

(1)   Where (at any time) a company has redeemed debentures previously issued, then—

   (a) unless provision to the contrary, whether express or implied, is contained in the articles or in any contract entered into by the company; or

   (b) unless the company has, by passing a resolution to that effect or by some other act, manifested its intention that the debentures shall be cancelled,

the company has, and is deemed always to have had, power to re-issue the debentures, either by re-issuing the same debentures or by issuing other debentures in their place.

(2)   On a re-issue of redeemed debentures, the person entitled to the debentures has, and is deemed always to have had, the same priorities as if the debentures had never been redeemed.

(3)   Where a company has (at any time) deposited any of its debentures to secure advances from time to time on current account or otherwise, the debentures are not deemed to have been redeemed by reason only of the company's account having ceased to be in debit while the debentures remained so deposited.

(4)   The re-issue of a debenture or the issue of another debenture in its place under the power which by this section is given to or deemed to be possessed by a company is to be treated as the issue of a new debenture for purposes of stamp duty; but it is not to be so treated for the purposes of any provision limiting the amount or number of debentures to be issued.

   This applies whenever the issue or re-issue was made.

(5)   A person lending money on the security of a debenture re-issued under this section which appears to be duly stamped may give the debenture in evidence in any proceedings for enforcing his security without payment of the stamp duty or any penalty in respect of it, unless he had notice (or, but for his negligence, might have discovered) that the debenture was not duly stamped; but in that case the company is liable to pay the proper stamp duty and penalty.

[196 Payment of debts out of assets subject to floating charge (England and Wales)]

[(1)   The following applies in the case of a company registered in England and Wales, where debentures of the company are secured by a charge which, as created, was a floating charge.

(2)   If possession is taken, by or on behalf of the holders of any of the debentures, of any property comprised in or subject to the charge, and the company is not at that time in course of being wound up, the company's preferential debts shall be paid out of assets coming to the hands of the person taking possession in priority to any claims for principal or interest in respect of the debentures.

(3)   "Preferential debts" means the categories of debts listed in Schedule 6 to the Insolvency Act; and for the purposes of that Schedule "the relevant date" is the date of possession being taken as above mentioned.

(4)   Payments made under this section shall be recouped, as far as may be, out of the assets of the company available for payment of general creditors.]

NOTES

Substituted, subject to transitional provisions, by the Insolvency Act 1986, ss 437, 439(1), Sch 11, Sch 13, Part I.

PART VI
DISCLOSURE OF INTERESTS IN SHARES

Individual and group acquisitions

198 Obligation of disclosure: the cases in which it may arise and "the relevant time"

(1)   Where a person either—
  (a) to his knowledge acquires an interest in shares comprised in a public company's relevant share capital, or ceases to be interested in shares so comprised (whether or not retaining an interest in other shares so comprised), or
  (b) becomes aware that he has acquired an interest in shares so comprised or that he has ceased to be interested in shares so comprised in which he was previously interested,

then in certain circumstances he comes under an obligation ("the obligation of disclosure") to make notification to the company [with respect to his interests (if any)], in its shares.

(2)   In relation to a public company, "relevant share capital" means the company's issued share capital of a class carrying rights to vote in all circumstances at general meetings of the company; and it is hereby declared for the avoidance of doubt that—
  (a) where a company's share capital is divided into different classes of shares, references in this Part to a percentage of the nominal value of its relevant share capital are to a percentage of the nominal value of the issued shares comprised in each of the classes taken separately, and
  (b) the temporary suspension of voting rights in respect of shares comprised in issued share capital of a company of any such class does not affect the application of this Part in relation to interests in those or any other shares comprised in that class.

(3)   Where, otherwise than in circumstances within subsection (1), a person—
  (a) is aware at the time when it occurs of any change of circumstances affecting facts relevant to the application of the next following section to an existing interest of his in shares comprised in a company's share capital of any description, or
  (b) otherwise becomes aware of any such facts (whether or not arising from any such change of circumstances),

then in certain circumstances he comes under the obligation of disclosure.

(4)   The existence of the obligation in a particular case depends (in part) on circumstances obtaining before and after whatever is in that case the relevant time; and that is—
  (a)   in a case within subsection (1)(a) or (3)(a), the time of the event or change of circumstances there mentioned, and
  (b)   in a case within subsection (1)(b) or (3)(b), the time at which the person became aware of the facts in question.

199 Interests to be disclosed

(1)   For the purposes of the obligation of disclosure, the interests to be taken into account are those in relevant share capital of the company concerned.

[(2)   Where a person is interested in shares comprised in relevant share capital, then—
  (a)   if in some or all of those shares he has interests which are material interests, he has a notifiable interest at any time when the aggregate nominal value of the shares in which those material interests subsist is equal to or more than 3 per cent of the nominal value of that share capital; and
  (b)   he has a notifiable interest at any time when, not having such an interest by virtue of paragraph (a), the aggregate nominal value of the shares in which he has interests (whether or not including material interests) is equal to or more than 10 per cent of the nominal value of the relevant share capital.

(2A)   For the purposes of this Part, a material interest is any interest other than—
  (a)   an interest which a person [who may lawfully] manage investments belonging to another has by virtue of having the management of such investments under an agreement in or evidenced in writing;
  (b)   an interest which a person has by virtue of being the operator of—
    (i)   an authorised unit trust scheme;
    (ii)   a recognised scheme; or
    (iii)   a UCITS (as defined in subsection (8));
  [(bb) an interest belonging to an [open-ended investment company];]
  (c)   an interest in shares in a listed company which, if that company were not listed, would fall to be disregarded by virtue of section 209(10); or
  (d)   an interest of another which a person is taken to have by virtue of the application of section 203 or 205, where the interest of that other person falls within paragraph [(a), (b), (bb) or (c)].]

(3)   All facts relevant to determining whether a person has a notifiable interest at any time (or the percentage level of his interest) are taken to be what he knows the facts to be at that time.

(4)   The obligation of disclosure arises under section 198(1) or (3) where the person has a notifiable interest immediately after the relevant time, but did not have such an interest immediately before that time.

(5)   The obligation also arises under section 198(1) [or (3)] where—

(a) the person had a notifiable interest immediately before the relevant time, but does not have such an interest immediately after it, or

(b) he had a notifiable interest immediately before that time, and has such an interest immediately after it, but the percentage levels of his interest immediately before and immediately after that time are not the same.

[[(6) For the purposes of subsection (2A), a person ("A") may lawfully manage investments belonging to another if—

(a) A can manage those investments in accordance with a permission which A has under Part 4 of the Financial Services and Markets Act 2000;

(b) A is an EEA firm of the kind mentioned in sub-paragraph (a) or (b) of paragraph 5 of Schedule 3 to that Act, and can manage those investments in accordance with its EEA authorisation;

(c) A can, in accordance with section 327 of that Act, manage those investments without contravening the prohibition contained in section 19 of that Act; or

(d) A can lawfully manage those investments in another Member State and would, if he were to manage those investments in the United Kingdom, require permission under Part 4 of that Act.

(7) References in this section to the management of investments must be read with—

(a) section 22 of the Financial Services and Markets Act 2000;

(b) any relevant order under that section; and

(c) Schedule 2 to that Act.]

(8) In this Part "UCITS" means a collective investment scheme which—

(a) is constituted in a member State other than the United Kingdom, and

(b) [is certified by the competent authority in that member State as complying with the conditions imposed] by Council Directive 85/611/EEC co-ordinating the laws, regulations and administrative provisions relating to undertakings for collective investment in transferable securities;

and [subsection (5) of section 264 of the Financial Services and Markets Act 2000] (meaning of "constituted in a member State") applies for the purposes of paragraph (a) of this subsection as it applies for the purposes of that section.]

NOTES

Sub-ss (2), (2A): substituted, for sub-s (2) as originally enacted, by SI 1993/1819, regs 2, 4(1).

Sub-s (2A): in para (a) words "who may lawfully" in square brackets substituted by SI 2001/3649, art 8(1), (2).

Date in force: 1 December 2001: see SI 2001/3649, art 1.

Sub-s (2A): para (bb) inserted by SI 1996/2827, reg 75, Sch 8, para 5.

Sub-s (2A): in para (bb) words "open-ended investment company" in square brackets substituted by SI 2001/1228, reg 84, Sch 7, Pt I, para 4(1), (2).

Date in force: 1 December 2001 (being the day on which the Financial Services and Markets Act 2000, s 19, came into force): see SI 2001/3538, art 2(1) and SI 2001/1228, reg 1(2)(c).

Sub-s (2A): in para (d) words "(a), (b), (bb) or (c)" in square brackets substituted by SI 2001/1228, reg 84, Sch 7, Pt I, para 4(1), (3).

Date in force: 1 December 2001 (being the day on which the Financial Services and Markets Act 2000, s 19, came into force): see SI 2001/3538, art 2(1) and SI 2001/1228, reg 1(2)(c).

Sub-s (5): words in square brackets substituted by SI 1993/1819, reg 4(2).

Sub-ss (6)–(8): inserted by SI 1993/1819, regs 2, 4(3).

Sub-ss (6), (7): substituted by SI 2001/3649, art 8(1), (3).

Date in force: 1 December 2001: see SI 2001/3649, art 1.

Sub-s (8): in para (b) words "is certified by the competent authority in that member State as complying with the conditions imposed" in square brackets substituted by SI 2001/3649, art 8(1), (4)(a).

Date in force: 1 December 2001: see SI 2001/3649, art 1.

Sub-s (8): words "subsection (5) of section 264 of the Financial Services and Markets Act 2000" in square brackets substituted by SI 2001/3649, art 8(1), (4)(b).

Date in force: 1 December 2001: see SI 2001/3649, art 1.

[200 "Percentage level" in relation to notifiable interests]

[(1) Subject to the qualifications mentioned below, "percentage level", in section 199(5)(b), means the percentage figure found by expressing the aggregate nominal value of all the shares comprised in the share capital concerned in which the person has material interests immediately before or (as the case may be) immediately after the relevant time as a percentage of the nominal value of that share capital and rounding that figure down, if it is not a whole number, to the next whole number.

(2) In relation to a notifiable interest which a person has when the aggregate nominal value of the shares in which he is interested is equal to or more than 10 per cent of the nominal value of that relevant share capital, subsection (1) shall have effect as if for the words "has material interests" there were substituted "is interested".

(3) Where the nominal value of the share capital is greater immediately after the relevant time than it was immediately before, the percentage level of the person's interest immediately before (as well as immediately after) that time is determined by reference to the larger amount.]

NOTES

Substituted by SI 1993/1819, regs 2, 5.

202 Particulars to be contained in notification

(1) Where notification is required by section 198 with respect to a person's interest (if any) in shares comprised in relevant share capital of a public company, the obligation to make the notification must . . . be performed within the period of [2 days] next following the day on which that obligation arises; and the notification must be in writing to the company.

(2) The notification must specify the share capital to which it relates, and must also—

[(a) subject to subsections (2A) and (2B), state the number of shares comprised in that share capital in which the person making the notification knows he had material interests immediately after the time when the obligation arose, or]

(b) in a case where the person no longer has a notifiable interest in shares comprised in that share capital, state that he no longer has that interest.

[(2A) Where, immediately after the relevant time, the aggregate nominal value of the shares in which the person making the notification is interested is equal to or more than 10 per cent of the nominal value of that relevant share capital, subsection (2)(a) shall have effect as if for the words "had material interests" there were substituted "was interested".

(2B) Nothing in subsection (2) or (2A) requires a notification to state, in relation to any shares, whether the interest of the person making the notification is (or is not) a material interest.]

[(3) A notification (other than one stating that a person no longer has a notifiable interest) shall include the following particulars, so far as known to the person making the notification at the date when it is made—

(a) the identity of each registered holder of shares to which the notification relates and the number of such shares held by each of them, and

(b) the number of such shares in which the interest of the person giving the notification is such an interest as is mentioned in section 208(5).]

(4) A person who has an interest in shares comprised in a company's relevant share capital, that interest being notifiable, is under obligation to notify the company in writing—

(a) of any particulars in relation to those shares which are specified in subsection (3), and

(b) of any change in those particulars,

of which in either case he becomes aware at any time after any interest notification date and before the first occasion following that date on which he comes under any further obligation of disclosure with respect to his interest in shares comprised in that share capital.

An obligation arising under this section must be performed within the period of [2 days] next following the day on which it arises.

(5) The reference in subsection (4) to an interest notification date, in relation to a person's interest in shares comprised in a public company's relevant share capital, is to either of the following—

(a) the date of any notification made by him with respect to his interest under this Part, and

(b) where he has failed to make a notification, the date on which the period allowed for making it came to an end.

(6) A person who at any time has an interest in shares which is notifiable is to be regarded under subsection (4) as continuing to have a notifiable interest in them unless and until he comes under obligation to make a notification stating that he no longer has such an interest in those shares.

NOTES

Sub-s (1): words omitted repealed and words in square brackets substituted, by the Companies Act 1989, ss 134(3), 212, Sch 24.

Sub-s (2): para (a) substituted by SI 1993/1819, regs 2, 6(1).

Sub-ss (2A), (2B): inserted by SI 1993/1819, regs 2, 6(2).
Sub-s (3): substituted by the Companies Act 1989, s 134(4).
Sub-s (4): words in square brackets substituted by the Companies Act 1989, s 134(3).

203 Notification of family and corporate interests

(1) For purposes of sections 198 to 202, a person is taken to be interested in any shares in which his spouse or any infant child or step-child of his is interested; and "infant" means, in relation to Scotland, [person under the age of 18 years].

(2) For those purposes, a person is taken to be interested in shares if a body corporate is interested in them and—
   (a) that body or its directors are accustomed to act in accordance with his directions or instructions, or
   (b) he is entitled to exercise or control the exercise of one-third or more of the voting power at general meetings of that body corporate.

(3) Where a person is entitled to exercise or control the exercise of one-third or more of the voting power at general meetings of a body corporate and that body corporate is entitled to exercise or control the exercise of any of the voting power at general meetings of another body corporate ("the effective voting power") then, for purposes of subsection (2)(b), the effective voting power is taken as exercisable by that person.

(4) For purposes of subsections (2) and (3), a person is entitled to exercise or control the exercise of voting power if—
   (a) he has a right (whether subject to conditions or not) the exercise of which would make him so entitled, or
   (b) he is under an obligation (whether or not so subject) the fulfilment of which would make him so entitled.

NOTES

Sub-s (1): words in square brackets substituted by the Age of Legal Capacity (Scotland) Act 1991, s 10, Sch 1, para 39.

204 Agreement to acquire interests in a particular company

(1) In certain circumstances the obligation of disclosure may arise from an agreement between two or more persons which includes provision for the acquisition by any one or more of them of interests in shares of a particular public company ("the target company"), being shares comprised in the relevant share capital company.

(2) This section applies to such an agreement if—
   (a) the agreement also includes provisions imposing obligations or restrictions on any one or more of the parties to it with respect to their use, retention or disposal of their interests in that company's shares acquired in pursuance of the agreement (whether or not together with any other interests of theirs in the company's shares to which the agreement relates), and
   (b) any interest in the company's shares is in fact acquired by any of the parties in pursuance of the agreement;

and in relation to such an agreement references below in this section, and in sections 205 and 206, to the target company are to the company which is the target company for that agreement in accordance with this and the previous subsection.

(3)   The reference in subsection (2)(a) to the use of interests in shares in the target company is to the exercise of any rights or of any control or influence arising from those interests (including the right to enter into any agreement for the exercise, or for control of the exercise, of any of those rights by another person).

(4)   Once any interest in shares in the target company has been acquired in pursuance of such an agreement as is mentioned above, this section continues to apply to that agreement irrespective of—

(a)   whether or not any further acquisitions of interests in the company's shares take place in pursuance of the agreement, and

(b)   any change in the persons who are for the time being parties to it, and

(c)   any variation of the agreement,

so long as the agreement continues to include provisions of any description mentioned in subsection (2)(a).

References in this subsection to the agreement include any agreement having effect (whether directly or indirectly) in substitution for the original agreement.

(5)   In this section, and also in references elsewhere in this Part to an agreement to which this section applies, "agreement" includes any agreement or arrangement; and references in this section to provisions of an agreement—

(a)   accordingly include undertakings, expectations or understandings operative under any arrangement, and

(b)   (without prejudice to the above) also include any provisions, whether express or implied and whether absolute or not.

(6)   However, this section does not apply to an agreement which is not legally binding unless it involves mutuality in the undertakings, expectations or understandings of the parties to it; nor does the section apply to an agreement to underwrite or sub-underwrite any offer of shares in a company, provided the agreement is confined to that purpose and any matters incidental to it.

205   Obligation of disclosure arising under s 204

(1)   In the case of an agreement to which section 204 applies, each party to the agreement is taken (for purposes of the obligation of disclosure) to be interested in all shares in the target company in which any other party to it is interested apart from the agreement (whether or not the interest of the other party in question was acquired, or includes any interest which was acquired, in pursuance of the agreement).

(2)   For those purposes, and also for those of the next section, an interest of a party to such an agreement in shares in the target company is an interest apart from the agreement if he is interested in those shares otherwise than by virtue of the application of section 204 and this section in relation to the agreement.

(3)   Accordingly, any such interest of the person (apart from the agreement) includes for those purposes any interest treated as his under section 203 or by the

application of section 204 and this section in relation to any other agreement with respect to shares in the target company to which he is a party.

(4) A notification with respect to his interest in shares in the target company made to that company under this Part by a person who is for the time being a party to an agreement to which section 204 applies shall—
- (a) state that the person making the notification is a party to such an agreement,
- (b) include the names and (so far as known to him) the addresses of the other parties to the agreement, identifying them as such, and
- (c) state whether or not any of the shares to which the notification relates are shares in which he is interested by virtue of section 204 and this section and, if so, the number of those shares.

(5) Where a person makes a notification to a company under this Part in consequence of ceasing to be interested in any shares of that company by virtue of the fact that he or any other person has ceased to be a party to an agreement to which section 204 applies, the notification shall include a statement that he or that other person has ceased to be a party to the agreement (as the case may require) and also (in the latter case) the name and (if known to him) the address of that other.

206 Obligation of persons acting together to keep each other informed

(1) A person who is a party to an agreement to which section 204 applies is subject to the requirements of this section at any time when—
- (a) the target company is a public company, and he knows it to be so, and
- (b) the shares in that company to which the agreement relates consist of or include shares comprised in relevant share capital of the company, and he knows that to be the case; and
- (c) he knows the facts which make the agreement one to which section 204 applies.

(2) Such a person is under obligation to notify every other party to the agreement, in writing, of the relevant particulars of his interest (if any) apart from the agreement in shares comprised in relevant share capital of the target company—
- (a) on his first becoming subject to the requirements of this section, and
- (b) on each occurrence after that time while he is still subject to those requirements of any event or circumstances within section 198(1) (as it applies to his case otherwise than by reference to interests treated as his under section 205 as applying to that agreement) [and
- (c) except in the circumstance mentioned in subsection (3A), the number of shares (if any) out of the number given under paragraph (a) in which he knows that, immediately after the time when the obligation to give the notice arose, he had interests (apart from the agreement) which were not material interests.]

(3) The relevant particulars to be notified under subsection (2) are—
- (a) the number of shares (if any) comprised in the target company's relevant share capital in which the person giving the notice would be required to state his interest [if he were under the wide obligation of disclosure with respect

to that interest] (apart from the agreement) immediately after the time when the obligation to give notice under subsection (2) arose, and

(b) the relevant particulars with respect to the registered ownership of those shares, so far as known to him at the date of the notice.

[(3A) The circumstance referred to in subsection (3)(c) is that the aggregate nominal value of the shares comprised in relevant share capital in which the person is interested (apart from the agreement) is equal to or more than 10 per cent of the nominal value of the relevant share capital.

(3B) For the purposes of subsection (3)(a) "the wide obligation of disclosure" means the obligation to disclose the number of shares in which the person concerned has any interest (material or otherwise).]

(4) A person who is for the time being subject to the requirements of this section is also under obligation to notify every other party to the agreement, in writing—

(a) of any relevant particulars with respect to the registered ownership of any shares comprised in relevant share capital of the target company in which he is interested apart from the agreement, and

(b) of any change in those particulars,

of which in either case he becomes aware at any time after any interest notification date and before the first occasion following that date on which he becomes subject to any further obligation to give notice under subsection (2) with respect to his interest in shares comprised in that share capital.

(5) The reference in subsection (4) to an interest notification date, in relation to a person's interest in shares comprised in the target company's relevant share capital, is to either of the following—

(a) the date of any notice given by him with respect to his interest under subsection (2), and

(b) where he has failed to give that notice, the date on which the period allowed by this section for giving the notice came to an end.

(6) A person who is a party to an agreement to which section 204 applies is under an obligation to notify each other party to the agreement, in writing, of his current address—

(a) on his first becoming subject to the requirements of this section, and

(b) on any change in his address occurring after that time and while he is still subject to those requirements.

(7) A reference to the relevant particulars with respect to the registered ownership of shares is to such particulars in relation to those shares as are mentioned in section 202(3)(a) or (b).

(8) A person's obligation to give any notice required by this section to any other person must be performed within the period of [2 days] next following the day on which that obligation arose.

NOTES

Sub-s (2): first words in square substituted and para (c) inserted by SI 1993/1819, reg 7(1).

Sub-s (3): in para (a) words in square brackets substituted, and para (c) and final word in para (b) inserted, by SI 1993/1819, regs 2, 7(1).

Sub-ss (3A), (3B): inserted by SI 1993/1819, regs 2, 7(2).
Sub-s (8): words in square brackets substituted by the Companies Act 1989, s 134(3).

208 Interests in shares which are to be notified

(1)   This section applies, subject to the section next following, in determining for purposes of sections 198 to 202 whether a person has a notifiable interest in shares.

(2)   A reference to an interest in shares is to be read as including an interest of any kind whatsoever in the shares; and accordingly there are to be disregarded any restraints or restrictions to which the exercise of any right attached to the interest is or may be subject.

(3)   Where property is held on trust and an interest in shares is comprised in the property, a beneficiary of the trust who apart from this subsection does not have an interest in the shares is to be taken as having such an interest.

(4)   A person is taken to have an interest in shares if—
  (a)   he enters into a contract for their purchase by him (whether for cash or other consideration), or
  (b)   not being the registered holder, he is entitled to exercise any right conferred by the holding of the shares or is entitled to control the exercise of any such right.

(5)   A person is taken to have an interest in shares if, otherwise than by virtue of having an interest under a trust—
  (a)   he has a right to call for delivery of the shares to himself or to his order, or
  (b)   he has a right to acquire an interest in shares or is under an obligation to take an interest in shares,

whether in any case the right or obligation is conditional or absolute.

(6)   For purposes of subsection (4)(b), a person is entitled to exercise or control the exercise of any right conferred by the holding of shares if he—
  (a)   has a right (whether subject to conditions or not) the exercise of which would make him so entitled, or
  (b)   is under an obligation (whether so subject or not) the fulfilment of which would make him so entitled.

(7)   Persons having a joint interest are taken each of them to have that interest.

(8)   It is immaterial that shares in which a person has an interest are unidentifiable.

Registration and investigation of share acquisitions and disposals

212 Company investigations

(1)   A public company may by notice in writing require a person whom the company knows or has reasonable cause to believe to be or, at any time during the 3 years immediately preceding the date on which the notice is issued, to have been interested in shares comprised in the company's relevant share capital—
  (a)   to confirm that fact or (as the case may be) to indicate whether or not it is the case, and

(b) where he holds or has during that time held an interest in shares so comprised, to give such further information as may be required in accordance with the following subsection.

(2) A notice under this section may require the person to whom it is addressed—

(a) to give particulars of his own past or present interest in shares comprised in relevant share capital of the company (held by him at any time during the 3-year period mentioned in subsection (1)),

(b) where the interest is a present interest and any other interest in the shares subsists or, in any case, where another interest in the shares subsisted during that 3-year period at any time when his own interest subsisted, to give (so far as lies within his knowledge) such particulars with respect to that other interest as may be required by the notice,

(c) where his interest is a past interest, to give (so far as lies within his knowledge) particulars of the identity of the person who held that interest immediately upon his ceasing to hold it.

(3) The particulars referred to in subsection (2)(a) and (b) include particulars of the identity of persons interested in the shares in question and of whether persons interested in the same shares are or were parties to any agreement to which section 204 applies or to any agreement or arrangement relating to the exercise of any rights conferred by the holding of the shares.

(4) A notice under this section shall require any information given in response to the notice to be given in writing within such reasonable time as may be specified in the notice.

(5) Sections 203 to 205 and 208 apply for the purpose of construing references in this section to persons interested in shares and to interests in shares respectively, as they apply in relation to sections 198 to 201 (but with the omission of any reference to section 209).

(6) This section applies in relation to a person who has or previously had, or is or was entitled to acquire, a right to subscribe for shares in a public company which would on issue be comprised in relevant share capital of that company as it applies in relation to a person who is or was interested in shares so comprised; and references above in this section to an interest in shares so comprised and to shares so comprised are to be read accordingly in any such case as including respectively any such right and shares which would on issue be so comprised.

214 Company investigation on requisition by members

(1) A company may be required to exercise its powers under section 212 on the requisition of members of the company holding at the date of the deposit of the requisition not less than one-tenth of such of the paid-up capital of the company as carries at that date the right of voting at general meetings of the company.

(2) The requisition must—

(a) state that the requisitionists are requiring the company to exercise its powers under section 212,

(b) specify the manner in which they require those powers to be exercised, and

(c) give reasonable grounds for requiring the company to exercise those powers in the manner specified,

and must be signed by the requisitionists and deposited at the company's registered office.

(3) The requisition may consist of several documents in like form each signed by one or more requisitionists.

(4) On the deposit of a requisition complying with this section it is the company's duty to exercise its powers under section 212 in the manner specified in the requisition.

(5) If default is made in complying with subsection (4), the company and every officer of it who is in default is liable to a fine.

216 Penalty for failure to provide information

(1) Where notice is served by a company under section 212 on a person who is or was interested in shares of the company and that person fails to give the company any information required by the notice within the time specified in it, the company may apply to the court for an order directing that the shares in question be subject to the restrictions of Part XV of this Act.

[(1A) On an application made under subsection (1) the court may make an interim order and any such order may be made unconditionally or on such terms as the court thinks fit.

(1B) If the court is satisfied that an order under subsection (1) may unfairly affect the rights of third parties in respect of shares then the court, for the purpose of protecting such rights and subject to such terms as it thinks fit, may direct that such acts by such persons or descriptions of persons and for such purposes as may be set out in the order, shall not constitute a breach of the restrictions of Part XV of this Act.]

(2) [An order under this section] may be made by the court notwithstanding any power contained in the applicant company's memorandum or articles enabling the company itself to impose similar restrictions on the shares in question.

(3) Subject to the following subsections, a person who fails to comply with a notice under section 212 or who, in purported compliance with such a notice, makes any statement which he knows to be false in a material particular or recklessly makes any statement which is false in a material particular is guilty of an offence and liable to imprisonment or a fine, or both.

Section 733(2) and (3) of this Act (liability of individuals for corporate default) apply to offences under this subsection.

(4) A person is not guilty of an offence by virtue of failing to comply with a notice under section 212 if he proves that the requirement to give the information was frivolous or vexatious.

(5)   A person is not obliged to comply with a notice under section 212 if he is for the time being exempted by the Secretary of State from the operation of that section; but the Secretary of State shall not grant any such exemption unless—

(a)   he has consulted with the Governor of the Bank of England, and

(b)   he (the Secretary of State) is satisfied that, having regard to any undertaking given by the person in question with respect to any interest held or to be held by him in any shares, there are special reasons why that person should not be subject to the obligations imposed by that section.

NOTES

Sub-ss (1A), (1B): inserted by SI 1991/1646, reg 4(a).
Sub-s (2): words in square brackets substituted by SI 1991/1646, reg 4(b).

219 Inspection of register and reports

(1)   Any register of interests in shares and any report which is required by section 215(7) to be available for inspection in accordance with this section shall, . . . be open to the inspection of any member of the company or of any other person without charge.

(2)   Any such member or other person may require a copy of any such register or report, or any part of it, on payment of [such fee as may be prescribed]; and the company shall cause any copy so required by a person to be sent to him before the expiration of the period of 10 days beginning with the day next following that on which the requirement is received by the company.

(3)   If an inspection required under this section is refused or a copy so required is not sent within the proper period, the company and every officer of it who is in default is liable to a fine and, for continued contravention, to a daily default fine.

(4)   In the case of a refusal of an inspection required under this section of any register or report, the court may by order compel an immediate inspection of it; and in the case of failure to send a copy required under this section, the court may by order direct that the copy required shall be sent to the person requiring it.

(5)   The Secretary of State may by regulations made by statutory instrument substitute a sum specified in the regulations for the sum for the time being mentioned in subsection (2).

NOTES

Sub-s (1): words omitted repealed by the Companies Act 1989, ss 143(5), 212, Sch 24.
Sub-s (2): words in square brackets substituted by the Companies Act 1989, s 143(5).

PART VII
ACCOUNTS AND AUDIT

Chapter I
Provisions Applying to Companies Generally

[Accounting records]

NOTES
Inserted by the Companies Act 1989, s 2.

[221 Duty to keep accounting records]

[(1)   Every company shall keep accounting records which are sufficient to show and explain the company's transactions and are such as to—
-   (a)   disclose with reasonable accuracy, at any time, the financial position of the company at that time, and
-   (b)   enable the directors to ensure that any balance sheet and profit and loss account prepared under this Part complies with the requirements of this Act.

(2)   The accounting records shall in particular contain—
-   (a)   entries from day to day of all sums of money received and expended by the company, and the matters in respect of which the receipt and expenditure takes place, and
-   (b)   a record of the assets and liabilities of the company.

(3)   If the company's business involves dealing in goods, the accounting records shall contain—
-   (a)   statements of stock held by the company at the end of each financial year of the company,
-   (b)   all statements of stocktakings from which any such statement of stock as is mentioned in paragraph (a) has been or is to be prepared, and
-   (c)   except in the case of goods sold by way of ordinary retail trade, statements of all goods sold and purchased, showing the goods and the buyers and sellers in sufficient detail to enable all these to be identified.

(4)   A parent company which has a subsidiary undertaking in relation to which the above requirements do not apply shall take reasonable steps to secure that the undertaking keeps such accounting records as to enable the directors of the parent company to ensure that any balance sheet and profit and loss account prepared under this Part complies with the requirements of this Act.

(5)   If a company fails to comply with any provision of this section, every officer of the company who is in default is guilty of an offence unless he shows that he acted honestly and that in the circumstances in which the company's business was carried on the default was excusable.

(6)   A person guilty of an offence under this section is liable to imprisonment or a fine, or both.]

NOTES
Except in relation to oversea companies (see note below), Part I of the Companies Act 1989 (ss 1–23) inserts new provisions in place of original ss 221–262 of this Act and amends the related Schedules (see s 1 of the 1989 Act).

Inserted by the Companies Act 1989, s 2.

[222 Where and for how long records to be kept]

[(1) A company's accounting records shall be kept at its registered office or such other place as the directors think fit, and shall at all times be open to inspection by the company's officers.

(2) If accounting records are kept at a place outside Great Britain, accounts and returns with respect to the business dealt with in the accounting records so kept shall be sent to, and kept at, a place in Great Britain, and shall at all times be open to such inspection.

(3) The accounts and returns to be sent to Great Britain shall be such as to—
  (a) disclose with reasonable accuracy the financial position of the business in question at intervals of not more than six months, and
  (b) enable the directors to ensure that the company's balance sheet and profit and loss account comply with the requirements of this Act.

(4) If a company fails to comply with any provision of subsections (1) to (3), every officer of the company who is in default is guilty of an offence, and liable to imprisonment or a fine or both, unless he shows that he acted honestly and that in the circumstances in which the company's business was carried on the default was excusable.

(5) Accounting records which a company is required by section 221 to keep shall be preserved by it—
  (a) in the case of a private company, for three years from the date on which they are made, and
  (b) in the case of a public company, for six years from the date on which they are made.

This is subject to any provision contained in rules made under section 411 of the Insolvency Act 1986 (company insolvency rules).

(6) An officer of a company is guilty of an offence, and liable to imprisonment or a fine or both, if he fails to take all reasonable steps for securing compliance by the company with subsection (5) or intentionally causes any default by the company under that subsection.]

NOTES
Except in relation to oversea companies (see note below), Part I of the Companies Act 1989 (ss 1–23) inserts new provisions in place of original ss 221–262 of this Act and amends the related Schedules (see s 1 of the 1989 Act).

Inserted by the Companies Act 1989, s 2.

[A company's financial year and accounting reference periods]

NOTES

Inserted by the Companies Act 1989, s 3.

[223 A company's financial year]

[(1)   A company's "financial year" is determined as follows.

(2)   Its first financial year begins with the first day of its first accounting reference period and ends with the last day of that period or such other date, not more than seven days before or after the end of that period, as the directors may determine.

(3)   Subsequent financial years begin with the day immediately following the end of the company's previous financial year and end with the last day of its next accounting reference period or such other date, not more than seven days before or after the end of that period, as the directors may determine.

(4)   In relation to an undertaking which is not a company, references in this Act to its financial year are to any period in respect of which a profit and loss account of the undertaking is required to be made up (by its constitution or by the law under which it is established), whether that period is a year or not.

(5)   The directors of a parent company shall secure that, except where in their opinion there are good reasons against it, the financial year of each of its subsidiary undertakings coincides with the company's own financial year.]

NOTES

Except in relation to oversea companies (see note below), Part I of the Companies Act 1989 (ss 1–23) inserts new provisions in place of original ss 221–262 of this Act and amends the related Schedules (see s 1 of the 1989 Act).

Inserted by the Companies Act 1989, s 3.

[224 Accounting reference periods and accounting reference date]

[(1)   A company's accounting reference periods are determined according to its accounting reference date.

(2)   A company [incorporated before 1st April 1996] may, at any time before the end of the period of nine months beginning with the date of its incorporation, by notice in the prescribed form given to the registrar specify its accounting reference date, that is, the date on which its accounting reference period ends in each calendar year.

(3)   Failing such notice, [the accounting reference date of such a company] is—
  (a)   in the case of a company incorporated before [1st April 1990], 31st March;
  (b)   in the case of a company incorporated after [1st April 1990], the last day of the month in which the anniversary of its incorporation falls.

[(3A)   The accounting reference date of a company incorporated on or after 1st April 1996 is the last day of the month in which the anniversary of its incorporation falls.]

(4)   A company's first accounting reference period is the period of more than six months, but not more than 18 months, beginning with the date of its incorporation and ending with its accounting reference date.

(5)   Its subsequent accounting reference periods are successive periods of twelve months beginning immediately after the end of the previous accounting reference period and ending with its accounting reference date.

(6)   This section has effect subject to the provisions of section 225 relating to the alteration of accounting reference dates and the consequences of such alteration.]

NOTES

Except in relation to oversea companies (see note below), Part I of the Companies Act 1989 (ss 1–23) inserts new provisions in place of original ss 221-262 of this Act and amends the related Schedules (see s 1 of the 1989 Act).

Inserted by the Companies Act 1989, s 3.

Sub-s (2): words in square brackets inserted by SI 1996/189, reg 2(2).

Sub-s (3): first words in square brackets substituted by SI 1996/189, reg 2(3); second and third words in square brackets substituted by SI 1990/355, art 15.

Sub-s (3A): inserted by SI 1996/189, reg 2(4).

[225 Alteration of accounting reference date]

[(1)   A company may by notice in the prescribed form given to the registrar specify a new accounting reference date [having effect in relation to—

(a)   the company's current accounting reference period and subsequent periods; or

(b)   the company's previous accounting reference period and subsequent periods.

A company's "previous accounting reference period" means that immediately preceding its current accounting reference period.]

(2)   . . .

(3)   The notice shall state whether the current or previous accounting reference period—

(a)   is to be shortened, so as to come to an end on the first occasion on which the new accounting reference date falls or fell after the beginning of the period, or

(b)   is to be extended, so as to come to an end on the second occasion on which that date falls or fell after the beginning of the period.

(4)   A notice under subsection (1) stating that the current [or previous] accounting reference period is to be extended is ineffective, except as mentioned below, if given less than five years after the end of an earlier accounting reference period of the company which was extended by virtue of this section.

This subsection does not apply—

[(a)   to a notice given by a company which is a subsidiary undertaking or parent undertaking of another EEA undertaking if the new accounting reference date coincides with that of the other EEA undertaking or, where that undertaking is not a company, with the last day of its financial year, or]

(b) where an administration order is in force under Part II of the Insolvency Act 1986,

or where the Secretary of State directs that it should not apply, which he may do with respect to a notice which has been given or which may be given.

(5) A notice under [subsection (1)] may not be given [in respect of a previous accounting reference period] if the period allowed for laying and delivering accounts and reports in relation to [that period] has already expired.

(6) An accounting reference period may not in any case, unless an administration order is in force under Part II of the Insolvency Act 1986, be extended so as to exceed 18 months and a notice under this section is ineffective if the current or previous accounting reference period as extended in accordance with the notice would exceed that limit.

[(7) In this section "EEA undertaking" means an undertaking established under the law of any part of the United Kingdom or the law of any other EEA State.]]

NOTES

Except in relation to oversea companies (see note below), Part I of the Companies Act 1989 (ss 1–23) inserts new provisions in place of ss 221–262 of this Act and amends the related Schedules (see s 1 of the 1989 Act).

Inserted by the Companies Act 1989, s 3.

Sub-s (1): words in square brackets substituted by SI 1996/189, reg 3(2).

Sub-s (2): repealed by SI 1996/189, reg 3(3).

Sub-s (4): first words in square brackets inserted, and para (a) substituted, by SI 1996/189, reg 3(4).

Sub-s (5): first and final words in square brackets substituted, and second words in square brackets inserted, by SI 1996/189, reg 3(5).

Sub-s (7): inserted by SI 1996/189, reg 3(6).

[Annual accounts]

NOTES

Inserted by the Companies Act 1989, s 4(1).

[226 Duty to prepare individual company accounts]

[(1) The directors of every company shall prepare for each financial year of the company—
(a) a balance sheet as at the last day of the year, and
(b) a profit and loss account.

Those accounts are referred to in this Part as the company's "individual accounts".

(2) The balance sheet shall give a true and fair view of the state of affairs of the company as at the end of the financial year; and the profit and loss account shall give a true and fair view of the profit or loss of the company for the financial year.

(3) A company's individual accounts shall comply with the provisions of Schedule 4 as to the form and content of the balance sheet and profit and loss account and additional information to be provided by way of notes to the accounts.

(4) Where compliance with the provisions of that Schedule, and the other provisions of this Act as to the matters to be included in a company's individual accounts or in notes to those accounts, would not be sufficient to give a true and fair view, the necessary additional information shall be given in the accounts or in a note to them.

(5) If in special circumstances compliance with any of those provisions is inconsistent with the requirement to give a true and fair view, the directors shall depart from that provision to the extent necessary to give a true and fair view.

Particulars of any such departure, the reasons for it and its effect shall be given in a note to the accounts.]

NOTES

Except in relation to oversea companies (see note below), Part I of the Companies Act 1989 (ss 1–23) inserts new provisions in place of original ss 221–262 of this Act and amends the related Schedules (see s 1 of the 1989 Act).

Inserted by the Companies Act 1989, s 4(1).

[227 Duty to prepare group accounts]

[(1) If at the end of a financial year a company is a parent company the directors shall, as well as preparing individual accounts for the year, prepare group accounts.

(2) Group accounts shall be consolidated accounts comprising—
  (a) a consolidated balance sheet dealing with the state of affairs of the parent company and its subsidiary undertakings, and
  (b) a consolidated profit and loss account dealing with the profit or loss of the parent company and its subsidiary undertakings.

(3) The accounts shall give a true and fair view of the state of affairs as at the end of the financial year, and the profit or loss for the financial year, of the undertakings included in the consolidation as a whole, so far as concerns members of the company.

(4) A company's group accounts shall comply with the provisions of Schedule 4A as to the form and content of the consolidated balance sheet and consolidated profit and loss account and additional information to be provided by way of notes to the accounts.

(5) Where compliance with the provisions of that Schedule, and the other provisions of this Act, as to the matters to be included in a company's group accounts or in notes to those accounts, would not be sufficient to give a true and fair view, the necessary additional information shall be given in the accounts or in a note to them.

(6) If in special circumstances compliance with any of those provisions is inconsistent with the requirement to give a true and fair view, the directors shall depart from that provision to the extent necessary to give a true and fair view.

Particulars of any such departure, the reasons for it and its effect shall be given in a note to the accounts.]

NOTES

Except in relation to oversea companies (see note below), Part I of the Companies Act 1989 (ss 1–23) inserts new provisions in place of original ss 221–262 of this Act and amends the related Schedules (see s 1 of the 1989 Act).

Inserted by the Companies Act 1989, s 5(1).

[231 Disclosure required in notes to accounts: related undertakings]

[(1) The information specified in Schedule 5 shall be given in notes to a company's annual accounts.

(2) Where the company is not required to prepare group accounts, the information specified in Part I of that Schedule shall be given; and where the company is required to prepare group accounts, the information specified in Part II of that Schedule shall be given.

(3) The information required by Schedule 5 need not be disclosed with respect to an undertaking which—

(a) is established under the law of a country outside the United Kingdom, or

(b) carries on business outside the United Kingdom,

if in the opinion of the directors of the company the disclosure would be seriously prejudicial to the business of that undertaking, or to the business of the company or any of its subsidiary undertakings, and the Secretary of State agrees that the information need not be disclosed.

This subsection does not apply in relation to the information required under [paragraph . . . 6, 9A, 20 or 28A] of that Schedule.

(4) Where advantage is taken of subsection (3), that fact shall be stated in a note to the company's annual accounts.

(5) If the directors of the company are of the opinion that the number of undertakings in respect of which the company is required to disclose information under any provision of Schedule 5 to this Act is such that compliance with that provision would result in information of excessive length being given, the information need only be given in respect of—

(a) the undertakings whose results or financial position, in the opinion of the directors, principally affected the figures shown in the company's annual accounts, and

(b) undertakings excluded from consolidation under section 229(3) or (4).

. . .

(6) If advantage is taken of subsection (5)—

(a) there shall be included in the notes to the company's annual accounts a statement that the information is given only with respect to such undertakings as are mentioned in that subsection, and

(b) the full information (both that which is disclosed in the notes to the accounts and that which is not) shall be annexed to the company's next annual return.

For this purpose the "next annual return" means that next delivered to the registrar after the accounts in question have been approved under section 233.

(7)   If a company fails to comply with subsection (6)(b), the company and every officer of it who is in default is liable to a fine and, for continued contravention, to a daily default fine.]

NOTES

Except in relation to oversea companies (see note below), Part I of the Companies Act 1989 (ss 1–23) inserts new provisions in place of original ss 221–262 of this Act and amends the related Schedules (see s 1 of the 1989 Act).

Inserted by the Companies Act 1989, s 6(1).

Sub-s (3): words in square brackets substituted by SI 1993/1820, reg 11(1); words omitted repealed, in relation to the annual accounts and annual report of any company for the financial year ending on or after 2 February 1996, by SI 1996/189, regs 15(1), 16(1), for savings see reg 16(2) thereof.

Sub-s (5): words omitted repealed, in relation to the annual accounts and annual report of any company for the financial year ending on or after 2 February 1996, by SI 1996/189, regs 15(1), 16(1); for savings see reg 16(2) thereof.

[232 Disclosure required in notes to accounts: emoluments and other benefits of directors and others]

[(1)   The information specified in Schedule 6 shall be given in notes to a company's annual accounts.

(2)   In that Schedule—

Part I relates to the emoluments of directors (including emoluments waived), pensions of directors and past directors, compensation for loss of office to directors and past directors and sums paid to third parties in respect of directors' services,

Part II relates to loans, quasi-loans and other dealings in favour of directors and connected persons, and

Part III relates to transactions, arrangements and agreements made by the company or a subsidiary undertaking for officers of the company other than directors.

(3)   It is the duty of any director of a company, and any person who is or has at any time in the preceding five years been an officer of the company, to give notice to the company of such matters relating to himself as may be necessary for the purposes of Part I Schedule 6.

(4)   A person who makes default in complying with subsection (3) commits an offence and is liable to a fine.]

NOTES

Except in relation to oversea companies (see note below), Part I of the Companies Act 1989 (ss 1–23) inserts new provisions in place of original ss 221–262 of this Act and amends the related Schedules (see s 1 of the 1989 Act).

Inserted by the Companies Act 1989, s 6(3).

[Approval and signing of accounts]

NOTES

Inserted by the Companies Act 1989, s 7.

[233 Approval and signing of accounts]

[(1)   A company's annual accounts shall be approved by the board of directors and signed on behalf of the board by a director of the company.

(2)   The signature shall be on the company's balance sheet.

(3)   Every copy of the balance sheet which is laid before the company in general meeting, or which is otherwise circulated, published or issued, shall state the name of the person who signed the balance sheet on behalf of the board.

(4)   The copy of the company's balance sheet which is delivered to the registrar shall be signed on behalf of the board by a director of the company.

(5)   If annual accounts are approved which do not comply with the requirements of this Act, every director of the company who is party to their approval and who knows that they do not comply or is reckless as to whether they comply is guilty of an offence and liable to a fine.

For this purpose every director of the company at the time the accounts are approved shall be taken to be a party to their approval unless he shows that he took all reasonable steps to prevent their being approved.

(6)   If a copy of the balance sheet—
  (a) is laid before the company, or otherwise circulated, published or issued, without the balance sheet having been signed as required by this section or without the required statement of the signatory's name being included, or
  (b) is delivered to the registrar without being signed as required by this section,

the company and every officer of it who is in default is guilty of an offence and liable to a fine.]

NOTES

Except in relation to oversea companies (see note below), Part I of the Companies Act 1989 (ss 1–23) inserts new provisions in place of original ss 221–262 of this Act and amends the related Schedules (see s 1 of the 1989 Act).

Inserted by the Companies Act 1989, s 7.

Sub-s (5): has effect in relation to annual accounts for financial years commencing on or after 23 December 1989: for further details see SI 1990/2569, art 6(2)–(4).

[Directors' report]

NOTES

Inserted by the Companies Act 1989, s 8(1).

[234 Duty to prepare director's report]

[(1) The directors of a company shall for each financial year prepare a report—

(a) containing a fair review of the development of the business of the company and its subsidiary undertakings during the financial year and of their position at the end of it, and

(b) stating the amount (if any) which they recommend should be paid as dividend . . .

(2) The report shall state the names of the persons who, at any time during the financial year, were directors of the company, and the principal activities of the company and its subsidiary undertakings in the course of the year and any significant change in those activities in the year.

(3) The report shall also comply with Schedule 7 as regards the disclosure of the matters mentioned there.

(4) In Schedule 7—

Part I relates to matters of a general nature, including changes in asset values, directors' shareholdings and other interests and contributions for political and charitable purposes,

Part II relates to the acquisition by a company of its own shares or a charge on them,

Part III relates to the employment, training and advancement of disabled persons,

. . .

Part V relates to the involvement of employees in the affairs, policy and performance of the company,

[Part VI relates to the company's policy [and practice] on the payment of creditors.]

(5) In the case of any failure to comply with the provisions of this part as to the preparation of a directors' report and the contents of the report, every person who was a director of the company immediately before the end of the period for laying and delivering accounts and reports for the financial year in question is guilty of an offence and liable to a fine.

(6) In proceedings against a person for an offence under this section it is a defence for him to prove that he took all reasonable steps for securing compliance with the requirements in question.]

NOTES

Except in relation to oversea companies (see note below), Part I of the Companies Act 1989 (ss 1–23) inserts new provisions in place of original ss 221–262 of this Act and amends the related Schedules (see s 1 of the 1989 Act).

Inserted by the Companies Act 1989, s 8(1).

Sub-s (1): in para (b) words omitted repealed by SI 1996/189, regs 5(2), 16(1).

Sub-s (4): entry omitted repealed, in relation to the annual accounts and annual report of any company for the financial year ending on or after 2 February 1996, by SI 1996/189 regs 5(3), 16(1); entry "Part VI" inserted, in relation to the annual accounts and annual report of any company for the financial year ending on or after 2 February 1996, by SI 1996/189, regs 5(3), 16(1), words in square brackets therein inserted by SI 1997/571, reg 2(1).

[234A Approval and signing of directors' report]

[(1)   The directors' report shall be approved by the board of directors and signed on behalf of the board by a director or the secretary of the company.

(2)   Every copy of the directors' report which is laid before the company in general meeting, or which is otherwise circulated, published or issued, shall state the name of the person who signed it on behalf of the board.

(3)   The copy of the directors' report which is delivered to the registrar shall be signed on behalf of the board by a director or the secretary of the company.

(4)   If a copy of the directors' report—
  (a)   is laid before the company, or otherwise circulated, published or issued, without the report having been signed as required by this section or without the required statement of the signatory's name being included, or
  (b)   is delivered to the registrar without being signed as required by this section,

the company and every officer of it who is in default is guilty of an offence and liable to a fine.]

NOTES

Except in relation to oversea companies (see note below), Part I of the Companies Act 1989 (ss 1–23) inserts new provisions in place of original ss 221–262 of this Act and amends the related Schedules (see s 1 of the 1989 Act).

Inserted by the Companies Act 1989, s 8(1).

[Auditors' report]

NOTES

Inserted by the Companies Act 1989, s 9.

[235 Auditors' report]

[(1)   A company's auditors shall make a report to the company's members on all annual accounts of the company of which copies are to be laid before the company in general meeting during their tenure of office.

(2)   The auditors' report shall state whether in the auditors' opinion the annual accounts have been properly prepared in accordance with this Act, and in particular whether a true and fair view is given—
  (a)   in the case of an individual balance sheet, of the state of affairs of the company as at the end of the financial year,
  (b)   in the case of an individual profit and loss account, of the profit or loss of the company for the financial year,
  (c)   in the case of group accounts, of the state of affairs at the end of the financial year, and the profit or loss for the financial year, of the undertakings included in the consolidation as a whole, so far as concerns members of the company.

(3)   The auditors shall consider whether the information given in the directors' report for the financial year for which the annual accounts are prepared is consistent with those accounts; and if they are of opinion that it is not they shall state that fact in their report.]

NOTES

Except in relation to oversea companies (see note below), Part I of the Companies Act 1989 (ss 1–23) inserts new provisions in place of original ss 221–262 of this Act and amends the related Schedules (see s 1 of the 1989 Act).

Inserted by the Companies Act 1989, s 9.

[236 Signature of auditors' report]

[(1)   The auditors' report shall state the names of the auditors and be signed by them.

(2)   Every copy of the auditors' report which is laid before the company in general meeting, or which is otherwise circulated, published or issued, shall state the names of the auditors.

(3)   The copy of the auditors' report which is delivered to the registrar shall state the names of the auditors and be signed by them.

(4)   If a copy of the auditors' report—
  (a)   is laid before the company, or otherwise circulated, published or issued, without the required statement of the auditors' names, or
  (b)   is delivered to the registrar without the required statement of the auditors' names or without being signed as required by this section,

the company and every officer of it who is in default is guilty of an offence and liable to a fine.

(5)   References in this section to signature by the auditors are, where the office of auditor is held by a body corporate or partnership, to signature in the name of the body corporate or partnership by a person authorised to sign on its behalf.]

NOTES

Except in relation to oversea companies (see note below), Part I of the Companies Act 1989 (ss 1–23) inserts new provisions in place of original ss 221–262 of this Act and amends the related Schedules (see s 1 of the 1989 Act).

Inserted by the Companies Act 1989, s 9.

[237 Duties of auditors]

[(1)   A company's auditors shall, in preparing their report, carry out such investigations as will enable them to form an opinion as to—
  (a)   whether proper accounting records have been kept by the company and proper returns adequate for their audit have been received from branches not visited by them, and
  (b)   whether the company's individual accounts are in agreement with the accounting records and returns.

(2)   If the auditors are of opinion that proper accounting records have not been kept, or that proper returns adequate for their audit have not been received from branches not visited by them, or if the company's individual accounts are not in agreement with the accounting records and returns, the auditors shall state that fact in their report.

(3)   If the auditors fail to obtain all the information and explanations which, to the best of their knowledge and belief, are necessary for the purposes of their audit, they shall state that fact in their report.

(4)   If the requirements of Schedule 6 (disclosure of information: emoluments and other benefits of directors and others) are not complied with in the annual accounts, the auditors shall include in their report, so far as they are reasonably able to do so, a statement giving the required particulars.

[(4A)   If the directors of the company have taken advantage of the exemption conferred by section 248 (exemption for small and medium-sized groups from the need to prepare group accounts) and in the auditors' opinion they were not entitled so to do, the auditors shall state that fact in their report.]]

NOTES

Except in relation to oversea companies (see note below), Part I of the Companies Act 1989 (ss 1–23) inserts new provisions in place of original ss 221–262 of this Act and amends the related Schedules (see s 1 of the 1989 Act).
Inserted by the Companies Act 1989, s 9.
Sub-s (4A): inserted by SI 1996/189, reg 6.

[Publication of accounts and reports]

NOTES

Inserted by the Companies Act 1989, s 10.

[238 Persons entitled to receive copies of accounts and reports]

[(1)   A copy of the company's annual accounts, together with a copy of the directors' report for that financial year and of the auditors' report on those accounts, shall be sent to—
   (a)   every member of the company,
   (b)   every holder of the company's debentures, and
   (c)   every person who is entitled to receive notice of general meetings,

not less than 21 days before the date of the meeting at which copies of those documents are to be laid in accordance with section 241.

(2)   Copies need not be sent—
   (a)   to a person who is not entitled to receive notices of general meetings and of whose address the company is unaware, or
   (b)   to more than one of the joint holders of shares or debentures none of whom is entitled to receive such notices, or
   (c)   in the case of joint holders of shares or debentures some of whom are, and some not, entitled to receive such notices, to those who are not so entitled.

(3)   In the case of a company not having a share capital, copies need not be sent to anyone who is not entitled to receive notices of general meetings of the company.

(4)   If copies are sent less than 21 days before the date of the meeting, they shall, notwithstanding that fact, be deemed to have been duly sent if it is so agreed by all the members entitled to attend and vote at the meeting.

[(4A)   References in this section to sending to any person copies of a company's annual accounts, of the directors' report and of the auditors' report include references to using electronic communications for sending copies of those documents to such address as may for the time being be notified to the company by that person for that purpose.

(4B)   For the purposes of this section copies of those documents are also to be treated as sent to a person where—
  (a)   the company and that person have agreed to his having access to the documents on a web site (instead of their being sent to him);
  (b)   the documents are documents to which that agreement applies; and
  (c)   that person is notified, in a manner for the time being agreed for the purpose between him and the company, of—
      (i)   the publication of the documents on a web site;
      (ii)   the address of that web site; and
      (iii) the place on that web site where the documents may be accessed, and how they may be accessed.

(4C)   For the purposes of this section documents treated in accordance with subsection (4B) as sent to any person are to be treated as sent to him not less than 21 days before the date of a meeting if, and only if—
  (a)   the documents are published on the web site throughout a period beginning at least 21 days before the date of the meeting and ending with the conclusion of the meeting; and
  (b)   the notification given for the purposes of paragraph (c) of that subsection is given not less than 21 days before the date of the meeting.

(4D)   Nothing in subsection (4C) shall invalidate the proceedings of a meeting where—
  (a)   any documents that are required to be published as mentioned in paragraph (a) of that subsection are published for a part, but not all, of the period mentioned in that paragraph; and
  (b)   the failure to publish those documents throughout that period is wholly attributable to circumstances which it would not be reasonable to have expected the company to prevent or avoid.

(4E)   A company may, notwithstanding any provision to the contrary in its articles, take advantage of any of subsections (4A) to (4D).]

(5)   If default is made in complying with this section, the company and every officer of it who is in default is guilty of an offence and liable to a fine.

(6)   Where copies are sent out under this section over a period of days, references elsewhere in this Act to the day on which copies are sent out shall be construed as references to the last day of that period.]

NOTES
Except in relation to oversea companies (see note below), Part I of the Companies Act 1989 (ss 1–23) inserts new provisions in place of original ss 221–262 of this Act and amends the related Schedules (see s 1 of the 1989 Act).
Inserted by the Companies Act 1989, s 10.
Sub-ss (4A)–(4E): inserted by SI 2000/3373, art 12.
Date in force: 22 December 2000: see SI 2000/3373, art 1(1).

[239 Right to demand copies of accounts and reports]

[(1) Any member of a company and any holder of a company's debentures is entitled to be furnished, on demand and without charge, with a copy of the company's last annual accounts and directors' report and a copy of the auditors' report on those accounts.

(2) The entitlement under this section is to a single copy of those documents, but that is in addition to any copy to which a person may be entitled under section 238.

[(2A) Any obligation by virtue of subsection (1) to furnish a person with a document may be complied with by using electronic communications for sending that document to such address as may for the time being be notified to the company by that person for that purpose.

(2B) A company may, notwithstanding any provision to the contrary in its articles, take advantage of subsection (2A).]

(3) If a demand under this section is not complied with within seven days, the company and every officer of it who is in default is guilty of an offence and liable to a fine and, for continued contravention, to a daily default fine.

(4) If in proceedings for such an offence the issue arises whether a person had already been furnished with a copy of the relevant document under this section, it is for the defendant to prove that he had.]

NOTES
Except in relation to oversea companies (see note below), Part I of the Companies Act 1989 (ss 1–23) inserts new provisions in place of original ss 221–262 of this Act and amends the related Schedules (see s 1 of the 1989 Act).
Inserted by the Companies Act 1989, s 10.
Sub-ss (2A), (2B): inserted by SI 2000/3373, art 13.
Date in force: 22 December 2000: see SI 2000/3373, art 1(1).

[240 Requirements in connection with publication of accounts]

[(1) If a company publishes any of its statutory accounts, they must be accompanied by the relevant auditors' report under section 235 [or, as the case may be, the relevant report made for the purposes of section 249A(2)].

(2) A company which is required to prepare group accounts for a financial year shall not publish its statutory individual accounts for that year without also publishing with them its statutory group accounts.

(3)   If a company publishes non-statutory accounts, it shall publish with them a statement indicating—

    (a)   that they are not the company's statutory accounts,

    (b)   whether statutory accounts dealing with any financial year with which the non-statutory accounts purport to deal have been delivered to the registrar,

    (c)   whether the company's auditors have made a report under section 235 on the statutory accounts for any such financial year [and, if no such report has been made, whether the company's reporting accountant has made a report for the purposes of section 249A(2) on the statutory accounts for any such financial year], and

    (d)   whether any [auditors'] report so made was qualified or contained a statement under section 237(2) or (3) (accounting records or returns inadequate, accounts not agreeing with records and returns or failure to obtain necessary information and explanations) [or whether any report made for the purposes of section 249A(2) was qualified];

and it shall not publish with the non-statutory accounts any auditors' report under section 235 [or any report made for the purposes of section 249A(2)].

(4)   For the purposes of this section a company shall be regarded as publishing a document if it publishes, issues or circulates it or otherwise makes it available for public inspection in a manner calculated to invite members of the public generally, or any class of members of the public, to read it.

(5)   References in this section to a company's statutory accounts are to its individual or group accounts for a financial year as required to be delivered to the registrar under section 242; and references to the publication by a company of "non-statutory accounts" are to the publication of—

    (a)   any balance sheet or profit and loss account relating to, or purporting to deal with, a financial year of the company, or

    (b)   an account in any form purporting to be a balance sheet or profit and loss account for the group consisting of the company and its subsidiary undertakings relating to, or purporting to deal with, a financial year of the company,

otherwise than as part of the company's statutory accounts.

(6)   A company which contravenes any provision of this section, and any officer of it who is in default, is guilty of an offence and liable to a fine.]

NOTES

Except in relation to oversea companies (see note below), Part I of the Companies Act 1989 (ss 1–23) inserts new provisions in place of original ss 221–262 of this Act and amends the related Schedules (see s 1 of the 1989 Act).

Inserted by the Companies Act 1989, s 10.

Sub-ss (1), (3): words in square brackets inserted by SI 1994/1935, reg 4, Sch 1, para 1.

[Laying and delivering of accounts and reports]

NOTES

Inserted by the Companies Act 1989, s 11.

[241 Accounts and reports to be laid before company in general meeting]

[(1)   The directors of a company shall in respect of each financial year lay before the company in general meeting copies of the company's annual accounts, the directors' report and the auditors' report on those accounts.

(2)   If the requirements of subsection (1) are not complied with before the end of the period allowed for laying and delivering accounts and reports, every person who immediately before the end of that period was a director of the company is guilty of an offence and liable to a fine and, for continued contravention, to a daily default fine.

(3)   It is a defence for a person charged with such an offence to prove that he took all reasonable steps for securing that those requirements would be complied with before the end of that period.

(4)   It is not a defence to prove that the documents in question were not in fact prepared as required by this Part.]

NOTES

Except in relation to oversea companies (see note below), Part I of the Companies Act 1989 (ss 1–23) inserts new provisions in place of original ss 221–262 of this Act and amends the related Schedules (see s 1 of the 1989 Act).

Inserted by the Companies Act 1989, s 11.

[242 Accounts and reports to be delivered to the registrar]

[(1)   The directors of a company shall in respect of each financial year deliver to the registrar a copy of the company's annual accounts together with a copy of the directors' report for that year and a copy of the auditors' report on those accounts.

[. . .] If any document comprised in those accounts or reports is in a language other than English [then, subject to section 710B(6) (delivery of certain Welsh documents without a translation))], the directors shall annex to the copy of that document delivered a translation of it into English, certified in the prescribed manner to be a correct translation.

(2)   If the requirements of subsection (1) are not complied with before the end of the period allowed for laying and delivering accounts and reports, every person who immediately before the end of that period was a director of the company is guilty of an offence and liable to a fine and, for continued contravention, to a daily default fine.

(3)   Further, if the directors of the company fail to make good the default within 14 days after the service of a notice on them requiring compliance, the court may on the application of any member or creditor of the company or of the registrar, make an order directing the directors (or any of them) to make good the default within such time as may be specified in the order.

The court's order may provide that all costs of and incidental to the application shall be borne by the directors.

(4) It is a defence for a person charged with an offence under this section to prove that he took all reasonable steps for securing that the requirements of subsection (1) would be complied with before the end of the period allowed for laying and delivering accounts and reports.

(5) It is not a defence in any proceedings under this section to prove that the documents in question were not in fact prepared as required by this Part.]

[242A Civil penalty for failure to deliver accounts]

[(1) Where the requirements of section 242(1) are not complied with before the end of the period allowed for laying and delivering accounts and reports, the company is liable to a civil penalty.

This is in addition to any liability of the directors under section 242.

(2) The amount of the penalty is determined by reference to the length of the period between the end of the period allowed for laying and delivering accounts and reports and the day on which the requirements are complied with, and whether the company is a public or private company, as follows:—

Length of period	Public company	Private company
Not more than 3 months.	£500	£100
More than 3 months but not more than 6 months.	£1,000	£250
More than 6 months but not more than 12 months.	£2,000	£500
More than 12 months.	£5,000	£1,000

(3) The penalty may be recovered by the registrar and shall be paid by him into the Consolidated Fund.

(4) It is not a defence in proceedings under this section to prove that the documents in question were not in fact prepared as required by this Part.]

[242B Delivery and publication of accounts in ECUs]

[(1)   The amounts set out in the annual accounts of a company may also be shown in the same accounts translated into ECUs.

(2)   When complying with section 242, the directors of a company may deliver to the registrar an additional copy of the company's annual accounts in which the amounts have been translated into ECUs.

(3)   In both cases—
  (a)   the amounts must have been translated at the relevant exchange rate prevailing on the balance sheet date, and
  (b)   that rate must be disclosed in the notes to the accounts.

(4)   For the purposes of section 240 any additional copy of the company's annual accounts delivered to the registrar under subsection (2) shall be treated as statutory accounts of the company and, in the case of such a copy, references in section 240 to the auditors' report under section 235 shall be read as references to the auditors' report on the annual accounts of which it is a copy.

(5)   In this section—
  "ECU" means a unit with a value equal to the value of the unit of account known as the ecu used in the European Monetary System, and
  "relevant exchange rate" means the rate of exchange used for translating the value of the ecu for the purposes of that System.]

NOTES

Except in relation to oversea companies (see note below), Part I of the Companies Act 1989 (ss 1–23) inserts new provisions in place of original ss 221–262 of this Act and amends the related Schedules (see s 1 of the 1989 Act).
Inserted by SI 1992/2452, reg 3.

[244 Period allowed for laying and delivering accounts and reports]

[(1)   The period allowed for laying and delivering accounts and reports is—
  (a)   for a private company, 10 months after the end of the relevant accounting reference period, and
  (b)   for a public company, 7 months after the end of that period.

This is subject to the following provisions of this section.

(2)   If the relevant accounting reference period is the company's first and is a period of more than 12 months, the period allowed is—
  (a)   10 months or 7 months, as the case may be, from the first anniversary of the incorporation of the company, or
  (b)   3 months from the end of the accounting reference period,
whichever last expires.

(3)   Where a company carries on business, or has interests, outside the United Kingdom, the Channel Islands and the Isle of Man, the directors may, in respect of any financial year, give to the registrar before the end of the period allowed by subsection (1) or (2) a notice in the prescribed form—
  (a)   stating that the company so carries on business or has such interests, and

(b) claiming a 3 month extension of the period allowed for laying and delivering accounts and reports;

and upon such a notice being given the period is extended accordingly.

(4) If the relevant accounting period is treated as shortened by virtue of a notice given by the company under section 225 (alteration of accounting reference date), the period allowed for laying and delivering accounts is that applicable in accordance with the above provisions or 3 months from the date of the notice under that section, whichever last expires.

(5) If for any special reason the Secretary of State thinks fit he may, on an application made before the expiry of the period otherwise allowed, by notice in writing to a company extend that period by such further period as may be specified in the notice.

(6) In this section "the relevant accounting reference period" means the accounting reference period by reference to which the financial year for the accounts in question was determined.]

NOTES

Except in relation to oversea companies (see note below), Part I of the Companies Act 1989 (ss 1–23) inserts new provisions in place of original ss 221–262 of this Act and amends the related Schedules (see s 1 of the 1989 Act).
Inserted by the Companies Act 1989, s 11.

[Revision of defective accounts and reports]

NOTES

Inserted by the Companies Act 1989, s 12.

[245 Voluntary revision of annual accounts or directors' report]

[(1) If it appears to the directors of a company that any annual accounts of the company, or any directors' report, did not comply with the requirements of this Act, they may prepare revised accounts or a revised report.

(2) Where copies of the previous accounts or report have been laid before the company in general meeting or delivered to the registrar, the revisions shall be confined to—
  (a) the correction of those respects in which the previous accounts or report did not comply with the requirements of this Act, and
  (b) the making of any necessary consequential alterations.

(3) The Secretary of State may make provision by regulations as to the application of the provisions of this Act in relation to revised annual accounts or a revised directors' report.

(4) The regulations may, in particular—
  (a) make different provision according to whether the previous accounts or report are replaced or are supplemented by a document indicating the corrections to be made;

(b) make provision with respect to the functions of the company's auditors [or reporting accountant] in relation to the revised accounts or report;

(c) require the directors to take such steps as may be specified in the regulations where the previous accounts or report have been—

(i) sent out to members and others under section 238(1),

(ii) laid before the company in general meeting, or

(iii) delivered to the registrar,

or where a summary financial statement based on the previous accounts or report has been sent to members under section 251;

(d) apply the provisions of this Act (including those creating criminal offences) subject to such additions, exceptions and modifications as are specified in the regulations.

(5) Regulations under this section shall be made by statutory instrument which shall be subject to annulment in pursuance of a resolution of either House of Parliament.]

NOTES

Except in relation to oversea companies (see note below), Part I of the Companies Act 1989 (ss 1–23) inserts new provisions in place of original ss 221–262 of this Act and amends the related Schedules (see s 1 of the 1989 Act).

Inserted by the Companies Act 1989, s 12.

Sub-s (4): words in square brackets inserted by SI 1994/1935, reg 4, Sch 1, para 2.

[245A Secretary of State's notice in respect of annual accounts]

[(1) Where copies of a company's annual accounts have been sent out under section 238, or a copy of a company's annual accounts has been laid before the company in general meeting or delivered to the registrar, and it appears to the Secretary of State that there is, or may be, a question whether the accounts comply with the requirements of this Act, he may give notice to the directors of the company indicating the respects in which it appears to him that such a question arises, or may arise.

(2) The notice shall specify a period of not less than one month for the directors to give him an explanation of the accounts or prepare revised accounts.

(3) If at the end of the specified period, or such longer period as he may allow, it appears to the Secretary of State that no satisfactory explanation of the accounts has been given and that the accounts have not been revised so as to comply with the requirements of this Act, he may if he thinks fit apply to the court.

(4) The provisions of this section apply equally to revised annual accounts, in which case the references to revised accounts shall be read as references to further revised accounts.]

NOTES

Except in relation to oversea companies (see note below), Part I of the Companies Act 1989 (ss 1–23) inserts new provisions in place of original ss 221–262 of this Act and amends the related Schedules (see s 1 of the 1989 Act).

Inserted by the Companies Act 1989, s 12, in relation to annual accounts for financial years commencing on or after 23 December 1989: for further details see SI 1990/2569, art 6(2)–(4).

[245B Application to court in respect of defective accounts]

[(1) An application may be made to the court—

(a) by the Secretary of State, after having complied with section 245A, or

(b) by a person authorised by the Secretary of State for the purposes of this section,

for a declaration or declarator that the annual accounts of a company do not comply with the requirements of this Act and for an order requiring the directors of the company to prepare revised accounts.

(2) Notice of the application, together with a general statement of the matters at issue in the proceedings, shall be given by the applicant to the registrar for registration.

(3) If the court orders the preparation of revised accounts, it may give directions with respect to—

(a) the auditing of the accounts,

(b) the revision of any directors' report or summary financial statement, and

(c) the taking of steps by the directors to bring the making of the order to the notice of persons likely to rely on the previous accounts,

and such other matters as the court thinks fit.

(4) If the court finds that the accounts did not comply with the requirements of this Act it may order that all or part of—

(a) the costs (or in Scotland expenses) of and incidental to the application, and

(b) any reasonable expenses incurred by the company in connection with or in consequence of the preparation of revised accounts,

shall be borne by such of the directors as were party to the approval of the defective accounts.

For this purpose every director of the company at the time the accounts were approved shall be taken to have been a party to their approval unless he shows that he took all reasonable steps to prevent their being approved.

(5) Where the court makes an order under subsection (4) it shall have regard to whether the directors party to the approval of the defective accounts knew or ought to have known that the accounts did not comply with the requirements of this Act, and it may exclude one or more directors from the order or order the payment of different amounts by different directors.

(6) On the conclusion of proceedings on an application under this section, the applicant shall give to the registrar for registration an office copy of the court order or, as the case may be, notice that the application has failed or been withdrawn.

(7) The provisions of this section apply equally to revised annual accounts, in which case the references to revised accounts shall be read as references to further revised accounts.]

NOTES

Except in relation to oversea companies (see note below), Part I of the Companies Act 1989 (ss 1–23) inserts new provisions in place of original ss 221–262 of this Act and amends the related Schedules (see s 1 of the 1989 Act).

Inserted by the Companies Act 1989, s 12, in relation to annual accounts for financial years commencing on or after 23 December 1989: for further details see SI 1990/2569, art 6(2)–(4).

[245C Other persons authorised to apply to court]

[(1)   The Secretary of State may authorise for the purposes of section 245B any person appearing to him—

  (a)   to have an interest in, and to have satisfactory procedures directed to securing, compliance by companies with the accounting requirements of this Act,

  (b)   to have satisfactory procedures for receiving and investigating complaints about the annual accounts of companies, and

  (c)   otherwise to be a fit and proper person to be authorised.

(2)   A person may be authorised generally or in respect of particular classes of case, and different persons may be authorised in respect of different classes of case.

(3)   The Secretary of State may refuse to authorise a person if he considers that his authorisation is unnecessary having regard to the fact that there are one or more other persons who have been or are likely to be authorised.

(4)   Authorisation shall be by order made by statutory instrument which shall be subject to annulment in pursuance of a resolution of either House of Parliament.

(5)   Where authorisation is revoked, the revoking order may make such provision as the Secretary of State thinks fit with respect to pending proceedings.

(6)   Neither a person authorised under this section, nor any officer, servant or member of the governing body of such a person, shall be liable in damages for anything done or purporting to be done for the purposes of or in connection with—

  (a)   the taking of steps to discover whether there are grounds for an application to the court,

  (b)   the determination whether or not to make such an application, or

  (c)   the publication of its reasons for any such decision,

unless the act or omission is shown to have been in bad faith.]

NOTES

Except in relation to oversea companies (see note below), Part I of the Companies Act 1989 (ss 1-23) inserts new provisions in place of original ss 221-262 of this Act and amends the related Schedules (see s 1 of the 1989 Act).

Inserted by the Companies Act 1989, s 12.

[Chapter II
Exemptions, Exceptions and Special Provisions]

NOTES

Inserted by the Companies Act 1989, s 13(1).

[Small and medium-sized companies and groups]

NOTES

Inserted by the Companies Act 1989, s 13(1).

[246 Special provisions for small companies]

[(1) Subject to section 247A, this section applies where a company qualifies as a small company in relation to a financial year.

(2) If the company's individual accounts for the year—
  (a) comply with the provisions of Schedule 8, or
  (b) fail to comply with those provisions only in so far as they comply instead with one or more corresponding provisions of Schedule 4,

they need not comply with the provisions or, as the case may be, the remaining provisions of Schedule 4; and where advantage is taken of this subsection, references in section 226 to compliance with the provisions of Schedule 4 shall be construed accordingly.

[(3) The company's individual accounts for the year—
  (a) may give the total of the aggregates required by paragraphs (a), (c) and (d) of paragraph 1(1) of Schedule 6 (emoluments and other benefits etc. of directors) instead of giving those aggregates individually; and
  (b) need not give the information required by—
      (i) paragraph 4 of Schedule 5 (financial years of subsidiary undertakings);
      (ii) paragraph 1(2)(b) of Schedule 6 (numbers of directors exercising share options and receiving shares under long term incentive schemes);
      (iii) paragraph 2 of Schedule 6 (details of highest paid director's emoluments etc); or
      (iv) paragraph 7 of Schedule 6 (excess retirement benefits of directors and past directors).]

(4) The directors' report for the year need not give the information required by—
  (a) section 234(1)(a) and (b) (fair review of business and amount to be paid as dividend);
  (b) paragraph 1(2) of Schedule 7 (statement of market value of fixed assets where substantially different from balance sheet amount);
  (c) paragraph 6 of Schedule 7 (miscellaneous disclosures); or
  (d) paragraph 11 of Schedule 7 (employee involvement).

(5) Notwithstanding anything in section 242(1), the directors of the company need not deliver to the registrar any of the following, namely—
  (a) a copy of the company's profit and loss account for the year;
  (b) a copy of the directors' report for the year; and
  (c) if they deliver a copy of a balance sheet drawn up as at the last day of the year which complies with the requirements of Schedule 8A, a copy of the company's balance sheet drawn up as at that day.

(6) Neither a copy of the company's accounts for the year delivered to the registrar under section 242(1), nor a copy of a balance sheet delivered to the registrar under subsection (5)(c), need give the information required by—

(a) paragraph 4 of Schedule 5 (financial years of subsidiary undertakings);

(b) paragraph 6 of Schedule 5 (shares of company held by subsidiary undertakings);

(c) Part I of Schedule 6 (directors' and chairman's emoluments, pensions and compensation for loss of office); or

(d) section 390A(3) (amount of auditors' remuneration).

(7) The provisions of section 233 as to the signing of the copy of the balance sheet delivered to the registrar apply to a copy of a balance sheet delivered under subsection (5)(c).

(8) Subject to subsection (9), each of the following, namely—

(a) accounts prepared in accordance with subsection (2) or (3),

(b) a report prepared in accordance with subsection (4), and

(c) a copy of accounts delivered to the registrar in accordance with subsection (5) or (6),

shall contain a statement in a prominent position on the balance sheet, in the report or, as the case may be, on the copy of the balance sheet, above the signature required by section 233, 234A or subsection (7), that they are prepared in accordance with the special provisions of this Part relating to small companies.

(9) Subsection (8) does not apply where [the directors of the company have taken advantage of the exemption from audit conferred by section 249AA (dormant companies)].]

NOTES

Except in relation to oversea companies (see note below), Part I of the Companies Act 1989 (ss 1–23) inserts new provisions in place of original ss 221–262 of this Act and amends the related Schedules (see s 1 of the 1989 Act).

Inserted by the Companies Act 1989, s 13(1).

Substituted by SI 1997/220, reg 2(1).

Date in force: this amendment applies to annual accounts approved by the board of directors on or after 1 March 1997, and to directors' and auditors' reports on such accounts: see SI 1997/220, reg 1(3); for transitional provision see reg 1(4) thereof.

Sub-s (3): substituted by SI 1997/570, reg 6(1).

Sub-s (9): words from "the directors of" to "249AA (dormant companies)" in square brackets substituted by SI 2000/1430, reg 8(1), (2).

Date in force: this amendment has effect in relation to annual accounts and reports in respect of financial years ending on or after 26 July 2000: see SI 2000/1430, reg 1(1), (2).

[246A Special provisions for medium-sized companies]

[(1) Subject to section 247A, this section applies where a company qualifies as a medium-sized company in relation to a financial year.

(2) The company's individual accounts for the year need not comply with the requirements of paragraph 36A of Schedule 4 (disclosure with respect to compliance with accounting standards).

(3) The company may deliver to the registrar a copy of the company's accounts for the year—

(a) which includes a profit and loss account in which the following items listed in the profit and loss account formats set out in Part I of Schedule 4 are combined as one item under the heading "gross profit or loss"—
Items 1, 2, 3 and 6 in Format 1;
Items 1 to 5 in Format 2;
Items A1, B1 and B2 in Format 3;
Items A1, A2 and B1 to B4 in Format 4;

(b) which does not contain the information required by paragraph 55 of Schedule 4 (particulars of turnover).

(4) A copy of accounts delivered to the registrar in accordance with subsection (3) shall contain a statement in a prominent position on the copy of the balance sheet, above the signature required by section 233, that the accounts are prepared in accordance with the special provisions of this Part relating to medium-sized companies.]

NOTES

Inserted by SI 1997/220, reg 3.

Date in force: this amendment applies to annual accounts approved by the board of directors on or after 1 March 1997, and to directors' and auditors' reports on such accounts: see SI 1997/220, reg 1(3); for transitional provision see reg 1(4) thereof.

[247 Qualification of company as small or medium-sized]

[(1) A company qualifies as small or medium-sized in relation to a financial year if the qualifying conditions are met—
(a) in the case of the company's first financial year, in that year, and
(b) in the case of any subsequent financial year, in that year and the preceding year.

(2) A company shall be treated as qualifying as small or medium-sized in relation to a financial year—
(a) if it so qualified in relation to the previous financial year under [subsection (1) above or was treated as so qualifying under paragraph (b) below]; or
(b) if it was treated as so qualifying in relation to the previous year by virtue of paragraph (a) and the qualifying conditions are met in the year in question.

(3) The qualifying conditions are met by a company in a year in which it satisfies two or more of the following requirements—

Small company
1 Turnover	[Not more than £2.8 million]
2 Balance sheet total	[Not more than £1.4 million]
3 Number of employees	Not more than 50

Medium-sized company
1 Turnover	[Not more than £11.2 million]
2 Balance sheet total	[Not more than £5.6 million]
3 Number of employees	Not more than 250.

(4) For a period which is a company's financial year but not in fact a year the maximum figures for turnover shall be proportionately adjusted.

(5) The balance sheet total means—
  (a) where in the company's accounts Format 1 of the balance sheet formats set out in Part I of Schedule 4 [or Part I of Schedule 8] is adopted, the aggregate of the amounts shown in the balance sheet under the headings corresponding to items A to D in that Format, and
  (b) where Format 2 is adopted, the aggregate of the amounts shown under the general heading "Assets".

(6) The number of employees means the average number of persons employed by the company in the year (determined on a [monthly] basis).

That number shall be determined by applying the method of calculation prescribed by paragraph 56(2) and (3) of Schedule 4 for determining the corresponding number required to be stated in a note to the company's accounts.]

NOTES

Except in relation to oversea companies (see note below), Part I of the Companies Act 1989 (ss 1–23) inserts new provisions in place of original ss 221–262 of this Act and amends the related Schedules (see s 1 of the 1989 Act).
Inserted by the Companies Act 1989, s 13(1).
Sub-s (2): in para (a) words in square brackets substituted by SI 1992/2452, reg 5(2).
Sub-s (3): words in square brackets substituted by SI 1992/2452, reg 5(3).
Sub-s (5): in para (a) words "or Part I of Schedule 8" in square brackets inserted by SI 1997/220, reg 7(2).
Date in force: this amendment applies to annual accounts approved by the board of directors on or after 1 March 1997, and to directors' and auditors' reports on such accounts: see SI 1997/220, reg 1(3); for transitional provision see reg 1(4) thereof.
Sub-s (6): word in square brackets substituted by SI 1996/189, reg 8.

[247A Cases in which special provisions do not apply]

[(1) Nothing in section 246 or 246A shall apply where—
  [(a) the company is, or was at any time within the financial year to which the accounts relate—
    (i) a public company,
    (ii) a person who has permission under Part 4 of the Financial Services and Markets Act 2000 to carry on one or more regulated activities, or
    (iii) a person who carries on insurance market activity;] or
  (b) the company is, or was at any time during that year, a member of an ineligible group.

(2) A group is ineligible if any of its members is—
  (a) a public company or a body corporate which (not being a company) has power under its constitution to offer its shares or debentures to the public and may lawfully exercise that power,
  [(b) a person who has permission under Part 4 of the Financial Services and Markets Act 2000 to carry on a regulated activity, or
  (c) a person who carries on an insurance market activity].

(3) A parent company shall not be treated as qualifying as a small company in relation to a financial year unless the group headed by it qualifies as a small group,

and shall not be treated as qualifying as a medium-sized company in relation to a financial year unless that group qualifies as a medium-sized group (see section 249).]

NOTES

Inserted by SI 1997/220, reg 4.

Date in force: this amendment applies to annual accounts approved by the board of directors on or after 1 March 1997, and to directors' and auditors' reports on such accounts: see SI 1997/220, reg 1(3); for transitional provision see reg 1(4) thereof.

Sub-s (1): para (a) substituted by SI 2001/3649, art 11(1), (2).

Date in force: 1 December 2001: see SI 2001/3649, art 1.

Sub-s (2): paras (b), (c) substituted, for paras (b)–(d) as originally enacted, by SI 2001/3649, art 11(1), (3).

Date in force: 1 December 2001: see SI 2001/3649, art 1.

[247B Special auditors' report]

[(1) This section applies where—
  (a) the directors of a company propose to deliver to the registrar copies of accounts ("abbreviated accounts") prepared in accordance with section 246(5) or (6) or 246A(3) ("the relevant provision"),
  (b) the directors have not taken advantage of the exemption from audit conferred by section 249A(1) or (2) [or section 249AA], . . .
  (c) . . ..

(2) If abbreviated accounts prepared in accordance with the relevant provision are delivered to the registrar, they shall be accompanied by a copy of a special report of the auditors stating that in their opinion—
  (a) the company is entitled to deliver abbreviated accounts prepared in accordance with that provision, and
  (b) the abbreviated accounts to be delivered are properly prepared in accordance with that provision.

(3) In such a case a copy of the auditors' report under section 235 need not be delivered, but—
  (a) if that report was qualified, the special report shall set out that report in full together with any further material necessary to understand the qualification; and
  (b) if that report contained a statement under—
    (i) section 237(2) (accounts, records or returns inadequate or accounts not agreeing with records and returns), or
    (ii) section 237(3) (failure to obtain necessary information and explanations),

the special report shall set out that statement in full.

(4) Section 236 (signature of auditors' report) applies to a special report under this section as it applies to a report under section 235.

(5) If abbreviated accounts prepared in accordance with the relevant provision are delivered to the registrar, references in section 240 (requirements in connection with publication of accounts) to the auditors' report under section 235 shall be read as references to the special auditors' report under this section.]

Inserted by SI 1997/220, reg 5.

Date in force: this amendment applies to annual accounts approved by the board of directors on or after 1 March 1997, and to directors' and auditors' reports on such accounts: see SI 1997/220, reg 1(3); for transitional provision see reg 1(4) thereof.

Sub-s (1): in para (b) words "or section 249AA" in square brackets inserted by SI 2000/1430, reg 8(2)(a).

Date in force: this amendment has effect in relation to annual accounts and reports in respect of financial years ending on or after 26 July 2000: see SI 2000/1430, reg 1(1), (2).

Sub-s (1): in para (b) word omitted repealed by SI 2000/1430, reg 8(2)(b).

Date in force: this amendment has effect in relation to annual acounts and reports in respect of financial years ending on or after 26 July 2000: see SI 2000/1430, reg 1(1), (2).

Sub-s (1): para (c) repealed by SI 2000/1430, reg 8(2)(c).

Date in force: this amendment has effect in relation to annual accounts and reports in respect of financial years ending on or after 26 July 2000: see SI 2000/1430, reg 1(1), (2).

[248 Exemption for small and medium-sized groups]

[(1)   A parent company need not prepare group accounts for a financial year in relation to which the group headed by that company qualifies as a small or medium-sized group and is not an ineligible group.

(2)   A group is ineligible if any of its members is—
- (a)   a public company or a body corporate which (not being a company) has power under its constitution to offer its shares or debentures to the public and may lawfully exercise that power,
- [(b)   a person who has permission under Part 4 of the Financial Services and Markets Act 2000 to carry on a regulated activity, or
- (c)   a person who carries on an insurance market activity].

(3), (4)   . . .]

Except in relation to oversea companies (see note below), Part I of the Companies Act 1989 (ss 1–23) inserts new provisions in place of original ss 221–262 of this Act and amends the related Schedules (see s 1 of the 1989 Act).

Inserted by the Companies Act 1989, s 13(3).

Sub-s (2): paras (b), (c) substituted, for paras (b)–(d) as originally enacted, by SI 2001/3649, art 12.

Date in force: 1 December 2001: see SI 2001/3649, art 1.

Sub-ss (3), (4): repealed, in relation to the annual accounts and annual report of any company for the financial year ending on or after 2 February 1996, by SI 1996/189, regs 9, 16.

[248A Group accounts prepared by small company]

[(1)   This section applies where a small company—
- (a)   has prepared individual accounts for a financial year in accordance with section 246(2) or (3), and
- (b)   is preparing group accounts in respect of the same year.

(2)   If the group accounts—

(a) comply with the provisions of Schedule 8, or

(b) fail to comply with those provisions only in so far as they comply instead with one or more corresponding provisions of Schedule 4,

they need not comply with the provisions or, as the case may be, the remaining provisions of Schedule 4; and where advantage is taken of this subsection, references in Schedule 4A to compliance with the provisions of Schedule 4 shall be construed accordingly.

(3) For the purposes of this section, Schedule 8 shall have effect as if, in each balance sheet format set out in that Schedule, for item B III there were substituted the following item—

"B III Investments

    1 Shares in group undertakings

    2 Interests in associated undertakings

    3 Other participating interests

    4 Loans to group undertakings and undertakings in which a participating interest is held

    5 Other investments other than loans

    6 Others."

(4) The group accounts need not give the information required by the provisions specified in section 246(3).

(5) Group accounts prepared in accordance with this section shall contain a statement in a prominent position on the balance sheet, above the signature required by section 233, that they are prepared in accordance with the special provisions of this Part relating to small companies.]

NOTES

Inserted by SI 1997/220, reg 6.

Date in force: this amendment applies to annual accounts approved by the board of directors on or after 1 March 1997, and to directors' and auditors' reports on such accounts: see SI 1997/220, reg 1(3); for transitional provision see reg 1(4) thereof.

[249 Qualification of group as small or medium-sized]

[(1) A group qualifies as small or medium-sized in relation to a financial year if the qualifying conditions are met—

(a) in the case of the parent company's first financial year, in that year, and

(b) in the case of any subsequent financial year, in that year and the preceding year.

(2) A group shall be treated as qualifying as small or medium-sized in relation to a financial year—

(a) if it so qualified in relation to the previous financial year under [subsection (1) above or was treated as so qualifying under paragraph (b) below]; or

(b) if it was treated as so qualifying in relation to the previous year by virtue of paragraph (a) and the qualifying conditions are met in the year in question.

(3) The qualifying conditions are met by a group in a year in which it satisfies two or more of the following requirements—

Small group

1. Aggregate turnover	[Not more than £2.8 million net (or £3.36 million gross)]
2. Aggregate balance sheet total	[Not more than £1.4 million net (or £1.68 million gross)]
3. Aggregate number of employees	Not more than 50

Medium-sized group

1. Aggregate turnover	[Not more than £11.2 million net (or £13.44 million gross)]
2. Aggregate balance sheet total	[Not more than £5.6 million net (or £6.72 million gross)]
3. Aggregate number of employees	Not more than 250.

(4)   The aggregate figures shall be ascertained by aggregating the relevant figures determined in accordance with section 247 for each member of the group.

In relation to the aggregate figures for turnover and balance sheet total, "net" means with the set-offs and other adjustments required by Schedule 4A in the case of group accounts and "gross" means without those set-offs and other adjustments; and a company may satisfy the relevant requirement on the basis of either the net or the gross figure.

(5)   The figures for each subsidiary undertaking shall be those included in its accounts for the relevant financial year, that is—

  (a)   if its financial year ends with that of the parent company, that financial year, and

  (b)   if not, its financial year ending last before the end of the financial year of the parent company.

(6)   If those figures cannot be obtained without disproportionate expense or undue delay, the latest available figures shall be taken.]

NOTES

Except in relation to oversea companies (see note below), Part I of the Companies Act 1989 (ss 1–23) inserts new provisions in place of original ss 221–262 of this Act and amends the related Schedules (see s 1 of the 1989 Act).
Inserted by the Companies Act 1989, s 13(3).
Sub-s (2): in para (a) words in square brackets substituted by SI 1992/2452, reg 6(2).
Sub-s (3): words in square brackets substituted by SI 1992/2542, reg 6(3), (4).

[Exemptions from audit for certain categories of small companies]

NOTES

Inserted by SI 1994 No 1935, reg 2.

[249A Exemptions from audit]

[(1)   Subject to section 249B, a company which meets the total exemption conditions set out below in respect of a financial year is exempt from the provisions of this Part relating to the audit of accounts in respect of that year.

(2)   Subject to section 249B, [a company which is a charity and] which meets the report conditions set out below in respect of a financial year is exempt from the provisions of this Part relating to the audit of accounts in respect of that year if the directors cause a report in respect of the company's individual accounts for that year to be prepared in accordance with section 249C and made to the company's members.

(3)   The total exemption conditions are met by a company in respect of a financial year if—

(a)   it qualifies as a small company in relation to that year for the purposes of section 246,

(b)   its turnover in that year is not more than [£1 million], and

(c)   its balance sheet total for that year is not more than £1.4 million.

[(3A)   In relation to any company which is a charity, subsection (3)(b) shall have effect with the substitution—

(a)   for the reference to turnover of a reference to gross income, and

(b)   for the reference to [£1 million] of a reference to £90,000.]

(4)   The report conditions are met by [a company which is a charity] in respect of a financial year if—

(a)   it qualifies as a small company in relation to that year for the purposes of section 246,

(b)   its [gross income] in that year is more than £90,000 but not more than [£250,000], and

(c)   its balance sheet total for that year is not more than £1.4 million.

(5)   . . .. . .

(6)   For a period which is a company's financial year but not in fact a year the maximum figures for turnover or gross income shall be proportionately adjusted.

[(6A)   A company is entitled to the exemption conferred by subsection (1) or (2) notwithstanding that it falls within paragraph (a) or (b) of [section 249AA(1)].]

(7)   In this section—

"balance sheet total" has the meaning given by section 247(5), and

"gross income" means the company's income from all sources, as shown in the company's income and expenditure account.]

NOTES

Except in relation to oversea companies (see note below), Part I of the Companies Act 1989 (ss 1–23) inserts new provisions in place of original ss 221–262 of this Act and amends the related Schedules (see s 1 of the 1989 Act).

Inserted by SI 1994/1935, reg 2.

Sub-s (2): words "a company which is a charity an" in square brackets substituted by SI 1997/936, reg 2(2).

Date in force: this amendment has effect in relation to the annual accounts of any company for any financial year ending on or after 15 June 1997: see SI 1997/936, reg 1(2).

Sub-s (3): in para (b) sum "£1 million" in square brackets substituted by SI 2000/1430, reg 2(1), (2).

Date in force: this amendment has effect in relation to annual accounts and reports in respect of financial years ending on or after 26 July 2000: see SI 2000/1430, reg 1(1), (2).

Sub-s (3A): inserted by SI 1997/936, reg 2(4).

Date in force: this amendment has effect in relation to the annual accounts of any company for any financial year ending on or after 15 June 1997: see SI 1997/936, reg 1(2).

Sub-s (3A): in para (b) sum "£1 million" in square brackets substituted by SI 2000/1430, reg 2(1), (2).

Date in force: this amendment has effect in relation to annual accounts and reports in respect of financial years ending on or after 26 July 2000: see SI 2000/1430, reg 1(1), (2).

Sub-s (4): words "a company which is a charity", "gross income" and "£250,000" in square brackets substituted by SI 1997/936, reg 2(5).

Date in force: these amendments have effect in relation to the annual accounts of any company for any financial year ending on or after 15 June 1997: see SI 1997/936, reg 1(2).

Sub-s (5): repealed by SI 1997/936, reg 2(6).

Date in force: this repeal has effect in relation to the annual accounts of any company for any financial year ending on or after 15 June 1997: see SI 1997/936, reg 1(2).

Sub-s (6A): inserted with retrospective effect by SI 1997/936, reg 2(7), (8).

Sub-s (6A): words "section 249AA(1)" in square brackets substituted by SI 2000/1430, reg 2(1), (3).

Date in force: this amendment has effect in relation to annual accounts and reports in respect of financial years ending on or after 26 July 2000: see SI 2000/1430, reg 1(1), (2).

[249AA Dormant companies]

[(1)   Subject to section 249B(2) to (5), a company is exempt from the provisions of this Part relating to the audit of accounts in respect of a financial year if—
   (a)   it has been dormant since its formation, or
   (b)   it has been dormant since the end of the previous financial year and subsection (2) applies.

(2)   This subsection applies if the company—
   (a)   is entitled in respect of its individual accounts for the financial year in question to prepare accounts in accordance with section 246, or would be so entitled but for the application of section 247A(1)(a)(i) or (b), and
   (b)   is not required to prepare group accounts for that year.

(3)   Subsection (1) does not apply if at any time in the financial year in question the company was—
   [(a)   a person who has permission under Part 4 of the Financial Services and Markets Act 2000 to carry on one or more regulated activities; or
   (b)   a person who carries on insurance market activity].

(4)   A company is "dormant" during any period in which it has no significant accounting transaction.

(5)   "Significant accounting transaction" means a transaction which—
   (a)   is required by section 221 to be entered in the company's accounting records; but
   (b)   is not a transaction to which subsection (6) or (7) applies.

(6)   This subsection applies to a transaction arising from the taking of shares in the company by a subscriber to the memorandum as a result of an undertaking of his in the memorandum.

(7)   This subsection applies to a transaction consisting of the payment of—

(a) a fee to the registrar on a change of name under section 28 (change of name),
(b) a fee to the registrar on the re-registration of a company under Part II (re-registration as a means of altering a company's status),
(c) a penalty under section 242A (penalty for failure to deliver accounts), or
(d) a fee to the registrar for the registration of an annual return under Chapter III of Part XI.]

NOTES

Inserted by SI 2000/1430, reg 3.

Date in force: this amendment has effect in relation to annual accounts and reports in respect of financial years ending on or after 26 July 2000: see SI 2000/1430, reg 1(1), (2).

Sub-s (3): paras (a), (b) substituted by SI 2001/3649, art 13.

Date in force: 1 December 2001: see SI 2001/3649, art 1.

[249B Cases where exemptions not available]

[(1) [Subject to [subsection (1A) to (1C)],] a company is not entitled to the exemption conferred by subsection (1) or (2) of section 249A in respect of a financial year if at any time within that year—
(a) it was a public company,
[(b) it was a person who had permission under Part 4 of the Financial Services and Markets Act 2000 to carry on a regulated activity,]
[(bb) it carried on an insurance market activity,]
(c) . . .
[(d) it was an appointed representative, within the meaning of section 39 of the Financial Services and Markets Act 2000,]
(e) it was a special register body as defined in section 117(1) of the Trade Union and Labour Relations (Consolidation) Act 1992 or an employers' association as defined in section 122 of that Act, or
(f) it was a parent company or a subsidiary undertaking.

[(1A) A company which, apart from this subsection, would fall within subsection (1)(f) by virtue of its being a subsidiary undertaking for any period within a financial year shall not be treated as so falling if it is dormant (within the meaning of [section 249AA]) throughout that period.]

[(1B) A company which, apart from this subsection, would fall within subsection (1)(f) by virtue of its being a parent company or a subsidiary undertaking for any period within a financial year, shall not be treated as so falling if throughout that period it was a member of a group meeting the conditions set out in subsection (1C).]

(1C) The conditions referred to in subsection (1B) are—
(a) that the group qualifies as a small group, in relation to the financial year within which the period falls, for the purposes of section 249 [(or if all bodies corporate in such group were companies, would so qualify)] and is not, and was not at any time within that year, an ineligible group within the meaning of section 248(2),

(b) that the group's aggregate turnover in that year (calculated in accordance with section 249) is[, where the company referred to in subsection (1B) is a charity,] not more than £350,000 net (or £420,000 gross) [or, where the company so referred to is not a charity, not more than £1 million net (or £1.2 million gross)], and

(c) that the group's aggregate balance sheet total for that year (calculated in accordance with section 249) is not more than £1.4 million net (or £1.68 million gross).]

(2) Any member or members holding not less in the aggregate than 10 per cent in nominal value of the company's issued share capital or any class of it or, if the company does not have a share capital, not less than 10 per cent in number of the members of the company, may, by notice in writing deposited at the registered office of the company during a financial year but not later than one month before the end of that year, require the company to obtain an audit of its accounts for that year.

(3) Where a notice has been deposited under subsection (2), the company is not entitled to the exemption conferred by subsection (1) or (2) of section 249A [or by subsection (1) of section 249AA] in respect of the financial year to which the notice relates.

(4) A company is not entitled to the exemption conferred by subsection (1) or (2) of section 249A [or by subsection (1) of section 249AA] unless its balance sheet contains a statement by the directors—

(a) [to the effect] that for the year in question the company was entitled to exemption under subsection (1) or (2) . . . of section 249A [or subsection (1) of section 249AA],

[(b) to the effect that members have not required the company to obtain an audit of its accounts for the year in question in accordance with subsection (2) of this section], and

(c) [to the effect] that the directors acknowledge their responsibilities for—

(i) ensuring that the company keeps accounting records which comply with section 221, and

(ii) preparing accounts which give a true and fair view of the state of affairs of the company as at the end of the financial year and of its profit or loss for the financial year in accordance with the requirements of section 226, and which otherwise comply with the requirements of this Act relating to accounts, so far as applicable to the company.

(5) The statement required by subsection (4) shall appear in the balance sheet [above the signature required by section 233].]

NOTES

Except in relation to oversea companies (see note below), Part I of the Companies Act 1989 (ss 1–23) inserts new provisions in place of original ss 221–262 of this Act and amends the related Schedules (see s 1 of the 1989 Act).

Inserted by SI 1994/1935, reg 2.

Sub-s (1): words in square brackets beginning with the words "Subject to" inserted by SI 1996/189, reg 10(2).

Sub-s (1): words "subsection (1A) to (1C)" in square brackets substituted by SI 1997/936, reg 3(2).

Date in force: this amendment has effect in relation to the annual accounts of any company for any financial year ending on or after 15 June 1997: see SI 1997/936, reg 1(2).

Sub-s (1): para (b) substituted by SI 2001/3649, art 14(1), (2).

Date in force: 1 December 2001: see SI 2001/3649, art 1.

Sub-s (1): para (bb) inserted by SI 2001/3649, art 14(1), (3).

Date in force: 1 December 2001: see SI 2001/3649, art 1.

Sub-s (1): para (c) repealed by SI 2001/1283, art 3(3)(a).

Date in force: 30 April 2001: see SI 2001/1283, art 1(1).

Sub-s (1): para (d) substituted by SI 2001/3649, art 14(1), (4).

Date in force: 1 December 2001: see SI 2001/3649, art 1.

Sub-s (1A): inserted by SI 1996/189, reg 10(3).

Sub-s (1A): words "section 249AA" in square brackets substituted by SI 2000/1430, reg 4(1), (2).

Date in force: this amendment has effect in relation to annual accounts and reports in respect of financial years ending on or after 26 July 2000: see SI 2000/1430, reg 1(1), (2).

Sub-ss (1B), (1C): inserted by SI 1997/936, reg 3(3).

Date in force: this amendment has effect in relation to the annual accounts of any company for any financial year ending on or after 15 June 1997: see SI 1997/936, reg 1(2).

Sub-s (1C): in para (a) words from "(or if all" to "would so qualify)" in square brackets inserted by SI 2000/1430, reg 4(1), (3)(a).

Date in force: this amendment has effect in relation to annual accounts and reports in respect of financial years ending on or after 26 July 2000: see SI 2000/1430, reg 1(1), (2).

Sub-s (1C): in para (b) words from ", where the company" to "is a charity," and from "or, where the company" to "or £1.2 million gross)" in square brackets inserted by SI 2000/1430, reg 4(3)(b)(i), (ii).

Date in force: this amendment has effect in relation to annual accounts and reports in respect of financial years ending on or after 26 July 2000: see SI 2000/1430, reg 1(1), (2).

Sub-s (3): words "or by subsection (1) of section 249AA" in square brackets inserted by SI 2000/1430, reg 4(1), (4).

Date in force: this amendment has effect in relation to annual accounts and reports in respect of financial years ending on or after 26 July 2000: see SI 2000/1430, reg 1(1), (2).

Sub-s (4): words "or by subsection (1) of section 249AA" in square brackets inserted by SI 2000/1430, reg 4(1), (5)(a).

Date in force: this amendment has effect in relation to annual accounts and reports in respect of financial years ending on or after 26 July 2000: see SI 2000/1430, reg 1(1), (2).

Sub-s (4): in para (a) words "to the effect" in square brackets inserted by SI 1996/189, reg 10(4).

Sub-s (4): in para (a) words omitted repealed by SI 2000/1430, reg 4(1), (5)(b).

Date in force: this amendment has effect in relation to annual accounts and reports in respect of financial years ending on or after 26 July 2000: see SI 2000/1430, reg 1(1), (2).

Sub-s (4): in para (a) words "or subsection (1) of section 249AA" in square brackets inserted by SI 2000/1430, reg 4(1), (5)(b).

Date in force: this amendment has effect in relation to annual accounts and reports in respect of financial years ending on or after 26 July 2000: see SI 2000/1430, reg 1(1), (2).

Sub-s (4): para (b) substituted by SI 2000/1430, reg 4(1), (5)(c).

Date in force: this amendment has effect in relation to annual accounts and reports in respect of financial years ending on or after 26 July 2000: see SI 2000/1430, reg 1(1), (2).

Sub-s (4): in para (c) words "to the effect" in square brackets inserted by SI 1996/189, reg 10(4).

Sub-s (5): words in square brackets substituted by SI 1996/189, reg 10(5).

[249C The report required for the purposes of section 249A(2)]

[(1) The report required for the purposes of section 249A(2) shall be prepared by a person (referred to in this Part as "the reporting accountant") who is eligible under section 249D.

(2) The report shall state whether in the opinion of the reporting accountant making it—

(a) the accounts of the company for the financial year in question are in agreement with the accounting records kept by the company under section 221, and

(b) having regard only to, and on the basis of, the information contained in those accounting records, those accounts have been drawn up in a manner consistent with the provisions of this Act specified in subsection (6), so far as applicable to the company.

(3) The report shall also state that in the opinion of the reporting accountant, having regard only to, and on the basis of, the information contained in the accounting records kept by the company under section 221, the company satisfied the requirements of subsection (4) of section 249A . . . for the financial year in question, and did not fall within section 249B(1)(a) to (f) at any time within that financial year.

(4) The report shall state the name of the reporting accountant and be signed by him.

(5) Where the reporting accountant is a body corporate or partnership, any reference to signature of the report, or any copy of the report, by the reporting accountant is a reference to signature in the name of the body corporate or partnership by a person authorised to sign on its behalf.

(6) The provisions referred to in subsection (2)(b) are—

(a) section 226(3) and Schedule 4,

(b) section 231 and paragraphs 7 to 9A and 13(1), (3) and (4) of Schedule 5, and

(c) section 232 and Schedule 6,

where appropriate as modified by [section 246(2) and (3)].]

NOTES

Except in relation to oversea companies (see note below), Part I of the Companies Act 1989 (ss 1–23) inserts new provisions in place of original ss 221–262 of this Act and amends the related Schedules (see s 1 of the 1989 Act).

Inserted by SI 1994/1935, reg 2.

Sub-s (3): words omitted repealed by SI 2000/1430, reg 8(3).

Date in force: this amendment has effect in relation to annual accounts and reports in respect of financial years ending on or after 26 July 2000: see SI 2000/1430, reg 1(1), (2).

Sub-s (6): words "section 246(2) and (3)" in square brackets substituted by SI 1997/220, reg 7(3).

Date in force: this amendment applies to annual accounts approved by the board of directors on or after 1 March 1997, and to directors' and auditors' reports on such accounts: see SI 1997/220, reg 1(3); for transitional provision see reg 1(4) thereof.

[249D The reporting accountant]

[(1) The reporting accountant shall be either—
(a) any member of a body listed in subsection (3) who, under the rules of the body—
  (i) is entitled to engage in public practice, and
  (ii) is not ineligible for appointment as a reporting accountant, or
(b) any person (whether or not a member of any such body) who—
  (i) is subject to the rules of any such body in seeking appointment or acting as auditor under Chapter V of Part XI, and
  (ii) under those rules, is eligible for appointment as auditor under that Chapter.

(1A) In subsection (1), references to the rules of a body listed in subsection (3) are to the rules (whether or not laid down by the body itself) which the body has power to enforce and which are relevant for the purposes of Part II of the Companies Act 1989 or this section.

This includes rules relating to the admission and expulsion of members of the body, so far as relevant for the purposes of that Part or this section.]

(2) An individual, a body corporate or a partnership may be appointed as a reporting accountant, and section 26 of the Companies Act 1989 (effect of appointment of partnership) shall apply to the appointment as reporting accountant of a partnership constituted under the law of England and Wales or Northern Ireland, or under the law of any other country or territory in which a partnership is not a legal person.

(3) The bodies referred to in [subsections (1) and (1A)] are—
(a) the Institute of Chartered Accountants in England and Wales,
(b) the Institute of Chartered Accountants of Scotland,
(c) the Institute of Chartered Accountants in Ireland,
(d) [the Association of Chartered Certified Accountants], . . .
(e) the Association of Authorised Public Accountants,
[(f) the Association of Accounting Technicians,
(g) the Association of International Accountants, and
(h) the Chartered Institute of Management Accountants.]

(4) A person is ineligible for appointment by a company as reporting accountant if he would be ineligible for appointment as an auditor of that company under section 27 of the Companies Act 1989 (ineligibility on ground of lack of independence).]

NOTES

Except in relation to oversea companies (see note below), Part I of the Companies Act 1989 (ss 1–23) inserts new provisions in place of original ss 221–262 of this Act and amends the related Schedules (see s 1 of the 1989 Act).

Inserted by SI 1994/1935, reg 2.

Sub-ss (1), (1A): substituted, for sub-s (1) as originally enacted, by SI 1995/589, reg 2.

Sub-s (3): words "subsections (1) and (1A)" in square brackets substituted by SI 1995/589, reg 2.

Sub-s (3): in para (d) words "the Association of Chartered Certified Accountants" in square brackets substituted by SI 1997/936, reg 4(2).

Date in force: this amendment has effect in relation to the annual accounts of any company for any financial year ending on or after 15 June 1997: see SI 1997/936, reg 1(2).

Sub-s (3): word omitted from the end of para (d) repealed by SI 1996/3080, reg 2.

Sub-s (3): paras (f)–(h) inserted by SI 1996/3080, reg 2.

[249E Effect of exemptions]

[(1) Where the directors of a company have taken advantage of the exemption conferred by section 249A(1) [or 249AA(1)]—

(a) sections 238 and 239 (right to receive or demand copies of accounts and reports) shall have effect with the omission of references to the auditors' report;

(b) no copy of an auditors' report need be delivered to the registrar or laid before the company in general meeting;

(c) subsections (3) to (5) of section 271 (accounts by reference to which distribution to be justified) shall not apply.

[(1A) Where the directors of a company have taken advantage of the exemption conferred by section 249AA, then for the purposes of that section the company shall be treated as a company entitled to prepare accounts in accordance with section 246 even though it is a member of an ineligible group.]

(2) Where the directors of a company have taken advantage of the exemption conferred by section 249A(2)—

(a) subsections (2) to (4) of section 236 (which require copies of the auditors' report to state the names of the auditors) shall have effect with the substitution for references to the auditors and the auditors' report of references to the reporting accountant and the report made for the purposes of section 249A(2) respectively;

(b) sections 238 and 239 (right to receive or demand copies of accounts and reports), section 241 (accounts and reports to be laid before company in general meeting) and section 242 (accounts and reports to be delivered to the registrar) shall have effect with the substitution for references to the auditors' report of references to the report made for the purposes of section 249A(2);

(c) subsections (3) to (5) of section 271 (accounts by reference to which distribution to be justified) shall not apply;

(d) section 389A(1) and (2) (rights to information) shall have effect with the substitution for references to the auditors of references to the reporting accountant.]

NOTES

Except in relation to oversea companies (see note below), Part I of the Companies Act 1989 (ss 1–23) inserts new provisions in place of original ss 221–262 of this Act and amends the related Schedules (see s 1 of the 1989 Act).

Inserted by SI 1994/1935, reg 2.

Sub-s (1): words "or section 249AA" in square brackets inserted by SI 2000/1430, reg 8(4).

Date in force: this amendment has effect in relation to annual accounts and reports in respect of financial years ending on or after 26 July 2000: see SI 2000/1430, reg 1(1), (2).

Sub-s (1A): inserted by SI 2000/1430, reg 8(5).

Date in force: this amendment has effect in relation to annual accounts and reports in respect of financial years ending on or after 26 July 2000: see SI 2000/1430, reg 1(1), (2).

[. . .]

NOTES
Inserted by the Companies Act 1989, s 14.
Repealed by SI 2000/1430, reg 8(6).
Date in force: this amendment has effect in relation to annual accounts and reports in respect of financial years ending on or after 26 July 2000: see SI 2000/1430, reg 1(1), (2).

[250 . . .]

. . .

NOTES
Inserted by the Companies Act 1989, s 14.
Repealed by SI 2000/1430, reg 8(6).
Date in force: this amendment has effect in relation to annual accounts and reports in respect of financial years ending on or after 26 July 2000: see SI 2000/1430, reg 1(1), (2).

[Listed public companies]

NOTES
Inserted by the Companies Act 1989, s 15.

[251 Provision of summary financial statement to shareholders]

[(1)   A public company whose shares [or debentures], or any class of whose shares [or debentures], are listed need not, in such cases as may be specified by regulations made by the Secretary of State, and provided any conditions so specified are complied with, send copies of the documents referred to in section 238(1) to [entitled persons], but may instead send them a summary financial statement.

[In this section—
"entitled persons ", in relation to a company, means such of the persons specified in paragraphs (a) to (c) of subsection (1) of section 238 as are or would apart from this section be entitled to be sent copies of those documents relating to the company which are referred to in that subsection;
["listed" means included in the official list by the competent authority for the purposes of Part 6 of the Financial services and Markets Act 2000 (official listing); and
"the official list" has the meaning given in section 103(1) of that Act].]

(2)   Copies of the documents referred to in section 238(1) shall, however, be sent to [any entitled person] who wishes to receive them; and the Secretary of State may by regulations make provision as to the manner in which it is to be ascertained [(whether before or after he becomes an entitled person)] whether [an entitled person] wishes to receive them.

[(2A)   References in this section to sending a summary financial statement to an entitled person include references to using electronic communications for sending the statement to such address as may for the time being be notified to the company by that person for that purpose.

(2B)   For the purposes of this section a summary financial statement is also to be treated as sent to an entitled person where—
  (a)   the company and that person have agreed to his having access to summary financial statements on a web site (instead of their being sent to him);
  (b)   the statement is a statement to which that agreement applies; and
  (c)   that person is notified, in a manner for the time being agreed for the purpose between him and the company, of—
      (i)   the publication of the statement on a web site;
      (ii)   the address of that web site; and
      (iii) the place on that web site where the statement may be accessed, and how it may be accessed.

(2C)   For the purposes of this section a statement treated in accordance with subsection (2B) as sent to an entitled person is to be treated as sent to him if, and only if—
  (a)   the statement is published on the web site throughout a period beginning at least 21 days before the date of the meeting at which the accounts and directors' report from which the statement is derived are to be laid and ending with the conclusion of that meeting; and
  (b)   the notification given for the purposes of paragraph (c) of that subsection is given not less than 21 days before the date of the meeting.

(2D)   Nothing in subsection (2C) shall invalidate the proceedings of a meeting where—
  (a)   any statement that is required to be published as mentioned in paragraph (a) of that subsection is published for a part, but not all, of the period mentioned in that paragraph; and
  (b)   the failure to publish that statement throughout that period is wholly attributable to circumstances which it would not be reasonable to have expected the company to prevent or avoid.

(2E)   A company may, notwithstanding any provision to the contrary in its articles, take advantage of any of subsections (2A) to (2D).]

(3)   The summary financial statement shall be derived from the company's annual accounts and the directors' report and shall be in such form and contain such information as may be specified by regulations made by the Secretary of State.

(4)   Every summary financial statement shall—
  (a)   state that it is only a summary of information in the company's annual accounts and the directors' report;
  (b)   contain a statement by the company's auditors of their opinion as to whether the summary financial statement is consistent with those accounts and that report and complies with the requirements of this section and regulations made under it;
  (c)   state whether the auditors' report on the annual accounts was unqualified or qualified, and if it was qualified set out the report in full together with any further material needed to understand the qualification;
  (d)   state whether the auditors' report on the annual accounts contained a statement under—

(i) section 237(2) (accounting records or returns inadequate or accounts not agreeing with records and returns), or

(ii) section 237(3) (failure to obtain necessary information and explanations),

and if so, set out the statement in full.

(5) Regulations under this section shall be made by statutory instrument which shall be subject to annulment in pursuance of a resolution of either House of Parliament.

(6) If default is made in complying with this section or regulations made under it, the company and every officer of it who is in default is guilty of an offence and liable to a fine.

(7) Section 240 (requirements in connection with publication of accounts) does not apply in relation to the provision to [entitled persons] of a summary financial statement in accordance with this section.]

NOTES

Except in relation to oversea companies (see note below), Part I of the Companies Act 1989 (ss 1–23) inserts new provisions in place of original ss 221–262 of this Act and amends the related Schedules (see s 1 of the 1989 Act).

Inserted by the Companies Act 1989, s 15.

Sub-s (1): words "or debentures" in square brackets in both places they occur inserted by SI 1992/3003, reg 3.

Sub-s (1): words "entitled persons" in square brackets substituted by SI 1992/3003, reg 3.

Sub-s (1): words in square brackets beginning with the words "In this section—" substituted by SI 1992/3003, reg 3.

Sub-s (1): definitions "listed" and "the official list" substituted, for definition "listed", by SI 2001/3649, art 15.

Date in force: 1 December 2001: see SI 2001/3649, art 1.

Sub-s (2): first and final words in square brackets substituted and second words in square brackets inserted by SI 1992/3003, reg 3(4).

Sub-ss (2A)–(2E): inserted by SI 2000/3373, art 14.

Date in force: 22 December 2000: see SI 2000/3373, art 1(1).

Sub-s (7): words in square brackets substituted by SI 1992/3003, reg 3(5).

[Private companies]

NOTES

Inserted by the Companies Act 1989, s 16.

[252 Election to dispense with laying of accounts and reports before general meeting]

[(1) A private company may elect (by elective resolution in accordance with section 379A) to dispense with the laying of accounts and reports before the company in general meeting.

(2) An election has effect in relation to the accounts and reports in respect of the financial year in which the election is made and subsequent financial years.

(3)   Whilst an election is in force, the references in the following provisions of this Act to the laying of accounts before the company in general meeting shall be read as references to the sending of copies of the accounts to members and others under section 238(1)—
  (a)   section 235(1) (accounts on which auditors are to report),
  (b)   section 270(3) and (4) (accounts by reference to which distributions are justified), and
  (c)   section 320(2) (accounts relevant for determining company's net assets for purposes of ascertaining whether approval required for certain transactions);

and the requirement in section 271(4) that the auditors' statement under that provision be laid before the company in general meeting shall be read as a requirement that it be sent to members and others along with the copies of the accounts sent to them under section 238(1).

(4)   If an election under this section ceases to have effect, section 241 applies in relation to the accounts and reports in respect of the financial year in which the election ceases to have effect and subsequent financial years.]

NOTES

  Except in relation to oversea companies (see note below), Part I of the Companies Act 1989 (ss 1–23) inserts new provisions in place of original ss 221–262 of this Act and amends the related Schedules (see s 1 of the 1989 Act).
  Inserted by the Companies Act 1989, s 16.

[253 Right of shareholder to require laying of accounts]

[(1)   Where an election under section 252 is in force, the copies of the accounts and reports sent out in accordance with section 238(1)—
  (a)   shall be sent not less than 28 days before the end of the period allowed for laying and delivering accounts and reports, and
  (b)   shall be accompanied, in the case of a member of the company, by a notice informing him of his right to require the laying of the accounts and reports before a general meeting;

and section 238(5) (penalty for default) applies in relation to the above requirements as to the requirements contained in that section.

(2)   Before the end of the period of 28 days beginning with the day on which the accounts and reports are sent out in accordance with section 238(1), any member or auditor of the company may by notice in writing deposited at the registered office of the company require that a general meeting be held for the purpose of laying the accounts and reports before the company.

[(2A)   The power of a member or auditor under subsection (2) to require the holding of a general meeting is exercisable not only by the deposit of a notice in writing but also by the transmission to the company at such address as may for the time being be specified for the purpose by or on behalf of the company of an electronic communication containing the requirement.]

(3)   If the directors do not within 21 days from the date of[—
  (a)   the deposit of a notice containing a requirement under subsection (2), or

(b) the receipt of such a requirement contained in an electronic communication, proceed]

duly to convene a meeting, the person who [required the holding of the meeting] may do so himself.

(4)   A meeting so convened shall not be held more than three months from that date and shall be convened in the same manner, as nearly as possible, as that in which meetings are to be convened by directors.

(5)   Where the directors do not duly convene a meeting, any reasonable expenses incurred by reason of that failure by the person who [required the holding of the meeting] shall be made good to him by the company, and shall be recouped by the company out of any fees, or other remuneration in respect of their services, due or to become due to such of the directors as were in default.

(6)   The directors shall be deemed not to have duly convened a meeting if they convene a meeting for a date more than 28 days after the date of the notice convening it.]

NOTES

Except in relation to oversea companies (see note below), Part I of the Companies Act 1989 (ss 1–23) inserts new provisions in place of original ss 221–262 of this Act and amends the related Schedules (see s 1 of the 1989 Act).

Inserted by the Companies Act 1989, s 16.

Sub-s (2A): inserted by SI 2000/3373, art 15(1), (2).

Date in force: 22 December 2000: see SI 2000/3373, art 1(1).

Sub-s (3): paras (a), (b) substituted by SI 2000/3373, art 15(1), (3)(a).

Date in force: 22 December 2000: see SI 2000/3373, art 1(1).

Sub-s (3): words "required the holding of the meeting" in square brackets substituted by SI 2000/3373, art 15(1), (3)(b).

Date in force: 22 December 2000: see SI 2000/3373, art 1(1).

Sub-s (5): words "required the holding of the meeting" in square brackets substituted by SI 2000/3373, art 15(1), (4).

Date in force: 22 December 2000: see SI 2000/3373, art 1(1).

[Unlimited companies]

NOTES

Inserted by the Companies Act 1989, s 17.

[254 Exemption from requirement to deliver accounts and reports]

[(1)   The directors of an unlimited company are not required to deliver accounts and reports to the registrar in respect of a financial year if the following conditions are met.

(2)   The conditions are that at no time during the relevant accounting reference period—
   (a)   has the company been, to its knowledge, a subsidiary undertaking of an undertaking which was then limited, or

(b)　have there been, to its knowledge, exercisable by or on behalf of two or more undertakings which were then limited, rights which if exercisable by one of them would have made the company a subsidiary undertaking of it, or

(c)　has the company been a parent company of an undertaking which was then limited.

The references above to an undertaking being limited at a particular time are to an undertaking (under whatever law established) the liability of whose members is at that time limited.

(3)　The exemption conferred by this section does not apply [if—

(a)　the company is a banking [or insurance] company or the parent company of a banking [or insurance] group, or

(b)　the company is a qualifying company within the meaning of the Partnerships and Unlimited Companies (Accounts) Regulations 1993, or

(c)] any time during the relevant accounting period the company carried on business as the promoter of a trading stamp scheme within the Trading Stamps Act 1964.

(4)　Where a company is exempt by virtue of this section from the obligation to deliver accounts, section 240 (requirements in connection with publication of accounts) has effect with the following modifications—

(a)　in subsection (3)(b) for the words from "whether statutory accounts" to "have been delivered to the registrar" substitute "that the company is exempt from the requirement to deliver statutory accounts", and

(b)　in subsection (5) for "as required to be delivered to the registrar under section 242" substitute "as prepared in accordance with this Part and approved by the board of directors".]

NOTES

Except in relation to oversea companies (see note below), Part I of the Companies Act 1989 (ss 1–23) inserts new provisions in place of original ss 221–262 of this Act and amends the related Schedules (see s 1 of the 1989 Act).

Inserted by the Companies Act 1989, s 17.

Sub-s (3): first words in square brackets originally inserted by SI 1991/2705, reg 6, Sch 2, substituted by 1993/1820, reg 10, words in square brackets therein inserted by SI 1993/3246, reg 5(1), Sch 2, para 2.

[Chapter III
Supplementary Provisions]

NOTES

Inserted by the Companies Act 1989, s 19.

[Accounting standards]

NOTES

Inserted by the Companies Act 1989, s 19.

256 Accounting standards

(1) In this Part "accounting standards" means statements of standard accounting practice issued by such body or bodies as may be prescribed by regulations.

(2) References in this Part to accounting standards applicable to a company's annual accounts are to such standards as are, in accordance with their terms, relevant to the company's circumstances and to the accounts.

(3) The Secretary of State may make grants to or for the purposes of bodies concerned with—
   (a) issuing accounting standards,
   (b) overseeing and directing the issuing of such standards, or
   (c) investigating departures from such standards or from the accounting requirements of this Act and taking steps to secure compliance with them.

(4) Regulations under this section may contain such transitional and other supplementary and incidental provisions as appear to the Secretary of State to be appropriate.]

NOTES
Inserted by the Companies Act 1989, s 19, as from 1 April 1990 subject to transitional provisions.

[Parent and subsidiary undertakings]

NOTES
Inserted by the Companies Act 1989, s 21(1).

[258 Parent and subsidiary undertakings]

[(1) The expressions "parent undertaking" and "subsidiary undertaking" in this Part shall be construed as follows; and a "parent company" means a parent undertaking which is a company.

(2) An undertaking is a parent undertaking in relation to another undertaking, a subsidiary undertaking, if—
   (a) it holds a majority of the voting rights in the undertaking, or
   (b) it is a member of the undertaking and has the right to appoint or remove a majority of its board of directors, or
   (c) it has the right to exercise a dominant influence over the undertaking—
      (i) by virtue of provisions contained in the undertaking's memorandum or articles, or
      (ii) by virtue of a control contract, or
   (d) it is a member of the undertaking and controls alone, pursuant to an agreement with other shareholders or members, a majority of the voting rights in the undertaking.

(3) For the purposes of subsection (2) an undertaking shall be treated as a member of another undertaking—
   (a) if any of its subsidiary undertakings is a member of that undertaking, or

(b) if any shares in that other undertaking are held by a person acting on behalf of the undertaking or any of its subsidiary undertakings.

(4) An undertaking is also a parent undertaking in relation to another undertaking, a subsidiary undertaking, if it has a participating interest in the undertaking and—
(a) it actually exercises a dominant influence over it, or
(b) it and the subsidiary undertaking are managed on a unified basis.

(5) A parent undertaking shall be treated as the parent undertaking of undertakings in relation to which any of its subsidiary undertakings are, or are to be treated as, parent undertakings; and references to its subsidiary undertakings shall be construed accordingly.

(6) Schedule 10A contains provisions explaining expressions used in this section and otherwise supplementing this section.]

NOTES

Except in relation to oversea companies (see note below), Part I of the Companies Act 1989 (ss 1–23) inserts new provisions in place of original ss 221–262 of this Act and amends the related Schedules (see s 1 of the 1989 Act).
Inserted by the Companies Act 1989, s 21(1).

[Other interpretation provisions]

NOTES
Inserted by the Companies Act 1989, s 22.

[259 Meaning of "undertaking" and related expressions]

[(1) In this Part "undertaking" means—
(a) a body corporate or partnership, or
(b) an unincorporated association carrying on a trade or business, with or without a view to profit.

(2) In this Part references to shares—
(a) in relation to an undertaking with a share capital, are to allotted shares;
(b) in relation to an undertaking with capital but no share capital, are to rights to share in the capital of the undertaking; and
(c) in relation to an undertaking without capital, are to interests—
(i) conferring any right to share in the profits or liability to contribute to the losses of the undertaking, or
(ii) giving rise to an obligation to contribute to the debts or expenses of the undertaking in the event of a winding up.

(3) Other expressions appropriate to companies shall be construed, in relation to an undertaking which is not a company, as references to the corresponding persons, officers, documents or organs, as the case may be, appropriate to undertakings of that description.

This is subject to provision in any specific context providing for the translation of such expressions.

(4)   References in this Part to "fellow subsidiary undertakings" are to undertakings which are subsidiary undertakings of the same parent undertaking but are not parent undertakings or subsidiary undertakings of each other.

(5)   In this Part "group undertaking", in relation to an undertaking, means an undertaking which is—
(a)   a parent undertaking or subsidiary undertaking of that undertaking, or
(b)   a subsidiary undertaking of any parent undertaking of that undertaking.]

NOTES

Except in relation to oversea companies (see note below), Part I of the Companies Act 1989 (ss 1–23) inserts new provisions in place of original ss 221–262 of this Act and amends the related Schedules (see s 1 of the 1989 Act).
Inserted by the Companies Act 1989, s 22.

[260 Participating interests]

[(1)   In this Part a "participating interest" means an interest held by an undertaking in the shares of another undertaking which it holds on a long-term basis for the purpose of securing a contribution to its activities by the exercise of control or influence arising from or related to that interest.

(2)   A holding of 20 per cent or more of the shares of an undertaking shall be presumed to be a participating interest unless the contrary is shown.

(3)   The reference in subsection (1) to an interest in shares includes—
(a)   an interest which is convertible into an interest in shares, and
(b)   an option to acquire shares or any such interest;

and an interest or option falls within paragraph (a) or (b) notwithstanding that the shares to which it relates are, until the conversion or the exercise of the option, unissued.

(4)   For the purposes of this section an interest held on behalf of an undertaking shall be treated as held by it.

(5)   For the purposes of this section as it applies in relation to the expression "participating interest" in section 258(4) (definition of "subsidiary undertaking")—
(a)   there shall be attributed to an undertaking any interests held by any of its subsidiary undertakings, and
(b)   the references in subsection (1) to the purpose and activities of an undertaking include the purposes and activities of any of its subsidiary undertakings and of the group as a whole.

(6)   In the balance sheet and profit and loss formats set out in Part I of Schedule 4, [Part I of Schedule 8, Schedule 8A,][Chapter I of Part I of Schedule 9 and Chapter I of Part I of Schedule 9A], "participating interest" does not include an interest in a group undertaking.

(7)   For the purposes of this section as it applies in relation to the expression "participating interest"—
(a)   in those formats as they apply in relation to group accounts, and

(b) in paragraph 20 of Schedule 4A (group accounts: undertakings to be accounted for as associated undertakings),

the references in subsection (1) to (4) to the interest held by, and the purposes and activities of, the undertaking concerned shall be construed as references to the interest held by, and the purposes and activities of, the group (within the meaning of paragraph 1 of that Schedule).]

NOTES

Except in relation to oversea companies (see note below), Part I of the Companies Act 1989 (ss 1–23) inserts new provisions in place of original ss 221–262 of this Act and amends the related Schedules (see s 1 of the 1989 Act).

Inserted by the Companies Act 1989, s 22.

Sub-s (6): words "Part I of Schedule 8, Schedule 8A," in square brackets inserted by SI 1997/220, reg 7(5).

Date in force: this amendment applies to annual accounts approved by the board of directors on or after 1 March 1997, and to directors' and auditors' reports on such accounts: see SI 1997/220, reg 1(3); for transitional provision see reg 1(4) thereof.

Sub-s (6): words "Chapter I of Part I of Schedule 9 and Chapter I of Part I of Schedule 9A" in square brackets substituted by SI 1993/3246, reg 5(1), Sch 2, para 4.

[262 Minor definitions

(1) In this Part—
"annual accounts" means—
(a) the individual accounts required by section 226, and
(b) any group accounts required by section 227,
(but see also section 230 (treatment of individual profit and loss account where group accounts prepared));
"annual report", in relation to a company, means the directors' report required by section 234;
"balance sheet date" means the date as at which the balance sheet was made up;
"capitalisation", in relation to work or costs, means treating that work or those costs as a fixed asset;
["credit institution" means a credit institution as defined in article 1 of the First Council Directive on the coordination of laws, regulations and administrative provisions relating to the taking up and pursuit of the business of credit institutions (77/780/EEC), that is to say an undertaking whose business is to receive deposits or other repayable funds from the public and to grant credits for its own account;]
[. . . . .]
"fixed assets" means assets of a company which are intended for use on a continuing basis in the company's activities, and "current assets" means assets not intended for such use;
"group" means a parent undertaking and its subsidiary undertakings;
"included in the consolidation", in relation to group accounts, or "included in consolidated group accounts", means that the undertaking is included in the accounts by the method of full (and not proportional) consolidation, and references to an undertaking excluded from consolidation shall be construed accordingly;
"purchase price", in relation to an asset of a company or any raw materials or consumables used in the production of such an asset, includes any consideration

(whether in cash or otherwise) given by the company in respect of that asset or those materials or consumables, as the case may be;

"qualified", in relation to an auditors' report, means that the report does not state the auditors' unqualified opinion that the accounts have been properly prepared in accordance with this Act or, in the case of an undertaking not required to prepare accounts in accordance with this Act, under any corresponding legislation under which it is required to prepare accounts;

"true and fair view" refers—

(a) in the case of individual accounts, to the requirement of section 226(2), and

(b) in the case of group accounts, to the requirement of section 227(3);

"turnover", in relation to a company, means the amounts derived from the provision of goods and services falling within the company's ordinary activities, after deduction of—

(i)   trade discounts,

(ii) value added tax, and

(iii) any other taxes based on the amounts so derived.

(2)   In the case of an undertaking not trading for profit, any reference in this Part to a profit and loss account is to an income and expenditure account; and references to profit and loss and, in relation to group accounts, to a consolidated profit and loss account shall be construed accordingly.

(3)   References in this Part to "realised profits" and "realised losses", in relation to a company's accounts, are to such profits or losses of the company as fall to be treated as realised in accordance with principles generally accepted, at the time when the accounts are prepared, with respect to the determination for accounting purposes of realised profits or losses.

This is without prejudice to—

(a) the construction of any other expression (where appropriate) by reference to accepted accounting principles or practice, or

(b) any specific provision for the treatment of profits or losses of any description as realised.]

NOTES

Inserted as noted to s 259.

Sub-s (1): definition "credit institution" substituted by the Companies Act 1985 (Disclosure of Branches and Bank Accounts) Regulations 1992, SI 1992/3178, regs 7, 8(b), subject to a transitional provision; definition "EEA State" (originally inserted, in relation to any financial year ending on or after 2 February 1996, by the Companies Act 1985 (Miscellaneous Accounting Amendments) Regulations 1996, SI 1996/189, regs 12(1), 16(1)), repealed by the Companies (Membership of Holding Company) (Dealers in Securities) Regulations 1997, SI 1997/2306, reg 4(2).

[262A Index of defined expressions]

[The following Table shows the provisions of this Part defining or otherwise explaining expressions used in this Part (other than expressions used only in the same section or paragraph)—

["the 1982 Act" (in Schedule 9A)	paragraph 81 of Part 1 of that Schedule]
accounting reference date and accounting reference period	section 224
accounting standards and applicable accounting standards	section 256
["address"	section 262(1)]
annual accounts (generally)	section 262(1)
(includes notes to the accounts)	section 261(2)
annual report	section 262(1)
associated undertaking (in Schedule 4A)	paragraph 20 of that Schedule
balance sheet (includes notes)	section 261(2)
balance sheet date	section 262(1)
[. . .	. . .]
banking group	[section 255A(4)]
[. . .	< . . . >]
capitalisation (in relation to work or costs)	section 262(1)
credit institution	section 262(1)
current assets	section 262(1)
[. . .	. . .]
fellow subsidiary undertaking	section 259(4)
[financial fixed assets (in Schedule 9)	paragraph 82 of Part I of that Schedule]
financial year	section 223
fixed assets	section 262(1)
["general business" (in Schedule 9A)	paragraph 81 of Part 1 of that Schedule]
group	section 262(1)
group undertaking	section 259(5)
[historical cost accounting rules	
—in Schedule 4	paragraph 29 of that Schedule
[—in Schedule 8	paragraph 29 of that Schedule]
—in Schedule 9	paragraph 39 of Part I of that Schedule
[—in Schedule 9A	paragraph 20(1) of Part 1 of that Schedule]]
included in the consolidation and related expressions	section 262(1)
individual accounts	section 262(1)
insurance group	[section 255A(5)]
land of freehold tenure and land of leasehold tenure (in relation to Scotland)	
—in Schedule 4	paragraph 93 of that Schedule
[—in Schedule 9	paragraph 86 of Part I of that Schedule]
—in [Schedule 9A]	[paragraph 85 of Part I of that Schedule]
lease, long lease and short lease	
—in Schedule 4	paragraph 83 of that Schedule
[—in Schedule 9	paragraph 82 of Part I of that Schedule]
—in [Schedule 9A]	[paragraph 81 of Part I of that Schedule]
listed investment	
—in Schedule 4	paragraph 84 of that Schedule
[—in Schedule 8	paragraph 54 of that Schedule]
—in [Schedule 9A]	[paragraph 81 of Part I of that Schedule]
[listed security (in Schedule 9)	paragraph 82 of Part I of that Schedule]
["long term business" (in Schedule 9A)	paragraph 81 of Part 1 of that Schedule]
["long term fund" (in Schedule 9A)	paragraph 81 of Part 1 of that Schedule]
notes to the accounts	section 261(1)

parent undertaking (and parent company)	section 258 and Schedule 10A
participating interest	section 260
[pension costs	
—in Schedule 4	paragraph 94(2) of that Schedule
—in Schedule 8	paragraph 59(2) of that Schedule
—in Schedule 9	paragraph 87(b) of Part I of that Schedule
—in Schedule 9A	paragraph 86(b) of Part I of that Schedule]
period allowed for laying and delivering accounts and reports	section 244
["policy holder" (in Schedule 9A)	paragraph 81 of Part 1 of that Schedule]
profit and loss account	
(includes notes)	section 261(2)
(in relation to a company not trading for profit)	section 262(2)
Provision	
—in Schedule 4	paragraphs 88 and 89 of that Schedule
[—in Schedule 8	paragraphs 57 and 58 of that Schedule]
[—in Schedule 9	paragraph 85 of Part I of that Schedule]
—in [Schedule 9A]	[paragraph 84 of Part I of that Schedule]
["provision for unexpired risks" (in Schedule 9A)	paragraph 81 of Part 1 of that Schedule;]
purchase price	section 262(1)
qualified	section 262(1)
realised losses and realised profits	section 262(3)
[repayable on demand (in Schedule 9)	paragraph 82 of Part I of that Schedule]
[reporting accountant	section 249C(1)]
reserve (in [Schedule 9A])	paragraph 32 of that Schedule
[sale and repurchase transaction (in Schedule 9)	paragraph 82 of Part I of that Schedule]
[sale and option to resell transaction (in Schedule 9)	paragraph 82 of Part I of that Schedule]
Shares	section 259(2)
[social security costs	
—in Schedule 4	paragraph 94(1) and (3) of that Schedule
[—in Schedule 8	paragraph 59(1) and (3) of that Schedule]
—in Schedule 9	paragraph 87(a) and (c) of Part I of that Schedule
[—in Schedule 9A	paragraph 86(a) and (c) of Part I of that Schedule]]
special provisions for banking and insurance companies and groups	sections 255 and 255A
subsidiary undertaking	section 258 and Schedule 10A
true and fair view	section 262(1)
turnover	section 262(1)
undertaking and related expressions	section 259(1) to (3)]

NOTES

Except in relation to oversea companies (see note below), Part I of the Companies Act 1989 (ss 1–23) inserts new provisions in place of original ss 221–262 of this Act and amends the related Schedules (see s 1 of the 1989 Act).

Inserted by the Companies Act 1989, s 22.

Entry "the 1982 Act (in Schedule 9A)" inserted by SI 1993/3246, reg 5(1), Sch 2, para 5(a).

Entry "address" inserted by SI 2000/3373, art 16(2).

Date in force: 22 December 2000: see SI 2000/3373, art 1(1).

First and second entries omitted inserted by SI 1991/2705, reg 6, Sch 2, para 3, repealed by SI 1994/233, reg 4(2).

In entry "banking group" words in square brackets in column 2 substituted by SI 1991/2705, reg 6, Sch 2, para 3.

Third entry omitted inserted, in relation to the annual accounts and annual report of any company for the financial year ending on or after 2 February 1996, by SI 1996/189, regs 12(2), 16(1), repealed by SI 1997/2306, reg 4(4).

Entry "financial fixed assets" inserted by SI 1991/2705, reg 6, Sch 2, para 3.

Entry "general business (in Schedule 9A)" inserted by SI 1993/3246, reg 5(1), Sch 2, para 5(a).

Entry "historical cost accounting rules" substituted by SI 1991/2705, reg 6, Sch 2, para 3.

In entry "historical cost accounting rules" words in square brackets relating to Schedule 8 inserted by SI 1997/220, reg 7(6)(a).

Date in force: this amendment applies to annual accounts approved by the board of directors on or after 1 March 1997, and to directors' and auditors' reports on such accounts: see SI 1997/220, reg 1(3); for transitional provision see reg 1(4) thereof.

In entry "historical cost accounting rules" words in square brackets relating to Schedule 9A inserted SI 1993/3246, reg 5(1), Sch 2, para 5(b).

In entry "insurance group" words in square brackets in column 2 substituted by SI 1991/2705, reg 6, Sch 2, para 3.

In entry "land of freehold tenure and land of leasehold tenure" first and second words in square brackets inserted by SI 1991/2705, reg 6, Sch 2, para 3, final words in square brackets substituted by SI 1993/3246, reg 5(1), Sch 2, para 5(c).

In entry "lease, long lease and short lease" first and second words in square brackets inserted by SI 1991/2705, reg 6, Sch 2, para 3, final words in square brackets substituted by SI 1993/3246, reg 5(1), Sch 2, para 5(d).

In entry "listed investment" words in square brackets relating to Schedule 8 inserted by SI 1997/220, reg 7(6)(b).

Date in force: this amendment applies to annual accounts approved by the board of directors on or after 1 March 1997, and to directors' and auditors' reports on such accounts: see SI 1997/220, reg 1(3); for transitional provision see reg 1(4) thereof.

In entry "listed investment" words "Schedule 9A" in square brackets substituted by SI 1991/2705, reg 6, Sch 2, para 3.

In entry "listed investment" words "paragraph 81 of Part I of that Schedule" substituted by SI 1993/3246, reg 5(1), Sch 2, para 5(e).

Entry "listed security" inserted by SI 1991/2705, reg 6, Sch 2, para 3.

Entry "long term business in Schedule 9A" inserted by SI 1993/3246, reg 5(1), Sch 2, para 5(a).

Entry "long term fund (in Schedule 9A)" inserted by SI 1993/3246, reg 5(1), Sch 2, para 5(a).

Entry "pension costs" substituted by SI 1997/220, reg 7(6)(c).

Date in force: this amendment applies to annual accounts approved by the board of directors on or after 1 March 1997, and to directors' and auditors' reports on such accounts: see SI 1997/220, reg 1(3); for transitional provision see reg 1(4) thereof.

Entry "policy holder (in Schedule 9A)" inserted by SI 1993/3246, reg 5(1), Sch 2, para 5(a).

In entry "provision" words in square brackets relating to Schedule 8 inserted by SI 1997/220, reg 7(6)(d).

Date in force: this amendment applies to annual accounts approved by the board of directors on or after 1 March 1997, and to directors' and auditors' reports on such accounts: see SI 1997/220, reg 1(3); for transitional provision see reg 1(4) thereof.

In entry "provision" words in square brackets relating to Schedule 9 inserted and words "Schedule 9A" substituted by SI 1991/2705, reg 6, Sch 2, para 3.

In entry "provision" words "paragraph 84 of Part I of that Schedule" in square brackets substituted by SI 1993/3246, reg 5(1), Sch 2, para 5(g).

Entry "provision for unexpired risks (in Schedule 9A)" inserted by SI 1993/3246, reg 5(1), Sch 2, para 5(a).

Entry "repayable on demand" inserted by SI 1991/2705, reg 6, Sch 2, para 3.

Entry "reporting accountant" inserted by SI 1994/1935, reg 4, Sch 1, para 3.

Entry "sale and repurchase transaction" inserted by SI 1991/2705, reg 6, Sch 2, para 3.

Entry "sale and option to resell transaction" inserted by SI 1991/2705, reg 6, Sch 2, para 3.

Entry "social security costs" substituted by SI 1991/2705, reg 6, Sch 2, para 3.

In entry "social security costs" words in square brackets relating to Schedule 8 inserted by SI 1997/220, reg 7(6)(e).

Date in force: this amendment applies to annual accounts approved by the board of directors on or after 1 March 1997, and to directors' and auditors' reports on such accounts: see SI 1997/220, reg 1(3); for transitional provision see reg 1(4) thereof.

In entry "social security costs" words in square brackets relating to Schedule 9A inserted SI 1993/3246, reg 5(1), Sch 2, para 5(h).

PART VIII
DISTRIBUTION OF PROFITS AND ASSETS

Limits of company's power of distribution

263 Certain distributions prohibited

(1)   A company shall not make a distribution except out of profits available for the purpose.

(2)   In this Part, "distribution" means every description of distribution of a company's assets to its members, whether in cash or otherwise, except distribution by way of—

  (a)   an issue of shares as fully or partly paid bonus shares,
  (b)   the redemption or purchase of any of the company's own shares out of capital (including the proceeds of any fresh issue of shares) or out of unrealised profits in accordance with Chapter VII of Part V,
  (c)   the reduction of share capital by extinguishing or reducing the liability of any of the members on any of the company's shares in respect of share capital not paid up, or by paying off paid up share capital, and
  (d)   a distribution of assets to members of the company on its winding up.

(3)   For purposes of this Part, a company's profits available for distribution are its accumulated, realised profits, so far as not previously utilised by distribution or capitalisation, less its accumulated, realised losses, so far as not previously written off in a reduction or reorganisation of capital duly made.

This is subject to the provision made by sections 265 and 266 for investment and other companies.

(4) A company shall not apply an unrealised profit in paying up debentures, or any amounts unpaid on its issued shares.

(5) Where the directors of a company are, after making all reasonable enquiries, unable to determine whether a particular profit made before 22nd December 1980 is realised or unrealised, they may treat the profit as realised; and where after making such enquiries they are unable to determine whether a particular loss so made is realised or unrealised, they may treat the loss as unrealised.

264 Restriction on distribution of assets

(1) A public company may only make a distribution at any time—
  (a) if at that time the amount of its net assets is not less than the aggregate of its called-up share capital and undistributable reserves, and
  (b) if, and to the extent that, the distribution does not reduce the amount of those assets to less than that aggregate.

This is subject to the provision made by sections 265 and 266 for investment and other companies.

(2) In subsection (1), "net assets" means the aggregate of the company's assets less the aggregate of its liabilities ("liabilities" to include any provision for liabilities or charges within paragraph 89 of Schedule 4).

(3) A company's undistributable reserves are—
  (a) the share premium account,
  (b) the capital redemption reserve,
  (c) the amount by which the company's accumulated, unrealised profits, so far as not previously utilised by capitalisation of a description to which this paragraph applies, exceed its accumulated, unrealised losses (so far as not previously written off in a reduction or reorganisation of capital duly made), and
  (d) any other reserve which the company is prohibited from distributing by any enactment (other than one contained in this Part) or by its memorandum or articles;

and paragraph (c) applies to every description of capitalisation except a transfer of profits of the company to its capital redemption reserve on or after 22nd December 1980.

(4) A public company shall not include any uncalled share capital as an asset in any accounts relevant for purposes of this section.

Relevant accounts

270 Distribution to be justified by reference to company's accounts

(1) This section and sections 271 to 276 below are for determining the question whether a distribution may be made by a company without contravening sections 263, 264 or 265.

(2)   The amount of a distribution which may be made is determined by reference to the following items as stated in the company's accounts—
  (a)   profits, losses, assets and liabilities,
  (b)   provisions of any of the kinds mentioned in paragraphs 88 and 89 of Schedule 4 (depreciation, diminution in value of assets, retentions to meet liabilities, etc), and
  (c)   share capital and reserves (including undistributable reserves).

(3)   Except in a case falling within the next subsection, the company's accounts which are relevant for this purpose are its last annual accounts, that is to say those prepared under Part VII which were laid in respect of the last preceding accounting reference period in respect of which accounts so prepared were laid; and for this purpose accounts are laid if section 241(1) has been complied with in relation to them.

(4)   In the following two cases—
  (a)   where the distribution would be found to contravene the relevant section if reference were made only to the company's last annual accounts, or
  (b)   where the distribution is proposed to be declared during the company's first accounting reference period, or before any accounts are laid in respect of that period,
the accounts relevant under this section (called "interim accounts" in the first case, and "initial accounts" in the second) are those necessary to enable a reasonable judgment to be made as to the amounts of the items mentioned in subsection (2) above.

(5)   The relevant section is treated as contravened in the case of a distribution unless the statutory requirements about the relevant accounts (that is, the requirements of this and the following three sections, as and where applicable) are complied with in relation to that distribution.

271   Requirements for last annual accounts

(1)   If the company's last annual accounts constitute the only accounts relevant under section 270, the statutory requirements in respect of them are as follows.

(2)   The accounts must have been properly prepared in accordance with this Act, or have been so prepared subject only to matters which are not material for determining, by reference to items mentioned in section 270(2), whether the distribution would contravene the relevant section; and, without prejudice to the foregoing—
  (a)   so much of the accounts as consists of a balance sheet must give a true and fair view of the state of the company's affairs as at the balance sheet date, and
  (b)   so much of the accounts as consists of a profit and loss account must give a true and fair view of the company's profit or loss for the period in respect of which the accounts were prepared.

(3)   The auditors must have made their report on the accounts under [section 235]; and the following subsection applies if the report is a qualified report, that is to say,

it is not a report without qualification to the effect that in the auditors' opinion the accounts have been properly prepared in accordance with this Act.

(4)   The auditors must in that case also have stated in writing (either at the time of their report or subsequently) whether, in their opinion, the matter in respect of which their report is qualified is material for determining, by reference to items mentioned in section 270(2), whether the distribution would contravene the relevant section; and a copy of the statement must have been laid before the company in general meeting.

(5)   A statement under subsection (4) suffices for purposes of a particular distribution not only if it relates to a distribution which has been proposed but also if it relates to distributions of any description which includes that particular distribution, notwithstanding that at the time of the statement it has not been proposed.

NOTES

Sub-s (3): words in square brackets substituted by the Companies Act 1989, s 23, Sch 10, Part I, para 4.

Supplementary

277 Consequences of unlawful distribution

(1)   Where a distribution, or part of one, made by a company to one of its members is made in contravention of this Part and, at the time of the distribution, he knows or has reasonable grounds for believing that it is so made, he is liable to repay it (or that part of it, as the case may be) to the company or (in the case of a distribution made otherwise than in cash) to pay the company a sum equal to the value of the distribution (or part) at that time.

(2)   The above is without prejudice to any obligation imposed apart from this section on a member of a company to repay a distribution unlawfully made to him; but this section does not apply in relation to—
(a)   financial assistance given by a company in contravention of section 151, or
(b)   any payment made by a company in respect of the redemption or purchase by the company of shares in itself.

(3)   Subsection (2) of this section is deemed included in Chapter VII of Part V for purposes of the Secretary of State's power to make regulations under section 179.

PART IX
A COMPANY'S MANAGEMENT; DIRECTORS AND SECRETARIES; THEIR QUALIFICATIONS, DUTIES AND RESPONSIBILITIES

Officers and registered office

282 Directors

(1)   Every company registered on or after 1st November 1929 (other than a private company) shall have at least two directors.

(2)   Every company registered before that date (other than a private company) shall have at least one director.

(3)   Every private company shall have at least one director.

283 Secretary

(1)   Every company shall have a secretary.

(2)   A sole director shall not also be secretary.

(3)   Anything required or authorised to be done by or to the secretary may, if the office is vacant or there is for any other reason no secretary capable of acting, be done by or to any assistant or deputy secretary or, if there is no assistant or deputy secretary capable of acting, by or to any officer of the company authorised generally or specially in that behalf by the directors.

(4)   No company shall—
   (a)   have as secretary to the company a corporation the sole director of which is a sole director of the company;
   (b)   have as sole director of the company a corporation the sole director of which is secretary to the company.

285 Validity of acts of directors

The acts of a director or manager are valid notwithstanding any defect that may afterwards be discovered in his appointment or qualification; and this provision is not excluded by section 292(2) (void resolution to appoint).

286 Qualifications of company secretaries

(1)   It is the duty of the directors of a public company to take all reasonable steps to secure that the secretary (or each joint secretary) of the company is a person who appears to them to have the requisite knowledge and experience to discharge the functions of secretary of the company and who—
   (a)   on 22nd December 1980 held the office of secretary or assistant or deputy secretary of the company; or
   (b)   for at least 3 of the 5 years immediately preceding his appointment as secretary held the office of secretary of a company other than a private company; or
   (c)   is a member of any of the bodies specified in the following subsection; or
   (d)   is a barrister, advocate or solicitor called or admitted in any part of the United Kingdom; or
   (e)   is a person who, by virtue of his holding or having held any other position or his being a member of any other body, appears to the directors to be capable of discharging those functions.

(2)   The bodies referred to in subsection (1)(c) are—
   (a)   the Institute of Chartered Accountants in England and Wales;
   (b)   the Institute of Chartered Accountants of Scotland;
   (c)   the Chartered Association of Certified Accountants;
   (d)   the Institute of Chartered Accountants in Ireland;

(e) the Institute of Chartered Secretaries and Administrators;

(f) the Institute of Cost and Management Accountants;

(g) the Chartered Institute of Public Finance and Accountancy.

[287 Registered office]

[(1) A company shall at all times have a registered office to which all communications and notices may be addressed.

(2) On incorporation the situation of the company's registered office is that specified in the statement sent to the registrar under section 10.

(3) The company may change the situation of its registered office from time to time by giving notice in the prescribed form to the registrar.

(4) The change takes effect upon the notice being registered by the registrar, but until the end of the period of 14 days beginning with the date on which it is registered a person may validly serve any document on the company at its previous registered office.

(5) For the purposes of any duty of a company—
   (a) to keep at its registered office, or make available for public inspection there, any register, index or other document, or
   (b) to mention the address of its registered office in any document,

a company which has given notice to the registrar of a change in the situation of its registered office may act on the change as from such date, not more than 14 days after the notice is given, as it may determine.

(6) Where a company unavoidably ceases to perform at its registered office any such duty as is mentioned in subsection (5)(a) in circumstances in which it was not practicable to give prior notice to the registrar of a change in the situation of its registered office, but—
   (a) resumes performance of that duty at other premises as soon as practicable, and
   (b) gives notice accordingly to the registrar of a change in the situation of its registered office within 14 days of doing so,

it shall not be treated as having failed to comply with that duty.

(7) In proceedings for an offence of failing to comply with any such duty as is mentioned in subsection (5), it is for the person charged to show that by reason of the matters referred to in that subsection or subsection (6) no offence was committed.]

NOTES

Substituted by the Companies Act 1989, s 136.

288 Register of directors and secretaries

(1) Every company shall keep at its registered office a register of its directors and secretaries; and the register shall, with respect to the particulars to be contained in it of those persons, comply with sections 289 and 290 below.

(2)   The company shall, within the period of 14 days from the occurrence of—

(a)   any change among its directors or in its secretary, or

(b)   any change in the particulars contained in the register,

send to the registrar of companies a notification in the prescribed form of the change and of the date on which it occurred; and a notification of a person having become a director or secretary, or one of joint secretaries, of the company shall contain a consent, signed by that person, to act in the relevant capacity.

(3)   The register shall . . . be open to the inspection of any member of the company without charge and of any other person on payment of [such fee as may be prescribed].

(4)   If an inspection required under this section is refused, or if default is made in complying with subsection (1) or (2), the company and every officer of it who is in default is liable to a fine and, for continued contravention, to a daily default fine.

(5)   In the case of a refusal of inspection of the register, the court may by order compel an immediate inspection of it.

[(5A)   Where a confidentiality order made under section 723B is in force in respect of a director or secretary of a company, subsections (3) and (5) shall not apply in relation to that part of the register of the company as contains particulars of the usual residential address of that individual.]

(6)   For purposes of this and the next section, a shadow director of a company is deemed a director and officer of it.

[(7)   . . .]

NOTES

Sub-s (3): words omitted repealed, and words in square brackets substituted, by the Companies Act 1989, ss 143(6), 212, Sch 24.

Sub-s (5A): inserted by SI 2002/912, reg 16, Sch 2, para 2(1), (2).

Date in force: 2 April 2002: see SI 2002/912, reg 1(2).

Sub-s (7): inserted by the Criminal Justice and Police Act 2001, s 45(1), (3).

Date in force: 2 April 2002: see the Criminal Justice and Police Act 2001, s 138(2), and SI 2002/533, art 3.

Sub-s (7): repealed by SI 2002/912, reg 16, Sch 2, para 2(1), (3).

Date in force: 2 April 2002: see SI 2002/912, reg 1(2).

Provisions governing appointment of directors

291 Share qualification of directors

(1)   It is the duty of every director who is by the company's articles required to hold a specified share qualification, and who is not already qualified, to obtain his qualification within 2 months after his appointment, or such shorter time as may be fixed by the articles.

(2)   For the purpose of any provision of the articles requiring a director or manager to hold any specified share qualification, the bearer of a share warrant is not deemed the holder of the shares specified in the warrant.

(3)   The office of director of a company is vacated if the director does not within 2 months from the date of his appointment (or within such shorter time as may be fixed by the articles) obtain his qualification, or if after the expiration of that period or shorter time he ceases at any time to hold his qualification.

(4)   A person vacating office under this section is incapable of being reappointed to be a director of the company until he has obtained his qualification.

(5)   If after the expiration of that period or shorter time any unqualified person acts as a director of the company, he is liable to a fine and, for continued contravention, to a daily default fine.

292 Appointment of directors to be voted on individually

(1)   At a general meeting of a public company, a motion for the appointment of two or more persons as directors of the company by a single resolution shall not be made, unless a resolution that it shall be so made has first been agreed to by the meeting without any vote being given against it.

(2)   A resolution moved in contravention of this section is void, whether or not its being so moved was objected to at the time; but where a resolution so moved is passed, no provision for the automatic reappointment of retiring directors in default of another appointment applies.

(3)   For purposes of this section, a motion for approving a person's appointment, or for nominating a person for appointment, is to be treated as a motion for his appointment.

(4)   Nothing in this section applies to a resolution altering the company's articles.

293 Age limit for directors

(1)   A company is subject to this section if—
   (a)   it is a public company, or
   (b)   being a private company, it is a subsidiary of a public company or of a body corporate registered under the law relating to companies for the time being in force in Northern Ireland as a public company.

(2)   No person is capable of being appointed a director of a company which is subject to this section if at the time of his appointment he has attained the age of 70.

(3)   A director of such a company shall vacate his office at the conclusion of the annual general meeting commencing next after he attains the age of 70; but acts done by a person as director are valid notwithstanding that it is afterwards discovered that his appointment had terminated under this subsection.

(4)   Where a person retires under subsection (3), no provision for the automatic reappointment of retiring directors in default of another appointment applies; and if at the meeting at which he retires the vacancy is not filled, it may be filled as a casual vacancy.

(5)   Nothing in subsections (2) to (4) prevents the appointment of a director at any age, or requires a director to retire at any time, if his appointment is or was made or approved by the company in general meeting; but special notice is required of a

resolution appointing or approving the appointment of a director for it to have effect under this subsection, and the notice of the resolution given to the company, and by the company to its members, must state, or have stated, the age of the person to whom it relates.

(6) A person reappointed director on retiring under subsection (3), or appointed in place of a director so retiring, is to be treated, for the purpose of determining the time at which he or any other director is to retire, as if he had become director on the day on which the retiring director was last appointed before his retirement.

Subject to this, the retirement of a director out of turn under subsection (3) is to be disregarded in determining when any other directors are to retire.

(7) In the case of a company first registered after the beginning of 1947, this section has effect subject to the provisions of the company's articles; and in the case of a company first registered before the beginning of that year—

(a) this section has effect subject to any alterations of the company's articles made after the beginning of that year; and

(b) if at the beginning of that year the company's articles contained provision for retirement of directors under an age limit, or for preventing or restricting appointments of directors over a given age, this section does not apply to directors to whom that provision applies.

Removal of directors

303 Resolution to remove director

(1) A company may by ordinary resolution remove a director before the expiration of his period of office, notwithstanding anything in its articles or in any agreement between it and him.

(2) Special notice is required of a resolution to remove a director under this section or to appoint somebody instead of a director so removed at the meeting at which he is removed.

(3) A vacancy created by the removal of a director under this section, if not filled at the meeting at which he is removed, may be filled as a casual vacancy.

(4) A person appointed director in place of a person removed under this section is treated, for the purpose of determining the time at which he or any other director is to retire, as if he had become director on the day on which the person in whose place he is appointed was last appointed a director.

(5) This section is not to be taken as depriving a person removed under it of compensation or damages payable to him in respect of the termination of his appointment as director or of any appointment terminating with that as director, or as derogating from any power to remove a director which may exist apart from this section.

304 Director's right to protest removal

(1) On receipt of notice of an intended resolution to remove a director under section 303, the company shall forthwith send a copy of the notice to the director concerned; and he (whether or not a member of the company) is entitled to be heard on the resolution at the meeting.

(2) Where notice is given of an intended resolution to remove a director under that section, and the director concerned makes with respect to it representations in writing to the company (not exceeding a reasonable length) and requests their notification to members of the company, the company shall, unless the representations are received by it too late for it to do so—
  (a) in any notice of the resolution given to members of the company state the fact of the representations having been made; and
  (b) send a copy of the representations to every member of the company to whom notice of the meeting is sent (whether before or after receipt of the representations by the company).

(3) If a copy of the representations is not sent as required by subsection (2) because received too late or because of the company's default, the director may (without prejudice to his right to be heard orally) require that the representations shall be read out at the meeting.

(4) But copies of the representations need not be sent out and the representations need not be read out at the meeting if, on the application either of the company or of any other person who claims to be aggrieved, the court is satisfied that the rights conferred by this section are being abused to secure needless publicity for defamatory matter.

(5) The court may order the company's costs on an application under this section to be paid in whole or in part by the director, notwithstanding that he is not a party to the application.

Other provisions about directors and officers

305 Directors' names on company correspondence, etc

(1) A company to which this section applies shall not state, in any form, the name of any of its directors (otherwise than in the text or as a signatory) on any business letter on which the company's name appears unless it states on the letter in legible characters [the name of every director in the company].

(2) This section applies to—
  (a) every company registered under this Act or under the former Companies Acts (except a company registered before 23rd November 1916); and
  (b) every company incorporated outside Great Britain which has an established place of business within Great Britain, unless it had established such a place of business before that date.

(3) If a company makes default in complying with this section, every officer of the company who is in default is liable for each offence to a fine; and for this purpose,

where a corporation is an officer of the company, any officer of the corporation is deemed an officer of the company.

[(4)   For the purposes of the obligation under subsection (1) to state the name of every director of the company, a person's "name" means—
  (a)   in the case of an individual, his Christian name (or other forename) and surname; and
  (b)   in the case of a corporation or Scottish firm, its corporate or firm name.

(5)   The initial or a recognised abbreviation of a person's Christian name or other forename may be stated instead of the full Christian name or other forename.

(6)   In the case of a peer, or an individual usually known by a title, the title may be stated instead of his Christian name (or other forename) and surname or in addition to either or both of them.

(7)   In this section "director" includes a shadow director and the reference in subsection (3) to an "officer" shall be construed accordingly.]

NOTES

Sub-s (1): words in square brackets substituted by the Companies Act 1989, s 145, Sch 19, para 4.

Sub-ss (4)–(7): substituted for sub-s (4), as originally enacted, by the Companies Act 1989, s 145, Sch 19, para 4.

309 Directors to have regard to interests of employees

(1)   The matters to which the directors of a company are to have regard in the performance of their functions include the interests of the company's employees in general, as well as the interests of its members.

(2)   Accordingly, the duty imposed by this section on the directors is owed by them to the company (and the company alone) and is enforceable in the same way as any other fiduciary duty owed to a company by its directors.

(3)   This section applies to shadow directors as it does to directors.

310 Provisions exempting officers and auditors from liability

(1)   This section applies to any provision, whether contained in a company's articles or in any contract with the company or otherwise, for exempting any officer of the company or any person (whether an officer or not) employed by the company as auditor from, or indemnifying him against, any liability which by virtue of any rule of law would otherwise attach to him in respect of any negligence, default, breach of duty or breach of trust of which he may be guilty in relation to the company.

(2)   Except as provided by the following subsection, any such provision is void.

[(3)   This section does not prevent a company—
  (a)   from purchasing and maintaining for any such officer or auditor insurance against any such liability, or

(b) from indemnifying any such officer or auditor against any liability incurred by him—

    (i) in defending any proceedings (whether civil or criminal) in which judgment is given in his favour or he is acquitted, or

    (ii) in connection with any application under section 144(3) or (4) (acquisition of shares by innocent nominee) or section 727 (general power to grant relief in case of honest and reasonable conduct) in which relief is granted to him by the court.]

NOTES

Sub-s (3): substituted by the Companies Act 1989, s 137(1).

PART X
ENFORCEMENT OF FAIR DEALING BY DIRECTORS

Restrictions on directors taking financial advantage

311 Prohibition on tax-free payments to directors

(1) It is not lawful for a company to pay a director remuneration (whether as director or otherwise) free of income tax, or otherwise calculated by reference to or varying with the amount of his income tax, or to or with any rate of income tax.

(2) Any provision contained in a company's articles, or in any contract, or in any resolution of a company or a company's directors, for payment to a director of remuneration as above mentioned has effect as if it provided for payment, as a gross sum subject to income tax, of the net sum for which it actually provides.

312 Payment to director for loss of office, etc

It is not lawful for a company to make to a director of the company any payment by way of compensation for loss of office, or as consideration for or in connection with his retirement from office, without particulars of the proposed payment (including its amount) being disclosed to members of the company and the proposal being approved by the company.

313 Company approval for property transfer

(1) It is not lawful, in connection with the transfer of the whole or any part of the undertaking or property of a company, for any payment to be made to a director of the company by way of compensation for loss of office, or as consideration for or in connection with his retirement from office, unless particulars of the proposed payment (including its amount) have been disclosed to members of the company and the proposal approved by the company.

(2) Where a payment unlawful under this section is made to a director, the amount received is deemed to be received by him in trust for the company.

314 Director's duty of disclosure on takeover, etc

(1) This section applies where, in connection with the transfer to any persons of all or any of the shares in a company, being a transfer resulting from—

    (a)   an offer made to the general body of shareholders; or

    (b)   an offer made by or on behalf of some other body corporate with a view to the company becoming its subsidiary or a subsidiary of its holding company; or

    (c)   an offer made by or on behalf of an individual with a view to his obtaining the right to exercise or control the exercise of not less than one-third of the voting power at any general meeting of the company; or

    (d)   any other offer which is conditional on acceptance to a given extent,

a payment is to be made to a director of the company by way of compensation for loss of office, or as consideration for or in connection with his retirement from office.

(2) It is in those circumstances the director's duty to take all reasonable steps to secure that particulars of the proposed payment (including its amount) are included in or sent with any notice of the offer made for their shares which is given to any shareholders.

(3) If—

    (a)   the director fails to take those steps, or

    (b)   any person who has been properly required by the director to include those particulars in or send them with the notice required by subsection (2) fails to do so,

he is liable to a fine.

315 Consequences of non-compliance with s 314

(1) If in the case of any such payment to a director as is mentioned in section 314(1)—

    (a)   his duty under that section is not complied with, or

    (b)   the making of the proposed payment is not, before the transfer of any shares in pursuance of the offer, approved by a meeting (summoned for the purpose) of the holders of the shares to which the offer relates and of other holders of shares of the same class as any of those shares,

any sum received by the director on account of the payment is deemed to have been received by him in trust for persons who have sold their shares as a result of the offer made; and the expenses incurred by him in distributing that sum amongst those persons shall be borne by him and not retained out of that sum.

(2) Where—

    (a)   the shareholders referred to in subsection (1)(b) are not all the members of the company, and

    (b)   no provision is made by the articles for summoning or regulating the meeting referred to in that paragraph,

the provisions of this Act and of the company's articles relating to general meetings of the company apply (for that purpose) to the meeting either without modification or with such modifications as the Secretary of State on the application of any person concerned may direct for the purpose of adapting them to the circumstances of the meeting.

(3) If at a meeting summoned for the purpose of approving any payment as required by subsection (1)(b) a quorum is not present and, after the meeting has been adjourned to a later date, a quorum is again not present, the payment is deemed for the purposes of that subsection to have been approved.

316 Provisions supplementing ss 312 to 315

(1) Where in proceedings for the recovery of any payment as having, by virtue of section 313(2) or 315(1) been received by any person in trust, it is shown that—
  (a) the payment was made in pursuance of any arrangement entered into as part of the agreement for the transfer in question, or within one year before or two years after that agreement or the offer leading to it; and
  (b) the company or any person to whom the transfer was made was privy to that arrangement,

the payment is deemed, except in so far as the contrary is shown, to be one to which the provisions mentioned above in this subsection apply.

(2) If in connection with any such transfer as is mentioned in any of sections 313 to 315—
  (a) the price to be paid to a director of the company whose office is to be abolished or who is to retire from office for any shares in the company held by him is in excess of the price which could at the time have been obtained by other holders of the like shares; or
  (b) any valuable consideration is given to any such director,

the excess or the money value of the consideration (as the case may be) is deemed for the purposes of that section to have been a payment made to him by way of compensation for loss of office or as consideration for or in connection with his retirement from office.

(3) References in sections 312 to 315 to payments made to a director by way of compensation for loss of office or as consideration for or in connection with his retirement from office, do not include any bona fide payment by way of damages for breach of contract or by way of pension in respect of past services.

  "Pension" here includes any superannuation allowance, superannuation gratuity or similar payment.

(4) Nothing in sections 313 to 315 prejudices the operation of any rule of law requiring disclosure to be made with respect to such payments as are there mentioned, or with respect to any other like payments made or to be made to a company's directors.

317 Directors to disclose interest in contracts

(1) It is the duty of a director of a company who is in any way, whether directly or indirectly, interested in a contract or proposed contract with the company to declare the nature of his interest at a meeting of the directors of the company.

(2) In the case of a proposed contract, the declaration shall be made—
   (a) at the meeting of the directors at which the question of entering into the contract is first taken into consideration; or
   (b) if the director was not at the date of that meeting interested in the proposed contract, at the next meeting of the directors held after he became so interested;

and, in a case where the director becomes interested in a contract after it is made, the declaration shall be made at the first meeting of the directors held after he becomes so interested.

(3) For purposes of this section, a general notice given to the directors of a company by a director to the effect that—
   (a) he is a member of a specified company or firm and is to be regarded as interested in any contract which may, after the date of the notice, be made with that company or firm; or
   (b) he is to be regarded as interested in any contract which may after the date of the notice be made with a specified person who is connected with him (within the meaning of section 346 below),

is deemed a sufficient declaration of interest in relation to any such contract.

(4) However, no such notice is of effect unless either it is given at a meeting of the directors or the director takes reasonable steps to secure that it is brought up and read at the next meeting of the directors after it is given.

(5) A reference in this section to a contract includes any transaction or arrangement (whether or not constituting a contract) made or entered into on or after 22nd December 1980.

(6) For purposes of this section, a transaction or arrangement of a kind described in section 330 (prohibition of loans, quasi-loans etc to directors) made by a company for a director of the company or a person connected with such a director is treated (if it would not otherwise be so treated, and whether or not it is prohibited by that section) as a transaction or arrangement in which that director is interested.

(7) A director who fails to comply with this section is liable to a fine.

(8) This section applies to a shadow director as it applies to a director, except that a shadow director shall declare his interest, not at a meeting of the directors, but by a notice in writing to the directors which is either—
   (a) a specific notice given before the date of the meeting at which, if he had been a director, the declaration would be required by subsection (2) to be made; or
   (b) a notice which under subsection (3) falls to be treated as a sufficient declaration of that interest (or would fall to be so treated apart from subsection (4)).

(9)   Nothing in this section prejudices the operation of any rule of law restricting directors of a company from having an interest in contracts with the company.

318 Directors' service contracts to be open to inspection

(1)   Subject to the following provisions, every company shall keep at an appropriate place—
  (a)   in the case of each director whose contract of service with the company is in writing, a copy of that contract;
  (b)   in the case of each director whose contract of service with the company is not in writing, a written memorandum setting out its terms; and
  (c)   in the case of each director who is employed under a contract of service with a subsidiary of the company, a copy of that contract or, if it is not in writing, a written memorandum setting out its terms.

(2)   All copies and memoranda kept by a company in pursuance of subsection (1) shall be kept at the same place.

(3)   The following are appropriate places for the purposes of subsection (1)—
  (a)   the company's registered office;
  (b)   the place where its register of members is kept (if other than its registered office);
  (c)   its principal place of business, provided that is situated in that part of Great Britain in which the company is registered.

(4)   Every company shall send notice in the prescribed form to the registrar of companies of the place where copies and memoranda are kept in compliance with subsection (1), and of any change in that place, save in a case in which they have at all times been kept at the company's registered office.

(5)   Subsection (1) does not apply to a director's contract of service with the company or with a subsidiary of it if that contract required him to work wholly or mainly outside the United Kingdom; but the company shall keep a memorandum—
  (a)   in the case of a contract of service with the company, giving the director's name and setting out the provisions of the contract relating to its duration;
  (b)   in the case of a contract of service with a subsidiary, giving the director's name and the name and place of incorporation of the subsidiary, and setting out the provisions of the contract relating to its duration,

at the same place as copies and memoranda are kept by the company in pursuance of subsection (1).

(6)   A shadow director is treated for purposes of this section as a director.

(7)   Every copy and memorandum required by subsection (1) or (5) to be kept shall . . . be open to inspection of any member of the company without charge.

(8)   If—
  (a)   default is made in complying with subsection (1) or (5), or
  (b)   an inspection required under subsection (7) is refused, or
  (c)   default is made for 14 days in complying with subsection (4),

the company and every officer of it who is in default is liable to a fine and, for continued contravention, to a daily default fine.

(9) In the case of a refusal of an inspection required under subsection (7) of a copy or memorandum, the court may by order compel an immediate inspection of it.

(10) Subsections (1) and (5) apply to a variation of a director's contract of service as they apply to the contract.

(11) This section does not require that there be kept a copy of, or memorandum setting out the terms of, a contract (or its variation) at a time when the unexpired portion of the term for which the contract is to be in force is less than 12 months, or at a time at which the contract can, within the next ensuing 12 months, be terminated by the company without payment of compensation.

NOTES

Sub-s (7): words omitted repealed by the Companies Act 1989, ss 143(7), 212, Sch 24.

319 Director's contract of employment for more than 5 years

(1) This section applies in respect of any term of an agreement whereby a director's employment with the company of which he is a director or, where he is the director of a holding company, his employment within the group is to continue, or may be continued, otherwise than at the instance of the company (whether under the original agreement or under a new agreement entered into in pursuance of it), for a period of more than 5 years during which the employment—
  (a) cannot be terminated by the company by notice; or
  (b) can be so terminated only in specified circumstances.

(2) In any case where—
  (a) a person is or is to be employed with a company under an agreement which cannot be terminated by the company by notice or can be so terminated only in specified circumstances; and
  (b) more than 6 months before the expiration of the period for which he is or is to be so employed, the company enters into a further agreement (otherwise than in pursuance of a right conferred by or under the original agreement on the other party to it) under which he is to be employed with the company or, where he is a director of a holding company, within the group,

this section applies as if to the period for which he is to be employed under that further agreement there were added a further period equal to the unexpired period of the original agreement.

(3) A company shall not incorporate in an agreement such a term as is mentioned in subsection (1), unless the term is first approved by a resolution of the company in general meeting and, in the case of a director of a holding company, by a resolution of that company in general meeting.

(4) No approval is required to be given under this section by any body corporate unless it is a company within the meaning of this Act, or is registered under section 680, or if it is a wholly-owned subsidiary of any body corporate, wherever incorporated.

(5)   A resolution of a company approving such a term as is mentioned in subsection (1) shall not be passed at a general meeting of the company unless a written memorandum setting out the proposed agreement incorporating the term is available for inspection by members of the company both—
  (a)   at the company's registered office for not less than 15 days ending with the date of the meeting; and
  (b)   at the meeting itself.

(6)   A term incorporated in an agreement in contravention of this section is, to the extent that it contravenes the section, void; and that agreement and, in a case where subsection (2) applies, the original agreement are deemed to contain a term entitling the company to terminate it at any time by the giving of reasonable notice.

(7)   In this section—
  (a)   "employment" includes employment under a contract for services; and
  (b)   "group", in relation to a director of a holding company, means the group which consists of that company and its subsidiaries;

and for purposes of this section a shadow director is treated as a director.

320 Substantial property transactions involving directors, etc

(1)   With the exceptions provided by the section next following, a company shall not enter into an arrangement—
  (a)   whereby a director of the company or its holding company, or a person connected with such a director, acquires or is to acquire one or more non-cash assets of the requisite value from the company; or
  (b)   whereby the company acquires or is to acquire one or more non-cash assets of the requisite value from such a director or a person so connected,

unless the arrangement is first approved by a resolution of the company in general meeting and, if the director or connected person is a director of its holding company or a person connected with such a director, by a resolution in general meeting of the holding company.

(2)   For this purpose a non-cash asset is of the requisite value if at the time the arrangement in question is entered into its value is not less than [£2,000] but (subject to that) exceeds [£100,000] or 10 per cent of the company's asset value, that is—
  (a)   except in a case falling within paragraph (b) below, the value of the company's net assets determined by reference to the accounts prepared and laid under Part VII in respect of the last preceding financial year in respect of which such accounts were so laid; and
  (b)   where no accounts have been so prepared and laid before that time, the amount of the company's called-up share capital.

(3)   For purposes of this section and sections 321 and 322, a shadow director is treated as a director.

NOTES
Sub-s (2): sums in square brackets substituted by SI 1990/1393, art 2.

321 Exceptions from s 320

(1)   No approval is required to be given under section 320 by any body corporate unless it is a company within the meaning of this Act or registered under section 680 or, if it is a wholly-owned subsidiary of any body corporate, wherever incorporated.

(2)   Section 320(1) does not apply to an arrangement for the acquisition of a non-cash asset—

(a)   if the asset is to be acquired by a holding company from any of its wholly-owned subsidiaries or from a holding company by any of its wholly-owned subsidiaries, or by one wholly-owned subsidiary of a holding company from another wholly-owned subsidiary of that same holding company, or

(b)   if the arrangement is entered into by a company which is being wound up, unless the winding up is a members' voluntary winding up.

(3)   Section 320(1)(a) does not apply to an arrangement whereby a person is to acquire an asset from a company of which he is a member, if the arrangement is made with that person in his character as a member.

[(4)   Section 320(1) does not apply to a transaction on a recognised investment exchange which is effected by a director, or a person connected with him, through the agency of a person who in relation to the transaction acts as an independent broker.

For this purpose an "independent broker" means—

(a)   in relation to a transaction on behalf of a director, a person who independently of the director selects the person with whom the transaction is to be effected, and

(b)   in relation to a transaction on behalf of a person connected with a director, a person who independently of that person or the director selects the person with whom the transaction is to be effected;

and "recognised", in relation to an investment exchange, means recognised under the [Financial Services and Markets Act 2000].]

NOTES

Sub-s (4): inserted by the Companies Act 1989, s 145, Sch 19, para 8.

Sub-s (4): words "Financial Services and Markets Act 2000" in square brackets substituted by SI 2001/3649, art 19.

Date in force: 1 December 2001: see SI 2001/3649, art 1.

322 Liabilities arising from contravention of s 320

(1)   An arrangement entered into by a company in contravention of section 320, and any transaction entered into in pursuance of the arrangement (whether by the company or any other person) is voidable at the instance of the company unless one or more of the conditions specified in the next subsection is satisfied.

(2)   Those conditions are that—

(a) restitution of any money or other asset which is the subject-matter of the arrangement or transaction is no longer possible or the company has been indemnified in pursuance of this section by any other person for the loss or damage suffered by it; or

(b) any rights acquired bona fide for value and without actual notice of the contravention by any person who is not a party to the arrangement or transaction would be affected by its avoidance; or

(c) the arrangement is, within a reasonable period, affirmed by the company in general meeting and, if it is an arrangement for the transfer of an asset to or by a director of its holding company or a person who is connected with such a director, is so affirmed with the approval of the holding company given by a resolution in general meeting.

(3) If an arrangement is entered into with a company by a director of the company or its holding company or a person connected with him in contravention of section 320, that director and the person so connected, and any other director of the company who authorised the arrangement or any transaction entered into in pursuance of such an arrangement, is liable—

(a) to account to the company for any gain which he has made directly or indirectly by the arrangement or transaction, and

(b) (jointly and severally with any other person liable under this subsection) to indemnify the company for any loss or damage resulting from the arrangement or transaction.

(4) Subsection (3) is without prejudice to any liability imposed otherwise than by that subsection, and is subject to the following two subsections; and the liability under subsection (3) arises whether or not the arrangement or transaction entered into has been avoided in pursuance of subsection (1).

(5) If an arrangement is entered into by a company and a person connected with a director of the company or its holding company in contravention of section 320, that director is not liable under subsection (3) if he shows that he took all reasonable steps to secure the company's compliance with that section.

(6) In any case, a person so connected and any such other director as is mentioned in subsection (3) is not so liable if he shows that, at the time the arrangement was entered into, he did not know the relevant circumstances constituting the contravention.

[322A Invalidity of certain transactions involving directors, etc]

[(1) This section applies where a company enters into a transaction to which the parties include—

(a) a director of the company or of its holding company, or

(b) a person connected with such a director or a company with whom such a director is associated,

and the board of directors, in connection with the transaction, exceed any limitation on their powers under the company's constitution.

(2) The transaction is voidable at the instance of the company.

(3)   Whether or not it is avoided, any such party to the transaction as is mentioned in subsection (1)(a) or (b), and any director of the company who authorised the transaction, is liable—

(a)   to account to the company for any gain which he has made directly or indirectly by the transaction, and

(b)   to idemnify the company for any loss or damage resulting from the transaction.

(4)   Nothing in the above provisions shall be construed as excluding the operation of any other enactment or rule of law by virtue of which the transaction may be called in question or any liability to the company may arise.

(5)   The transaction ceases to be voidable if—

(a)   restitution of any money or other asset which was the subject-matter of the transaction is no longer possible, or

(b)   the company is indemnified for any loss or damage resulting from the transaction, or

(c)   rights acquired bona fide for value and without actual notice of the directors' exceeding their powers by a person who is not party to the transaction would be affected by the avoidance, or

(d)   the transaction is ratified by the company in general meeting, by ordinary or special resolution or otherwise as the case may require.

(6)   A person other than a director of the company is not liable under subsection (3) if he shows that at the time the transaction was entered into he did not know that the directors were exceeding their powers.

(7)   This section does not affect the operation of section 35A in relation to any party to the transaction not within subsection (1)(a) or (b).

But where a transaction is voidable by virtue of this section and valid by virtue of that section in favour of such a person, the court may, on the application of that person or of the company, make such order affirming, severing or setting aside the transaction, on such terms, as appear to the court to be just.

(8)   In this section "transaction" includes any act; and the reference in subsection (1) to limitations under the company's constitution includes limitations deriving—

(a)   from a resolution of the company in general meeting or a meeting of any class of shareholders, or

(b)   from any agreement between the members of the company or of any class of shareholders.]

NOTES
Inserted by the Companies Act 1989, s 109(1).

[322B Contracts with sole members who are directors]

[(1)   Subject to subsection (2), where a private company limited by shares or by guarantee having only one member enters into a contract with the sole member of the company and the sole member is also a director of the company, the company shall, unless the contract is in writing, ensure that the terms of the contract are either set out in a written memorandum or are recorded in the minutes of the first meeting of the directors of the company following the making of the contract.

(2)   Subsection (1) shall not apply to contracts entered into in the ordinary course of the company's business.

(3)   For the purposes of this section a sole member who is a shadow director is treated as a director.

(4)   If a company fails to comply with subsection (1), the company and every officer of it who is in default is liable to a fine.

(5)   Subject to subsection (6), nothing in this section shall be construed as excluding the operation of any other enactment or rule of law applying to contracts between a company and a director of that company.

(6)   Failure to comply with subsection (1) with respect to a contract shall not affect the validity of that contract.]

NOTES

Inserted by SI 1992/1699, reg 2(b), Schedule, para 3(1).

Share dealings by directors and their families

323 Prohibition on directors dealing in share options

(1)   It is an offence for a director of a company to buy—
  (a)   a right to call for delivery at a specified price and within a specified time of a specified number of relevant shares or a specified amount of relevant debentures; or
  (b)   a right to make delivery at a specified price and within a specified time of a specified number of relevant shares or a specified amount of relevant debentures; or
  (c)   a right (as he may elect) to call for delivery at a specified price and within a specified time or to make delivery at a specified price and within a specified time of a specified number of relevant shares or a specified amount of relevant debentures.

(2)   A person guilty of an offence under subsection (1) is liable to imprisonment or a fine, or both.

(3)   In subsection (1)—
  (a)   "relevant shares", in relation to a director of a company, means shares in the company or in any other body corporate, being the company's subsidiary or holding company, or a subsidiary of the company's holding company, being shares as respects which there has been granted a listing on a stock exchange (whether in Great Britain or elsewhere);
  (b)   "relevant debentures", in relation to a director of a company, means debentures of the company or of any other body corporate, being the company's subsidiary or holding company or a subsidiary of the company's holding company, being debentures as respects which there has been granted such a listing; and

(c)   "price" includes any consideration other than money.

(4)   This section applies to a shadow director as to a director.

(5)   This section is not to be taken as penalising a person who buys a right to subscribe for shares in, or debentures of, a body corporate or buys debentures of a body corporate that confer upon the holder of them a right to subscribe for, or to convert the debentures (in whole or in part) into, shares of that body.

324 Duty of director to disclose shareholdings in own company

(1)   A person who becomes a director of a company and at the time when he does so is interested in shares in, or debentures of, the company or any other body corporate, being the company's subsidiary or holding company or a subsidiary of the company's holding company, is under obligation to notify the company in writing—
  (a)   of the subsistence of his interests at that time; and
  (b)   of the number of shares of each class in, and the amount of debentures of each class of, the company or other such body corporate in which each interest of his subsists at that time.

(2)   A director of a company is under obligation to notify the company in writing of the occurrence, while he is a director, of any of the following events—
  (a)   any event in consequence of whose occurrence he becomes, or ceases to be, interested in shares in, or debentures of, the company or any other body corporate, being the company's subsidiary or holding company or a subsidiary of the company's holding company;
  (b)   the entering into by him of a contract to sell any such shares or debentures;
  (c)   the assignment by him of a right granted to him by the company to subscribe for shares in, or debentures of, the company; and
  (d)   the grant to him by another body corporate, being the company's subsidiary or holding company or a subsidiary of the company's holding company, of a right to subscribe for shares in, or debentures of, that other body corporate, the exercise of such a right granted to him and the assignment by him of such a right so granted;

and notification to the company must state the number or amount, and class, of shares or debentures involved.

(3)   Schedule 13 has effect in connection with subsections (1) and (2) above; and of that Schedule—
  (a)   Part I contains rules for the interpretation of, and otherwise in relation to, those subsections and applies in determining, for purposes of those subsections, whether a person has an interest in shares or debentures;
  (b)   Part II applies with respect to the periods within which obligations imposed by the subsections must be fulfilled; and
  (c)   Part III specifies certain circumstances in which obligations arising from subsection (2) are to be treated as not discharged;

and subsections (1) and (2) are subject to any exceptions for which provision may be made by regulations made by the Secretary of State by statutory instrument.

(4)   Subsection (2) does not require the notification by a person of the occurrence of an event whose occurrence comes to his knowledge after he has ceased to be a director.

(5)   An obligation imposed by this section is treated as not discharged unless the notice by means of which it purports to be discharged is expressed to be given in fulfilment of that obligation.

(6)   This section applies to shadow directors as to directors; but nothing in it operates so as to impose an obligation with respect to shares in a body corporate which is the wholly-owned subsidiary of another body corporate.

(7)   A person who—
   (a)   fails to discharge, within the proper period, an obligation to which he is subject under subsection (1) or (2), or
   (b)   in purported discharge of an obligation to which he is so subject, makes to the company a statement which he knows to be false, or recklessly makes to it a statement which is false,

is guilty of an offence and liable to imprisonment or a fine, or both.

(8)   Section 732 (restriction on prosecutions) applies to an offence under this section.

325 Register of directors' interests notified under s 324

(1)   Every company shall keep a register for the purposes of section 324.

(2)   Whenever a company receives information from a director given in fulfilment of an obligation imposed on him by that section, it is under obligation to enter in the register, against the director's name, the information received and the date of the entry.

(3)   The company is also under obligation, whenever it grants to a director a right to subscribe for shares in, or debentures of, the company to enter in the register against his name—
   (a)   the date on which the right is granted,
   (b)   the period during which, or time at which, it is exercisable,
   (c)   the consideration for the grant (or, if there is no consideration, that fact), and
   (d)   the description of shares or debentures involved and the number or amount of them, and the price to be paid for them (or the consideration, if otherwise than in money).

(4)   Whenever such a right as is mentioned above is exercised by a director, the company is under obligation to enter in the register against his name that fact (identifying the right), the number or amount of shares or debentures in respect of which it is exercised and, if they were registered in his name, that fact and, if not, the name or names of the person or persons in whose name or names they were registered, together (if they were registered in the names of two persons or more) with the number or amount of the shares or debentures registered in the name of each of them.

(5)   Part IV of Schedule 13 has effect with respect to the register to be kept under this section, to the way in which entries in it are to be made, to the right of inspection, and generally.

(6)   For purposes of this section, a shadow director is deemed a director.

329 Duty to notify stock exchange of matters notified under preceding sections

(1)   Whenever a company whose shares or debentures are listed on a [recognised investment exchange other than an overseas investment exchange . . .] is notified of any matter by a director in consequence of the fulfilment of an obligation imposed by section 324 or 328, and that matter relates to shares or debentures so listed, the company is under obligation to notify [that investment exchange] of that matter; and [the investment exchange] may publish, in such manner as it may determine, any information received by it under this subsection.

(2)   An obligation imposed by subsection (1) must be fulfilled before the end of the day next following that on which it arises; but there is disregarded for this purpose a day which is a Saturday or a Sunday or a bank holiday in any part of Great Britain.

(3)   If default is made in complying with this section, the company and every officer of it who is in default is guilty of an offence and liable to a fine and, for continued contravention, to a daily default fine.

   Section 732 (restriction on prosecutions) applies to an offence under this section.

[(4)   In subsection (1) "recognised investment exchange" and "overseas investment exchange" have the same meaning as in Part 18 of the Financial Services and Markets Act 2000.]

NOTES

   Sub-s (1): words in square brackets substituted by the Financial Services Act 1986, s 212(2), Sch 16, para 20.
   Sub-s (1): words omitted repealed by SI 2001/3649, art 20(1), (2).
   Date in force: 1 December 2001: see SI 2001/3649, art 1.
   Sub-s (4): inserted by SI 2001/3649, art 20(1), (3).
   Date in force: 1 December 2001: see SI 2001/3649, art 1.

Restrictions on a company's power to make loans, etc, to directors and persons connected with them

330 General restriction on loans, etc, to directors and persons connected with them

(1)   The prohibitions listed below in this section are subject to the exceptions in sections 332 to 338.

(2)   A company shall not—
   (a)   make a loan to a director of the company or of its holding company;

(b) enter into any guarantee or provide any security in connection with a loan made by any person to such a director.

(3) A relevant company shall not—
   (a) make a quasi-loan to a director of the company or of its holding company;
   (b) make a loan or a quasi-loan to a person connected with such a director;
   (c) enter into a guarantee or provide any security in connection with a loan or quasi-loan made by any other person for such a director or a person so connected.

(4) A relevant company shall not—
   (a) enter into a credit transaction as creditor for such a director or a person so connected;
   (b) enter into any guarantee or provide any security in connection with a credit transaction made by any other person for such a director or a person so connected.

(5) For purposes of sections 330 to 346, a shadow director is treated as a director.

(6) A company shall not arrange for the assignment to it, or the assumption by it, of any rights, obligations or liabilities under a transaction which, if it had been entered into by the company, would have contravened subsection (2), (3) or (4); but for the purposes of sections 330 to 347 the transaction is to be treated as having been entered into on the date of the arrangement.

(7) A company shall not take part in any arrangement whereby—
   (a) another person enters into a transaction which, if it had been entered into by the company, would have contravened any of subsections (2), (3), (4) or (6); and
   (b) that other person, in pursuance of the arrangement, has obtained or is to obtain any benefit from the company or its holding company or a subsidiary of the company or its holding company.

331 Definitions for ss 330 ff

(1) The following subsections apply for the interpretation of sections 330 to 346.

(2) "Guarantee" includes indemnity, and cognate expressions are to be construed accordingly.

(3) A quasi-loan is a transaction under which one party ("the creditor") agrees to pay, or pays otherwise than in pursuance of an agreement, a sum for another ("the borrower") or agrees to reimburse, or reimburses otherwise than in pursuance of an agreement, expenditure incurred by another party for another ("the borrower")—
   (a) on terms that the borrower (or a person on his behalf) will reimburse the creditor; or
   (b) in circumstances giving rise to a liability on the borrower to reimburse the creditor.

(4) Any reference to the person to whom a quasi-loan is made is a reference to the borrower; and the liabilities of a borrower under a quasi-loan include the liabilities of any person who has agreed to reimburse the creditor on behalf of the borrower.

(5) . . .

(6) "Relevant company" means a company which—
    (a) is a public company, or
    (b) is a subsidiary of a public company, or
    (c) is a subsidiary of a company which has as another subsidiary a public company, or
    (d) has a subsidiary which is a public company.

(7) A credit transaction is a transaction under which one party ("the creditor")—
    (a) supplies any goods or sells any land under a hire-purchase agreement or a conditional sale agreement;
    (b) leases or hires any land or goods in return for periodical payments;
    (c) otherwise disposes of land or supplies goods or services on the understanding that payment (whether in a lump sum or instalments or by way of periodical payments or otherwise) is to be deferred.

(8) "Services" means anything other than goods or land.

(9) A transaction or arrangement is made "for" a person if—
    (a) in the case of a loan or quasi-loan, it is made to him;
    (b) in the case of a credit transaction, he is the person to whom goods or services are supplied, or land is sold or otherwise disposed of, under the transaction;
    (c) in the case of a guarantee or security, it is entered into or provided in connection with a loan or quasi-loan made to him or a credit transaction made for him;
    (d) in the case of an arrangement within subsection (6) or (7) of section 330, the transaction to which the arrangement relates was made for him; and
    (e) in the case of any other transaction or arrangement for the supply or transfer of, or of any interest in, goods, land or services, he is the person to whom the goods, land or services (or the interest) are supplied or transferred.

(10) "Conditional sale agreement" means the same as in the Consumer Credit Act 1974.

NOTES

Sub-s (5): repealed by the Banking Act 1987, s 108(2), Sch 7, Part I.

332 Short-term quasi-loans

(1) Subsection (3) of section 330 does not prohibit a company ("the creditor") from making a quasi-loan to one of its directors or to a director of its holding company if—
    (a) the quasi-loan contains a term requiring the director or a person on his behalf to reimburse the creditor his expenditure within 2 months of its being incurred; and
    (b) the aggregate of the amount of that quasi-loan and of the amount outstanding under each relevant quasi-loan does not exceed [£5,000].

(2) A quasi-loan is relevant for this purpose if it was made to the director by virtue of this section by the creditor or its subsidiary or, where the director is a director of

the creditor's holding company, any other subsidiary of that company; and "the amount outstanding" is the amount of the outstanding liabilities of the person to whom the quasi-loan was made.

NOTES

Sub-s (1): in para (b) sum in square brackets substituted by the Companies Act 1989, s 138.

333 Inter-company loans in same group

In the case of a relevant company which is a member of a group of companies (meaning a holding company and its subsidiaries), paragraphs (b) and (c) of section 330(3) do not prohibit the company from—

(a)   making a loan or quasi-loan to another member of that group; or

(b)   entering into a guarantee or providing any security in connection with a loan or quasi-loan made by any person to another member of the group,

by reason only that a director of one member of the group is associated with another.

334 Loans of small amounts

Without prejudice to any other provision of sections 332 to 338, paragraph (a) of section 330(2) does not prohibit a company from making a loan to a director of the company or of its holding company if the aggregate of the relevant amounts does not exceed [£5,000].

NOTES

Sum in square brackets substituted by the Companies Act 1989, s 138.

335 Minor and business transactions

(1)   Section 330(4) does not prohibit a company from entering into a transaction for a person if the aggregate of the relevant amounts does not exceed [£10,000].

(2)   Section 330(4) does not prohibit a company from entering into a transaction for a person if—

(a)   the transaction is entered into by the company in the ordinary course of its business; and

(b)   the value of the transaction is not greater, and the terms on which it is entered into are no more favourable, in respect of the person for whom the transaction is made, than that or those which it is reasonable to expect the company to have offered to or in respect of a person of the same financial standing but unconnected with the company.

NOTES

Sub-s (1): sum in square brackets substituted by SI 1990/1393, art 2.

336 Transactions at behest of holding company

The following transactions are excepted from the prohibitions of section 330—
  (a) a loan or quasi-loan by a company to its holding company, or a company entering into a guarantee or providing any security in connection with a loan or quasi-loan made by any person to its holding company;
  (b) a company entering into a credit transaction as creditor for its holding company, or entering into a guarantee or providing any security in connection with a credit transaction made by any other person for its holding company.

337 Funding of director's expenditure on duty to company

(1) A company is not prohibited by section 330 from doing anything to provide a director with funds to meet expenditure incurred or to be incurred by him for the purposes of the company or for the purpose of enabling him properly to perform his duties as an officer of the company.

(2) Nor does the section prohibit a company from doing any thing to enable a director to avoid incurring such expenditure.

(3) Subsections (1) and (2) apply only if one of the following conditions is satisfied—
  (a) the thing in question is done with prior approval of the company given at a general meeting at which there are disclosed all the matters mentioned in the next subsection;
  (b) that thing is done on condition that, if the approval of the company is not so given at or before the next annual general meeting, the loan is to repaid, or any other liability arising under any such transaction discharged, within 6 months from the conclusion of that meeting;

but those subsections do not authorise a relevant company to enter into any transaction if the aggregate of the relevant amounts exceeds [£20,000].

(4) The matters to be disclosed under subsection (3)(a) are—
  (a) the purpose of the expenditure incurred or to be incurred, or which would otherwise be incurred, by the director,
  (b) the amount of the funds to be provided by the company, and
  (c) the extent of the company's liability under any transaction which is or is connected with the thing in question.

NOTES
Sub-s (3): sum in square brackets substituted by SI 1990/1393, art 2.

338 Loan or quasi-loan by money-lending company

(1) There is excepted from the prohibitions in section 330—
  (a) a loan or quasi-loan made by a money-lending company to any person; or
  (b) a money-lending company entering into a guarantee in connection with any other loan or quasi-loan.

(2) "Money-lending company" means a company whose ordinary business includes the making of loans or quasi-loans, or the giving of guarantees in connection with loans or quasi-loans.

(3) Subsection (1) applies only if both the following conditions are satisfied—
  (a) the loan or quasi-loan in question is made by the company, or it enters into the guarantee, in the ordinary course of the company's business; and
  (b) the amount of the loan or quasi-loan, or the amount guaranteed, is not greater, and the terms of the loan, quasi-loan or guarantee are not more favourable, in the case of the person to whom the loan or quasi-loan is made or in respect of whom the guarantee is entered into, than that or those which it is reasonable to expect that company to have offered to or in respect of a person of the same financial standing but unconnected with the company.

(4) But subsection (1) does not authorise a relevant company (unless it is [a banking company]) to enter into any transaction if the aggregate of the relevant amounts exceeds [£100,000].

(5) In determining that aggregate, a company which a director does not control is deemed not to be connected with him.

(6) The condition specified in subsection (3)(b) does not of itself prevent a company from making a loan to one of its directors or a director of its holding company—
  (a) for the purpose of facilitating the purchase, for use as that director's only or main residence, of the whole or part of any dwelling-house together with any land to be occupied and enjoyed with it;
  (b) for the purpose of improving a dwelling-house or part of a dwelling-house so used or any land occupied and enjoyed with it;
  (c) in substitution for any loan made by any person and falling within paragraph (a) or (b) of this subsection,

if loans of that description are ordinarily made by the company to its employees and on terms no less favourable than those on which the transaction in question is made, and the aggregate of the relevant amounts does not exceed [£100,000].

NOTES

Sub-s (4): words in square brackets substituted by the Companies Act 1989, s 23, Sch 10, Part I, para 10; sum in square brackets substituted by the Companies Act 1989, s 138.

Sub-s (6): sum in square brackets substituted by the Companies Act 1989, s 138.

339 "Relevant amounts" for purposes of ss 334 ff

(1) This section has effect for defining the "relevant amounts" to be aggregated under sections 334, 335(1), 337(3) and 338(4); and in relation to any proposed transaction or arrangement and the question whether it falls within one or other of the exceptions provided by those sections, "the relevant exception" is that exception; but where the relevant exception is the one provided by section 334 (loan of small amount), references in this section to a person connected with a director are to be disregarded.

(2)   Subject as follows, the relevant amounts in relation to a proposed transaction or arrangement are—

   (a) the value of the proposed transaction or arrangement,

   (b) the value of any existing arrangement which—

      (i) falls within subsection (6) or (7) of section 330, and

      (ii) also falls within subsection (3) of this section, and

      (iii) was entered into by virtue of the relevant exception by the company or by a subsidiary of the company or, where the proposed transaction or arrangement is to be made for a director of its holding company or a person connected with such a director, by that holding company or any of its subsidiaries;

   (c) the amount outstanding under any other transaction—

      (i) falling within subsection (3) below, and

      (ii) made by virtue of the relevant exception, and

      (iii) made by the company or by a subsidiary of the company or, where the proposed transaction or arrangement is to be made for a director of its holding company or a person connected with such a director, by that holding company or any of its subsidiaries.

(3)   A transaction falls within this subsection if it was made—

   (a) for the director for whom the proposed transaction or arrangement is to be made, or for any person connected with that director; or

   (b) where the proposed transaction or arrangement is to be made for a person connected with a director of a company, for that director or any person connected with him;

and an arrangement also falls within this subsection if it relates to a transaction which does so.

(4)   But where the proposed transaction falls within section 338 and is one which [a banking company] proposes to enter into under subsection (6) of that section (housing loans, etc), any other transaction or arrangement which apart from this subsection would fall within subsection (3) of this section does not do so unless it was entered into in pursuance of section 338(6).

(5)   A transaction entered into by a company which is (at the time of that transaction being entered into) a subsidiary of the company which is to make the proposed transaction, or is a subsidiary of that company's holding company, does not fall within subsection (3) if at the time when the question arises (that is to say, the question whether the proposed transaction or arrangement falls within any relevant exception), it no longer is such a subsidiary.

(6)   Values for purposes of subsection (2) of this section are to be determined in accordance with the section next following; and "the amount outstanding" for purposes of subsection (2)(c) above is the value of the transaction less any amount by which that value has been reduced.

NOTES

Sub-s (4): words in square brackets substituted by the Companies Act 1989, s 23, Sch 10, Part I, para 10.

340 "Value" of transactions and arrangements

(1) This section has effect for determining the value of a transaction or arrangement for purposes of sections 330 to 339.

(2) The value of a loan is the amount of its principal.

(3) The value of a quasi-loan is the amount, or maximum amount, which the person to whom the quasi-loan is made is liable to reimburse the creditor.

(4) The value of a guarantee or security is the amount guaranteed or secured.

(5) The value of an arrangement to which section 330(6) or (7) applies is the value of the transaction to which the arrangement relates less any amount by which the liabilities under the arrangement or transaction of the person for whom the transaction was made have been reduced.

(6) The value of a transaction or arrangement not falling within subsections (2) to (5) above is the price which it is reasonable to expect could be obtained for the goods, land or services to which the transaction or arrangement relates if they had been supplied (at the time the transaction or arrangement is entered into) in the ordinary course of business and on the same terms (apart from price) as they have been supplied, or are to be supplied, under the transaction or arrangement in question.

(7) For purposes of this section, the value of a transaction or arrangement which is not capable of being expressed as a specific sum of money (because the amount of any liability arising under the transaction or arrangement is unascertainable, or for any other reason), whether or not any liability under the transaction or arrangement has been reduced, is deemed to exceed [£100,000].

NOTES

Sub-s (7): sum in square brackets substituted by SI 1990/1393, art 2.

341 Civil remedies for breach of s 330

(1) If a company enters into a transaction or arrangement in contravention of section 330, the transaction or arrangement is voidable at the instance of the company unless—
  (a) restitution of any money or any other asset which is the subject matter of the arrangement or transaction is no longer possible, or the company has been indemnified in pursuance of subsection (2)(b) below for the loss or damage suffered by it, or
  (b) any rights acquired bona fide for value and without actual notice of the contravention by a person other than the person for whom the transaction or arrangement was made would be affected by its avoidance.

(2) Where an arrangement or transaction is made by a company for a director of the company or its holding company or a person connected with such a director in contravention of section 330, that director and the person so connected and any other director of the company who authorised the transaction or arrangement (whether or not it has been avoided in pursuance of subsection (1)) is liable—

(a) to account to the company for any gain which he has made directly or indirectly by the arrangement or transaction; and

(b) (jointly and severally with any other person liable under this subsection) to indemnify the company for any loss or damage resulting from the arrangement or transaction.

(3)   Subsection (2) is without prejudice to any liability imposed otherwise than by that subsection, but is subject to the next two subsections.

(4)   Where an arrangement or transaction is entered into by a company and a person connected with a director of the company or its holding company in contravention of section 330, that director is not liable under subsection (2) of this section if he shows that he took all reasonable steps to secure the company's compliance with that section.

(5)   In any case, a person so connected and any such other director as is mentioned in subsection (2) is not so liable if he shows that, at the time the arrangement or transaction was entered into, he did not know the relevant circumstances constituting the contravention.

342 Criminal penalties for breach of s 330

(1)   A director of a relevant company who authorises or permits the company to enter into a transaction or arrangement knowing or having reasonable cause to believe that the company was thereby contravening section 330 is guilty of an offence.

(2)   A relevant company which enters into a transaction or arrangement for one of its directors or for a director of its holding company in contravention of section 330 is guilty of an offence.

(3)   A person who procures a relevant company to enter into a transaction or arrangement knowing or having reasonable cause to believe that the company was thereby contravening section 330 is guilty of an offence.

(4)   A person guilty of an offence under this section is liable to imprisonment or a fine, or both.

(5)   A relevant company is not guilty of an offence under subsection (2) if it shows that, at the time the transaction or arrangement was entered into, it did not know the relevant circumstances.

Supplementary

346 "Connected persons", etc

(1)   This section has effect with respect to references in this Part to a person being "connected" with a director of a company, and to a director being "associated with" or "controlling" a body corporate.

(2)   A person is connected with a director of a company if, but only if, he (not being himself a director of it) is—

(a) that director's spouse, child or step-child; or

(b) except where the context otherwise requires, a body corporate with which the director is associated; or

(c) a person acting in his capacity as trustee of any trust the beneficiaries of which include—
(i) the director, his spouse or any children or step-children of his, or
(ii) a body corporate with which he is associated,
or of a trust whose terms confer a power on the trustees that may be exercised for the benefit of the director, his spouse, or any children or step-children of his, or any such body corporate; or

(d) a person acting in his capacity as partner of that director or of any person who, by virtue of paragraph (a), (b) or (c) of this subsection, is connected with that director; or

(e) a Scottish firm in which—
(i) that director is a partner,
(ii) a partner is a person who, by virtue of paragraph (a), (b) or (c) above, is connected with that director, or
(iii) a partner is a Scottish firm in which that director is a partner or in which there is a partner who, by virtue of paragraph (a), (b) or (c) above, is connected with that director.

(3) In subsection (2)—
(a) a reference to the child or step-child of any person includes an illegitimate child of his, but does not include any person who has attained the age of 18; and
(b) paragraph (c) does not apply to a person acting in his capacity as trustee under an employees' share scheme or a pension scheme.

(4) A director of a company is associated with a body corporate if, but only if, he and the persons connected with him, together—
(a) are interested in shares comprised in the equity share capital of that body corporate of a nominal value equal to at least one-fifth of that share capital; or
(b) are entitled to exercise or control the exercise of more than one-fifth of the voting power at any general meeting of that body.

(5) A director of a company is deemed to control a body corporate if, but only if—
(a) he or any person connected with him is interested in any part of the equity share capital of that body or is entitled to exercise or control the exercise of any part of the voting power at any general meeting of that body; and
(b) that director, the persons connected with him and the other directors of that company, together, are interested in more than one-half of that share capital or are entitled to exercise or control the exercise of more than one-half of that voting power.

(6) For purposes of subsections (4) and (5)—
(a) a body corporate with which a director is associated is not to be treated as connected with that director unless it is also connected with him by virtue of subsection (2)(c) or (d); and

(b)   a trustee of a trust the beneficiaries of which include (or may include) a body corporate with which a director is associated is not to be treated as connected with a director by reason only of that fact.

(7)   The rules set out in Part I of Schedule 13 apply for the purposes of subsections (4) and (5).

(8)   References in those subsections to voting power the exercise of which is controlled by a director include voting power whose exercise is controlled by a body corporate controlled by him; but this is without prejudice to other provisions of subsections (4) and (5).

PART XI
COMPANY ADMINISTRATION AND PROCEDURE

Chapter I
Company Identification

349 Company's name to appear in its correspondence, etc

(1)   Every company shall have its name mentioned in legible characters—
   (a)   in all business letters of the company,
   (b)   in all its notices and other official publications,
   (c)   in all bills of exchange, promissory notes, endorsements, cheques and orders for money or goods purporting to be signed by or on behalf of the company, and
   (d)   in all its bills of parcels, invoices, receipts and letters of credit.

(2)   If a company fails to comply with subsection (1) it is liable to a fine.

(3)   If an officer of a company or a person on its behalf—
   (a)   issues or authorises the issue of any business letter of the company, or any notice or other official publication of the company, in which the company's name is not mentioned as required by subsection (1), or
   (b)   issues or authorises the issue of any bill of parcels, invoice, receipt or letter of credit of the company in which its name is not so mentioned,

he is liable to a fine.

(4)   If an officer of a company or a person on its behalf signs or authorises to be signed on behalf of the company any bill of exchange, promissory note, endorsement, cheque or order for money or goods in which the company's name is not mentioned as required by subsection (1), he is liable to a fine; and he is further personally liable to the holder of the bill of exchange, promissory note, cheque or order for money or goods for the amount of it (unless it is duly paid by the company).

351 Particulars in correspondence etc

(1)   Every company shall have the following particulars mentioned in legible characters in all business letters and order forms of the company, that is to say—

(a) the company's place of registration and the number with which it is registered,

(b) the address of its registered office,

(c) in the case of an investment company (as defined in section 266), the fact that it is such a company, and

(d) in the case of a limited company exempt from the obligation to use the word "limited" as part of its name, the fact that it is a limited company.

(2) If in the case of a company having a share capital there is on the stationery used for any such letters, or on the company's order forms, a reference to the amount of share capital, the reference must be to paid-up share capital.

(3), (4) . . .

(5) As to contraventions of this section, the following applies—

(a) if a company fails to comply with subsection (1) or (2), it is liable to a fine,

(b) if an officer of a company or a person on its behalf issues or authorises the issue of any business letter or order form not complying with those subsections, he is liable to a fine, . . .

(c) . . .

NOTES

Sub-ss (3), (4): repealed by the Welsh Language Act 1993, s 31.

Sub-s (5): para (c) and the word immediately preceding it omitted by the Welsh Language Act 1993, s 35(1), Sch 2.

Chapter II
Register of Members

352 Obligation to keep and enter up register

(1) Every company shall keep a register of its members and enter in it the particulars required by this section.

(2) There shall be entered in the register—

(a) the names and addresses of the members;

(b) the date on which each person was registered as a member; and

(c) the date at which any person ceased to be a member.

(3) The following applies in the case of a company having a share capital—

(a) with the names and addresses of the members there shall be entered a statement—

(i) of the shares held by each member, distinguishing each share by its number (so long as the share has a number) and, where the company has more than one class of issued shares, by its class, and

(ii) of the amount paid or agreed to be considered as paid on the shares of each member;

(b) where the company has converted any of its shares into stock and given notice of the conversion to the registrar of companies, the register shall show the amount and class of stock held by each member, instead of the amount of shares and the particulars relating to shares specified in paragraph (a).

(4)   In the case of a company which does not have a share capital but has more than one class of members, there shall be entered in the register, with the names and addresses of the members, the class to which each member belongs.

(5)   If a company makes default in complying with this section, the company and every officer of it who is in default is liable to a fine and, for continued contravention, to a daily default fine.

(6)   An entry relating to a former member of the company may be removed from the register after the expiration of 20 years from the date on which he ceased to be a member.

(7)   Liability incurred by a company from the making or deletion of an entry in its register of members, or from a failure to make or delete any such entry, is not enforceable more than 20 years after the date on which the entry was made or deleted or, in the case of any such failure, the failure first occurred.

This is without prejudice to any lesser period of limitation.

[352A Statement that company has only one member]

[(1)   If the number of members of a private company limited by shares or by guarantee falls to one there shall upon the occurrence of that event be entered in the company's register of members with the name and address of the sole member—
  (i)   a statement that the company has only one member, and
  (ii)   the date on which the company became a company having only one member.

(2)   If the membership of a private company limited by shares or by guarantee increases from one to two or more members there shall upon the occurrence of that event be entered in the company's register of members, with the name and address of the person who was formerly the sole member, a statement that the company has ceased to have only one member together with the date on which that event occurred.

(3)   If a company makes default in complying with this section, the company and every officer of it who is in default is liable to a fine and, for continued contravention, to a daily default fine.]

NOTES

Inserted by SI 1992/1699, reg 2(b), Schedule, para 4(1).

356 Inspection of register and index

(1)   Except when the register of members is closed under the provisions of this Act, the register and the index of members' names shall . . . be open to the inspection of any member of the company without charge, and of any other person on payment of [such fee as may be prescribed].

(2)   . . .

(3)   Any member of the company or other person may require a copy of the register, or of any part of it, on payment of [such fee as may be prescribed]; and the company shall cause any copy so required by a person to be sent to him within 10

days beginning with the day next following that on which the requirement is received by the company.

(4) . . .

(5) If an inspection required under this section is refused, or if a copy so required is not sent within the proper period, the company and every officer of it who is in default is liable in respect of each offence to a fine.

(6) In the case of such refusal or default, the court may by order compel an immediate inspection of the register and index, or direct that the copies required be sent to the persons requiring them.

NOTES

Sub-s (1): words omitted repealed, and words in square brackets substituted, by the Companies Act 1989, ss 143(8), 212, Sch 24.

Sub-ss (2), (4): repealed by the Companies Act 1989, ss 143(8), 212, Sch 24.

Sub-s (3): words in square brackets substituted by the Companies Act 1989, s 143(8).

359 Power of court to rectify register

(1) If—
  (a) the name of any person is, without sufficient cause, entered in or omitted from a company's register of members, or
  (b) default is made or unnecessary delay takes place in entering on the register the fact of any person having ceased to be a member,

the person aggrieved, or any member of the company, or the company, may apply to the court for rectification of the register.

(2) The court may either refuse the application or may order rectification of the register and payment by the company of any damages sustained by any party aggrieved.

(3) On such an application the court may decide any question relating to the title of a person who is a party to the application to have his name entered in or omitted from the register, whether the question arises between members or alleged members, or between members or alleged members on the one hand and the company on the other hand, and generally may decide any question necessary or expedient to be decided for rectification of the register.

(4) In the case of a company required by this Act to send a list of its members to the registrar of companies, the court, when making an order for rectification of the register, shall by its order direct notice of the rectification to be given to the registrar.

360 Trusts not to be entered on register in England and Wales

No notice of any trust, expressed, implied or constructive, shall be entered on the register, or be receivable by the registrar, in the case of companies registered in England and Wales.

361 Register to be evidence

The register of members is prima facie evidence of any matters which are by this Act directed or authorised to be inserted in it.

Chapter III
Annual Return

[363 Duty to deliver annual returns]

[(1)   Every company shall deliver to the registrar successive annual returns each of which is made up to a date not later than the date which is from time to time the company's "return date", that is—
  (a)   the anniversary of the company's incorporation, or
  (b)   if the company's last return delivered in accordance with this Chapter was made up to a different date, the anniversary of that date.

(2)   Each return shall—
  (a)   be in the prescribed form,
  (b)   contain the information required by or under the following provisions of this Chapter, and
  (c)   be signed by a director or the secretary of the company;

and it shall be delivered to the registrar within 28 days after the date to which it is made up.

(3)   If a company fails to deliver an annual return in accordance with this Chapter before the end of the period of 28 days after a return date, the company is guilty of an offence and liable to a fine and, in the case of continued contravention, to a daily default fine.

The contravention continues until such time as an annual return made up to that return date and complying with the requirements of subsection (2) (except as to date of delivery) is delivered by the company to the registrar.

(4)   Where a company is guilty of an offence under subsection (3), every director or secretary of the company is similarly liable unless he shows that he took all reasonable steps to avoid the commission or continuation of the offence.

(5)   The references in this section to a return being delivered "in accordance with this Chapter" are—
  (a)   in relation to a return made [on or after 1st October 1990], to a return with respect to which all the requirements of subsection (2) are complied with;
  (b)   in relation to a return made before [1 October 1990] , to a return with respect to which the formal and substantive requirements of this Chapter as it then had effect were complied with, whether or not the return was delivered in time.]

NOTES

Substituted by the Companies Act 1989, s 139(1).
Sub-s (5): words in square brackets substituted by SI 1990/1707, art 7.

[364 Contents of annual return: general]

[(1)   Every annual return shall state the date to which it is made up and shall contain the following information—

(a)   the address of the company's registered office;

(b)   the type of company it is and its principal business activities;

(c)   the name and address of the company secretary;

(d)   the name and address of every director of the company;

(e)   in the case of each individual director—

(i)   his nationality, date of birth and business occupation; . . .

(ii) . . .

(f)   . . .

(g)   if the register of members is not kept at the company's registered office, the address of the place where it is kept;

(h)   if any register of debenture holders (or a duplicate of any such register or a part of it) is not kept at the company's registered office, the address of the place where it is kept;

(i)   . . ..

(2)   The information as to the company's type shall be given by reference to the classification scheme prescribed for the purposes of this section.

(3)   The information as to the company's principal business activities may be given by reference to one or more categories of any prescribed system of classifying business activities.

(4)   A person's "name" and "address" mean, respectively—

(a)   in the case of an individual, his Christian name (or other forename) and surname and his usual residential address;

(b)   in the case of a corporation or a Scottish firm, its corporate or firm name and its registered or principal office.

(5)   In the case of a peer, or an individual usually known by a title, the title may be stated instead of his Christian name (or other forename) and surname or in addition to either or both of them.

(6)   Where all the partners in a firm are joint secretaries, the name and principal office of the firm may be stated instead of the names and addresses of the partners.]

NOTES

Substituted by the Companies Act 1989, s 139(1).

Sub-s (1): para (e)(ii) and word omitted immediately preceding it repealed by SI 1999/2322, reg 2(a).

Date in force: 13 September 1999: see SI 1999/2322, reg 1.

Sub-s (1): para (f) repealed by SI 1999/2322, reg 2(b).

Date in force: 13 September 1999: see SI 1999/2322, reg 1.

Sub-s (1): para (i) repealed by SI 1999/2322, reg 2(c).

Date in force: 13 September 1999: see SI 1999/2322, reg 1.

[364A Contents of annual return: particulars of share capital and shareholders]

[(1)   The annual return of a company having a share capital shall contain the following information with respect to its share capital and members.

(2)   The return shall state the total number of issued shares of the company at the date to which the return is made up and the aggregate nominal value of those shares.

(3)   The return shall state with respect to each class of shares in the company—
  (a) the nature of the class, and
  (b) the total number and aggregate nominal value of issued shares of that class at the date to which the return is made up.

(4)   The return shall contain a list of the names and addresses of every person who—
  (a) is a member of the company on the date to which the return is made up, or
  (b) has ceased to be a member of the company since the date to which the last return was made up (or, in the case of the first return, since the incorporation of the company);

and if the names are not arranged in alphabetical order the return shall have annexed to it an index sufficient to enable the name of any person in the list to be easily found.

(5)   The return shall also state—
  (a) the number of shares of each class held by each member of the company at the date to which the return is made up, and
  (b) the number of shares of each class transferred since the date to which the last return was made up (or, in the case of the first return, since the incorporation of the company) by each member or person who has ceased to be a member, and the dates of registration of the transfers.

(6)   The return may, if either of the two immediately preceding returns has given the full particulars required by subsections (4) and (5), give only such particulars as relate to persons ceasing to be or becoming members since the date of the last return and to shares transferred since that date.

(7)   Subsections (4) and (5) do not require the inclusion of particulars entered in an overseas branch register if copies of those entries have not been received at the company's registered office by the date to which the return is made up.

Those particulars shall be included in the company's next annual return after they are received.

(8)   Where the company has converted any of its shares into stock, the return shall give the corresponding information in relation to that stock, stating the amount of stock instead of the number or nominal value of shares.]

NOTES
Inserted by the Companies Act 1989, s 139(1), (2).

Chapter IV
Meetings and Resolutions

Meetings

366 Annual general meeting

(1)   Every company shall in each year hold a general meeting as its annual general meeting in addition to any other meetings in that year, and shall specify the meeting as such in the notices calling it.

(2)   However, so long as a company holds its first annual general meeting within 18 months of its incorporation, it need not hold it in the year of its incorporation or in the following year.

(3)   Not more than 15 months shall elapse between the date of one annual general meeting of a company and that of the next.

(4)   If default is made in holding a meeting in accordance with this section, the company and every officer of it who is in default is liable to a fine.

[366A Election by private company to dispense with annual general meetings]

[(1)   A private company may elect (by elective resolution in accordance with section 379A) to dispense with the holding of annual general meetings.

(2)   An election has effect for the year in which it is made and subsequent years, but does not affect any liability already incurred by reason of default in holding an annual general meeting.

(3)   In any year in which an annual general meeting would be required to be held but for the election, and in which no such meeting has been held, any member of the company may, by notice to the company not later than three months before the end of the year, require the holding of an annual general meeting in that year.

[(3A)   The power of a member under subsection (3) to require the holding of an annual general meeting is exercisable not only by the giving of a notice but also by the transmission to the company at such address as may for the time being be specified for the purpose by or on behalf of the company of an electronic communication containing the requirement.]

(4)   If such a notice is given [or electronic communication is transmitted], the provisions of section 366(1) and (4) apply with respect to the calling of the meeting and the consequences of default.

(5)   If the election ceases to have effect, the company is not obliged under section 366 to hold an annual general meeting in that year if, when the election ceases to have effect, less than three months of the year remains.

This does not affect any obligation of the company to hold an annual general meeting in that year in pursuance of a notice given [or electronic communication is transmitted] under subsection (3).]

[(5A) In this section, "address" includes any number or address used for the purposes of electronic communications.]

NOTES

Inserted by the Companies Act 1989, s 115(2).

Sub-s (3A): inserted by SI 2000/3373, art 17(1), (2).

Date in force: 22 December 2000: see SI 2000/3373, art 1(1).

Sub-s (4): words "or electronic communication is transmitted" in square brackets inserted by SI 2000/3373, art 17(1), (3).

Date in force: 22 December 2000: see SI 2000/3373, art 1(1).

Sub-s (5): words "or electronic communication is transmitted" in square brackets inserted by SI 2000/3373, art 17(1), (4).

Date in force: 22 December 2000: see SI 2000/3373, art 1(1).

Sub-s (5A): inserted by SI 2000/3373, art 17(1), (5).

Date in force: 22 December 2000: see SI 2000/3373, art 1(1).

367 Secretary of State's power to call meeting in default

(1)   If default is made in holding a meeting in accordance with section 366, the Secretary of State may, on the application of any member of the company, call, or direct the calling of, a general meeting of the company and give such ancillary or consequential directions as he thinks expedient, including directions modifying or supplementing, in relation to the calling, holding and conduct of the meeting, the operation of the company's articles.

(2)   The directions that may be given under subsection (1) include a direction that one member of the company present in person or by proxy shall be deemed to constitute a meeting.

(3)   If default is made in complying with directions of the Secretary of State under subsection (1), the company and every officer of it who is in default is liable to a fine.

(4)   A general meeting held under this section shall, subject to any directions of the Secretary of State, be deemed to be an annual general meeting of the company; but, where a meeting so held is not held in the year in which the default in holding the company's annual general meeting occurred, the meeting so held shall not be treated as the annual general meeting for the year in which it is held unless at that meeting the company resolves that it be so treated.

(5)   Where a company so resolves, a copy of the resolution shall, within 15 days after its passing, be forwarded to the registrar of companies and recorded by him; and if default is made in complying with this subsection, the company and every officer of it who is in default is liable to a fine and, for continued contravention, to a daily default fine.

368 Extraordinary general meeting on members' requisition

(1)   The directors of a company shall, on a members' requisition, forthwith proceed duly to convene an extraordinary general meeting of the company.

This applies notwithstanding anything in the company's articles.

(2)   A members' requisition is a requisition of—
  (a)   members of the company holding at the date of the deposit of the requisition not less than one-tenth of such of the paid-up capital of the company as at that date carries the right of voting at general meetings of the company; or
  (b)   in the case of a company not having a share capital, members of it representing not less than one-tenth of the total voting rights of all the members having at the date of deposit of the requisition a right to vote at general meetings.

(3)   The requisition must state the objects of the meeting, and must be signed by the requisitionists and deposited at the registered office of the company, and may consist of several documents in like form each signed by one or more requisitionists.

(4)   If the directors do not within 21 days from the date of the deposit of the requisition proceed duly to convene a meeting, the requisitionists, or any of them representing more than one half of the total voting rights of all of them, may themselves convene a meeting, but any meeting so convened shall not be held after the expiration of 3 months from that date.

(5)   A meeting convened under this section by requisitionists shall be convened in the same manner, as nearly as possible, as that in which meetings are to be convened by directors.

(6)   Any reasonable expenses incurred by the requisitionists by reason of the failure of the directors duly to convene a meeting shall be repaid to the requisitionists by the company, and any sum so repaid shall be retained by the company out of any sums due or to become due from the company by way of fees or other remuneration in respect of their services to such of the directors as were in default.

(7)   In the case of a meeting at which a resolution is to be proposed as a special resolution, the directors are deemed not to have duly convened the meeting if they do not give the notice required for special resolutions by section 378(2).

[(8)   The directors are deemed not to have duly convened a meeting if they convene a meeting for a date more than 28 days after the date of the notice convening the meeting.]

NOTES
  Sub-s (8): inserted by the Companies Act 1989, s 145, Sch 19, para 9.

369 Length of notice for calling meetings

(1)   A provision of a company's articles is void in so far as it provides for the calling of a meeting of the company (other than an adjourned meeting) by a shorter notice than—
  (a)   in the case of the annual general meeting, 21 days' notice in writing; and
  (b)   in the case of a meeting other than an annual general meeting or a meeting for the passing of a special resolution—
    (i)   7 days' notice in writing in the case of an unlimited company, and
    (ii)   otherwise, 14 days' notice in writing.

(2)   Save in so far as the articles of a company make other provision in that behalf (not being a provision avoided by subsection (1)), a meeting of the company (other than an adjourned meeting) may be called—
(a)   in the case of the annual general meeting, by 21 days' notice in writing; and
(b)   in the case of a meeting other than an annual general meeting or a meeting for the passing of a special resolution—
(i)   by 7 days' notice in writing in the case of an unlimited company, and
(ii) otherwise, 14 days' notice in writing.

(3)   Notwithstanding that a meeting is called by shorter notice than that specified in subsection (2) or in the company's articles (as the case may be), it is deemed to have been duly called if it is so agreed—
(a)   in the case of a meeting called as the annual general meeting, by all the members entitled to attend and vote at it; and
(b)   otherwise, by the requisite majority.

(4)   The requisite majority for this purpose is a majority in number of the members having a right to attend and vote at the meeting, being a majority—
(a)   together holding not less than 95 per cent in nominal value of the shares giving a right to attend and vote at the meeting; or
(b)   in the case of a company not having a share capital, together representing not less than 95 per cent of the total voting rights at that meeting of all the members.

[A private company may elect (by elective resolution in accordance with section 379A) that the above provisions shall have effect in relation to the company as if for the references to 95 per cent there were substituted references to such lesser percentage, but not less than 90 per cent, as may be specified in the resolution or subsequently determined by the company in general meeting.]

[(4A)   For the purposes of this section the cases in which notice in writing of a meeting is to be taken as given to a person include any case in which notice of the meeting is sent using electronic communications to such address as may for the time being be notified by that person to the company for that purpose.

(4B)   For the purposes of this section a notice in writing of a meeting is also to be treated as given to a person where—
(a)   the company and that person have agreed that notices of meetings required to be given to that person may instead be accessed by him on a web site;
(b)   the meeting is a meeting to which that agreement applies;
(c)   that person is notified, in a manner for the time being agreed between him and the company for the purpose, of—
(i)   the publication of the notice on a web site;
(ii) the address of that web site; and
(iii) the place on that web site where the notice may be accessed, and how it may be accessed;
and
(d)   the notice continues to be published on that web site throughout the period beginning with the giving of that notification and ending with the conclusion of the meeting;

and for the purposes of this section a notice treated in accordance with this subsection as given to any person is to be treated as so given at the time of the notification mentioned in paragraph (c).

(4C) A notification given for the purposes of subsection (4B)(c) must—
   (a) state that it concerns a notice of a company meeting served in accordance with this Act,
   (b) specify the place, date and time of the meeting, and
   (c) state whether the meeting is to be an annual or extraordinary general meeting.

(4D) Nothing in subsection (4B) shall invalidate the proceedings of a meeting where—
   (a) any notice that is required to be published as mentioned in paragraph (d) of that subsection is published for a part, but not all, of the period mentioned in that paragraph; and
   (b) the failure to publish that notice throughout that period is wholly attributable to circumstances which it would not be reasonable to have expected the company to prevent or avoid.

(4E) A company may, notwithstanding any provision to the contrary in a company's articles, take advantage of any of subsections (4A) to (4D).

(4F) In so far as the articles of the company do not provide for notices and notifications to be served using electronic communications, the provisions of Table A (as for the time being in force) as to such service shall apply.

(4G) In this section, "address" includes any number or address used for the purposes of electronic communications.]

NOTES

Sub-s (4): words in square brackets inserted by the Companies Act 1989, s 115(3).
Sub-ss (4A)–(4G): inserted by SI 2000/3373, art 18.
Date in force: 22 December 2000: see SI 2000/3373, art 1(1).

370 General provisions as to meetings and votes

(1) The following provisions have effect in so far as the articles of the company do not make other provision in that behalf.

(2) Notice of the meeting of a company shall be served on every member of it in the manner in which notices are required to be served by Table A (as for the time being in force).

(3) Two or more members holding not less than one-tenth of the issued share capital or, if the company does not have a share capital, not less than 5 per cent in number of the members of the company may call a meeting.

(4) Two members personally present are a quorum.

(5) Any member elected by the members present at a meeting may be chairman of it.

(6)   In the case of a company originally having a share capital, every member has one vote in respect of each share or each £10 of stock held by him; and in any other case every member has one vote.

[370A Quorum at meetings of the sole member]

[Notwithstanding any provision to the contrary in the articles of a private company limited by shares or by guarantee having only one member, one member present in person or by proxy shall be a quorum.]

NOTES

Inserted by SI 1992/1699, reg 2(b), Schedule, para 5.

371 Power of court to order meeting

(1)   If for any reason it is impracticable to call a meeting of a company in any manner in which meetings of that company may be called, or to conduct the meeting in manner prescribed by the articles or this Act, the court may, either of its own motion or on the application—
  (a)   of any director of the company, or
  (b)   of any member of the company who would be entitled to vote at the meeting,
order a meeting to be called, held and conducted in any manner the court thinks fit.

(2)   Where such an order is made, the court may give such ancillary or consequential directions as it thinks expedient; and these may include a direction that one member of the company present in person or by proxy be deemed to constitute a meeting.

(3)   A meeting called, held and conducted in accordance with an order under subsection (1) is deemed for all purposes a meeting of the company duly called, held and conducted.

372 Proxies

(1)   Any member of a company entitled to attend and vote at a meeting of it is entitled to appoint another person (whether a member or not) as his proxy to attend and vote instead of him; and in the case of a private company a proxy appointed to attend and vote instead of a member has also the same right as the member to speak at the meeting.

(2)   But, unless the articles otherwise provide—
  (a)   subsection (1) does not apply in the case of a company not having a share capital; and
  (b)   a member of a private company is not entitled to appoint more than one proxy to attend on the same occasion; and
  (c)   a proxy is not entitled to vote except on a poll.

[(2A)   The appointment of a proxy may, notwithstanding any provision to the contrary in a company's articles, be contained in an electronic communication sent to such address as may be notified by or on behalf of the company for that purpose.

(2B)   In so far as the articles of the company do not make other provision in that behalf, the appointment of a proxy may be contained in an electronic communication in accordance with the provisions of Table A (as for the time being in force).]

(3)   In the case of a company having a share capital, in every notice calling a meeting of the company there shall appear with reasonable prominence a statement that a member entitled to attend and vote is entitled to appoint a proxy or, where that is allowed, one or more proxies to attend and vote instead of him, and that a proxy need not also be a member.

(4)   If default is made in complying with subsection (3) as respects any meeting, every officer of the company who is in default is liable to a fine.

(5)   A provision contained in a company's articles is void in so far as it would have the effect of requiring [the appointment of a proxy or any] document necessary to show the validity of, or otherwise relating to, the appointment of a proxy, to be received by the company or any other person more than 48 hours before a meeting or adjourned meeting in order that the appointment may be effective.

(6)   If for the purpose of any meeting of a company invitations to appoint as proxy a person or one of a number of persons specified in the invitations are issued at the company's expense to some only of the members entitled to be sent a notice of the meeting and to vote at it by proxy, then every officer of the company who knowingly and wilfully authorises or permits their issue in that manner is liable to a fine.

However, an officer is not so liable by reason only of the issue to a member at his request . . . of a form of appointment naming the proxy, or of a list of persons willing to act as proxy, if the form or list is available on request . . . to every member entitled to vote at the meeting by proxy.

[(6A)   In this section, "address" includes any number or address used for the purposes of electronic communications.]

(7)   This section applies to meetings of any class of members of a company as it applies to general meetings of the company.

NOTES

Sub-ss (2A), (2B): inserted by SI 2000/3373, art 19(1), (2).
Date in force: 22 December 2000: see SI 2000/3373, art 1(1).
Sub-s (5): words "the appointment of a proxy or any" in square brackets substituted by SI 2000/3373, art 19(1), (3).
Date in force: 22 December 2000: see SI 2000/3373, art 1(1).
Sub-s (6): words omitted repealed by SI 2000/3373, art 19(1), (4).
Date in force: 22 December 2000: see SI 2000/3373, art 1(1).
Sub-s (6A): inserted by SI 2000/3373, art 19(1), (5).
Date in force: 22 December 2000: see SI 2000/3373, art 1(1).

373 Right to demand a poll

(1)   A provision contained in a company's articles is void in so far as it would have the effect either—

(a) of excluding the right to demand a poll at a general meeting on any question other than the election of the chairman of the meeting or the adjournment of the meeting; or

(b) of making ineffective a demand for a poll on any such question which is made either—

  (i) by not less than 5 members having the right to vote at the meeting; or

  (ii) by a member or members representing not less than one-tenth of the total voting rights of all the members having the right to vote at the meeting; or

  (iii) by a member or members holding shares in the company conferring a right to vote at the meeting, being shares on which an aggregate sum has been paid up equal to not less than one-tenth of the total sum paid up on all the shares conferring that right.

(2) [The appointment of] a proxy to vote at a meeting of a company is deemed also to confer authority to demand or join in demanding a poll; and for the purposes of subsection (1) a demand by a person as proxy for a member is the same as a demand by the member.

NOTES

Sub-s (2): words "The appointment of" in square brackets substituted by SI 2000/3373, art 20.

Date in force: 22 December 2000: see SI 2000/3373, art 1(1).

Resolutions

376 Circulation of members' resolutions

(1) Subject to the section next following, it is the duty of a company, on the requisition in writing of such number of members as is specified below and (unless the company otherwise resolves) at the expense of the requisitionists—

(a) to give to members of the company entitled to receive notice of the next annual general meeting notice of any resolution which may properly be moved and is intended to be moved at that meeting;

(b) to circulate to members entitled to have notice of any general meeting sent to them any statement of not more than 1,000 words with respect to the matter referred to in any proposed resolution or the business to be dealt with at that meeting.

(2) The number of members necessary for a requisition under subsection (1) is—

(a) any number representing not less than one-twentieth of the total voting rights of all the members having at the date of the requisition a right to vote at the meeting to which the requisition relates; or

(b) not less than 100 members holding shares in the company on which there has been paid up an average sum, per member, of not less than £100.

(3) Notice of any such resolution shall be given, and any such statement shall be circulated, to members of the company entitled to have notice of the meeting sent to them, by serving a copy of the resolution or statement on each such member in any manner permitted for service of notice of the meeting.

(4)   Notice of any such resolution shall be given to any other member of the company by giving notice of the general effect of the resolution in any manner permitted for giving him notice of meetings of the company.

(5)   For compliance with subsections (3) and (4), the copy must be served, or notice of the effect of the resolution be given (as the case may be) in the same manner and (so far as practicable) at the same time as notice of the meeting; and, where it is not practicable for it to be served or given at the same time, it must be served or given as soon as practicable thereafter.

(6)   The business which may be dealt with at an annual general meeting includes any resolution of which notice is given in accordance with this section; and for purposes of this subsection notice is deemed to have been so given notwithstanding the accidental omission, in giving it, of one or more members. This has effect notwithstanding anything in the company's articles.

(7)   In the event of default in complying with this section, every officer of the company who is in default is liable to a fine.

377 In certain cases, compliance with s 376 not required

(1)   A company is not bound under section 376 to give notice of a resolution or to circulate a statement unless—
  (a)   a copy of the requisition signed by the requisitionists (or two or more copies which between them contain the signatures of all the requisitionists) is deposited at the registered office of the company—
      (i)   in the case of a requisition requiring notice of a resolution, not less than 6 weeks before the meeting, and
      (ii)   otherwise, not less than one week before the meeting; and
  (b)   there is deposited or tendered with the requisition a sum reasonably sufficient to meet the company's expenses in giving effect to it.

(2)   But if, after a copy of a requisition requiring notice of a resolution has been deposited at the company's registered office, an annual general meeting is called for a date 6 weeks or less after the copy has been deposited, the copy (though not deposited within the time required by subsection (1)) is deemed properly deposited for the purposes of that subsection.

(3)   The company is also not bound under section 376 to circulate a statement if, on the application either of the company or of any other person who claims to be aggrieved, the court is satisfied that the rights conferred by that section are being abused to secure needless publicity for defamatory matter; and the court may order the company's costs on such an application to be paid in whole or in part by the requisitionists, notwithstanding that they are not parties to the application.

378 Extraordinary and special resolutions

(1)   A resolution is an extraordinary resolution when it has been passed by a majority of not less than three-fourths of such members as (being entitled to do so) vote in person or, where proxies are allowed, by proxy, at a general meeting of

which notice specifying the intention to propose the resolution as an extraordinary resolution has been duly given.

(2)   A resolution is a special resolution when it has been passed by such a majority as is required for the passing of an extraordinary resolution and at a general meeting of which not less than 21 days' notice, specifying the intention to propose the resolution as a special resolution, has been duly given.

(3)   If it is so agreed by a majority in number of the members having the right to attend and vote at such a meeting, being a majority—

(a)   together holding not less than 95 per cent in nominal value of the shares giving that right; or

(b)   in the case of a company not having a share capital, together representing not less than 95 per cent of the total voting rights at that meeting of all the members,

a resolution may be proposed and passed as a special resolution at a meeting of which less than 21 days' notice has been given.

[A private company may elect (by elective resolution in accordance with section 379A) that the above provisions shall have effect in relation to the company as if for the references to 95 per cent there were substituted references to such lesser percentage, but not less than 90 per cent, as may be specified in the resolution or subsequently determined by the company in general meeting.]

(4)   At any meeting at which an extraordinary resolution or a special resolution is submitted to be passed, a declaration by the chairman that the resolution is carried is, unless a poll is demanded, conclusive evidence of the fact without proof of the number or proportion of the votes recorded in favour of or against the resolution.

(5)   In computing the majority on a poll demanded on the question that an extraordinary resolution or a special resolution be passed, reference is to be had to the number of votes cast for and against the resolution.

(6)   For purposes of this section, notice of a meeting is deemed duly given, and the meeting duly held, when the notice is given and the meeting held in the manner provided by this Act or the company's articles.

NOTES

Sub-s (3): words in square brackets inserted by the Companies Act 1989, s 115(3).

379 Resolution requiring special notice

(1)   Where by any provision of this Act special notice is required of a resolution, the resolution is not effective unless notice of the intention to move it has been given to the company at least 28 days before the meeting at which it is moved.

(2)   The company shall give its members notice of any such resolution at the same time and in the same manner as it gives notice of the meeting or, if that is not practicable, shall give them notice either by advertisement in a newspaper having an appropriate circulation or in any other mode allowed by the company's articles, at least 21 days before the meeting.

(3)   If, after notice of the intention to move such a resolution has been given to the company, a meeting is called for a date 28 days or less after the notice has been given, the notice is deemed properly given, though not given within the time required.

[379A Elective resolution of private company]

[(1)   An election by a private company for the purposes of—
  (a)   section 80A (election as to duration of authority to allot shares),
  (b)   section 252 (election to dispense with laying of accounts and reports before general meeting),
  (c)   section 366A (election to dispense with holding of annual general meeting),
  (d)   section 369(4) or 378(3) (election as to majority required to authorise short notice of meeting), or
  (e)   section 386 (election to dispense with appointment of auditors annually),

shall be made by resolution of the company in general meeting in accordance with this section.

Such a resolution is referred to in this Act as an "elective resolution".

(2)   An elective resolution is not effective unless—
  (a)   at least 21 days' notice in writing is given of the meeting, stating that an elective resolution is to be proposed and stating the terms of the resolution, and
  (b)   the resolution is agreed to at the meeting, in person or by proxy, by all the members entitled to attend and vote at the meeting.

[(2A)   An elective resolution is effective notwithstanding the fact that less than 21 days' notice in writing of the meeting is given if all the members entitled to attend and vote at the meeting so agree.]

[(2B)   For the purposes of this section, notice in writing of the meeting is to be taken as given to a person where notice of the meeting is sent using electronic communications to such address as may for the time being be notified by that person to the company for that purpose.

(2C)   For the purposes of this section a notice in writing of the meeting is also to be treated as given to a person where—
  (a)   the company and that person have agreed that notices of meetings required to be given to that person may instead be accessed by him on a web site;
  (b)   the meeting is a meeting to which that agreement applies;
  (c)   that person is notified, in a manner for the time being agreed between him and the company for the purpose, of—
    (i)   the publication of the notice on a web site;
    (ii)   the address of that web site; and
    (iii) the place on that web site where the notice may be accessed, and how it may be accessed; and
  (d)   the notice continues to be published on that web site throughout the period beginning with the giving of that notification and ending with the conclusion of the meeting;

and for the purposes of this section a notice treated in accordance with this subsection as given to any person is to be treated as so given at the time of the notification mentioned in paragraph (c).

(2D)   A notification given for the purposes of subsection (2C)(c) must—
   (a)   state that it concerns a notice of a company meeting at which an elective resolution is to be proposed, and
   (b)   specify the place, date and time of the meeting.

(2E)   Nothing in subsection (2C) shall invalidate the proceedings of a meeting where—
   (a)   any notice that is required to be published as mentioned in paragraph (d) of that subsection is published for a part, but not all, of the period mentioned in that paragraph; and
   (b)   the failure to publish that notice throughout that period is wholly attributable to circumstances which it would not be reasonable to have expected the company to prevent or avoid.

(2F)   In so far as the articles of the company do not provide for notices and notifications to be served using electronic communications, the provisions of Table A (as for the time being in force) as to such service shall apply.]

(3)   The company may revoke an elective resolution by passing an ordinary resolution to that effect.

(4)   An elective resolution shall cease to have effect if the company is re-registered as a public company.

(5)   An elective resolution may be passed or revoked in accordance with this section, and the provisions referred to in [subsections (1) and (2B) to (2E)] have effect, notwithstanding any contrary provision in the company's articles of association.

[(5A)   In this section, "address" includes any number or address used for the purposes of electronic communications.]]

NOTES

Inserted by the Companies Act 1989, s 116(1).
Sub-s (2A): inserted by SI 1996/1471, art 2.
Sub-ss (2B)–(2F): inserted by SI 2000/3373, art 21(1), (2).
Date in force: 22 December 2000: see SI 2000/3373, art 1(1).
Sub-s (5): words "subsections (1) and (2B) to (2E)" in square brackets substituted by SI 2000/3373, art 21(1), (3).
Date in force: 22 December 2000: see SI 2000/3373, art 1(1).
Sub-s (5A): inserted by SI 2000/3373, art 21(1), (4).
Date in force: 22 December 2000: see SI 2000/3373, art 1(1).

380 Registration, etc of resolutions and agreements

(1)   A copy of every resolution or agreement to which this section applies shall, within 15 days after it is passed or made, be forwarded to the registrar of companies and recorded by him; and it must be either a printed copy or else a copy in some other form approved by the registrar.

(2) Where articles have been registered, a copy of every such resolution or agreement for the time being in force shall be embodied in or annexed to every copy of the articles issued after the passing of the resolution or the making of the agreement.

(3) Where articles have not been registered, a printed copy of every such resolution or agreement shall be forwarded to any member at his request on payment of 5 pence or such less sum as the company may direct.

(4) This section applies to—
  (a) special resolutions;
  (b) extraordinary resolutions;
  [(bb) an elective resolution or a resolution revoking such a resolution;]
  (c) resolutions or agreements which have been agreed to by all the members of a company but which, if not so agreed to, would not have been effective for their purpose unless (as the case may be) they had been passed as special resolutions or as extraordinary resolutions;
  (d) resolutions or agreements which have been agreed to by all the members of some class of shareholders but which, if not so agreed to, would not have been effective for their purpose unless they had been passed by some particular majority or otherwise in some particular manner, and all resolutions or agreements which effectively bind all the members of any class of shareholders though not agreed to by all those members;
  (e) a resolution passed by the directors of a company in compliance with a direction under section 31(2) (change of name on Secretary of State's direction);
  (f) a resolution of a company to give, vary, revoke or renew an authority to the directors for the purposes of section 80 (allotment of relevant securities);
  (g) a resolution of the directors passed under section 147(2) (alteration of memorandum on company ceasing to be a public company, following acquisition of its own shares);
  (h) a resolution conferring, varying, revoking or renewing authority under section 166 (market purchase of company's own shares);
  (j) a resolution for voluntary winding up, passed under [section 84(1)(a) of the Insolvency Act];
  (k) a resolution passed by the directors of an old public company, under section 2(1) of the Consequential Provisions Act, that the company should be re-registered as a public company;
  [(l) a resolution of the directors passed by virtue of regulation [16(2) of the Uncertificated Securities Regulations 2001 (which allows title to a company's shares to be evidenced and transferred without written instrument); and
  (m) a resolution of a company passed by virtue of regulation 16(6) of the Uncertificated Securities Regulations 2001 (which prevents or reverses a resolution of the directors under regulation 16(2) of those Regulations)].

(5) If a company fails to comply with subsection (1), the company and every officer of it who is in default is liable to a fine and, for continued contravention, to a daily default fine.

(6)   If a company fails to comply with subsection (2) or (3), the company and every officer of it who is in default is liable to a fine.

(7)   For purposes of subsections (5) and (6), a liquidator of a company is deemed an officer of it.

NOTES

Sub-s (4): para (bb) inserted by the Companies Act 1989, s 116(3).

Sub-s (4): in para (j) words "section 84(1)(a) of the Insolvency Act" in square brackets substituted by the Insolvency Act 1986, s 439(1), Sch 13, Pt I; for transitional provisions see s 437, Sch 11 thereof.

Sub-s (4): paras (l), (m) inserted by SI 2001/3755, reg 51, Sch 7, Pt 1, para 10.

Date in force: 26 November 2001: see SI 2001/3755, reg 1.

[Written resolutions of private companies]

NOTES

Inserted by the Companies Act 1989, s 113(2).

[381A Written resolutions of private companies]

[(1)   Anything which in the case of a private company may be done—
  (a)   by resolution of the company in general meeting, or
  (b)   by resolution of a meeting of any class of members of the company,

may be done, without a meeting and without any previous notice being required, by resolution in writing signed by or on behalf of all the members of the company who at the date of the resolution would be entitled to attend and vote at such meeting.

(2)   The signatures need not be on a single document provided each is on a document which accurately states the terms of the resolution.

(3)   The date of the resolution means when the resolution is signed by or on behalf of the last member to sign.

(4)   A resolution agreed to in accordance with this section has effect as if passed—
  (a)   by the company in general meeting, or
  (b)   by a meeting of the relevant class of members of the company,

as the case may be; and any reference in any enactment to a meeting at which a resolution is passed or to members voting in favour of a resolution shall be construed accordingly.

(5)   Any reference in any enactment to the date of passing of a resolution is, in relation to a resolution agreed to in accordance with this section, a reference to the date of the resolution, . . .

(6)   A resolution may be agreed to in accordance with this section which would otherwise be required to be passed as a special, extraordinary or elective resolution; and any reference in any enactment to a special, extraordinary or elective resolution includes such a resolution.

(7)   This section has effect subject to the exceptions specified in Part I of Schedule 15A; and in relation to certain descriptions of resolution under this section

the procedural requirements of this Act have effect with the adaptations specified in Part II of that Schedule.]

NOTES

Inserted by the Companies Act 1989, s 113(2).
Sub-s (5): words omitted repealed by SI 1996/1471, art 3(2)(a), (3).

[381B Rights of auditors in relation to written resolution]

[(1)   If a director or secretary of a company—
   (a)   knows that it is proposed to seek agreement to a resolution in accordance with section 381A, and
   (b)   knows the terms of the resolution,

he shall, if the company has auditors, secure that a copy of the resolution is sent to them, or that they are otherwise notified of its contents, at or before the time the resolution is supplied to a member for signature.

(2)   A person who fails to comply with subsection (1) is liable to a fine.

(3)   In any proceedings for an offence under this section it is a defence for the accused to prove—
   (a)   that the circumstances were such that it was not practicable for him to comply with subsection (1), or
   (b)   that he believed on reasonable grounds that a copy of the resolution had been sent to the company's auditors or that they had otherwise been informed of its contents.

(4)   Nothing in this section affects the validity of any resolution.]

NOTES

Inserted by the Companies Act 1989, s 113(2).
Substituted by SI 1996/1471, art 3(1), (3)

[381C Written resolutions: supplementary provisions]

[(1)   Sections 381A and 381B have effect notwithstanding any provision of the company's memorandum or articles[, but do not prejudice any power conferred by any such provision.]

(2)   Nothing in those sections affects any enactment or rule of law as to—
   (a)   things done otherwise than by passing a resolution, or
   (b)   cases in which a resolution is treated as having been passed, or a person is precluded from alleging that a resolution has not been duly passed.]

NOTES

Inserted by the Companies Act 1989, s 113(2).
Sub-s (1): words in square brackets inserted by SI 1996/1471, art 4.

382 Minutes of meetings

(1) Every company shall cause minutes of all proceedings of general meetings, all proceedings at meetings of its directors and, where there are managers, all proceedings at meetings of its managers to be entered in books kept for that purpose.

(2) Any such minute, if purporting to be signed by the chairman of the meeting at which the proceedings were had, or by the chairman of the next succeeding meeting, is evidence of the proceedings.

(3) Where a shadow director by means of a notice required by section 317(8) declares an interest in a contract or proposed contract, this section applies—
    (a) if it is a specific notice under paragraph (a) of that subsection, as if the declaration had been made at the meeting there referred to, and
    (b) otherwise, as if it had been made at the meeting of the directors next following the giving of the notice;

and the making of the declaration is in either case deemed to form part of the proceedings at the meeting.

(4) Where minutes have been made in accordance with this section of the proceedings at any general meeting of the company or meeting of directors or managers, then, until the contrary is proved, the meeting is deemed duly held and convened, and all proceedings had at the meeting to have been duly had; and all appointments of directors, managers or liquidators are deemed valid.

(5) If a company fails to comply with subsection (1), the company and every officer of it who is in default is liable to a fine and, for continued contravention, to a daily default fine.

[382A Recording of written resolutions]

[(1) Where a written resolution is agreed to in accordance with section 381A which has effect as if agreed by the company in general meeting, the company shall cause a record of the resolution (and of the signatures) to be entered in a book in the same way as minutes of proceedings of a general meeting of the company.

(2) Any such record, if purporting to be signed by a director of the company or by the company secretary, is evidence of the proceedings in agreeing to the resolution; and where a record is made in accordance with this section, then, until the contrary is proved, the requirements of this Act with respect to those proceedings shall be deemed to be complied with.

(3) Section 382(5) (penalties) applies in relation to a failure to comply with subsection (1) above as it applies in relation to a failure to comply with subsection (1) of that section; and section 383 (inspection of minute books) applies in relation to a record made in accordance with this section as it applies in relation to the minutes of a general meeting.]

NOTES

Inserted by the Companies Act 1989, s 113(3).

[382B Recording of decisions by the sole member]

[(1)   Where a private company limited by shares or by guarantee has only one member and he takes any decision which may be taken by the company in general meeting and which has effect as if agreed by the company in general meeting, he shall (unless that decision is taken by way of a written resolution) provide the company with a written record of that decision.

(2)   If the sole member fails to comply with subsection (1) he shall be liable to a fine.

(3)   Failure by the sole member to comply with subsection (1) shall not affect the validity of any decision referred to in that subsection.]

NOTES

Inserted by SI 1992/1699, reg 2(b), Schedule, para 6(1).

383 Inspection of minute books

(1)   The books containing the minutes of proceedings of any general meeting of a company held on or after 1st November 1929 shall be kept at the company's registered office, and shall . . . be open to the inspection of any member without charge.

(2)   . . .

(3)   Any member shall be entitled [on payment of such fee as may be prescribed] to be furnished, within 7 days after he has made a request in that behalf to the company, with a copy of any such minutes as are referred to above, . . .

(4)   If an inspection required under this section is refused or if a copy required under this section is not sent within the proper time, the company and every officer of it who is in default is liable in respect of each offence to a fine.

(5)   In the case of any such refusal or default, the court may by order compel an immediate inspection of the books in respect of all proceedings of general meetings, or direct that the copies required be sent to the persons requiring them.

NOTES

Sub-s (1): words omitted repealed by the Companies Act 1989, ss 143(9), 212, Sch 24.
Sub-s (2): repealed by the Companies Act 1989, ss 143(9), 212, Sch 24.
Sub-s (3): words omitted repealed and words in square brackets inserted by the Companies Act 1989, ss 143(9), 212, Sch 24.

Chapter V
Auditors

[Appointment of auditors]

NOTES

Inserted by the Companies Act 1989, s 119(1).

[384 Duty to appoint auditors]

[(1) Every company shall appoint an auditor or auditors in accordance with this Chapter.

This is subject to section 388A ([certain companies] exempt from obligation to appoint auditors).

(2) Auditors shall be appointed in accordance with section 385 (appointment at general meeting at which accounts are laid), except in the case of a private company which has elected to dispense with the laying of accounts in which case the appointment shall be made in accordance with section 385A.

(3) References in this Chapter to the end of the time for appointing auditors are to the end of the time within which an appointment must be made under section 385(2) or 385A(2), according to whichever of those sections applies.

(4) Sections 385 and 385A have effect subject to section 386 under which a private company may elect to dispense with the obligation to appoint auditors annually.]

NOTES

Sections 118–123 of the Companies Act 1989 insert new provisions in place of original ss 384–394 of this Act (with the exception of s 389); see s 118 of the 1989 Act.

Inserted by the Companies Act 1989, s 119(1).

Sub-s (1): words in square brackets substituted by SI 1994/1935, reg 4, Sch 1, para 4.

[385 Appointment at general meeting at which accounts laid]

[(1) This section applies to every public company and to a private company which has not elected to dispense with the laying of accounts.

(2) The company shall, at each general meeting at which accounts are laid, appoint an auditor or auditors to hold office from the conclusion of that meeting until the conclusion of the next general meeting at which accounts are laid.

(3) The first auditors of the company may be appointed by the directors at any time before the first general meeting of the company at which accounts are laid; and auditors so appointed shall hold office until the conclusion of that meeting.

(4) If the directors fail to exercise their powers under subsection (3), the powers may be exercised by the company in general meeting.]

NOTES

Sections 118–123 of the Companies Act 1989 insert new provisions in place of original ss 384–394 of this Act (with the exception of s 389); see s 118 of the 1989 Act.

Inserted by the Companies Act 1989, s 119(1).

[385A Appointment by private company which is not obliged to lay accounts]

[(1) This section applies to a private company which has elected in accordance with section 252 to dispense with the laying of accounts before the company in general meeting.

(2)   Auditors shall be appointed by the company in general meeting before the end of the period of 28 days beginning with the day on which copies of the company's annual accounts for the previous financial year are sent to members under section 238 or, if notice is given under section 253(2) requiring the laying of the accounts before the company in general meeting, the conclusion of that meeting.

Auditors so appointed shall hold office from the end of that period or, as the case may be, the conclusion of that meeting until the end of the time for appointing auditors for the next financial year.

(3)   The first auditors of the company may be appointed by the directors at any time before—
  (a)   the end of the period of 28 days beginning with the day on which copies of the company's first annual accounts are sent to members under section 238, or
  (b)   if notice is given under section 253(2) requiring the laying of the accounts before the company in general meeting, the beginning of that meeting;

and auditors so appointed shall hold office until the end of that period or, as the case may be, the conclusion of that meeting.

(4)   If the directors fail to exercise their powers under subsection (3), the powers may be exercised by the company in general meeting.

(5)   Auditors holding office when the election is made shall, unless the company in general meeting determines otherwise, continue to hold office until the end of the time for appointing auditors for the next financial year; and auditors holding office when an election ceases to have effect shall continue to hold office until the conclusion of the next general meeting of the company at which accounts are laid.]

NOTES

Sections 118–123 of the Companies Act 1989 insert new provisions in place of original ss 384–394 of this Act (with the exception of s 389); see s 118 of the 1989 Act.

Inserted by the Companies Act 1989, s 119(1).

[386 Election by private company to dispense with annual appointment]

[(1)   A private company may elect (by elective resolution in accordance with section 379A) to dispense with the obligation to appoint auditors annually.

(2)   When such an election is in force the company's auditors shall be deemed to be re-appointed for each succeeding financial year on the expiry of the time for appointing auditors for that year, unless—
  [(a)   the directors of the company have taken advantage of the exemption conferred by section 249A or 249AA, or]
  (b)   a resolution has been passed under section 393 to the effect that their appointment should be brought to an end.

(3)   If the election ceases to be in force, the auditors then holding office shall continue to hold office—

(a) where section 385 then applies, until the conclusion of the next general meeting of the company at which accounts are laid;

(b) where section 385A then applies, until the end of the time for appointing auditors for the next financial year under that section.

(4) No account shall be taken of any loss of the opportunity of further deemed re-appointment under this section in ascertaining the amount of any compensation or damages payable to an auditor on his ceasing to hold office for any reason.]

NOTES

Sections 118–123 of the Companies Act 1989 insert new provisions in place of original ss 384–394 of this Act (with the exception of s 389); see s 118 of the 1989 Act.

Inserted by the Companies Act 1989, s 119(1).

Sub-s (2): para (a) substituted by SI 2000/1430, reg 8(8).

Date in force: this amendment has effect in relation to annual accounts and reports in respect of financial years ending on or after 26 July 2000: see SI 2000/1430, reg 1(1), (2).

[388A Certain companies exempt from obligation to appoint auditors]

[(1) A company which by virtue of section 249A (certain categories of small company) or [section 249AA] (dormant companies) is exempt from the provisions of Part VII relating to the audit of accounts is also exempt from the obligation to appoint auditors.

(2) The following provisions apply if a company which has been exempt from those provisions ceases to be so exempt.

(3) Where section 385 applies (appointment at general meeting at which accounts are laid), the directors may appoint auditors at any time before the next meeting of the company at which accounts are to be laid; and auditors so appointed shall hold office until the conclusion of that meeting.

(4) Where section 385A applies (appointment by private company not obliged to lay accounts), the directors may appoint auditors at any time before—

(a) the end of the period of 28 days beginning with the day on which copies of the company's annual accounts are next sent to members under section 238, or

(b) if notice is given under section 253(2) requiring the laying of the accounts before the company in general meeting, the beginning of that meeting;

and auditors so appointed shall hold office until the end of that period or, as the case may be, the conclusion of that meeting.

(5) If the directors fail to exercise their powers under subsection (3) or (4), the powers may be exercised by the company in general meeting.]

NOTES

Sections 118–123 of the Companies Act 1989 insert new provisions in place of original ss 384–394 of this Act (with the exception of s 389); see s 118 of the 1989 Act.

Inserted by the Companies Act 1989, s 119(4).

Substituted by SI 1994/1935, reg 3.

Sub-s (1): words "section 249AA" in square brackets substituted by SI 2000/1430, reg 8(9).

Date in force: this amendment has effect in relation to annual accounts and reports in respect of financial years ending on or after 26 July 2000: see SI 2000/1430, reg 1(1), (2).

[Rights of auditors]

NOTES
Inserted by the Companies Act 1989, s 120(1).

[389A Rights to information]

[(1)   The auditors of a company have a right of access at all times to the company's books, accounts and vouchers, and are entitled to require from the company's officers such information and explanations as they think necessary for the performance of their duties as auditors.

(2)   An officer of a company commits an offence if he knowingly or recklessly makes to the company's auditors a statement (whether written or oral) which—

  (a)   conveys or purports to convey any information or explanations which the auditors require, or are entitled to require, as auditors of the company, and

  (b)   is misleading, false or deceptive in a material particular.

A person guilty of an offence under this subsection is liable to imprisonment or a fine, or both.

(3)   A subsidiary undertaking which is a body corporate incorporated in Great Britain, and the auditors of such an undertaking, shall give to the auditors of any parent company of the undertaking such information and explanations as they may reasonably require for the purposes of their duties as auditors of that company.

If a subsidiary undertaking fails to comply with this subsection, the undertaking and every officer of it who is in default is guilty of an offence and liable to a fine; and if an auditor fails without reasonable excuse to comply with this subsection he is guilty of an offence and liable to a fine.

(4)   A parent company having a subsidiary undertaking which is not a body corporate incorporated in Great Britain shall, if required by its auditors to do so, take all such steps as are reasonably open to it to obtain from the subsidiary undertaking such information and explanations as they may reasonably require for the purposes of their duties as auditors of that company.

If a parent company fails to comply with this subsection, the company and every officer of it who is in default is guilty of an offence and liable to a fine.

(5)   Section 734 (criminal proceedings against unincorporated bodies) applies to an offence under subsection (3).]

NOTES
Sections 118–123 of the Companies Act 1989 insert new provisions in place of original ss 384–394 of this Act (with the exception of s 389); see s 118 of the 1989 Act.
Inserted by the Companies Act 1989, s 120(1).

[390 Right to attend company meetings, &c]

[(1) A company's auditors are entitled—
- (a) to receive all notices of, and other communications relating to, any general meeting which a member of the company is entitled to receive;
- (a) to attend any general meeting of the company; and
- (b) to be heard at any general meeting which they attend on any part of the business of the meeting which concerns them as auditors.

[(1A) Subsections (4A) to (4G) of section 369 (electronic communication of notices of meetings) apply for the purpose of determining whether notice of a meeting is received by the company's auditors as they apply in determining whether such a notice is given to any person.]

(2) In relation to a written resolution proposed to be agreed to by a private company in accordance with section 381A, the company's auditors are entitled—
- (a) to receive all such communications relating to the resolution as, by virtue of any provision of Schedule 15A, are required to be supplied to a member of the company,
- (b)–(d). .

(3) The right to attend or be heard at a meeting is exercisable in the case of a body corporate or partnership by an individual authorised by it in writing to act as its representative at the meeting.]

NOTES
Sections 118–123 of the Companies Act 1989 insert new provisions in place of original ss 384–394 of this Act (with the exception of s 389); see s 118 of the 1989 Act.
Inserted by the Companies Act 1989, s 120(1).
Sub-s (1A): inserted by SI 2000/3373, art 31(3).
Date in force: 22 December 2000: see SI 2000/3373, art 1(1).
Sub-s (2): paras (b)–(d) repealed by SI 1996/1471, art 3(2)(b), (3).

[Remuneration of auditors]

NOTES
Inserted by the Companies Act 1989, s 121.

[390A Remuneration of auditors]

[(1) The remuneration of auditors appointed by the company in general meeting shall be fixed by the company in general meeting or in such manner as the company in general meeting may determine.

(2) The remuneration of auditors appointed by the directors of the Secretary of State shall be fixed by the directors of the Secretary of State, as the case may be.

(3) There shall be stated in a note to the company's annual accounts the amount of the remuneration of the company's auditors in their capacity as such.

(4) For the purposes of this section "remuneration" includes sums paid in respect of expenses.

(5)   This section applies in relation to benefits in kind as to payments in cash, and in relation to any such benefit references to its amount are to its estimated money value.

The nature of any such benefit shall also be disclosed.]

NOTES

Sections 118–123 of the Companies Act 1989 insert new provisions in place of original ss 384–394 of this Act (with the exception of s 389); see s 118 of the 1989 Act.
Inserted by the Companies Act 1989, s 121.

[390B Remuneration of auditors or their associates for non-audit work]

[(1)   The Secretary of State may make provision by regulations for securing the disclosure of the amount of any remuneration received or receivable by a company's auditors or their associates in respect of services other than those of auditors in their capacity as such.

(2)   The regulations may—
   (a)   provide that "remuneration" includes sums paid in respect of expenses,
   (b)   apply in relation to benefits in kind as to payments in cash, and in relation to any such benefit require disclosure of its nature and its estimated money value,
   (c)   define "associate" in relation to an auditor,
   (d)   require the disclosure of remuneration in respect of services rendered to associated undertakings of the company, and
   (e)   define "associated undertaking" for that purpose.

(3)   The regulations may require the auditors to disclose the relevant information in their report or require the relevant information to be disclosed in a note to the company's accounts and require the auditors to supply the directors of the company with such information as is necessary to enable that disclosure to be made.

(4)   The regulations may make different provision for different cases.

(5)   Regulations under this section shall be made by statutory instrument which shall be subject to annulment in pursuance of a resolution of either House of Parliament.]

NOTES

Sections 118–123 of the Companies Act 1989 insert new provisions in place of original ss 384–394 of this Act (with the exception of s 389); see s 118 of the 1989 Act.
Inserted by the Companies Act 1989, s 121.

[Removal, resignation, &c of auditors]

NOTES

Inserted by the Companies Act 1989, s 122(1).

[391 Removal of auditors]

[(1)   A company may by ordinary resolution at any time remove an auditor from office, notwithstanding anything in any agreement between it and him.

(2)   Where a resolution removing an auditor is passed at a general meeting of a company, the company shall within 14 days give notice of that fact in the prescribed form to the registrar.

If a company fails to give the notice required by this subsection, the company and every officer of it who is in default is guilty of an offence and liable to a fine and, for continued contravention, to a daily default fine.

(3)   Nothing in this section shall be taken as depriving a person removed under it of compensation or damages payable to him in respect of the termination of his appointment as auditor or of any appointment terminating with that as auditor.

(4)   An auditor of a company who has been removed has, notwithstanding his removal, the rights conferred by section 390 in relation to any general meeting of the company—

(a)   at which his term of office would otherwise have expired, or

(b)   at which it is proposed to fill the vacancy caused by his removal.

In such a case the references in that section to matters concerning the auditors as auditors shall be construed as references to matters concerning him as a former auditor.]

NOTES

Sections 118–123 of the Companies Act 1989 insert new provisions in place of original ss 384–394 of this Act (with the exception of s 389); see s 118 of the 1989 Act.

Inserted by the Companies Act 1989, s 122(1).

[391A Rights of auditors who are removed or not re-appointed]

[(1)   Special notice is required for a resolution at a general meeting of a company—

(a)   removing an auditor before the expiration of his term of office, or

(b)   appointing as auditor a person other than a retiring auditor.

(2)   On receipt of notice of such an intended resolution the company shall forthwith send a copy of it to the person proposed to be removed or, as the case may be, to the person proposed to be appointed and to the retiring auditor.

(3)   The auditor proposed to be removed or (as the case may be) the retiring auditor may make with respect to the intended resolution representations in writing to the company (not exceeding a reasonable length) and request their notification to members of the company.

(4)   The company shall (unless the representations are received by it too late for it to do so)—

(a)   in any notice of the resolution given to members of the company, state the fact of the representations having been made, and

(b) send a copy of the representations to every member of the company to whom notice of the meeting is or has been sent.

(5) If a copy of any such representations is not sent out as required because received too late or because of the company's default, the auditor may (without prejudice to his right to be heard orally) require that the representations be read out at the meeting.

(6) Copies of the representations need not be sent out and the representations need not be read at the meeting if, on the application either of the company or of any other person claiming to be aggrieved, the court is satisfied that the rights conferred by this section are being abused to secure needless publicity for defamatory matter; and the court may order the company's costs on the application to be paid in whole or in part by the auditor, notwithstanding that he is not a party to the application.]

NOTES

Sections 118–123 of the Companies Act 1989 insert new provisions in place of original ss 384–394 of this Act (with the exception of s 389); see s 118 of the 1989 Act.

Inserted by the Companies Act 1989, s 122(1).

[392 Resignation of auditors]

[(1) An auditor of a company may resign his office by depositing a notice in writing to that effect at the company's registered office.

The notice is not effective unless it is accompanied by the statement required by section 394.

(2) An effective notice of resignation operates to bring the auditor's term of office to an end as of the date on which the notice is deposited or on such later date as may be specified in it.

(3) The company shall within 14 days of the deposit of a notice of resignation send a copy of the notice to the registrar of companies.

If default is made in complying with this subsection, the company and every officer of it who is in default is guilty of an offence and liable to a fine and, for continued contravention, a daily default fine.]

NOTES

Sections 118–123 of the Companies Act 1989 insert new provisions in place of original ss 384–394 of this Act (with the exception of s 389); see s 118 of the 1989 Act.

Inserted by the Companies Act 1989, s 122(1).

[392A Rights of resigning auditors]

[(1) This section applies where an auditor's notice of resignation is accompanied by a statement of circumstances which he considers should be brought to the attention of members or creditors of the company.

(2) He may deposit with the notice a signed requisition calling on the directors of the company forthwith duly to convene an extraordinary general meeting of the

company for the purpose of receiving and considering such explanation of the circumstances connected with his resignation as he may wish to place before the meeting.

(3) He may request the company to circulate to its members—
    (a) before the meeting convened on his requisition, or
    (b) before any general meeting at which his term of office would otherwise have expired or at which it is proposed to fill the vacancy caused by his resignation,

a statement in writing (not exceeding a reasonable length) of the circumstances connected with his resignation.

(4) The company shall (unless the statement is received too late for it to comply)—
    (a) in any notice of the meeting given to members of the company, state the fact of the statement having been made, and
    (b) send a copy of the statement to every member of the company to whom notice of the meeting is or has been sent.

(5) If the directors do not within 21 days from the date of the deposit of a requisition under this section proceed duly to convene a meeting for a day not more than 28 days after the date on which the notice convening the meeting is given, every director who failed to take all reasonable steps to secure that a meeting was convened as mentioned above is guilty of an offence and liable to a fine.

(6) If a copy of the statement mentioned above is not sent out as required because received too late or because of the company's default, the auditor may (without prejudice to his right to be heard orally) require that the statement be read out at the meeting.

(7) Copies of a statement need not be sent out and the statement need not be read out at the meeting if, on the application either of the company or of any other person who claims to be aggrieved, the court is satisfied that the rights conferred by this section are being abused to secure needless publicity for defamatory matter; and the court may order the company's costs on such an application to be paid in whole or in part by the auditor, notwithstanding that he is not a party to the application.

(8) An auditor who has resigned has, notwithstanding his resignation, the rights conferred by section 390 in relation to any such general meeting of the company as is mentioned in subsection (3)(a) or (b).

In such a case the references in that section to matters concerning the auditors as auditors shall be construed as references to matters concerning him as a former auditor.]

NOTES
Sections 118–123 of the Companies Act 1989 insert new provisions in place of original ss 384–394 of this Act (with the exception of s 389); see s 118 of the 1989 Act.
Inserted by the Companies Act 1989, s 122(1).

[394 Statement by person ceasing to hold office as auditors]

[(1)   Where an auditor ceases for any reason to hold office, he shall deposit at the company's registered office a statement of any circumstances connected with his ceasing to hold office which he considers should be brought to the attention of the members or creditors of the company or, if he considers that there are no such circumstances, a statement that there are none.

(2)   In the case of resignation, the statement shall be deposited along with the notice of resignation; in the case of failure to seek re-appointment, the statement shall be deposited not less than 14 days before the end of the time allowed for next appointing auditors; in any other case, the statement shall be deposited not later than the end of the period of 14 days beginning with the date on which he ceases to hold office.

(3)   If the statement is of circumstances which the auditor considers should be brought to the attention of the members or creditors of the company, the company shall within 14 days of the deposit of the statement either—
  (a)   send a copy of it to every person who under section 238 is entitled to be sent copies of the accounts, or
  (b)   apply to the court.

(4)   The company shall if it applies to the court notify the auditor of the application.

(5)   Unless the auditor receives notice of such an application before the end of the period of 21 days beginning with the day on which he deposited the statement, he shall within a further seven days send a copy of the statement to the registrar.

(6)   If the court is satisfied that the auditor is using the statement to secure needless publicity for defamatory matter—
  (a)   it shall direct that copies of the statement need not be sent out, and
  (b)   it may further order the company's costs on the application to be paid in whole or in part by the auditor, notwithstanding that he is not a party to the application;

and the company shall within 14 days of the court's decision send to the persons mentioned in subsection (3)(a) a statement setting out the effect of the order.

(7)   If the court is not so satisfied, the company shall within 14 days of the court's decision—
  (a)   send copies of the statement to the persons mentioned in subsection (3)(a), and
  (b)   notify the auditor of the court's decision;

and the auditor shall within seven days of receiving such notice send a copy of the statement to the registrar.]

NOTES

Sections 118–123 of the Companies Act 1989 insert new provisions in place of original ss 384–394 of this Act (with the exception of s 389); see s 118 of the 1989 Act.
Inserted by the Companies Act 1989, s 123(1).

[394A Offences of failing to comply with s 394]

[(1)   If a person ceasing to hold office as auditor fails to comply with section 394 he is guilty of an offence and liable to a fine.

(2)   In proceedings for an offence under subsection (1) it is a defence for the person charged to show that he took all reasonable steps and exercised all due diligence to avoid the commission of the offence.

(3)   Sections 733 (liability of individuals for corporate default) and 734 (criminal proceedings against unincorporated bodies) apply to an offence under subsection (1).

(4)   If a company makes default in complying with section 394, the company and every officer of it who is in default is guilty of an offence and liable to a fine and, for continued contravention, to a daily default fine.]

NOTES

Sections 118–123 of the Companies Act 1989 insert new provisions in place of original ss 384–394 of this Act (with the exception of s 389); see s 118 of the 1989 Act.
Inserted by the Companies Act 1989, s 123(1).

PART XII
REGISTRATION OF CHARGES

Chapter I
Registration of Charges (England and Wales)

NOTES

Prospectively repealed by virtue of the Companies Act 1989, s 92, as from a day to be appointed.

[Registration in the company charges register]

NOTES

Inserted by the Companies Act 1989, s 93.
Date in force: to be appointed: see the Companies Act 1989, s 215(2).

395 Certain charges void if not registered [395 Introductory provisions]

(1) Subject to the provisions of this Chapter, a charge created by a company registered in England and Wales and being a charge to which this section applies is, so far as any security on the company's property or undertaking is conferred by the charge, void against the liquidator [or administrator] and any creditor of the company, unless the prescribed particulars of the charge together with the instrument (if any) by which the charge is created or evidenced, are delivered to or received by the registrar of companies for registration in the manner required by this Chapter within 21 days after the date of the charge's creation.

(2) Subsection (1) is without prejudice to any contract or obligation for repayment of the money secured by the charge; and when a charge becomes void under this section, the money secured by it immediately becomes payable.

[(1) The purpose of this Part is to secure the registration of charges on a company's property.

(2) In this Part—

"charge" means any form of security interest (fixed or floating) over property, other than an interest arising by operation of law; and

"property", in the context of what is the subject of a charge, includes future property.

(3) It is immaterial for the purposes of this Part where the property subject to a charge is situated.

(4) References in this Part to "the registrar" are—

    (a)   in relation to a company registered in England and Wales, to the registrar of companies for England and Wales, and

    (b)   in relation to a company registered in Scotland, to the registrar of companies for Scotland;

and references to registration, in relation to a charge, are to registration in the register kept by him under this Part.]

NOTES

Part IV of the Companies Act 1989 (ss 92–107) inserts new provisions in place of original ss 395–424 of this Act, as from a day to be appointed; see s 92 of the 1989 Act.

New provision in square brackets prospectively inserted by the Companies Act 1989, s 93, as from a day to be appointed.

Original sub-s (1): words in square brackets inserted by the Insolvency Act 1985, s 109, Sch 6, para 10.

396 Charges which have to be registered [396 Charges requiring registration]

(1) Section 395 applies to the following charges—

    (a) a charge for the purpose of securing any issue of debentures,

    (b) a charge on uncalled share capital of the company,

    (c) a charge created or evidenced by an instrument which, if executed by an individual, would require registration as a bill of sale,

    (d) a charge on land (wherever situated) or any interest in it, but not including a charge for any rent or other periodical sum issuing out of the land,

    (e) a charge on book debts of the company,

    (f) a floating charge on the Company's undertaking or property,

    (g) a charge on calls made but not paid,

    (h) a charge on a ship or aircraft, or any share in a ship,

    (j) a charge on goodwill, [or on any intellectual property].

(2) Where a negotiable instrument has been given to secure the payment of any book debts of a company, the deposit of the instrument for the purpose of securing

an advance to the company is not, for purposes of sections 395, to be treated as a charge on those book debts.

(3) The holding of debentures entitling the holder to a charge on land is not for purposes of this section deemed to be an interest in land.

[(3A) The following are "intellectual property" for the purposes of this section—
  (a) any patent, trade mark, < . . . > registered design, copyright or design right;
  (b) any licence under or in respect of any such right.]

(4) In this Chapter, "charge" includes mortgage.

[(1)   The charges requiring registration under this Part are—
  (a)   a charge on land or any interest in land, other than—
    (i)   in England and Wales, a charge for rent or any other periodical sum issuing out of the land,
    (ii)   in Scotland, a charge for any rent, *ground annual* or other periodical sum payable in respect of the land;
  (b)   a charge on goods or any interest in goods, other than a charge under which the chargee is entitled to possession either of the goods or of a document of title to them;
  (c)   a charge on intangible movable property (in Scotland, incorporeal moveable property) of any of the following descriptions—
    (i)   goodwill,
    (ii)   intellectual property,
    (iii)   book debts (whether book debts of the company or assigned to the company),
    (iv)   uncalled share capital of the company or calls made but not paid;
  (d)   a charge for securing an issue of debentures; or
  (e)   a floating charge on the whole or part of the company's property.

(2)   The descriptions of charge mentioned in subsection (1) shall be construed as follows—
  (a)   a charge on a debenture forming part of an issue or series shall not be treated as falling within paragraph (a) or (b) by reason of the fact that the debenture is secured by a charge on land or goods (or on an interest in land or goods);
  (b)   in paragraph (b) "goods" means any tangible movable property (in Scotland, corporeal moveable property) other than money;
  (c)   a charge is not excluded from paragraph (b) because the chargee is entitled to take possession in case of default or on the occurrence of some other event;
  (d)   in paragraph (c)(ii) "intellectual property" means—
    (i)   any patent, trade mark, . . . registered design, copyright or design right, or
    (ii)   any licence under or in respect of any such right;
  (e)   a debenture which is part of an issue or series shall not be treated as a book debt for the purposes of paragraph (c)(iii);
  (f)   the deposit by way of security of a negotiable instrument given to secure the payment of book debts shall not be treated for the purposes of paragraph (c)(iii) as a charge on book debts;

(g) a shipowner's lien on subfreights shall not be treated as a charge on book debts for the purposes of paragraph (c)(iii) or as a floating charge for the purposes of paragraph (e).

(3) Whether a charge is one requiring registration under this Part shall be determined—

(a) in the case of a charge created by a company, as at the date the charge is created, and

(b) in the case of a charge over property acquired by a company, as at the date of the acquisition.

(4) The Secretary of State may by regulations amend subsections (1) and (2) so as to add any description of charge to, or remove any description of charge from, the charges requiring registration under this Part.

(5) Regulations under this section shall be made by statutory instrument which shall be subject to annulment in pursuance of a resolution of either House of Parliament.

(6) In the following provisions of this Part references to a charge are, unless the context otherwise requires, to a charge requiring registration under this Part.

Where a charge not otherwise requiring registration relates to property by virtue of which it requires to be registered and to other property, the references are to the charge so far as it relates to property of the former description.]

NOTES

Part IV of the Companies Act 1989 (ss 92–107) inserts new provisions in place of original ss 395–424 of this Act, as from a day to be appointed; see s 92 of the 1989 Act.

New provision in square brackets prospectively inserted by the Companies Act 1989, s 93, as from a day to be appointed.

Original sub-s (1): in para (j), words in square brackets substituted by the Copyright, Designs and Patents Act 1988, s 303(1), Sch 7, para 31(2).

Sub-s (3A): inserted by the Copyright, Designs and Patents Act 1988, s 303(1), Sch 7, para 31(2); words omitted repealed by the Trade Marks Act 1994, s 106(2), Sch 5.

New sub-s (1): in para (a)(ii) words ", ground annual" in italics repealed by the Abolition of Feudal Tenure etc (Scotland) Act 2000, s 76(1), (2), Sch 12, para 46(1)–(4), Sch 13.

Date in force: this repeal shall have effect on the coming into force of the Companies Act 1989, s 92: see the Abolition of Feudal Tenure etc (Scotland) Act 2000, Sch 12, para 46(2)–(4).

New sub-s (2): words omitted repealed by the Trade Marks Act 1994, s 106(2).

397 Formalities of registration (debentures) [397 The companies charges register]

(1) Where a series of debentures containing, or giving by reference to another instrument, any charge to the benefit of which the debenture holders of that series are entitled pari passu is created by a company, it is for purposes of section 395 sufficient if there are delivered to or received by the registrar, within 21 days after the execution of the deed containing the charge (or, if there is no such deed, after the execution of any debentures of the series), the following particulars in the prescribed form—

(a) the total amount secured by the whole series, and

(b) the dates of the resolutions authorising the issue of the series and the date of the covering deed (if any) by which the security is created or defined, and

(c) a general description of the property charged, and

(d) the names of the trustees (if any) for the debenture holders,

together with the deed containing the charge or, if there is no such deed, one of the debentures of the series:

Provided that there shall be sent to the registrar of companies, for entry in the register, particulars in the prescribed form of the date and amount of each issue of debentures of the series, but any omission to do this does not affect the validity of any of those debentures.

(2) Where any commission, allowance or discount has been paid or made either directly or indirectly by a company to a person in consideration of his—

(a) subscribing or agreeing to subscribe, whether absolutely or conditionally, for debentures of the company, or

(b) procuring or agreeing to procure subscriptions, whether absolute or conditional, for such debentures,

the particulars required to be sent for registration under section 395 shall include particulars as to the amount or rate per cent of the commission, discount or allowance so paid or made, but omission to do this does not affect the validity of the debentures issued.

(3) The deposit of debentures as security for a debt of the company is not, for the purposes of subsection (2), treated as the issue of the debentures at a discount.

[(1) The registrar shall keep for each company a register, in such form as he thinks fit, of charges on property of the company.

(2) The register shall consist of a file containing with respect to each charge the particulars and other information delivered to the registrar under the provisions of this Part.

(3) Any person may require the registrar to provide a certificate stating the date on which any specified particulars of, or other information relating to, a charge were delivered to him.

(4) The certificate shall be signed by the registrar or authenticated by his official seal.

(5) The certificate shall be conclusive evidence that the specified particulars or other information were delivered to the registrar no later than the date stated in the certificate; and it shall be presumed unless the contrary is proved that they were not delivered earlier than that date.]

NOTES

Part IV of the Companies Act 1989 (ss 92–107) inserts new provisions in place of original ss 395–424 of this Act, as from a day to be appointed; see s 92 of the 1989 Act.

New provision in square brackets prospectively inserted by the Companies Act 1989, s 94, as from a day to be appointed.

398 Verification of charge on property outside United Kingdom [398 Company's duty to deliver particulars of charge for registration]

(1) In the case of a charge created out of the United Kingdom comprising property situated outside the United Kingdom, the delivery to and the receipt by the registrar of companies of a copy (verified in the prescribed manner) of the instrument by which the charge is created or evidenced has the same effect for purposes of sections 395 to 398 as the delivery and receipt of the instrument itself.

(2) In that case, 21 days after the date on which the instrument or copy could, in due course of post (and if despatched with due diligence), have been received in the United Kingdom are substituted for the 21 days mentioned in section 395(2) (or as the case may be, section 397(1)) as the time within which the particulars and instrument or copy are to be delivered to the registrar.

(3) Where a charge is created in the United Kingdom but comprises property outside the United Kingdom, the instrument creating or purporting to create the charge may be sent for registration under section 395 notwithstanding that further proceedings may be necessary to make the charge valid or effectual according to the law of the country in which the property is situated.

(4) Where a charge comprises property situated in Scotland or Northern Ireland and registration in the country where the property is situated is necessary to make the charge valid or effectual according to the law of that country, the delivery to and receipt by the registrar of a copy (verified in the prescribed manner) of the instrument by which the charge is created or evidenced, together with a certificate in the prescribed form stating that the charge was presented for registration in Scotland or Northern Ireland (as the case may be) on the date on which it was so presented has, for purposes of sections 395 to 398, the same effect as the delivery and receipt of the instrument itself.

[(1) It is the duty of a company which creates a charge, or acquires property subject to a charge—

    (a) to deliver the prescribed particulars of the charge, in the prescribed form, to the registrar for registration, and

    (b) to do so within 21 days after the date of the charge's creation or, as the case may be, the date of the acquisition;

but particulars of a charge may be delivered for registration by any person interested in the charge.

(2) Where the particulars are delivered for registration by a person other than the company concerned, that person is entitled to recover from the company the amount of any fees paid by him to the registrar in connection with the registration.

(3) If a company fails to comply with subsection (1), then, unless particulars of the charge have been delivered for registration by another person, the company and every officer of it who is in default is liable to a fine.

(4) Where prescribed particulars in the prescribed form are delivered to the registrar for registration, he shall file the particulars in the register and shall note, in such form as he thinks fit, the date on which they were delivered to him.

(5)   The registrar shall send to the company and any person appearing from the particulars to be the chargee, and if the particulars were delivered by another person interested in the charge to that person, a copy of the particulars filed by him and of the note made by him as to the date on which they were delivered.]

NOTES

Part IV of the Companies Act 1989 (ss 92–107) inserts new provisions in place of original ss 395–424 of this Act, as from a day to be appointed; see s 92 of the 1989 Act.

New provision in square brackets prospectively inserted by the Companies Act 1989, s 95, as from a day to be appointed.

399 Company's duty to register charges it creates [399 Effect of failure to deliver particulars for registration]

(1)   It is a company's duty to send to the registrar of companies for registration the particulars of every charge created by the company and of the issues of debentures of a series requiring registration under sections 395 to 398; but registration of any such charge may be effected on the application of any person interested in it.

(2)   Where registration is effected on the application of some person other than the company, that person is entitled to recover from the company the amount of any fees properly paid by him to the registrar on the registration.

(3)   If a company fails to comply with subsection (1), then, unless the registration has been effected on the application of some other person, the company and every officer of it who is in default is liable to a fine and, for continued contravention, to a daily default fine.

[(1)   Where a charge is created by a company and no prescribed particulars in the prescribed form are delivered for registration within the period of 21 days after the date of the charge's creation, the charge is void against—
  (a)   an administrator or liquidator of the company, and
  (b)   any person who for value acquires an interest in or right over property subject to the charge,

where the relevant event occurs after the creation of the charge, whether before or after the end of the 21 day period.

This is subject to section 400 (late delivery of particulars).

(2)   In this Part "the relevant event" means—
  (a)   in relation to the voidness of a charge as against an administrator or liquidator, the beginning of the insolvency proceedings, and
  (b)   in relation to the voidness of a charge as against a person acquiring an interest in or right over property subject to a charge, the acquisition of that interest or right;

and references to "a relevant event" shall be construed accordingly.

(3)   Where a relevant event occurs on the same day as the charge is created, it shall be presumed to have occurred after the charge is created unless the contrary is proved.]

NOTES

Part IV of the Companies Act 1989 (ss 92–107) inserts new provisions in place of ss 395–424 of this Act, as from a day to be appointed; see s 92 of the 1989 Act.

New provision in square brackets prospectively inserted by the Companies Act 1989, s 95, as from a day to be appointed.

400 Charges existing on property acquired [400 Late delivery of particulars]

(1) This section applies where a company registered in England and Wales acquires property which is subject to a charge of any such kind as would, if it had been created by the company after the acquisition of the property, have been required to be registered under this Chapter.

(2) The company shall cause the prescribed particulars of the charge, together with a copy (certified in the prescribed manner to be a correct copy) of the instrument (if any) by which the charge was created or is evidenced, to be delivered to the registrar of companies for registration in manner required by this Chapter within 21 days after the date on which the acquisition is completed.

(3) However, if the property is situated and the charge was created outside Great Britain, 21 days after the date on which the copy of the instrument could in due course of post, and if despatched with due diligence, have been received in the United Kingdom is substituted for the 21 days above-mentioned as the time within which the particulars and copy of the instrument are to be delivered to the registrar.

(4) If default is made in complying with this section, the company and every officer of it who is in default is liable to a fine and, for continued contravention, to a daily default fine.

[(1) Where prescribed particulars of a charge created by a company, in the prescribed form, are delivered for registration more than 21 days after the date of the charge's creation, section 399(1) does not apply in relation to relevant events occurring after the particulars are delivered.

(2) However, where in such a case—
 (a) the company is at the date of delivery of the particulars unable to pay its debts, or subsequently becomes unable to pay its debts in consequence of the transaction under which the charge is created, and
 (b) insolvency proceedings begin before the end of the relevant period beginning with the date of delivery of the particulars,

the charge is void as against the administrator or liquidator.

(3) For this purpose—
 (a) the company is "unable to pay its debts" in the circumstances specified in section 123 of the Insolvency Act 1986; and
 (b) the "relevant period" is—
  (i) two years in the case of a floating charge created in favour of a person connected with the company (within the meaning of section 249 of that Act),

(ii) one year in the case of a floating charge created in favour of a person not so connected, and

(iii) six months in any other case.

(4) Where a relevant event occurs on the same day as the particulars are delivered, it shall be presumed to have occurred before the particulars are delivered unless the contrary is proved.]

NOTES

Part IV of the Companies Act 1989 (ss 92–107) inserts new provisions in place of original ss 395–424 of this Act, as from a day to be appointed; see s 92 of the 1989 Act.

New provision in square brackets prospectively inserted by the Companies Act 1989, s 95, as from a day to be appointed.

401 Register of charges to be kept by registrar of companies [401 Delivery of further particulars]

(1) The registrar of companies shall keep, with respect to each company, a register in the prescribed form of all the charges requiring registration under this Chapter; and he shall enter in the register with respect to such charges the following particulars—

(a) in the case of a charge to the benefit of which the holders of a series of debentures are entitled, the particulars specified in section 397(1),

(b) in the case of any other charge—

(i) if it is a charge created by the company, the date of its creation, and if it is a charge which was existing on property acquired by the company, the date of the acquisition of the property, and

(ii) the amount secured by the charge, and

(iii) short particulars of the property charged, and

(iv) the persons entitled to the charge.

(2) The registrar shall give a certificate of the registration of any charge registered in pursuance of this Chapter, stating the amount secured by the charge.

The certificate—

(a) shall be either signed by the registrar, or authenticated by his official seal, and

(b) is conclusive evidence that the requirements of this Chapter as to registration have been satisfied.

(3) The register kept in pursuance of this section shall be open to inspection by any person.

[(1) Further particulars of a charge, supplementing or varying the registered particulars, may be delivered to the registrar for registration at any time.

(2) Further particulars must be in the prescribed form signed by or on behalf of both the company and the chargee.

(3) Where further particulars are delivered to the registrar for registration and appear to him to be duly signed, he shall file the particulars in the register and shall note, in such form as he thinks fit, the date on which they were delivered to him.

(4) The registrar shall send to the company and any person appearing from the particulars to be the chargee, and if the particulars were delivered by another person interested in the charge to that other person, a copy of the further particulars filed by him and of the note made by him as to the date on which they were delivered.]

NOTES

Part IV of the Companies Act 1989 (ss 92–107) inserts new provisions in place of original ss 395–424 of this Act, as from a day to be appointed; see s 92 of the 1989 Act.

New provision in square brackets prospectively inserted by the Companies Act 1989, s 96, as from a day to be appointed.

402 Endorsement of certificate on debentures [402 Effect of omissions and errors in registered particulars]

(1) The company shall cause a copy of every certificate of registration given under section 401 to be endorsed on every debenture or certificate of debenture stock which is issued by the company, and the payment of which is secured by the charge so registered.

(2) But this does not require a company to cause a certificate of registration of any charge so given to be endorsed on any debenture or certificate of debenture stock issued by the company before the charge was created.

(3) If a person knowingly and wilfully authorises or permits the delivery of a debenture or certificate of debenture stock which under this section is required to have endorsed on it a copy of a certificate of registration, without the copy being so endorsed upon it, he is liable (without prejudice to any other liability) to a fine.

[(1) Where the registered particulars of a charge created by a company are not complete and accurate, the charge is void, as mentioned below, to the extent that rights are not disclosed by the registered particulars which would be disclosed if they were complete and accurate.

(2) The charge is void to that extent, unless the court on the application of the chargee orders otherwise, as against—
(a) an administrator or liquidator of the company, and
(b) any person who for value acquires an interest in or right over property subject to the charge,

where the relevant event occurs at a time when the particulars are incomplete or inaccurate in a relevant respect.

(3) Where a relevant event occurs on the same day as particulars or further particulars are delivered, it shall be presumed to have occurred before those particulars are delivered unless the contrary is proved.

(4) The court may order that the charge is effective as against an administrator or liquidator of the company if it is satisfied—
(a) that the omission or error is not likely to have misled materially to his prejudice any unsecured creditor of the company, or

(b) that no person became an unsecured creditor of the company at a time when the registered particulars of the charge were incomplete or inaccurate in a relevant respect.

(5) The court may order that the charge is effective as against a person acquiring an interest in or right over property subject to the charge if it is satisfied that he did not rely, in connection with the acquisition, on registered particulars which were incomplete or inaccurate in a relevant respect.

(6) For the purposes of this section an omission or inaccuracy with respect to the name of the chargee shall not be regarded as a failure to disclose the rights of the chargee.]

NOTES

Part IV of the Companies Act 1989 (ss 92–107) inserts new provisions in place of original ss 395–424 of this Act, as from a day to be appointed; see s 92 of the 1989 Act.

New provision in square brackets prospectively inserted by the Companies Act 1989, s 97, as from a day to be appointed.

403 Entries of satisfaction and release [403 Memorandum of charge ceasing to affect company's property]

(1) [Subject to subsection (1A), the registrar] of companies, on receipt of a statutory declaration in the prescribed form verifying, with respect to a registered charge,—

(a) *that the debt for which the charge was given has been paid or satisfied in whole or in part, or*

(b) *that part of the property or undertaking charged has been released from the charge or has ceased to form part of the company's property or undertaking,*

may enter on the register a memorandum of satisfaction in whole or in part, or of the fact that part of the property or undertaking has been released from the charge or has ceased to form part of the company's property or undertaking (as the case may be).

[(1A) The registrar of companies may make any such entry as is mentioned in subsection (1) where, instead of receiving such a statutory declaration as is mentioned in that subsection, he receives a statement by a director, secretary, administrator or administrative receiver of the company which is contained in an electronic communication and that statement—

(a) *verifies the matters set out in paragraph (a) or (b) of that subsection,*

(b) *contains a description of the charge,*

(c) *states the date of creation of the charge and the date of its registration under this Chapter,*

(d) *states the name and address of the chargee or, in the case of a debenture, trustee, and*

(e) *where paragraph (b) of subsection (1) applies, contains short particulars of the property or undertaking which has been released from the charge, or which has ceased to form part of the company's property or undertaking (as the case may be).]*

(2) Where the registrar enters a memorandum of satisfaction in whole, he shall if required furnish the company with a copy of it.

[*(2A) Any person who makes a false statement under subsection (1A) which he knows to be false or does not believe to be true is liable to imprisonment or a fine, or both.*]

[(1) Where a charge of which particulars have been delivered ceases to affect the company's property, a memorandum to that effect may be delivered to the registrar for registration.

(2) The memorandum must be in the prescribed form signed by or on behalf of both the company and the chargee.

(3) Where a memorandum is delivered to the registrar for registration and appears to him to be duly signed, he shall file it in the register, and shall note, in such form as he thinks fit, the date on which it was delivered to him.

(4) The registrar shall send to the company and any person appearing from the memorandum to be the chargee, and if the memorandum was delivered by another person interested in the charge to that person, a copy of the memorandum filed by him and of the note made by him as to the date on which it was delivered.

(5) If a duly signed memorandum is delivered in a case where the charge in fact continues to affect the company's property, the charge is void as against—
  (a) an administrator or liquidator of the company, and
  (b) any person who for value acquires an interest in or right over property subject to the charge,
where the relevant event occurs after the delivery of the memorandum.

(6) Where a relevant event occurs on the same day as the memorandum is delivered, it shall be presumed to have occurred before the memorandum is delivered unless the contrary is proved.]

NOTES

Part IV of the Companies Act 1989 (ss 92–107) inserts new provisions in place of original ss 395–424 of this Act, as from a day to be appointed; see s 92 of the 1989 Act.

New provision in square brackets prospectively inserted by the Companies Act 1989, s 98, as from a day to be appointed.

Sub-s (1): words "Subject to subsection (1A), the registrar" in square brackets substituted by SI 2000/3373, art 22(1), (2).

Date in force: 22 December 2000: see SI 2000/3373, art 1(1).

Sub-s (1A): inserted by SI 2000/3373, art 22(1), (3).

Date in force: 22 December 2000: see SI 2000/3373, art 1(1).

Sub-s (2A): inserted by SI 2000/3373, art 22(1), (4).

Date in force: 22 December 2000: see SI 2000/3373, art 1(1).

[Further provisions with respect to voidness of charges]

NOTES

Prospectively inserted by the Companies Act 1989, s 99, as from a day to be appointed.

404 Rectification of register of charges [404 Exclusion of voidness as against unregistered charges]

(1) The following applies if the court is satisfied that the omission to register a charge within the time required by this Chapter or that the omission or mis-statement of any particular with respect to any such charge or in a memorandum of satisfaction was accidental, or due to inadvertence or to some other sufficient cause, or is not of a nature to prejudice the position of creditors or shareholders of the company, or that on other grounds it is just and equitable to grant relief.

(2) The court may, on the application of the company or a person interested, and on such terms and conditions as seem to the court just and expedient, order that the time for registration shall be extended or, as the case may be, that the omission or mis-statement shall be rectified.

[(1)   A charge is not void by virtue of this Part as against a subsequent charge unless some or all of the relevant particulars of that charge are duly delivered for registration—

    (a)   within 21 days after the date of its creation, or

    (b)   before complete and accurate relevant particulars of the earlier charge are duly delivered for registration.

(2)   Where relevant particulars of the subsequent charge so delivered are incomplete or inaccurate, the earlier charge is void as against that charge only to the extent that rights are disclosed by registered particulars of the subsequent charge duly delivered for registration before the corresponding relevant particulars of the earlier charge.

(3)   The relevant particulars of a charge for the purposes of this section are those prescribed particulars relating to rights inconsistent with those conferred by or in relation to the other charge.]

NOTES

Part IV of the Companies Act 1989 (ss 92–107) inserts new provisions in place of original ss 395–424 of this Act, as from a day to be appointed; see s 92 of the 1989 Act.

New provision in square brackets prospectively inserted by the Companies Act 1989, s 99, as from a day to be appointed.

405 Registration of enforcement of security [405 Restrictions on voidness by virtue of this Part]

(1) If a person obtains an order for the appointment of a receiver or manager of a company's property, or appoints such a receiver or manager under powers contained in an instrument, he shall within 7 days of the order or of the appointment under those powers, give notice of the fact to the registrar of companies; and the registrar shall enter the fact in the register of charges.

(2) Where a person appointed receiver or manager of a company's property under powers contained in an instrument ceases to act as such receiver or manager, he shall, on so ceasing, give the registrar notice to that effect, and the registrar shall enter the fact in the register of charges.

(3) A notice under this section shall be in the prescribed form.

(4) If a person makes default in complying with the requirements of this section, he is liable to a fine and, for continued contravention, to a daily default fine.

[(1) A charge is not void by virtue of this Part as against a person acquiring an interest in or right over property where the acquisition is expressly subject to the charge.

(2) Nor is a charge void by virtue of this Part in relation to any property by reason of a relevant event occurring after the company which created the charge has disposed of the whole of its interest in that property.]

NOTES

Part IV of the Companies Act 1989 (ss 92–107) inserts new provisions in place of original ss 395–424 of this Act, as from a day to be appointed; see s 92 of the 1989 Act.

New provision in square brackets prospectively inserted by the Companies Act 1989, s 99, as from a day to be appointed.

406 Companies to keep copies of instruments creating charges [406 Effect of exercise of power of sale]

(1) Every company shall cause a copy of every instrument creating a charge requiring registration under this Chapter to be kept at its registered office.

(2) In the case of a series of uniform debentures, a copy of one debenture of the series is sufficient.

[(1) A chargee exercising a power of sale may dispose of property to a purchaser freed from any interest or right arising from the charge having become void to any extent by virtue of this Part—
   (a) against an administrator or liquidator of the company, or
   (b) against a person acquiring a security interest over property subject to the charge;

and a purchaser is not concerned to see or inquire whether the charge has become so void.

(2) The proceeds of the sale shall be held by the chargee in trust to be applied—
   First, in discharge of any sum effectively secured by prior incumbrances to which the sale is not made subject;
   Second, in payment of all costs, charges and expenses properly incurred by him in connection with the sale, or any previous attempted sale, of the property;
   Third, in discharge of any sum effectively secured by the charge and incumbrances ranking *pari passu* with the charge;
   Fourth, in discharge of any sum effectively secured by incumbrances ranking after the charge;

and any residue is payable to the company or to a person authorised to give a receipt for the proceeds of the sale of the property.

(3) For the purposes of subsection (2)—
   (a) prior incumbrances include any incumbrance to the extent that the charge is void as against it by virtue of this Part; and

(b) no sum is effectively secured by a charge to the extent that it is void as against an administrator or liquidator of the company.

(4) In this section—

(a) references to things done by a chargee include things done by a receiver appointed by him, whether or not the receiver acts as his agent;

(b) "power of sale" includes any power to dispose of, or grant an interest out of, property for the purpose of enforcing a charge (but in relation to Scotland does not include the power to grant a lease), and references to "sale" shall be construed accordingly; and

(c) "purchaser" means a person who in good faith and for valuable consideration acquires an interest in property.

(5) The provisions of this section as to the order of application of the proceeds of sale have effect subject to any other statutory provision (in Scotland, any other statutory provision or rule of law) applicable in any case.

(6) Where a chargee exercising a power of sale purports to dispose of property freed from any such interest or right as is mentioned in subsection (1) to a person other than a purchaser, the above provisions apply, with any necessary modifications, in relation to a disposition to a purchaser by that person or any successor in title of his.

(7) In Scotland, subsections (2) and (7) of section 27 of the Conveyancing and Feudal Reform (Scotland) Act 1970 apply to a chargee unable to obtain a discharge for any payment which he is required to make under subsection (2) above as they apply to a creditor in the circumstances mentioned in those subsections.]

NOTES

Part IV of the Companies Act 1989 (ss 92–107) inserts new provisions in place of original ss 395–424 of this Act, as from a day to be appointed; see s 92 of the 1989 Act.

New provision in square brackets prospectively inserted by the Companies Act 1989, s 99, as from a day to be appointed.

407 Company's register of charges [407 Effect of voidness on obligation secured]

(1) Every limited company shall keep at its registered office a register of charges and enter in it all charges specifically affecting property of the company and all floating charges on the company's undertaking or any of its property.

(2) The entry shall in each case give a short description of the property charged, the amount of the charge and, except in the case of securities to bearer, the names of the persons entitled to it.

(3) If an officer of the company knowingly and wilfully authorises or permits the omission of an entry required to be made in pursuance of this section, he is liable to a fine.

[(1) Where a charge becomes void to any extent by virtue of this Part, the whole of the sum secured by the charge is payable forthwith on demand; and this applies notwithstanding that the sum secured by the charge is also the subject of other security.

(2) Where the charge is to secure the repayment of money, the references in subsection (1) to the sum secured include any interest payable.]

NOTES

Part IV of the Companies Act 1989 (ss 92–107) inserts new provisions in place of original ss 395–424 of this Act, as from a day to be appointed; see s 92 of the 1989 Act.

New provision in square brackets prospectively inserted by the Companies Act 1989, s 99, as from a day to be appointed.

[Additional information to be registered]

NOTES

Prospectively inserted by the Companies Act 1989, s 100, as from a day to be appointed.

408 Right to inspect instruments which create charges, etc
[408 Particulars of taking up of issue of debentures]

(1) The copies of instruments creating any charge requiring registration under this Chapter with the registrar of companies, and the register of charges kept in pursuance of section 407, shall be open during business hours (but subject to such reasonable restrictions as the company in general meeting may impose, so that not less than 2 hours in each day be allowed for inspection) to the inspection of any creditor or member of the company without fee.

(2) The register of charges shall also be open to the inspection of any other person on payment of such fee, not exceeding 5 pence, for each inspection, as the company may prescribe.

(3) If inspection of the copies referred to, or of the register, is refused, every officer of the company who is in default is liable to a fine and, for continued contravention, to a daily default fine.

(4) If such a refusal occurs in relation to a company registered in England and Wales, the court may by order compel an immediate inspection of the copies or register.

[(1) Where particulars of a charge for securing an issue of debentures have been delivered for registration, it is the duty of the company—
  (a) to deliver to the registrar for registration particulars in the prescribed form of the date on which any debentures of the issue are taken up, and of the amount taken up, and
  (b) to do so before the end of the period of 21 days after the date on which they are taken up.

(2) Where particulars in the prescribed form are delivered to the registrar for registration under this section, he shall file them in the register.

(3) If a company fails to comply with subsection (1), the company and every officer of it who is in default is liable to a fine.]

NOTES

Part IV of the Companies Act 1989 (ss 92–107) inserts new provisions in place of original ss 395–424 of this Act, as from a day to be appointed; see s 92 of the 1989 Act.

New provision in square brackets prospectively inserted by the Companies Act 1989, s 100, as from a day to be appointed.

PART XIII
ARRANGEMENTS AND RECONSTRUCTIONS

425 Power of company to compromise with creditors and members

(1) Where a compromise or arrangement is proposed between a company and its creditors, or any class of them, or between the company and its members, or any class of them, the court may on the application of the company or any creditor or member of it, or in the case of a company being wound up [or an administration order being in force in relation to a company, of the liquidator or administrator], order a meeting of the creditors or class of creditors, or of the members of the company or class of members (as the case may be), to be summoned in such manner as the court directs.

(2) If a majority in number representing three-fourths in value of the creditors or class of creditors or members or class of members (as the case may be), present and voting either in person or by proxy at the meeting, agree to any compromise or arrangement, the compromise or arrangement, if sanctioned by the court, is binding on all creditors or the class of creditors or on the members or class of members (as the case may be), and also on the company or, in the case of a company in the course of being wound up, on the liquidator and contributories of the company.

(3) The court's order under subsection (2) has no effect until an office copy of it has been delivered to the registrar of companies for registration; and a copy of every such order shall be annexed to every copy of the company's memorandum issued after the order has been made or, in the case of a company not having a memorandum, of every copy so issued of the instrument constituting the company or defining its constitution.

(4) If a company makes default in complying with subsection (3), the company and every officer of it who is in default is liable to a fine.

(5) An order under subsection (1) pronounced in Scotland by the judge acting as vacation judge in pursuance of section 4 of the Administration of Justice (Scotland) Act 1933 is not subject to review, reduction, suspension or stay of execution.

(6) In this section and the next—
  (a) "company" means any company liable to be wound up under this Act, and
  (b) "arrangement" includes a reorganisation of the company's share capital by the consolidation of shares of different classes or by the division of shares into shares of different classes, or by both of those methods.

Sub-s (1): words in square brackets substituted by the Insolvency Act 1985, s 109, Sch 6, para 11.

426 Information as to compromise to be circulated

(1) The following applies where a meeting of creditors or any class of creditors, or of members or any class of members, is summoned under section 425.

(2) With every notice summoning the meeting which is sent to a creditor or member there shall be sent also a statement explaining the effect of the compromise or arrangement and in particular stating any material interests of the directors of the company (whether as directors or as members or as creditors of the company or otherwise) and the effect on those interests of the compromise or arrangement, in so far as it is different from the effect on the like interests of other persons.

(3) In every notice summoning the meeting which is given by advertisement there shall be included either such a statement as above-mentioned or a notification of the place at which, and the manner in which, creditors or members entitled to attend the meeting may obtain copies of the statement.

(4) Where the compromise or arrangement affects the rights of debenture holders of the company, the statement shall give the like explanation as respects the trustees of any deed for securing the issue of the debentures as it is required to give as respects the company's directors.

(5) Where a notice given by advertisement includes a notification that copies of a statement explaining the effect of the compromise or arrangement proposed can be obtained by creditors or members entitled to attend the meeting, every such creditor or member shall, on making application in the manner indicated by the notice, be furnished by the company free of charge with a copy of the statement.

(6) If a company makes default in complying with any requirement of this section, the company and every officer of it who is in default is liable to a fine; and for this purpose a liquidator [or administrator] of the company and a trustee of a deed for securing the issue of debentures of the company is deemed an officer of it.

However, a person is not liable under this subsection if he shows that the default was due to the refusal of another person, being a director or trustee for debenture holders, to supply the necessary particulars of his interests.

(7) It is the duty of any director of the company, and of any trustee for its debenture holders, to give notice to the company of such matters relating to himself as may be necessary for purposes of this section; and any person who makes default in complying with this subsection is liable to a fine.

Sub-s (6): words in square brackets inserted by the Insolvency Act 1985, s 109, Sch 6, para 12.

427 Provisions for facilitating company reconstruction or amalgamation

(1) The following applies where application is made to the court under section 425 for the sanctioning of a compromise or arrangement proposed between a company and any such persons as are mentioned in that section.

(2) If it is shown—

  (a) that the compromise or arrangement has been proposed for the purposes of, or in connection with, a scheme for the reconstruction of any company or companies, or the amalgamation of any two or more companies, and

  (b) that under the scheme the whole or any part of the undertaking or the property of any company concerned in the scheme ("a transferor company") is to be transferred to another company ("the transferee company"),

the court may, either by the order sanctioning the compromise or arrangement or by any subsequent order, make provision for all or any of the following matters.

(3) The matters for which the court's order may make provision are—

  (a) the transfer to the transferee company of the whole or any part of the undertaking and of the property or liabilities of any transferor company,

  (b) the allotting or appropriation by the transferee company of any shares, debentures, policies or other like interests in that company which under the compromise or arrangement are to be allotted or appropriated by that company to or for any person,

  (c) the continuation by or against the transferee company of any legal proceedings pending by or against any transferor company,

  (d) the dissolution, without winding up, of any transferor company,

  (e) the provision to be made for any persons who, within such time and in such manner as the court directs, dissent from the compromise or arrangement,

  (f) such incidental, consequential and supplemental matters as are necessary to secure that the reconstruction or amalgamation is fully and effectively carried out.

(4) If an order under this section provides for the transfer of property or liabilities, then—

  (a) that property is by virtue of the order transferred to, and vests in, the transferee company, and

  (b) those liabilities are, by virtue of the order, transferred to and become liabilities of that company;

and property (if the order so directs) vests freed from any charge which is by virtue of the compromise or arrangement to cease to have effect.

(5) Where an order is made under this section, every company in relation to which the order is made shall cause an office copy of the order to be delivered to the registrar of companies for registration within 7 days after its making; and if default is made in complying with this subsection, the company and every officer of it who is in default is liable to a fine and, for continued contravention, to a daily default fine.

(6) In this section the expression "property" includes property, rights and powers of every description; the expression "liabilities" includes duties and "company" includes only a company as defined in section 735(1).

[427A Application of ss 425–427 to mergers and divisions of public companies]

[(1) Where—
  (a) a compromise or arrangement is proposed between a public company and any such persons as are mentioned in section 425(1) for the purposes of, or in connection with, a scheme for the reconstruction of any company or companies or the amalgamation of any two or more companies,
  (b) the circumstances are as specified in any of the Cases described in subsection (2), and
  (c) the consideration for the transfer or each of the transfers envisaged in the Case in question is to be shares in the transferee company or any of the transferee companies receivable by members of the transferor company or transferor companies, with or without any cash payment to members,

sections 425 to 427 shall, as regards that compromise or arrangement, have effect subject to the provisions of this section and Schedule [15B].

(2) The Cases referred to in subsection (1) are as follows—

Case 1

Where under the scheme the undertaking, property and liabilities of the company in respect of which the compromise or arrangement in question is proposed are to be transferred to another public company, other than one formed for the purpose of, or in connection with, the scheme.

Case 2

Where under the scheme the undertaking, property and liabilities of each of two or more public companies concerned in the scheme, including the company in respect of which the compromise or arrangement in question is proposed, are to be transferred to a company (whether or not a public company) formed for the purpose of, or in connection with, the scheme.

Case 3

Where under the scheme the undertaking, property and liabilities of the company in respect of which the compromise or arrangement in question is proposed are to be divided among and transferred to two or more companies each of which is either—
  (a) a public company, or
  (b) a company (whether or not a public company) formed for the purposes of, or in connection with, the scheme.

(3) Before sanctioning any compromise or arrangement under section 425(2) the court may, on the application of any pre-existing transferee company or any member or creditor of it or, an administration order being in force in relation to the company, the administrator, order a meeting of the members of the company or any class of

them or of the creditors of the company or any class of them to be summoned in such manner as the court directs.

(4) This section does not apply where the company in respect of which the compromise or arrangement is proposed is being wound up.

(5) This section does not apply to compromises or arrangements in respect of which an application has been made to the court for an order under section 425(1) before 1st January 1988.

(6) Where section 427 would apply in the case of a scheme but for the fact that the transferee company or any of the transferee companies is a company within the meaning of Article 3 of the Companies (Northern Ireland) Order 1986 (and thus not within the definition of "company" in subsection (6) of section 427), section 427 shall apply notwithstanding that fact.

(7) In the case of a scheme mentioned in subsection (1), for a company within the meaning of Article 3 of the Companies (Northern Ireland) Order 1986, the reference in section 427(5) to the registrar of companies shall have effect as a reference to the registrar as defined in Article 2 of that Order.

(8) In this section and Schedule [15B]—
   "transferor company" means a company whose undertaking, property and liabilities are to be transferred by means of a transfer envisaged in any of the Cases specified in subsection (2);
   "transferee company" means a company to which a transfer envisaged in any of those Cases is to be made;
   "pre-existing transferee company" means a transferee company other than one formed for the purpose of, or in connection with, the scheme;
   "compromise or arrangement" means a compromise or arrangement to which subsection (1) applies;
   "the scheme" means the scheme mentioned in subsection (1)(a);
   "company" includes only a company as defined in section 735(1) except that, in the case of a transferee company, it also includes a company as defined in Article 3 of the Companies (Northern Ireland) Order 1986 (referred to in these definitions as a "Northern Ireland company");
   "public company" means, in relation to a transferee company which is a Northern Ireland company, a public company within the meaning of article 12 of the Companies (Northern Ireland) Order 1986;
   "the registrar of companies" means, in relation to a transferee company which is a Northern Ireland company, the registrar as defined in Article 2 of the Companies (Northern Ireland) Order 1986;
   "the Gazette" means, in relation to a transferee company which is a Northern Ireland company, the Belfast Gazette;
   "Case 1 Scheme", "Case 2 Scheme" and "Case 3 Scheme" mean a scheme of the kind described in Cases 1, 2 and 3 of subsection (2) respectively;
   "property" and "liabilities" have the same meaning as in section 427.]

NOTES
Inserted by SI 1987/1991, reg 2, Schedule.
Sub-ss (1), (8): figures in square brackets substituted by the Companies Act 1989, s 114(2).

[PART XIIIA
TAKEOVER OFFERS]

NOTES

Inserted by the Financial Services Act 1986, s 172, Sch 12.

[428 "Takeover offers"]

[(1)   In this Part of this Act "a takeover offer" means an offer to acquire all the shares, or all the shares of any class or classes, in a company (other than shares which at the date of the offer are already held by the offeror), being an offer on terms which are the same in relation to all the shares to which the offer relates or, where those shares include shares of different classes, in relation to all the shares of each class.

(2)   In subsection (1) "shares" means shares which have been allotted on the date of the offer but a takeover offer may include among the shares to which it relates all or any shares that are subsequently allotted before a date specified in or determined in accordance with the terms of the offer.

(3)   The terms offered in relation to any shares shall for the purposes of this section be treated as being the same in relation to all the shares or, as the case may be, all the shares of a class to which the offer relates notwithstanding any variation permitted by subsection (4).

(4)   A variation is permitted by this subsection where—
  (a)   the law of a country or territory outside the United Kingdom precludes an offer of consideration in the form or any of the forms specified in the terms in question or precludes it except after compliance by the offeror with conditions with which he is unable to comply or which he regards as unduly onerous; and
  (b)   the variation is such that the persons to whom an offer of consideration in that form is precluded are able to receive consideration otherwise than in that form but of substantially equivalent value.

(5)   The reference in subsection (1) to shares already held by the offeror includes a reference to shares which he has contracted to acquire but that shall not be construed as including shares which are the subject of a contract binding the holder to accept the offer when it is made, being a contract entered into by the holder either for no consideration and under seal or for no consideration other than a promise by the offeror to make the offer.

(6)   In the application of subsection (5) to Scotland, the words "and under seal" shall be omitted.

(7)   Where the terms of an offer make provision for their revision and for acceptances on the previous terms to be treated as acceptances on the revised terms, the revision shall not be regarded for the purposes of this Part of this Act as the making of a fresh offer and references in this Part of this Act to the date of the offer shall accordingly be construed as references to the date on which the original offer was made.

(8)   In this Part of this Act "the offeror" means, subject to section 430D, the person making a takeover offer and "the company" means the company whose shares are the subject of the offer.]

NOTES

Substituted, together with ss 429–430F, for original ss 428–430, by the Financial Services Act 1986, s 172, Sch 12.

[429 Right of offeror to buy out minority shareholders]

[(1)   If, in a case in which a takeover offer does not relate to shares of different classes, the offeror has by virtue of acceptances of the offer acquired or contracted to acquire not less than nine-tenths in value of the shares to which the offer relates he may give notice to the holder of any shares to which the offer relates which the offeror has not acquired or contracted to acquire that he desires to acquire those shares.

(2)   If, in a case in which a takeover offer relates to shares of different classes, the offeror has by virtue of acceptances of the offer acquired or contracted to acquire not less than nine-tenths in value of the shares of any class to which the offer relates, he may give notice to the holder of any shares of that class which the offeror has not acquired or contracted to acquire that he desires to acquire those shares.

(3)   No notice shall be given under subsection (1) or (2) unless the offeror has acquired or contracted to acquire the shares necessary to satisfy the minimum specified in that subsection before the end of the period of four months beginning with the date of the offer; and no such notice shall be given after the end of the period of two months beginning with the date on which he has acquired or contracted to acquire shares which satisfy that minimum.

(4)   Any notice under this section shall be given in the prescribed manner; and when the offeror gives the first notice in relation to an offer he shall send a copy of it to the company together with a statutory declaration by him in the prescribed form stating that the conditions for the giving of the notice are satisfied.

(5)   Where the offeror is a company (whether or not a company within the meaning of this Act) the statutory declaration shall be signed by a director.

(6)   Any person who fails to send a copy of a notice or a statutory declaration as required by subsection (4) or makes such a declaration for the purposes of that subsection knowing it to be false or without having reasonable grounds for believing it to be true shall be liable to imprisonment or a fine, or both, and for continued failure to send the copy or declaration, to a daily default fine.

(7)   If any person is charged with an offence for failing to send a copy of a notice as required by subsection (4) it is a defence for him to prove that he took reasonable steps for securing compliance with that subsection.

(8)   Where during the period within which a takeover offer can be accepted the offeror acquires or contracts to acquire any of the shares to which the offer relates but otherwise than by virtue of acceptances of the offer, then, if—

(a) the value of the consideration for which they are acquired or contracted to be acquired ("the acquisition consideration") does not at that time exceed the value of the consideration specified in the terms of the offer; or

(b) those terms are subsequently revised so that when the revision is announced the value of the acquisition consideration, at the time mentioned in paragraph (a) above, no longer exceeds the value of the consideration specified in those terms,

the offeror shall be treated for the purposes of this section as having acquired or contracted to acquire those shares by virtue of acceptances of the offer; but in any other case those shares shall be treated as excluded from those to which the offer relates.]

NOTES

Substituted, together with ss 428, 430–430F, for original ss 428–430, by the Financial Services Act 1986, s 172, Sch 12.

[430 Effect of notice under s 429]

[(1) The following provisions shall, subject to section 430C, have effect where a notice is given in respect of any shares under section 429.

(2) The offeror shall be entitled and bound to acquire those shares on the terms of the offer.

(3) Where the terms of an offer are such as to give the holder of any shares a choice of consideration the notice shall give particulars of the choice and state—

(a) that the holder of the shares may within six weeks from the date of the notice indicate his choice by a written communication sent to the offeror at an address specified in the notice; and

(b) which consideration specified in the offer is to be taken as applying in default of his indicating a choice as aforesaid;

and the terms of the offer mentioned in subsection (2) shall be determined accordingly.

(4) Subsection (3) applies whether or not any time-limit or other conditions applicable to the choice under the terms of the offer can still be complied with; and if the consideration chosen by the holder of the shares—

(a) is not cash and the offeror is no longer able to provide it;

(b) was to have been provided by a third party who is no longer bound or able to provide it,

the consideration shall be taken to consist of an amount of cash payable by the offeror which at the date of the notice is equivalent to the chosen consideration.

(5) At the end of six weeks from the date of the notice the offeror shall forthwith—

(a) send a copy of the notice to the company; and

(b) pay or transfer to the company the consideration for the shares to which the notice relates.

(6) If the shares to which the notice relates are registered the copy of the notice sent to the company under subsection (5)(a) shall be accompanied by an instrument of transfer executed on behalf of the shareholder by a person appointed by the offeror; and on receipt of that instrument the company shall register the offeror as the holder of those shares.

(7) If the shares to which the notice relates are transferable by the delivery of warrants or other instruments the copy of the notice sent to the company under subsection (5)(a) shall be accompanied by a statement to that effect; and the company shall on receipt of the statement issue the offeror with warrants or other instruments in respect of the shares and those already in issue in receipt of the shares shall become void.

(8) Where the consideration referred to in paragraph (b) of subsection (5) consists of shares or securities to be allotted by the offeror the reference in that paragraph to the transfer of the consideration shall be construed as a reference to the allotment of the shares or securities to the company.

(9) Any sum received by a company under paragraph (b) of subsection (5) and any other consideration received under that paragraph shall be held by the company on trust for the person entitled to the shares in respect of which the sum or other consideration was received.

(10) Any sum received by a company under paragraph (e) of subsection (5), and any dividend or other sum accruing from any other consideration received by a company under that paragraph, shall be paid into a separate bank account, being an account the balance on which bears interest at an appropriate rate and can be withdrawn by such notice (if any) as is appropriate.

(11) Where after reasonable enquiry made at such intervals as are reasonable the person entitled to any consideration held on trust by virtue of subsection (9) cannot be found and twelve years have elapsed since the consideration was received or the company is wound up the consideration (together with any interest, dividend or other benefit that has accrued from it) shall be paid into court.

(12) In relation to a company registered in Scotland, subsections (13) and (14) shall apply in place of subsection (11).

(13) Where after reasonable enquiry made at such intervals as are reasonable the person entitled to any consideration held on trust by virtue of subsection (9) cannot be found and twelve years have elapsed since the consideration was received or the company is wound up—

    (a) the trust shall terminate;

    (b) the company or, as the case may be, the liquidator shall sell any consideration other than cash and any benefit other than cash that has accrued from the consideration; and

    (c) a sum representing—

        (i) the consideration so far as it is cash;

        (ii) the proceeds of any sale under paragraph (b) above; and

        (iii) any interest, dividend or other benefit that has accrued from the consideration,

    shall be deposited in the name of the Accountant of Court in a bank account such as is referred to in subsection (10) and the receipt for the deposit shall be transmitted to the Account of Court.

(14)   Section 58 of the Bankruptcy (Scotland) Act 1985 (so far as consistent with this Act) shall apply with any necessary modifications to sums deposited under subsection (13) as that section applies to sums deposited under section 57(1)(a) of that Act.

(15)   The expenses of any such enquiry as is mentioned in subsection (11) or (13) may be defrayed out of the money or other property held on trust for the person or persons to whom the enquiry relates.]

NOTES

Substituted, together with ss 428, 429, 430A–430F, for original ss 428–430, by the Financial Services Act 1986, s 172, Sch 12.

[430A Right of minority shareholder to be bought out by offeror]

[(1)   If a takeover offer relates to all the shares in a company and at any time before the end of the period within which the offer can be accepted—

    (a) the offeror has by virtue of acceptances of the offer acquired or contracted to acquire some (but not all) of the shares to which the offer relates; and

    (b) those shares, with or without any other shares in the company which he has acquired or contracted to acquire, amount to not less than nine-tenths in value of all the shares in the company,

the holder of any shares to which the offer relates who has not accepted the offer may by a written communication addressed to the offeror require him to acquire those shares.

(2)   If a takeover offer relates to shares of any class or classes and at any time before the end of the period within which the offer can be accepted—

    (a) the offeror has by virtue of acceptances of the offer required or contracted to acquire some (but not all) of the shares of any class to which the offer relates; and

    (b) those shares, with or without any other shares of that class which he has acquired or contracted to acquire, amount to not less than nine-tenths in value of all the shares of that class,

the holder of any shares of that class who has not accepted the offer may by a written communication addressed to the offeror require him to acquire those shares.

(3)   Within one month of the time specified in subsection (1) or, as the case may be, subsection (2) the offeror shall give any shareholder who has not accepted the offer notice in the prescribed manner of the rights that are exercisable by him under that subsection; and if the notice is given before the end of the period mentioned in that subsection it shall state that the offer is still open for acceptance.

(4)   A notice under subsection (3) may specify a period for the exercise of the rights conferred by this section and in that event the rights shall not be exercisable after the end of that period; but no such period shall end less than three months after the end of the period within which the offer can be accepted.

(5)　Subsection (3) does not apply if the offeror has given the shareholder a notice in respect of the shares in question under section 429.

(6)　If the offeror fails to comply with subsection (3) he and, if the offeror is a company, every officer of the company who is in default or to whose neglect the failure is attributable, shall be liable to a fine and, for continued contravention, to a daily default fine.

(7)　If an offeror other than a company is charged with an offence for failing to comply with subsection (3) it is a defence for him to prove that he took all reasonable steps for securing compliance with that subsection.]

NOTES

Substituted, together with ss 428–430, 430B–430F, for original ss 428–430, by the Financial Services Act 1986, s 172, Sch 12.

[430B　Effect of requirement under s 430A]

[(1)　The following provisions shall, subject to section 430C, have effect where a shareholder exercises his rights in respect of any shares under section 430A.

(2)　The offeror shall be entitled and bound to acquire those shares on the terms of the offer or on such other terms as may be agreed.

(3)　Where the terms of an offer are such as to give the holder of shares a choice of consideration the holder of the shares may indicate his choice when requiring the offeror to acquire them and the notice given to the holder under section 430A(3)—

    (a)　shall give particulars of the choice and of the rights conferred by this subsection; and

    (b)　may state which consideration specified in the offer is to be taken as applying in default of his indicating a choice;

and the terms of the offer mentioned in subsection (2) shall be determined accordingly.

(4)　Subsection (3) applies whether or not any time-limit or other conditions applicable to the choice under the terms of the offer can still be complied with; and if the consideration chosen by the holder of the shares—

    (a)　is not cash and the offeror is no longer able to provide it; or

    (b)　was to have been provided by a third party who is no longer bound or able to provide it,

the consideration shall be taken to consist of an amount of cash payable by the offeror which at the date when the holder of the shares requires the offeror to acquire them is equivalent to the chosen consideration.]

NOTES

Substituted, together with ss 428–430A, 430C–430F, for original ss 428–430, by the Financial Services Act 1986, s 172, Sch 12.

[430C Applications to the court]

[(1)   Where a notice is given under section 429 to the holder of any shares the court may, on an application made by him within six weeks from the date on which the notice was given—
  (a)   order that the offeror shall not be entitled and bound to acquire the shares; or
  (b)   specify terms of acquisition different from those of the offer.

(2)   If an application to the court under subsection (1) is pending at the end of the period mentioned in subsection (5) of section 430 that subsection shall not have effect until the application has been disposed of.

(3)   Where the holder of any shares exercises his rights under section 430A the court may, on an application made by him or the offeror, order that the terms on which the offeror is entitled and bound to acquire the shares shall be such as the court thinks fit.

(4)   No order for costs or expenses shall be made against a shareholder making an application under subsection (1) or (3) unless the court considers—
  (a)   that the application was unnecessary, improper or vexatious; or
  (b)   that there has been unreasonable delay in making the application or unreasonable conduct on his part in conducting the proceedings on the application.

(5)   Where a takeover offer has not been accepted to the extent necessary for entitling the offeror to give notices under subsection (1) or (2) of section 429 the court may, on the application of the offeror, make an order authorising him to give notices under that subsection if satisfied—
  (a)   that the offeror has after reasonable enquiry been unable to trace one or more of the persons holding shares to which the offer relates;
  (b)   that the shares which the offeror has acquired or contracted to acquire by virtue of acceptances of the offer, together with the shares held by the person or persons mentioned in paragraph (a), amount to not less than the minimum specified in that subsection; and
  (c)   that the consideration offered is fair and reasonable;
but the court shall not make an order under this subsection unless it considers that it is just and equitable to do so having regard, in particular, to the number of shareholders who have been traced but who have not accepted the offer.]

NOTES

Substituted, together with ss 428–430B, 430D–430F, for original ss 428–430, by the Financial Services Act 1986, s 172, Sch 12.

[430D Joint offers]

[(1)   A takeover offer may be made by two or more persons jointly and in that event this Part of this Act has effect with the following modifications.

(2)   The conditions for the exercise of the rights conferred by sections 429 and 430A shall be satisfied by the joint offerors acquiring or contracting to acquire the necessary shares jointly (as respects acquisitions by virtue of acceptances of the

offer) and either jointly or separately (in other cases); and, subject to the following provisions, the rights and obligations of the offeror under those sections and sections 430 and 430B shall be respectively joint rights and joint and several obligations of the joint offerors.

(3)   It shall be a sufficient compliance with any provision of those sections requiring or authorising a notice or other document to be given or sent by or to the joint offerors that it is given or sent by or to any of them; but the statutory declaration required by section 429(4) shall be made by all of them and, in the case of a joint offeror being a company, signed by a director of that company.

(4)   in sections 428, 430(8) and 430E references to the offeror shall be construed as references to the joint offerors or any of them.

(5)   In section 430(6) and (7) references to the offeror shall be construed as references to the joint offerors or such of them as they may determine.

(6)   In sections 430(4)(a) and 430B(4)(a) references to the offeror being no longer able to provide the relevant consideration shall be construed as references to none of the joint offerors being able to do so.

(7)   In section 430C references to the offeror shall be construed as references to the joint offerors except that any application under subsection (3) or (5) may be made by any of them and the reference in subsection (5)(a) to the offeror having been unable to trace one or more of the persons holding shares shall be construed as a reference to none of the offerors having been able to do so.]

NOTES

   Substituted, together with ss 428–430C, 430E, 430F, for original ss 428–430, by the Financial Services Act 1986, s 172, Sch 12.

[430E Associates]

[(1)   The requirement in section 428(1) that a takeover offer must extend to all the shares, or all the shares of any class or classes, in a company shall be regarded as satisfied notwithstanding that the offer does not extend to shares which associates of the offeror hold or have contracted to acquire; but, subject to subsection (2), shares which any such associate holds or has contracted to acquire, whether at the time when the offer is made or subsequently, shall be disregarded for the purposes of any reference in this Part of this Act to the shares to which a takeover offer relates.

(2)   Where during the period within which a takeover offer can be accepted any associate of the offeror acquires or contracts to acquire any of the shares to which the offer relates, then, if the condition specified in subsection (8)(a) or (b) of section 429 is satisfied as respects those shares they shall be treated for the purposes of that section as shares to which the offer relates.

(3)   In section 430A(1)(b) and (2)(b) the reference to shares which the offeror has acquired or contracted to acquire shall include a reference to shares which any associate of his has acquired or contracted to acquire.

(4)   In this section "associate", in relation to an offeror means—
   (a)   a nominee of the offeror;

(b) a holding company, subsidiary or fellow subsidiary of the offeror or a nominee of such a holding company, subsidiary or fellow subsidiary;

(c) a body corporate in which the offeror is substantially interested; or

(d) any person who is, or is a nominee of, a party to an agreement with the offeror for the acquisition of, or of an interest in, the shares which are the subject of the takeover offer, being an agreement which includes provisions imposing obligations or restrictions such as are mentioned in section 204(2)(a).

(5) For the purposes of subsection (4)(b) a company is a fellow subsidiary of another body corporate if both are subsidiaries of the same body corporate but neither is a subsidiary of the other.

(6) For the purposes of subsection (4)(c) an offeror has a substantial interest in a body corporate if—

(a) that body or its directors are accustomed to act in accordance with his directions or instructions; or

(b) he is entitled to exercise or control the exercise of one-third or more of the voting power at general meetings of that body.

(7) Subsections (5) and (6) of section 204 shall apply to subsection (4)(d) above as they apply to that section and subsections (3) and (4) of section 203 shall apply for the purposes of subsection (6) above as they apply for the purposes of subsection (2)(b) of that section.

(8) Where the offeror is an individual his associates shall also include his spouse and any minor child or step-child of his.]

NOTES

Substituted, together with ss 428–430D, 430F, for original ss 428–430, by the Financial Services Act 1986, s 172, Sch 12.

[430F Convertible securities]

[(1) For the purposes of this Part of this Act securities of a company shall be treated as shares in the company if they are convertible into or entitle the holder to subscribe for such shares; and references to the holder of shares or a shareholder shall be construed accordingly.

(2) Subsection (1) shall not be construed as requiring any securities to be treated—

(a) as shares of the same class as those into which they are convertible or for which the holder is entitled to subscribe; or

(b) as shares of the same class as other securities by reason only that the shares into which they are convertible or for which the holder is entitled to subscribe are of the same class.]

NOTES

Substituted, together with ss 428–430A–430E, for original ss 428–430, by the Financial Services Act 1986, s 172, Sch 12.

PART XIV
INVESTIGATION OF COMPANIES AND THEIR AFFAIRS; REQUISITION OF DOCUMENTS

Appointment and functions of inspectors

431 Investigation of a company on its own application or that of its members

(1) The Secretary of State may appoint one or more competent inspectors to investigate the affairs of a company and to report on them in such manner as he may direct.

(2) The appointment may be made—
  (a) in the case of a company having a share capital, on the application either of not less than 200 members or of members holding not less than one tenth of the shares issued,
  (b) in the case of a company not having a share capital, on the application of not less than one fifth in number of the persons on the company's register of members, and
  (c) in any case, on application of the company.

(3) The application shall be supported by such evidence as the Secretary of State may require for the purpose of showing that the applicant or applicants have good reason for requiring the investigation.

(4) The Secretary of State may, before appointing inspectors, require the applicant or applicants to give security, to an amount not exceeding £5,000, or such other sum as he may by order specify, for payment of the costs of the investigation.

An order under this subsection shall be made by statutory instrument subject to annulment in pursuance of a resolution of either House of Parliament.

432 Other company investigations

(1) The Secretary of State shall appoint one or more competent inspectors to investigate the affairs of a company and report on them in such manner as he directs, if the court by order declares that its affairs ought to be so investigated.

(2) The Secretary of State may make such an appointment if it appears to him that there are circumstances suggesting—
  (a) that the company's affairs are being or have been conducted with intent to defraud its creditors or the creditors of any other person, or otherwise for a fraudulent or unlawful purpose, or in a manner which is unfairly prejudicial to some part of its members, or
  (b) that any actual or proposed act or omission of the company (including an act or omission on its behalf) is or would be so prejudicial, or that the company was formed for any fraudulent or unlawful purpose, or
  (c) that persons concerned with the company's formation or the management of its affairs have in connection therewith been guilty of fraud, misfeasance or other misconduct towards it or towards its members, or

(d)   that the company's members have not been given all the information with respect to its affairs which they might reasonably expect.

[(2A)   Inspectors may be appointed under subsection (2) on terms that any report they may make is not for publication; and in such a case, the provisions of section 437(3) (availability and publication of inspectors' reports) do not apply.]

(3)   Subsections (1) and (2) are without prejudice to the powers of the Secretary of State under section 431; and the power conferred by subsection (2) is exercisable with respect to a body corporate notwithstanding that it is in course of being voluntarily wound up.

(4)   The reference in subsection (2)(a) to a company's members includes any person who is not a member but to whom shares in the company have been transferred or transmitted by operation of law.

NOTES

Sub-s (2A): inserted by the Companies Act 1989, s 55.

434 Production of documents and evidence to inspectors

(1)   When inspectors are appointed under section 431 or 432, it is the duty of all officers and agents of the company, and of all officers and agents of any other body corporate whose affairs are investigated under section 433(1)—
   (a)   to produce to the inspectors all [documents] of or relating to the company or, as the case may be, the other body corporate which are in their custody or power,
   (b)   to attend before the inspectors when required to do so, and
   (c)   otherwise to give the inspectors all assistance in connection with the investigation which they are reasonably able to give.

[(2)   If the inspectors consider that an officer or agent of the company or other body corporate, or any other person, is or may be in possession of information relating to a matter which they believe to be relevant to the investigation, they may require him—
   (a)   to produce to them any documents in his custody or power relating to that matter,
   (b)   to attend before them, and
   (c)   otherwise to give them all assistance in connection with the investigation which he is reasonably able to give;

and it is that person's duty to comply with the requirement.]

[(3)   An inspector may for the purposes of the investigation examine any person on oath, and may administer an oath accordingly.]

(4)   In this section a reference to officers or to agents includes past, as well as present, officers or agents (as the case may be); and "agents", in relation to a company or other body corporate, includes its bankers and solicitors and persons employed by it as auditors, whether these persons are or are not officers of the company or other body corporate.

(5) An answer given by a person to a question put to him in exercise of powers conferred by this section (whether as it has effect in relation to an investigation under any of sections 431 to 433, or as applied by any other section in this Part) may be used in evidence against him.

[(5A) However, in criminal proceedings in which that person is charged with an offence to which this subsection applies—
  (a) no evidence relating to the answer may be adduced, and
  (b) no question relating to it may be asked,

by or on behalf of the prosecution, unless evidence relating to it is adduced, or a question relating to it is asked, in the proceedings by or on behalf of that person.

(5B) Subsection (5A) applies to any offence other than—
  (a) an offence under section 2 or 5 of the Perjury Act 1911 (false statements made on oath otherwise than in judicial proceedings or made otherwise than on oath); or
  (b) an offence under section 44(1) or (2) of the Criminal Law (Consolidation) (Scotland) Act 1995 (false statements made on oath or otherwise than on oath).]

[(6) In this section "documents" includes information recorded in any form; and, in relation to information recorded otherwise than in legible form, the power to require its production includes power to require the production of a copy of the information in legible form[, or in a form from which it can readily be produced in visible and legible form].]

NOTES

Sub-s (1): word in square brackets substituted by the Companies Act 1989, s 56(2).
Sub-ss (2), (3): substituted by the Companies Act 1989, s 56(3), (4).
Sub-ss (5A), (5B): inserted by the Youth Justice and Criminal Evidence Act 1999, s 59, Sch 3, paras 4, 5.
Date in force (in relation to England and Wales): 14 April 2000: see SI 2000/1034, arts 2(a), 3.
Date in force (in relation to Scotland): 1 January 2001: see SSI 2000/445, art 2.
Sub-s (6): inserted by the Companies Act 1989, s 56(5).
Sub-s (6): words from ", or in a" to "and legible form" in square brackets inserted by the Criminal Justice and Police Act 2001, s 70, Sch 2, Pt 2, para 17.
Date in force: to be appointed: see the Criminal Justice and Police Act 2001, s 138(2).

436 Obstruction of inspectors treated as contempt of court

[(1) If any person—
  (a) fails to comply with section 434(1)(a) or (c),
  (b) refuses to comply with a requirement under section 434(1)(b) or (2), or
  (c) refuses to answer any question put to him by the inspectors for the purposes of the investigation,

the inspectors may certify that fact in writing to the court.]

(3) The court may thereupon enquire into the case; and, after hearing any witnesses who may be produced against or on behalf of the alleged offender and

after hearing any statement which may be offered in defence, the court may punish the offender in like manner as if he had been guilty of contempt of the court.

NOTES

Sub-s (1): substituted, for original sub-ss (1), (2), by the Companies Act 1989, s 56(6).

437 Inspectors' reports

(1) The inspectors may, and if so directed by the Secretary of State shall, make interim reports to the Secretary of State, and on the conclusion of their investigation shall make a final report to him.

Any such report shall be written or printed, as the Secretary of State directs.

[(1A) Any persons who have been appointed under section 431 or 432 may at any time and, if the Secretary of State directs them to do so, shall inform him of any matters coming to their knowledge as a result of their investigations.]

[(1B) If it appears to the Secretary of State that matters have come to light in the course of the inspectors' investigation which suggest that a criminal offence has been committed, and those matters have been referred to the appropriate prosecuting authority, he may direct the inspectors to take no further steps in the investigation or to take only such further steps as are specified in the direction.

(1C) Where an investigation is the subject of a direction under subsection (1B), the inspectors shall make a final report to the Secretary of State only where—
  (a) they were appointed under section 432(1) (appointment in pursuance of an order of the court), or
  (b) the Secretary of State directs them to do so.]

(2) If the inspectors were appointed under section 432 in pursuance of an order of the court, the Secretary of State shall furnish a copy of any report of theirs to the court.

(3) In any case the Secretary of State may, if he thinks fit—
  (a) forward a copy of any report made by the inspectors to the company's registered office,
  (b) furnish a copy on request and on payment of the prescribed fee to—
    (i) any member of the company or other body corporate which is the subject of the report,
    (ii) any person whose conduct is referred to in the report,
    (iii) the auditors of that company or body corporate,
    (iv) the applicants for the investigation,
    (v) any other person whose financial interests appear to the Secretary of State to be affected by the matters dealt with in the report, whether as a creditor of the company or body corporate, or otherwise, and
  (c) cause any such report to be printed and published.

NOTES

Sub-s (1A): inserted by the Financial Services Act 1986, s 182, Sch 13, para 7.
Sub-ss (1B), (1C): inserted by the Companies Act 1989, s 57.

441 Inspectors' report to be evidence

(1)   A copy of any report of inspectors appointed under [this Part], certified by the Secretary of State to be a true copy, is admissible in any legal proceedings as evidence of the opinion of the inspectors in relation to any matter contained in the report [and, in proceedings on an application under [section 8 of the Company Directors Disqualification Act 1986], as evidence of any fact stated therein].

(2)   A document purporting to be such a certificate as is mentioned above shall be received in evidence and be deemed to be such a certificate, unless the contrary is proved.

NOTES

Sub-s (1): first words in square brackets substituted by the Companies Act 1989, s 61; second words in square brackets inserted by the Insolvency Act 1985, ss 109, 235, Sch 6, para 3, Sch 9, Part II, words in square brackets therein substituted by the Insolvency Act 1986, s 439(1), Sch 13, Part I.

Other powers of investigation available to the Secretary of State

442 Power to investigate company ownership

(1)   Where it appears to the Secretary of State that there is good reason to do so, he may appoint one or more competent inspectors to investigate and report on the membership of any company, and otherwise with respect to the company, for the purpose of determining the true persons who are or have been financially interested in the success or failure (real or apparent) of the company or able to control or materially to influence its policy.

(2)   The appointment of inspectors under this section may define the scope of their investigation (whether as respects the matter or the period to which it is to extend or otherwise) and in particular may limit the investigation to matters connected with particular shares or debentures.

[(3)   If an application for investigation under this section with respect to particular shares or debentures of a company is made to the Secretary of State by members of the company, and the number of applicants or the amount of shares held by them is not less than that required for an application for the appointment of inspectors under section 431(2)(a) or (b), then, subject to the following provisions, the Secretary of State shall appoint inspectors to conduct the investigation applied for.

(3A)   The Secretary of State shall not appoint inspectors if he is satisfied that the application is vexatious; and where inspectors are appointed their terms of appointment shall exclude any matter in so far as the Secretary of State is satisfied that it is unreasonable for it to be investigated.

(3B)   The Secretary of State may, before appointing inspectors, require the applicant or applicants to give security, to an amount not exceeding £5,000, or such other sum as he may by order specify, for payment of the costs of the investigation.

An order under this subsection shall be made by statutory instrument which shall be subject to annulment in pursuance of a resolution of either House of Parliament.

(3C)   If on an application under subsection (3) it appears to the Secretary of State that the powers conferred by section 444 are sufficient for the purposes of investigating the matters which inspectors would be appointed to investigate, he may instead conduct the investigation under that section.]

(4)   Subject to the terms of their appointment, the inspectors' powers extend to the investigation of any circumstances suggesting the existence of an arrangement or understanding which, though not legally binding, is or was observed or likely to be observed in practice and which is relevant to the purposes of the investigation.

NOTES

Sub-ss (3)–(3C): substituted for original sub-s (3) by the Companies Act 1989, s 62.

443 Provisions applicable on investigation under s 442

(1)   For purposes of an investigation under section 442, sections 433(1), 434, 436 and 437 apply with the necessary modifications of references to the affairs of the company or to those of any other body corporate, subject however to the following subsections.

(2)   Those sections apply to—
   (a)   all persons who are or have been, or whom the inspector has reasonable cause to believe to be or have been, financially interested in the success or failure or the apparent success or failure of the company or any other body corporate whose membership is investigated with that of the company, or able to control or materially influence its policy (including persons concerned only on behalf of others), and
   (b)   any other person whom the inspector has reasonable cause to believe possesses information relevant to the investigation,

as they apply in relation to officers and agents of the company or the other body corporate (as the case may be).

(3)   If the Secretary of State is of opinion that there is good reason for not divulging any part of a report made by virtue of section 442 and this section, he may under section 437 disclose the report with the omission of that part; and he may cause to be kept by the registrar of companies a copy of the report with that part omitted or, in the case of any other such report, a copy of the whole report.

(4)   . . .

NOTES

Sub-s (4): repealed by the Companies Act 1989, s 212, Sch 24.

444 Power to obtain information as to those interested in shares, etc

(1)   If it appears to the Secretary of State that there is good reason to investigate the ownership of any shares in or debentures of a company and that it is unnecessary to appoint inspectors for the purpose, he may require any person whom he has reasonable cause to believe to have or to be able to obtain any information as to the present and past interests in those shares or debentures and the names and addresses of the persons interested and of any persons who act or have acted on

their behalf in relation to the shares or debentures to give any such information to the Secretary of State.

(2) For this purpose a person is deemed to have an interest in shares or debentures if he has any right to acquire or dispose of them or of any interest in them, or to vote in respect of them, or if his consent is necessary for the exercise of any of the rights of other persons interested in them, or if other persons interested in them can be required, or are accustomed, to exercise their rights in accordance with his instructions.

(3) A person who fails to give information required of him under this section, or who in giving such information makes any statement which he knows to be false in a material particular, or recklessly makes any statement which is false in a material particular, is liable to imprisonment or a fine, or both.

445 Power to impose restrictions on shares and debentures

(1) If in connection with an investigation under either section 442 or 444 it appears to the Secretary of State that there is difficulty in finding out the relevant facts about any shares (whether issued or to be issued), he may by order direct that the shares shall until further order be subject to the restrictions of Part XV of this Act.

[(1A) If the Secretary of State is satisfied that an order under subsection (1) may unfairly affect the rights of third parties in respect of shares then the Secretary of State, for the purpose of protecting such rights and subject to such terms as he thinks fit, may direct that such acts by such persons òr descriptions of persons and for such purposes as may be set out in the order, shall not constitute a breach of the restrictions of Part XV of this Act.]

(2) This section, and Part XV in its application to orders under it, apply in relation to debentures as in relation to shares [save that subsection (1A) shall not so apply].

NOTES

Sub-s (1A): inserted by SI 1991/1646, reg 5(a).
Sub-s (2): words in square brackets inserted by SI 1991/1646, reg 5(b).

446 Investigation of share dealings

(1) If it appears to the Secretary of State that there are circumstances suggesting that contraventions may have occurred, in relation to a company's shares or debentures, of section 323 or 324 (taken with Schedule 13), or of subsections (3) to (5) of section 328 (restrictions on share dealing by directors and their families; obligation of director to disclose shareholding in his own company), he may appoint one or more competent inspectors to carry out such investigations as are requisite to establish whether or not such contraventions have occurred and to report the result of their investigations to him.

(2) The appointment of inspectors under this section may limit the period to which their investigation is to extend or confine it to shares or debentures of a particular class, or both.

(3) For purposes of an investigation under this section, sections 434 [to 437] apply—
  (a) with the substitution, for references to any other body corporate whose affairs are investigated under section 433(1), of a reference to any other body corporate which is, or has at any relevant time been, the company's subsidiary or holding company, or a subsidiary of its holding company, . . .
  (b) . . .

[(4) Sections 434 to 436 apply for the purposes of an investigation under this section to the following persons as they apply to officers of the company or of the other body corporate—
  (a) an authorised person;
  (b) a relevant professional;
  (c) a person not falling within paragraph (a) or (b) who may carry on a regulated activity without contravening the prohibition imposed by section 19 of the Financial Services and Markets Act 2000; and
  (d) in relation to an authorised person, to a relevant professional or to a person falling within paragraph (c)—
    (i) if it is a body corporate, any person who is or has been an officer of it;
    (ii) if it is a partnership, any person who is or has been a partner in it;
    (iii) if it is an unincorporated association, any person who is or has been a member of its governing body or an officer of it.

(4A) In subsection (4)—
  "authorised person" has the meaning given in section 31(2) of the Financial Services and Markets Act 2000;
  "relevant professional" means a member of a profession in relation to which a body has been designated under section 326(1) of that Act, and, in relation to such a profession, "member" has the meaning given in section 325(2) of that Act.]

(5)–(7) < . . . >

NOTES

Sub-s (3): words in square brackets substituted by the Financial Services Act 1986, s 182, Sch 13, para 8; words omitted repealed by the Companies Act 1989, s 212, Sch 24.
Sub-ss (4), (4A): substituted, for sub-s (4) as originally enacted, by SI 2001/3649, art 21. Date in force: 1 December 2001: see SI 2001/3649, art 1.
Sub-ss (5), (6): repealed by the Financial Services Act 1986, ss 182, 212(3), Sch 13, para 8, Sch 17, Part I.
Sub-s (7): repealed by the Companies Act 1989, s 212, Sch 24.

Requisition and seizure of books and papers

447 Secretary of State's power to require production of documents

(1) . . .

(2) The Secretary of State may at any time, if he thinks there is good reason to do so, give directions to [a company] requiring it, at such time and place as may be specified in the directions, to produce such [documents] as may be so specified.

(3)   The Secretary of State may at any time, if he thinks there is good reason to do so, authorise an officer of his [or any other competent person], on producing (if so required) evidence of his authority, to require [a company] to produce to him (the officer [or other person]) forthwith any [documents] which [he (the officer or other person)] may specify.

(4)   Where by virtue of subsection (2) or (3) the Secretary of State or an officer of his [or other person] has power to require the production of [documents] from [a company], he or the officer [or other person] has the like power to require production of those [documents] from any person who appears to him or the officer to be in possession of them; but where any such person claims a lien on [documents] produced by him, the production is without prejudice to the lien.

(5)   The power under this section to require [a company] or other person to produce [documents] includes power—
  (a)   if the [documents] are produced—
    (i)   to take copies of them or extracts from them, and
    (ii)   to require that person, or any other person who is a present or past officer of, or is or was at any time employed by, [the company] in question, to provide an explanation of any of them;
  (b)   if the [documents] are not produced, to require the person who was required to produce them to state, to the best of his knowledge and belief, where they are.

(6)   If the requirement to produce [documents] or provide an explanation or make a statement is not complied with, [the company] or other person on whom the requirement was so imposed is guilty of an offence and liable to a fine.

[Sections 732 (restriction on prosecutions), 733 (liability of individuals for corporate default) and 734 (criminal proceedings against unincorporated bodies) apply to this offence.]

(7)   However, where a person is charged with an offence under subsection (6) in respect of a requirement to produce any [documents], it is a defence to prove that they were not in his possession or under his control and that it was not reasonably practicable for him to comply with the requirement.

(8)   A statement made by a person in compliance with such a requirement may be used in evidence against him.

[(8A)   However, in criminal proceedings in which that person is charged with an offence to which this subsection applies—
  (a)   no evidence relating to the statement may be adduced, and
  (b)   no question relating to it may be asked,
by or on behalf of the prosecution, unless evidence relating to it is adduced, or a question relating to it is asked, in the proceedings by or on behalf of that person.

(8B)   Subsection (8A) applies to any offence other than—
  (a)   an offence under subsection (6) or section 451;
  (b)   an offence under section 5 of the Perjury Act 1911 (false statements made otherwise than on oath); or

(c) an offence under section 44(2) of the Criminal Law (Consolidation) (Scotland) Act 1995 (false statements made otherwise than on oath).]

[(9) In this section "documents" includes information recorded in any form; and, in relation to information recorded otherwise than in legible form, the power to require its production includes power to require the production of a copy of it in legible form[, or in a form from which it can readily be produced in visible and legible form].]

449 Provision for security of information obtained

(1) No information or document relating to a [company] which has been obtained under section 447 . . . shall, without the previous consent in writing of that [company], be published or disclosed, except to a competent authority, unless the publication or disclosure is required—

[(a) with a view to the institution of or otherwise for the purposes of criminal proceedings;]

[(ba) with a view to the institution of, or otherwise for the purposes of, any proceedings on an application under [section 6, 7 or 8 of the Company Directors Disqualification Act 1986];]

[(c) for the purposes of enabling or assisting any inspector appointed under this Part. . . to discharge his functions;]

[(cc) for the purpose of enabling or assisting any person authorised to exercise powers [section 447 of this Act] or section 84 of the Companies Act 1989 to discharge his functions;]

[(cd) for the purposes of enabling or assisting a person appointed under—

(i) section 167 of the Financial Services and Markets Act 2000 (general investigations),

(ii) section 168 of that Act (investigations in particular cases),

(iii) section 169(1)(b) of that Act (investigation in support of overseas regulator),

(iv) section 284 of that Act (investigations into affairs of certain collective investment schemes), or

(v) regulations made as a result of section 262(2)(k) of that Act (investigations into open-ended investment companies),

to conduct an investigation to discharge his functions;]

[(d) for the purpose of enabling or assisting the [Secretary of State or the Treasury to exercise any of their functions], under this Act, the [insider dealing legislation], *the Prevention of Fraud (Investments) Act 1958*, . . . the Insolvency Act 1986, the Company Directors Disqualification Act 1986[, Part 2, 3 or 7 of the Companies Act 1989 or the Financial Services and Markets Act 2000;]

(dd) for the purpose of enabling or assisting the Department of Economic Development for Northern Ireland to exercise any powers conferred on it by the enactments relating to companies or insolvency or for the purpose of enabling or assisting any inspector appointed by it under the enactments relating to companies to discharge his functions]

[(de). . .

(df) . . .]

[(dg)for the purpose of enabling or assisting the Occupational Pensions Regulatory Authority to discharge their functions under the Pension Schemes Act 1993 or the Pensions Act 1995 or any enactment in force in Northern Ireland corresponding to either of them,]

(e) . . .

[(f) for the purpose of enabling or assisting the Bank of England to discharge its functions,]

[(fa) for the purposes of enabling or assisting the Financial Services Authority to discharge its functions under the legislation relating to friendly societies or to industrial and provident societies, under the Building Societies Act 1986, under Part 7 of the Companies Act 1989 or under the Financial Services and Markets Act 2000;

(fb) for the purposes of enabling or assisting the competent authority for the purposes of Part 6 of the Financial Services and Markets Act 2000 to discharge its functions under that Part;

(g) for the purposes of enabling or assisting a body corporate established in accordance with section 212(1) of the Financial Services and Markets Act 2000 (compensation scheme manager) to discharge its functions;

(h) for the purposes of any proceedings before the Financial Services Tribunal by virtue of the Financial Services and Markets Act 2000 (Transitional Provisions) (Partly Completed Procedures) Order 2001;

(ha) with a view to the institution of, or otherwise for the purposes of, proceedings before the Financial Services and Markets Tribunal;

(hb) for the purpose of enabling or assisting a recognised investment exchange or a recognised clearing house to discharge its functions as such;

(hc) for the purpose of enabling or assisting a body designated under section 326(1) of the Financial Services and Markets Act 2000 (designated professional bodies) to discharge its functions in its capacity as a body designated under that section;]

[(hh)for the purpose of enabling or assisting a body established by order under section 46 of the Companies Act 1989 to discharge its functions under Part II of that Act, or of enabling or assisting a recognised supervisory or qualifying body within the meaning of that Part to discharge its functions as such;]

[(i) . . .]

[(j) . . .

(k) for the purpose of enabling or assisting an official receiver to discharge his functions under the enactments relating to insolvency or for the purpose of enabling or assisting a body which is for the time being a recognised professional body for the purposes of section 391 of the Insolvency Act 1986 to discharge its functions as such,

(l) with a view to the institution of, or otherwise for the purposes of, any disciplinary proceedings relating to the exercise by a solicitor, auditor, accountant, valuer or actuary of his professional duties,]

[(ll) with a view to the institution of, or otherwise for the purposes of, any disciplinary proceedings relating to the discharge by a public servant of his duties;]

[(m) for the purpose of enabling or assisting an overseas regulatory authority to exercise its regulatory functions].

[[(1A) In subsection (1)—

[(aa) in paragraph (hb) "recognised investment exchange" and "recognised clearing house" has the same meaning as in section 285 of the Financial Services and Markets Act 2000;]

(a) in paragraph (ll) "public servant" means an officer or servant of the Crown or of any public or other authority for the time being designated for the purposes of that paragraph by the Secretary of State by order made by statutory instrument; and

(b) in paragraph (m) "overseas regulatory authority" and "regulatory functions" have the same meaning as in section 82 of the Companies Act 1989.]

(1B) Subject to subsection (1C), subsection (1) shall not preclude publication or disclosure for the purpose of enabling or assisting any public or other authority for the time being [designated for the purposes of this subsection] by the Secretary of State by an order in a statutory instrument to discharge any functions which are specified in the order.

(1C) An order under subsection (1B) designating an authority for the purpose of that subsection may—

(a) impose conditions subject to which the publication or disclosure of any information or document is permitted by that subsection; and

(b) otherwise restrict the circumstances in which that subsection permits publication or disclosure.

(1D) . . .]

(2) A person who publishes or discloses any information or document in contravention of this section is guilty of an offence and liable to imprisonment or a fine, or both.

[Sections 732 (restriction on prosecutions), 733 (liability of individuals for corporate default) and 734 (criminal proceedings against unincorporated bodies) apply to this offence.]

[(3) For the purposes of this section each of the following is a competent authority—

(a) the Secretary of State,

(b) an inspector appointed under this Part . . .,

[(ba) a person appointed under—

    (i) section 167 of the Financial Services and Markets Act 2000 (general investigations),

    (ii) section 168 of that Act (investigations in particular cases),

    (iii) section 169(1)(b) of that Act (investigation in support of overseas regulator),

    (iv) section 284 of that Act (investigations into affairs of certain collective investment schemes), or

    (v) regulations made as a result of section 262(2)(k) of that Act (investigations into open-ended investment companies),

    to conduct an investigation;]

(c) any person authorised to exercise powers [under section 447 of this Act] or section 84 of the Companies Act 1989,

(d) the Department of Economic Development in Northern Ireland,

(e) the Treasury,

(f) the Bank of England,

(g) the Lord Advocate,

(h) the Director of Public Prosecutions, and the Director of Public Prosecutions for Northern Ireland,

[(ha) the Financial Services Authority;]

(l) any constable,

(m) any procurator fiscal,

[(n) the Scottish Ministers].

(3A) Any information which may by virtue of this section be disclosed to a competent authority may be disclosed to any officer or servant of the authority.]

[(4) A statutory instrument containing an order under [subsection (1A)(a) or (1B)] is subject to annulment in pursuance of a resolution of either House of Parliament.]

NOTES

Sub-s (1): word "company", in both places where it occurs, substituted by the Companies Act 1989, s 65(2)(a).

Sub-s (1): words omitted repealed by the Companies Act 1989, s 212, Sch 24.

Sub-s (1): para (a) substituted, for paras (a), (b) as originally enacted, by the Financial Services Act 1986, s 182, Sch 13, para 9.

Sub-s (1): para (ba) inserted by the Insolvency Act 1985, s 109, Sch 6, para 4.

Sub-s (1): in para (ba) words "section 6, 7 or 8 of the Company Directors Disqualification Act 1986" in square brackets substituted by the Insolvency Act 1986, s 439(1), Sch 13, Pt I.

Sub-s (1): para (c) substituted by the Companies Act 1989, s 65(2)(b).

Sub-s (1): in para (c) words omitted repealed by SI 2001/3649, art 22(1), (2)(a).

Date in force: 1 December 2001: see SI 2001/3649, art 1.

Sub-s (1): para (cc) inserted by the Companies Act 1989, s 65(2)(c).

Sub-s (1): in para (cc) words "section 447 of this Act" in square brackets substituted by SI 2001/3649, art 22(1), (3).

Date in force: 1 December 2001: see SI 2001/3649, art 1.

Sub-s (1): para (cd) inserted by SI 2001/3649, art 22(1), (4).

Date in force: 1 December 2001: see SI 2001/3649, art 1.

Sub-s (1): paras (d), (dd) substituted, for para (d) as originally enacted, by the Financial Services Act 1986, s 182, Sch 13, para 9.

Sub-s (1): in para (d) words "Secretary of State or the Treasury to exercise any of their functions" in square brackets substituted by SI 1992/1315, art 10(1), Sch 4, para 1.

Sub-s (1): in para (d) words "insider dealing legislation" substituted by the Criminal Justice Act 1993, s 79(13), Sch 5, Pt I.

Sub-s (1): in para (d) words "the Prevention of Fraud (Investments) Act 1958" in italics repealed for certain purposes, and prospectively repealed for remaining purposes as from a day to be appointed, by the Financial Services Act 1986, s 212(3), Sch 17, Pt I.

Sub-s (1): in para (d) words omitted repealed by SI 2001/3649, art 22(1), (2)(b).

Date in force: 1 December 2001: see SI 2001/3649, art 1.

Sub-s (1): in para (d) words ", Part 2, 3 or 7 of the Companies Act 1989 or the Financial Services and Markets Act 2000;" in square brackets substituted by SI 2001/3649, art 22(1), (5).

Date in force: 1 December 2001: see SI 2001/3649, art 1.

Sub-s (1): paras (de), (df) inserted by the Friendly Societies Act 1992, s 120, Sch 21, para 7(1).

Sub-s (1): paras (de), (df) repealed by SI 2001/3649, art 22(1), (2)(c).

Date in force: 1 December 2001: see SI 2001/3649, art 1.

Sub-s (1): para (dg) inserted by the Pensions Act 1995, s 122, Sch 3, para 12.

Sub-s (1): para (e) repealed by the Companies Act 1989, ss 65(2)(e), 212, Sch 24.

Sub-s (1): paras (f), (fa) substituted, for para (f) (as inserted by the Financial Services Act 1986, s 182, Sch 13, para 9), by the Bank of England Act 1998, s 23, Sch 5, para 62(2).

Date in force: 1 June 1998: see SI 1998/1120, art 2.

Sub-s (1): paras (fa), (fb), (g), (h), (ha)–(hc) substituted, for para (fa) (as substituted by the Bank of England Act 1998, s 23, Sch 5 para 62(2)) and paras (g) (h) (inserted by the Financial Services Act 1986, s 182, Sch 13, para 9), by SI 2001/3649, art 22(1), (6).

Date in force: 1 December 2001: see SI 2001/3649, art 1.

Sub-s (1): para (hh) inserted by the Companies Act 1989, s 65(2)(g).

Date in force (for certain purposes): 21 February 1990: see SI 1990/142, art 4(a).

Date in force (for certain purposes): 25 April 1991: see SI 1991/878, art 2, Schedule.

Date in force (for remaining purposes): to be appointed: see the Companies Act 1989, s 215(2).

Sub-s (1): para (i) inserted by the Financial Services Act 1986, s 182, Sch 13, para 9.

Sub-s (1): para (i) repealed by SI 2001/3649, art 22(1), (2)(d).

Date in force: 1 December 2001: see SI 2001/3649, art 1.

Sub-s (1): paras (j)–(l) inserted by the Financial Services Act 1986, s 182, Sch 13, para 9.

Sub-s (1): para (j) repealed by SI 2001/1283, art 3(3)(b).

Date in force: 30 April 2001: see SI 2001/1283, art 1(1).

Sub-s (1): para (ll) inserted by the Companies Act 1989, s 65(2)(h).

Sub-s (1): para (m) inserted by the Financial Services Act 1986, s 182, Sch 13, para 9, substituted by the Companies Act 1989, s 65(2)(i).

Sub-s (1A): inserted by the Financial Services Act 1986, s 182, Sch 13, para 9; substituted by the Companies Act 1989, s 65(3).

Sub-s (1A): para (aa) inserted by SI 2001/3649, art 22(1), (7).

Date in force: 1 December 2001: see SI 2001/3649, art 1.

Sub-s (1B): inserted by the Financial Services Act 1986, s 182, Sch 13, para 9; words in square brackets substituted by the Companies Act 1989, s 65(4).

Sub-ss (1C), (1D): inserted by the Financial Services Act 1986, s 182, Sch 13, para 9.

Sub-s (1D): repealed by SI 2001/3649, art 22(1), (8).

Date in force: 1 December 2001: see SI 2001/3649, art 1.

Sub-s (2): words in square brackets substituted by the Companies Act 1989, s 65(5).

Sub-s (3): originally substituted, together with sub-s (4), for sub-s (3) as originally enacted, by the Financial Services Act 1986, s 182, Sch 13, para 9; further substituted, together with sub-s (3A), by the Companies Act 1989, s 65(6).

Sub-s (3): in para (b) words omitted repealed by SI 2001/3649, art 22(1), (9).

Date in force: 1 December 2001: see SI 2001/3649, art 1.

Sub-s (3): para (ba) inserted by SI 2001/3649, art 22(1), (10).

Date in force: 1 December 2001: see SI 2001/3649, art 1.

Sub-s (3): in para (c) words "under section 447 of this Act" in square brackets substituted by SI 2001/3649, art 22(1), (11).

Date in force: 1 December 2001: see SI 2001/3649, art 1.

Sub-s (3): para (ha) substituted, for para (ha) (as inserted by the Bank of England Act 1998, s 23, Sch 5, para 62(3), paras (i), (j), (k) as originally enacted, and para (jj) (as inserted by the Friendly Societies Act 1992, s 120, Sch 21, para 7(2)), by SI 2001/3649, art 22(1), (12).

Date in force: 1 December 2001: see SI 2001/3649, art 1.

Sub-s (3): para (n) inserted by SI 1999/1820, art 4, Sch 2, Pt I, para 78.

Date in force: 1 July 1999: see SI 1999/1820, art 1(2).

Sub-s (3A): substituted, together with sub-s (3), for sub-s (3) as previously in force, by the Companies Act 1989, s 65(6).

Sub-s (4): substituted, together with sub-s (3), for sub-s (3) as originally enacted, by the Financial Services Act 1986, s 182, Sch 13, para 9; words in square brackets substituted by the Companies Act 1989, s 65(7).

450 Punishment for destroying, mutilating etc company documents

(1)   [An officer of a company]. . . who—
- (a)   destroys, mutilates or falsifies, or is privy to the destruction, mutilation or falsification of a document affecting or relating to the [company's] property or affairs, or
- (b)   makes, or is privy to the making of, a false entry in such a document,

is guilty of an offence, unless he proves that he had no intention to conceal the state of affairs of [the company] or to defeat the law.

[(1A)   Subsection (1) applies to an officer of an authorised insurance company which is not a body corporate as it applies to an officer of a company.]

(2)   Such a person as above mentioned who fraudulently either parts with, alters or makes an omission in any such document or is privy to fraudulent parting with, fraudulent altering or fraudulent making of an omission in, any such document, is guilty of an offence.

(3)   A person guilty of an offence under this section is liable to imprisonment or a fine, or both.

[(4)   Sections 732 (restriction on prosecutions), 733 (liability of individuals for corporate default) and 734 (criminal proceedings against unincorporated bodies) apply to an offence under this section.]

[(5)   In this section "document" includes information recorded in any form.]

NOTES
Sub-s (1): words in square brackets substituted by the Companies Act 1989, s 66(2).

Sub-s (1): words omitted repealed by SI 2001/3649, art 23(1), (2).

Date in force: 1 December 2001: see SI 2001/3649, art 1.

Sub-s (1A): inserted by SI 2001/3649, art 23(1), (3).

Date in force: 1 December 2001: see SI 2001/3649, art 1.

Sub-s (4): substituted by the Companies Act 1989, s 66(3).

Sub-s (5): inserted by the Companies Act 1989, s 66(4).

451 Punishment for furnishing false information

A person who, in purported compliance with a requirement imposed under section 447 to provide an explanation or make a statement, provides or makes an explanation or statement which he knows to be false in a material particular or recklessly provides or makes an explanation or statement which is so false, is guilty of an offence and liable to imprisonment or a fine, or both.

[Sections 732 (restriction on prosecutions), 733 (liability of individuals for corporate default) and 734 (criminal proceedings against unincorporated bodies) apply to this offence.]

NOTES

Words in square brackets substituted by the Companies Act 1989, s 67.

[451A Disclosure of information by Secretary of State or inspector]

[(1)   This section applies to information obtained under sections 434 to 446.

(2)   The Secretary of State may, if he thinks fit—
  (a)   disclose any information to which this section applies to any person to whom, or for any purpose for which, disclosure is permitted under section 449, or
  (b)   authorise or require an inspector appointed under this Part to disclose such information to any such person or for any such purpose.

[(3)   Information to which this section applies may also be disclosed by an inspector appointed under this Part to—
  (a)   another inspector appointed under this Part;
  (b)   a person appointed under—
      (i)   section 167 of the Financial Services and Markets Act 2000 (general investigations),
      (ii)   section 168 of that Act (investigations in particular cases),
      (iii)   section 169(1)(b) of that Act (investigation in support of overseas regulator);
      (iv)   section 284 of that Act (investigations into affairs of certain collective investment schemes), or
      (v)   regulations made as a result of section 262(2)(k) of that Act (investigations into open-ended investment companies),
      to conduct an investigation; or
  (c)   a person authorised to exercise powers under—
      (i)   section 447 of this Act; or
      (ii)   section 84 of the Companies Act 1989 (exercise of powers to assist overseas regulatory authority).]

(4)   Any information which may by virtue of subsection (3) be disclosed to any person may be disclosed to any officer or servant of that person.

(5)   The Secretary of State may, if he thinks fit, disclose any information obtained under section 444 to—

(a) the company whose ownership was the subject of the investigation,

(b) any member of the company,

(c) any person whose conduct was investigated in the course of the investigation,

(d) the auditors of the company, or

(e) any person whose financial interests appear to the Secretary of State to be affected by matters covered by the investigation.]

NOTES

Inserted by the Financial Services Act 1986, s 182, Sch 13, para 10.

Substituted by the Companies Act 1989, s 68.

Sub-s (3): substituted by SI 2001/3649, art 24.

Date in force: 1 December 2001: see SI 2001/3649, art 1.

Supplementary

452 Privileged information

(1) Nothing in sections 431 to 446 requires the disclosure to the Secretary of State or to an inspector appointed by him—

(a) by any person of information which he would in an action in the High Court or the Court of Session be entitled to refuse to disclose on grounds of legal professional privilege except, if he is a lawyer, the name and address of his client,

(b) . . .

[(1A) Nothing in section 434, 443 or 446 requires a person (except as mentioned in subsection (1B) below) to disclose information or produce documents in respect of which he owes an obligation of confidence by virtue of carrying on the business of banking unless—

(a) the person to whom the obligation of confidence is owed is the company or other body corporate under investigation,

(b) the person to whom the obligation of confidence is owed consents to the disclosure or production, or

(c) the making of the requirement is authorised by the Secretary of State.

(1B) Subsection (1A) does not apply where the person owing the obligation of confidence is the company or other body corporate under investigation under section 431, 432 or 433.]

(2) Nothing in sections 447 to 451 compels the production by any person of a document which he would in an action in the High Court or the Court of Session be entitled to refuse to produce on grounds of legal professional privilege, or authorises the taking of possession of any such document which is in the person's possession.

(3) The Secretary of State shall not under section 447 require, or authorise an officer of his [or other person] to require, the production by a person carrying on the business of banking of a document relating to the affairs of a customer of his unless either it appears to the Secretary of State that it is necessary to do so for the purpose of investigating the affairs of the first-mentioned person, [or the customer is—

(a) a person on whom a requirement has been imposed under that section, or

(b) a person on whom a requirement has been imposed to produce information or documents has been imposed by the Secretary of State, or by a person appointed by the Secretary of State to conduct an investigation, under section 171 or 173 of the Financial Services and Markets Act 2000].

NOTES

Sub-s (1): para (b) repealed by the Companies Act 1989, ss 69(2), 212, Sch 24.
Sub-ss (1A), (1B): inserted by the Companies Act 1989, s 69(3).
Sub-s (3): words "or other person" in square brackets inserted by the Companies Act 1989, s 69(4).
Sub-s (3): words from "or the customer" to "Financial Services and Markets Act 2000" in square brackets substituted by SI 2001/3649, art 25.
Date in force: 1 December 2001: see SI 2001/3649, art 1.

453 Investigation of oversea companies

[(1) The provisions of this Part apply to bodies corporate incorporated outside Great Britain which are carrying on business in Great Britain, or have at any time carried on business there, as they apply to companies under this Act; but subject to the following exceptions, adaptations and modifications.

(1A) The following provisions do not apply to such bodies—
(a) section 431 (investigation on application of company or its members),
(b) section 438 (power to bring civil proceedings on the company's behalf),
(c) sections 442 to 445 (investigation of company ownership and power to obtain information as to those interested in shares, &c), and
(d) section 446 (investigation of share dealings).

(1B) The other provisions of this Part apply to such bodies subject to such adaptations and modifications as may be specified by regulations made by the Secretary of State.]

(2) Regulations under this section shall be made by statutory instrument subject to annulment in pursuance of a resolution of either House of Parliament.

NOTES

Sub-ss (1), (1A), (1B): substituted for sub-s (1), as originally enacted, by the Companies Act 1989, s 70.

PART XV
ORDERS IMPOSING RESTRICTIONS ON SHARES (SECTIONS 210, 216, 445)

454 Consequence of order imposing restrictions

(1) So long as any shares are directed to be subject to the restrictions of this Part [then, subject to any directions made in relation to an order pursuant to sections 210(5A), 216(1B), 445(1A) or 456(1A) or subject in the case of an interim order pursuant to section 216(1A) to the terms of that order]—
(a) any transfer of those shares or, in the case of unissued shares, any transfer of the right to be issued with them, and any issue of them, is void;
(b) no voting rights are exercisable in respect of the shares;

    (c)   no further shares shall be issued in right of them or in pursuance of any offer made to their holder; and

    (d)   except in a liquidation, no payment shall be made of any sums due from the company on the shares, whether in respect of capital or otherwise.

(2)   Where shares are subject to the restrictions of subsection (1)(a), any agreement to transfer the shares or, in the case of unissued shares, the right to be issued with them is void (except [such agreement or right as may be made or exercised under the terms of directions made by the Secretary of State or the court under sections 210(5A), 216(1B), 445(1A), 456(1A) or of an interim order made under section 216(1A) or] an agreement to [transfer] the shares on the making of an order under section 456(3)(b) below).

(3)   Where shares are subject to the restrictions of subsection (1)(c) or (d), an agreement to transfer any right to be issued with other shares in right of those shares, or to receive any payment on them (otherwise than in a liquidation) is void (except [such agreement or right as may be made or exercised under the terms of directions made by the Secretary of State or the court under sections 210(5A), 216(1B), 445(1A), 456(1A) or of an interim order made under section 216(1A) or] an agreement to transfer any such right on the [transfer] of the shares on the making of an order under section 456(3)(b) below).

NOTES

Sub-s (1): words in square brackets inserted by SI 1991/1646, reg 6(a).

Sub-ss (2), (3): first words in square brackets inserted by SI 1991/1646, reg 6(b), (c); final words in square brackets substituted by the Companies Act 1989, s 145, Sch 19, para 10(2).

455 Punishment for attempted evasion of restrictions

(1)   [Subject to the terms of any directions made under sections 210(5A), 216(1B) or 445(1A) or 456 or of an interim order made under section 216(1A)] a person is liable to a fine if he—

    (a)   exercises or purports to exercise any right to dispose of any shares which, to his knowledge, are for the time being subject to the restrictions of this Part or of any right to be issued with any such shares, or

    (b)   votes in respect of any such shares (whether as holder or proxy), or appoints a proxy to vote in respect of them, or

    (c)   being the holder of any such shares, fails to notify of their being subject to those restrictions any person whom he does not know to be aware of that fact but does know to be entitled (apart from the restrictions) to vote in respect of those shares whether as holder or as proxy, or

    (d)   being the holder of any such shares, or being entitled to any right to be issued with other shares in right of them, or to receive any payment on them (otherwise than in a liquidation), enters into any agreement which is void under section 454(2) or (3).

(2)   [Subject to the terms of any directions made under sections 210(5A), 216(1B), 445(1A) or 456 or of an interim order made under section 216(1A)] if shares in a company are issued in contravention of the restrictions, the company and every officer of it who is in default is liable to a fine.

(3) Section 732 (restriction on prosecutions) applies to an offence under this section.

Sub-ss (1), (2): words in square brackets inserted by SI 1991/1646, reg 7(a), (b).

456 Relaxation and removal of restrictions

(1) Where shares in a company are by order made subject to the restrictions of this Part, application may be made to the court for an order directing that the shares be no longer so subject.

[(1A) Where the court is satisfied that an order subjecting the shares to the restrictions of this Part unfairly affects the rights of third parties in respect of shares then the court, for the purpose of protecting such rights and subject to such terms as it thinks fit and in addition to any order it may make under subsection (1), may direct on an application made under that subsection that such acts by such persons or descriptions of persons and for such purposes, as may be set out in the order, shall not constitute a breach of the restrictions of Part XV of this Act.

Subsection (3) does not apply to an order made under this subsection.]

(2) If the order applying the restrictions was made by the Secretary of State, or he has refused to make an order disapplying them, the application may be made by any person aggrieved; and if the order was made by the court under section 216 (non-disclosure of share holding), it may be made by any such person or by the company.

(3) Subject as follows, an order of the court or the Secretary of State directing that shares shall cease to be subject to the restrictions may be made only if—
  (a) the court or (as the case may be) the Secretary of State is satisfied that the relevant facts about the shares have been disclosed to the company and no unfair advantage has accrued to any person as a result of the earlier failure to make that disclosure, or
  (b) the shares are to be [transferred for valuable consideration] and the court (in any case) or the Secretary of State (if the order was made under section 210 or 445) approves the [transfer].

(4) [Without prejudice to the power of the court to give directions under subsection (1A),] where shares in a company are subject to the restrictions, the court may on application order the shares to be sold, subject to the court's approval as to the sale, and may also direct that the shares shall cease to be subject to the restrictions.

An application to the court under this subsection may be made by the Secretary of State (unless the restrictions were imposed by court order under section 216), or by the company.

(5) Where an order has been made under subsection (4), the court may on application make such further order relating to the sale or transfer of the shares as it thinks fit.

An application to the court under this subsection may be made—

(a) by the Secretary of State (unless the restrictions on the shares were imposed by court order under section 216), or
(b) by the company, or
(c) by the person appointed by or in pursuance of the order to effect the sale, or
(d) by any person interested in the shares.

(6) An order (whether of the Secretary of State or the court) directing that shares shall cease to be subject to the restrictions of this Part, if it is—
(a) expressed to be made with a view to permitting a transfer of the shares, or
(b) made under subsection (4) of this section,
may continue the restrictions mentioned in paragraphs (c) and (d) of section 454(1), either in whole or in part, so far as they relate to any right acquired or offer made before the transfer.

(7) Subsection (3) does not apply to an order directing that shares shall cease to be subject to any restrictions which have been continued in force in relation to those shares under subsection (6).

NOTES
Sub-s (1A): inserted by SI 1991/1646, reg 8(a).
Sub-s (3): in para (b) words in square brackets substituted by the Companies Act 1989, s 145, Sch 19, para 10(1).
Sub-s (4): words in square brackets inserted by SI 1991/1646, reg 8(b).

457 Further provisions on sale by court order of restricted shares

(1) Where shares are sold in pursuance of an order of the court under section 456(4) the proceeds of sale, less the costs of the sale, shall be paid into court for the benefit of the persons who are beneficially interested in the shares; and any such person may apply to the court for the whole or part of those proceeds to be paid to him.

(2) On application under subsection (1) the court shall (subject as provided below) order the payment to the applicant of the whole of the proceeds of sale together with any interest thereon or, if any other person had a beneficial interest in the shares at the time of their sale, such proportion of those proceeds and interest as is equal to the proportion which the value of the applicant's interest in the shares bears to the total value of the shares.

(3) On granting an application for an order under section 456(4) or (5) the court may order that the applicant's costs be paid out of the proceeds of sale; and if that order is made, the applicant is entitled to payment of his costs out of those proceeds before any person interested in the shares in question receives any part of those proceeds.

PART XVI
FRAUDULENT TRADING BY A COMPANY

458 Punishment for fraudulent trading

If any business of a company is carried on with intent to defraud creditors of the company or creditors of any other person, or for any fraudulent purpose, every person who was knowingly a party to the carrying on of the business in that manner is liable to imprisonment or a fine, or both.

This applies whether or not the company has been, or is in the course of being, wound up.

PART XVII
PROTECTION OF COMPANY'S MEMBERS AGAINST UNFAIR PREJUDICE

459 Order on application of company member

(1) A member of a company may apply to the court by petition for an order under this Part on the ground that the company's affairs are being or have been conducted in a manner which is [unfairly prejudicial to the interests of its members generally or of some part of its members] (including at least himself) or that any actual or proposed act or omission of the company (including an act or omission on its behalf) is or would be so prejudicial.

(2) The provisions of this Part apply to a person who is not a member of a company but to whom shares in the company have been transferred or transmitted by operation of law, as those provisions apply to a member of the company; and references to a member or members are to be construed accordingly.

[(3) In this section (and so far as applicable for the purposes of this section, in section 461(2)) "company" means any company within the meaning of this Act or any company which is not such a company but is a statutory water company within the meaning of [the Statutory Water Companies Act 1991].]

NOTES

Sub-s (1): words in square brackets substituted by the Companies Act 1989, s 145, Sch 19, para 11.

Sub-s (3): inserted by the Water Act 1989, s 190, Sch 25, para 71; words in square brackets therein substituted by the Water Consolidation (Consequential Provisions) Act 1991, s 2, Sch 1, para 40(2).

461 Provisions as to petitions and orders under this Part

(1) If the court is satisfied that a petition under this Part is well founded, it may make such order as it thinks fit for giving relief in respect of the matters complained of.

(2) Without prejudice to the generality of subsection (1), the court's order may—
  (a) regulate the conduct of the company's affairs in the future,

(b) require the company to refrain from doing or continuing an act complained of by the petitioner or to do an act which the petitioner has complained it has omitted to do,

(c) authorise civil proceedings to be brought in the name and on behalf of the company by such person or persons and on such terms as the court may direct,

(d) provide for the purchase of the shares of any members of the company by other members or by the company itself and, in the case of a purchase by the company itself, the reduction of the company's capital accordingly.

(3) If an order under this Part requires the company not to make any, or any specified, alteration in the memorandum or articles, the company does not then have power without leave of the court to make any such alteration in breach of that requirement.

(4) Any alteration in the company's memorandum or articles made by virtue of an order under this Part is of the same effect as if duly made by resolution of the company, and the provisions of this Act apply to the memorandum or articles as so altered accordingly.

(5) An office copy of an order under this Part altering, or giving leave to alter, a company's memorandum or articles shall, within 14 days from the making of the order or such longer period as the court may allow, be delivered by the company to the registrar of companies for registration; and if a company makes default in complying with this subsection, the company and every officer of it who is in default is liable to a fine and, for continued contravention, to a daily default fine.

[(6) The power under [section 411 of the Insolvency Act] to make rules shall, so far as it relates to a winding-up petition, apply for the purposes of a petition under this Part.]

NOTES

Sub-s (6): substituted by the Insolvency Act 1985, s 109, Sch 6, para 24; words in square brackets substituted by the Insolvency Act 1986, s 439(1), Sch 13, Part I.

Chapter VI
Matters Arising Subsequent to Winding Up

651 Power of court to declare dissolution of company void

(1) Where a company has been dissolved, the court may . . ., on an application made for the purpose by the liquidator of the company or by any other person appearing to the court to be interested, make an order, on such terms as the court thinks fit, declaring the dissolution to have been void.

(2) Thereupon such proceedings may be taken as might have been taken if the company had not been dissolved.

(3) It is the duty of the person on whose application the order was made, within 7 days after its making (or such further time as the court may allow), to deliver to the registrar of companies for registration an office copy of the order.

If the person fails to do so, he is liable to a fine and, for continued contravention, to a daily default fine.

[(4) Subject to the following provisions, an application under this section may not be made after the end of the period of two years from the date of the dissolution of the company.

(5) An application for the purposes of bringing proceedings against the company—
    (a) for damages in respect of personal injuries (including any sum claimed by virtue of section 1(2)(c) of the Law Reform (Miscellaneous Provisions) Act 1934 (funeral expenses)), or
    (b) for damages under the Fatal Accidents Act 1976 or the Damages (Scotland) Act 1976,

may be made at any time; but no order shall be made on such an application if it appears to the court that the proceedings would fail by virtue of any enactment as to the time within which proceedings must be brought.

(6) Nothing in subsection (5) affects the power of the court on making an order under this section to direct that the period between the dissolution of the company and the making of the order shall not count for the purposes of any such enactment.

(7) In subsection (5)(a) "personal injuries" includes any disease and any impairment of a person's physical or mental condition.]

NOTES

Sub-s (1): words omitted repealed by the Companies Act 1989, ss 141(2), 212, Sch 24.

Sub-ss (4)–(7): inserted by the Companies Act 1989, s 141(3); for effect see s 141(4), (5) thereof.

652 Registrar may strike defunct company off register

(1) If the registrar of companies has reasonable cause to believe that a company is not carrying on business or in operation, he may send to the company by post a letter inquiring whether the company is carrying on business or in operation.

(2) If the registrar does not within one month of sending the letter receive any answer to it, he shall within 14 days after the expiration of that month send to the company by post a registered letter referring to the first letter, and stating that no answer to it has been received, and that if an answer is not received to the second letter within one month from its date, a notice will be published in the Gazette with a view to striking the company's name off the register.

(3) If the registrar either receives an answer to the effect that the company is not carrying on business or in operation, or does not within one month after sending the second letter receive any answer, he may publish in the Gazette, and send to the company by post, a notice that at the expiration of 3 months from the date of that notice the name of the company mentioned in it will, unless cause is shown to the contrary, be struck off the register and the company will be dissolved.

(4) If, in a case where a company is being wound up, the registrar has reasonable cause to believe either that no liquidator is acting, or that the affairs of the company are fully wound up, and the returns required to be made by the liquidator have not

been made for a period of 6 consecutive months, the registrar shall publish in the Gazette and send to the company or the liquidator (if any) a like notice as is provided in subsection (3).

(5)   At the expiration of the time mentioned in the notice the registrar may, unless cause to the contrary is previously shown by the company, strike its name off the register, and shall publish notice of this in the Gazette; and on the publication of that notice in the Gazette the company is dissolved.

(6)   However—
  (a)   the liability (if any) of every director, managing officer and member of the company continues and may be enforced as if the company had not been dissolved, and
  (b)   nothing in subsection (5) affects the power of the court to wind up a company the name of which has been struck off the register.

(7)   A notice to be sent to a liquidator under this section may be addressed to him at his last known place of business; and a letter or notice to be sent under this section to a company may be addressed to the company at its registered office or, if no office has been registered, to the care of some officer of the company.

If there is no officer of the company whose name and address are known to the registrar of companies, the letter or notice may be sent to each of the persons who subscribed the memorandum, addressed to him at the address mentioned in the memorandum.

[652A Registrar may strike private company off register on application]

[(1)   On application by a private company, the registrar of companies may strike the company's name off the register.

(2)   An application by a company under this section shall—
  (a)   be made on its behalf by its directors or by a majority of them,
  (b)   be in the prescribed form, and
  (c)   contain the prescribed information.

(3)   The registrar shall not strike a company off under this section until after the expiration of 3 months from the publication by him in the Gazette of a notice—
  (a)   stating that he may exercise his power under this section in relation to the company, and
  (b)   inviting any person to show cause why he should not do so.

(4)   Where the registrar strikes a company off under this section, he shall publish notice of that fact in the Gazette.

(5)   On the publication in the Gazette of a notice under subsection (4), the company to which the notice relates is dissolved.

(6)   However, the liability (if any) of every director, managing officer and member of the company continues and may be enforced as if the company had not been dissolved.

(7)   Nothing in this section affects the power of the court to wind up a company the name of which has been struck off the register.]

NOTES

Inserted by the Deregulation and Contracting Out Act 1994, s 13(1), Sch 5, para 2.

[652B   Duties in connection with making application under section 652A]

[(1)   A person shall not make an application under section 652A on behalf of a company if, at any time in the previous 3 months, the company has—

(a)   changed its name,

(b)   traded or otherwise carried on business,

(c)   made a disposal for value of property or rights which, immediately before ceasing to trade or otherwise carry on business, it held for the purpose of disposal for gain in the normal course of trading or otherwise carrying on business, or

(d)   engaged in any other activity, except one which is—

    (i)   necessary or expedient for the purpose of making an application under section 652A, or deciding whether to do so,

    (ii)   necessary or expedient for the purpose of concluding the affairs of the company,

    (iii)   necessary or expedient for the purpose of complying with any statutory requirement, or

    (iv)   specified by the Secretary of State by order for the purposes of this sub-paragraph.

(2)   For the purposes of subsection (1), a company shall not be treated as trading or otherwise carrying on business by virtue only of the fact that it makes a payment in respect of a liability incurred in the course of trading or otherwise carrying on business.

(3)   A person shall not make an application under section 652A on behalf of a company at a time when any of the following is the case—

(a)   an application has been made to the court under section 425 on behalf of the company for the sanctioning of a compromise or arrangement and the matter has not been finally concluded;

(b)   a voluntary arrangement in relation to the company has been proposed under Part I of the Insolvency Act 1986 and the matter has not been finally concluded;

(c)   an administration order in relation to the company is in force under Part II of that Act or a petition for such an order has been presented and not finally dealt with or withdrawn;

(d)   the company is being wound up under Part IV of that Act, whether voluntarily or by the court, or a petition under that Part for the winding up of the company by the court has been presented and not finally dealt with or withdrawn;

(e)   there is a receiver or manager of the company's property;

(f)   the company's estate is being administered by a judicial factor.

(4)   For the purposes of subsection (3)(a), the matter is finally concluded if—
  (a)   the application has been withdrawn,
  (b)   the application has been finally dealt with without a compromise or arrangement being sanctioned by the court, or
  (c)   a compromise or arrangement has been sanctioned by the court and has, together with anything required to be done under any provision made in relation to the matter by order of the court, been fully carried out.

(5)   For the purposes of subsection (3)(b), the matter is finally concluded if—
  (a)   no meetings are to be summoned under section 3 of the Insolvency Act 1986,
  (b)   meetings summoned under that section fail to approve the arrangement with no, or the same, modifications,
  (c)   an arrangement approved by meetings summoned under that section, or in consequence of a direction under section 6(4)(b) of that Act, has been fully implemented, or
  (d)   the court makes an order under subsection (5) of section 6 of that Act revoking approval given at previous meetings and, if the court gives any directions under subsection (6) of that section, the company has done whatever it is required to do under those directions.

(6)   A person who makes an application under section 652A on behalf of a company shall secure that a copy of the application is given, within 7 days from the day on which the application is made, to every person who, at any time on that day, is—
  (a)   a member of the company,
  (b)   an employee of the company,
  (c)   a creditor of the company,
  (d)   a director of the company,
  (e)   a manager or trustee of any pension fund established for the benefit of employees of the company, or
  (f)   a person of a description specified for the purposes of this paragraph by regulations made by the Secretary of State.

(7)   Subsection (6) shall not require a copy of the application to be given to a director who is a party to the application.

(8)   The duty imposed by subsection (6) shall cease to apply if the application is withdrawn before the end of the period for giving the copy application.

(9)   The Secretary of State may by order amend subsection (1) for the purpose of altering the period in relation to which the doing of the things mentioned in paragraphs (a) to (d) of that subsection is relevant.]

NOTES

Inserted by the Deregulation and Contracting Out Act 1994, s 13(1), Sch 5, para 2.

[652C Directors' duties following application under section 652A]

[(1)   Subsection (2) applies in relation to any time after the day on which a company makes an application under section 652A and before the day on which the application is finally dealt with or withdrawn.

(2)   A person who is a director of the company at the end of a day on which a person other than himself becomes—
- (a)   a member of the company,
- (b)   an employee of the company,
- (c)   a creditor of the company,
- (d)   a director of the company,
- (e)   a manager or trustee of any pension fund established for the benefit of employees of the company, or
- (f)   a person of a description specified for the purposes of this paragraph by regulations made by the Secretary of State,

shall secure that a copy of the application is given to that person within 7 days from that day.

(3)   The duty imposed by subsection (2) shall cease to apply if the application is finally dealt with or withdrawn before the end of the period for giving the copy application.

(4)   Subsection (5) applies where, at any time on or after the day on which a company makes an application under section 652A and before the day on which the application is finally dealt with or withdrawn—
- (a)   the company—
  - (i)   changes its name,
  - (ii)   trades or otherwise carries on business,
  - (iii) makes a disposal for value of any property or rights other than those which it was necessary or expedient for it to hold for the purpose of making, or proceeding with, an application under section 652A, or
  - (iv) engages in any other activity, except one to which subsection (6) applies;
- (b)   an application is made to the court under section 425 on behalf of the company for the sanctioning of a compromise or arrangement;
- (c)   a voluntary arrangement in relation to the company is proposed under Part I of the Insolvency Act 1986;
- (d)   a petition is presented for the making of an administration order under Part II of that Act in relation to the company;
- (e)   there arise any of the circumstances in which, under section 84(1) of that Act, the company may be voluntarily wound up;
- (f)   a petition is presented for the winding up of the company by the court under Part IV of that Act;
- (g)   a receiver or manager of the company's property is appointed; or
- (h)   a judicial factor is appointed to administer the company's estate.

(5)   A person who, at the end of a day on which an event mentioned in any of paragraphs (a) to (h) of subsection (4) occurs, is a director of the company shall secure that the company's application is withdrawn forthwith.

(6)   This subsection applies to any activity which is—
  (a)   necessary or expedient for the purpose of making, or proceeding with, an application under section 652A,
  (b)   necessary or expedient for the purpose of concluding affairs of the company which are outstanding because of what has been necessary or expedient for the purpose of making, or proceeding with, such an application,
  (c)   necessary or expedient for the purpose of complying with any statutory requirement, or
  (d)   specified by the Secretary of State by order for the purposes of this subsection.

(7)   For the purposes of subsection (4)(a), a company shall not be treated as trading or otherwise carrying on business by virtue only of the fact that it makes a payment in respect of a liability incurred in the course of trading or otherwise carrying on business.]

NOTES

Inserted by the Deregulation and Contracting Out Act 1994, s 13(1), Sch 5, para 2.

[652D   Sections 652B and 652C: supplementary provisions]

[(1)   For the purposes of sections 652B(6) and 652C(2), a document shall be treated as given to a person if it is delivered to him or left at his proper address or sent by post to him at that address.

(2)   For the purposes of subsection (1) and section 7 of the Interpretation Act 1978 (which relates to the service of documents by post) in its application to that subsection, the proper address of any person shall be his last known address, except that—
  (a)   in the case of a body corporate, other than one to which subsection (3) applies, it shall be the address of its registered or principal office,
  (b)   in the case of a partnership, other than one to which subsection (3) applies, it shall be the address of its principal office, and
  (c)   in the case of a body corporate or partnership to which subsection (3) applies, it shall be the address of its principal office in the United Kingdom.

(3)   This subsection applies to a body corporate or partnership which—
  (a)   is incorporated or formed under the law of a country or territory outside the United Kingdom, and
  (b)   has a place of business in the United Kingdom.

(4)   Where a creditor of the company has more than one place of business, subsection (1) shall have effect, so far as concerns the giving of a document to him, as if for the words from "delivered" to the end there were substituted "left, or sent by post to him, at each place of business of his with which the company has had dealings in relation to a matter by virtue of which he is a creditor of the company."

(5)   Any power to make an order or regulations under section 652B or 652C shall—
  (a)   include power to make different provision for different cases or classes of case,

(b) include power to make such transitional provisions as the Secretary of State considers appropriate, and

(c) be exercisable by statutory instrument subject to annulment in pursuance of a resolution of either House of Parliament.

(6) For the purposes of sections 652B and 652C, an application under section 652A is withdrawn if notice of withdrawal in the prescribed form is given to the registrar of companies.

(7) In sections 652B and 652C, "disposal" includes part disposal.

(8) In sections 652B and 652C and this section, "creditor" includes a contingent or prospective creditor.]

NOTES

Inserted by the Deregulation and Contracting Out Act 1994, s 13(1), Sch 5, para 2.

[652E Sections 652B and 652C: enforcement]

[(1) A person who breaches or fails to perform a duty imposed on him by section 652B or 652C is guilty of an offence and liable to a fine.

(2) A person who fails to perform a duty imposed on him by section 652B(6) or 652C(2) with the intention of concealing the making of the application in question from the person concerned is guilty of an offence and liable to imprisonment or a fine, or both.

(3) In any proceedings for an offence under subsection (1) consisting of breach of a duty imposed by section 652B(1) or (3), it shall be a defence for the accused to prove that he did not know, and could not reasonably have known, of the existence of the facts which led to the breach.

(4) In any proceedings for an offence under subsection (1) consisting of failure to perform the duty imposed by section 652B(6), it shall be a defence for the accused to prove that he took all reasonable steps to perform the duty.

(5) In any proceedings for an offence under subsection (1) consisting of failure to perform a duty imposed by section 652C(2) or (5), it shall be a defence for the accused to prove—

(a) that at the time of the failure he was not aware of the fact that the company had made an application under section 652A, or

(b) that he took all reasonable steps to perform the duty.]

NOTES

Inserted by the Deregulation and Contracting Out Act 1994, s 13(1), Sch 5, para 2.

[652F Other offences connected with section 652A]

[(1) Where a company makes an application under section 652A, any person who, in connection with the application, knowingly or recklessly furnishes any information to the registrar of companies which is false or misleading in a material particular is guilty of an offence and liable to a fine.

(2)   Any person who knowingly or recklessly makes an application to the registrar of companies which purports to be an application under section 652A, but which is not, is guilty of an offence and liable to a fine.]

NOTES

Inserted by the Deregulation and Contracting Out Act 1994, s 13(1), Sch 5, para 2.

653 Objection to striking off by person aggrieved

(1)   [Subsection (2)] applies if a company or any member or creditor of it feels aggrieved by the company having been struck off the register [under section 652.]

(2)   The court, on an application by the company or the member or creditor made before the expiration of 20 years from publication in the Gazette of notice under section 652, may, if satisfied that the company was at the time of the striking off carrying on business or in operation, or otherwise that it is just that the company be restored to the register, order the company's name to be restored.

[(2A)   Subsections (2B) and (2D) apply if a company has been struck off the register under section 652A.

(2B)   The court, on an application by a notifiable person made before the expiration of 20 years from publication in the Gazette of notice under section 652A(4), may, if satisfied—

(a)   that any duty under section 652B or 652C with respect to the giving to that person of a copy of the company's application under section 652A was not performed,

(b)   that the making of the company's application under section 652A involved a breach of duty under section 652B(1) or (3), or

(c)   that it is for some other reason just to do so,

order the company's name to be restored to the register.

(2C)   In subsection (2B), "notifiable person" means a person to whom a copy of the company's application under section 652A was required to be given under section 652B or 652C.

(2D)   The court, on an application by the Secretary of State made before the expiration of 20 years from publication in the Gazette of notice under section 652A(4), may, if satisfied that it is in the public interest to do so, order the company's name to be restored.]

(3)   On an office copy of [an order under subsection (2), (2B) or (2D)] being delivered to the registrar of companies for registration the company [to which the order relates] is deemed to have continued in existence as if its name had not been struck off; and the court may by the order give such directions and make such provisions as seem just for placing the company and all other persons in the same position (as nearly as may be) as if the company's name had not been struck off.

NOTES

Sub-ss (1), (3): first words in square brackets substituted and final words in square brackets inserted, by the Deregulation and Contracting Out Act 1994, s 13(1), Sch 5, para 3(2), (4).

Sub-ss (2A)–(2D): inserted by the Deregulation and Contracting Out Act 1994, s 13(1), Sch 5, para 3(3).

654 Property of dissolved company to be bona vacantia

(1)   When a company is dissolved, all property and rights whatsoever vested in or held on trust for the company immediately before its dissolution (including leasehold property, but not including property held by the company on trust for any other person) are deemed to be bona vacantia and—

    (a)   accordingly belong to the Crown, or to the Duchy of Lancaster or to the Duke of Cornwall for the time being (as the case may be), and

    (b)   vest and may be dealt with in the same manner as other bona vacantia accruing to the Crown, to the Duchy of Lancaster or to the Duke of Cornwall.

(2)   Except as provided by the section next following, the above has effect subject and without prejudice to any order made by the court under section 651 or 653.

[Chapter IV
Winding Up etc]

NOTES

Inserted by SI 1992/3179, reg 3(1), Sch 2, para 19.

PART XXIV
THE REGISTRAR OF COMPANIES, HIS FUNCTIONS AND OFFICES

[709 Inspection, &c of records kept by the registrar]

[(1)   [Subject to section 723B,] any person may inspect any records kept by the registrar for the purposes of the Companies Acts and may require—

    (a)   a copy, in such form as the registrar considers appropriate, of any information contained in those records, or

    (b)   a certified copy of, or extract from, any such record.

(2)   The right of inspection extends to the originals of documents delivered to the registrar in legible form only where the record kept by the registrar of the contents of the document is illegible or unavailable.

(3)   A copy of or extract from a record kept at any of the offices for the registration of companies in England and Wales or Scotland, certified in writing by the registrar (whose official position it is unnecessary to prove) to be an accurate record of the contents of any document delivered to him under the Companies Acts, is in all legal proceedings admissible in evidence as of equal validity with the original document and as evidence of any fact stated therein of which direct oral evidence would be admissible.

   . . .

(4) Copies of or extracts from records furnished by the registrar may, instead of being certified by him in writing to be an accurate record, be sealed with his official seal.

(5) No process for compelling the production of a record kept by the registrar shall issue from any court except with the leave of the court; and any such process shall bear on it a statement that it is issued with the leave of the court.]

NOTES

Substituted, together with ss 710, 710A, for ss 709, 710 as originally enacted, by the Companies Act 1989, s 126(2).

Sub-s (1): words "Subject to section 723B," in square brackets inserted by the Criminal Justice and Police Act 2001, s 45(1), (4).

Date in force: 2 April 2002: see the Criminal Justice and Police Act 2001, s 138(2), and SI 2002/533, art 3.

Sub-s (3): words omitted repealed by the Youth Justice and Criminal Evidence Act 1999, s 67(3), Sch 6.

Date in force: 14 April 2000: see SI 2000/1034, art 2(c).

711 Public notice by registrar of receipt and issue of certain documents

(1) The registrar of companies shall cause to be published in the Gazette notice of the issue or receipt by him of documents of any of the following descriptions (stating in the notice the name of the company, the description of document and the date of issue or receipt)—

  (a) any certificate of incorporation of a company,
  (b) any document making or evidencing an alteration in a company's memorandum or articles,
  (c) any notification of a change among the directors of a company,
  (d) any copy of a resolution of a public company which gives, varies, revokes or renews an authority for the purposes of section 80 (allotment of relevant securities),
  (e) any copy of a special resolution of a public company passed under section 95(1), (2) or (3) (disapplication of pre-emption rights),
  (f) any report under section 103 or 104 as to the value of a non-cash asset,
  (g) any statutory declaration [or statement] delivered under section 117 (public company share capital requirements),
  (h) any notification (given under section 122) of the redemption of shares,
  (j) any statement or notice delivered by a public company under section 128 (registration of particulars of special rights),
  (k) any documents delivered by a company under [section 242(1) (accounts and reports)],
  (l) a copy of any resolution or agreement to which section 380 applies and which—
    (i) states the rights attached to any shares in a public company, other than shares which are in all respects uniform (for purposes of section 128) with shares previously allotted, or
    (ii) varies rights attached to any shares in a public company, or

           (iii) assigns a name or other designation, or a new name or designation, to any class of shares in a public company,

(m) any return of allotments of a public company,

(n) any notice of a change in the situation of a company's registered office,

(p) any copy of a winding-up order in respect of a company,

(q) any order for the dissolution of a company on a winding up,

(r) any return by a liquidator of the final meeting of a company on a winding up,

[(s) any copy of a draft of the terms of a scheme delivered to the registrar of companies under paragraph 2(1) of Schedule 15A,

(t) any copy of an order under section 425(2) or section 427 in respect of a compromise or arrangement to which section 427A(1) applies,]

[(u) any return delivered under paragraph 1, 7 or 8 of Schedule 21A (branch registration),

(v) any document delivered under paragraph 1 or 8 of that Schedule,

(w) any notice under section 695A(3) of the closure of a branch,

(x) any document delivered under Schedule 21C (accounts and reports of foreign credit and financial institutions),

(y) any document delivered under Schedule 21D (accounts and reports of oversea companies subject to branch registration, other than credit and financial institutions),

(z) any return delivered under section 703P (particulars of winding up of oversea companies subject to branch registration).]

(2) In section 42 "official notification" means—

(a) in relation to anything stated in a document of any of the above descriptions, the notification of that document in the Gazette under this section, and

(b) in relation to the appointment of a liquidator in a voluntary winding up, the notification of it in the Gazette under [section 109 of the Insolvency Act];

and "officially notified" is to be construed accordingly.

NOTES

Sub-s (1): in para (g) words "or statement" in square brackets inserted by SI 2000/3373, art 31(5).

Date in force: 22 December 2000: see SI 2000/3373, art 1(1).

Sub-s (1): in para (k) words "section 242(1) (accounts and reports)" in square brackets substituted by the Companies Act 1989, s 23, Sch 10, Pt I, para 14.

Sub-s (1): paras (s), (t) inserted by SI 1987/1991, reg 2.

Sub-s (1): paras (u)–(z) inserted by SI 1992/3179, reg 4, Sch 3, para 7.

Sub-s (2): words in square brackets substituted, subject to transitional provisions, by the Insolvency Act 1986, ss 437, 439(1), Sch 11, Sch 13, Part I.

[711A Exclusion of deemed notice]

[(1) A person shall not be taken to have notice of any matter merely because of its being disclosed in any document kept by the registrar of companies (and thus available for inspection) or made available by the company for inspection.

(2) This does not affect the question whether a person is affected by notice of any matter by reason of a failure to make such inquiries as ought reasonably to be made.

(3) In this section "document" includes any material which contains information.

(4) Nothing in this section affects the operation of—

   (a) section 416 of this Act (under which a person taking a charge over a company's property is deemed to have notice of matters disclosed on the companies charges register), or

   (b) section 198 of the Law of Property Act 1925 as it applies by virtue of section 3(7) of the Land Charges Act 1972 (under which the registration of certain land charges under Part XII, or Chapter III of Part XXIII, of this Act is deemed to constitute actual notice for all purposes connected with the land affected).]

NOTES

Inserted by the Companies Act 1989, s 142(1).
Date in force: to be appointed: see the Companies Act 1989, s 215(2).

[715A Interpretation]

[(1) In this Part—

"document" includes information recorded in any form; and

"legible", in the context of documents in legible or non-legible form, means capable of being read with the naked eye.

(2) References in this Part to delivering a document include sending, forwarding, producing or (in the case of a notice) giving it.]

NOTES

Inserted by the Companies Act 1989, s 127(1).

PART XXV

MISCELLANEOUS AND SUPPLEMENTARY PROVISIONS

716 Prohibition of partnerships with more than 20 members

(1) No company, association or partnership consisting of more than 20 persons shall be formed for the purpose of carrying on any business that has for its object the acquisition of gain by the company, association or partnership, or by its individual members, unless it is registered as a company under this Act, [is incorporated by virtue of regulations made under section 262 of the Financial Services and Markets Act 2000] or is formed in pursuance of some other Act of Parliament, or of letters patent.

(2) However, this does not prohibit the formation—

   (a) for the purpose of carrying on practice as solicitors, of a partnership consisting of persons each of whom is a solicitor;

   (b) for the purpose of carrying on practice as accountants, of [a partnership which is eligible for appointment as a company auditor under section 25 of the Companies Act 1989];

(c) for the purpose of carrying on business as members of a recognised stock exchange, of a partnership consisting of persons each of whom is a member of that stock exchange;

[(d) for any purpose prescribed by regulations (which may include a purpose mentioned above), of a partnership of a description so prescribed;]

[(e) of an open-ended investment company within the meaning of the Open-Ended Investment Companies Regulations 2001].

[. . .]

[(3) In subsection (2)(a) "solicitor"—

(a) in relation to England and Wales, means solicitor of the Supreme Court, and

(b) in relation to Scotland, means a person enrolled or deemed enrolled as a solicitor in pursuance of the Solicitors (Scotland) Act 1980.

(4) In subsection (2)(c) "recognised stock exchange" means—

(a) The International Stock Exchange of the United Kingdom and the Republic of Ireland Limited, and

(b) any other stock exchange for the time being recognised for the purposes of this section by the Secretary of State by order made by statutory instrument.]

(5) Subsection (1) does not apply in relation to any body of persons for the time being approved for the purposes of the Marine and Aviation Insurance (War Risks) Act 1952 by the Secretary of State, being a body the objects of which are or include the carrying on of business by way of the re-insurance of risks which may be re-insured under any agreement for the purpose mentioned in section 1(1)(b) of that Act.

NOTES

Sub-s (1): words "is incorporated by virtue of regulations made under section 262 of the Financial Services and Markets Act 2000" in square brackets inserted by the Financial Services and Markets Act 2000, s 263.

Date in force: 1 December 2001: see SI 2001/3538, art 2(1).

Sub-s (2): in para (b) words from "a partnership which" to "Companies Act 1989" in square brackets substituted by SI 1991/1997, reg 2, Schedule, para 53(3).

Sub-s (2): para (d) inserted by the Companies Act 1989, s 145, Sch 19, para 15(2).

Sub-s (2): para (e) inserted by SI 1996/2827, reg 75, Sch 8, para 8.

Sub-s (2): para (e) substituted by SI 2001/1228, reg 84, Sch 7, Pt I, para 7.

Date in force: 1 December 2001 (being the date on which the Financial Services and Markets Act 2000, s 19, came into force): see SI 2001/3538, art 2(1) and SI 2001/1228, reg 1(2)(c).

Sub-s (2): words omitted (inserted by the Financial Services Act 1986, s 212(2), Sch 16, para 22) repealed by the Companies Act 1989, ss 145, 212, Sch 19, para 15(2), Sch 24.

Sub-ss (3), (4): substituted by the Companies Act 1989, s 145, Sch 19, para 15(3).

719 Power of company to provide for employees on cessation or transfer of business

(1) The powers of a company include (if they would not otherwise do so apart from this section) power to make the following provision for the benefit of persons employed or formerly employed by the company or any of its subsidiaries, that is to

say, provision in connection with the cessation or the transfer to any person of the whole or part of the undertaking of the company or that subsidiary.

(2)   The power conferred by subsection (1) is exercisable notwithstanding that its exercise is not in the best interests of the company.

(3)   The power which a company may exercise by virtue only of subsection (1) shall only be exercised by the company if sanctioned—

(a)   in a case not falling within paragraph (b) or (c) below, by an ordinary resolution of the company, or

(b)   if so authorised by the memorandum or articles, a resolution of the directors, or

(c)   if the memorandum or articles require the exercise of the power to be sanctioned by a resolution of the company of some other description for which more than a simple majority of the members voting is necessary, with the sanction of a resolution of that description;

and in any case after compliance with any other requirements of the memorandum or articles applicable to its exercise.

(4)   Any payment which may be made by a company under this section may, if made before the commencement of any winding up of the company, be made out of profits of the company which are available for dividend.

727 Power of court to grant relief in certain cases

(1)   If in any proceedings for negligence, default, breach of duty or breach of trust against an officer of a company or a person employed by a company as auditor (whether he is or is not an officer of the company) it appears to the court hearing the case that that officer or person is or may be liable in respect of the negligence, default, breach of duty or breach of trust, but that he has acted honestly and reasonably, and that having regard to all the circumstances of the case (including those connected with his appointment) he ought fairly to be excused for the negligence, default, breach of duty or breach of trust, that court may relieve him, either wholly or partly, from his liability on such terms as it thinks fit.

(2)   If any such officer or person as above-mentioned has reason to apprehend that any claim will or might be made against him in respect of any negligence, default, breach of duty or breach of trust, he may apply to the court for relief; and the court on the application has the same power to relieve him as under this section it would have had if it had been a court before which proceedings against that person for negligence, default, breach of duty or breach of trust had been brought.

(3)   Where a case to which subsection (1) applies is being tried by a judge with a jury, the judge, after hearing the evidence, may, if he is satisfied that the defendant or defender ought in pursuance of that subsection to be relieved either in whole or in part from the liability sought to be enforced against him, withdraw the case in whole or in part from the jury and forthwith direct judgment to be entered for the defendant or defender on such terms as to costs or otherwise as the judge may think proper.

PART XXVI
INTERPRETATION

735 "Company", etc

(1) In this Act—
- (a) "company" means a company formed and registered under this Act, or an existing company;
- (b) "existing company" means a company formed and registered under the former Companies Acts, but does not include a company registered under the Joint Stock Companies Acts, the Companies Act 1862 or the Companies (Consolidation) Act 1908 in what was then Ireland;
- (c) "the former Companies Acts" means the Joint Stock Companies Acts, the Companies Act 1862, the Companies (Consolidation) Act 1908, the Companies Act 1929 and the Companies Acts 1948 to 1983.

(2) "Public company" and "private company" have the meanings given by section 1(3).

(3) "The Joint Stock Companies Acts" means the Joint Stock Companies Act 1856, the Joint Stock Companies Acts 1856, 1857, the Joint Stock Banking Companies Act 1857 and the Act to enable Joint Stock Banking Companies to be formed on the principle of limited liability, or any one or more of those Acts (as the case may require), but does not include the Joint Stock Companies Act 1844.

(4) The definitions in this section apply unless the contrary intention appears.

[735A Relationship of this Act to Insolvency Act]

[(1) In this Act "the Insolvency Act" means the Insolvency Act 1986; and in the following provisions of this Act, namely, sections 375(1)(b), 425(6)(a), . . . 460(2), 675, 676, 677, 699(1), 728 and Schedule 21, paragraph 6(1), the words "this Act" are to be read as including Parts I to VII of that Act, sections 411, 413, 414, 416 and 417 in Part XV of that Act, and also the Company Directors Disqualifications Act 1986.

(2) In [sections 704(5), (7) and (8)], 706(1), [707B(1)], [707A(1),] 708(1)(a) and (4), [709(1) and (3),] [710A], 713(1), 729 and 732(3) references to the Companies Acts include Parts I to VII of the Insolvency Act, sections 411, 413, 414, 416 and 417 in Part XV of that Act, and also the Company Directors Disqualification Act 1986.

(3) Subsections (1) and (2) apply unless the contrary intention appears.]

NOTES

Inserted by the Insolvency Act 1986, s 439(1), Sch 13, Part II.
Sub-s (1): words omitted repealed by the Companies Act 1989, s 212, Sch 24.
Sub-s (2): words "sections 704(5), (7) and (8)" in square brackets substituted by the Deregulation and Contracting Out Act 1994, s 76, Sch 16, para 9.
Sub-s (2): reference to "707B(1)" in square brackets substituted by SI 2000/3373, art 31(4)(b).
Date in force: 22 December 2000: see SI 2000/3373, art 1(1).

Sub-s (2): reference to "707A(1)," in square brackets inserted by the Companies Act 1989, s 127(5).

Sub-s (2): words "709(1) and (3)," in square brackets substituted by the Companies Act 1989, s 127(5).

Sub-s (2): reference to "710A" in square brackets inserted by the Companies Act 1989, s 127(5).

[735B Relationship of this Act to [Part 6 of the Financial Services and Markets Act 2000]]

[In [sections 704(5), (7) and (8)], 706(1), 707(1), 707A(1), 708(1)(a) and (4), 709(1) and (3), 710A and 713(1) references to the Companies Acts include [Part 6 of the Financial Services and Markets Act 2000].]

NOTES

Section heading: words "Part 6 of the Financial Services and Markets Act 2000" in square brackets substituted by SI 2001/3649, art 28.

Date in force: 1 December 2001: see SI 2001/3649, art 1.

Inserted by the Companies Act 1989, s 127(6).

Words "sections 704(5), (7) and (8)" in square brackets substituted by the Deregulation and Contracting Out Act 1994, s 76, Sch 16, para 10.

Words "Part 6 of the Financial Services and Markets Act 2000" in square brackets substituted by SI 2001/3649, art 28.

Date in force: 1 December 2001: see SI 2001/3649, art 1.

[736 "Subsidiary", "holding company" and "wholly owned subsidiary"]

[(1) A company is a "subsidiary" of another company, its "holding company", if that other company—

(a) holds a majority of the voting rights in it, or

(b) is a member of it and has the right to appoint or remove a majority of its board of directors, or

(c) is a member of it and controls alone, pursuant to an agreement with other shareholders or members, a majority of the voting rights in it,

or if it is a subsidiary of a company which is itself a subsidiary of that other company.

(2) A company is a "wholly-owned subsidiary" of another company if it has no members except that other and that other's wholly-owned subsidiaries or persons acting on behalf of that other or its wholly-owned subsidiaries.

(3) In this section "company" includes any body corporate.]

NOTES

Substituted, together with s 736A, for s 736 as originally enacted, by the Companies Act 1989, s 144(1).

[736A Provisions supplementing s 736]

[(1)   The provisions of this section explain expressions used in section 736 and otherwise supplement that section.

(2)   In section 736(1)(a) and (c) the references to the voting rights in a company are to the rights conferred on shareholders in respect of their shares or, in the case of a company not having a share capital, on members, to vote at general meetings of the company on all, or substantially all, matters.

(3)   In section 736(1)(b) the reference to the right to appoint or remove a majority of the board of directors is to the right to appoint or remove directors holding a majority of the voting rights at meetings of the board on all, or substantially all, matters; and for the purposes of that provision—
  (a)   a company shall be treated as having the right to appoint to a directorship if—
    (i)   a person's appointment to it follows necessarily from his appointment as director of the company, or
    (ii)   the directorship is held by the company itself; and
  (b)   a right to appoint or remove which is exercisable only with the consent or concurrence of another person shall be left out of account unless no other person has a right to appoint or, as the case may be, remove in relation to that directorship.

(4)   Rights which are exercisable only in certain circumstances shall be taken into account only—
  (a)   when the circumstances have arisen, and for so long as they continue to obtain, or
  (b)   when the circumstances are within the control of the person having the rights;

and rights which are normally exercisable but are temporarily incapable of exercise shall continue to be taken into account.

(5)   Rights held by a person in a fiduciary capacity shall be treated as not held by him.

(6)   Rights held by a person as nominee for another shall be treated as held by the other; and rights shall be regarded as held as nominee for another if they are exercisable only on his instructions or with his consent or concurrence.

(7)   Rights attached to shares held by way of security shall be treated as held by the person providing the security—
  (a)   where apart from the right to exercise them for the purpose of preserving the value of the security, or of realising it, the rights are exercisable only in accordance with his instructions;
  (b)   where the shares are held in connection with the granting of loans as part of normal business activities and apart from the right to exercise them for the purpose of preserving the value of the security, or of realising it, the rights are exercisable only in his interests.

(8)   Rights shall be treated as held by a company if they are held by any of its subsidiaries; and nothing in subsection (6) or (7) shall be construed as requiring rights held by a company to be treated as held by any of its subsidiaries.

(9)   For the purposes of subsection (7) rights shall be treated as being exercisable in accordance with the instructions or in the interests of a company if they are exercisable in accordance with the instructions of or, as the case may be, in the interests of—

   (a)   any subsidiary or holding company of that company, or

   (b)   any subsidiary of a holding company of that company.

(10)   The voting rights in a company shall be reduced by any rights held by the company itself.

(11)   References in any provision of subsections (5) to (10) to rights held by a person include rights falling to be treated as held by him by virtue of any other provision of those subsections but not rights which by virtue of any such provision are to be treated as not held by him.

(12)   In this section "company" includes any body corporate.]

NOTES

Substituted, together with new s 736, for s 736 as originally enacted, by the Companies Act 1989, s 144(1).

[736B Power to amend ss 736 and 736A]

[(1)   The Secretary of State may by regulations amend sections 736 and 736A so as to alter the meaning of the expressions "holding company", "subsidiary" or "wholly-owned subsidiary".

(2)   The regulations may make different provision for different cases or classes of case and may contain such incidental and supplementary provisions as the Secretary of State thinks fit.

(3)   Regulations under this section shall be made by statutory instrument which shall be subject to annulment in pursuance of a resolution of either House of Parliament.

(4)   Any amendment made by regulations under this section does not apply for the purposes of enactments outside the Companies Acts unless the regulations so provide.

(5)   So much of section 23(3) of the Interpretation Act 1978 as applies section 17(2)(a) of that Act (effect of repeal and re-enactment) to deeds, instruments and documents other than enactments shall not apply in relation to any repeal and re-enactment effected by regulations made under this section.]

NOTES

Inserted by the Companies Act 1989, s 144(3).

737 "Called-up share capital"

(1)   In this Act, "called-up share capital", in relation to a company, means so much of its share capital as equals the aggregate amount of the calls made on its shares (whether or not those calls have been paid), together with any share capital paid up without being called and any share capital to be paid on a specified future date under the articles, the terms of allotment of the relevant shares or any other arrangements for payment of those shares.

(2)   "Uncalled share capital" is to be construed accordingly.

(3)   The definitions in this section apply unless the contrary intention appears.

738 "Allotment" and "paid up"

(1)   In relation to an allotment of shares in a company, the shares are to be taken for the purposes of this Act to be allotted when a person acquires the unconditional right to be included in the company's register of members in respect of those shares.

(2)   For purposes of this Act, a share in a company is deemed paid up (as to its nominal value or any premium on it) in cash, or allotted for cash, if the consideration for the allotment or payment up is cash received by the company, or is a cheque received by it in good faith which the directors have no reason for suspecting will not be paid, or is a release of a liability of the company for a liquidated sum, or is an undertaking to pay cash to the company at a future date.

(3)   In relation to the allotment or payment up of any shares in a company, references in this Act (except sections 89 to 94) to consideration other than cash and to the payment up of shares and premiums on shares otherwise than in cash include the payment of, or any undertaking to pay, cash to any person other than the company.

(4)   For the purpose of determining whether a share is or is to be allotted for cash, or paid up in cash, "cash" includes foreign currency.

739 "Non-cash asset"

(1)   In this Act "non-cash asset" means any property or interest in property other than cash; and for this purpose "cash" includes foreign currency.

(2)   A reference to the transfer or acquisition of a non-cash asset includes the creation or extinction of an estate or interest in, or a right over, any property and also the discharge of any person's liability, other than a liability for a liquidated sum.

741 "Director" and "shadow director"

(1)   In this Act, "director" includes any person occupying the position of director, by whatever name called.

(2)   In relation to a company, "shadow director" means a person in accordance with whose directions or instructions the directors of the company are accustomed to act.

However, a person is not deemed a shadow director by reason only that the directors act on advice given by him in a professional capacity.

(3)   For the purposes of the following provisions of this Act, namely—
section 309 (directors' duty to have regard to interests of employees),
section 319 (directors' long-term contracts of employment),
sections 320 to 322 (substantial property transactions involving directors), . . .
[section 322B (contracts with sole members who are directors), and]
sections 330 to 346 (general restrictions on power of companies to make loans,
etc, to directors and others connected with them),

(being provisions under which shadow directors are treated as directors), a body corporate is not to be treated as a shadow director of any of its subsidiary companies by reason only that the directors of the subsidiary are accustomed to act in accordance with its directions or instructions.

NOTES

Sub-s (3): word omitted repealed, and words in square brackets inserted, by SI 1992/1699, reg 2(b), Schedule, para 3(2).

744 Expressions used generally in this Act

In this Act, unless the contrary intention appears, the following definitions apply—
"agent" does not include a person's counsel acting as such;
. . .
"articles" means, in relation to a company, its articles of association, as originally framed or as altered by resolution, including (so far as applicable to the company) regulations contained in or annexed to any enactment relating to companies passed before this Act, as altered by or under any such enactment;
[. . .]
"authorised minimum" has the meaning given by section 118;
"bank holiday" means a holiday under the Banking and Financial Dealings Act 1971;
[. . .]
"books and papers" and "books or papers" include accounts, deeds, writings and documents;
["communication" means the same as in the Electronic Communications Act 2000;]
"the Companies Acts" means this Act, the [insider dealing legislation] and the Consequential Provisions Act;
"the Consequential Provisions Act" means the Companies Consolidation (Consequential Provisions) Act 1985;
"the court", in relation to a company, means the court having jurisdiction to wind up the company;
"debenture" includes debenture stock, bonds and any other securities of a company, whether constituting a charge on the assets of the company or not;
"document" includes summons, notice, order, and other legal process, and registers;
["EEA State" means a State which is a Contracting Party to the Agreement on the European Economic Area signed at Oporto on 2nd May 1992 as adjusted by the Protocol signed at Brussels on 17th March 1993;]

["electronic communication" means the same as in the Electronic Communications Act 2000;]

"equity share capital" means, in relation to a company, its issued share capital excluding any part of that capital which, neither as respects dividends nor as respects capital, carries any right to participate beyond a specified amount in a distribution;

"expert" has the meaning given by section 62;

"floating charge" includes a floating charge within the meaning given by section 462;

"the Gazette" means, as respects companies registered in England and Wales, the London Gazette and, as respects companies registered in Scotland, the Edinburgh Gazette;

. . .

"hire-purchase agreement" has the same meaning as in the Consumer Credit Act 1974;

["the insider dealing legislation" means Part V of the Criminal Justice Act 1993 (insider dealing).]

["insurance market activity" has the meaning given in section 316(3) of the Financial Services and Markets Act 2000;]

. . .

"joint stock company" has the meaning given by section 683;

"memorandum", in relation to a company, means its memorandum of association, as originally framed or as altered in pursuance of any enactment;

"number", in relation to shares, includes amount, where the context admits of the reference to shares being construed to include stock;

"officer", in relation to a body corporate, includes a director, manager or secretary;

"official seal", in relation to the registrar of companies, means a seal prepared under section 704(4) for the authentication of documents required for or in connection with the registration of companies;

"oversea company" means—

(a) a company incorporated elsewhere than in Great Britain which, after the commencement of this Act, establishes a place of business in Great Britain, and

(b) a company so incorporated which has, before that commencement, established a place of business and continues to have an established place of business in Great Britain at that commencement;

"place of business" includes a share transfer or share registration office;

"prescribed" means—

(a) as respects provisions of this Act relating to winding up, prescribed by general rules . . ., and

(b) otherwise, prescribed by statutory instrument made by the Secretary of State;

"prospectus" means any prospectus, notice, circular, advertisement, or other invitation, offering to the public for subscription or purchase any shares in or debentures of a company;

"prospectus issued generally" means a prospectus issued to persons who are not existing members of the company or holders of its debentures;

. . .

. . .

["regulated activity" has the meaning given in section 22 of the Financial Services and Markets Act 2000;]

"the registrar of companies" and "the registrar" mean the registrar or other officer performing under this Act the duty of registration of companies in England and Wales or in Scotland, as the case may require;

"share" means share in the share capital of a company, and includes stock (except where a distinction between shares and stock is express or implied); and

"undistributable reserves" has the meaning given by section 264(3).

NOTES

Definition "annual return" (omitted) repealed by the Companies Act 1989, s 212, Sch 24.

Definition "authorised institution" (omitted) inserted by the Banking Act 1987, s 108(1), Sch 6, para 18(8).

Definition "authorised institution" (omitted) repealed by the Companies Act 1989, ss 23, 212, Sch 10, Pt I, para 16, Sch 24.

Definition "authorised minimum" repealed by the Companies Act 1989, s 212, Sch 24, as from a day to be appointed.

Definition "banking company" (omitted) inserted by the Companies Act 1989, s 23, Sch 10, Pt I, para 16.

Definition "banking company" (omitted) repealed by SI 2001/3649, art 30(a).

Date in force: 1 December 2001: see SI 2001/3649, art 1.

Definition "communication" inserted by SI 2000/3373, art 29.

Date in force: 22 December 2000: see SI 2000/3373, art 1(1).

In definition "Companies Acts" words "insider dealing legislation" in square brackets substituted by the Criminal Justice Act 1993, s 79(13), Sch 5, para 4.

Definition "EEA State" inserted by SI 1997/2306, reg 4(1).

Definition "electronic communication" inserted by SI 2000/3373, art 29.

Date in force: 22 December 2000: see SI 2000/3373, art 1(1).

Definition "expert" repealed by the Companies Act 1989, s 212, Sch 24, as from a day to be appointed.

Definition "floating charge" repealed by the Companies Act 1989, s 212, Sch 24, as from a day to be appointed.

Definition "general rules" (omitted) repealed by the Insolvency Act 1985, s 235(3), Sch 10, Pt II.

Definition "the insider dealing legislation" inserted by the Criminal Justice Act 1993, s 79(13), Sch 5, para 4.

Definition "insurance market activity" inserted by SI 2001/3649, art 30(b).

Date in force: 1 December 2001: see SI 2001/3649, art 1.

Definition "insurance company" (omitted) repealed by SI 2001/3649, art 30(a).

Date in force: 1 December 2001: see SI 2001/3649, art 1.

Definition "joint stock company" repealed by the Companies Act 1989, s 212, Sch 24, as from a day to be appointed.

In definition "prescribed" words omitted repealed by the Insolvency Act 1985, s 235(3), Sch 10, Pt II.

Definition "prospectus issued generally" repealed for certain purposes and for remaining purposes as from a day to be appointed by the Financial Services Act 1986, s 212(3), Sch 17, Pt I; for purposes see SI 1988/740, Schedule.

Definition "recognised bank" (omitted) repealed by the Banking Act 1987, s 108, Sch 6, para 18(8), Sch 7, Pt I.

Definition "recognised stock exchange" (omitted) repealed by the Financial Services Act 1986, s 212(3), Sch 17, Pt I.

Definition "regulated activity" inserted by SI 2001/3649, art 30(c).

Date in force: 1 December 2001: see SI 2001/3649, art 1.

Definition "undistributable reserves" repealed by the Companies Act 1989, s 212, Sch 24, as from a day to be appointed.

SCHEDULE 1
PARTICULARS OF DIRECTORS ETC TO BE CONTAINED IN STATEMENT UNDER SECTION 10

Section 10

Directors

1   Subject as provided below, the statement under section 10(2) shall contain the following particulars with respect to each person named as director—

(a)   in the case of an individual, his present [name], any former [name], his usual residential address, his nationality, his business occupation (if any), particulars of any other directorships held by him, or which have been held by him [and his date of birth;]

(b)   in the case of a corporation [or Scottish firm], its corporate [or firm] name and registered or principal office.

2   (1) It is not necessary for the statement to contain particulars of a directorship—

(a)   which has not been held by a director at any time during the 5 years preceding the date on which the statement is delivered to the registrar,

(b)   which is held by a director in a company which—

(i)   is dormant or grouped with the company delivering the statement, and

(ii)   if he also held that directorship for any period during those 5 years, was for the whole of that period either dormant or so grouped,

(c)   which was held by a director for any period during those 5 years in a company which for the whole of that period was either dormant or grouped with the company delivering the statement.

(2)   For these purposes, "company" includes any body corporate incorporated in Great Britain; and—

(a)   [section 249AA(3)] applies as regards whether and when a company is or has been "dormant", and

(b)   a company is treated as being or having been at any time grouped with another company if at that time it is or was a company of which that other is or was a wholly-owned subsidiary, or if it is or was a wholly-owned subsidiary of the other or of another company of which that other is or was a wholly-owned subsidiary.

Secretaries

3   (1) The statement shall contain the following particulars with respect to the person named as secretary or, where there are to be joint secretaries, with respect to each person named as one of them—

(a)   in the case of an individual, his present [name], any former [name] and his usual residential address,

(b)   in the case of a corporation or a Scottish firm, its corporate or firm name and registered or principal office.

(2)   However, if all the partners in a firm are joint secretaries, the name and principal office of the firm may be stated instead of the particulars otherwise required by this paragraph.

Interpretation

[4   In paragraphs 1(a) and 3(1)(a) above—
   (a)   "name" means a person's Christian name (or other forename) and surname, except that in the case of a peer, or an individual usually known by a title, the title may be stated instead of his Christian name (or other forename) and surname or in addition to either or both of them; and
   (b)   the reference to a former name does not include—
      (i)   in the case of a peer, or an individual normally known by a British title, the name by which he was known previous to the adoption of or succession to the title, or
      (ii)   in the case of any person, a former name which was changed or disused before he attained the age of 18 years or which has been changed or disused for 20 years or more, or
      (iii) in the case of a married woman, the name by which she was known previous to the marriage.]

[5   Where a confidentiality order made under section 723B is in force in respect of any individual named as a director or secretary, paragraphs 1(a) and 3(1)(a) have effect as if the references to the usual residential address of the individual were references to the address for the time being notified by him under regulations made under sections 723B to 723F to any companies or oversea companies of which he is a director, secretary or permanent representative, or, if he is not such a director, secretary or permanent representative either the address specified in his application for a confidentiality order under regulations made under section 723B or the address last notified by him under regulations made under sections 723B to 723F as the case may be.]

NOTES

Para 1: first, second and third words in square brackets substituted, and fourth and final words in square brackets inserted, by the Companies Act 1989, s 145, Sch 19, para 7(2), (3).

Para 2: in sub-para (2)(a) words "section 249AA(3)" in square brackets substituted by SI 2000/1430, reg 8(10).

Date in force: this amendment has effect in relation to annual accounts and reports in respect of financial years ending on or after 26 July 2000: see SI 2000/1430, reg 1(1), (2).

Para 3: words in square brackets substituted by the Companies Act 1989, s 145, Sch 19, para 7(4).

Para 4: substituted by the Companies Act 1989, s 145, Sch 19, para 7(5).

Para 5: inserted by SI 2002/912, reg 16, Sch 2, para 7.

Date in force: 2 April 2002: see SI 2002/912, reg 1(2).

PART XXVII
FINAL PROVISIONS

SCHEDULE 4
FORM AND CONTENT OF COMPANY ACCOUNTS

Section 226

PART I
GENERAL RULES AND FORMATS

Section A
General Rules

1 (1) Subject to the following provisions of this Schedule—

(a) every balance sheet of a company shall show the items listed in either of the balance sheet formats set out below in section B of this Part; and

(b) every profit and loss account of a company shall show the items listed in any one of the profit and loss account formats so set out;

in either case in the order and under the headings and sub-headings given in the format adopted.

(2) Sub-paragraph (1) above is not to be read as requiring the heading or sub-heading for any item to be distinguished by any letter or number assigned to that item in the format adopted.

2 (1) Where in accordance with paragraph 1 a company's balance sheet or profit and loss account for any financial year has been prepared by reference to one of the formats set out in section B below, the directors of the company shall adopt the same format in preparing the accounts for subsequent financial years of the company unless in their opinion there are special reasons for a change.

(2) Particulars of any change in the format adopted in preparing a company's balance sheet or profit and loss account in accordance with paragraph 1 shall be disclosed, and the reasons for the change shall be explained, in a note to the accounts in which the new format is first adopted.

3 (1) Any item required in accordance with paragraph 1 to be shown in a company's balance sheet or profit and loss account may be shown in greater detail than required by the format adopted.

(2) A company's balance sheet or profit and loss account may include an item representing or covering the amount of any asset or liability, income or expenditure not otherwise covered by any of the items listed in the format adopted, but the following shall not be treated as assets in any company's balance sheet—

(a) preliminary expenses;

(b) expenses of and commission on any issue of shares or debentures; and

(c) costs of research.

(3) In preparing a company's balance sheet or profit and loss account the directors of the company shall adapt the arrangement and headings and sub-headings otherwise required by paragraph 1 in respect of items to which an Arabic number is assigned in the format adopted, in any case where the special nature of the company's business requires such adaptation.

(4) Items to which Arabic numbers are assigned in any of the formats set out in section B below may be combined in a company's accounts for any financial year if either—

(a)   their individual amounts are not material to assessing the state of affairs or profit or loss of the company for that year; or

(b)   the combination facilitates that assessment;

but in a case within paragraph (b) the individual amounts of any items so combined shall be disclosed in a note to the accounts.

(5)   Subject to paragraph 4(3) below, a heading or sub-heading corresponding to an item listed in the format adopted in preparing a company's balance sheet or profit and loss account shall not be included if there is no amount to be shown for that item in respect of the financial year to which the balance sheet or profit and loss account relates.

(6)   Every profit and loss account of a company shall show the amount of the company's profit or loss on ordinary activities before taxation.

(7)   Every profit and loss account of a company shall show separately as additional items—

(a)   any amount set aside or proposed to be set aside to, or withdrawn or proposed to be withdrawn from, reserves; . . .

(b)   the aggregate amount of any dividends paid and proposed.

[(c)   if it is not shown in the notes to the accounts, the aggregate amount of any dividends proposed.]

4   (1)   In respect of every item shown in a company's balance sheet or profit and loss account the corresponding amount for the financial year immediately preceding that to which the balance sheet or profit and loss account relates shall also be shown.

(2)   Where that corresponding amount is not comparable with the amount to be shown for the item in question in respect of the financial year to which the balance sheet or profit and loss account relates, the former amount shall be adjusted and particulars of the adjustment and the reasons for it shall be disclosed in a note to the accounts.

(3)   Paragraph 3(5) does not apply in any case where an amount can be shown for the item in question in respect of the financial year immediately preceding that to which the balance sheet or profit and loss account relates, and that amount shall be shown under the heading or sub-heading required by paragraph 1 for that item.

5   Amounts in respect of items representing assets or income may not be set off against amounts in respect of items representing liabilities or expenditure (as the case may be), or vice versa.

Section B
The Required Formats for Accounts

PRELIMINARY

6   References in this Part of this Schedule to the items listed in any of the formats set out below are to those items read together with any of the notes following the formats which apply to any of those items, and the requirement imposed by paragraph 1 to show the items listed in any such format in the order adopted in the format is subject to any provision in those notes for alternative positions for any particular items.

7   A number in brackets following any item in any of the formats set out below is a reference to the note of that number in the notes following the formats.

8   In the notes following the formats—

(a)   the heading of each note gives the required heading or sub-heading for the item to which it applies and a reference to any letters and numbers assigned to that item in the formats set out below (taking a reference in the case of Format 2 of the balance sheet formats to the item listed under "Assets" or under "Liabilities" as the case may require); and

(b) references to a numbered format are to the balance sheet format or (as the case may require) to the profit and loss account format of that number set out below.

BALANCE SHEET FORMATS

Format 1

A. Called up share capital not paid (1)

B. Fixed assets
I Intangible assets
    1. Development costs
    2. Concessions, patents, licences, trade marks and similar rights and assets (2)
    3. Goodwill (3)
    4. Payments on account
II Tangible assets
    1. Land and buildings
    2. Plant and machinery
    3. Fixtures, fittings, tools and equipment
    4. Payments on account and assets in course of construction
III Investments
    1. Shares in [group undertakings]
    2. Loans to [group undertakings]
    3. [Participating interests]
    4. Loans to [undertakings in which the company has a participating interest]
    5. Other investments other than loans
    6. Other loans
    7. Own shares (4)

C. Current assets
I Stocks
    1. Raw materials and consumables
    2. Work in progress
    3. Finished goods and goods for resale
    4. Payments on account
II Debtors (5)
    1. Trade debtors
    2. Amounts owed by [group undertakings]
    3. Amounts owed by [undertakings in which the company has a participating interest]
    4. Other debtors
    5. Called up share capital not paid (1)
    6. Prepayments and accrued income (6)
III Investments
    1. Shares in [group undertakings]
    2. Own shares (4)
    3. Other investments
IV Cash at bank and in hand

D. Prepayments and accrued income (6).

E. Creditors: amounts falling due within one year
    1. Debenture loans (7)

      2. Bank loans and overdrafts
      3. Payments received on account (8)
      4. Trade creditors
      5. Bills of exchange payable
      6. Amounts owed to [group undertakings]
      7. Amounts owed to [undertakings in which the company has a participating interest]
      8. Other creditors including taxation and social security (9)
      9. Accruals and deferred income (10)

F. Net current assets (liabilities) (11)

G. Total assets less current liabilities

H. Creditors: amounts falling due after more than one year
      1. Debenture loans (7)
      2. Bank loans and overdrafts
      3. Payments received on account (8)
      4. Trade creditors
      5. Bills of exchange payable
      6. Amounts owed to [group undertakings]
      7. Amounts owed to [undertakings in which the company has a participating interest]
      8. Other creditors including taxation and social security (9)
      9. Accruals and deferred income (10)

I. Provisions for liabilities and charges
      1. Pensions and similar obligations
      2. Taxation, including deferred taxation
      3. Other provisions

J. Accruals and deferred income (10)

K. Capital and reserves
  I Called up share capital (12)
  II Share premium account
  III Revaluation reserve
  IV Other reserves
      1. Capital redemption reserve
      2. Reserve for own shares
      3. Reserves provided for by the articles of association
      4. Other reserves
  V Profit and loss account

BALANCE SHEET FORMATS

Format 2

ASSETS

A. Called up share capital not paid (1)

B. Fixed assets
  I Intangible assets
      1. Development costs
      2. Concessions, patents, licences, trade marks and similar rights and assets (2)
      3. Goodwill (3)
      4. Payments on account
  II Tangible assets
      1. Land and buildings

2. Plant and machinery
3. Fixtures, fittings, tools and equipment
4. Payments on account and assets in course of construction
III Investments
  1. Shares in [group undertakings]
  2. Loans to [group undertakings]
  3. [Participating interests]
  4. Loans to [undertakings in which the company has a participating interest]
  5. Other investments other than loans
  6. Other loans
  7. Own shares (4)

C. Current assets
  I Stocks
    1. Raw materials and consumables
    2. Work in progress
    3. Finished goods and goods for resale
    4. Payments on account
  II Debtors (5)
    1. Trade debtors
    2. Amounts owed by [group undertakings]
    3. Amounts owed by [undertakings in which the company has a participating interest]
    4. Other debtors
    5. Called up share capital not paid (1)
    6. Prepayments and accrued income (6)
  III Investments
    1. Shares in [group undertakings]
    2. Own shares (4)
    3. Other investments
  IV Cash at bank and in hand

D. Prepayments and accrued income (6)

LIABILITIES

A. Capital and reserves
  I Called up share capital (12)
  II Share premium account
  III Revaluation reserve
  IV Other reserves
    1. Capital redemption reserve
    2. Reserve for own shares
    3. Reserves provided for by the articles of association
    4. Other reserves
  V Profit and loss account

B. Provisions for liabilities and charges
  1. Pensions and similar obligations
  2. Taxation including deferred taxation
  3. Other provisions

C. Creditors (13)
  1. Debenture loans (7)
  2. Bank loans and overdrafts
  3. Payments received on account (8)

4. Trade creditors
5. Bills of exchange payable
6. Amounts owed to [group undertakings]
7. Amounts owed to [undertakings in which the company has a participating interest]
8. Other creditors including taxation and social security (9)
9. Accruals and deferred income (10)

D. Accruals and deferred income (10)

NOTES ON THE BALANCE SHEET FORMATS

(1)   Called up share capital not paid
  (Formats 1 and 2, items A and C.II.5.)
      This item may be shown in either of the two positions given in Formats 1 and 2.

(2)   Concessions, patents, licences, trade marks and similar rights and assets
  (Formats 1 and 2, item B.I.2.)
      Amounts in respect of assets shall only be included in a company's balance sheet
      under this item if either—
        (a)   the assets were acquired for valuable consideration and are not required to
              be shown under goodwill; or
        (b)   the assets in question were created by the company itself.

(3)   Goodwill
  (Formats 1 and 2, item B.I.3.)
      Amounts representing goodwill shall only be included to the extent that the goodwill
      was acquired for valuable consideration.

(4)   Own shares
  (Formats 1 and 2, items B.III.7 and C.III.2.)
      The nominal value of the shares held shall be shown separately.

(5)   Debtors
  (Formats 1 and 2, items C.II.1 to 6.)
      The amount falling due after more than one year shall be shown separately for each
      item included under debtors.

(6)   Prepayments and accrued income
  (Formats 1 and 2, items C.II.6 and D.)
      This item may be shown in either of the two positions given in Formats 1 and 2.

(7)   Debenture loans
  (Format 1, items E.1 and H.1 and Format 2, item C.1.)
      The amount of any convertible loans shall be shown separately.

(8)   Payments received on account
  (Format 1, items E.3 and H.3 and Format 2, item C.3.)
      Payments received on account of orders shall be shown for each of these items in so
      far as they are not shown as deductions from stocks.

(9)   Other creditors including taxation and social security
  (Format 1, items E.8 and H.8 and Format 2, item C.8.)
      The amount for creditors in respect of taxation and social security shall be shown
      separately from the amount for other creditors.

(10)   Accruals and deferred income
  (Format 1, items E.9, H.9 and J and Format 2, items C.9 and D.)

The two positions given for this item in Format 1 at E.9 and H.9 are an alternative to the position at J, but if the item is not shown in a position corresponding to that at J it may be shown in either or both of the other two positions (as the case may require).

The two positions given for this item in Format 2 are alternatives.

(11)   Net current assets (liabilities)
   (Format 1, item F.)

In determining the amount to be shown for this item any amount shown under "prepayments and accrued income" shall be taken into account wherever shown.

(12)   Called up share capital
   (Format 1, item K.I and Format 2, item A.I.)

The amount of allotted share capital and the amount of called up share capital which has been paid up shall be shown separately.

(13)   Creditors
   (Format 2, items C.1 to 9.)

Amounts falling due within one year and after one year shall be shown separately for each of these items [and for the aggregate of all of these items].

PROFIT AND LOSS ACCOUNT FORMATS

Format 1
(see note (17) below)

1   Turnover

2   Cost of sales (14)

3   Gross profit or loss

4   Distribution costs (14)

5   Administrative expenses (14)

6   Other operating income

7   Income from shares in [group undertakings]

8   Income from [participating interests]

9   Income from other fixed asset investments (15)

10   Other interest receivable and similar income (15)

11   Amounts written off investments

12   Interest payable and similar charges (16)

13   Tax on profit or loss on ordinary activities

14   Profit or loss on ordinary activities after taxation

15   Extraordinary income

16   Extraordinary charges

17   Extraordinary profit or loss

18   Tax on extraordinary profit or loss

19   Other taxes not shown under the above items

20 Profit or loss for the financial year

Format 2

1 Turnover

2 Change in stocks of finished goods and in work in progress

3 Own work capitalised

4 Other operating income

5 (a) Raw materials and consumables

    (b) Other external charges

6 Staff costs:

    (a) wages and salaries

    (b) social security costs

    (c) other pension costs

7 (a) Depreciation and other amounts written off tangible and intangible fixed assets

    (b) Exceptional amounts written off current assets

8 Other operating charges

9 Income from shares in [group undertakings]

10 Income from [participating interests]

11 Income from other fixed asset investments (15)

12 Other interest receivable and similar income (15)

13 Amounts written off investments

14 Interest payable and similar charges (16)

15 Tax on profit or loss on ordinary activities

16 Profit or loss on ordinary activities after taxation

17 Extraordinary income

18 Extraordinary charges

19 Extraordinary profit or loss

20 Tax on extraordinary profit or loss

21 Other taxes not shown under the above items

22 Profit or loss for the financial year

PROFIT AND LOSS ACCOUNT FORMATS

PROFIT AND LOSS ACCOUNT FORMATS

Format 3
(see note (17) below)

A. Charges

1 Cost of sales (14)

2 Distribution costs (14)

3 Administrative expenses (14)

4 Amounts written off investments

5 Interest payable and similar charges (16)

6 Tax on profit or loss on ordinary activities

7 Profit or loss on ordinary activities after taxation

8 Extraordinary charges

9 Tax on extraordinary profit or loss

10 Other taxes not shown under the above items

11 Profit or loss for the financial year

B. Income

1 Turnover

2 Other operating income

3 Income from shares in [group undertakings]

4 Income from [participating interests]

5 Income from other fixed asset investments (15)

6 Other interest receivable and similar income (15)

7 Profit or loss on ordinary activities after taxation

8 Extraordinary income

9 Profit or loss for the financial year

PROFIT AND LOSS ACCOUNT FORMATS

Format 4

A. Charges

1 Reduction in stocks of finished goods and in work in progress

2 (a) Raw materials and consumables

   (b) Other external charges

3   Staff costs:

    (a)   wages and salaries

    (b)   social security costs

    (c)   other pension costs

4   (a)   Depreciation and other amounts written off tangible and intangible fixed assets

    (b)   Exceptional amounts written off current assets

5   Other operating charges

6   Amounts written off investments

7   Interest payable and similar charges (16)

8   Tax on profit or loss on ordinary activities

9   Profit or loss on ordinary activities after taxation

10   Extraordinary charges

11   Tax on extraordinary profit or loss

12   Other taxes not shown under the above items

13   Profit or loss for the financial year

B. Income

1   Turnover

2   Increase in stocks of finished goods and in work in progress

3   Own work capitalised

4   Other operating income

5   Income from shares in [group undertakings]

6   Income from [participating interests]

7   Income from other fixed asset investments (15)

8   Other interest receivable and similar income (15)

9   Profit or loss on ordinary activities after taxation

10   Extraordinary income

11   Profit or loss for the financial year

NOTES ON THE PROFIT AND LOSS ACCOUNT FORMATS

(14)   Cost of sales: distribution costs: administrative expenses
    (Format 1, items 2, 4 and 5 and Format 3, items A.1, 2 and 3.)
        These items shall be stated after taking into account any necessary provisions for depreciation or diminution in value of assets.

(15)   Income from other fixed asset investments: other interest receivable and similar income
    (Format 1, items 9 and 10: Format 2, items 11 and 12: Format 3, items B.5 and 6: Format 4, items B.7 and 8.)
        Income and interest derived from [group undertakings] shall be shown separately from income and interest derived from other sources.

(16) Interest payable and similar charges
(Format 1, item 12: Format 2, item 14: Format 3, item A.5: Format 4, item A.7.)
The amount payable to [group undertakings] shall be shown separately.

(17) Formats 1 and 3
The amount of any provisions for depreciation and diminution in value of tangible and intangible fixed assets falling to be shown under items 7(a) and A.4(a) respectively in Formats 2 and 4 shall be disclosed in a note to the accounts in any case where the profit and loss account is prepared by reference to Format 1 or Format 3.

NOTES

Para 3: in sub-para (7) word omitted repealed and para (c) inserted, in relation to the annual accounts and annual report of any company for the financial year ending on or after 2 February 1996, by SI 1996/189, regs 14(1), 16(1), Sch 1, para 2.

Para 8: words in square brackets substituted by the Companies Act 1989, s 4(2), Sch 1, paras 2–4; in note (13) words in square brackets substituted, in relation to the annual accounts and annual report of any company for the financial year ending on or after 2 February 1996, by SI 1996/189, regs 14(1), 16(1), Sch 1, para 3.

PART II
ACCOUNTING PRINCIPLES AND RULES

Section A
Accounting Principles

PRELIMINARY

9 Subject to paragraph 15 below, the amounts to be included in respect of all items shown in a company's accounts shall be determined in accordance with the principles set out in paragraphs 10 to 14.

ACCOUNTING PRINCIPLES

10 The company shall be presumed to be carrying on business as a going concern.

[11 Accounting policies shall be applied consistently within the same accounts and from one financial year to the next.]

12 The amount of any item shall be determined on a prudent basis, and in particular—
(a) only profits realised at the balance sheet date shall be included in the profit and loss account; and
(b) all liabilities and losses which have arisen or are likely to arise in respect of the financial year to which the accounts relate or a previous financial year shall be taken into account, including those which only become apparent between the balance sheet date and the date on which it is signed on behalf of the board of directors in pursuance of [section 233] of this Act.

13 All income and charges relating to the financial year to which the accounts relate shall be taken into account, without regard to the date of receipt or payment.

14 In determining the aggregate amount of any item the amount of each individual asset or liability that falls to be taken into account shall be determined separately.

DEPARTURE FROM THE ACCOUNTING PRINCIPLES

15 If it appears to the directors of a company that there are special reasons for departing from any of the principles stated above in preparing the company's accounts in respect of any financial year they may do so, but particulars of the departure, the reasons for it and its effect shall be given in a note to the accounts.

Section B
Historical Cost Accounting Rules

PRELIMINARY

16 Subject to section C of this Part of this Schedule, the amounts to be included in respect of all items shown in a company's accounts shall be determined in accordance with the rules set out in paragraphs 17 to 28.

FIXED ASSETS

General rules

17 Subject to any provision for depreciation or diminution in value made in accordance with paragraph 18 or 19 the amount to be included in respect of any fixed asset shall be its purchase price or production cost.

18 In the case of any fixed asset which has a limited useful economic life, the amount of—
  (a) its purchase price or production cost; or
  (b) where it is estimated that any such asset will have a residual value at the end of the period of its useful economic life, its purchase price or production cost less that estimated residual value;

shall be reduced by provisions for depreciation calculated to write off that amount systematically over the period of the asset's useful economic life.

19 (1) Where a fixed asset investment of a description falling to be included under item B.III of either of the balance sheet formats set out in Part I of this Schedule has diminished in value provisions for diminution in value may be made in respect of it and the amount to be included in respect of it may be reduced accordingly; and any such provisions which are not shown in the profit and loss account shall be disclosed (either separately or in aggregate) in a note to the accounts.

(2) Provisions for diminution in value shall be made in respect of any fixed asset which has diminished in value if the reduction in its value is expected to be permanent (whether its useful economic life is limited or not), and the amount to be included in respect of it shall be reduced accordingly; and any such provisions which are not shown in the profit and loss account shall be disclosed (either separately or in aggregate) in a note to the accounts.

(3) Where the reasons for which any provision was made in accordance with sub-paragraph (1) or (2) have ceased to apply to any extent, that provision shall be written back to the extent that it is no longer necessary; and any amounts written back in accordance with this sub-paragraph which are not shown in the profit and loss account shall be disclosed (either separately or in aggregate) in a note to the accounts.

Rules for determining particular fixed asset items

20 (1) Notwithstanding that an item in respect of "development costs" is included under "fixed assets" in the balance sheet formats set out in Part I of this Schedule, an amount may only be included in a company's balance sheet in respect of development costs in special circumstances.

(2) If any amount is included in a company's balance sheet in respect of development costs the following information shall be given in a note to the accounts—
  (a) the period over which the amount of those costs originally capitalised is being or is to be written off; and
  (b) the reasons for capitalising the development costs in question.

21 (1) The application of paragraphs 17 to 19 in relation to goodwill (in any case where goodwill is treated as an asset) is subject to the following provisions of this paragraph.

(2) Subject to sub-paragraph (3) below, the amount of the consideration for any goodwill acquired by a company shall be reduced by provisions for depreciation calculated to write off that amount systematically over a period chosen by the directors of the company.

(3) The period chosen shall not exceed the useful economic life of the goodwill in question.

(4) In any case where any goodwill acquired by a company is shown or included as an asset in the company's balance sheet the period chosen for writing off the consideration for that goodwill and the reasons for choosing that period shall be disclosed in a note to the accounts.

CURRENT ASSETS

22 Subject to paragraph 23, the amount to be included in respect of any current asset shall be its purchase price or production cost.

23 (1) If the net realisable value of any current asset is lower than its purchase price or production cost the amount to be included in respect of that asset shall be the net realisable value.

(2) Where the reasons for which any provision for diminution in value was made in accordance with sub-paragraph (1) have ceased to apply to any extent, that provision shall be written back to the extent that it is no longer necessary.

MISCELLANEOUS AND SUPPLEMENTARY PROVISIONS

Excess of money owed over value received as an asset item

24 (1) Where the amount repayable on any debt owed by a company is greater than the value of the consideration received in the transaction giving rise to the debt, the amount of the difference may be treated as an asset.

(2) Where any such amount is so treated—
  (a) it shall be written off by reasonable amounts each year and must be completely written off before repayment of the debt; and
  (b) if the current amount is not shown as a separate item in the company's balance sheet it must be disclosed in a note to the accounts.

Assets included at a fixed amount

25 (1) Subject to the following sub-paragraph, assets which fall to be included—
  (a) amongst the fixed assets of a company under the item "tangible assets"; or

(b) amongst the current assets of a company under the item "raw materials and consumables";

may be included at a fixed quantity and value.

(2) Sub-paragraph (1) applies to assets of a kind which are constantly being replaced, where—

(a) their overall value is not material to assessing the company's state of affairs; and

(b) their quantity, value and composition are not subject to material variation.

Determination of purchase price or production cost

26 (1) The purchase price of an asset shall be determined by adding to the actual price paid any expenses incidental to its acquisition.

(2) The production cost of an asset shall be determined by adding to the purchase price of the raw materials and consumables used the amount of the costs incurred by the company which are directly attributable to the production of that asset.

(3) In addition, there may be included in the production cost of an asset—

(a) a reasonable proportion of the costs incurred by the company which are only indirectly attributable to the production of that asset, but only to the extent that they relate to the period of production; and

(b) interest on capital borrowed to finance the production of that asset, to the extent that it accrues in respect of the period of production;

provided, however, in a case within paragraph (b) above, that the inclusion of the interest in determining the cost of that asset and the amount of the interest so included is disclosed in a note to the accounts.

(4) In the case of current assets distribution costs may not be included in production costs.

27 (1) Subject to the qualification mentioned below, the purchase price or production cost of—

(a) any assets which fall to be included under any item shown in a company's balance sheet under the general item "stocks"; and

(b) any assets which are fungible assets (including investments);

may be determined by the application of any of the methods mentioned in sub-paragraph (2) below in relation to any such assets of the same class.

The method chosen must be one which appears to the directors to be appropriate in the circumstances of the company.

(2) Those methods are—

(a) the method known as "first in, first out" (FIFO);

(b) the method known as "last in, first out" (LIFO);

(c) a weighted average price; and

(d) any other method similar to any of the methods mentioned above.

(3) Where in the case of any company—

(a) the purchase price or production cost of assets falling to be included under any item shown in the company's balance sheet has been determined by the application of any method permitted by this paragraph; and

(b) the amount shown in respect of that item differs materially from the relevant alternative amount given below in this paragraph;

the amount of that difference shall be disclosed in a note to the accounts.

(4)   Subject to sub-paragraph (5) below, for the purposes of sub-paragraph (3)(b) above, the relevant alternative amount, in relation to any item shown in a company's balance sheet, is the amount which would have been shown in respect of that item if assets of any class included under that item at an amount determined by any method permitted by this paragraph had instead been included at their replacement cost as at the balance sheet date.

(5)   The relevant alternative amount may be determined by reference to the most recent actual purchase price or production cost before the balance sheet date of assets of any class included under the item in question instead of by reference to their replacement cost as at that date, but only if the former appears to the directors of the company to constitute the more appropriate standard of comparison in the case of assets of that class.

(6)   For the purposes of this paragraph, assets of any description shall be regarded as fungible if assets of that description are substantially indistinguishable one from another.

Substitution of original stated amount where price or cost unknown

28   Where there is no record of the purchase price or production cost of any asset of a company or of any price, expenses or costs relevant for determining its purchase price or production cost in accordance with paragraph 26, or any such record cannot be obtained without unreasonable expense or delay, its purchase price or production cost shall be taken for the purposes of paragraphs 17 to 23 to be the value ascribed to it in the earliest available record of its value made on or after its acquisition or production by the company.

Section C
Alternative Accounting Rules

PRELIMINARY

29   (1)   The rules set out in section B are referred to below in this Schedule as the historical cost accounting rules.

(2)   Those rules, with the omission of paragraphs 16, 21 and 25 to 28, are referred to below in this Part of this Schedule as the depreciation rules; and references below in this Schedule to the historical cost accounting rules do not include the depreciation rules as they apply by virtue of paragraph 32.

30   Subject to paragraphs 32 to 34, the amounts to be included in respect of assets of any description mentioned in paragraph 31 may be determined on any basis so mentioned.

ALTERNATIVE ACCOUNTING RULES

31   (1)   Intangible fixed assets, other than goodwill, may be included at their current cost.

(2)   Tangible fixed assets may be included at a market value determined as at the date of their last valuation or at their current cost.

(3)   Investments of any description falling to be included under item B.III of either of the balance sheet formats set out in Part I of this Schedule may be included either—
   (a)   at a market value determined as at the date of their last valuation; or
   (b)   at a value determined on any basis which appears to the directors to be appropriate in the circumstances of the company;

but in the latter case particulars of the method of valuation adopted and of the reasons for adopting it shall be disclosed in a note to the accounts.

(4)   Investments of any description falling to be included under item C.III of either of the balance sheet formats set out in Part I of this Schedule may be included at their current cost.

(5)   Stocks may be included at their current cost.

APPLICATION OF THE DEPRECIATION RULES

32   (1)   Where the value of any asset of a company is determined on any basis mentioned in paragraph 31, that value shall be, or (as the case may require) be the starting point for determining, the amount to be included in respect of that asset in the company's accounts, instead of its purchase price or production cost or any value previously so determined for that asset; and the depreciation rules shall apply accordingly in relation to any such asset with the substitution for any reference to its purchase price or production cost of a reference to the value most recently determined for that asset on any basis mentioned in paragraph 31.

(2)   The amount of any provision for depreciation required in the case of any fixed asset by paragraph 18 or 19 as it applies by virtue of sub-paragraph (1) is referred to below in this paragraph as the adjusted amount, and the amount of any provision which would be required by that paragraph in the case of that asset according to the historical cost accounting rules is referred to as the historical cost amount.

(3)   Where sub-paragraph (1) applies in the case of any fixed asset the amount of any provision for depreciation in respect of that asset—
  (a)   included in any item shown in the profit and loss account in respect of amounts written off assets of the description in question; or
  (b)   taken into account in stating any item so shown which is required by note (14) of the notes on the profit and loss account formats set out in Part I of this Schedule to be stated after taking into account any necessary provisions for depreciation or diminution in value of assets included under it;

may be the historical cost amount instead of the adjusted amount, provided that the amount of any difference between the two is shown separately in the profit and loss account or in a note to the accounts.

ADDITIONAL INFORMATION TO BE PROVIDED IN CASE OF DEPARTURE FROM HISTORICAL COST ACCOUNTING RULES

33   (1)   This paragraph applies where the amounts to be included in respect of assets covered by any items shown in a company's accounts have been determined on any basis mentioned in paragraph 31.

(2)   The items affected and the basis of valuation adopted in determining the amounts of the assets in question in the case of each such item shall be disclosed in a note to the accounts.

(3)   In the case of each balance sheet item affected (except stocks) either—
  (a)   the comparable amounts determined according to the historical cost accounting rules; or
  (b)   the differences between those amounts and the corresponding amounts actually shown in the balance sheet in respect of that item;

shall be shown separately in the balance sheet or in a note to the accounts.

(4)   In sub-paragraph (3) above, references in relation to any item to the comparable amounts determined as there mentioned are references to—
  (a)   the aggregate amount which would be required to be shown in respect of that item if the amounts to be included in respect of all the assets covered by that item were determined according to the historical cost accounting rules; and

(b)   the aggregate amount of the cumulative provisions for depreciation or diminution in value which would be permitted or required in determining those amounts according to those rules.

REVALUATION RESERVE

34   (1)   With respect to any determination of the value of an asset of a company on any basis mentioned in paragraph 31, the amount of any profit or loss arising from that determination (after allowing, where appropriate, for any provisions for depreciation or diminution in value made otherwise than by reference to the value so determined and any adjustments of any such provisions made in the light of that determination) shall be credited or (as the case may be) debited to a separate reserve ("the revaluation reserve").

(2)   The amount of the revaluation reserve shall be shown in the company's balance sheet under a separate sub-heading in the position given for the item "revaluation reserve" in Format 1 or 2 of the balance sheet formats set out in Part I of this Schedule, but need not be shown under that name.

[(3)   An amount may be transferred
  [(a)   from the revaluation reserve—
       (i)   to the profit and loss account, if the amount was previously charged to that account or represents realised profit, or
       (ii)   on capitalisation,
  (b)   to or from the revaluation reserve in respect of the taxation relating to any profit or loss credited or debited to the reserve;]

and the revaluation reserve shall be reduced to the extent that the amounts transferred to it are no longer necessary for the purposes of the valuation method used.

(3A)   In [sub-paragraph (3)(a)(ii)] "capitalisation", in relation to an amount standing to the credit of the revaluation reserve, means applying it in wholly or partly paying up unissued shares in the company to be allotted to members of the company as fully or partly paid shares.

(3B)   The revaluation reserve shall not be reduced except as mentioned in this paragraph.]

(4)   The treatment for taxation purposes of amounts credited or debited to the revaluation reserve shall be disclosed in a note to the accounts.

NOTES

Para 11: substituted by the Companies Act 1989, s 4(2), Sch 1, para 5.

Para 12: in sub-para (b) words in square brackets substituted by the Companies Act 1989, s 23, Sch 10, Part I, para 20.

Para 34: sub-paras (3), (3A), (3B) substituted, for sub-para (3), as originally enacted, by the Companies Act 1989, s 4(2), Sch 1, para 6; in sub-paras (3), (3A) words in square brackets substituted, in relation to the annual accounts and annual report of any company for the financial year ending on or after 2 February 1996, by SI 1996/189, regs 14(1), 16(1), Sch 1, para 4.

PART III
NOTES TO THE ACCOUNTS

PRELIMINARY

35   Any information required in the case of any company by the following provisions of this Part of this Schedule shall (if not given in the company's accounts) be given by way of a note to those accounts.

DISCLOSURE OF ACCOUNTING POLICIES

36   The accounting policies adopted by the company in determining the amounts to be included in respect of items shown in the balance sheet and in determining the profit or loss of the company shall be stated (including such policies with respect to the depreciation and diminution in value of assets).

[36A   It shall be stated whether the accounts have been prepared in accordance with applicable accounting standards and particulars of any material departure from those standards and the reasons for it shall be given.]

INFORMATION SUPPLEMENTING THE BALANCE SHEET

37   Paragraphs 38 to 51 require information which either supplements the information given with respect to any particular items shown in the balance sheet or is otherwise relevant to assessing the company's state of affairs in the light of the information so given.

SHARE CAPITAL AND DEBENTURES

38   (1)   The following information shall be given with respect to the company's share capital—
  (a)   the authorised share capital; and
  (b)   where shares of more than one class have been allotted, the number and aggregate nominal value of shares of each class allotted.

(2)   In the case of any part of the allotted share capital that consists of redeemable shares, the following information shall be given—
  (a)   the earliest and latest dates on which the company has power to redeem those shares;
  (b)   whether those shares must be redeemed in any event or are liable to be redeemed at the option of the company or of the shareholder; and
  (c)   whether any (and, if so, what) premium is payable on redemption.

39   If the company has allotted any shares during the financial year, the following information shall be given—
  (a)   . . .
  (b)   the classes of shares allotted; and
  (c)   as respects each class of shares, the number allotted, their aggregate nominal value, and the consideration received by the company for the allotment.

40   (1)   With respect to any contingent right to the allotment of shares in the company the following particulars shall be given—
  (a)   the number, description and amount of the shares in relation to which the right is exercisable;
  (b)   the period during which it is exercisable; and
  (c)   the price to be paid for the shares allotted.

(2)   In sub-paragraph (1) above "contingent right to the allotment of shares" means any option to subscribe for shares and any other right to require the allotment of shares to any person whether arising on the conversion into shares of securities of any other description or otherwise.

41   (1)   If the company has issued any debentures during the financial year to which the accounts relate, the following information shall be given—

(a)   . . .

(b)   the classes of debentures issued; and

(c)   as respects each class of debentures, the amount issued and the consideration received by the company for the issue.

(2)   . . .

(3)   Where any of the company's debentures are held by a nominee of or trustee for the company, the nominal amount of the debentures and the amount at which they are stated in the accounting records kept by the company in accordance with section 221 of this Act shall be stated.

FIXED ASSETS

42   (1)   In respect of each item which is or would but for paragraph 3(4)(b) be shown under the general item "fixed assets" in the company's balance sheet the following information shall be given—

(a)   the appropriate amounts in respect of that item as at the date of the beginning of the financial year and as at the balance sheet date respectively;

(b)   the effect on any amount shown in the balance sheet in respect of that item of—

(i)   any revision of the amount in respect of any assets included under that item made during that year on any basis mentioned in paragraph 31;

(ii)   acquisitions during that year of any assets;

(iii)   disposals during that year of any assets; and

(iv)   any transfers of assets of the company to and from that item during that year.

(2)   The reference in sub-paragraph (1)(a) to the appropriate amounts in respect of any item as at any date there mentioned is a reference to amounts representing the aggregate amounts determined, as at that date, in respect of assets falling to be included under that item on either of the following bases, that is to say—

(a)   on the basis of purchase price or production cost (determined in accordance with paragraphs 26 and 27); or

(b)   on any basis mentioned in paragraph 31,

(leaving out of account in either case any provisions for depreciation or diminution in value).

(3)   In respect of each item within sub-paragraph (1)—

(a)   the cumulative amount of provisions for depreciation or diminution in value of assets included under that item as at each date mentioned in sub-paragraph (1)(a);

(b)   the amount of any such provisions made in respect of the financial year;

(c)   the amount of any adjustments made in respect of any such provisions during that year in consequence of the disposal of any assets; and

(d)   the amount of any other adjustments made in respect of any such provisions during that year;

shall also be stated.

43   Where any fixed assets of the company (other than listed investments) are included under any item shown in the company's balance sheet at an amount determined on any basis mentioned in paragraph 31, the following information shall be given—

(a) the years (so far as they are known to the directors) in which the assets were severally valued and the several values; and

(b) in the case of assets that have been valued during the financial year, the names of the persons who valued them or particulars of their qualifications for doing so and (whichever is stated) the bases of valuation used by them.

44 In relation to any amount which is or would but for paragraph 3(4)(b) be shown in respect of the item "land and buildings" in the company's balance sheet there shall be stated—

(a) how much of that amount is ascribable to land of freehold tenure and how much to land of leasehold tenure; and

(b) how much of the amount ascribable to land of leasehold tenure is ascribable to land held on long lease and how much to land held on short lease.

INVESTMENTS

45 (1) In respect of the amount of each item which is or would but for paragraph 3(4)(b) be shown in the company's balance sheet under the general item "investments" (whether as fixed assets or as current assets) there shall be stated—

(a) how much of that amount is ascribable to listed investments; . . .

(b) . . .

(2) Where the amount of any listed investments is stated for any item in accordance with sub-paragraph (1)(a), the following amounts shall also be stated—

(a) the aggregate market value of those investments where it differs from the amount so stated; and

(b) both the market value and the stock exchange value of any investments of which the former value is, for the purposes of the accounts, taken as being higher than the latter.

RESERVES AND PROVISIONS

46 (1) Where any amount is transferred—

(a) to or from any reserves; or

(b) to any provisions for liabilities and charges; or

(c) from any provision for liabilities and charges otherwise than for the purpose for which the provision was established;

and the reserves or provisions are or would but for paragraph 3(4)(b) be shown as separate items in the company's balance sheet, the information mentioned in the following sub-paragraph shall be given in respect of the aggregate of reserves or provisions included in the same item.

(2) That information is—

(a) the amount of the reserves or provisions as at the date of the beginning of the financial year and as at the balance sheet date respectively;

(b) any amounts transferred to or from the reserves or provisions during that year; and

(c) the source and application respectively of any amounts so transferred.

(3) Particulars shall be given of each provision included in the item "other provisions" in the company's balance sheet in any case where the amount of that provision is material.

PROVISION FOR TAXATION

[**47** The amount of any provision for deferred taxation shall be stated separately from the amount of any provision for other taxation.]

DETAILS OF INDEBTEDNESS

48   [(1)   In respect of each item shown under "creditors" in the company's balance sheet there shall be stated the aggregate of the following amounts, that is to say—

  (a)   the amount of any debts included under that item which are payable or repayable otherwise than by instalments and fall due for payment or repayment after the end of the period of five years beginning with the day next following the end of the financial year; and

  [(b)   in the case of any debts so included which are payable or repayable by instalments, the amount of any instalments which fall due for payment after the end of that period]].

(2)   Subject to sub-paragraph (3), in relation to each debt falling to be taken into account under sub-paragraph (1), the terms of payment or repayment and the rate of any interest payable on the debt shall be stated.

(3)   If the number of debts is such that, in the opinion of the directors, compliance with sub-paragraph (2) would result in a statement of excessive length, it shall be sufficient to give a general indication of the terms of payment or repayment and the rates of any interest payable on the debts.

(4)   In respect of each item shown under "creditors" in the company's balance sheet there shall be stated—

  (a)   the aggregate amount of any debts included under that item in respect of which any security has been given by the company; and

  (b)   an indication of the nature of the securities so given.

(5)   References above in this paragraph to an item shown under "creditors" in the company's balance sheet include references, where amounts falling due to creditors within one year and after more than one year are distinguished in the balance sheet—

  (a)   in a case within sub-paragraph (1), to an item shown under the latter of those categories; and

  (b)   in a case within sub-paragraph (4), to an item shown under either of those categories;

and references to items shown under "creditors" include references to items which would but for paragraph 3(4)(b) be shown under that heading.

49   If any fixed cumulative dividends on the company's shares are in arrear, there shall be stated—

  (a)   the amount of the arrears; and

  (b)   the period for which the dividends or, if there is more than one class, each class of them are in arrear.

GUARANTEES AND OTHER FINANCIAL COMMITMENTS

50   (1)   Particulars shall be given of any charge on the assets of the company to secure the liabilities of any other person, including, where practicable, the amount secured.

(2)   The following information shall be given with respect to any other contingent liability not provided for—

  (a)   the amount or estimated amount of that liability;

  (b)   its legal nature; and

  (c)   whether any valuable security has been provided by the company in connection with that liability and if so, what.

(3)   There shall be stated, where practicable—

  (a)   the aggregate amount or estimated amount of contracts for capital expenditure, so far as not provided for;

(b) . . .

(4) Particulars shall be given of—
  (a) any pension commitments included under any provision shown in the company's balance sheet; and
  (b) any such commitments for which no provision has been made;

and where any such commitment relates wholly or partly to pensions payable to past directors of the company separate particulars shall be given of that commitment so far as it relates to such pensions.

(5) Particulars shall also be given of any other financial commitments which—
  (a) have not been provided for; and
  (b) are relevant to assessing the company's state of affairs.

(6) . . .

MISCELLANEOUS MATTERS

51 (1) Particulars shall be given of any case where the purchase price or production cost of any asset is for the first time determined under paragraph 28.

(2) Where any outstanding loans made under the authority of section 153(4)(b)[, (bb)] or (c) or section 155 of this Act (various cases of financial assistance by a company for purchase of its own shares) are included under any item shown in the company's balance sheet, the aggregate amount of those loans shall be disclosed for each item in question.

(3) . . .

INFORMATION SUPPLEMENTING THE PROFIT AND LOSS ACCOUNT

52 Paragraphs 53 to 57 require information which either supplements the information given with respect to any particular items shown in the profit and loss account or otherwise provides particulars of income or expenditure of the company or of circumstances affecting the items shown in the profit and loss account.

SEPARATE STATEMENT OF CERTAIN ITEMS OF INCOME AND EXPENDITURE

53 (1) Subject to the following provisions of this paragraph, each of the amounts mentioned below shall be stated.

(2) The amount of the interest on or any similar charges in respect of—
  (a) bank loans and overdrafts, . . .; and
  (b) loans of any other kind made to the company.

 This sub-paragraph does not apply to interest or charges on loans to the company from [group undertakings], but, with that exception, it applies to interest or charges on all loans, whether made on the security of debentures or not.

(3)–(6) . . .

(7) . . .

PARTICULARS OF TAX

54 (1) . . .

(2)   Particulars shall be given of any special circumstances which affect liability in respect of taxation of profits, income or capital gains for the financial year or liability in respect of taxation of profits, income or capital gains for succeeding financial years.

(3)   The following amounts shall be stated—
   (a)   the amount of the charge for United Kingdom corporation tax;
   (b)   if that amount would have been greater but for relief from double taxation, the amount which it would have been but for such relief;
   (c)   the amount of the charge for United Kingdom income tax; and
   (d)   the amount of the charge for taxation imposed outside the United Kingdom of profits, income and (so far as charged to revenue) capital gains.

These amounts shall be stated separately in respect of each of the amounts which is or would but for paragraph 3(4)(b) be shown under the following items in the profit and loss account, that is to say "tax on profit or loss on ordinary activities" and "tax on extraordinary profit or loss".

Particulars of turnover

55   (1)   If in the course of the financial year the company has carried on business of two or more classes that, in the opinion of the directors, differ substantially from each other, there shall be stated in respect of each class (describing it)—
   (a)   the amount of the turnover attributable to that class;
   (b)   . . .

(2)   If in the course of the financial year the company has supplied markets that, in the opinion of the directors, differ substantially from each other, the amount of the turnover attributable to each such market shall also be stated.

In this paragraph "market" means a market delimited by geographical bounds.

(3)   In analysing for the purposes of this paragraph the source (in terms of business or in terms of market) of turnover . . ., the directors of the company shall have regard to the manner in which the company's activities are organised.

(4)   For the purposes of this paragraph—
   (a)   classes of business which, in the opinion of the directors, do not differ substantially from each other shall be treated as one class; and
   (b)   markets which, in the opinion of the directors, do not differ substantially from each other shall be treated as one market;

and any amounts properly attributable to one class of business or (as the case may be) to one market which are not material may be included in the amount stated in respect of another.

(5)   Where in the opinion of the directors the disclosure of any information required by this paragraph would be seriously prejudicial to the interests of the company, that information need not be disclosed, but the fact that any such information has not been disclosed must be stated.

Particulars of staff

56   (1)   The following information shall be given with respect to the employees of the company—
   (a)   the average number of persons employed by the company in the financial year; and
   (b)   the average number of persons so employed within each category of persons employed by the company.

(2)   The average number required by sub-paragraph (1)(a) or (b) shall be determined by dividing the relevant annual number by the number of [months] in the financial year.

(3)   The relevant annual number shall be determined by ascertaining for each [month] in the financial year—

(a)   for the purposes of sub-paragraph (1)(a), the number of persons employed under contracts of service by the company in that [month] (whether throughout the [month] or not);

(b)   for the purposes of sub-paragraph (1)(b), the number of persons in the category in question of persons so employed;

and, in either case, adding together all the [monthly] numbers.

(4)   In respect of all persons employed by the company during the financial year who are taken into account in determining the relevant annual number for the purposes of sub-paragraph (1)(a) there shall also be stated the aggregate amounts respectively of—

(a)   wages and salaries paid or payable in respect of that year to those persons;

(b)   social security costs incurred by the company on their behalf; and

(c)   other pension costs so incurred;

save in so far as those amounts or any of them are stated in the profit and loss account.

(5)   The categories of persons employed by the company by reference to which the number required to be disclosed by sub-paragraph (1)(b) is to be determined shall be such as the directors may select, having regard to the manner in which the company's activities are organised.

MISCELLANEOUS MATTERS

57   (1)   Where any amount relating to any preceding financial year is included in any item in the profit and loss account, the effect shall be stated.

(2)   Particulars shall be given of any extraordinary income or charges arising in the financial year.

(3)   The effect shall be stated of any transactions that are exceptional by virtue of size or incidence though they fall within the ordinary activities of the company.

GENERAL

58   (1)   Where sums originally denominated in foreign currencies have been brought into account under any items shown in the balance sheet or profit and loss account, the basis on which those sums have been translated into sterling shall be stated.

(2)   Subject to the following sub-paragraph, in respect of every item stated in a note to the accounts the corresponding amount for the financial year immediately preceding that to which the accounts relate shall also be stated and where the corresponding amount is not comparable, it shall be adjusted and particulars of the adjustment and the reasons for it shall be given.

(3)   Sub-paragraph (2) does not apply in relation to any amounts stated by virtue of any of the following provisions of this Act—

[(a)   paragraph 13 of Schedule 4A (details of accounting treatment of acquisitions),

(b)   paragraphs 2, 8(3), 16, 21(1)(d), 22(4) and (5), 24(3) and (4) and 27(3) and (4) of Schedule 5 (shareholdings in other undertakings),

(c)   Parts II and III of Schedule 6 (loans and other dealings in favour of directors and others), and

(d)   paragraphs 42 and 46 above (fixed assets and reserves and provisions).]

[DORMANT COMPANIES ACTING AS AGENTS

58A Where the directors of a company take advantage of the exemption conferred by section 249AA, and the company has during the financial year in question acted as an agent for any person, the fact that it has so acted must be stated.]

NOTES

Para 36A: inserted by the Companies Act 1989, s 4(2), Sch 1, para 7.

Para 39: sub-para (a) repealed, in relation to the annual accounts and annual report of any company for the financial year ending on or after 2 February 1996, by SI 1996/189, regs 14(1), 16(1), Sch 1, para 5.

Para 41: sub-paras (1)(a), (2) repealed, in relation to the annual accounts and annual report of any company for the financial year ending on or after 2 February 1996, by SI 1996/189, regs 14(1), 16(1), Sch 1, para 6.

Para 45: in sub-para (1) words in square brackets substituted by the Financial Services Act 1986, s 212(2), Sch 16, para 23, sub-para (1)(b), and word omitted following sub-para (1)(a), repealed, in relation to the annual accounts and annual report of any company for the financial year ending on or after 2 February 1996, by SI 1996/189, regs 14(1), 16(1), Sch 1, para 7.

Para 47: substituted by the Companies Act 1989, s 4(2), Sch 1, para 8.

Para 48: sub-para (1) substituted, in relation to the annual accounts and annual report of any company for the financial year ending on or after 2 February 1996, by SI 1996/189, regs 14(1), 16(1), Sch 1, para 8.

Para 48: sub-para (1)(b) substituted by SI 1997/220, reg 7(9).

Date in force: this amendment applies to annual accounts approved by the board of directors on or after 1 March 1997, and to directors' and auditors' reports on such accounts: see SI 1997/220, reg 1(3); for transitional provision see reg 1(4) thereof.

Para 50: sub-para (3)(b) repealed, in relation to the annual accounts and annual report of any company for the financial year ending on or after 2 February 1996, by SI 1996/189, regs 14(1), 16(1), Sch 1, para 9; sub-para (6) repealed by the Companies Act 1989, s 212, Sch 24.

Para 51: in sub-para (2) item in square brackets inserted by the Companies Act 1989, s 4(2), Sch 1, para 9; sub-para (3) repealed, in relation to the annual accounts and annual report of any company for the financial year ending on or after 2 February 1996, by SI 1996/189, regs 14(1), 16(1), Sch 1, para 10.

Para 53: in sub-para (2)(a) words omitted repealed, and sub-paras (3)–(6) repealed, in relation to the annual accounts and annual report of any company for the financial year ending on or after 2 February 1996, by SI 1996/189, regs 14(1), 16(1), Sch 1, para 11; in sub-para (2) words in square brackets substituted, and sub-para (7) repealed, by the Companies Act 1989, ss 4(2), 212, Sch 1, para 2, Sch 24.

Para 54: sub-para (1) repealed, in relation to the annual accounts and annual report of any company for the financial year ending on or after 2 February 1996, by SI 1996/189, regs 14(1), 16(1), Sch 1, para 12.

Para 55: sub-para (1)(b) repealed, and in sub-para (3) words omitted repealed, in relation to the annual accounts and annual report of any company for the financial year ending on or after 2 February 1996, by SI 1996/189, regs 14(1), 16(1), Sch 1, para 13.

Para 56: words in square brackets substituted, in relation to the annual accounts and annual report of any company for the financial year ending on or after 2 February 1996, by SI 1996/189, regs 14(1), 16(1), Sch 1, para 14.

Para 58: in sub-para (3), paras (a)–(d) substituted for paras (a)–(c) as originally enacted, by the Companies Act 1989, s 4(2), Sch 1, para 10.

Para 58A: inserted by SI 2000/1430, reg 5.

Date in force: this amendment has effect in relation to annual accounts and reports in respect of financial years ending on or after 26 July 2000: see SI 2000/1430, reg 1(1), (2).

PART VII
INTERPRETATION OF SCHEDULE

76   The following paragraphs apply for the purposes of this Schedule and its interpretation.

77–81   . . .

Historical cost accounting rules

82   References to the historical cost accounting rules shall be read in accordance with paragraph 29.

Leases

83   (1)   "Long lease" means a lease in the case of which the portion of the term for which it was granted remaining unexpired at the end of the financial year is not less than 50 years.

(2)   "Short lease" means a lease which is not a long lease.

(3)   "Lease" includes an agreement for a lease.

Listed investments

[84   (1)   "Listed investment" means an investment as respects which there has been granted a listing on—
  (a)   a recognised investment exchange other than an overseas investment exchange; or
  (b)   a stock exchange of repute outside Great Britain.

(2)   "Recognised investment exchange" and "overseas investment exchange" have the meaning given in Part 18 of the Financial Services and Markets Act 2000.]

Loans

85   A loan is treated as falling due for repayment, and an instalment of a loan is treated as falling due for payment, on the earliest date on which the lender could require repayment or (as the case may be) payment, if he exercised all options and rights available to him.

Materiality

86   Amounts which in the particular context of any provision of this Schedule are not material may be disregarded for the purposes of that provision.

Notes to the accounts

87   < . . . >

Provisions

88   (1)   References to provisions for depreciation or diminution in value of assets are to any amount written off by way of providing for depreciation or diminution in value of assets.

(2)   Any reference in the profit and loss account formats set out in Part I of this Schedule to the depreciation of, or amounts written off, assets of any description is to any provision for depreciation or diminution in value of assets of that description.

89   References to provisions for liabilities or charges are to any amount retained as reasonably necessary for the purpose of providing for any liability or loss which is either likely to be incurred, or certain to be incurred but uncertain as to amount or as to the date on which it will arise.

90–92   . . .

Scots land tenure

93   In the application of this Schedule to Scotland, "land of freehold tenure" means land in respect of which the company *is the proprietor of the dominium utile or, in the case of land not held on feudal tenure,* is the owner; "land of leasehold tenure" means land of which the company is the tenant under a lease*; and the reference to ground-rents, rates and other outgoings includes feu-duty and ground annual.*

Staff costs

94   (1)   "Social security costs" means any contributions by the company to any state social security or pension scheme, fund or arrangement.

[(2)   "Pension costs" includes any costs incurred by the company in respect of any pension scheme established for the purpose of providing pensions for persons currently or formerly employed by the company, any sums set aside for the future payment of pensions directly by the company to current or former employees and any pensions paid directly to such persons without having first been set aside.]

(3)   Any amount stated in respect of [the item "social security costs"] or in respect of the item "wages and salaries" in the company's profit and loss account shall be determined by reference to payments made or costs incurred in respect of all persons employed by the company during the financial year who are taken into account in determining the relevant annual number for the purposes of paragraph 56(1)(a).

Turnover

95   . . .

NOTES

Paras 77–81: repealed by the Companies Act 1989, s 212, Sch 24.

Para 84: substituted by SI 2001/3649, art 32.

Date in force: 1 December 2001: see SI 2001/3649, art 1.

Paras 87, 90–92, 95: repealed by the Companies Act 1989, s 212, Sch 24.

Para 93: words "is the proprietor of the dominium utile or, in the case of land not held on feudal tenure," and words from "; and the reference" to "and ground annual" in italics repealed by the Abolition of Feudal Tenure etc (Scotland) Act 2000, s 76(1), (2), Sch 12, para 46(1), (5), Sch 13.

Date in force: to be appointed: see the Abolition of Feudal Tenure etc (Scotland) Act 2000, ss 71, 77(2).

Para 94: sub-para (2) substituted, and in sub-para (3) words in square brackets substituted, in relation to the annual accounts and annual report of any company for the financial year ending on or after 2 February 1996, by SI 1996/189, regs 14(1), 16(1), Sch 1, para 16.

SCHEDULE 6
[DISCLOSURE OF INFORMATION: EMOLUMENTS AND OTHER BENEFITS OF DIRECTORS AND OTHERS]

NOTES

Heading substituted by the Companies Act 1989, s 6(4), Sch 4, para 2.

[PART I
CHAIRMAN'S AND DIRECTORS' EMOLUMENTS, PENSIONS AND COMPENSATION FOR
LOSS OF OFFICE]

NOTES

Inserted by the Companies Act 1989, s 6(4), Sch 4, para 3.

[[Aggregate amount of directors' emoluments etc

1 (1) Subject to sub-paragraph (2), the following shall be shown, namely—

(a) the aggregate amount of emoluments paid to or receivable by directors in respect of qualifying services;

(b) the aggregate of the amount of gains made by directors on the exercise of share options;

(c) the aggregate of the following, namely—

(i) the amount of money paid to or receivable by directors under long term incentive schemes in respect of qualifying services; and

(ii) the net value of assets (other than money and share options) received or receivable by directors under such schemes in respect of such services;

(d) the aggregate value of any company contributions paid, or treated as paid, to a pension scheme in respect of directors' qualifying services, being contributions by reference to which the rate or amount of any money purchase benefits that may become payable will be calculated; and

(e) in the case of each of the following, namely—

(i) money purchase schemes; and

(ii) defined benefit schemes,

the number of directors (if any) to whom retirement benefits are accruing under such schemes in respect of qualifying services.

(2) In the case of a company which is not a listed company—

(a) sub-paragraph (1) shall have effect as if paragraph (b) were omitted and, in paragraph (c)(ii), "assets" did not include shares; and

(b) the number of each of the following (if any) shall be shown, namely—

(i) the directors who exercised share options; and

(ii) the directors in respect of whose qualifying services shares were received or receivable under long term incentive schemes.

(3) In this paragraph "emoluments" of a director—

(a) includes salary, fees and bonuses, sums paid by way of expenses allowance (so far as they are chargeable to United Kingdom income tax) and, subject to paragraph (b), the estimated money value of any other benefits received by him otherwise than in cash; but

(b) does not include any of the following, namely—

(i) the value of any share options granted to him or the amount of any gains made on the exercise of any such options;

(ii) any company contributions paid, or treated as paid, in respect of him under any pension scheme or any benefits to which he is entitled under any such scheme; or

(iii) any money or other assets paid to or received or receivable by him under any long term incentive scheme.

(4)   In this paragraph "long term incentive scheme" means any agreement or arrangement under which money or other assets may become receivable by a director and which includes one or more qualifying conditions with respect to service or performance which cannot be fulfilled within a single financial year; and for this purpose the following shall be disregarded, namely—

- (a)   bonuses the amount of which falls to be determined by reference to service or performance within a single financial year;
- (b)   compensation for loss of office, payments for breach of contract and other termination payments; and
- (c)   retirement benefits.

(5)   In this paragraph—

"amount", in relation to a gain made on the exercise of a share option, means the difference between—

- (a)   the market price of the shares on the day on which the option was exercised; and
- (b)   the price actually paid for the shares;

"company contributions", in relation to a pension scheme and a director, means any payments (including insurance premiums) made, or treated as made, to the scheme in respect of the director by a person other than the director;

"defined benefits" means retirement benefits payable under a pension scheme which are not money purchase benefits;

"defined benefit scheme", in relation to a director, means a pension scheme which is not a money purchase scheme;

["listed company" means a company—

- (a)   whose securities have been admitted to the official list in accordance with the provisions of Part 6 of the Financial Services and Markets Act 2000; or
- (b)   dealings in whose securities are permitted on any recognised investment exchange approved by the Treasury in accordance with regulations made under section 2(2) of the European Communities Act 1972 with respect to dealings in unlisted securities;]

"money purchase benefits", in relation to a director, means retirement benefits payable under a pension scheme the rate or amount of which is calculated by reference to payments made, or treated as made, by the director or by any other person in respect of the director and which are not average salary benefits;

"money purchase scheme", in relation to a director, means a pension scheme under which all of the benefits that may become payable to or in respect of the director are money purchase benefits;

"net value", in relation to any assets received or receivable by a director, means value after deducting any money paid or other value given by the director in respect of those assets;

["the official list" has the meaning given in section 103(1) of the Financial Services and Markets Act 2000;]

"qualifying services", in relation to any person, means his services as a director of the company, and his services while director of the company—

- (a)   as director of any of its subsidiary undertakings; or
- (b)   otherwise in connection with the management of the affairs of the company or any of its subsidiary undertakings;

["recognised investment exchange" has the same meaning as in the Financial Services and Markets Act 2000;]

"shares" means shares (whether allotted or not) in the company, or any undertaking which is a group undertaking in relation to the company, and includes a share warrant as defined by section 188(1);

"share option" means a right to acquire shares;

"value", in relation to shares received or receivable by a director on any day, means the market price of the shares on that day.

(6) For the purposes of this paragraph—

(a) any information, other than the aggregate amount of gains made by directors on the exercise of share options, shall be treated as shown if it is capable of being readily ascertained from other information which is shown; and

(b) emoluments paid or receivable or share options granted in respect of a person's accepting office as a director shall be treated as emoluments paid or receivable or share options granted in respect of his services as a director.

(7) Where a pension scheme provides for any benefits that may become payable to or in respect of any director to be whichever are the greater of—

(a) money purchase benefits as determined by or under the scheme; and

(b) defined benefits as so determined,

the company may assume for the purposes of this paragraph that those benefits will be money purchase benefits, or defined benefits, according to whichever appears more likely at the end of the financial year.

(8) For the purpose of determining whether a pension scheme is a money purchase or defined benefit scheme, any death in service benefits provided for by the scheme shall be disregarded.]

[Details of highest paid director's emoluments etc

2 (1) Where the aggregates shown under paragraph 1(1)(a), (b) and (c) total £200,000 or more, the following shall be shown, namely—

(a) so much of the total of those aggregates as is attributable to the highest paid director; and

(b) so much of the aggregate mentioned in paragraph 1(1)(d) as is so attributable.

(2) Where sub-paragraph (1) applies and the highest paid director has performed qualifying services during the financial year by reference to which the rate or amount of any defined benefits that may become payable will be calculated, there shall also be shown—

(a) the amount at the end of the year of his accrued pension; and

(b) where applicable, the amount at the end of the year of his accrued lump sum.

(3) Subject to sub-paragraph (4), where sub-paragraph (1) applies in the case of a company which is not a listed company, there shall also be shown—

(a) whether the highest paid director exercised any share options; and

(b) whether any shares were received or receivable by that director in respect of qualifying services under a long term incentive scheme.

(4) Where the highest paid director has not been involved in any of the transactions specified in sub-paragraph (3), that fact need not be stated.

(5) In this paragraph—

"accrued pension" and "accrued lump sum", in relation to any pension scheme and any director, mean respectively the amount of the annual pension, and the amount of the lump sum, which would be payable under the scheme on his attaining normal pension age if—

(a) he had left the company's service at the end of the financial year;

(b) there were no increase in the general level of prices in Great Britain during the period beginning with the end of that year and ending with his attaining that age;

(c) no question arose of any commutation of the pension or inverse commutation of the lump sum; and

(d)   any amounts attributable to voluntary contributions paid by the director to the scheme, and any money purchase benefits which would be payable under the scheme, were disregarded;

"the highest paid director" means the director to whom is attributable the greatest part of the total of the aggregates shown under paragraph 1(1)(a), (b) and (c);

"normal pension age", in relation to any pension scheme and any director, means the age at which the director will first become entitled to receive a full pension on retirement of an amount determined without reduction to take account of its payment before a later age (but disregarding any entitlement to pension upon retirement in the event of illness, incapacity or redundancy).

(6)   Sub-paragraphs (4) to (8) of paragraph 1 apply for the purposes of this paragraph as they apply for the purposes of that paragraph.]

[Excess retirement benefits of directors and past directors

7   (1)   Subject to sub-paragraph (2), there shall be shown the aggregate amount of—
- (a)   so much of retirement benefits paid to or receivable by directors under pension schemes; and
- (b)   so much of retirement benefits paid to or receivable by past directors under such schemes,

as (in each case) is in excess of the retirement benefits to which they were respectively entitled on the date on which the benefits first became payable or 31st March 1997, whichever is the later.

(2)   Amounts paid or receivable under a pension scheme need not be included in the aggregate amount if—
- (a)   the funding of the scheme was such that the amounts were or, as the case may be, could have been paid without recourse to additional contributions; and
- (b)   amounts were paid to or receivable by all pensioner members of the scheme on the same basis;

and in this sub-paragraph "pensioner member", in relation to a pension scheme, means any person who is entitled to the present payment of retirement benefits under the scheme.

(3)   In this paragraph—
- (a)   references to retirement benefits include benefits otherwise than in cash; and
- (b)   in relation to so much of retirement benefits as consists of a benefit otherwise than in cash, references to their amount are to the estimated money value of the benefit;

and the nature of any such benefit shall also be disclosed.]

Compensation to directors for loss of office

8   (1)   There shall be shown the aggregate amount of any compensation to directors or past directors in respect of loss of office.

(2)   This amount includes compensation received or receivable by a director or past director for—
- (a)   loss of office as director of the company, or
- (b)   loss, while director of the company or on or in connection with his ceasing to be a director of it, of—
  - (i)   any other office in connection with the management of the company's affairs, or
  - (ii)   any office as director or otherwise in connection with the management of the affairs of any subsidiary undertaking of the company; . . .

(3) References to compensation include benefits otherwise than in cash; and in relation to such compensation references to its amount are to the estimated money value of the benefit.

The nature of any such compensation shall be disclosed.

[(4) In this paragraph, references to compensation for loss of office include the following, namely—
- (a) compensation in consideration for, or in connection with, a person's retirement from office; and
- (b) where such a retirement is occasioned by a breach of the person's contract with the company or with a subsidiary undertaking of the company—
  - (i) payments made by way of damages for the breach; or
  - (ii) payments made by way of settlement or compromise of any claim in respect of the breach.

(5) Sub-paragraph (6)(a) of paragraph 1 applies for the purposes of this paragraph as it applies for the purposes of that paragraph.]

Sums paid to third parties in respect of directors' services

9 (1) There shall be shown the aggregate amount of any consideration paid to or receivable by third parties for making available the services of any person—
- (a) as a director of the company, or
- (b) while director of the company—
  - (i) as director of any of its subsidiary undertakings, or
  - (ii) otherwise in connection with the management of the affairs of the company or any of its subsidiary undertakings.

(2) The reference to consideration includes benefits otherwise than in cash; and in relation to such consideration the reference to its amount is to the estimated money value of the benefit.

The nature of any such consideration shall be disclosed.

(3) The reference to third parties is to persons other than—
- (a) the director himself or a person connected with him or body corporate controlled by him, and
- (b) the company or any of its subsidiary undertakings.

Supplementary

10 (1) The following applies with respect to the amounts to be shown under [this Part of this schedule].

(2) The amount in each case includes all relevant sums paid by or receivable from—
- (a) the company; and
- (b) the company's subsidiary undertakings; and
- (c) any other person,

except sums to be accounted for to the company or any of its subsidiary undertakings or, by virtue of sections 314 and 315 of this Act (duty of directors to make disclosure on company takeover; consequence of non-compliance), to past or present members of the company or any of its subsidiaries or any class of those members.

(3) . . .

(4) References to amounts paid to or receivable by a person include amounts paid to or receivable by a person connected with him or a body corporate controlled by him (but not so as to require an amount to be counted twice).

11 (1) The amounts to be shown for any financial year under [this Part of this Schedule] are the sums receivable in respect of that year (whenever paid) or, in the case of sums not receivable in respect of a period, the sums paid during that year.

(2) But where—
- (a) any sums are not shown in a note to the accounts for the relevant financial year on the ground that the person receiving them is liable to account for them as mentioned in paragraph 10(2), but the liability is thereafter wholly or partly released or is not enforced within a period of 2 years; or
- (b) any sums paid by way of expenses allowance are charged to United Kingdom income tax after the end of the relevant financial year,

those sums shall, to the extent to which the liability is released or not enforced or they are charged as mentioned above (as the case may be), be shown in a note to the first accounts in which it is practicable to show them and shall be distinguished from the amounts to be shown apart from this provision.

12 Where it is necessary to do so for the purpose of making any distinction required by the preceding paragraphs in an amount to be shown in compliance with this Part of this Schedule, the directors may apportion any payments between the matters in respect of which these have been paid or are receivable in such manner as they think appropriate.

Interpretation

13 (1) The following applies for the interpretation of this Part of this Schedule.

(2) A reference to a subsidiary undertaking of the company—
- (a) in relation to a person who is or was, while a director of the company, a director also, by virtue of the company's nomination (direct or indirect) of any other undertaking, includes (subject to the following sub-paragraph) that undertaking, whether or not it is or was in fact a subsidiary undertaking of the company, and
- (b) for the purposes of paragraphs 1 to 7 . . . is to an undertaking which is a subsidiary undertaking at the time the services were rendered, and for the purposes of paragraph 8 to a subsidiary undertaking immediately before the loss of office as director.

[(3) The following definitions apply—
- (a) "pension scheme" has the meaning assigned to "retirement benefits scheme" by section 611 of the Income and Corporation Taxes Act 1988;
- (b) "retirement benefits" has the meaning assigned to relevant benefits by section 612(1) of that Act.]

(4) References in this Part of this Schedule to a person being "connected" with a director, and to a director "controlling" a body corporate, shall be construed in accordance with section 346.

Supplementary

14 This Part of this Schedule requires information to be given only so far as it is contained in the company's books and papers or the company has the right to obtain it from the persons concerned.]

NOTES

Inserted by the Companies Act 1989, s 6(4), Sch 4, para 3.
Para 1: substituted by SI 1997/570, reg 2.
Para 1: in sub-para (5) definition "listed company" substituted by SI 2001/3649, art 33(1), (2).

Date in force: 1 December 2001: see SI 2001/3649, art 1.

Para 1: in sub-para (5) definition "the official list" inserted by SI 2001/3649, art 33(1), (3).

Date in force: 1 December 2001: see SI 2001/3649, art 1.

Para 1: in sub-para (5) definition "recognised investment exchange" inserted by SI 2001/3649, art 33(1), (4).

Date in force: 1 December 2001: see SI 2001/3649, art 1.

Para 2: substituted, for paras 2–6 as originally enacted, by SI 1997/570, reg 3(1).

Para 7: substituted by SI 1997/570, reg 4.

Para 8: words omitted repealed and sub-paras (4), (5) substituted for sub-para (4) as originally enacted by SI 1997/570, reg 5(1), (2).

Para 10: words in square brackets substituted and sub-para (3) repealed by SI 1997/570, reg 6(2).

Para 11: words in square brackets substituted by SI 1997/570, reg 6(3).

Para 13: in sub-para (2) words omitted repealed and sub-para (3) substituted by SI 1997/570, regs 6(4), (5).

[PART II
LOANS, QUASI-LOANS AND OTHER DEALINGS IN FAVOUR OF DIRECTORS]

NOTES

Heading substituted, and renumbered as Part II, by the Companies Act 1989, s 6(4), Sch 4, para 4.

[15]   [The group accounts of a holding company, or if it is not required to prepare group accounts its individual accounts,] shall contain the particulars required by this Schedule of—

(a)   any transaction or arrangement of a kind described in section 330 entered into by the company or by a subsidiary of the company for a person who at any time during the financial year was a director of the company or its holding company, or was connected with such a director;

(b)   an agreement by the company or by a subsidiary of the company to enter into any such transaction or arrangement for a person who was at any time during the financial year a director of the company or its holding company, or was connected with such a director; and

(c)   any other transaction or arrangement with the company or a subsidiary of it in which a person who at any time during the financial year was a director of the company or its holding company had, directly or indirectly, a material interest.

[16]   The accounts prepared by a company other than a holding company shall contain the particulars required by this Schedule of—

(a)   any transaction or arrangement of a kind described in section 330 entered into by the company for a person who at any time during the financial year was a director of it or of its holding company or was connected with such a director;

(b)   an agreement by the company to enter into any such transaction or arrangement for a person who at any time during the financial year was a director of the company or its holding company or was connected with such a director; and

(c)   any other transaction or arrangement with the company in which a person who at any time during the financial year was a director of the company or of its holding company had, directly or indirectly, a material interest.

[17]   (1)   For purposes of paragraphs [15](c) and [16](c), a transaction or arrangement between a company and a director of it or of its holding company, or a person connected with such a director, is to be treated (if it would not otherwise be so) as a transaction, arrangement or agreement in which that director is interested.

(2)   An interest in such a transaction or arrangement is not "material" for purposes of those sub-paragraphs if in the board's opinion it is not so; but this is without prejudice to the question whether or not such an interest is material in a case where the board have not considered the matter.

"The board" here means the directors of the company preparing the accounts, or a majority of those directors, but excluding in either case the director whose interest it is.

[18]   Paragraphs [15] and [16] do not apply in relation to the following transactions, arrangements and agreements—
   (a)   a transaction, arrangement or agreement between one company and another in which a director of the former or of its subsidiary or holding company is interested only by virtue of his being a director of the latter;
   (b)   a contract of service between a company and one of its directors or a director of its holding company, or between a director of a company and any of that company's subsidiaries;
   (c)   a transaction, arrangement or agreement which was not entered into during the financial year and which did not subsist at any time during that year.

[19]   Paragraphs [15] and [16] apply whether or not—
   (a)   the transaction or arrangement was prohibited by section 330;
   (b)   the person for whom it was made was a director of the company or was connected with a director of it at the time it was made;
   (c)   in the case of a transaction or arrangement made by a company which at any time during a financial year is a subsidiary of another company, it was a subsidiary of that other company at the time the transaction or arrangement was made.

[20]   Neither paragraph [15](c) nor paragraph [16](c) applies in relation to any transaction or arrangement if—
   (a)   each party to the transaction or arrangement which is a member of the same group of companies (meaning a holding company and its subsidiaries) as the company entered into the transaction or arrangement in the ordinary course of business, and
   (b)   the terms of the transaction or arrangement are not less favourable to any such party than it would be reasonable to expect if the interest mentioned in that sub-paragraph had not been an interest of a person who was a director of the company or of its holding company.

[21]   Neither paragraph [15](c) nor paragraph [16](c) applies in relation to any transaction or arrangement if—
   (a)   the company is a member of a group of companies (meaning a holding company and its subsidiaries), and
   (b)   either the company is a wholly-owned subsidiary or no body corporate (other than the company or a subsidiary of the company) which is a member of the group of companies which includes the company's ultimate holding company was a party to the transaction or arrangement, and
   (c)   the director in question was at some time during the relevant period associated with the company, and
   (d)   the material interest of the director in question in the transaction or arrangement would not have arisen if he had not been associated with the company at any time during the relevant period.

The particulars required by this Part

[22]   (1)   Subject to the next paragraph, the particulars required by this Part are those of the principal terms of the transaction, arrangement or agreement.

(2)   Without prejudice to the generality of sub-paragraph (1), the following particulars are required—

(a)   a statement of the fact either that the transaction, arrangement or agreement was made or subsisted (as the case may be) during the financial year;

(b)   the name of the person for whom it was made and, where that person is or was connected with a director of the company or of its holding company, the name of that director;

(c)   in a case where paragraph [15](c) or [16](c) applies, the name of the director with the material interest and the nature of that interest;

(d)   in the case of a loan or an agreement for a loan or an arrangement within section 330(6) or (7) of this Act relating to a loan—

(i)   the amount of the liability of the person to whom the loan was or was agreed to be made, in respect of principal and interest, at the beginning and at the end of the financial year;

(ii)   the maximum amount of that liability during that year;

(iii) the amount of any interest which, having fallen due, has not been paid; and

(iv) the amount of any provision (within the meaning of Schedule 4 to this Act) made in respect of any failure or anticipated failure by the borrower to repay the whole or part of the loan or to pay the whole or part of any interest on it;

(e)   in the case of a guarantee or security or an arrangement within section 330(6) relating to a guarantee or security—

(i)   the amount for which the company (or its subsidiary) was liable under the guarantee or in respect of the security both at the beginning and at the end of the financial year;

(ii)   the maximum amount for which the company (or its subsidiary) may become so liable; and

(iii) any amount paid and any liability incurred by the company (or its subsidiary) for the purpose of fulfilling the guarantee or discharging the security (including any loss incurred by reason of the enforcement of the guarantee or security); and

(f)   in the case of any transaction, arrangement or agreement other than those mentioned in sub-paragraphs (d) and (e), the value of the transaction or arrangement or (as the case may be) the value of the transaction or arrangement to which the agreement relates.

[23]   In paragraph [22](2) above, sub-paragraphs (c) to (f) do not apply in the case of a loan or quasi-loan made or agreed to be made by a company to or for a body corporate which is either—

(a)   a body corporate of which that company is a wholly-owned subsidiary, or

(b)   a wholly-owned subsidiary of a body corporate of which that company is a wholly-owned subsidiary, or

(c)   a wholly-owned subsidiary of that company,

if particulars of that loan, quasi-loan or agreement for it would not have been required to be included in that company's annual accounts if the first-mentioned body corporate had not been associated with a director of that company at any time during the relevant period.

[Excluded transactions]

[24]   (1)   In relation to a company's accounts for a financial year, compliance with this Part is not required in the case of transactions of a kind mentioned in the following sub-paragraph which are made by the company or a subsidiary of it for a person who at any time during that financial year was a director of the company or of its holding company, or was connected with such a director, if the aggregate of the values of each transaction, arrangement or agreement so made for that director or any person connected with him, less the amount (if

any) by which the liabilities of the person for whom the transaction or arrangement was made has been reduced, did not at any time during the financial year exceed £5,000.

(2) The transactions in question are—
  (a) credit transactions,
  (b) guarantees provided or securities entered into in connection with credit transactions,
  (c) arrangements within subsection (6) or (7) of section 330 relating to credit transactions,
  (d) agreements to enter into credit transactions.

[25] In relation to a company's accounts for a financial year, compliance with this Part is not required by virtue of paragraph [15](c) or [16](c) in the case of any transaction or arrangement with a company or any of its subsidiaries in which a director of the company or its holding company had, directly or indirectly, a material interest if—
  (a) the value of each transaction or arrangement within paragraph [15](c) or [16](c) (as the case may be) in which that director had (directly or indirectly) a material interest and which was made after the commencement of the financial year with the company or any of its subsidiaries, and
  (b) the value of each such transaction or arrangement which was made before the commencement of the financial year less the amount (if any) by which the liabilities of the person for whom the transaction or arrangement was made have been reduced,

did not at any time during the financial year exceed in the aggregate £1,000 or, if more, did not exceed £5,000 or 1 per cent of the value of the net assets of the company preparing the accounts in question as at the end of the financial year, whichever is the less.

For this purpose a company's net assets are the aggregate of its assets, less the aggregate of its liabilities ("liabilities" to include any provision for liabilities or charges within paragraph 89 of Schedule 4).

[26] Section 345 of this Act (power of Secretary of State to alter sums by statutory instrument subject to negative resolution in Parliament) applies as if the money sums specified in paragraph [24] or [25] above were specified in Part X.

Interpretation

[27] [(1)] The following provisions of this Act apply for purposes of this Part of this Schedule—
  (a) section 331(2), . . . and (7), as regards the meaning of "guarantee", . . . and "credit transaction";
  (b) section 331(9), as to the interpretation of references to a transaction or arrangement being made "for" a person;
  (c) section 340, in assigning values to transactions and arrangements, and
  (d) section 346, as to the interpretation of references to a person being "connected with" a director of a company.

[(2) In this Part of this Schedule "director" includes a shadow director.]

NOTES

Part heading: renumbered as such and heading substituted by the Companies Act 1989, s 6(4), Sch 4, para 4(1).

Para 15: renumbered by the Companies Act 1989, s 6(4), Sch 4, para 4(2); words in square brackets substituted by the Companies Act 1989, s 6(4), Sch 4, para 4(4).

Paras 16–23, 25, 26: renumbered, and para references therein substituted by, or by virtue of the Companies Act 1989, s 6(4), Sch 4, para 4(2).

Para 4 as originally enacted repealed by the Companies Act 1989, s 6(4), Sch 4, para 4(3).

Para 24: renumbered, and heading substituted, by the Companies Act 1989, s 6(4), Sch 4, paras 4(2), (5).

Para 27: renumbered, sub-para (1) numbered and sub-para (2) inserted, by the Companies Act 1989, s 6(4), Sch 4, para 4(2), (5); words omitted repealed by the Banking Act 1987, s 108(2), Sch 7, Part I.

[PART III
OTHER TRANSACTIONS, ARRANGEMENTS AND AGREEMENTS]

NOTES

Heading substituted, and renumbered as Part III, by the Companies Act 1989, s 6(4), Sch 4, paras 2, 6(1).

[28] This Part of this Schedule applies in relation to the following classes of transactions, arrangements and agreements—

(a) loans, guarantees and securities relating to loans, arrangements of a kind described in subsection (6) or (7) of section 330 of this Act relating to loans and agreements to enter into any of the foregoing transactions and arrangements;

(b) quasi-loans, guarantees and securities relating to quasi-loans arrangements of a kind described in either of those subsections relating to quasi-loans and agreements to enter into any of the foregoing transactions and arrangements;

(c) credit transactions, guarantees and securities relating to credit transactions, arrangements of a kind described in either of those subsections relating to credit transactions and agreements to enter into any of the foregoing transactions and arrangements.

[29] (1) To comply with this Part of this Schedule, the accounts must contain a statement, in relation to transactions, arrangements and agreements [made by the company or a subsidiary of it for persons who at any time during the financial year were officers of the company (but not directors or shadow directors)], of—

(a) the aggregate amounts outstanding at the end of the financial year under transactions, arrangements and agreements within sub-paragraphs (a), (b) and (c) respectively of paragraph [28] above, and

(b) the numbers of officers for whom the transactions, arrangements and agreements falling within each of those sub-paragraphs were made.

(2) This paragraph does not apply to transactions, arrangements and agreements made by the company or any of its subsidiaries for an officer of the company if the aggregate amount outstanding at the end of the financial year under the transactions, arrangements and agreements so made for that officer does not exceed £2,500.

(3) Section 345 of this Act (power of Secretary of State to alter money sums by statutory instrument subject to negative resolution in Parliament) applies as if the money sum specified above in this paragraph were specified in Part X.

[30] The following provisions of this Act apply for purposes of this Part—

(a) section 331(2), (3), . . . and (7), as regards the meaning of "guarantee", "quasi-loan", . . . and "credit transaction", and

(b) section 331(9), as to the interpretation of references to a transaction or arrangement being made "for" a person;

and "amount outstanding" means the amount of the outstanding liabilities of the person for whom the transaction, arrangement or agreement was made or, in the case of a guarantee or security, the amount guaranteed or secured.

Part heading: renumbered as such and heading substituted by the Companies Act 1989, s 6(4), Sch 4, paras 2, 6(1).

Para 28: renumbered by the Companies Act 1989, s 6(4), Sch 4, para 6(2).

Para 29: renumbered, and words in square brackets substituted by, or by virtue of, the Companies Act 1989, s 6(4), Sch 4, paras 6(2), (3).

Para 30: renumbered by the Companies Act 1989, s 6(4), Sch 4, para 6(2); words omitted repealed by the Banking Act 1987, s 108(2), Sch 7, Part I.

SCHEDULE 7
MATTERS TO BE DEALT WITH IN DIRECTORS' REPORT

Section 234

PART I
MATTERS OF A GENERAL NATURE

Asset values

1 (1) . . .

(2) If, in the case of [such of the fixed assets of the company or of any of its subsidiary undertakings] as consist in interests in land, their market value (as at the end of the financial year) differs substantially from the amount at which they are included in the balance sheet, and the difference is, in the directors' opinion, of such significance as to require that the attention of members of the company or of holders of its debentures should be drawn to it, the report shall indicate the difference with such degree of precision as is practicable.

Directors' interests

[**2** (1) The information required by paragraphs 2A and 2B shall be given in the directors' report, or by way of notes to the company's annual accounts, with respect to each person who at the end of the financial year was a director of the company.

(2) In those paragraphs—
  (a) "the register" means the register of directors' interests kept by the company under section 325; and
  (b) references to a body corporate being in the same group as the company are to its being a subsidiary or holding company, or another subsidiary of a holding company, of the company.

2A (1) It shall be stated with respect to each director whether, according to the register, he was at the end of the financial year interested in shares in or debentures of the company or any other body corporate in the same group.

(2) If he was so interested, there shall be stated the number of shares in and amount of debentures of each body (specifying it) in which, according to the register, he was then interested.

(3) If a director was interested at the end of the financial year in shares in or debentures of the company or any other body corporate in the same group—
  (a) it shall also be stated whether, according to the register, he was at the beginning of the financial year (or, if he was not then a director, when he became one) interested in shares in or debentures of the company or any other body corporate in the same group, and

(b)   if he was so interested, there shall be stated the number of shares in and amount of debentures of each body (specifying it) in which, according to the register, he was then interested.

(4)   In this paragraph references to an interest in shares or debentures have the same meaning as in section 324; and references to the interest of a director include any interest falling to be treated as his for the purposes of that section.

(5)   The reference above to the time when a person became a director is, in the case of a person who became a director on more than one occasion, to the time when he first became a director.

2B   (1)   It shall be stated with respect to each director whether, according to the register, any right to subscribe for shares in or debentures of the company or another body corporate in the same group was during the financial year granted to, or exercised by, the director or a member of his immediate family.

(2)   If any such right was granted to, or exercised by, any such person during the financial year, there shall be stated the number of shares in and amount of debentures of each body (specifying it) in respect of which, according to the register, the right was granted or exercised.

(3)   A director's "immediate family" means his or her spouse and infant children; and for this purpose "children" includes step-children, and "infant", in relation to Scotland, means pupil or minor.

(4)   The reference above to a member of the director's immediate family does not include a person who is himself or herself a director of the company.]

[Political donations and expenditure

3   (1)   If—
(a)   the company (not being the wholly-owned subsidiary of a company incorporated in Great Britain) has in the financial year—
    (i)   made any donation to any registered party or to any other EU political organisation, or
    (ii)   incurred any EU political expenditure, and
(b)   the amount of the donation or expenditure, or (as the case may be) the aggregate amount of all donations and expenditure falling within paragraph (a), exceeded £200,

the directors' report for the year shall contain the particulars specified in sub-paragraph (2).

(2)   Those particulars are—
(a)   as respects donations falling within sub-paragraph (1)(a)(i)—
    (i)   the name of each registered party or other organisation to whom any such donation has been made, and
    (ii)   the total amount given to that party or organisation by way of such donations in the financial year; and
(b)   as respects expenditure falling within sub-paragraph (1)(a)(ii), the total amount incurred by way of such expenditure in the financial year.

(3)   If—
(a)   at the end of the financial year the company has subsidiaries which have, in that year, made any donations or incurred any such expenditure as is mentioned in sub-paragraph (1)(a), and
(b)   it is not itself the wholly-owned subsidiary of a company incorporated in Great Britain,

the directors' report for the year is not, by virtue of sub-paragraph (1), required to contain the particulars specified in sub-paragraph (2); but, if the total amount of any such donations or expenditure (or both) made or incurred in that year by the company and the subsidiaries between them exceeds £200, the directors' report for the year shall contain those particulars in relation to each body by whom any such donation or expenditure has been made or incurred.

(4)   Any expression used in this paragraph which is also used in Part XA of this Act has the same meaning as in that Part.

4   (1)   If the company (not being the wholly-owned subsidiary of a company incorporated in Great Britain) has in the financial year made any contribution to a non-EU political party, the directors' report for the year shall contain—
  (a)   a statement of the amount of the contribution, or
  (b)   (if it has made two or more such contributions in the year) a statement of the total amount of the contributions.

(2)   If—
  (a)   at the end of the financial year the company has subsidiaries which have, in that year, made any such contributions as are mentioned in sub-paragraph (1), and
  (b)   it is not itself the wholly-owned subsidiary of a company incorporated in Great Britain,

the directors' report for the year is not, by virtue of sub-paragraph (1), required to contain any such statement as is there mentioned, but it shall instead contain a statement of the total amount of the contributions made in the year by the company and the subsidiaries between them.

(3)   In this paragraph "contribution", in relation to an organisation, means—
  (a)   any gift of money to the organisation (whether made directly or indirectly);
  (b)   any subscription or other fee paid for affiliation to, or membership of, the organisation; or
  (c)   any money spent (otherwise than by the organisation or a person acting on its behalf) in paying any expenses incurred directly or indirectly by the organisation.

(4)   In this paragraph "non-EU political party" means any political party which carries on, or proposes to carry on, its activities wholly outside the member States.

Charitable donations

5   (1)   If—
  (a)   the company (not being the wholly-owned subsidiary of a company incorporated in Great Britain) has in the financial year given money for charitable purposes, and
  (b)   the money given exceeded £200 in amount,

the directors' report for the year shall contain, in the case of each of the purposes for which money has been given, a statement of the amount of money given for that purpose.

(2)   If—
  (a)   at the end of the financial year the company has subsidiaries which have, in that year, given money for charitable purposes, and
  (b)   it is not itself the wholly-owned subsidiary of a company incorporated in Great Britain,

sub-paragraph (1) does not apply to the company; but, if the amount given in that year for charitable purposes by the company and the subsidiaries between them exceeds £200, the directors' report for the year shall contain, in the case of each of the purposes for which money has been given by the company and the subsidiaries between them, a statement of the amount of money given for that purpose.

(3) Money given for charitable purposes to a person who, when it was given, was ordinarily resident outside the United Kingdom is to be left out of account for the purposes of this paragraph.

(4) For the purposes of this paragraph "charitable purposes" means purposes which are exclusively charitable, and as respects Scotland "charitable" is to be construed as if it were contained in the Income Tax Acts.]

[5A . . .]

Miscellaneous

6   The directors' report shall contain—
- (a)   particulars of any important events affecting the company or any of its [subsidiary undertakings] which have occurred since the end of the financial year,
- (b)   an indication of likely future developments in the business of the company and of its [subsidiary undertakings], . . .
- (c)   an indication of the activities (if any) of the company and its [subsidiary undertakings] in the field of research and development[, and
- (d)   (unless the company is an unlimited company) an indication of the existence of branches (as defined in section 698(2)) of the company outside the United Kingdom.]

NOTES

Para 1: sub-para (1) repealed, and in sub-para (2) words in square brackets substituted, in relation to the annual accounts and annual report of any company for the financial year ending on or after 2 February 1996, by SI 1996/189, regs 14(4)(a), 15(3), 16(1).

Paras 2, 2A, 2B: substituted, for para 2 as originally enacted, by the Companies Act 1989, s 8(2), Sch 5, para 3.

Paras 3–5: substituted by the Political Parties, Elections and Referendums Act 2000, s 140; for transitional provisions see Sch 23, Pt II, para 13 thereto.

Date in force: 16 February 2001: see SI 2001/222, art 2, Sch 1, Pt I.

Para 5A: inserted by the Companies Act 1989, s 137(2); repealed, in relation to the annual accounts and annual report of any company for the financial year ending on or after 2 February 1996, by SI 1996/189, regs 14(4)(b), 16(1).

Para 6: in sub-paras (a), (c), words in square brackets substituted by the Companies Act 1989, s 8(2), Sch 5, para 2(2); in sub-para (b), words in square brackets substituted by the Companies Act 1989, s 8(2), Sch 5, para 2(2), word omitted repealed and sub-para (d) inserted by SI 1992/3178, reg 3.

PART II
DISCLOSURE REQUIRED BY COMPANY ACQUIRING ITS OWN SHARES, ETC

7   This Part of this Schedule applies where shares in a company—
- (a)   are purchased by the company or are acquired by it by forfeiture or surrender in lieu of forfeiture, or in pursuance of section 143(3) of this Act (acquisition of own shares by company limited by shares), or
- (b)   are acquired by another person in circumstances where paragraph (c) or (d) of section 146(1) applies (acquisition by company's nominee, or by another with company financial assistance, the company having a beneficial interest), or
- (c)   are made subject to a lien or other charge taken (whether expressly or otherwise) by the company and permitted by section 150(2) or (4), or section 6(3) of the Consequential Provisions Act (exceptions from general rule against a company having a lien or charge on its own shares).

8   The directors' report with respect to a financial year shall state—

(a)   the number and nominal value of the shares so purchased, the aggregate amount of the consideration paid by the company for such shares and the reasons for their purchase;

(b)   the number and nominal value of the shares so acquired by the company, acquired by another person in such circumstances and so charged respectively during the financial year;

(c)   the maximum number and nominal value of shares which, having been so acquired by the company, acquired by another person in such circumstances or so charged (whether or not during that year) are held at any time by the company or that other person during that year;

(d)   the number and nominal value of the shares so acquired by the company, acquired by another person in such circumstances or so charged (whether or not during that year) which are disposed of by the company or that other person or cancelled by the company during that year;

(e)   where the number and nominal value of the shares of any particular description are stated in pursuance of any of the preceding sub-paragraphs, the percentage of the called-up share capital which shares of that description represent;

(f)   where any of the shares have been so charged the amount of the charge in each case; and

(g)   where any of the shares have been disposed of by the company or the person who acquired them in such circumstances for money or money's worth the amount or value of the consideration in each case.

PART III
DISCLOSURE CONCERNING EMPLOYMENT, ETC, OF DISABLED PERSONS

9   (1)   This Part of this Schedule applies to the directors' report where the average number of persons employed by the company in each week during the financial year exceeded 250.

(2)   That average number is the quotient derived by dividing, by the number of weeks in the financial year, the number derived by ascertaining, in relation to each of those weeks, the number of persons who, under contracts of service, were employed in the week (whether throughout it or not) by the company, and adding up the numbers ascertained.

(3)   The directors' report shall in that case contain a statement describing such policy as the company has applied during the financial year—

(a)   for giving full and fair consideration to applications for employment by the company made by disabled persons, having regard to their particular aptitudes and abilities,

(b)   for continuing the employment of, and for arranging appropriate training for, employees of the company who have become disabled persons during the period when they were employed by the company, and

(c)   otherwise for the training, career development and promotion of disabled persons employed by the company.

(4)   In this Part—

(a)   "employment" means employment other than employment to work wholly or mainly outside the United Kingdom, and "employed" and "employee" shall be construed accordingly; and

(b)   "disabled person" means the same as in the [Disability Discrimination Act 1995].

NOTES

Sub-para (4): in the definition "disabled person" words in square brackets substituted by the Disability Discrimination Act 1995, s 70(4), Sch 6, para 4.

PART IV

. . .

. . .

NOTES

Repealed by SI 1996/189, regs 14(4), 15(3).

PART V
EMPLOYEE INVOLVEMENT

11 (1) This Part of this Schedule applies to the directors' report where the average number of persons employed by the company in each week during the financial year exceeded 250.

(2) That average number is the quotient derived by dividing by the number of weeks in the financial year the number derived by ascertaining, in relation to each of those weeks, the number of persons who, under contracts of service, were employed in the week (whether throughout it or not) by the company, and adding up the numbers ascertained.

(3) The directors' report shall in that case contain a statement describing the action that has been taken during the financial year to introduce, maintain or develop arrangements aimed at—

(a) providing employees systematically with information on matters of concern to them as employees,

(b) consulting employees or their representatives on a regular basis so that the views of employees can be taken into account in making decisions which are likely to affect their interests,

(c) encouraging the involvement of employees in the company's performance through an employees' share scheme or by some other means,

(d) achieving a common awareness on the part of all employees of the financial and economic factors affecting the performance of the company.

(4) In sub-paragraph (3) "employee" does not include a person employed to work wholly or mainly outside the United Kingdom; and for the purposes of sub-paragraph (2) no regard is to be had to such a person.

[PART VI
POLICY AND PRACTICE ON PAYMENT OF CREDITORS]

NOTES

Inserted, in relation to the annual accounts and annual report of any company for the financial year ending on or after 2 February 1996, by SI 1996/189, regs 14(5), 16(1).

Substituted with savings by SI 1997/571, reg 2(2); for savings see reg 3 thereof.

[12 (1) This Part of this Schedule applies to the directors' report for a financial year if—

(a) the company was at any time within the year a public company, or

(b) the company did not quality as small or medium-sized in relation to the year by virtue of section 247 and was at any time within the year a member of a group of which the parent company was a public company.

(2) The report shall state, with respect to the next following financial year—

(a) whether in respect of some or all of its suppliers it is the company's policy to follow any code or standard on payment practice and, if so, the name of the code or standard and the place where information about, and copies of, the code or standard can be obtained,

(b) whether in respect of some or all of its suppliers it is the company's policy—

(i) to settle the terms of payment with those suppliers when agreeing the terms of each transaction,

(ii) to ensure that those suppliers are made aware of the terms of payment, and

(iii) to abide by the terms of payment,

(c) where the company's policy is not as mentioned in paragraph (a) or (b) in respect of some or all of its suppliers, what its policy is with respect to the payment of those suppliers;

and if the company's policy is different for different suppliers or classes of suppliers, the report shall identify the suppliers to which the different policies apply.

In this sub-paragraph references to the company's suppliers are references to persons who are or may become its suppliers.

(3) The report shall also state the number of days which bears to the number of days in the financial year the same proportion as X bears to Y where—

X = the aggregate of the amounts which were owed to trade creditors at the end of the year; and

Y = the aggregate of the amounts in which the company was invoiced by suppliers during the year.

(4) For the purposes of sub-paragraphs (2) and (3) a person is a supplier of the company at any time if—

(a) at that time, he is owed an amount in respect of goods or services supplied, and

(b) that amount would be included under the heading corresponding to item E.4 (trade creditors) in Format 1 if—

(i) the company's accounts fell to be prepared as at that time,

(ii) those accounts were prepared in accordance with Schedule 4, and

(iii) that Format were adopted.

(5) For the purpose of sub-paragraph (3), the aggregate of the amounts which at the end of the financial year were owed to trade creditors shall be taken to be—

(a) where in the company's accounts Format 1 of the balance sheet formats set out in Part I of Schedule 4 is adopted, the amount shown under the heading corresponding to item E.4 (trade creditors) in that Format,

(b) where Format 2 is adopted, the amount which, under the heading corresponding to item C.4 (trade creditors) in that Format, is shown as falling due within one year, and

(c) where the company's accounts are prepared in accordance with Schedule 9 or 9A, the amount which would be shown under the heading corresponding to item E.4 (trade creditors) in Format 1 if the company's accounts were prepared in accordance with Schedule 4 and that Format were adopted.]

NOTES

Inserted, in relation to the annual accounts and annual report of any company for the financial year ending on or after 2 February 1996, by SI 1996/189, regs 14(5), 16(1).

Substituted by SI 1997/571, reg 2(2); for transitional provision see reg 3 thereof.

Date in force: 4 March 1997: see SI 1997/571, reg 1(2).

[SCHEDULE 8
FORM AND CONTENT OF ACCOUNTS PREPARED BY SMALL COMPANIES]

Sections 247, 249, 250, 253, 254

NOTES

Part heading: inserted by SI 1992/2452, reg 4(3), Schedule, para 1(5).

[PART I
GENERAL RULES AND FORMATS]

[Section A
General Rules

1 (1) Subject to the following provisions of this Schedule—

(a) every balance sheet of a small company shall show the items listed in either of the balance sheet formats set out below in section B of this Part; and

(b) every profit and loss account of a small company shall show the items listed in any one of the profit and loss account formats so set out;

in either case in the order and under the headings and sub-headings given in the format adopted.

(2) Sub-paragraph (1) above is not to be read as requiring the heading or sub-heading for any item to be distinguished by any letter or number assigned to that item in the format adopted.

2 (1) Where in accordance with paragraph 1 a small company's balance sheet or profit and loss account for any financial year has been prepared by reference to one of the formats set out in section B below, the directors of the company shall adopt the same format in preparing the accounts for subsequent financial years of the company unless in their opinion there are special reasons for a change.

(2) Particulars of any change in the format adopted in preparing a small company's balance sheet or profit and loss account in accordance with paragraph 1 shall be disclosed, and the reasons for the change shall be explained, in a note to the accounts in which the new format is first adopted.

3 (1) Any item required in accordance with paragraph 1 to be shown in a small company's balance sheet or profit and loss account may he shown in greater detail than required by the format adopted.

(2) A small company's balance sheet or profit and loss account may include an item representing or covering the amount of any asset or liability, income or expenditure not otherwise covered by any of the items listed in the format adopted, but the following shall not be treated as assets in any small company's balance sheet—

(a) preliminary expenses;

(b) expenses of and commission on any issue of shares or debentures; and

(c) costs of research.

(3) In preparing a small company's balance sheet or profit and loss account the directors of the company shall adapt the arrangement and headings and sub-headings otherwise required by paragraph 1 in respect of items to which an Arabic number is assigned in the format adopted, in any case where the special nature of the company's business requires such adaptation.

(4) Items to which Arabic numbers are assigned in any of the formats set out in section B below may be combined in a small company's accounts for any financial year if either—

(a) their individual amounts are not material to assessing the state of affairs or profit or loss of the company for that year; or

(b) the combination facilitates that assessment;

but in a case within paragraph (b) the individual amounts of any items so combined shall be disclosed in a note to the accounts.

(5)   Subject to paragraph 4(3) below, a heading or sub-heading corresponding to an item listed in the format adopted in preparing a small company's balance sheet or profit and loss account shall not be included if there is no amount to be shown for that item in respect of the financial year to which the balance sheet or profit and loss account relates.

(6)   Every profit and loss account of a small company shall show the amount of the company's profit or loss on ordinary activities before taxation.

(7)   Every profit and loss account of a small company shall show separately as additional items—
  (a)   any amount set aside or proposed to be set aside to, or withdrawn or proposed to be withdrawn from, reserves;
  (b)   the aggregate amount of any dividends paid and proposed.

4   (1)   In respect of every item shown in a small company's balance sheet or profit and loss account the corresponding amount for the financial year immediately preceding that to which the balance sheet or profit and loss account relates shall also be shown.

(2)   Where that corresponding amount is not comparable with the amount to be shown for the item in question in respect of the financial year to which the balance sheet or profit and loss account relates, the former amount shall be adjusted and particulars of the adjustment and the reasons for it shall be disclosed in a note to the accounts.

(3)   Paragraph 3(5) does not apply in any case where an amount can be shown for the item in question in respect of the financial year immediately preceding that to which the balance sheet or profit and loss account relates, and that amount shall be shown under the heading or sub-heading required by paragraph 1 for that item.

5   Amounts in respect of items representing assets or income may not be set off against amounts in respect of items representing liabilities or expenditure (as the case may be), or vice versa.

Section B
The Required Formats For Accounts

PRELIMINARY

6   References in this Part of this Schedule to the items listed in any of the formats set out below are to those items read together with any of the notes following the formats which apply to any of those items, and the requirement imposed by paragraph 1 to show the items listed in any such format in the order adopted in the format is subject to any provision in those notes for alternative positions for any particular items.

7   A number in brackets following any item in any of the formats set out below is a reference to the note of that number in the notes following the formats.

8   In the notes following the formats—
  (a)   the heading of each note gives the required heading or sub-heading for the item to which it applies and a reference to any letters and numbers assigned to that item in the formats set out below (taking a reference in the case of Format 2 of the balance sheet formats to the item listed under "Assets" or under "Liabilities" as the case may require); and
  (b)   references to a numbered format are to the balance sheet format or (as the case may require) to the profit and loss account format of that number set out below.

BALANCE SHEET FORMATS

Format 1

A Called up share capital not paid (1)

B Fixed assets
  I Intangible assets
      1 Goodwill (2)
      2 Other intangible assets (3)
  II Tangible assets
      1 Land and buildings
      2 Plant and machinery etc
  III Investments
      1 Shares in group undertakings and participating interests
      2 Loans to group undertakings and undertakings in which the company has a
        participating interest
      3 Other investments other than loans
      4 Other investments (4)

C Current assets
  I Stocks
      1 Stocks
      2 Payments on account
  II Debtors (5)
      1 Trade debtors
      2 Amounts owed by group undertakings and undertakings in which the company has
        a participating interest
      3 Other debtors
  III Investments
      1 Shares in group undertakings
      2 Other investments
  IV Cash at bank and in hand

D Prepayments and accrued income (6)

E Creditors: amounts falling due within one year
  1 Bank loans and overdrafts
  2 Trade creditors
  3 Amounts owed to group undertakings and undertakings in which the company has a
participating interest
  4 Other creditors (7)

F Net current assets (liabilities) (8)

G Total assets less current liabilities

H Creditors: amounts falling due after more than one year
  1 Bank loans and overdrafts
  2 Trade creditors
  3 Amounts owed to group undertakings and undertakings in which the company has a
participating interest
  4 Other creditors (7)

I Provisions for liabilities and charges

J Accruals and deferred income (7)

K Capital and reserves
  I Called up share capital (9)
  II Share premium account
  III Revaluation reserve
  IV Other reserves
  V Profit and loss account

BALANCE SHEET FORMATS

Format 2

ASSETS

A Called up share capital not paid (1)

B Fixed assets
  I Intangible assets
    1 Goodwill (2)
    2 Other intangible assets (3)
  II Tangible assets
    1 Land and buildings
    2 Plant and machinery etc
  III Investments
    1 Shares in group undertakings and participating interests
    2 Loans to group undertakings and undertakings in which the company has a participating interest
    3 Other investments other than loans
    4 Other investments (4)

C Current assets
  I Stocks
    1 Stocks
    2 Payments on account
  II Debtors (5)
    1 Trade debtors
    2 Amounts owed by group undertakings and undertakings in which the company has a participating interest
    3 Other debtors
  III Investments
    1 Shares in group undertakings
    2 Other investments
  IV Cash at bank and in hand

D Prepayments and accrued income (6)

LIABILITIES

A Capital and reserves
  I Called up share capital (9)
  II Share premium account
  III Revaluation reserve
  IV Other reserves
  V Profit and loss account

B Provisions for liabilities and charges

C Creditors (10)
   1 Bank loans and overdrafts
   2 Trade creditors
   3 Amounts owed to group undertakings and undertakings in which the company has a participating interest
   4 Other creditors (7)

D Accruals and deferred income (7)

NOTES ON THE BALANCE SHEET FORMATS

(1) Called up share capital not paid

(Formats 1 and 2, items A and C II 3.)

This item may either be shown at item A or included under item C II 3 in Format 1 or 2.

(2) Goodwill

(Formats 1 and 2, item B I 1.)

Amounts representing goodwill shall only be included to the extent that the goodwill was acquired for valuable consideration.

(3) Other intangible assets

(Formats 1 and 2, item B I 2.)

Amounts in respect of concessions, patents, licences, trade marks and similar rights and assets shall only be included in a company's balance sheet under this item if either—
  (a) the assets were acquired for valuable consideration and are not required to be shown under goodwill; or
  (b) the assets in question were created by the company itself.

(4) Others: Other investments

(Formats 1 and 2, items B III 4 and C III 2.)

Where amounts in respect of own shares held are included under either of these items, the nominal value of such shares shall be shown separately.

(5) Debtors

(Formats 1 and 2, items C II 1 to 3.)

The amount falling due after more than one year shall be shown separately for each item included under debtors unless the aggregate amount of debtors falling due after more than one year is disclosed in the notes to the accounts.

(6) Prepayments and accrued income

(Formats 1 and 2, item D.)

This item may alternatively be included under item C II 3 in Format 1 or 2.

(7) Other creditors

(Format 1, items E 4, H 4 and J and Format 2, items C 4 and D.)

There shall be shown separately—
  (a) the amount of any convertible loans, and
  (b) the amount for creditors in respect of taxation and social security.

Payments received on account of orders shall be included in so far as they are not shown as deductions from stocks.

In Format 1, accruals and deferred income may be shown under item J or included under item E 4 or H 4, or both (as the case may require). In Format 2, accruals and deferred income may be shown under item D or within item C 4 under Liabilities.

(8) Net current assets (liabilities)

(Format 1, item F.)

In determining the amount to be shown under this item any prepayments and accrued income shall be taken into account wherever shown.

(9) Called up share capital

(Format 1, item K I and Format 2, item A I.)

The amount of allotted share capital and the amount of called up share capital which has been paid up shall be shown separately.

(10) Creditors

(Format 2, items C I to 4.)

Amounts falling due within one year and after one year shall be shown separately for each of these items and for the aggregate of all of these items unless the aggregate amount of creditors falling due within one year and the aggregate amount of creditors falling due after more than one year is disclosed in the notes to the accounts.

PROFIT AND LOSS ACCOUNT FORMATS

Format 1
(see note (14) below)

1   Turnover
2   Cost of sales (11)
3   Gross profit or loss
4   Distribution costs (11)
5   Administrative expenses (11)
6   Other operating income
7   Income from shares in group undertakings
8   Income from participating interests
9   Income from other fixed asset investments (12)
10   Other interest receivable and similar income (12)
11   Amounts written off investments
12   Interest payable and similar charges (13)
13   Tax on profit or loss on ordinary activities
14   Profit or loss on ordinary activities after taxation
15   Extraordinary income
16   Extraordinary charges

17 Extraordinary profit or loss

18 Tax on extraordinary profit or loss

19 Other taxes not shown under the above items

20 Profit or loss for the financial year

PROFIT AND LOSS ACCOUNT FORMATS

Format 2

1 Turnover

2 Change in stocks of finished goods and in work in progress

3 Own work capitalised

4 Other operating income

5 (a) Raw materials and consumables

    (b) Other external charges

6 Staff costs:

    (a) wages and salaries

    (b) social security costs

    (c) other pension costs

7 (a) Depreciation and other amounts written off tangible and intangible fixed assets

    (b) Exceptional amounts written off current assets

8 Other operating charges

9 Income from shares in group undertakings

10 Income from participating interests

11 Income from other fixed asset investments (12)

12 Other interest receivable and similar income (12)

13 Amounts written off investments

14 Interest payable and similar charges (13)

15 Tax on profit or loss on ordinary activities

16 Profit or loss on ordinary activities after taxation

17 Extraordinary income

18 Extraordinary charges

19 Extraordinary profit or loss

20 Tax on extraordinary profit or loss

21 Other taxes not shown under the above items

22 Profit or loss for the financial year

PROFIT AND LOSS ACCOUNT FORMATS

Format 3
(see note (14) below)

A Charges

1   Cost of sales (11)

2   Distribution costs (11)

3   Administrative expenses (11)

4   Amounts written off investments

5   Interest payable and similar charges (13)

6   Tax on profit or loss on ordinary activities

7   Profit or loss on ordinary activities after taxation

8   Extraordinary charges

9   Tax on extraordinary profit or loss

10   Other taxes not shown under the above items

11   Profit or loss for the financial year

B Income

1   Turnover

2   Other operating income

3   Income from shares in group undertakings

4   Income from participating interests

5   Income from other fixed asset investments (12)

6   Other interest receivable and similar income (12)

7   Profit or loss on ordinary activities after taxation

8   Extraordinary income

9   Profit or loss for the financial year

PROFIT AND LOSS ACCOUNT FORMATS

Format 4

A Charges

1   Reduction in stocks of finished goods and in work in progress

2   (a)   Raw materials and consumables

     (b)   Other external charges

3 Staff costs:

   (a) wages and salaries

   (b) social security costs

   (c) other pension costs

4 (a) Depreciation and other amounts written off tangible and intangible fixed assets

   (b) Exceptional amounts written off current assets

5 Other operating charges

6 Amounts written off investments

7 Interest payable and similar charges (13)

8 Tax on profit or loss on ordinary activities

9 Profit or loss on ordinary activities after taxation

10 Extraordinary charges

11 Tax on extraordinary profit or loss

12 Other taxes not shown under the above items

13 Profit or loss for the financial year

B Income

1 Turnover

2 Increase in stocks of finished goods and in work in progress

3 Own work capitalised

4 Other operating income

5 Income from shares in group undertakings

6 Income from participating interests

7 Income from other fixed asset investments (12)

8 Other interest receivable and similar income (12)

9 Profit or loss on ordinary activities after taxation

10 Extraordinary income

11 Profit or loss for the financial year

NOTES ON THE PROFIT AND LOSS ACCOUNT FORMATS

(11) Cost of sales: distribution costs: administrative expenses

(Format 1, items 2, 4 and 5 and Format 3, items A 1, 2 and 3.)

These items shall be stated after taking into account any necessary provisions for depreciation or diminution in value of assets.

(12) Income from other fixed asset investments: other interest receivable and similar income

(Format 1, items 9 and 10: Format 2, items 11 and 12: Format 3, items B 5 and 6: Format

4, items B 7 and 8.)

Income and interest derived from group undertakings shall be shown separately from income and interest derived from other sources.

(13) Interest payable and similar charges

(Format 1, item 12: Format 2, item 14: Format 3, item A 5: Format 4, item A 7.)

The amount payable to group undertakings shall be shown separately.

(14) Formats 1 and 3

The amount of any provisions for depreciation and diminution in value of tangible and intangible fixed assets falling to be shown under items 7(a) and A 4(a) respectively in Formats 2 and 4 shall be disclosed in a note to the accounts in any case where the profit and loss account is prepared by reference to Format 1 or Format 3.]

NOTES

Original Part I substituted by the Companies Act 1989, s 13(2), Sch 6; renumbered as Part III, section A by SI 1992/2452, reg 4(3), Schedule, para 1(1).

New Part I inserted by SI 1992/2452, reg 4(3), Schedule, para 2.

Substituted, together with Parts II–IV, for existing Parts I–III by SI 1997/220, reg 2(2), Sch 1.

Date in force: this amendment applies to annual accounts approved by the board of directors on or after 1 March 1997, and to directors' and auditors' reports on such accounts: see SI 1997/220, reg 1(3); for transitional provision see reg 1(4) thereof.

[PART II
ACCOUNTING PRINCIPLES AND RULES]

[Section A
Accounting Principles

PRELIMINARY

9 Subject to paragraph 15 below, the amounts to be included in respect of all items shown in a small company's accounts shall be determined in accordance with the principles set out in paragraphs 10 to 14.

ACCOUNTING PRINCIPLES

10 The company shall be presumed to be carrying on business as a going concern.

11 Accounting policies shall be applied consistently within the same accounts and from one financial year to the next.

12 The amount of any item shall be determined on a prudent basis, and in particular—
  (a) only profits realised at the balance sheet date shall be included in the profit and loss account; and
  (b) all liabilities and losses which have arisen or are likely to arise in respect of the financial year to which the accounts relate or a previous financial year shall be taken into account, including those which only become apparent between the balance sheet date and the date on which it is signed on behalf of the board of directors in pursuance of section 233 of this Act.

13   All income and charges relating to the financial year to which the accounts relate shall be taken into account, without regard to the date of receipt or payment.

14   In determining the aggregate amount of any item the amount of each individual asset or liability that falls to be taken into account shall be determined separately.

DEPARTURE FROM THE ACCOUNTING PRINCIPLES

15   If it appears to the directors of a small company that there are special reasons for departing from any of the principles stated above in preparing the company's accounts in respect of any financial year they may do so, but particulars of the departure, the reasons for it and its effect shall be given in a note to the accounts.

Section B
Historical Cost Accounting Rules

PRELIMINARY

16   Subject to section C of this Part of this Schedule, the amounts to be included in respect of all items shown in a small company's accounts shall be determined in accordance with the rules set out in paragraphs 17 to 28.

FIXED ASSETS

General rules

17   Subject to any provision for depreciation or diminution in value made in accordance with paragraph 18 or 19 the amount to be included in respect of any fixed asset shall be its purchase price or production cost.

18   In the case of any fixed asset which has a limited useful economic life, the amount of—
  (a)   its purchase price or production cost; or
  (b)   where it is estimated that any such asset will have a residual value at the end of the period of its useful economic life, its purchase price or production cost less that estimated residual value;

shall be reduced by provisions for depreciation calculated to write off that amount systematically over the period of the asset's useful economic life.

19   (1)   Where a fixed asset investment of a description falling to be included under item B III of either of the balance sheet formats set out in Part I of this Schedule has diminished in value provisions for diminution in value may be made in respect of it and the amount to be included in respect of it may be reduced accordingly; and any such provisions which are not shown in the profit and loss account shall be disclosed (either separately or in aggregate) in a note to the accounts.

(2)   Provisions for diminution in value shall be made in respect of any fixed asset which has diminished in value if the reduction in its value is expected to be permanent (whether its useful economic life is limited or not), and the amount to be included in respect of it shall be reduced accordingly; and any such provisions which are not shown in the profit and loss account shall be disclosed (either separately or in aggregate) in a note to the accounts.

(3)   Where the reasons for which any provision was made in accordance with sub-paragraph (1) or (2) have ceased to apply to any extent, that provision shall be written back to the extent that it is no longer necessary; and any amounts written back in accordance with this

sub-paragraph which are not shown in the profit and loss account shall be disclosed (either separately or in aggregate) in a note to the accounts.

Rules for determining particular fixed asset items

20 (1) Notwithstanding that an item in respect of "development costs" is included under "fixed assets" in the balance sheet formats set out in Part I of this Schedule, an amount may only be included in a small company's balance sheet in respect of development costs in special circumstances.

(2) If any amount is included in a small company's balance sheet in respect of development costs the following information shall be given in a note to the accounts—
   (a) the period over which the amount of those costs originally capitalised is being or is to be written off; and
   (b) the reasons for capitalising the development costs in question.

21 (1) The application of paragraphs 17 to 19 in relation to goodwill (in any case where goodwill is treated as an asset) is subject to the following provisions of this paragraph.

(2) Subject to sub-paragraph (3) below, the amount of the consideration for any goodwill acquired by a small company shall be reduced by provisions for depreciation calculated to write off that amount systematically over a period chosen by the directors of the company.

(3) The period chosen shall not exceed the useful economic life of the goodwill in question.

(4) In any case where any goodwill acquired by a small company is shown or included as an asset in the company's balance sheet the period chosen for writing off the consideration for that goodwill and the reasons for choosing that period shall be disclosed in a note to the accounts.

CURRENT ASSETS

22 Subject to paragraph 23, the amount to be included in respect of any current asset shall be its purchase price or production cost.

23 (1) If the net realisable value of any current asset is lower than its purchase price or production cost the amount to be included in respect of that asset shall be the net realisable value.

(2) Where the reasons for which any provision for diminution in value was made in accordance with sub-paragraph (1) have ceased to apply to any extent, that provision shall be written back to the extent that it is no longer necessary.

MISCELLANEOUS AND SUPPLEMENTARY PROVISIONS

Excess of money owed over value received as an asset item

24 (1) Where the amount repayable on any debt owed by a small company is greater than the value of the consideration received in the transaction giving rise to the debt, the amount of the difference may be treated as an asset.

(2) Where any such amount is so treated—
   (a) it shall be written off by reasonable amounts each year and must be completely written off before repayment of the debt; and
   (b) if the current amount is not shown as a separate item in the company's balance sheet it must be disclosed in a note to the accounts.

Assets included at a fixed amount

25 (1) Subject to the following sub-paragraph, assets which fall to be included—

(a) amongst the fixed assets of a small company under the item "tangible assets"; or

(b) amongst the current assets of a small company under the item "raw materials and consumables";

may be included at a fixed quantity and value.

(2) Sub-paragraph (1) applies to assets of a kind which are constantly being replaced, where—

(a) their overall value is not material to assessing the company's state of affairs; and

(b) their quantity, value and composition are not subject to material variation.

Determination of purchase price or production cost

26 (1) The purchase price of an asset shall be determined by adding to the actual price paid any expenses incidental to its acquisition.

(2) The production cost of an asset shall be determined by adding to the purchase price of the raw materials and consumables used the amount of the costs incurred by the company which are directly attributable to the production of that asset.

(3) In addition, there may be included in the production cost of an asset—

(a) a reasonable proportion of the costs incurred by the company which are only indirectly attributable to the production of that asset, but only to the extent that they relate to the period of production; and

(b) interest on capital borrowed to finance the production of that asset, to the extent that it accrues in respect of the period of production;

provided, however, in a case within paragraph (b) above, that the inclusion of the interest in determining the cost of that asset and the amount of the interest so included is disclosed in a note to the accounts.

(4) In the case of current assets distribution costs may not be included in production costs.

27 (1) Subject to the qualification mentioned below, the purchase price or production cost of—

(a) any assets which fall to be included under any item shown in a small company's balance sheet under the general item "stocks"; and

(b) any assets which are fungible assets (including investments);

may be determined by the application of any of the methods mentioned in sub-paragraph (2) below in relation to any such assets of the same class.

The method chosen must be one which appears to the directors to be appropriate in the circumstances of the company.

(2) Those methods are—

(a) the method known as "first in, first out" (FIFO);

(b) the method known as "last in, first out" (LIFO);

(c) a weighted average price; and

(d) any other method similar to any of the methods mentioned above.

(3) For the purposes of this paragraph, assets of any description shall be regarded as fungible if assets of that description are substantially indistinguishable one from another.

Substitution of original stated amount where price or cost unknown

28

Where there is no record of the purchase price or production cost of any asset of a small company or of any price, expenses or costs relevant for determining its purchase price or production cost in accordance with paragraph 26, or any such record cannot be obtained without unreasonable expense or delay, its purchase price or production cost shall be taken for the purposes of paragraphs 17 to 23 to be the value ascribed to it in the earliest available record of its value made on or after its acquisition or production by the company.

Section C
Alternative Accounting Rules

PRELIMINARY

29　(1)　The rules set out in section B are referred to below in this Schedule as the historical cost accounting rules.

(2)　Those rules, with the omission of paragraphs 16, 21 and 25 to 28, are referred to below in this Part of this Schedule as the depreciation rules; and references below in this Schedule to the historical cost accounting rules do not include the depreciation rules as they apply by virtue of paragraph 32.

30　Subject to paragraphs 32 to 34, the amounts to be included in respect of assets of any description mentioned in paragraph 31 may be determined on any basis so mentioned.

ALTERNATIVE ACCOUNTING RULES

31　(1)　Intangible fixed assets, other than goodwill, may be included at their current cost.

(2)　Tangible fixed assets may be included at a market value determined as at the date of their last valuation or at their current cost.

(3)　Investments of any description falling to be included under item B III of either of the balance sheet formats set out in Part I of this Schedule may be included either—
(a)　at a market value determined as at the date of their last valuation; or
(b)　at a value determined on any basis which appears to the directors to be appropriate in the circumstances of the company;

but in the latter case particulars of the method of valuation adopted and of the reasons for adopting it shall be disclosed in a note to the accounts.

(4)　Investments of any description falling to be included under item C III of either of the balance sheet formats set out in Part I of this Schedule may be included at their current cost.

(5)　Stocks may be included at their current cost.

APPLICATION OF THE DEPRECIATION RULES

32　(1)　Where the value of any asset of a small company is determined on any basis mentioned in paragraph 31, that value shall be, or (as the case may require) be the starting point for determining, the amount to be included in respect of that asset in the company's accounts, instead of its purchase price or production cost or any value previously so determined for that asset; and the depreciation rules shall apply accordingly in relation to any such asset with the substitution for any reference to its purchase price or production cost of a reference to the value most recently determined for that asset on any basis mentioned in paragraph 31.

(2)   The amount of any provision for depreciation required in the case of any fixed asset by paragraph 18 or 19 as it applies by virtue of sub-paragraph (1) is referred to below in this paragraph as the adjusted amount, and the amount of any provision which would be required by that paragraph in the case of that asset according to the historical cost accounting rules is referred to as the historical cost amount.

(3)   Where sub-paragraph (1) applies in the case of any fixed asset the amount of any provision for depreciation in respect of that asset—

(a)   included in any item shown in the profit and loss account in respect of amounts written off assets of the description in question; or

(b)   taken into account in stating any item so shown which is required by note (11) of the notes on the profit and loss account formats set out in Part I of this Schedule to be stated after taking into account any necessary provision for depreciation or diminution in value of assets included under it;

may be the historical cost amount instead of the adjusted amount, provided that the amount of any difference between the two is shown separately in the profit and loss account or in a note to the accounts.

ADDITIONAL INFORMATION TO BE PROVIDED IN CASE OF DEPARTURE FROM HISTORICAL COST ACCOUNTING RULES

33   (1)   This paragraph applies where the amounts to be included in respect of assets covered by any items shown in a small company's accounts have been determined on any basis mentioned in paragraph 31.

(2)   The items affected and the basis of valuation adopted in determining the amounts of the assets in question in the case of each such item shall be disclosed in a note to the accounts.

(3)   In the case of each balance sheet item affected (except stocks) either—

(a)   the comparable amounts determined according to the historical cost accounting rules; or

(b)   the differences between those amounts and the corresponding amounts actually shown in the balance sheet in respect of that item;

shall be shown separately in the balance sheet or in a note to the accounts.

(4)   In sub-paragraph (3) above, references in relation to any item to the comparable amounts determined as there mentioned are references to—

(a)   the aggregate amount which would be required to be shown in respect of that item if the amounts to be included in respect of all the assets covered by that item were determined according to the historical cost accounting rules; and

(b)   the aggregate amount of the cumulative provisions for depreciation or diminution in value which would be permitted or required in determining those amounts according to those rules.

REVALUATION RESERVE

34   (1)   With respect to any determination of the value of an asset of a small company on any basis mentioned in paragraph 31, the amount of any profit or loss arising from that determination (after allowing, where appropriate, for any provisions for depreciation or diminution in value made otherwise than by reference to the value so determined and any adjustments of any such provisions made in the light of that determination) shall be credited or (as the case may be) debited to a separate reserve ("the revaluation reserve").

(2) The amount of the revaluation reserve shall be shown in the company's balance sheet under a separate sub-heading in the position given for the item "revaluation reserve" in Format 1 or 2 of the balance sheet formats set out in Part I of this Schedule, but need not be shown under that name.

(3) An amount may be transferred—
 (a) from the revaluation reserve—
 (i) to the profit and loss account, if the amount was previously charged to that account or represents realised profit, or
 (ii) on capitalisation,
 (b) to or from the revaluation reserve in respect of the taxation relating to any profit or loss credited or debited to the reserve;

and the revaluation reserve shall be reduced to the extent that the amounts transferred to it are no longer necessary for the purposes of the valuation method used.

(4) In sub-paragraph (3)(a)(ii) "capitalisation", in relation to an amount standing to the credit of the revaluation reserve, means applying it in wholly or partly paying up unissued shares in the company to be allotted to members of the company as fully or partly paid shares.

(5) The revaluation reserve shall not be reduced except as mentioned in this paragraph.

(6) The treatment for taxation purposes of amounts credited or debited to the revaluation reserve shall be disclosed in a note to the accounts.]

NOTES

Original Part II substituted by the Companies Act 1989, s 13(2), Sch 6; renumbered as Part III, section B by SI 1992/2452, reg 4(3), Schedule, para 1(1).

New Part II inserted by SI 1992/2452, reg 4(3), Schedule, para 3.

Substituted, together with Parts I, III, IV for existing Parts I–III by SI 1997/220, reg 2(2), Sch 1.

Date in force: this amendment applies to annual accounts approved by the board of directors on or after 1 March 1997, and to directors' and auditors' reports on such accounts: see SI 1997/220, reg 1(3); for transitional provision see reg 1(4) thereof.

[PART III
NOTES TO THE ACCOUNTS]

[PRELIMINARY

35 Any information required in the case of any small company by the following provisions of this Part of this Schedule shall (if not given in the company's accounts) be given by way of a note to those accounts.

DISCLOSURE OF ACCOUNTING POLICIES

36 The accounting policies adopted by the company in determining the amounts to be included in respect of items shown in the balance sheet and in determining the profit or loss of the company shall be stated (including such policies with respect to the depreciation and diminution in value of assets).

INFORMATION SUPPLEMENTING THE BALANCE SHEET

37   Paragraphs 38 to 47 require information which either supplements the information given with respect to any particular items shown in the balance sheet or is otherwise relevant to assessing the company's state of affairs in the light of the information so given.

Share capital and debentures

38   (1)   The following information shall be given with respect to the company's share capital—
- (a)   the authorised share capital; and
- (b)   where shares of more than one class have been allotted, the number and aggregate nominal value of shares of each class allotted.

(2)   In the case of any part of the allotted share capital that consists of redeemable shares, the following information shall be given—
- (a)   the earliest and latest dates on which the company has power to redeem those shares;
- (b)   whether those shares must be redeemed in any event or are liable to be redeemed at the option of the company or of the shareholder; and
- (c)   whether any (and, if so, what) premium is payable on redemption.

39   If the company has allotted any shares during the financial year, the following information shall be given—
- (a)   the classes of shares allotted; and
- (b)   as respects each class of shares, the number allotted, their aggregate nominal value, and the consideration received by the company for the allotment.

Fixed assets

40   (1)   In respect of each item which is or would but for paragraph 3(4)(b) be shown under the general item "fixed assets" in the company's balance sheet the following information shall be given—
- (a)   the appropriate amounts in respect of that item as at the date of the beginning of the financial year and as at the balance sheet date respectively;
- (b)   the effect on any amount shown in the balance sheet in respect of that item of—
  - (i)   any revision of the amount in respect of any assets included under that item made during that year on any basis mentioned in paragraph 31;
  - (ii)   acquisitions during that year of any assets;
  - (iii)   disposals during that year of any assets; and
  - (iv)   any transfers of assets of the company to and from that item during that year.

(2)   The reference in sub-paragraph (1)(a) to the appropriate amounts in respect of any item as at any date there mentioned is a reference to amounts representing the aggregate amounts determined, as at that date, in respect of assets falling to be included under that item on either of the following bases, that is to say—
- (a)   on the basis of purchase price or production cost (determined in accordance with paragraphs 26 and 27); or
- (b)   on any basis mentioned in paragraph 31,

(leaving out of account in either case any provisions for depreciation or diminution in value).

(3)   In respect of each item within sub-paragraph (1)—
- (a)   the cumulative amount of provisions for depreciation or diminution in value of assets included under that item as at each date mentioned in sub-paragraph (1)(a);
- (b)   the amount of any such provisions made in respect of the financial year;

(c)   the amount of any adjustments made in respect of any such provisions during that year in consequence of the disposal of any assets; and

(d)   the amount of any other adjustments made in respect of any such provisions during that year;

shall also be stated.

41   Where any fixed assets of the company (other than listed investments) are included under any item shown in the company's balance sheet at an amount determined on any basis mentioned in paragraph 31, the following information shall be given—

(a)   the years (so far as they are known to the directors) in which the assets were severally valued and the several values; and

(b)   in the case of assets that have been valued during the financial year, the names of the persons who valued them or particulars of their qualifications for doing so and (whichever is stated) the bases of valuation used by them.

Investments

42   (1)   In respect of the amount of each item which is or would but for paragraph 3(4)(b) be shown in the company's balance sheet under the general item "investments" (whether as fixed assets or as current assets) there shall be stated how much of that amount is ascribable to listed investments.

(2)   Where the amount of any listed investments is stated for any item in accordance with sub-paragraph (1), the following amounts shall also be stated—

(a)   the aggregate market value of those investments where it differs from the amount so stated; and

(b)   both the market value and the stock exchange value of any investments of which the former value is, for the purposes of the accounts, taken as being higher than the latter.

Reserves and provisions

43   (1)   Where any amount is transferred—

(a)   to or from any reserves; or

(b)   to any provisions for liabilities and charges; or

(c)   from any provision for liabilities and charges otherwise than for the purpose for which the provision was established;

and the reserves or provisions are or would but for paragraph 3(4)(b) be shown as separate items in the company's balance sheet, the information mentioned in the following sub-paragraph shall be given in respect of the aggregate of reserves or provisions included in the same item.

(2)   That information is—

(a)   the amount of the reserves or provisions as at the date of the beginning of the financial year and as at the balance sheet date respectively;

(b)   any amounts transferred to or from the reserves or provisions during that year; and

(c)   the source and application respectively of any amounts so transferred.

(3)   Particulars shall be given of each provision included in the item "other provisions" in the company's balance sheet in any case where the amount of that provision is material.

Details of indebtedness

44   (1)   For the aggregate of all items shown under "creditors" in the company's balance sheet there shall be stated the aggregate of the following amounts, that is to say—

(a) the amount of any debts included under "creditors" which are payable or repayable otherwise than by instalments and fall due for payment or repayment after the end of the period of five years beginning with the day next following the end of the financial year; and

(b) in the case of any debts so included which are payable or repayable by instalments, the amount of any instalments which fall due for payment after the end of that period.

(2) In respect of each item shown under "creditors" in the company's balance sheet there shall be stated the aggregate amount of any debts included under that item in respect of which any security has been given by the company.

(3) References above in this paragraph to an item shown under "creditors" in the company's balance sheet include references, where amounts falling due to creditors within one year and after more than one year are distinguished in the balance sheet—

(a) in a case within sub-paragraph (1), to an item shown under the latter of those categories; and

(b) in a case within sub-paragraph (2), to an item shown under either of those categories;

and references to items shown under "creditors" include references to items which would but for paragraph 3(4)(b) be shown under that heading.

45 If any fixed cumulative dividends on the company's shares are in arrear, there shall be stated—

(a) the amount of the arrears; and

(b) the period for which the dividends or, if there is more than one class, each class of them are in arrear.

Guarantees and other financial commitments

46 (1) Particulars shall be given of any charge on the assets of the company to secure the liabilities of any other person, including, where practicable, the amount secured.

(2) The following information shall be given with respect to any other contingent liability not provided for—

(a) the amount or estimated amount of that liability;

(b) its legal nature; and

(c) whether any valuable security has been provided by the company in connection with that liability and if so, what.

(3) There shall be stated, where practicable, the aggregate amount or estimated amount of contracts for capital expenditure, so far as not provided for.

(4) Particulars shall be given of—

(a) any pension commitments included under any provision shown in the company's balance sheet; and

(b) any such commitments for which no provision has been made;

and where any such commitment relates wholly or partly to pensions payable to past directors of the company separate particulars shall be given of that commitment so far as it relates to such pensions.

(5) Particulars shall also be given of any other financial commitments which—

(a) have not been provided for; and

(b) are relevant to assessing the company's state of affairs.

(6) Commitments within any of sub-paragraphs (1) to (5) which are undertaken on behalf of or for the benefit of—

(a) any parent undertaking or fellow subsidiary undertaking, or

(b) any subsidiary undertaking of the company,

shall be stated separately from the other commitments within that sub-paragraph, and commitments within paragraph (a) shall also be stated separately from those within paragraph (b).

Miscellaneous matters

47 Particulars shall be given of any case where the purchase price or production cost of any asset is for the first time determined under paragraph 28.

INFORMATION SUPPLEMENTING THE PROFIT AND LOSS ACCOUNT

48 Paragraphs 49 and 50 require information which either supplements the information given with respect to any particular items shown in the profit and loss account or otherwise provides particulars of income or expenditure of the company or of circumstances affecting the items shown in the profit and loss account.

Particulars of turnover

49 (1) If the company has supplied geographical markets outside the United Kingdom during the financial year in question, there shall be stated the percentage of its turnover that, in the opinion of the directors, is attributable to those markets.

(2) In analysing for the purposes of this paragraph the source of turnover, the directors of the company shall have regard to the manner in which the company's activities are organised.

Miscellaneous matters

50 (1) Where any amount relating to any preceding financial year is included in any item in the profit and loss account, the effect shall be stated.

(2) Particulars shall be given of any extraordinary income or charges arising in the financial year.

(3) The effect shall be stated of any transactions that are exceptional by virtue of size or incidence though they fall within the ordinary activities of the company.

GENERAL

51 (1) Where sums originally denominated in foreign currencies have been brought into account under any items shown in the balance sheet or profit and loss account, the basis on which those sums have been translated into sterling shall be stated.

(2) Subject to the following sub-paragraph, in respect of every item stated in a note to the accounts the corresponding amount for the financial year immediately preceding that to which the accounts relate shall also be stated and where the corresponding amount is not comparable, it shall be adjusted and particulars of the adjustment and the reasons for it shall be given.

(3) Sub-paragraph (2) does not apply in relation to any amounts stated by virtue of any of the following provisions of this Act—

(a) paragraph 13 of Schedule 4A (details of accounting treatment of acquisitions),

(b) paragraphs 2, 8(3), 16, 21(1)(d), 22(4) and (5), 24(3) and (4) and 27(3) and (4) of Schedule 5 (shareholdings in other undertakings),

(c)   Parts II and III of Schedule 6 (loans and other dealings in favour of directors and others), and

(d)   paragraphs 40 and 43 above (fixed assets and reserves and provisions).]

[Dormant Companies Acting as Agents]

[51A   Where the directors of a company take advantage of the exemption conferred by section 249AA, and the company has during the financial year in question acted as an agent for any person, the fact that it has so acted must be stated.]

NOTES

Substituted, together with Parts I, II, IV, for existing Parts I–III by SI 1997/220, reg 2(2), Sch 1.

Date in force: this amendment applies to annual accounts approved by the board of directors on or after 1 March 1997, and to directors' and auditors' reports on such accounts: see SI 1997/220, reg 1(3); for transitional provision see reg 1(4) thereof.

Para 51A: inserted by SI 2000/1430, reg 6.

Date in force: this amendment has effect in relation to annual accounts and reports in respect of financial years ending on or after 26 July 2000: see SI 2000/1430, reg 1(1), (2).

[PART IV
INTERPRETATION OF SCHEDULE]

[52   The following paragraphs apply for the purposes of this Schedule and its interpretation.

Historical cost accounting rules

53   References to the historical cost accounting rules shall be read in accordance with paragraph 29.

Listed investments

[54   (1)   "Listed investment" means an investment as respects which there has been granted a listing on—

(a)   a recognised investment exchange other than an overseas investment exchange; or

(b)   a stock exchange of repute outside Great Britain.

(2)   "Recognised investment exchange" and "overseas investment exchange" have the meaning given in Part 18 of the Financial Services and Markets Act 2000.]

Loans

55   A loan is treated as falling due for repayment, and an instalment of a loan is treated as falling due for payment, on the earliest date on which the lender could require repayment or (as the case may be) payment, if he exercised all options and rights available to him.

Materiality

56   Amounts which in the particular context of any provision of this Schedule are not material may be disregarded for the purposes of that provision.

Provisions

57   (1)   References to provisions for depreciation or diminution in value of assets are to any amount written off by way of providing for depreciation or diminution in value of assets.

(2) Any reference in the profit and loss account formats set out in Part I of this Schedule to the depreciation of, or amounts written off, assets of any description is to any provision for depreciation or diminution in value of assets of that description.

58 References to provisions for liabilities or charges are to any amount retained as reasonably necessary for the purpose of providing for any liability or loss which is either likely to be incurred, or certain to be incurred but uncertain as to amount or as to the date on which it will arise.

Staff costs

59 (1) "Social security costs" means any contributions by the company to any state social security or pension scheme, fund or arrangement.

(2) "Pension costs" includes any costs incurred by the company in respect of any pension scheme established for the purpose of providing pensions for persons currently or formerly employed by the company, any sums set aside for the future payment of pensions directly by the company to current or former employees and any pensions paid directly to such persons without having first been set aside.

(3) Any amount stated in respect of the item "social security costs" or in respect of the item "wages and salaries" in the company's profit and loss account shall be determined by reference to payments made or costs incurred in respect of all persons employed by the company during the financial year under contracts of service.]

NOTES

Substituted, together with Parts I–III, for existing Parts I–III by SI 1997/220, reg 2(2), Sch 1.

Date in force: this amendment applies to annual accounts approved by the board of directors on or after 1 March 1997, and to directors' and auditors' reports on such accounts: see SI 1997/220, reg 1(3); for transitional provision see reg 1(4) thereof.

Para 54: substituted by SI 2001/3649, art 34.

Date in force: 1 December 2001: see SI 2001/3649, art 1.

[SCHEDULE 8A
FORM AND CONTENT OF ABBREVIATED ACCOUNTS OF SMALL COMPANIES DELIVERED TO REGISTRAR]

Section 246

[PART I
BALANCE SHEET FORMATS]

[1 A small company may deliver to the registrar a copy of the balance sheet showing the items listed in either of the balance sheet formats set out in paragraph 2 below in the order and under the headings and sub-headings given in the format adopted, but in other respects corresponding to the full balance sheet.

2 The formats referred to in paragraph 1 are as follows—

BALANCE SHEET FORMATS

Format 1

A Called up share capital not paid

B Fixed assets
  I Intangible assets
  II Tangible assets
  III Investments

C Current assets
  I Stocks
  II Debtors (1)
  III Investments
  IV Cash at bank and in hand

D Prepayments and accrued income

E Creditors: amounts falling due within one year

F Net current assets (liabilities)

G Total assets less current liabilities

H Creditors: amounts falling due after more than one year

I Provisions for liabilities and charges

J Accruals and deferred income

K Capital and reserves
  I Called up share capital
  II Share premium account
  III Revaluation reserve
  IV Other reserves
  V Profit and loss account

BALANCE SHEET FORMATS

Format 2

ASSETS

A Called up share capital not paid

B Fixed assets
  I Intangible assets
  II Tangible assets
  III Investments

C Current assets
  I Stocks
  II Debtors (1)
  III Investments
  IV Cash at bank and in hand

D Prepayments and accrued income

LIABILITIES

A Capital and reserves
  I Called up share capital
  II Share premium account
  III Revaluation reserve
  IV Other reserves
  V Profit and loss account

B Provisions for liabilities and charges

C Creditors (2)

D Accruals and deferred income

NOTES ON THE BALANCE SHEET FORMATS

(1) Debtors

(Formats 1 and 2, item C II.)

The aggregate amount of debtors falling due after more than one year shall be shown separately, unless it is disclosed in the notes to the accounts.

(2) Creditors

(Format 2, Liabilities item C.)

The aggregate amount of creditors falling due within one year and of creditors falling due after more than one year shall be shown separately, unless it is disclosed in the notes to the accounts.]

NOTES

Inserted by SI 1997/220, reg 2(3), Sch 2.

Date in force: this amendment applies to annual accounts approved by the board of directors on or after 1 March 1997, and to directors' and auditors' reports on such accounts: see SI 1997/220, reg 1(3); for transitional provision see reg 1(4) thereof.

[PART II
NOTES TO THE ACCOUNTS]

[PRELIMINARY

3 Any information required in the case of any small company by the following provisions of this Part of this Schedule shall (if not given in the company's accounts) be given by way of a note to those accounts.

DISCLOSURE OF ACCOUNTING POLICIES

4 The accounting policies adopted by the company in determining the amounts to be included in respect of items shown in the balance sheet and in determining the profit or loss of the company shall be stated (including such policies with respect to the depreciation and diminution in value of assets).

INFORMATION SUPPLEMENTING THE BALANCE SHEET

Share capital and debentures

5 (1) The following information shall be given with respect to the company's share capital—

   (a) the authorised share capital; and

   (b) where shares of more than one class have been allotted, the number and aggregate nominal value of shares of each class allotted.

(2) In the case of any part of the allotted share capital that consists of redeemable shares, the following information shall be given—

   (a) the earliest and latest dates on which the company has power to redeem those shares;

   (b) whether those shares must be redeemed in any event or are liable to be redeemed at the option of the company or of the shareholder; and

   (c) whether any (and, if so, what) premium is payable on redemption.

6 If the company has allotted any shares during the financial year, the following information shall be given—

   (a) the classes of shares allotted; and

   (b) as respects each class of shares, the number allotted, their aggregate nominal value, and the consideration received by the company for the allotment.

Fixed assets

7 (1) In respect of each item to which a letter or Roman number is assigned under the general item "fixed assets" in the company's balance sheet the following information shall be given—

   (a) the appropriate amounts in respect of that item as at the date of the beginning of the financial year and as at the balance sheet date respectively;

   (b) the effect on any amount shown in the balance sheet in respect of that item of—

   (i) any revision of the amount in respect of any assets included under that item made during that year on any basis mentioned in paragraph 31 of Schedule 8;

   (ii) acquisitions during that year of any assets;

   (iii) disposals during that year of any assets; and

   (iv) any transfers of assets of the company to and from that item during that year.

(2) The reference in sub-paragraph (1)(a) to the appropriate amounts in respect of any item as at any date there mentioned is a reference to amounts representing the aggregate amounts determined, as at that date, in respect of assets falling to be included under that item on either of the following bases, that is to say—

   (a) on the basis of purchase price or production cost (determined in accordance with paragraphs 26 and 27 of Schedule 8); or

   (b) on any basis mentioned in paragraph 31 of that Schedule,

(leaving out of account in either case any provisions for depreciation or diminution in value).

(3) In respect of each item within sub-paragraph (1)—

   (a) the cumulative amount of provisions for depreciation or diminution in value of assets included under that item as at each date mentioned in sub-paragraph (1)(a);

   (b) the amount of any such provisions made in respect of the financial year;

   (c) the amount of any adjustments made in respect of any such provisions during that year in consequence of the disposal of any assets; and

   (d) the amount of any other adjustments made in respect of any such provisions during that year;

shall also be stated.

Details of indebtedness

8 (1) For the aggregate of all items shown under "creditors" in the company's balance sheet there shall be stated the aggregate of the following amounts, that is to say—

(a) the amount of any debts included under "creditors" which are payable or repayable otherwise than by instalments and fall due for payment or repayment after the end of the period of five years beginning with the day next following the end of the financial year; and

(b) in the case of any debts so included which are payable or repayable by instalments, the amount of any instalments which fall due for payment after the end of that period.

(2) In respect of each item shown under "creditors" in the company's balance sheet there shall be stated the aggregate amount of any debts included under that item, in respect of which any security has been given by the company.

GENERAL

9 (1) Where sums originally denominated in foreign currencies have been brought into account under any items shown in the balance sheet or profit and loss account, the basis on which those sums have been translated into sterling shall be stated.

(2) Subject to the following sub-paragraph, in respect of every item required to be stated in a note to the accounts by or under any provision of this Act, the corresponding amount for the financial year immediately preceding that to which the accounts relate shall also be stated and where the corresponding amount is not comparable, it shall be adjusted and particulars of the adjustment and the reasons for it shall be given.

(3) Sub-paragraph (2) does not apply in relation to any amounts stated by virtue of any of the following provisions of this Act—

(a) paragraph 13 of Schedule 4A (details of accounting treatment of acquisitions),

(b) paragraphs 2, 8(3), 16, 21(1)(d), 22(4) and (5), 24(3) and (4) and 27(3) and (4) of Schedule 5 (shareholdings in other undertakings),

(c) Parts II and III of Schedule 6 (loans and other dealings in favour of directors and others), and

(d) paragraph 7 above (fixed assets).]

[Dormant Companies Acting as Agents]

[9A Where the directors of a company take advantage of the exemption conferred by section 249AA, and the company has during the financial year in question acted as an agent for any person, the fact that it has so acted must be stated.]

NOTES

Inserted by SI 1997/220, reg 2(3), Sch 2.

Date in force: this amendment applies to annual accounts approved by the board of directors on or after 1 March 1997, and to directors' and auditors' reports on such accounts: see SI 1997/220, reg 1(3); for transitional provision see reg 1(4) thereof.

Para 9A: inserted by SI 2000/1430, reg 7.

Date in force: this amendment has effect in relation to annual accounts and reports in respect of financial years ending on or after 26 July 2000: see SI 2000/1430, reg 1(1), (2).

SCHEDULE 13
Provisions Supplementing and Interpreting Sections 324–328

PART I
RULES FOR INTERPRETATION OF THE SECTIONS AND ALSO SECTION 346(4) AND (5)

1   (1)   A reference to an interest in shares or debentures is to be read as including any interest of any kind whatsoever in shares or debentures.

(2)   Accordingly, there are to be disregarded any restraints or restrictions to which the exercise of any right attached to the interest is or may be subject.

2   Where property is held on trust and any interest in shares or debentures is comprised in the property, any beneficiary of the trust who (apart from this paragraph) does not have an interest in the shares or debentures is to be taken as having such an interest; but this paragraph is without prejudice to the following provisions of this Part of this Schedule.

3   (1)   A person is taken to have an interest in shares or debentures if—
- (a)   he enters into a contract for their purchase by him (whether for cash or other consideration), or
- (b)   not being the registered holder, he is entitled to exercise any right conferred by the holding of the shares or debentures, or is entitled to control the exercise of any such right.

(2)   For purposes of sub-paragraph (1)(b), a person is taken to be entitled to exercise or control the exercise of a right conferred by the holding of shares or debentures if he—
- (a)   has a right (whether subject to conditions or not) the exercise of which would make him so entitled, or
- (b)   is under an obligation (whether or not so subject) the fulfilment of which would make him so entitled.

(3)   A person is not by virtue of sub-paragraph (1)(b) taken to be interested in shares or debentures by reason only that he—
- (a)   has been appointed a proxy to vote at a specified meeting of a company or of any class of its members and at any adjournment of that meeting, or
- (b)   has been appointed by a corporation to act as its representative at any meeting of a company or of any class of its members.

4   A person is taken to be interested in shares or debentures if a body corporate is interested in them and—
- (a)   that body corporate or its directors are accustomed to act in accordance with his directions or instructions, or
- (b)   he is entitled to exercise or control the exercise of one-third or more of the voting power at general meetings of that body corporate.

As this paragraph applies for the purposes of section 346(4) and (5), "more than one-half" is substituted for "one-third or more".

5   Where a person is entitled to exercise or control the exercise of one-third or more of the voting power at general meetings of a body corporate, and that body corporate is entitled to exercise or control the exercise of any of the voting power at general meetings of another body corporate ("the effective voting power"), then, for purposes of paragraph 4(b), the effective voting power is taken to be exercisable by that person.

As this paragraph applies for the purposes of section 346(4) and (5), "more than one-half" is substituted for "one-third or more".

6 (1) A person is taken to have an interest in shares or debentures if, otherwise than by virtue of having an interest under a trust—

(a) he has a right to call for delivery of the shares or debentures to himself or to his order, or

(b) he has a right to acquire an interest in shares or debentures or is under an obligation to take an interest in shares or debentures;

whether in any case the right or obligation is conditional or absolute.

(2) Rights or obligations to subscribe for shares or debentures are not to be taken, for purposes of sub-paragraph (1), to be rights to acquire, or obligations to take, an interest in shares or debentures.

This is without prejudice to paragraph 1.

7 Persons having a joint interest are deemed each of them to have that interest.

8 It is immaterial that shares or debentures in which a person has an interest are unidentifiable.

9 So long as a person is entitled to receive, during the lifetime of himself or another, income from trust property comprising shares or debentures, an interest in the shares or debentures in reversion or remainder or (as regards Scotland) in fee, are to be disregarded.

10 A person is to be treated as uninterested in shares or debentures if, and so long as, he holds them under the law in force in England and Wales as a bare trustee or as a custodian trustee, or under the law in force in Scotland, as a simple trustee.

11 [(1)] There is to be disregarded an interest of a person subsisting by virtue of—

[(a) any unit trust scheme which is an authorised unit trust scheme . . .]

(b) a scheme made under section 22 [or 22A] of the Charities Act 1960 [or section 24 or 25 of the Charities Act 1993], section 11 of the Trustee Investments Act 1961 or section 1 of the Administration of Justice Act 1965; or

(c) the scheme set out in the Schedule to the Church Funds Investment Measure 1958.

[(2) "Unit trust scheme" and "authorised unit trust scheme" have the meaning given in section 237 of the Financial Services and Markets Act 2000.]

12 There is to be disregarded any interest—

(a) of the Church of Scotland General Trustees or of the Church of Scotland Trust in shares or debentures held by them;

(b) of any other person in shares or debentures held by those Trustees or that Trust otherwise than as simple trustees.

"The Church of Scotland General Trustees" are the body incorporated by the order confirmed by the Church of Scotland (General Trustees) Order Confirmation Act 1921; and "the Church of Scotland Trust" is the body incorporated by the order confirmed by the Church of Scotland Trust Order Confirmation Act 1932.

13 Delivery to a person's order of shares or debentures in fulfilment of a contract for the purchase of them by him or in satisfaction of a right of his to call for their delivery, or failure to deliver shares or debentures in accordance with the terms of such a contract or on which such a right falls to be satisfied, is deemed to constitute an event in consequence of the occurrence of which he ceases to be interested in them, and so is the lapse of a person's right to call for delivery of shares or debentures.

NOTES

Para 11: sub-para (1) numbered as such by SI 2001/3649, art 37(1), (2).
Date in force: 1 December 2001: see SI 2001/3649, art 1.

Para 11: sub-para (1)(a) substituted by the Financial Services Act 1986, s 212(2), Sch 16, para 25.

Para 11: in sub-para (1)(a) words omitted repealed by SI 2001/3649, art 37(1), (3).

Date in force: 1 December 2001: see SI 2001/3649, art 1.

Para 11: in sub-para (1)(b) words "or 22A" in square brackets inserted by the Charities Act 1992, s 78(1), Sch 6, para 11.

Para 11: in sub-para (1)(b) words "or section 24 or 25 of the Charities Act 1993" in square brackets inserted by the Charities Act 1993, s 98(1), Sch 6, para 20(3).

Para 11: sub-para (2) inserted by SI 2001/3649, art 37(1), (4).

Date in force: 1 December 2001: see SI 2001/3649, art 1.

PART II
PERIODS WITHIN WHICH OBLIGATIONS IMPOSED BY SECTION 324 MUST BE FULFILLED

14 (1) An obligation imposed on a person by section 324(1) to notify an interest must, if he knows of the existence of the interest on the day on which he becomes a director, be fulfilled before the expiration of the period of 5 days beginning with the day following that day.

(2) Otherwise, the obligation must be fulfilled before the expiration of the period of 5 days beginning with the day following that on which the existence of the interest comes to his knowledge.

15 (1) An obligation imposed on a person by section 324(2) to notify the occurrence of an event must, if at the time at which the event occurs he knows of its occurrence and of the fact that its occurrence gives rise to the obligation, be fulfilled before the expiration of the period of 5 days beginning with the day following that on which the event occurs.

(2) Otherwise, the obligation must be fulfilled before the expiration of a period of 5 days beginning with the day following that on which the fact that the occurrence of the event gives rise to the obligation comes to his knowledge.

16 In reckoning, for purposes of paragraphs 14 and 15, any period of days, a day that is a Saturday or Sunday, or a bank holiday in any part of Great Britain, is to be disregarded.

PART III
CIRCUMSTANCES IN WHICH OBLIGATION IMPOSED BY SECTION 324 IS NOT DISCHARGED

17 (1) Where an event of whose occurrence a director is, by virtue of section 324(2)(a), under obligation to notify a company consists of his entering into a contract for the purchase by him of shares or debentures, the obligation is not discharged in the absence of inclusion in the notice of a statement of the price to be paid by him under the contract.

(2) An obligation imposed on a director by section 324(2)(b) is not discharged in the absence of inclusion in the notice of the price to be received by him under the contract.

18 (1) An obligation imposed on a director by virtue of section 324(2)(c) to notify a company is not discharged in the absence of inclusion in the notice of a statement of the consideration for the assignment (or, if it be the case that there is no consideration, that fact).

(2) Where an event of whose occurrence a director is, by virtue of section 324(2)(d), under obligation to notify a company consists in his assigning a right, the obligation is not discharged in the absence of inclusion in the notice of a similar statement.

19 (1) Where an event of whose occurrence a director is, by virtue of section 324(2)(d), under obligation to notify a company consists in the grant to him of a right to subscribe for shares or debentures, the obligation is not discharged in the absence of inclusion in the notice of a statement of—

(a) the date on which the right was granted,
(b) the period during which or the time at which the right is exercisable,
(c) the consideration for the grant (or, if it be the case that there is no consideration, that fact), and
(d) the price to be paid for the shares or debentures.

(2) Where an event of whose occurrence a director is, by section 324(2)(d), under obligation to notify a company consists in the exercise of a right granted to him to subscribe for shares or debentures, the obligation is not discharged in the absence of inclusion in the notice of a statement of—

(a) the number of shares or amount of debentures in respect of which the right was exercised, and
(b) if it be the case that they were registered in his name, that fact, and, if not, the name or names of the person or persons in whose name or names they were registered, together (if they were registered in the names of 2 persons or more) with the number or amount registered in the name of each of them.

20 In this Part, a reference to price paid or received includes any consideration other than money.

PART IV
PROVISIONS WITH RESPECT TO REGISTER OF DIRECTORS' INTERESTS TO BE KEPT UNDER SECTION 325

21 The register must be so made up that the entries in it against the several names appear in chronological order.

22 An obligation imposed by section 325(2) to (4) must be fulfilled before the expiration of the period of 3 days beginning with the day after that on which the obligation arises; but in reckoning that period, a day which is a Saturday or Sunday or a bank holiday in any part of Great Britain is to be disregarded.

23 The nature and extent of an interest recorded in the register of a director in any shares or debentures shall, if he so requires, be recorded in the register.

24 The company is not, by virtue of anything done for the purposes of section 325 or this Part of this Schedule, affected with notice of, or put upon enquiry as to, the rights of any person in relation to any shares or debentures.

25 The register shall—

(a) if the company's register of members is kept at its registered office, be kept there;
(b) if the company's register of members is not so kept, be kept at the company's registered office or at the place where its register of members is kept;

and shall . . . be open to the inspection of any member of the company without charge and of any other person on payment of [such fee as may be prescribed.]

26 (1) Any member of the company or other person may require a copy of the register, or of any part of it, on payment of [such fee as may be prescribed].

(2) The company shall cause any copy so required by a person to be sent to him within the period of 10 days beginning with the day after that on which the requirement is received by the company.

27   The company shall send notice in the prescribed form to the registrar of companies of the place where the register is kept and of any change in that place, save in a case in which it has at all times been kept at its registered office.

28   Unless the register is in such a form as to constitute in itself an index, the company shall keep an index of the names inscribed in it, which shall—

(a)   in respect of each name, contain a sufficient indication to enable the information entered against it to be readily found; and

(b)   be kept at the same place as the register;

and the company shall, within 14 days after the date on which a name is entered in the register, make any necessary alteration in the index.

29   The register shall be produced at the commencement of the company's annual general meeting and remain open and accessible during the continuance of the meeting to any person attending the meeting.

NOTES

Para 25: words omitted repealed and words in square brackets substituted by the Companies Act 1989, ss 143(10), 212, Sch 24.

Para 26: words omitted repealed and words in square brackets substituted by the Companies Act 1989, s 143(10).

[SCHEDULE 15A
WRITTEN RESOLUTIONS OF PRIVATE COMPANIES]

NOTES

Inserted by the Companies Act 1989, s 114(1).

Section 381A(7)

[PART I
EXCEPTIONS]

NOTES

Inserted by the Companies Act 1989, s 114(1).

1   Section 381A does not apply to—

(a)   a resolution under section 303 removing a director before the expiration of his period of office, or

(b)   a resolution under section 391 removing an auditor before the expiration of his term of office.]

NOTES

Inserted by the Companies Act 1989, s 114(1).

[PART II
ADAPTATION OF PROCEDURAL REQUIREMENTS]

NOTES

Inserted by the Companies Act 1989, s 114(1).

[Introductory

2 (1) In this Part of this Schedule (which adapts certain requirements of this Act in relation to proceedings under section 381A)—

(a) a "written resolution" means a resolution agreed to, or proposed to be agreed to, in accordance with that section, and

(b) a "relevant member" means a member by whom, or on whose behalf, the resolution is required to be signed in accordance with that section.

(2) A written resolution is not effective if any of the requirements of this Part of this Schedule is not complied with.

Section 95 (disapplication of pre-emption rights)

3 (1) The following adaptations have effect in relation to a written resolution under section 95(2) (disapplication of pre-emption rights), or renewing a resolution under that provision.

(2) So much of section 95(5) as requires the circulation of a written statement by the directors with a notice of meeting does not apply, but such a statement must be supplied to each relevant member at or before the time at which the resolution is supplied to him for signature.

(3) Section 95(6) (offences) applies in relation to the inclusion in any such statement of matter which is misleading, false or deceptive in a material particular.

Section 155 (financial assistance for purchase of company's own shares or those of holding company)

4 In relation to a written resolution giving approval under section 155(4) or (5) (financial assistance for purchase of company's own shares or those of holding company), section 157(4)(a) (documents to be available at meeting) does not apply, but the documents referred to in that provision must be supplied to each relevant member at or before the time at which the resolution is supplied to him for signature.

Sections 164, 165 and 167 (authority for off-market purchase or contingent purchase contract of company's own shares)

5 (1) The following adaptations have effect in relation to a written resolution—

(a) conferring authority to make an off-market purchase of the company's own shares under section 164(2),

(b) conferring authority to vary a contract for an off-market purchase of the company's own shares under section 164(7), or

(c) varying, revoking or renewing any such authority under section 164(3).

(2) Section 164(5) (resolution ineffective if passed by exercise of voting rights by member holding shares to which the resolution relates) does not apply; but for the purposes of section 381A(1) a member holding shares to which the resolution relates shall not be regarded as a member who would be entitled to attend and vote.

(3) Section 164(6) (documents to be available at company's registered office and at meeting) does not apply, but the documents referred to in that provision and, where that provision applies by virtue of section 164(7), the further documents referred to in that provision must be supplied to each relevant member at or before the time at which the resolution is supplied to him for signature.

(4)   The above adaptations also have effect in relation to a written resolution in relation to which the provisions of section 164(3) to (7) apply by virtue of—
  (a)   section 165(2) (authority for contingent purchase contract), or
  (b)   section 167(2) (approval of release of rights under contract approved under section 164 or 165).

Section 173 (approval for payment out of capital)

6   (1)   The following adaptations have effect in relation to a written resolution giving approval under section 173(2) (redemption or purchase of company's own shares out of capital).

(2)   Section 174(2) (resolution ineffective if passed by exercise of voting rights by member holding shares to which the resolution relates) does not apply; but for the purposes of section 381A(1) a member holding shares to which the resolution relates shall not be regarded as a member who would be entitled to attend and vote.

(3)   Section 174(4) (documents to be available at meeting) does not apply, but the documents referred to in that provision must be supplied to each relevant member at or before the time at which the resolution is supplied to him for signature.

Section 319 (approval of director's service contract)

7   In relation to a written resolution approving any such term as is mentioned in section 319(1) (director's contract of employment for more than five years), section 319(5) (documents to be available at company's registered office and at meeting) does not apply, but the documents referred to in that provision must be supplied to each relevant member at or before the time at which the resolution supplied to him for signature.

Section 337 (funding of director's expenditure in performing his duties)

8   In relation to a written resolution giving approval under section 337(3)(a) (funding a director's expenditure in performing his duties), the requirement of that provision that certain matters be disclosed at the meeting at which the resolution is passed does not apply, but those matters must be disclosed to each relevant member at or before the time at which the resolution is supplied to him for signature.]

NOTES

Inserted by the Companies Act 1989, s 114(1).

[SCHEDULE 15B
PROVISIONS SUBJECT TO WHICH SS 425–427 HAVE EFFECT IN THEIR APPLICATION TO MERGERS AND DIVISIONS OF PUBLIC COMPANIES]

NOTES

Inserted by SI 1987/1991, reg 2, Schedule.
Renumbered by the Companies Act 1989, s 114(2).

Section 427A

[Meetings of transferee company

1   Subject to paragraphs 10(1), 12(4) and 14(2), the court shall not sanction a compromise or arrangement under section 425(2) unless a majority in number representing three-fourths in value of each class of members of every pre-existing transferee company concerned in the scheme, present and voting either in person or by proxy at a meeting, agree to the scheme.

Draft terms of merger

2 (1) The court shall not sanction the compromise or arrangement under section 425(2) unless—

    (a)   a draft of the proposed terms of the scheme (from here on referred to as the "draft terms") has been drawn up and adopted by the directors of all the transferor and pre-existing transferee companies concerned in the scheme,

    (b)   subject to paragraph 11(3), in the case of each of those companies the directors have delivered a copy of the draft terms to the registrar of companies and the registrar has published in the Gazette notice of receipt by him of a copy of the draft terms from that company, and

    (c)   subject to paragraphs 10 to 14, that notice was so published at least one month before the date of any meeting of that company summoned under section 425(1) or for the purposes of paragraph 1.

(2) Subject to paragraph 12(2), the draft terms shall give particulars of at least the following matters—

    (a)   in respect of each transferor company and transferee company concerned in the scheme, its name, the address of its registered office and whether it is a company limited by shares or a company limited by guarantee and having a share capital;

    (b)   the number of shares in any transferee company to be allotted to members of any transferor company for a given number of their shares (from here on referred to as the "share exchange ratio") and the amount of any cash payment;

    (c)   the terms relating to the allotment of shares in any transferee company;

    (d)   the date from which the holding of shares in a transferee company will entitle the holders to participate in profits, and any special conditions affecting that entitlement;

    (e)   the date from which the transactions of any transferor company are to be treated for accounting purposes as being those of any transferee company;

    (f)   any rights or restrictions attaching to shares or other securities in any transferee company to be allotted under the scheme to the holders of shares to which any special rights or restrictions attach, or of other securities, in any transferor company, or the measures proposed concerning them;

    (g)   any amount or benefit paid or given or intended to be paid or given to any of the experts referred to in paragraph 5 or to any director of a transferor company or pre-existing transferee company, and the consideration for the payment of benefit.

(3) Where the scheme is a Case 3 Scheme the draft terms shall also—

    (a)   give particulars of the property and liabilities to be transferred (to the extent these are known to the transferor company) and their allocation among the transferee companies;

    (b)   make provision for the allocation among and transfer to the transferee companies of any other property and liabilities which the transferor company has or may subsequently acquire; and

    (c)   specify the allocation to members of the transferor company of shares in the transferee companies and the criteria upon which that allocation is based.

Documents and information to be made available

3 Subject to paragraphs 10 to 14, the court shall not sanction the compromise or arrangement under section 425(2) unless—

(a) in the case of each transferor company and each pre-existing transferee company the directors have drawn up and adopted a report complying with paragraph 4 (from here on referred to as a "directors' report");

(b) where the scheme is a Case 3 Scheme, the directors of the transferor company have reported to every meeting of the members or any class of members of that company summoned under section 425(1), and to the directors of each transferee company, any material changes in the property and liabilities of the transferor company between the date when the draft terms were adopted and the date of the meeting in question;

(c) where the directors of a transferor company have reported to the directors of a transferee company such a change as is mentioned in sub-paragraph (b) above, the latter have reported that change to every meeting of the members or any class of members of that transferee company summoned for the purposes of paragraph 1, or have sent a report of that change to every member who would have been entitled to receive a notice of such a meeting;

(d) a report complying with paragraph 5 has been drawn up on behalf of each transferor company and pre-existing transferee company (from here on referred to as an "expert's report");

(e) the members of any transferor company or transferee company were able to inspect at the registered office of that company copies of the documents listed in paragraph 6(1) in relation to every transferor company and pre-existing transferee company concerned in the scheme during a period beginning one month before, and ending on, the date of the first meeting of the members or any class of members of the first-mentioned transferor or transferee company summoned either under section 425(1) or for the purposes of paragraph 1 and those members were able to obtain copies of those documents or any part of them on request during that period free of charge; and

(f) the memorandum and articles of association of any transferee company which is not a pre-existing transferee company, or a draft thereof, has been approved by ordinary resolution of every transferor company concerned in the scheme.

Directors' report

4 (1) The directors' report shall consist of—

(a) the statement required by section 426, and

(b) insofar as that statement does not contain the following matters, a further statement—

(i) setting out the legal and economic grounds for the draft terms, and in particular for the share exchange ratio, and, where the scheme is a Case 3 Scheme, for the criteria upon which the allocation to the members of the transferor company of shares in the transferee companies was based, and

(ii) specifying any special valuation difficulties.

(2) Where the scheme is a Case 3 Scheme the directors' report shall also state whether a report has been made to the transferee company under section 103 (non-cash consideration to be valued before allotment) and, if so, whether that report has been delivered to the registrar of companies.

Expert's report

5 (1) Except where a joint expert is appointed under sub-paragraph (2) below, an expert's report shall consist of a separate written report on the draft terms to the members of one transferor company or pre-existing transferee company concerned in the scheme drawn up by a separate expert appointed on behalf of that company.

(2)   The court may, on the joint application of all the transferor companies and pre-existing transferee companies concerned in the scheme, approve the appointment of a joint expert to draw up a single report on behalf of all those companies.

(3)   An expert shall be independent of any of the companies concerned in the scheme, that is to say a person qualified at the time of the report to be appointed, or to continue to be, an auditor of those companies.

(4)   However, where it appears to an expert that a valuation is reasonably necessary to enable him to draw up the report, and it appears to him to be reasonable for that valuation, or part of it, to be made (or for him to accept such a valuation) by another person who—
   (a)   appears to him to have the requisite knowledge and experience to make the valuation or that part of it; and
   (b)   is not an officer or servant of any of the companies concerned in the scheme or any other body corporate which is one of those companies' subsidiary or holding company or a subsidiary of one of those companies' holding company or a partner or employee of such an officer or servant,

he may arrange for or accept such a valuation, together with a report which will enable him to make his own report under this paragraph.

(5)   The reference in sub-paragraph (4) above to an officer or servant does not include an auditor.

(6)   Where any valuation is made by a person other than the expert himself, the latter's report shall state that fact and shall also—
   (a)   state the former's name and what knowledge and experience he has to carry out the valuation, and
   (b)   describe so much of the undertaking, property and liabilities as were valued by the other person, and the method used to value them, and specify the date of the valuation.

(7)   An expert's report shall—
   (a)   indicate the method or methods used to arrive at the share exchange ratio proposed;
   (b)   give an opinion as to whether the method or methods used are reasonable in all the circumstances of the case, indicate the values arrived at using each such method and (if there is more than one method) give an opinion on the relative importance attributed to such methods in arriving at the value decided on;
   (c)   describe any special valuation difficulties which have arisen;
   (d)   state whether in the expert's opinion the share exchange ratio is reasonable; and
   (e)   in the case of a valuation made by a person other than himself, state that it appeared to himself reasonable to arrange for it to be so made or to accept a valuation so made.

(8)   Each expert has the right of access to all such documents of all the transferor companies and pre-existing transferee companies concerned in the scheme, and the right to require from the companies' officers all such information, as he thinks necessary for the purpose of making his report.

Inspection of documents

6   (1)   The documents referred to in paragraph 3(e) are, in relation to any company,—
   (a)   the draft terms;
   (b)   the directors' report [referred to in paragraph 4 above];
   (c)   the expert's report;

[(d)   the company's annual accounts, together with the relevant directors' report and auditors' report, for the last three financial years ending on or before the relevant date; and

(e)   if the last of those financial years ended more than six months before the relevant date, an accounting statement in the form described in the following provisions.]

[In paragraphs (d) and (e) "the relevant date" means one month before the first meeting of the company summoned under section 425(1) or for the purposes of paragraph 1.]

[(2)   The accounting statement shall consist of—

(a)   a balance sheet dealing with the state of the affairs of the company as at a date not more than three months before the draft terms were adopted by the directors, and

(b)   where the company would be required to prepare group accounts if that date were the last day of a financial year, a consolidated balance sheet dealing with the state of affairs of the company and its subsidiary undertakings as at that date.

(3)   The requirements of this Act as to balance sheets forming part of a company's annual accounts, and the matters to be included in notes thereto, apply to any balance sheet required for the accounting statement, with such modifications as are necessary by reason of its being prepared otherwise than as at the last day of a financial year.

(4)   Any balance sheet required for the accounting statement shall be approved by the board of directors and signed on behalf of the board by a director of the company.

(5)   In relation to a company within the meaning of Article 3 of the Companies (Northern Ireland) Order 1986, the references in this paragraph to the requirements of this Act shall be construed as reference to the corresponding requirements of that Order.]

Transferor company holding its own shares

7   The court shall not sanction under section 425(2) a compromise or arrangement under which any shares in a transferee company are to be allotted to a transferor company or its nominee in respect of shares in that transferor company held by it or its nominee.

Securities other than shares to which special rights are attached

8   (1)   Where any security of a transferor company to which special rights are attached is held by a person other than as a member or creditor of the company, the court shall not sanction a compromise or arrangement under section 425(2) unless under the scheme that person is to receive rights in a transferee company of equivalent value.

(2)   Sub-paragraph (1) above shall not apply in the case of any such security where—

(a)   the holder has agreed otherwise; or

(b)   the holder is, or under the scheme is to be, entitled to have the security purchased by a transferee company involved in the scheme on terms which the court considers reasonable.

Date and consequences of the compromise or arrangement

9   (1)   The following provisions of this paragraph shall apply where the court sanctions a compromise or arrangement.

(2)   The court shall in the order sanctioning the compromise or arrangement or in a subsequent order under section 427 fix a date on which the transfer or transfers to the transferee company or transferee companies of the undertaking, property and liabilities of the transferor company shall take place; and any such order which provide for the dissolution of the transferor company shall fix the same date for the dissolution.

(3) If it is necessary for the transferor company to take any steps to ensure that the undertaking, property and liabilities are fully transferred, the court shall fix a date, not later than six months after the date fixed under sub-paragraph (2) above, by which such steps must be taken and for that purpose may postpone the dissolution of the transferor company until that date.

(4) The court may postpone or further postpone the date fixed under sub-paragraph (3) above if it is satisfied that the steps there mentioned cannot be completed by the date (or latest date) fixed under that sub-paragraph.

Exceptions

10   (1) The court may sanction a compromise or arrangement under section 425(2) notwithstanding that—
- (a)   any meeting otherwise required by paragraph 1 has not been summoned by a pre-existing transferee company ("the relevant company"), and
- (b)   paragraphs 2(1)(c) and 3(e) have not been complied with in respect of that company,

if the court is satisfied that the conditions specified in sub-paragraph (2) below have been complied with.

(2)   Subject to paragraphs 11(3) and 12(3), the conditions mentioned in sub-paragraph (1) above are—
- (a)   that the publication of notice of receipt of the draft terms by the registrar of companies referred to in paragraph 2(1)(b) took place in respect of the relevant company at least one month before the date of any meeting of members of any transferor company concerned in the scheme summoned under section 425(1);
- (b)   that the members of the relevant company were able to inspect at the registered office of that company the documents listed in paragraph 6(1) in relation to every transferor company and transferee company concerned in the scheme during a period ("the relevant period") beginning one month before, and ending on, the date of any such meeting, and that they were able to obtain copies of those documents or any part of them on request during that period free of charge; and
- (c)   that one or more members of the relevant company, who together held not less than five per cent. of the paid-up capital of that company which carried the right to vote at general meetings of the company, would have been able during the relevant period to require that a meeting of each class of members be called for the purpose of deciding whether or not to agree to the scheme but that no such requisition had been made.

11   (1)   The following sub-paragraphs apply where the scheme is a Case 3 Scheme.

(2)   Sub-paragraphs (a) to (d) of paragraph 3 shall not apply and sub-paragraph (e) of that paragraph shall not apply as regards the documents listed in paragraph 6(1)(b), (c) and (e), if all members holding shares in, and all persons holding other securities of, any of the transferor companies and pre-existing transferee companies concerned in the scheme on the date of the application to the court under section 425(1), being shares or securities which as at that date carry the right to vote in general meetings of the company, so agree.

(3)   The court may by order direct in respect of any transferor company or pre-existing transferee company that the requirements relating to—
- (a)   delivering copies of the draft terms and publication of notice of receipt of the draft terms under paragraph 2(1)(b) and (c), or
- (b)   inspection under paragraph 3(e),

shall not apply, and may by order direct that paragraph 10 shall apply to any pre-existing transferee company with the omission of sub-paragraph (2)(a) and (b) of that paragraph.

(4)   The court shall not make any order under sub-paragraph (3) above unless it is satisfied that the following conditions will be fulfilled—

(a)   that the members of the company will have received or will have been able to obtain free of charge copies of the documents listed in paragraph 6(1) in time to examine them before the date of the first meeting of the members or any class of members of the company summoned under section 425(1) or for the purposes of paragraph 1;

(b)   in the case of a pre-existing transferee company, where in the circumstances described in paragraph 10 no meeting is held, that the members of that company will have received or will have been able to obtain free of charge copies of those documents in time to require a meeting under paragraph 10(2)(c);

(c)   that the creditors of the company will have received or will have been able to obtain free of charge copies of the draft terms in time to examine them before the date of the meeting of the members or any class of members of the company, or, in the circumstances referred to in paragraph (b) above, at the same time as the members of the company; and

(d)   that no prejudice would be caused to the members or creditors of any transferor company or transferee company concerned in the scheme by making the order in question.

Transferee company or companies holding shares in the transferor company

12   (1)   Where the scheme is a Case 1 Scheme and in the case of every transferor company concerned—

(a)   the shares in that company, and

(b)   such securities of that company (other than shares) as carry the right to vote at general meetings of that company,

are all held by or on behalf of the transferee company, section 427A and this Schedule shall apply subject to the following sub-paragraphs.

(2)   The draft terms need not give particulars of the matters mentioned in paragraph 2(2)(b), (c) or (d).

(3)   Section 426 and sub-paragraphs (a) and (d) of paragraph 3 shall not apply, and sub-paragraph (e) of that paragraph shall not apply as regards the documents listed in paragraph 6(1)(b) and (c).

(4)   The court may sanction the compromise or arrangement under section 425(2) notwithstanding that—

(a)   any meeting otherwise required by section 425 or paragraph 1 has not been summoned by any company concerned in the scheme, and

(b)   paragraphs 2(1)(c) and 3(e) have not been complied with in respect of that company,

if it is satisfied that the conditions specified in the following sub-paragraphs have been complied with.

(5)   The conditions mentioned in the previous sub-paragraph are—

(a)   that the publication of notice of receipt of the draft terms by the registrar of companies referred to in paragraph 2(1)(b) took place in respect of every transferor company and transferee company concerned in the scheme at least one month before the date of the order under section 425(2) ("the relevant date");

(b)   that the members of the transferee company were able to inspect at the registered office of that company copies of the documents listed in paragraphs 6(1)(a), (d) and (e) in relation to every transferor company or transferee company concerned in the scheme during a period ("the relevant period") beginning one month before, and ending on, the relevant date and that they were able to obtain copies of those documents or any part of them on request during that period free of charge; and

(c)   that one or more members of the transferee company who together held not less than five per cent. of the paid-up capital of the company which carried the right to vote at general meetings of the company would have been able during the relevant period to require that a meeting of each class of members be called for the purpose of deciding whether or not to agree to the scheme but that no such requisition has been made.

13   (1)   Where the scheme is a Case 3 Scheme and—

(a)   the shares in the transferor company, and

(b)   such securities of that company (other than shares) as carry the right to vote at general meetings of that company,

are all held by or on behalf of one or more transferee companies, section 427A and this Schedule shall apply subject to the following sub-paragraphs.

(2)   The court may sanction a compromise or arrangement under section 425(2) notwithstanding that—

(a)   any meeting otherwise required by section 425 has not been summoned by the transferor company, and

(b)   paragraphs 2(1)(c) and 3(b) and (e) have not been complied with in respect of that company,

if it is satisfied that the conditions specified in the following sub-paragraph have been complied with.

(3)   The conditions referred to in the previous sub-paragraph are—

(a)   the conditions set out in paragraph 12(5)(a) and (c);

(b)   that the members of the transferor company and every transferee company concerned in the scheme were able to inspect at the registered office of the company of which they were members copies of the documents listed in paragraph 6(1) in relation to every such company during a period beginning one month before, and ending on, the date of the order under section 425(2) ("the relevant date"), and that they were able to obtain copies of those documents or any part of them on request during that period free of charge; and

(c)   that the directors of the transferor company have sent to every member who would have been entitled to receive a notice of the meeting (had it been called), and to the directors of each transferee company, a report of any material changes in the property and liabilities of the transferor company between the date when the draft terms were adopted and a date one month before the relevant date.

14   (1)   Where the scheme is a Case 1 Scheme and in the case of every transferor company concerned ninety per cent or more (but not all) of—

(a)   the shares in that company, and

(b)   such securities of that company (other than shares) as carry the right to vote at general meetings of that company,

are held by or on behalf of the transferee company, section 427A and this Schedule shall apply subject to the following sub-paragraphs.

(2)   The court may sanction a compromise or arrangement under section 425(2) notwithstanding that—

(a)   any meeting otherwise required by paragraph 1 has not been summoned by the transferee company, and

(b)   paragraphs 2(1)(c) and 3(e) have not been complied with in respect of that company, if the court is satisfied that the conditions specified in the following sub-paragraph have been complied with.

(3) The conditions referred to in the previous sub-paragraph are the same conditions as those specified in paragraph 10(2), save that for this purpose the condition contained in paragraph 10(2)(b) shall be treated as referring only to the documents listed in paragraph 6(1)(a), (d) and (e).

Liability of transferee companies for the default of another

15 (1) Where the scheme is a Case 3 Scheme, each transferee company shall be jointly and severally liable, subject to sub-paragraph (2) below, for any liability transferred to any other transferee company under the scheme to the extent that that other company has made default in satisfying that liability, but so that no transferee company shall be so liable for an amount greater than the amount arrived at by calculating the value at the time of the transfer of the property transferred to it under the scheme less the amount at that date of the liabilities so transferred.

(2) If a majority in number representing three-fourths in value of the creditors or any class of creditors of the transferor company present and voting either in person or by proxy at a meeting summoned under section 425(1) so agree, sub-paragraph (1) above shall not apply in respect of the liabilities of the creditors or that class of creditors.]

NOTES

Inserted by SI 1987/1991, reg 2, Schedule.

Para 6: words in square brackets in sub-para (1)(b), and words following sub-para (1)(e), inserted, and sub-paras (1)(d), (e) and (2)–(5) substituted, by the Companies Act 1989, s 23, Sch 10, Pt I, para 22.

Business Names Act 1985

1985 CHAPTER 7

ARRANGEMENT OF SECTIONS

An Act to consolidate certain enactments relating to the names under which persons may carry on business in Great Britain

[11th March 1985]

1 Persons subject to this Act

(1) This Act applies to any person who has a place of business in Great Britain and who carries on business in Great Britain under a name which—

  (a) in the case of a partnership, does not consist of the surnames of all partners who are individuals and the corporate names of all partners who are bodies corporate without any addition other than an addition permitted by this Act;

  (b) in the case of an individual, does not consist of his surname without any addition other than one so permitted;

  (c) in the case of a company, being a company which is capable of being wound up under the Companies Act 1985, does not consist of its corporate name without any addition other than one so permitted;

  [(d) in the case of a limited liability partnership, does not consist of its corporate name without any addition other than one so permitted].

(2) The following are permitted additions for the purposes of subsection (1)—

  (a) in the case of a partnership, the forenames of individual partners or the initials of those forenames or, where two or more individual partners have the same surname, the addition of "s" at the end of that surname; or

  (b) in the case of an individual, his forename or its initial;

  (c) in any case, any addition merely indicating that the business is carried on in succession to a former owner of the business.

NOTES

Sub-s (1): para (d) inserted by SI 2001/1090, reg 9(1), Sch 5, para 10.
Date in force: 6 April 2001: see SI 2001/1090, reg 1.

2 Prohibition of use of certain business names

(1) Subject to the following subsections, a person to whom this Act applies shall not, without the written approval of the Secretary of State, carry on business in Great Britain under a name which—

  (a) would be likely to give the impression that the business is connected with Her Majesty's Government[, with any part of the Scottish Administration,] or with any local authority; or

  (b) includes any word or expression for the time being specified in regulations made under this Act.

(2) Subsection (1) does not apply to the carrying on of a business by a person—

  (a) to whom the business has been transferred on or after 26th February 1982; and

  (b) who carries on the business under the name which was its lawful business name immediately before that transfer,

during the period of 12 months beginning with the date of that transfer.

(3)   Subsection (1) does not apply to the carrying on of a business by a person who—

(a)   carried on that business immediately before 26th February 1982; and

(b)   continues to carry it on under the name which immediately before that date was its lawful business name.

(4)   A person who contravenes subsection (1) is guilty of an offence.

NOTES

Sub-s (1): in para (a) words ", with any part of the Scottish Administration," in square brackets inserted by SI 1999/1820, art 4, Sch 2, Pt I, para 79.

Date in force: 1 July 1999: see SI 1999/1820, art 1(2).

3 Words and expressions requiring Secretary of State's approval

(1)   The Secretary of State may by regulations—

(a)   specify words or expressions for the use of which as or as part of a business name his approval is required by section 2(1)(b); and

(b)   in relation to any such word or expression, specify a Government department or other body as the relevant body for purposes of the following subsection.

(2)   Where a person to whom this Act applies proposes to carry on a business under a name which is or includes any such word or expression, and a Government department or other body is specified under subsection (1)(b) in relation to that word or expression, that person shall—

(a)   request (in writing) the relevant body to indicate whether (and if so why) it has any objections to the proposal; and

(b)   submit to the Secretary of State a statement that such a request has been made and a copy of any response received from the relevant body.

4 Disclosure required of persons using business names

(1)   A person to whom this Act applies shall—

(a)   [subject to subsections (3) and (3A)], state in legible characters on all business letters, written orders for goods or services to be supplied to the business, invoices and receipts issued in the course of the business and written demands for payment of debts arising in the course of the business—

(i)   in the case of a partnership, the name of each partner,

(ii)   in the case of an individual, his name,

(iii) in the case of a company, its corporate name, . . .

[(iiia) In the case of a limited liability partnership, its corporate name and the name of each member, and]

(iv) in relation to each person so named, an address in Great Britain at which service of any document relating in any way to the business will be effective; and

(b)   in any premises where the business is carried on and to which the customers of the business or suppliers of any goods or services to the business have access, display in a prominent position so that it may easily be read by such customers or suppliers a notice containing such names and addresses.

(2)   A person to whom this Act applies shall secure that the names and addresses required by subsection (1)(a) to be stated on his business letters, or which would have been so required but for [subsection (3) or (3A)], are immediately given, by written notice to any person with whom anything is done or discussed in the course of the business and who asks for such names and addresses.

(3)   Subsection (1)(a) does not apply in relation to any document issued by a partnership of more than 20 persons which maintains at its principal place of business a list of the names of all the partners if—

(a)   none of the names of the partners appears in the document otherwise than in the text or as a signatory; and

(b)   the document states in legible characters the address of the partnership's principal place of business and that the list of the partners' names is open to inspection at that place.

[(3A)   Subsection (1)(a) does not apply in relation to any document issued by a limited liability partnership with more than 20 members which maintains at its principal place of business a list of the names of all the members if—

(a)   none of the names of the members appears in the document otherwise than in the text or as a signatory; and

(b)   the document states in legible characters the address of the principal place of business of the limited liability partnership and that the list of the members' names is open to inspection at that place.]

(4)   Where a partnership maintains a list of the partners' names for purposes of subsection (3), any person may inspect the list during office hours.

[(4A)   Where a limited liability partnership maintains a list of the members' names for the purposes of subsection (3A), any person may inspect the list during office hours.]

(5)   The Secretary of State may by regulations require notices under subsection (1)(b) or (2) to be displayed or given in a specified form.

(6)   A person who without reasonable excuse contravenes subsection (1) or (2), or any regulations made under subsection (5), is guilty of an offence.

(7)   Where an inspection required by a person in accordance with subsection (4) [or (4A)] is refused, any partner of the partnership concerned[, or any member of the limited liability partnership concerned,] who without reasonable excuse refused that inspection, or permitted it to be refused, is guilty of an offence.

NOTES

Sub-s (1): in para (a) words "subject to subsections (3) and (3A)" in square brackets substituted by SI 2001/1090, reg 9(1), Sch 5, para 11(1), (2).
Date in force: 6 April 2001: see SI 2001/1090, reg 1.
Sub-s (1): in para (a)(iii) word omitted repealed by SI 2001/1090, reg 9(1), Sch 5, para 11(1), (2).
Date in force: 6 April 2001: see SI 2001/1090, reg 1.
Sub-s (1): para (a)(iiia) inserted by SI 2001/1090, reg 9(1), Sch 5, para 11(1), (2).
Date in force: 6 April 2001: see SI 2001/1090, reg 1.
Sub-s (2): words "subsection (3) or (3A)" in square brackets substituted by SI 2001/1090, reg 9(1), Sch 5, para 11(1), (3).

Date in force: 6 April 2001: see SI 2001/1090, reg 1.
Sub-s (3A): inserted by SI 2001/1090, reg 9(1), Sch 5, para 11(1), (4).
Date in force: 6 April 2001: see SI 2001/1090, reg 1.
Sub-s (4A): inserted by SI 2001/1090, reg 9(1), Sch 5, para 11(1), (5).
Date in force: 6 April 2001: see SI 2001/1090, reg 1.
Sub-s (7): words "or (4A)" and ", or any member of the limited liability partnership concerned," in square brackets inserted by SI 2001/1090, reg 9(1), Sch 5, para 11(1), (6).
Date in force: 6 April 2001: see SI 2001/1090, reg 1.

5 Civil remedies for breach of s 4

(1)   Any legal proceedings brought by a person to whom this Act applies to enforce a right arising out of a contract made in the course of a business in respect of which he was, at the time the contract was made, in breach of subsection (1) or (2) of section 4 shall be dismissed if the defendant (or, in Scotland, the defender) to the proceedings shows—

(a)   that he has a claim against the plaintiff (pursuer) arising out of that contract which he has been unable to pursue by reason of the latter's breach of section 4(1) or (2), or

(b)   that he has suffered some financial loss in connection with the contract by reason of the plaintiff's (pursuer's) breach of section 4(1) or (2),

unless the court before which the proceedings are brought is satisfied that it is just and equitable to permit the proceedings to continue.

(2)   This section is without prejudice to the right of any person to enforce such rights as he may have against another person in any proceedings brought by that person.

6 Regulations

(1)   Regulations under this Act shall be made by statutory instrument and may contain such transitional provisions and savings as the Secretary of State thinks appropriate, and may make different provision for different cases or classes of case.

(2)   In the case of regulations made under section 3, the statutory instrument containing them shall be laid before Parliament after the regulations are made and shall cease to have effect at the end of the period of 28 days beginning with the day on which they were made (but without prejudice to anything previously done by virtue of them or to the making of new regulations) unless during that period they are approved by a resolution of each House of Parliament.

In reckoning this period of 28 days, no account is to be taken of any time during which Parliament is dissolved or prorogued, or during which both Houses are adjourned for more than 4 days.

(3)   In the case of regulations made under section 4, the statutory instrument containing them is subject to annulment in pursuance of a resolution of either House of Parliament.

7 Offences

(1)   Offences under this Act are punishable on summary conviction.

(2)   A person guilty of an offence under this Act is liable to a fine not exceeding one-fifth of the statutory maximum.

(3)   If after a person has been convicted summarily of an offence under section 2 or 4(6) the original contravention is continued, he is liable on a second or subsequent summary conviction of the offence to a fine not exceeding one-fiftieth of the statutory maximum for each day on which the contravention is continued (instead of to the penalty which may be imposed on the first conviction of the offence).

(4)   Where an offence under section 2 or 4(6) or (7) committed by a body corporate is proved to have been committed with the consent or connivance of, or to be attributable to any neglect on the part of, any director, manager, secretary or other similar officer of the body corporate, or any person who was purporting to act in any such capacity, he as well as the body corporate is guilty of the offence and liable to be proceeded against and punished accordingly.

(5)   Where the affairs of a body corporate are managed by its members, subsection (4) applies in relation to the acts and defaults of a member in connection with his functions of management as if he were a director of the body corporate.

(6)   For purposes of the following provisions of the Companies Act 1985—
  (a)   section 731 (summary proceedings under the Companies Acts), and
  (b)   section 732(3) (legal professional privilege),

this Act is to be treated as included in those Acts.

8 Interpretation

(1)   The following definitions apply for purposes of this Act—
  "business" includes a profession;
  "initial" includes any recognised abbreviation of a name;
  "lawful business name", in relation to a business, means a name under which the business was carried on without contravening section 2(1) of this Act or section 2 of the Registration of Business Names Act 1916;
  "local authority" means any local authority within the meaning of the Local Government Act 1972 or the Local Government (Scotland) Act 1973, the Common Council of the City of London or the Council of the Isles of Scilly;
  "partnership" includes a foreign partnership;
  . . .
  and "surname", in relation to a peer or person usually known by a British title different from his surname, means the title by which he is known.

(2)   Any expression used in this Act and also in the Companies Act 1985 has the same meaning in this Act as in that.

NOTES

Sub-s (1): definition omitted repealed by the Statute Law (Repeals) Act 1993.

9 Northern Ireland

This Act does not extend to Northern Ireland.

10 Commencement

This Act comes into force on 1st July 1985.

11 Citation

This Act may be cited as the Business Names Act 1985.

Insolvency Act 1986

1986 CHAPTER 45

ARRANGEMENT OF SECTIONS

THE FIRST GROUP OF PARTS
COMPANY INSOLVENCY; COMPANIES WINDING UP

PART I
COMPANY VOLUNTARY ARRANGEMENTS

The proposal

PART II
ADMINISTRATION ORDERS

Making etc of administration order

CHAPTER VII
LIQUIDATORS

CHAPTER VIII
PROVISIONS OF GENERAL APPLICATION IN WINDING UP

PART XIV
PUBLIC ADMINISTRATION (ENGLAND AND WALES)

PART XVI
PROVISIONS AGAINST DEBT AVOIDANCE (ENGLAND AND WALES ONLY)

PART XVIII
INTERPRETATION

An Act to consolidate the enactments relating to company insolvency and winding up (including the winding up of companies that are not insolvent, and of unregistered companies); enactments relating to the insolvency and bankruptcy of individuals; and other enactments bearing on those two subject matters, including the functions and qualification of insolvency practitioners, the public administration of insolvency, the penalisation and redress of malpractice and wrongdoing, and the avoidance of certain transactions at an undervalue

[25th July 1986]

THE FIRST GROUP OF PARTS
COMPANY INSOLVENCY; COMPANIES WINDING UP

PART I
COMPANY VOLUNTARY ARRANGEMENTS

The proposal

1 Those who may propose an arrangement

(1)   The directors of a company (other than one for which an administration order is in force, or which is being wound up) may make a proposal under this Part to the company and to its creditors for a composition in satisfaction of its debts or a

scheme of arrangement of its affairs (from here on referred to, in either case, as a "voluntary arrangement").

(2) A proposal under this Part is one which provides for some person ("the nominee") to act in relation to the voluntary arrangement either as trustee or otherwise for the purpose of supervising its implementation; and the nominee must be a person who is qualified to act as an insolvency practitioner *in relation to the company* [or authorised to act as nominee, in relation to the voluntary arrangement].

(3) Such a proposal may also be made—
    (a) where an administration order is in force in relation to the company, by the administrator, and
    (b) where the company is being wound up, by the liquidator.

[(4) In this Part a reference to a company includes a reference to a company in relation to which a proposal for a voluntary arrangement may be made by virtue of Article 3 of the EC Regulation.]

NOTES

Sub-s (2): words "in relation to the company" in italics repealed and subsequent words in square brackets substituted by the Insolvency Act 2000, s 2(a), Sch 2, Pt I, paras 1, 2.
Date in force: to be appointed: see the Insolvency Act 2000, s 16(1).
Sub-s (4): inserted by SI 2002/1240, regs 3, 4.
Date in force: 31 May 2002: see SI 2002/1240, reg 1.

[1A Moratorium]

[(1) Where the directors of an eligible company intend to make a proposal for a voluntary arrangement, they may take steps to obtain a moratorium for the company.

(2) The provisions of Schedule A1 to this Act have effect with respect to—
    (a) companies eligible for a moratorium under this section,
    (b) the procedure for obtaining such a moratorium,
    (c) the effects of such a moratorium, and
    (d) the procedure applicable (in place of sections 2 to 6 and 7) in relation to the approval and implementation of a voluntary arrangement where such a moratorium is or has been in force.]

NOTES

Inserted by the Insolvency Act 2000, s 1, Sch 1, paras 1, 2.
Date in force: to be appointed: see the Insolvency Act 2000, s 16(1).

2 Procedure where nominee is not the liquidator or administrator

(1) This section applies where the nominee under section 1 is not the liquidator or administrator of the company [and the directors do not propose to take steps to obtain a moratorium under section 1A for the company].

(2) The nominee shall, within 28 days (or such longer period as the court may allow) after he is given notice of the proposal for a voluntary arrangement, submit a report to the court stating—

(a) [whether, in his opinion, the proposed voluntary arrangement has a reasonable prospect of being approved and implemented,

(aa)] whether, in his opinion, meetings of the company and of its creditors should be summoned to consider the proposal, and

(b) if in his opinion such meetings should be summoned, the date on which, and time and place at which, he proposes the meetings should be held.

(3) For the purposes of enabling the nominee to prepare his report, the person intending to make the proposal shall submit to the nominee—

(a) a document setting out the terms of the proposed voluntary arrangement, and

(b) a statement of the company's affairs containing—

(i) such particulars of its creditors and of its debts and other liabilities and of its assets as may be prescribed, and

(ii) such other information as may be prescribed.

(4) The court may, on an application made by the person intending to make the proposal, in a case where the nominee has failed to submit the report required by this section, direct that the nominee be replaced as such by another person qualified to act as an insolvency practitioner in relation to the company.

[(4) The court may—

(a) on an application made by the person intending to make the proposal, in a case where the nominee has failed to submit the report required by this section or has died, or

(b) on an application made by that person or the nominee, in a case where it is impracticable or inappropriate for the nominee to continue to act as such,

direct that the nominee be replaced as such by another person qualified to act as an insolvency practitioner, or authorised to act as nominee, in relation to the voluntary arrangement.]

NOTES

Sub-s (1): words from "and the directors" to "for the company" in square brackets inserted by the Insolvency Act 2000, s 1, Sch 1, paras 1, 3.

Date in force: to be appointed: see the Insolvency Act 2000, s 16(1).

Sub-s (2): in para (a) words from "whether, in his" to "approved and implemented," and subsequent reference to "(aa)" in square brackets inserted by the Insolvency Act 2000, s 2(a), Sch 2, Pt I, paras 1, 3(a).

Date in force: to be appointed: see the Insolvency Act 2000, s 16(1).

Sub-s (4): substituted by the Insolvency Act 2000, s 2(a), Sch 2, Pt I, paras 1, 3(b).

Date in force: to be appointed: see the Insolvency Act 2000, s 16(1).

3 Summoning of meetings

(1) Where the nominee under section 1 is not the liquidator or administrator, and it has been reported to the court that such meetings as are mentioned in section 2(2) should be summoned, the person making the report shall (unless the court otherwise directs) summon those meetings for the time, date and place proposed in the report.

(2) Where the nominee is the liquidator or administrator, he shall summon meetings of the company and of its creditors to consider the proposal for such a time, date and place as he thinks fit.

(3)   The persons to be summoned to a creditors' meeting under this section are every creditor of the company of whose claim and address the person summoning the meeting is aware.

Consideration and implementation of proposal

4 Decisions of meetings

(1)   The meetings summoned under section 3 shall decide whether to approve the proposed voluntary arrangement (with or without modifications).

(2)   The modifications may include one conferring the functions proposed to be conferred on the nominee on another person qualified to act as an insolvency practitioner *in relation to the company* [or authorised to act as nominee, in relation to the voluntary arrangement].

But they shall not include any modification by virtue of which the proposal ceases to be a proposal such as is mentioned in section 1.

(3)   A meeting so summoned shall not approve any proposal or modification which affects the right of a secured creditor of the company to enforce his security, except with the concurrence of the creditor concerned.

(4)   Subject as follows, a meeting so summoned shall not approve any proposal or modification under which—

    (a)   any preferential debt of the company is to be paid otherwise than in priority to such of its debts as are not preferential debts, or

    (b)   a preferential creditor of the company is to be paid an amount in respect of a preferential debt that bears to that debt a smaller proportion than is borne to another preferential debt by the amount that is to be paid in respect of that other debt.

However, the meeting may approve such a proposal or modification with the concurrence of the preferential creditor concerned.

(5)   Subject as above, each of the meetings shall be conducted in accordance with the rules.

(6)   After the conclusion of either meeting in accordance with the rules, the chairman of the meeting shall report the result of the meeting to the court, and, immediately after reporting to the court, shall give notice of the result of the meeting to such persons as may be prescribed.

(7)   References in this section to preferential debts and preferential creditors are to be read in accordance with section 386 in Part XII of this Act.

NOTES

Sub-s (2): words "in relation to the company" in italics repealed and subsequent words in square brackets substituted by the Insolvency Act 2000, s 2(a), Sch 2, Pt I, paras 1, 4.

Date in force: to be appointed: see the Insolvency Act 2000, s 16(1).

[4A Approval of arrangement]

[(1)   This section applies to a decision, under section 4, with respect to the approval of a proposed voluntary arrangement.

(2)   The decision has effect if, in accordance with the rules—
    (a)   it has been taken by both meetings summoned under section 3, or
    (b)   (subject to any order made under subsection (4)) it has been taken by the creditors' meeting summoned under that section.

(3)   If the decision taken by the creditors' meeting differs from that taken by the company meeting, a member of the company may apply to the court.

(4)   An application under subsection (3) shall not be made after the end of the period of 28 days beginning with—
    (a)   the day on which the decision was taken by the creditors' meeting, or
    (b)   where the decision of the company meeting was taken on a later day, that day.

(5)   Where a member of a regulated company, within the meaning given by paragraph 44 of Schedule A1, applies to the court under subsection (3), the Financial Services Authority is entitled to be heard on the application.

(6)   On an application under subsection (3), the court may—
    (a)   order the decision of the company meeting to have effect instead of the decision of the creditors' meeting, or
    (b)   make such other order as it thinks fit.]

NOTES

Inserted by the Insolvency Act 2000, s 2(a), Sch 2, Pt I, paras 1, 5.
Date in force: to be appointed: see the Insolvency Act 2000, s 16(1).

5 Effect of approval

(1)   This section has effect where each of the meetings summoned under section 3 approves the proposed voluntary arrangement either with the same modifications or without modifications.

[(1)   This section applies where a decision approving a voluntary arrangement has effect under section 4A.]

(2)   The *approved* voluntary arrangement—
    (a)   takes effect as if made by the company at the creditors' meeting, and
    (b)   *binds every person who in accordance with the rules had notice of, and was entitled to vote at, that meeting (whether or not he was present or represented at the meeting) as if he were a party to the voluntary arrangement.*
    [(b)   binds every person who in accordance with the rules—
        (i)   was entitled to vote at that meeting (whether or not he was present or represented at it), or
        (ii)   would have been so entitled if he had had notice of it,
    as if he were a party to the voluntary arrangement.

(2A)   If—
   (a)   when the arrangement ceases to have effect any amount payable under the arrangement to a person bound by virtue of subsection (2)(b)(ii) has not been paid, and
   (b)   the arrangement did not come to an end prematurely,

the company shall at that time become liable to pay to that person the amount payable under the arrangement.]

(3)   Subject as follows, if the company is being wound up or an administration order is in force, the court may do one or both of the following, namely—
   (a)   by order stay or sist all proceedings in the winding up or discharge the administration order;
   (b)   give such directions with respect to the conduct of the winding up or the administration as it thinks appropriate for facilitating the implementation of the *approved* voluntary arrangement.

(4)   The court shall not make an order under subsection (3)(a)—
   (a)   at any time before the end of the period of 28 days beginning with the first day on which each of the reports required by section 4(6) has been made to the court, or
   (b)   at any time when an application under the next section or an appeal in respect of such an application is pending, or at any time in the period within which such an appeal may be brought.

NOTES

Sub-s (1): substituted by the Insolvency Act 2000, s 2(a), Sch 2, Pt I, paras 1, 6(a).
Date in force: to be appointed: see the Insolvency Act 2000, s 16(1).
Sub-s (2): word "approved" in italics repealed by the Insolvency Act 2000, ss 2(a), 15(1), Sch 2, Pt I, paras 1, 6(b), Sch 5.
Date in force: to be appointed: see the Insolvency Act 2000, s 16(1).
Sub-s (2): para (b) substituted, by subsequent para (b) and sub-s (2A), by the Insolvency Act 2000, s 2(a), Sch 2, Pt I, paras 1, 6(c).
Date in force: to be appointed: see the Insolvency Act 2000, s 16(1).
Sub-s (3): in para (b) word "approved" in italics repealed by the Insolvency Act 2000, s 2(a), Sch 2, Pt I, paras 1, 6(b), s 15(1), Sch 5.
Date in force: to be appointed: see the Insolvency Act 2000, s 16(1).

6 Challenge of decisions

(1)   Subject to this section, an application to the court may be made, by any of the persons specified below, on one or both of the following grounds, namely—
   (a)   that a voluntary arrangement *approved at the meetings summoned under section 3* [which has effect under section 4A] unfairly prejudices the interests of a creditor, member or contributory of the company;
   (b)   that there has been some material irregularity at or in relation to either of the meetings.

(2)   The persons who may apply under this section are—
   (a)   a person entitled, in accordance with the rules, to vote at either of the meetings;

[(aa) a person who would have been entitled, in accordance with the rules, to vote at the creditors' meeting if he had had notice of it;]

(b)   the nominee or any person who has replaced him under section 2(4) or 4(2); and

(c)   if the company is being wound up or an administration order is in force, the liquidator or administrator.

(3)   An application under this section shall not be made

[(a)] after the end of the period of 28 days beginning with the first day on which each of the reports required by section 4(6) has been made to the court [or

(b)   in the case of a person who was not given notice of the creditors' meeting, after the end of the period of 28 days beginning with the day on which he became aware that the meeting had taken place,

but (subject to that) an application made by a person within subsection (2)(aa) on the ground that the voluntary arrangement prejudices his interests may be made after the arrangement has ceased to have effect, unless it came to an end prematurely].

(4)   Where on such an application the court is satisfied as to either of the grounds mentioned in subsection (1), it may do one or both of the following, namely—

(a)   revoke or suspend *the approvals given by the meetings* [any decision approving the voluntary arrangement which has effect under section 4A] or, in a case falling within subsection (1)(b), any *approval given by the meeting in question* [decision taken by the meeting in question which has effect under that section];

(b)   give a direction to any person for the summoning of further meetings to consider any revised proposal the person who made the original proposal may make or, in a case falling within subsection (1)(b), a further company or (as the case may be) creditors' meeting to reconsider the original proposal.

(5)   Where at any time after giving a direction under subsection (4)(b) for the summoning of meetings to consider a revised proposal the court is satisfied that the person who made the original proposal does not intend to submit a revised proposal, the court shall revoke the direction and revoke or suspend any *approval given at the previous meetings* [decision approving the voluntary arrangement which has effect under section 4A].

(6)   In a case where the court, on an application under this section with respect to any meeting—

(a)   gives a direction under subsection (4)(b), or

(b)   revokes or suspends an approval under subsection (4)(a) or (5),

the court may give such supplemental directions as it thinks fit and, in particular, directions with respect to things done *since the meeting under any voluntary arrangement approved by the meeting* [under the voluntary arrangement since it took effect].

(7)   Except in pursuance of the preceding provisions of this section, *an approval given* [a decision taken] at a meeting summoned under section 3 is not invalidated by any irregularity at or in relation to the meeting.

NOTES

Sub-s (1): in para (a) words "approved at the meetings summoned under section 3" in italics repealed and subsequent words in square brackets substituted by the Insolvency Act 2000, s 2(a), Sch 2, Pt I, paras 1, 7(1), (2).

Date in force: to be appointed: see the Insolvency Act 2000, s 16(1).

Sub-s (2): para (aa) inserted by the Insolvency Act 2000, s 2(a), Sch 2, Pt I, paras 1, 7(1), (3).

Date in force: to be appointed: see the Insolvency Act 2000, s 16(1).

Sub-s (3): reference to "(a)" in square brackets inserted by the Insolvency Act 2000, s 2(a), Sch 2, Pt I, paras 1, 7(1), (4)(a).

Date in force: to be appointed: see the Insolvency Act 2000, s 16(1).

Sub-s (3): para (b) and word "or" immediately preceding it and words from "but (subject to that)" to "an end prematurely" in square brackets inserted by the Insolvency Act 2000, s 2(a), Sch 2, Pt I, paras 1, 7(1), (4)(b).

Date in force: to be appointed: see the Insolvency Act 2000, s 16(1).

Sub-s (4): in para (a) words "the approvals given by the meetings" in italics repealed and subsequent words ins quare brackets substituted by the Insolvency Act 2000, s 2(a), Sch 2, Pt I, paras 1, 7(1), (5)(a).

Date in force: to be appointed: see the Insolvency Act 2000, s 16(1).

Sub-s (4): in para (a) words "approval given by the meeting in question" in italics repealed and subsequent words in square brackets substituted by the Insolvency Act 2000, s 2(a), Sch 2, Pt I, paras 1, 7(1), (5)(b).

Date in force: to be appointed: see the Insolvency Act 2000, s 16(1).

Sub-s (5): words "approval given at the previous meetings" in italics repealed and subsequent words in square brackets substituted by the Insolvency Act 2000, s 2(a), Sch 2, Pt I, paras 1, 7(1), (6).

Date in force: to be appointed: see the Insolvency Act 2000, s 16(1).

Sub-s (6): words "since the meeting under any voluntary arrangement approved by the meeting" in italics repealed and subsequent words in square brackets substituted by the Insolvency Act 2000, s 2(a), Sch 2, Pt I, paras 1, 7(1), (7).

Date in force: to be appointed: see the Insolvency Act 2000, s 16(1).

Sub-s (7): words "an approval given" in italics repealed and subsequent words in square brackets substituted by the Insolvency Act 2000, s 2(a), Sch 2, Pt I, paras 1, 7(1), (8).

Date in force: to be appointed: see the Insolvency Act 2000, s 16(1).

[6A False representations, etc]

[(1) If, for the purpose of obtaining the approval of the members or creditors of a company to a proposal for a voluntary arrangement, a person who is an officer of the company—

(a) makes any false representation, or

(b) fraudulently does, or omits to do, anything,

he commits an offence.

(2) Subsection (1) applies even if the proposal is not approved.

(3) For purposes of this section "officer" includes a shadow director.

(4) A person guilty of an offence under this section is liable to imprisonment or a fine, or both.]

NOTES
Inserted by the Insolvency Act 2000, s 2(a), Sch 2, Pt I, paras 1, 8.
Date in force: to be appointed: see the Insolvency Act 2000, s 16(1).

7 Implementation of proposal

(1)   This section applies where a voluntary arrangement *approved by the meetings summoned under section 3 has taken effect* [has effect under section 4A].

(2)   The person who is for the time being carrying out in relation to the voluntary arrangement the functions conferred—

    (a)   by virtue of the approval on the nominee, or

    [(a)   on the nominee by virtue of the approval given at one or both of the meetings summoned under section 3]

    (b)   by virtue of section 2(4) or 4(2) on a person other than the nominee,

shall be known as the supervisor of the voluntary arrangement.

(3)   If any of the company's creditors or any other person is dissatisfied by any act, omission or decision of the supervisor, he may apply to the court; and on the application the court may—

    (a)   confirm, reverse or modify any act or decision of the supervisor,

    (b)   give him directions, or

    (c)   make such other order as it thinks fit.

(4)   The supervisor—

    (a)   may apply to the court for directions in relation to any particular matter arising under the voluntary arrangement, and

    (b)   is included among the persons who may apply to the court for the winding up of the company or for an administration order to be made in relation to it.

(5)   The court may, whenever—

    (a)   it is expedient to appoint a person to carry out the functions of the supervisor, and

    (b)   it is inexpedient, difficult or impracticable for an appointment to be made without the assistance of the court,

make an order appointing a person who is qualified to act as an insolvency practitioner *in relation to the company* [or authorised to act as supervisor, in relation to the voluntary arrangement], either in substitution for the existing supervisor or to fill a vacancy.

(6)   The power conferred by subsection (5) is exercisable so as to increase the number of persons exercising the functions of supervisor or, where there is more than one person exercising those functions, so as to replace one or more of those persons.

NOTES
Sub-s (1): words "approved by the meetings summoned under section 3 has taken effect" in italics repealed and subsequent words in square brackets substituted by the Insolvency Act 2000, s 2(a), Sch 2, Pt I, paras 1, 9(a).
Date in force: to be appointed: see the Insolvency Act 2000, s 16(1).

Sub-s (2): para (a) substituted by the Insolvency Act 2000, s 2(a), Sch 2, Pt I, paras 1, 9(b).
Date in force: to be appointed: see the Insolvency Act 2000, s 16(1).
Sub-s (5): words "in relation to the company" in italics repealed and subsequent words in square brackets substituted by the Insolvency Act 2000, s 2(a), Sch 2, Pt I, paras 1, 9(c).
Date in force: to be appointed: see the Insolvency Act 2000, s 16(1).

[7A Prosecution of delinquent officers of company]

[(1) This section applies where a moratorium under section 1A has been obtained for a company or the approval of a voluntary arrangement in relation to a company has taken effect under section 4A or paragraph 36 of Schedule A1.

(2) If it appears to the nominee or supervisor that any past or present officer of the company has been guilty of any offence in connection with the moratorium or, as the case may be, voluntary arrangement for which he is criminally liable, the nominee or supervisor shall forthwith—

(a) report the matter to the appropriate authority, and

(b) provide the appropriate authority with such information and give the authority such access to and facilities for inspecting and taking copies of documents (being information or documents in the possession or under the control of the nominee or supervisor and relating to the matter in question) as the authority requires.

In this subsection, "the appropriate authority" means—

(i) in the case of a company registered in England and Wales, the Secretary of State, and

(ii) in the case of a company registered in Scotland, the Lord Advocate.

(3) Where a report is made to the Secretary of State under subsection (2), he may, for the purpose of investigating the matter reported to him and such other matters relating to the affairs of the company as appear to him to require investigation, exercise any of the powers which are exercisable by inspectors appointed under section 431 or 432 of the Companies Act to investigate a company's affairs.

(4) For the purpose of such an investigation any obligation imposed on a person by any provision of the Companies Act to produce documents or give information to, or otherwise to assist, inspectors so appointed is to be regarded as an obligation similarly to assist the Secretary of State in his investigation.

(5) An answer given by a person to a question put to him in exercise of the powers conferred by subsection (3) may be used in evidence against him.

(6) However, in criminal proceedings in which that person is charged with an offence to which this subsection applies—

(a) no evidence relating to the answer may be adduced, and

(b) no question relating to it may be asked,

by or on behalf of the prosecution, unless evidence relating to it is adduced, or a question relating to it is asked, in the proceedings by or on behalf of that person.

(7) Subsection (6) applies to any offence other than—

(a) an offence under section 2 or 5 of the Perjury Act 1911 (false statements made on oath otherwise than in judicial proceedings or made otherwise than on oath), or

(b) an offence under section 44(1) or (2) of the Criminal Law (Consolidation) (Scotland) Act 1995 (false statements made on oath or otherwise than on oath).

(8) Where a prosecuting authority institutes criminal proceedings following any report under subsection (2), the nominee or supervisor, and every officer and agent of the company past and present (other than the defendant or defender), shall give the authority all assistance in connection with the prosecution which he is reasonably able to give.

For this purpose—
"agent" includes any banker or solicitor of the company and any person employed by the company as auditor, whether that person is or is not an officer of the company,
"prosecuting authority" means the Director of Public Prosecutions, the Lord Advocate or the Secretary of State.

(9) The court may, on the application of the prosecuting authority, direct any person referred to in subsection (8) to comply with that subsection if he has failed to do so.]

NOTES

Inserted by the Insolvency Act 2000, s 2(a), Sch 2, Pt I, paras 1, 10.
Date in force: to be appointed: see the Insolvency Act 2000, s 16(1).

[7B Arrangements coming to an end prematurely]

[For the purposes of this Part, a voluntary arrangement the approval of which has taken effect under section 4A or paragraph 36 of Schedule A1 comes to an end prematurely if, when it ceases to have effect, it has not been fully implemented in respect of all persons bound by the arrangement by virtue of section 5(2)(b)(i) or, as the case may be, paragraph 37(2)(b)(i) of Schedule A1.]

NOTES

Inserted by the Insolvency Act 2000, s 2(a), Sch 2, Pt I, paras 1, 10.
Date in force: to be appointed: see the Insolvency Act 2000, s 16(1).

PART II
ADMINISTRATION ORDERS

Making etc of administration order

8 Power of court to make order

(1) Subject to this section, if the court—
  (a) is satisfied that a company is or is likely to become unable to pay its debts (within the meaning given to that expression by section 123 of this Act), and
  (b) considers that the making of an order under this section would be likely to achieve one or more of the purposes mentioned below,

the court may make an administration order in relation to the company.

[(1A)   For the purposes of a petition presented by the Financial Services Authority alone or together with any other party, an authorised deposit taker who defaults in an obligation to pay any sum due and payable in respect of a relevant deposit is deemed to be unable to pay its debts as mentioned in subsection (1).

(1B)   In subsection (1A)—
   (a)   "authorised deposit taker" means a person who has permission under Part 4 of the Financial Services and Markets Act 2000 to accept deposits, but excludes a person who has such permission only for the purpose of carrying on another regulated activity in accordance with that permission; and
   (b)   "relevant deposit" must be read with—
      (i)   section 22 of the Financial Services and Markets Act 2000,
      (ii)   any relevant order under that section, and
      (iii)   Schedule 2 to that Act,

but any restriction on the meaning of deposit which arises from the identity of the person making it is to be disregarded.]

(2)   An administration order is an order directing that, during the period for which the order is in force, the affairs, business and property of the company shall be managed by a person ("the administrator") appointed for the purpose by the court.

(3)   The purposes for whose achievement an administration order may be made are—
   (a)   the survival of the company, and the whole or any part of its undertaking, as a going concern;
   (b)   the approval of a voluntary arrangement under Part I;
   (c)   the sanctioning under section 425 of the Companies Act of a compromise or arrangement between the company and any such persons as are mentioned in that section; and
   (d)   a more advantageous realisation of the company's assets than would be effected on a winding up;

and the order shall specify the purpose or purposes for which it is made.

[(4)   An administration order shall not be made in relation to a company after it has gone into liquidation.

(5)   An administration order shall not be made against a company if—
   (a)   it has permission under Part 4 of the Financial Services and Markets Act 2000 to effect or carry out contracts of insurance in the United Kingdom;
   (b)   it continues to have a liability in respect of a deposit which was held by it in accordance with the Banking Act 1979 or the Banking Act 1987.

(6)   Subsection (5)(a) must be read with—
   (a)   section 22 of the Financial Services and Markets Act 2000;
   (b)   any relevant order under that section; and
   (c)   Schedule 2 to that Act.]

[(7)   In this Part a reference to a company includes a reference to a company in relation to which an administration order may be made by virtue of Article 3 of the EC Regulation.]

NOTES
Sub-ss (1A), (1B): inserted by SI 2001/3649, art 303.
Date in force: 1 December 2001: see SI 2001/3649, art 1.
Sub-ss (4)–(6): substituted, for sub-s (4) as originally enacted, by SI 2001/3649, art 304.
Date in force: 1 December 2001: see SI 2001/3649, art 1.
Sub-s (7): inserted by SI 2002/1240, regs 3, 5.
Date in force: 31 May 2002: see SI 2002/1240, reg 1.

9 Application for order

(1) An application to the court for an administration order shall be by petition presented either by the company or the directors, or by a creditor or creditors (including any contingent or prospective creditor or creditors), [or by [a justices' chief executive] in the exercise of the power conferred by section 87A of the Magistrates' Courts Act 1980 (enforcement of fines imposed on companies)] or by all or any of those parties, together or separately.

(2)   Where a petition is presented to the court—
  (a)   notice of the petition shall be given forthwith to any person who has appointed, or is or may be entitled to appoint, an administrative receiver of the company, and to such other persons as may be prescribed, and
  (b)   the petition shall not be withdrawn except with the leave of the court.

(3)   Where the court is satisfied that there is an administrative receiver of the company, the court shall dismiss the petition unless it is also satisfied either—
  (a)   that the person by whom or on whose behalf the receiver was appointed has consented to the making of the order, or
  (b)   that, if an administration order were made, any security by virtue of which the receiver was appointed would—
    [(i)   be void against the administrator to any extent by virtue of the provisions of Part XII of the Companies Act 1985 (registration of company charges),]
    (i) [(ii)] be liable to be released or discharged under sections 238 to 240 in Part VI (transactions at an undervalue and preferences),
    (ii) [(iii)] be avoided under section 245 in that Part (avoidance of floating charges), or
    (iii) [(iv)] be challengeable under section 242 (gratuitous alienations) or 243 (unfair preferences) in that Part, or under any rule of law in Scotland.

(4)   Subject to subsection (3), on hearing a petition the court may dismiss it, or adjourn the hearing conditionally or unconditionally, or make an interim order or any other order that it thinks fit.

(5)   Without prejudice to the generality of subsection (4), an interim order under that subsection may restrict the exercise of any powers of the directors or of the company (whether by reference to the consent of the court or of a person qualified to act as an insolvency practitioner in relation to the company, or otherwise).

NOTES
Sub-s (1): words from "or by" to "imposed on companies)" in square brackets inserted by the Criminal Justice Act 1988, s 62(2)(a).

Sub-s (1): words "a justices' chief executive" in square brackets substituted by the Access to Justice Act 1999, s 90(1), Sch 13, para 133.

Date in force: 1 April 2001: see SI 2001/916, art 2(a)(ii).

Sub-s (3): in para (b) sub-para (i) in square brackets prospectively inserted, and original sub-paras (i)–(iii) prospectively re-numbered, by the Companies Act 1989, s 107, Sch 16, para 3(2), as from a day to be appointed.

10 Effect of application

(1) During the period beginning with the presentation of a petition for an administration order and ending with the making of such an order or the dismissal of the petition—

    (a) no resolution may be passed or order made for the winding up of the company;

    [(aa) no landlord or other person to whom rent is payable may exercise any right of forfeiture by peaceable re-entry in relation to premises let to the company in respect of a failure by the company to comply with any term or condition of its tenancy of such premises, except with the leave of the court and subject to such terms as the court may impose;]

    (b) no steps may be taken to enforce any security over the company's property, or to repossess goods in the company's possession under any hire-purchase agreement, except with the leave of the court and subject to such terms as the court may impose; and

    (c) no other proceedings and no execution or other legal process may be commenced or continued, and no distress may be levied, against the company or its property except with the leave of the court and subject to such terms as aforesaid.

(2) Nothing in subsection (1) requires the leave of the court—

    (a) for the presentation of a petition for the winding up of the company,

    (b) for the appointment of an administrative receiver of the company, or

    (c) for the carrying out by such a receiver (whenever appointed) of any of his functions.

(3) Where—

    (a) a petition for an administration order is presented at a time when there is an administrative receiver of the company, and

    (b) the person by or on whose behalf the receiver was appointed has not consented to the making of the order,

the period mentioned in subsection (1) is deemed not to begin unless and until that person so consents.

(4) References in this section and the next to hire-purchase agreements include conditional sale agreements, chattel leasing agreements and retention of title agreements.

(5) In the application of this section and the next to Scotland, references to execution being commenced or continued include references to diligence being carried out or continued, and references to distress being levied shall be omitted.

NOTES
Sub-s (1): para (aa) inserted by the Insolvency Act 2000, s 9(1), (2).

Date in force: 2 April 2001 (except in relation to a petition for an administration order presented before that date): see SI 2001/766, arts 2(1)(b), 3(1).

11 Effect of order

(1)   On the making of an administration order—
  (a)   any petition for the winding up of the company shall be dismissed, and
  (b)   any administrative receiver of the company shall vacate office.

(2)   Where an administration order has been made, any receiver of part of the company's property shall vacate office on being required to do so by the administrator.

(3)   During the period for which an administration order is in force—
  (a)   no resolution may be passed or order made for the winding up of the company;
  (b)   no administrative receiver of the company may be appointed;
  [(ba) no landlord or other person to whom rent is payable may exercise any right of forfeiture by peaceable re-entry in relation to premises let to the company in respect of a failure by the company to comply with any term or condition of its tenancy of such premises, except with the consent of the administrator or the leave of the court and subject (where the court gives leave) to such terms as the court may impose;]
  (c)   no other steps may be taken to enforce any security over the company's property, or to repossess goods in the company's possession under any hire-purchase agreement, except with the consent of the administrator or the leave of the court and subject (where the court gives leave) to such terms as the court may impose; and
  (d)   no other proceedings and no execution or other legal process may be commenced or continued, and no distress may be levied, against the company or its property except with the consent of the administrator or the leave of the court and subject (where the court gives leave) to such terms as aforesaid.

(4)   Where at any time an administrative receiver of the company has vacated office under subsection (1)(b), or a receiver of part of the company's property has vacated office under subsection (2)—
  (a)   his remuneration and any expenses properly incurred by him, and
  (b)   any indemnity to which he is entitled out of the assets of the company,
shall be charged on and (subject to subsection (3) above) paid out of any property of the company which was in his custody or under his control at that time in priority to any security held by the person by or on whose behalf he was appointed.

(5)   Neither an administrative receiver who vacates office under subsection (1)(b) nor a receiver who vacates office under subsection (2) is required on or after so vacating office to take any steps for the purpose of complying with any duty imposed on him by section 40 or 59 of this Act (duty to pay preferential creditors).

NOTES

Sub-s (3): para (ba) inserted by the Insolvency Act 2000, s 9(1), (3).

Date in force: 2 April 2001 (except in relation to a petition for an administration order presented before that date): see SI 2001/766, arts 2(1)(b), 3(1).

Administrators

13 Appointment of administrator

(1) The administrator of a company shall be appointed either by the administration order or by an order under the next subsection.

(2) If a vacancy occurs by death, resignation or otherwise in the office of the administrator, the court may by order fill the vacancy.

(3) An application for an order under subsection (2) may be made—
  (a) by any continuing administrator of the company; or
  (b) where there is no such administrator, by a creditors' committee established under section 26 below; or
  (c) where there is no such administrator and no such committee, by the company or the directors or by any creditor or creditors of the company.

14 General powers

(1) The administrator of a company—
  (a) may do all such things as may be necessary for the management of the affairs, business and property of the company, and
  (b) without prejudice to the generality of paragraph (a), has the powers specified in Schedule 1 to this Act;

and in the application of that Schedule to the administrator of a company the words "he" and "him" refer to the administrator.

(2) The administrator also has power—
  (a) to remove any director of the company and to appoint any person to be a director of it, whether to fill a vacancy or otherwise, and
  (b) to call any meeting of the members or creditors of the company.

(3) The administrator may apply to the court for directions in relation to any particular matter arising in connection with the carrying out of his functions.

(4) Any power conferred on the company or its officers, whether by this Act or the Companies Act or by the memorandum or articles of association, which could be exercised in such a way as to interfere with the exercise by the administrator of his powers is not exercisable except with the consent of the administrator, which may be given either generally or in relation to particular cases.

(5) In exercising his powers the administrator is deemed to act as the company's agent.

(6) A person dealing with the administrator in good faith and for value is not concerned to inquire whether the administrator is acting within his powers.

15 Power to deal with charged property, etc

(1)   The administrator of a company may dispose of or otherwise exercise his powers in relation to any property of the company which is subject to a security to which this subsection applies as if the property were not subject to the security.

(2)   Where, on an application by the administrator, the court is satisfied that the disposal (with or without other assets) of—

(a)   any property of the company subject to a security to which this subsection applies, or

(b)   any goods in the possession of the company under a hire-purchase agreement,

would be likely to promote the purpose or one or more of the purposes specified in the administration order, the court may by order authorise the administrator to dispose of the property as if it were not subject to the security or to dispose of the goods as if all rights of the owner under the hire-purchase agreement were vested in the company.

(3)   Subsection (1) applies to any security which, as created, was a floating charge; and subsection (2) applies to any other security.

(4)   Where property is disposed of under subsection (1), the holder of the security has the same priority in respect of any property of the company directly or indirectly representing the property disposed of as he would have had in respect of the property subject to the security.

(5)   It shall be a condition of an order under subsection (2) that—

(a)   the net proceeds of the disposal, and

(b)   where those proceeds are less than such amount as may be determined by the court to be the net amount which would be realised on a sale of the property or goods in the open market by a willing vendor, such sums as may be required to make good the deficiency,

shall be applied towards discharging the sums secured by the security or payable under the hire-purchase agreement.

(6)   Where a condition imposed in pursuance of subsection (5) relates to two or more securities, that condition requires the net proceeds of the disposal and, where paragraph (b) of that subsection applies, the sums mentioned in that paragraph to be applied towards discharging the sums secured by those securities in the order of their priorities.

(7)   An office copy of an order under subsection (2) shall, within 14 days after the making of the order, be sent by the administrator to the registrar of companies.

(8)   If the administrator without reasonable excuse fails to comply with subsection (7), he is liable to a fine and, for continued contravention, to a daily default fine.

(9)   References in this section to hire-purchase agreements include conditional sale agreements, chattel leasing agreements and retention of title agreements.

17 General duties

(1) The administrator of a company shall, on his appointment, take into his custody or under his control all the property to which the company is or appears to be entitled.

(2) The administrator shall manage the affairs, business and property of the company—
  (a) at any time before proposals have been approved (with or without modifications) under section 24 below, in accordance with any directions given by the court, and
  (b) at any time after proposals have been so approved, in accordance with those proposals as from time to time revised, whether by him or a predecessor of his.

(3) The administrator shall summon a meeting of the company's creditors if—
  (a) he is requested, in accordance with the rules, to do so by one-tenth, in value, of the company's creditors, or
  (b) he is directed to do so by the court.

18 Discharge or variation of administration order

(1) The administrator of a company may at any time apply to the court for the administration order to be discharged, or to be varied so as to specify an additional purpose.

(2) The administrator shall make an application under this section if—
  (a) it appears to him that the purpose or each of the purposes specified in the order either has been achieved or is incapable of achievement, or
  (b) he is required to do so by a meeting of the company's creditors summoned for the purpose in accordance with the rules.

(3) On the hearing of an application under this section, the court may by order discharge or vary the administration order and make such consequential provision as it thinks fit, or adjourn the hearing conditionally or unconditionally, or make an interim order or any other order it thinks fit.

(4) Where the administration order is discharged or varied the administrator shall, within 14 days after the making of the order effecting the discharge or variation, send an office copy of that order to the registrar of companies.

(5) If the administrator without reasonable excuse fails to comply with subsection (4), he is liable to a fine and, for continued contravention, to a daily default fine.

19 Vacation of office

(1) The administrator of a company may at any time be removed from office by order of the court and may, in the prescribed circumstances, resign his office by giving notice of his resignation to the court.

(2) The administrator shall vacate office if—
  (a) he ceases to be qualified to act as an insolvency practitioner in relation to the company, or

(b) the administration order is discharged.

(3) Where at any time a person ceases to be administrator, the [following] subsections apply.

(4) His remuneration and any expenses properly incurred by him shall be charged on and paid out of any property of the company which is in his custody or under his control at that time in priority to any security to which section 15(1) then applies.

(5) Any sums payable in respect of debts or liabilities incurred, while he was administrator, under contracts entered into . . . by him or a predecessor of his in the carrying out of his or the predecessor's functions shall be charged on and paid out of any such property as is mentioned in subsection (4) in priority to any charge arising under that subsection.

[(6) Any sums payable in respect of liabilities incurred, while he was administrator, under contracts of employment adopted by him or a predecessor of his in the carrying out of his or the predecessor's functions shall, to the extent that the liabilities are qualifying liabilities, be charged on and paid out of any such property as is mentioned in subsection (4) and enjoy the same priority as any sums to which subsection (5) applies.]

For this purpose, the administrator is not to be taken to have adopted a contract of employment by reason of anything done or omitted to be done within 14 days after his appointment.

[(7) For the purposes of subsection (6), a liability under a contract of employment is a qualifying liability if—
    (a) it is a liability to pay a sum by way of wages or salary or contribution to an occupational pension scheme, and
    (b) it is in respect of services rendered wholly or partly after the adoption of the contract.

(8) There shall be disregarded for the purposes of subsection (6) so much of any qualifying liability as represents payment in respect of services rendered before the adoption of the contract.

(9) For the purposes of subsections (7) and (8)—
    (a) wages or salary payable in respect of a period of holiday or absence from work through sickness or other good cause are deemed to be wages or (as the case may be) salary in respect of services rendered in that period, and
    (b) a sum payable in lieu of holiday is deemed to be wages or (as the case may be) salary in respect of services rendered in the period by reference to which the holiday entitlement arose.

(10) In subsection (9)(a), the reference to wages or salary payable in respect of a period of holiday includes any sums which, if they had been paid, would have been treated for the purposes of the enactments relating to social security as earnings in respect of that period.]

NOTES

Sub-s (3): word in square brackets substituted in relation to contracts of employment adopted on or after 15 March 1994, by the Insolvency Act 1994, s 1(2).

Sub-s (5): words omitted repealed in relation to contracts of employment adopted on or after 15 March 1994, by the Insolvency Act 1994, s 1(3).

Sub-s (6): words in square brackets inserted in relation to contracts of employment adopted on or after 15 March 1994, by the Insolvency Act 1994, s 1(4).

Sub-ss (7)–(10): inserted in relation to contracts of employment adopted on or after 15 March 1994, by the Insolvency Act 1994, s 1(6).

20 Release of administrator

(1) A person who has ceased to be the administrator of a company has his release with effect from the following time, that is to say—

(a) in the case of a person who has died, the time at which notice is given to the court in accordance with the rules that he has ceased to hold office;

(b) in any other case, such time as the court may determine.

(2) Where a person has his release under this section, he is, with effect from the time specified above, discharged from all liability both in respect of acts or omissions of his in the administration and otherwise in relation to his conduct as administrator.

(3) However, nothing in this section prevents the exercise, in relation to a person who has had his release as above, of the court's powers under section 212 in Chapter X of Part IV (summary remedy against delinquent directors, liquidators, etc.).

Ascertainment and investigation of company's affairs

21 Information to be given by administrator

(1) Where an administration order has been made, the administrator shall—

(a) forthwith send to the company and publish in the prescribed manner a notice of the order, and

(b) within 28 days after the making of the order, unless the court otherwise directs, send such a notice to all creditors of the company (so far as he is aware of their addresses).

(2) Where an administration order has been made, the administrator shall also, within 14 days after the making of the order, send an office copy of the order to the registrar of companies and to such other persons as may be prescribed.

(3) If the administrator without reasonable excuse fails to comply with this section, he is liable to a fine and, for continued contravention, to a daily default fine.

22 Statement of affairs to be submitted to administrator

(1) Where an administration order has been made, the administrator shall forthwith require some or all of the persons mentioned below to make out and submit to him a statement in the prescribed form as to the affairs of the company.

(2) The statement shall be verified by affidavit by the persons required to submit it and shall show—

(a) particulars of the company's assets, debts and liabilities;

(b) the names and addresses of its creditors;

(c) the securities held by them respectively;

(d) the dates when the securities were respectively given; and

(e) such further or other information as may be prescribed.

(3) The persons referred to in subsection (1) are—

(a) those who are or have been officers of the company;

(b) those who have taken part in the company's formation at any time within one year before the date of the administration order;

(c) those who are in the company's employment or have been in its employment within that year, and are in the administrator's opinion capable of giving the information required;

(d) those who are or have been within that year officers of or in the employment of a company which is, or within that year was, an officer of the company.

In this subsection "employment" includes employment under a contract for services.

(4) Where any persons are required under this section to submit a statement of affairs to the administrator, they shall do so (subject to the next subsection) before the end of the period of 21 days beginning with the day after that on which the prescribed notice of the requirement is given to them by the administrator.

(5) The administrator, if he thinks fit, may—

(a) at any time release a person from an obligation imposed on him under subsection (1) or (2), or

(b) either when giving notice under subsection (4) or subsequently, extend the period so mentioned;

and where the administrator has refused to exercise a power conferred by this subsection, the court, if it thinks fit, may exercise it.

(6) If a person without reasonable excuse fails to comply with any obligation imposed under this section, he is liable to a fine and, for continued contravention, to a daily default fine.

Administrator's proposals

23 Statement of proposals

(1) Where an administration order has been made, the administrator shall, within 3 months (or such longer period as the court may allow) after the making of the order—

(a) send to the registrar of companies and (so far as he is aware of their addresses) to all creditors a statement of his proposals for achieving the purpose or purposes specified in the order, and

(b) lay a copy of the statement before a meeting of the company's creditors summoned for the purpose on not less than 14 days' notice.

(2) The administrator shall also, within 3 months (or such longer period as the court may allow) after the making of the order, either—

(a) send a copy of the statement (so far as he is aware of their addresses) to all members of the company, or

(b) publish in the prescribed manner a notice stating an address to which members of the company should write for copies of the statement to be sent to them free of charge.

(3) If the administrator without reasonable excuse fails to comply with this section, he is liable to a fine and, for continued contravention, to a daily default fine.

24 Consideration of proposals by creditors' meeting

(1) A meeting of creditors summoned under section 23 shall decide whether to approve the administrator's proposals.

(2) The meeting may approve the proposals with modifications, but shall not do so unless the administrator consents to each modification.

(3) Subject as above, the meeting shall be conducted in accordance with the rules.

(4) After the conclusion of the meeting in accordance with the rules, the administrator shall report the result of the meeting to the court and shall give notice of that result to the registrar of companies and to such persons as may be prescribed.

(5) If a report is given to the court under subsection (4) that the meeting has declined to approve the administrator's proposals (with or without modifications), the court may by order discharge the administration order and make such consequential provision as it thinks fit, or adjourn the hearing conditionally or unconditionally, or make an interim order or any other order that it thinks fit.

(6) Where the administration order is discharged, the administrator shall, within 14 days after the making of the order effecting the discharge, send an office copy of that order to the registrar of companies.

(7) If the administrator without reasonable excuse fails to comply with subsection (6), he is liable to a fine and, for continued contravention, to a daily default fine.

Miscellaneous

26 Creditors' committee

(1) Where a meeting of creditors summoned under section 23 has approved the administrator's proposals (with or without modifications), the meeting may, if it thinks fit, establish a committee ("the creditor's committee") to exercise the functions conferred on it by or under this Act.

(2) If such a committee is established, the committee may, on giving not less than 7 days' notice, require the administrator to attend before it at any reasonable time and furnish it with such information relating to the carrying out of his functions as it may reasonably require.

27 Protection of interests of creditors and members

(1)   At any time when an administration order is in force, a creditor or member of the company may apply to the court by petition for an order under this section on the ground—

(a)   that the company's affairs, business and property are being or have been managed by the administrator in a manner which is unfairly prejudicial to the interests of its creditors or members generally, or of some part of its creditors or members (including at least himself), or

(b)   that any actual or proposed act or omission of the administrator is or would be so prejudicial.

(2)   On an application or an order under this section the court may, subject as follows, make such order as it thinks fit for giving relief in respect of the matters complained of, or adjourn the hearing conditionally or unconditionally, or make an interim order or any other order that it thinks fit.

(3)   An order under this section shall not prejudice or prevent—

(a)   the implementation of a voluntary arrangement approved under *section 4 in* Part I, or any compromise or arrangement sanctioned under section 425 of the Companies Act; or

(b)   where the application for the order was made more than 28 days after the approval of any proposals or revised proposals under section 24 or 25, the implementation of those proposals or revised proposals.

(4)   Subject as above, an order under this section may in particular—

(a)   regulate the future management by the administrator of the company's affairs, business and property;

(b)   require the administrator to refrain from doing or continuing an act complained of by the petitioner, or to do an act which the petitioner has complained he has omitted to do;

(c)   require the summoning of a meeting of creditors or members for the purpose of considering such matters as the court may direct;

(d)   discharge the administration order and make such consequential provision as the court thinks fit.

(5)   Nothing in section 15 or 16 is to be taken as prejudicing applications to the court under this section.

(6)   Where the administration order is discharged, the administrator shall, within 14 days after the making of the order effecting the discharge, send an office copy of that order to the registrar of companies; and if without reasonable excuse he fails to comply with this subsection, he is liable to a fine and, for continued contravention, to a daily default fine.

NOTES

Sub-s (3): in para (a) words "section 4 in" in italics repealed by the Insolvency Act 2000, ss 1, 15(1), Sch 1, paras 1, 5, Sch 5.

Date in force: to be appointed: see the Insolvency Act 2000, s 16(1).

PART III
RECEIVERSHIP

CHAPTER I
RECEIVERS AND MANAGERS (ENGLAND AND WALES)

Preliminary and general provisions

29 Definitions

(1)   It is hereby declared that, except where the context otherwise requires—
  (a)   any reference in the Companies Act or this Act to a receiver or manager of the property of a company, or to a receiver of it, includes a receiver or manager, or (as the case may be) a receiver of part only of that property and a receiver only of the income arising from the property or from part of it; and
  (b)   any reference in the Companies Act or this Act to the appointment of a receiver or manager under powers contained in an instrument includes an appointment made under powers which, by virtue of any enactment, are implied in and have effect as if contained in an instrument.

(2)   In this Chapter "administrative receiver" means—
  (a)   a receiver or manager of the whole (or substantially the whole) of a company's property appointed by or on behalf of the holders of any debentures of the company secured by a charge which, as created, was a floating charge, or by such a charge and one or more other securities; or
  (b)   a person who would be such a receiver or manager but for the appointment of some other person as the receiver of part of the company's property.

Receivers and managers appointed out of court

33 Time for which appointment is effective

(1)   The appointment of a person as a receiver or manager of a company's property under powers contained in an instrument—
  (a)   is of no effect unless it is accepted by that person before the end of the business day next following that on which the instrument of appointment is received by him or on his behalf, and
  (b)   subject to this, is deemed to be made at the time at which the instrument of appointment is so received.

(2)   This section applies to the appointment of two or more persons as joint receivers or managers of a company's property under powers contained in an instrument, subject to such modifications as may be prescribed by the rules.

34 Liability for invalid appointment

Where the appointment of a person as the receiver or manager of a company's property under powers contained in an instrument is discovered to be invalid (whether by virtue of the invalidity of the instrument or otherwise), the court may order the person by whom or on whose behalf the appointment was made to indemnify the person appointed against any liability which arises solely by reason of the invalidity of the appointment.

35 Application to court for directions

(1)   A receiver or manager of the property of a company appointed under powers contained in an instrument, or the persons by whom or on whose behalf a receiver or manager has been so appointed, may apply to the court for directions in relation to any particular matter arising in connection with the performance of the functions of the receiver or manager.

(2)   On such an application, the court may give such directions, or may make such order declaring the rights of persons before the court or otherwise, as it thinks just.

37 Liability for contracts, etc

(1)   A receiver or manager appointed under powers conferred in an instrument (other than an administrative receiver) is, to the same extent as if he had been appointed by order of the court—
   (a)   personally liable on any contract entered into by him in the performance of his functions (except in so far as the contract otherwise provides) and on any contract of employment adopted by him in the performance of those functions, and
   (b)   entitled in respect of that liability to indemnity out of the assets.

(2)   For the purposes of subsection (1)(a), the receiver or manager is not to be taken to have adopted a contract of employment by reason of anything done or omitted to be done within 14 days after his appointment.

(3)   Subsection (1) does not limit any right to indemnity which the receiver or manager would have apart from it, nor limit his liability on contracts entered into without authority, nor confer any right to indemnity in respect of that liability.

(4)   Where at any time the receiver or manager so appointed vacates office—
   (a)   his remuneration and any expenses properly incurred by him, and
   (b)   any indemnity to which he is entitled out of the assets of the company,

shall be charged on and paid out of any property of the company which is in his custody or under his control at that time in priority to any charge or other security held by the person by or on whose behalf he was appointed.

40 Payment of debts out of assets subject to floating charge

(1)   The following applies, in the case of a company, where a receiver is appointed on behalf of the holders of any debentures of the company secured by a charge which, as created, was a floating charge.

(2)   If the company is not at the time in course of being wound up, its preferential debts (within the meaning given to that expression by section 386 in Part XII) shall

be paid out of the assets coming to the hands of the receiver in priority to any claims for principal or interest in respect of the debentures.

(3)   Payments made under this section shall be recouped, as far as may be, out of the assets of the company available for payment of general creditors.

Administrative receivers: general

42 General powers

(1)   The powers conferred on the administrative receiver of a company by the debentures by virtue of which he was appointed are deemed to include (except in so far as they are inconsistent with any of the provisions of those debentures) the powers specified in Schedule 1 to this Act.

(2)   In the application of Schedule 1 to the administrative receiver of a company—
 (a)   the words "he" and "him" refer to the administrative receiver, and
 (b)   references to the property of the company are to the property of which he is or, but for the appointment of some other person as the receiver of part of the company's property, would be the receiver or manager.

(3)   A person dealing with the administrative receiver in good faith and for value is not concerned to inquire whether the receiver is acting within his powers.

43 Power to dispose of charged property, etc

(1)   Where, on an application by the administrative receiver, the court is satisfied that the disposal (with or without other assets) of any relevant property which is subject to a security would be likely to promote a more advantageous realisation of the company's assets than would otherwise be effected, the court may by order authorise the administrative receiver to dispose of the property as if it were not subject to the security.

(2)   Subsection (1) does not apply in the case of any security held by the person by or on whose behalf the administrative receiver was appointed, or of any security to which a security so held has priority.

(3)   It shall be a condition of an order under this section that—
 (a)   the net proceeds of the disposal, and
 (b)   where those proceeds are less than such amount as may be determined by the court to be the net amount which would be realised on a sale of the property in the open market by a willing vendor, such sums as may be required to make good the deficiency,
shall be applied towards discharging the sums secured by the security.

(4)   Where a condition imposed in pursuance of subsection (3) relates to two or more securities, that condition shall require the net proceeds of the disposal and, where paragraph (b) of that subsection applies, the sums mentioned in that paragraph to be applied towards discharging the sums secured by those securities in the order of their priorities.

(5)   An office copy of an order under this section shall, within 14 days of the making of the order, be sent by the administrative receiver to the registrar of companies.

(6)   If the administrative receiver without reasonable excuse fails to comply with subsection (5), he is liable to a fine and, for continued contravention, to a daily default fine.

(7)   In this section "relevant property", in relation to the administrative receiver, means the property of which he is or, but for the appointment of some other person as the receiver of part of the company's property, would be the receiver or manager.

44 Agency and liability for contracts

(1)   The administrative receiver of a company—
  (a)   is deemed to be the company's agent, unless and until the company goes into liquidation;
  (b)   is personally liable on any contract entered into by him in the carrying out of his functions (except in so far as the contract otherwise provides) and[, to the extent of any qualifying liability,] on any contract of employment adopted by him in the carrying out of those functions; and
  (c)   is entitled in respect of that liability to an indemnity out of the assets of the company.

(2)   For the purposes of subsection (1)(b) the administrative receiver is not to be taken to have adopted a contract of employment by reason of anything done or omitted to be done within 14 days after his appointment.

[(2A)   For the purposes of subsection (1)(b), a liability under a contract of employment is a qualifying liability if—
  (a)   it is a liability to pay a sum by way of wages or salary or contribution to an occupational pension scheme,
  (b)   it is incurred while the administrative receiver is in office, and
  (c)   it is in respect of services rendered wholly or partly after the adoption of the contract.

(2B)   Where a sum payable in respect of a liability which is a qualifying liability for the purposes of subsection (1)(b) is payable in respect of services rendered partly before and partly after the adoption of the contract, liability under subsection (1)(b) shall only extend to so much of the sum as is payable in respect of services rendered after the adoption of the contract.

(2C)   For the purposes of subsections (2A) and (2B)—
  (a)   wages or salary payable in respect of a period of holiday or absence from work through sickness or other good cause are deemed to be wages or (as the case may be) salary in respect of services rendered in that period, and
  (b)   a sum payable in lieu of holiday is deemed to be wages or (as the case may be) salary in respect of services rendered in the period by reference to which the holiday entitlement arose.

(2D)   In subsection (2C)(a), the reference to wages or salary payable in respect of a period of holiday includes any sums which, if they had been paid, would have been treated for the purposes of the enactments relating to social security as earnings in respect of that period.]

(3)   This section does not limit any right to indemnity which the administrative receiver would have apart from it, nor limit his liability on contracts entered into or adopted without authority, nor confer any right to indemnity in respect of that liability.

NOTES

Sub-s (1): words in square brackets inserted in relation to contracts of employment adopted on or after 15 March 1994, by the Insolvency Act 1994, s 2(2).

Sub-ss (2A)–(2D): inserted in relation to contracts of employment adopted on or after 15 March 1994, by the Insolvency Act 1994, s 2(3).

45 Vacation of office

(1)   An administrative receiver of a company may at any time be removed from office by order of the court (but not otherwise) and may resign his office by giving notice of his resignation in the prescribed manner to such persons as may be prescribed.

(2)   An administrative receiver shall vacate office if he ceases to be qualified to act as an insolvency practitioner in relation to the company.

(3)   Where at any time an administrative receiver vacates office—
    (a)   his remuneration and any expenses properly incurred by him, and
    (b)   any indemnity to which he is entitled out of the assets of the company,

shall be charged on and paid out of any property of the company which is in his custody or under his control at that time in priority to any security held by the person by or on whose behalf he was appointed.

(4)   Where an administrative receiver vacates office otherwise than by death, he shall, within 14 days after his vacation of office, send a notice to that effect to the registrar of companies.

(5)   If an administrative receiver without reasonable excuse fails to comply with subsection (4), he is liable to a fine *and, for continued contravention, to a daily default fine.*

NOTES

Sub-s (5): words in italics prospectively repealed by the Companies Act 1989, ss 107, 212, Sch 16, para 3(3), Sch 24, as from a day to be appointed.

Administrative receivers: ascertainment and investigation of company's affairs

46 Information to be given by administrative receiver

(1)   Where an administrative receiver is appointed, he shall—
    (a)   forthwith send to the company and publish in the prescribed manner a notice of his appointment, and

(b) within 28 days after his appointment, unless the court otherwise directs, send such a notice to all the creditors of the company (so far as he is aware of their addresses).

(2) This section and the next do not apply in relation to the appointment of an administrative receiver to act—
(a) with an existing administrative receiver, or
(b) in place of an administrative receiver dying or ceasing to act,

except that, where they apply to an administrative receiver who dies or ceases to act before they have been fully complied with, the references in this section and the next to the administrative receiver include (subject to the next subsection) his successor and any continuing administrative receiver.

(3) If the company is being wound up, this section and the next apply notwithstanding that the administrative receiver and the liquidator are the same person, but with any necessary modifications arising from that fact.

(4) If the administrative receiver without reasonable excuse fails to comply with this section, he is liable to a fine and, for continued contravention, to a daily default fine.

47 Statement of affairs to be submitted

(1) Where an administrative receiver is appointed, he shall forthwith require some or all of the persons mentioned below to make out and submit to him a statement in the prescribed form as to the affairs of the company.

(2) A statement submitted under this section shall be verified by affidavit by the persons required to submit it and shall show—
(a) particulars of the company's assets, debts and liabilities;
(b) the names and addresses of its creditors;
(c) the securities held by them respectively;
(d) the dates when the securities were respectively given; and
(e) such further or other information as may be prescribed.

(3) The persons referred to in subsection (1) are—
(a) those who are or have been officers of the company;
(b) those who have taken part in the company's formation at any time within one year before the date of the appointment of the administrative receiver;
(c) those who are in the company's employment, or have been in its employment within that year, and are in the administrative receiver's opinion capable of giving the information required;
(d) those who are or have been within that year officers of or in the employment of a company which is, or within that year was, an officer of the company.

In this subsection "employment" includes employment under a contract for services.

(4) Where any persons are required under this section to submit a statement of affairs to the administrative receiver, they shall do so (subject to the next subsection)

before the end of the period of 21 days beginning with the day after that on which the prescribed notice of the requirement is given to them by the administrative receiver.

(5) The administrative receiver, if he thinks fit, may—

    (a) at any time release a person from an obligation imposed on him under subsection (1) or (2), or

    (b) either when giving notice under subsection (4) or subsequently, extend the period so mentioned;

and where the administrative receiver has refused to exercise a power conferred by this subsection, the court, if it thinks fit, may exercise it.

(6) If a person without reasonable excuse fails to comply with any obligation imposed under this section, he is liable to a fine and, for continued contravention, to a daily default fine.

48 Report by administrative receiver

(1) Where an administrative receiver is appointed, he shall, within 3 months (or such longer period as the court may allow) after his appointment, send to the registrar of companies, to any trustees for secured creditors of the company and (so far as he is aware of their addresses) to all such creditors a report as to the following matters, namely—

    (a) the events leading up to his appointment, so far as he is aware of them;

    (b) the disposal or proposed disposal by him of any property of the company and the carrying on or proposed carrying on by him of any business of the company;

    (c) the amounts of principal and interest payable to the debenture holders by whom or on whose behalf he was appointed and the amounts payable to preferential creditors; and

    (d) the amount (if any) likely to be available for the payment of other creditors.

(2) The administrative receiver shall also, within 3 months (or such longer period as the court may allow) after his appointment, either—

    (a) send a copy of the report (so far as he is aware of their addresses) to all unsecured creditors of the company; or

    (b) publish in the prescribed manner a notice stating an address to which unsecured creditors of the company should write for copies of the report to be sent to them free of charge,

and (in either case), unless the court otherwise directs, lay a copy of the report before a meeting of the company's unsecured creditors summoned for the purpose on not less than 14 days' notice.

(3) The court shall not give a direction under subsection (2) unless—

    (a) the report states the intention of the administrative receiver to apply for the direction, and

    (b) a copy of the report is sent to the persons mentioned in paragraph (a) of that subsection, or a notice is published as mentioned in paragraph (b) of that subsection, not less than 14 days before the hearing of the application.

(4)   Where the company has gone or goes into liquidation, the administrative receiver—

  (a)   shall, within 7 days after his compliance with subsection (1) or, if later, the nomination or appointment of the liquidator, send a copy of the report to the liquidator, and

  (b)   where he does so within the time limited for compliance with subsection (2), is not required to comply with that subsection.

(5)   A report under this section shall include a summary of the statement of affairs made out and submitted to the administrative receiver under section 47 and of his comments (if any) upon it.

(6)   Nothing in this section is to be taken as requiring any such report to include any information the disclosure of which would seriously prejudice the carrying out by the administrative receiver of his functions.

(7)   Section 46(2) applies for the purposes of this section also.

(8)   If the administrative receiver without reasonable excuse fails to comply with this section, he is liable to a fine and, for continued contravention, to a default fine.

49 Committee of creditors

(1)   Where a meeting of creditors is summoned under section 48, the meeting may, if it thinks fit, establish a committee ("the creditors' committee") to exercise the functions conferred on it by or under this Act.

(2)   If such a committee is established, the committee may, on giving not less than 7 days' notice, require the administrative receiver to attend before it at any reasonable time and furnish it with such information relating to the carrying out by him of his functions as it may reasonably require.

PART IV
WINDING UP OF COMPANIES REGISTERED UNDER THE COMPANIES ACTS

CHAPTER I
PRELIMINARY

Modes of winding up

73 Alternative modes of winding up

(1)   The winding up of a company, within the meaning given to that expression by section 735 of the Companies Act, may be either voluntary (Chapters II, III, IV and V in this Part) or by the court (Chapter VI).

(2)   This Chapter, and Chapters VII to X, relate to winding up generally, except where otherwise stated.

Contributories

74 Liability as contributories of present and past members

(1)   When a company is wound up, every present and past member is liable to contribute to its assets to any amount sufficient for payment of its debts and liabilities, and the expenses of the winding up, and for the adjustment of the rights of the contributories among themselves.

(2)   This is subject as follows—
   (a)   a past member is not liable to contribute if he has ceased to be a member for one year or more before the commencement of the winding up;
   (b)   a past member is not liable to contribute in respect of any debt or liability of the company contracted after he ceased to be a member;
   (c)   a past member is not liable to contribute, unless it appears to the court that the existing members are unable to satisfy the contributions required to be made by them in pursuance of the Companies Act and this Act;
   (d)   in the case of a company limited by shares, no contribution is required from any member exceeding the amount (if any) unpaid on the shares in respect of which he is liable as a present or past member;
   (e)   nothing in the Companies Act or this Act invalidates any provision contained in a policy of insurance or other contract whereby the liability of individual members on the policy or contract is restricted, or whereby the funds of the company are alone made liable in respect of the policy or contract;
   (f)   a sum due to any member of the company (in his character of a member) by way of dividends, profits or otherwise is not deemed to be a debt of the company, payable to that member in a case of competition between himself and any other creditor not a member of the company, but any such sum may be taken into account for the purpose of the final adjustment of the rights of the contributories among themselves.

(3)   In the case of a company limited by guarantee, no contribution is required from any member exceeding the amount undertaken to be contributed by him to the company's assets in the event of its being wound up; but if it is a company with a share capital, every member of it is liable (in addition to the amount so undertaken to be contributed to the assets), to contribute to the extent of any sums unpaid on shares held by him.

76 Liability of past directors and shareholders

(1)   This section applies where a company is being wound up and—
   (a)   it has under Chapter VII of Part V of the Companies Act (redeemable shares; purchase by a company of its own shares) made a payment out of capital in respect of the redemption or purchase of any of its own shares (the payment being referred to below as "the relevant payment"), and
   (b)   the aggregate amount of the company's assets and the amounts paid by way of contribution to its assets (apart from this section) is not sufficient for payment of its debts and liabilities, and the expenses of the winding up.

(2)   If the winding up commenced within one year of the date on which the relevant payment was made, then—

(a)   the person from whom the shares were redeemed or purchased, and

(b)   the directors who signed the statutory declaration made in accordance with section 173(3) of the Companies Act for purposes of the redemption or purchase (except a director who shows that he had reasonable grounds for forming the opinion set out in the declaration),

are, so as to enable that insufficiency to be met, liable to contribute to the following extent to the company's assets.

(3)   A person from whom any of the shares were redeemed or purchased is liable to contribute an amount not exceeding so much of the relevant payment as was made by the company in respect of his shares; and the directors are jointly and severally liable with that person to contribute that amount.

(4)   A person who has contributed any amount to the assets in pursuance of this section may apply to the court for an order directing any other person jointly and severally liable in respect of that amount to pay him such amount as the court thinks just and equitable.

(5)   Sections 74 and 75 do not apply in relation to liability accruing by virtue of this section.

(6)   This section is deemed included in Chapter VII of Part V of the Companies Act for the purposes of the Secretary of State's power to make regulations under section 179 of that Act.

79 Meaning of "contributory"

(1)   In this Act and the Companies Act the expression "contributory" means every person liable to contribute to the assets of a company in the event of its being wound up, and for the purposes of all proceedings for determining, and all proceedings prior to the final determination of, the persons who are to be deemed contributories, includes any person alleged to be a contributory.

(2)   The reference in subsection (1) to persons liable to contribute to the assets does not include a person so liable by virtue of a declaration by the court under section 213 (imputed responsibility for company's fraudulent trading) or section 214 (wrongful trading) in Chapter X of this Part.

(3)   A reference in a company's articles to a contributory does not (unless the context requires) include a person who is a contributory only by virtue of section 76.

This subsection is deemed included in Chapter VII of Part V of the Companies Act for the purposes of the Secretary of State's power to make regulations under section 179 of that Act.

80 Nature of contributory's liability

The liability of a contributory creates a debt (in England and Wales in the nature of a specialty) accruing due from him at the time when his liability commenced, but payable at the times when calls are made for enforcing the liability.

CHAPTER II
VOLUNTARY WINDING UP (INTRODUCTORY AND GENERAL)

Resolutions for, and commencement of, voluntary winding up

84 Circumstances in which company may be wound up voluntarily

(1)   A company may be wound up voluntarily—
  (a)   when the period (if any) fixed for the duration of the company by the articles expires, or the event (if any) occurs, on the occurrence of which the articles provide that the company is to be dissolved, and the company in general meeting has passed a resolution requiring it to be wound up voluntarily;
  (b)   if the company resolves by special resolution that it be wound up voluntarily;
  (c)   if the company resolves by extraordinary resolution to the effect that it cannot by reason of its liabilities continue its business, and that it is advisable to wind up.

(2)   In this Act the expression "a resolution for voluntary winding up" means a resolution passed under any of the paragraphs of subsection (1).

(3)   A resolution passed under paragraph (a) of subsection (1), as well as a special resolution under paragraph (b) and an extraordinary resolution under paragraph (c), is subject to section 380 of the Companies Act (copy of resolution to be forwarded to registrar of companies within 15 days).

[(4)   This section has effect subject to section 43 of the Commonhold and Leasehold Reform Act 2002.]

NOTES

Sub-s (4): inserted by the Commonhold and Leasehold Reform Act 2002, s 68, Sch 5, para 6.

Date in force: to be appointed: see the Commonhold and Leasehold Reform Act 2002, s 181(1).

85 Notice of resolution to wind up

(1)   When a company has passed a resolution for voluntary winding up, it shall, within 14 days after the passing of the resolution, give notice of the resolution by advertisement in the Gazette.

(2)   If default is made in complying with this section, the company and every officer of it who is in default is liable to a fine and, for continued contravention, to a daily default fine.

For the purposes of this subsection the liquidator is deemed an officer of the company.

86 Commencement of winding up

A voluntary winding up is deemed to commence at the time of the passing of the resolution for voluntary winding up.

Consequences of resolution to wind up

87 Effect on business and status of company

(1)   In case of a voluntary winding up, the company shall from the commencement of the winding up cease to carry on its business, except so far as may be required for its beneficial winding up.

(2)   However, the corporate state and corporate powers of the company, notwith-standing anything to the contrary in its articles, continue until the company is dissolved.

88 Avoidance of share transfers, etc after winding-up resolution

Any transfer of shares, not being a transfer made to or with the sanction of the liquidator, and any alteration in the status of the company's members, made after the commencement of a voluntary winding up, is void.

Declaration of solvency

89 Statutory declaration of solvency

(1)   Where it is proposed to wind up a company voluntarily, the directors (or, in the case of a company having more than two directors, the majority of them) may at a directors' meeting make a statutory declaration to the effect that they have made a full inquiry into the company's affairs and that, having done so, they have formed the opinion that the company will be able to pay its debts in full, together with interest at the official rate (as defined in section 251), within such period, not exceeding 12 months from the commencement of the winding up, as may be specified in the declaration.

(2)   Such a declaration by the directors has no effect for purposes of this Act unless—

   (a)   it is made within the 5 weeks immediately preceding the date of the passing of the resolution for winding up, or on that date but before the passing of the resolution, and

   (b)   it embodies a statement of the company's assets and liabilities as at the latest practicable date before the making of the declaration.

(3)   The declaration shall be delivered to the registrar of companies before the expiration of 15 days immediately following the date on which the resolution for winding up is passed.

(4)   A director making a declaration under this section without having reasonable grounds for the opinion that the company will be able to pay its debts in full, together with interest at the official rate, within the period specified is liable to imprisonment or a fine, or both.

(5)   If the company is wound up in pursuance of a resolution passed within 5 weeks after the making of the declaration, and its debts (together with interest at the official rate) are not paid or provided for in full within the period specified, it is to

be presumed (unless the contrary is shown) that the director did not have reasonable grounds for his opinion.

(6) If a declaration required by subsection (3) to be delivered to the registrar is not so delivered within the time prescribed by that subsection, the company and every officer in default is liable to a fine and, for continued contravention, to a daily default fine.

90 Distinction between "members'" and "creditors'" voluntary winding up

A winding up in the case of which a directors' statutory declaration under section 89 has been made is a "members' voluntary winding up"; and a winding up in the case of which such a declaration has not been made is a "creditors' voluntary winding up".

CHAPTER III
MEMBERS' VOLUNTARY WINDING UP

91 Appointment of liquidator

(1) In a members' voluntary winding up, the company in general meeting shall appoint one or more liquidators for the purpose of winding up the company's affairs and distributing its assets.

(2) On the appointment of a liquidator all the powers of the directors cease, except so far as the company in general meeting or the liquidator sanctions their continuance.

94 Final meeting prior to dissolution

(1) As soon as the company's affairs are fully wound up, the liquidator shall make up an account of the winding up, showing how it has been conducted and the company's property has been disposed of, and thereupon shall call a general meeting of the company for the purpose of laying before it the account, and giving an explanation of it.

(2) The meeting shall be called by advertisement in the Gazette, specifying its time, place and object and published at least one month before the meeting.

(3) Within one week after the meeting, the liquidator shall send to the registrar of companies a copy of the account, and shall make a return to him of the holding of the meeting and of its date.

(4) If the copy is not sent or the return is not made in accordance with subsection (3), the liquidator is liable to a fine and, for continued contravention, to a daily default fine.

(5) If a quorum is not present at the meeting, the liquidator shall, in lieu of the return mentioned above, make a return that the meeting was duly summoned and that no quorum was present; and upon such a return being made, the provisions of subsection (3) as to the making of the return are deemed complied with.

(6)   If the liquidator fails to call a general meeting of the company as required by subsection (1), he is liable to a fine.

95 Effect of company's insolvency

(1)   This section applies where the liquidator is of the opinion that the company will be unable to pay its debts in full (together with interest at the official rate) within the period stated in the directors' declaration under section 89.

(2)   The liquidator shall—
    (a)   summon a meeting of creditors for a day not later than the 28th day after the day on which he formed that opinion;
    (b)   send notices of the creditors' meeting to the creditors by post not less than 7 days before the day on which that meeting is to be held;
    (c)   cause notice of the creditors' meeting to be advertised once in the Gazette and once at least in 2 newspapers circulating in the relevant locality (that is to say the locality in which the company's principal place of business in Great Britain was situated during the relevant period); and
    (d)   during the period before the day on which the creditors' meeting is to be held, furnish creditors free of charge with such information concerning the affairs of the company as they may reasonably require;

and the notice of the creditors' meeting shall state the duty imposed by paragraph (d) above.

(3)   The liquidator shall also—
    (a)   make out a statement in the prescribed form as to the affairs of the company;
    (b)   lay that statement before the creditors' meeting; and
    (c)   attend and preside at that meeting.

(4)   The statement as to the affairs of the company shall be verified by affidavit by the liquidator and shall show—
    (a)   particulars of the company's assets, debts and liabilities;
    (b)   the names and addresses of the company's creditors;
    (c)   the securities held by them respectively;
    (d)   the dates when the securities were respectively given; and
    (e)   such further or other information as may be prescribed.

(5)   Where the company's principal place of business in Great Britain was situated in different localities at different times during the relevant period, the duty imposed by subsection (2)(c) applies separately in relation to each of those localities.

(6)   Where the company had no place of business in Great Britain during the relevant period, references in subsections (2)(c) and (5) to the company's principal place of business in Great Britain are replaced by references to its registered office.

(7)   In this section "the relevant period" means the period of 6 months immediately preceding the day on which were sent the notices summoning the company meeting at which it was resolved that the company be wound up voluntarily.

(8)   If the liquidator without reasonable excuse fails to comply with this section, he is liable to a fine.

96 Conversion to creditors' voluntary winding up

As from the day on which the creditors' meeting is held under section 95, this Act has effect as if—

(a) the directors' declaration under section 89 had not been made; and

(b) the creditors' meeting and the company meeting at which it was resolved that the company be wound up voluntarily were the meetings mentioned in section 98 in the next Chapter;

and accordingly the winding up becomes a creditors' voluntary winding up.

CHAPTER IV
CREDITORS' VOLUNTARY WINDING UP

97 Application of this Chapter

(1) Subject as follows, this Chapter applies in relation to a creditors' voluntary winding up.

(2) Sections 98 and 99 do not apply where, under section 96 in Chapter III, a members' voluntary winding up has become a creditors' voluntary winding up.

98 Meeting of creditors

(1) The company shall—

(a) cause a meeting of its creditors to be summoned for a day not later than the 14th day after the day on which there is to be held the company meeting at which the resolution for voluntary winding up is to be proposed;

(b) cause the notices of the creditors' meeting to be sent by post to the creditors not less than 7 days before the day on which that meeting is to be held; and

(c) cause notice of the creditors' meeting to be advertised once in the Gazette and once at least in two newspapers circulating in the relevant locality (that is to say the locality in which the company's principal place of business in Great Britain was situated during the relevant period).

(2) The notice of the creditors' meeting shall state either—

(a) the name and address of a person qualified to act as an insolvency practitioner in relation to the company who, during the period before the day on which that meeting is to be held, will furnish creditors free of charge with such information concerning the company's affairs as they may reasonably require; or

(b) a place in the relevant locality where, on the two business days falling next before the day on which that meeting is to be held, a list of the names and addresses of the company's creditors will be available for inspection free of charge.

(3) Where the company's principal place of business in Great Britain was situated in different localities at different times during the relevant period, the duties imposed by subsections (1)(c) and (2)(b) above apply separately in relation to each of those localities.

(4)　Where the company had no place of business in Great Britain during the relevant period, references in subsections (1)(c) and (3) to the company's principal place of business in Great Britain are replaced by references to its registered office.

(5)　In this section "the relevant period" means the period of 6 months immediately preceding the day on which were sent the notices summoning the company meeting at which it was resolved that the company be wound up voluntarily.

(6)　If the company without reasonable excuse fails to comply with subsection (1) or (2), it is guilty of an offence and liable to a fine.

99 Directors to lay statement of affairs before creditors

(1)　The directors of the company shall—
- (a)　make out a statement in the prescribed form as to the affairs of the company;
- (b)　cause that statement to be laid before the creditors' meeting under section 98; and
- (c)　appoint one of their number to preside at that meeting;

and it is the duty of the director so appointed to attend the meeting and preside over it.

(2)　The statement as to the affairs of the company shall be verified by affidavit by some or all of the directors and shall show—
- (a)　particulars of the company's assets, debts and liabilities;
- (b)　the names and addresses of the company's creditors;
- (c)　the securities held by them respectively;
- (d)　the dates when the securities were respectively given; and
- (e)　such further or other information as may be prescribed.

(3)　If—
- (a)　the directors without reasonable excuse fail to comply with subsection (1) or (2); or
- (b)　any director without reasonable excuse fails to comply with subsection (1), so far as requiring him to attend and preside at the creditors' meeting,

the directors are or (as the case may be) the director is guilty of an offence and liable to a fine.

100 Appointment of liquidator

(1)　The creditors and the company at their respective meetings mentioned in section 98 may nominate a person to be liquidator for the purpose of winding up the company's affairs and distributing its assets.

(2)　The liquidator shall be the person nominated by the creditors or, where no person has been so nominated, the person (if any) nominated by the company.

(3)　In the case of different persons being nominated, any director, member or creditor of the company may, within 7 days after the date on which the nomination was made by the creditors, apply to the court for an order either—
- (a)　directing that the person nominated as liquidator by the company shall be liquidator instead of or jointly with the person nominated by the creditors, or

(b) appointing some other person to be liquidator instead of the person nominated by the creditors.

101 Appointment of liquidation committee

(1) The creditors at the meeting to be held under section 98 or at any subsequent meeting may, if they think fit, appoint a committee ("the liquidation committee") of not more than 5 persons to exercise the functions conferred on it by or under this Act.

(2) If such a committee is appointed, the company may, either at the meeting at which the resolution for voluntary winding up is passed or at any time subsequently in general meeting, appoint such number of persons as they think fit to act as members of the committee, not exceeding 5.

(3) However, the creditors may, if they think fit, resolve that all or any of the persons so appointed by the company ought not to be members of the liquidation committee; and if the creditors so resolve—

(a) the persons mentioned in the resolution are not then, unless the court otherwise directs, qualified to act as members of the committee; and

(b) on any application to the court under this provision the court may, if it thinks fit, appoint other persons to act as such members in place of the persons mentioned in the resolution.

(4) In Scotland, the liquidation committee has, in addition to the powers and duties conferred and imposed on it by this Act, such of the powers and duties of commissioners on a bankrupt estate as may be conferred and imposed on liquidation committees by the rules.

103 Cesser of directors' powers

On the appointment of a liquidator, all the powers of the directors cease, except so far as the liquidation committee (or, if there is no such committee, the creditors) sanction their continuance.

106 Final meeting prior to dissolution

(1) As soon as the company's affairs are fully wound up, the liquidator shall make up an account of the winding up, showing how it has been conducted and the company's property has been disposed of, and thereupon shall call a general meeting of the company and a meeting of the creditors for the purpose of laying the account before the meetings and giving an explanation of it.

(2) Each such meeting shall be called by advertisement in the Gazette specifying the time, place and object of the meeting, and published at least one month before it.

(3) Within one week after the date of the meetings (or, if they are not held on the same date, after the date of the later one) the liquidator shall send to the registrar of companies a copy of the account, and shall make a return to him of the holding of the meetings and of their dates.

(4)   If the copy is not sent or the return is not made in accordance with subsection (3), the liquidator is liable to a fine and, for continued contravention, to a daily default fine.

(5)   However, if a quorum is not present at either such meeting, the liquidator shall, in lieu of the return required by subsection (3), make a return that the meeting was duly summoned and that no quorum was present; and upon such return being made the provisions of that subsection as to the making of the return are, in respect of that meeting, deemed complied with.

(6)   If the liquidator fails to call a general meeting of the company or a meeting of the creditors as required by this section, he is liable to a fine.

CHAPTER V
PROVISIONS APPLYING TO BOTH KINDS OF VOLUNTARY WINDING UP

107 Distribution of company's property

Subject to the provisions of this Act as to preferential payments, the company's property in a voluntary winding up shall on the winding up be applied in satisfaction of the company's liabilities pari passu and, subject to that application, shall (unless the articles otherwise provide) be distributed among the members according to their rights and interests in the company.

108 Appointment or removal of liquidator by the court

(1)   If from any cause whatever there is no liquidator acting, the court may appoint a liquidator.

(2)   The court may, on cause shown, remove a liquidator and appoint another.

109 Notice by liquidator of his appointment

(1)   The liquidator shall, within 14 days after his appointment, publish in the Gazette and deliver to the registrar of companies for registration a notice of his appointment in the form prescribed by statutory instrument made by the Secretary of State.

(2)   If the liquidator fails to comply with this section, he is liable to a fine and, for continued contravention, to a daily default fine.

110 Acceptance of shares, etc, as consideration for sale of company property

(1)   This section applies, in the case of a company proposed to be, or being, wound up voluntarily, where the whole or part of the company's business or property is proposed to be transferred or sold
  [(a)] to another company ("the transferee company"), whether or not the latter is a company within the meaning of the Companies Act[, or
  (b) to a limited liability partnership (the "transferee limited liability partnership")].

(2)   With the requisite sanction, the liquidator of the company being, or proposed to be, wound up ("the transferor company") may receive, in compensation or part compensation for the transfer or [sale—

(a)   in the case of the transferee company, shares, policies or other like interests in the transferee company for distribution among the members of the transferor company, or

(b)   in the case of the transferee limited liability partnership, membership in the transferee limited liability partnership for distribution among the members of the transferor company].

(3)   The sanction requisite under subsection (2) is—

(a)   in the case of a members' voluntary winding up, that of a special resolution of the company, conferring either a general authority on the liquidator or an authority in respect of any particular arrangement, and

(b)   in the case of a creditors' voluntary winding up, that of either the court or the liquidation committee.

(4)   Alternatively to subsection (2), the liquidator may (with that sanction) enter into any other arrangement whereby the members of the transferor [company may—

(a)   in the case of the transferee company, in lieu of receiving cash, shares, policies or other like interests (or in addition thereto) participate in the profits of, or receive any other benefit from, the transferee company, or

(b)   in the case of the transferee limited liability partnership, in lieu of receiving cash or membership (or in addition thereto), participate in some other way in the profits of, or receive any other benefit from, the transferee limited liability partnership].

(5)   A sale or arrangement in pursuance of this section is binding on members of the transferor company.

(6)   A special resolution is not invalid for purposes of this section by reason that it is passed before or concurrently with a resolution for voluntary winding up or for appointing liquidators; but, if an order is made within a year for winding up the company by the court, the special resolution is not valid unless sanctioned by the court.

NOTES

Sub-s (1): reference to "(a)" in square brackets inserted in relation to England and Wales by SI 2001/1090, reg 9(1), (2)(a), Sch 5, para 15(1), (2), and in relation to Scotland by SSI 2001/128, reg 5, Sch 4, para 1(1), (2).
    Date in force (in relation to England and Wales): 6 April 2001: see SI 2001/1090, reg 1.
    Date in force (in relation to Scotland): 6 April 2001: see SSI 2001/128, reg 1(1).
    Sub-s (1): para (b) and word ", or" immediately preceding it inserted in relation to England and Wales by SI 2001/1090, reg 9(1), (2)(a), Sch 5, para 15(1), (2), and in relation to Scotland by SSI 2001/128, reg 5, Sch 4, para 1(1), (2).
    Date in force (in relation to England and Wales): 6 April 2001: see SI 2001/1090, reg 1.
    Date in force (in relation to Scotland): 6 April 2001: see SSI 2001/128, reg 1(1).
    Sub-s (2): words from "sale—" to "the transferor company" in square brackets substituted in relation to England and Wales by SI 2001/1090, reg 9(1), (2)(a), Sch 5, para 15(1), (3), and in relation to Scotland by SSI 2001/128, reg 5, Sch 4, para 1(1), (3).
    Date in force (in relation to England and Wales): 6 April 2001: see SI 2001/1090, reg 1.
    Date in force (in relation to Scotland): 6 April 2001: see SSI 2001/128, reg 1(1).

Sub-s (4): words from "company may—" to "limited liability partnership" in square brackets substituted in relation to England and Wales by SI 2001/1090, reg 9(1), (2)(a), Sch 5, para 15(1), (4), and (subject to minor variation) in relation to Scotland by SSI 2001/128, reg 5, Sch 4, para 1(1), (4) (for the exact text as substituted in relation to Scotland see the said sub-para (4)).

Date in force (in relation to England and Wales): 6 April 2001: see SI 2001/1090, reg 1.
Date in force (in relation to Scotland): 6 April 2001: see SSI 2001/128, reg 1(1).

111 Dissent from arrangement under s 110

(1) This section applies in the case of a voluntary winding up where, for the purposes of section 110(2) or (4), there has been passed a special resolution of the transferor company providing the sanction requisite for the liquidator under that section.

(2) If a member of the transferor company who did not vote in favour of the special resolution expresses his dissent from it in writing, addressed to the liquidator and left at the company's registered office within 7 days after the passing of the resolution, he may require the liquidator either to abstain from carrying the resolution into effect or to purchase his interest at a price to be determined by agreement or by arbitration under this section.

(3) If the liquidator elects to purchase the member's interest, the purchase money must be paid before the company is dissolved and be raised by the liquidator in such manner as may be determined by special resolution.

(4) For purposes of an arbitration under this section, the provisions of the Companies Clauses Consolidation Act 1845 or, in the case of a winding up in Scotland, the Companies Clauses Consolidation (Scotland) Act 1845 with respect to the settlement of disputes by arbitration are incorporated with this Act, and—
  (a) in the construction of those provisions this Act is deemed the special Act and "the company" means the transferor company, and
  (b) any appointment by the incorporated provisions directed to be made under the hand of the secretary or any two of the directors may be made in writing by the liquidator (or, if there is more than one liquidator, then any two or more of them).

112 Reference of questions to court

(1) The liquidator or any contributory or creditor may apply to the court to determine any question arising in the winding up of a company, or to exercise, as respects the enforcing of calls or any other matter, all or any of the powers which the court might exercise if the company were being wound up by the court.

(2) The court, if satisfied that the determination of the question or the required exercise of power will be just and beneficial, may accede wholly or partially to the application on such terms and conditions as it thinks fit, or may make such other order on the application as it thinks just.

(3)   A copy of an order made by virtue of this section staying the proceedings in the winding up shall forthwith be forwarded by the company, or otherwise as may be prescribed, to the registrar of companies, who shall enter it in his records relating to the company.

114 No liquidator appointed or nominated by company

(1)   This section applies where, in the case of a voluntary winding up, no liquidator has been appointed or nominated by the company.

(2)   The powers of the directors shall not be exercised, except with the sanction of the court or (in the case of a creditors' voluntary winding up) so far as may be necessary to secure compliance with sections 98 (creditors' meeting) and 99 (statement of affairs), during the period before the appointment or nomination of a liquidator of the company.

(3)   Subsection (2) does not apply in relation to the powers of the directors—
   (a)   to dispose of perishable goods and other goods the value of which is likely to diminish if they are not immediately disposed of, and
   (b)   to do all such other things as may be necessary for the protection of the company's assets.

(4)   If the directors of the company without reasonable excuse fail to comply with this section, they are liable to a fine.

115 Expenses of voluntary winding up

All expenses properly incurred in the winding up, including the remuneration of the liquidator, are payable out of the company's assets in priority to all other claims.

116 Saving for certain rights

The voluntary winding up of a company does not bar the right of any creditor or contributory to have it wound up by the court; but in the case of an application by a contributory the court must be satisfied that the rights of the contributories will be prejudiced by a voluntary winding up.

CHAPTER VI
WINDING UP BY THE COURT

Jurisdiction (England and Wales)

117 High Court and county court jurisdiction

(1)   The High Court has jurisdiction to wind up any company registered in England and Wales.

(2)   Where the amount of a company's share capital paid up or credited as paid up does not exceed £120,000, then (subject to this section) the county court of the district in which the company's registered office is situated has concurrent jurisdiction with the High Court to wind up the company.

(3)   The money sum for the time being specified in subsection (2) is subject to increase or reduction by order under section 416 in Part XV.

(4)   The Lord Chancellor may by order in a statutory instrument exclude a county court from having winding-up jurisdiction, and for the purposes of that jurisdiction may attach its district, or any part thereof, to any other county court, and may by statutory instrument revoke or vary any such order.

In exercising the powers of this section, the Lord Chancellor shall provide that a county court is not to have winding-up jurisdiction unless it has for the time being jurisdiction for the purposes of Parts VIII to XI of this Act (individual insolvency).

(5)   Every court in England and Wales having winding-up jurisdiction has for the purposes of that jurisdiction all the powers of the High Court; and every prescribed officer of the court shall perform any duties which an officer of the High Court may discharge by order of a judge of that court or otherwise in relation to winding up.

(6)   For the purposes of this section, a company's "registered office" is the place which has longest been its registered office during the 6 months immediately preceding the presentation of the petition for winding up.

[(7)   This section is subject to Article 3 of the EC Regulation (jurisdiction under EC Regulation).]

NOTES

Sub-s (7): inserted by SI 2002/1240, regs 3, 6.
Date in force: 31 May 2002: see SI 2002/1240, reg 1.

Grounds and effect of winding-up petition

122 Circumstances in which company may be wound up by the court

(1)   A company may be wound up by the court if—
  (a)   the company has by special resolution resolved that the company be wound up by the court,
  (b)   being a public company which was registered as such on its original incorporation, the company has not been issued with a certificate under section 117 of the Companies Act (public company share capital require-ments) and more than a year has expired since it was so registered,
  (c)   it is an old public company, within the meaning of the Consequential Provisions Act,
  (d)   the company does not commence its business within a year from its incorporation or suspends its business for a whole year,
  (e)   [except in the case of a private company limited by shares or by guarantee,] the number of members is reduced below 2,
  (f)   the company is unable to pay its debts,
  [(fa) at the time at which a moratorium for the company under section 1A comes to an end, no voluntary arrangement approved under Part I has effect in relation to the company,]
  (g)   the court is of the opinion that it is just and equitable that the company should be wound up.

(2) In Scotland, a company which the Court of Session has jurisdiction to wind up may be wound up by the Court if there is subsisting a floating charge over property comprised in the company's property and undertaking, and the court is satisfied that the security of the creditor entitled to the benefit of the floating charge is in jeopardy.

For this purpose a creditor's security is deemed to be in jeopardy if the Court is satisfied that events have occurred or are about to occur which render it unreasonable in the creditor's interests that the company should retain power to dispose of the property which is subject to the floating charge.

NOTES

Sub-s (1): in para (e) words in square brackets inserted by SI 1992/1699, reg 2(b), Schedule, para 8.

Sub-s (1): para (fa) inserted by the Insolvency Act 2000, s 1, Sch 1, paras 1, 6.

Date in force: to be appointed: see the Insolvency Act 2000, s 16(1).

123 Definition of inability to pay debts

(1) A company is deemed unable to pay its debts—

    (a) if a creditor (by assignment or otherwise) to whom the company is indebted in a sum exceeding £750 then due has served on the company, by leaving it at the company's registered office, a written demand (in the prescribed form) requiring the company to pay the sum so due and the company has for 3 weeks thereafter neglected to pay the sum or to secure or compound for it to the reasonable satisfaction of the creditor, or

    (b) if, in England and Wales, execution or other process issued on a judgment, decree or order of any court in favour of a creditor of the company is returned unsatisfied in whole or in part, or

    (c) if, in Scotland, the induciae of a charge for payment on an extract decree, or an extract registered bond, or an extract registered protest, have expired without payment being made, or

    (d) if, in Northern Ireland, a certificate of unenforceability has been granted in respect of a judgment against the company, or

    (e) if it is proved to the satisfaction of the court that the company is unable to pay its debts as they fall due.

(2) A company is also deemed unable to pay its debts if it is proved to the satisfaction of the court that the value of the company's assets is less than the amount of its liabilities, taking into account its contingent and prospective liabilities.

(3) The money sum for the time being specified in subsection (1)(a) is subject to increase or reduction by order under section 416 in Part XV.

124 Application for winding up

(1) Subject to the provisions of this section, an application to the court for the winding up of a company shall be by petition presented either by the company, or the directors, or by any creditor or creditors (including any contingent or prospective creditor or creditors), contributory or contributories[, or by a liquidator (within the meaning of Article 2(b) of the EC Regulation) appointed in proceedings by virtue of

Article 3(1) of the EC Regulation or a temporary administrator (within the meaning of Article 38 of the EC Regulation)] [or by [a justices' chief executive] in the exercise of the power conferred by section 87A of the Magistrates' Courts Act 1980 (enforcement of fines imposed on companies)], or by all or any of those parties, together or separately.

(2)   Except as mentioned below, a contributory is not entitled to present a winding-up petition unless either—
  (a)   the number of members is reduced below 2, or
  (b)   the shares in respect of which he is a contributory, or some of them, either were originally allotted to him, or have been held by him, and registered in his name, for at least 6 months during the 18 months before the commencement of the winding up, or have devolved on him through the death of a former holder.

(3)   A person who is liable under section 76 to contribute to a company's assets in the event of its being wound up may petition on either of the grounds set out in section 122(1)(f) and (g), and subsection (2) above does not then apply; but unless the person is a contributory otherwise than under section 76, he may not in his character as contributory petition on any other ground.

This subsection is deemed included in Chapter VII of Part V of the Companies Act (redeemable shares; purchase by a company of its own shares) for the purposes of the Secretary of State's power to make regulations under section 179 of that Act.

[(3A)   A winding-up petition on the ground set out in section 122(1)(fa) may only be presented by one or more creditors]

(4)   A winding-up petition may be presented by the Secretary of State—
  (a)   if the ground of the petition is that in section 122(1)(b) or (c), or
  [(b)   in a case falling within section 124A below.]

(5)   Where a company is being wound up voluntarily in England and Wales, a winding-up petition may be presented by the official receiver attached to the court as well as by any other person authorised in that behalf under the other provisions of this section; but the court shall not make a winding-up order on the petition unless it is satisfied that the voluntary winding up cannot be continued with due regard to the interests of the creditors or contributories.

NOTES

Sub-s (1): words from ", or by a" to "the EC Regulation)" in square brackets inserted by SI 2002/1240, regs 3, 8.

Date in force: 31 May 2002: see SI 2002/1240, reg 1.

Sub-s (1): words from "or by" to "imposed on companies)" in square brackets inserted by the Criminal Justice Act 1988, s 62(2).

Sub-s (1): words "a justices' chief executive" in square brackets substituted by the Access to Justice Act 1999, s 90(1), Sch 13, para 133.

Date in force: 1 April 2001: see SI 2001/916, art 2(a)(ii).

Sub-s (3A): inserted by the Insolvency Act 2000, s 1, Sch 1, paras 1, 7.

Date in force: to be appointed: see the Insolvency Act 2000, s 16(1).

Sub-s (4): para (b) substituted by the Companies Act 1989, s 60(2).

[124A Petition for winding up on grounds of public interest]

[(1) Where it appears to the Secretary of State from—
(a) any report made or information obtained under Part XIV of the Companies Act 1985 (company investigations, &c.),
[(b) any report made by inspectors under—
(i) section 167, 168, 169 or 284 of the Financial Services and Markets Act 2000, or
(ii) where the company is an open-ended investment company (within the meaning of that Act), regulations made as a result of section 262(2)(k) of that Act;
(bb) any information or documents obtained under section 165, 171, 172, 173 or 175 of that Act,]
(c) any information obtained under section 2 of the Criminal Justice Act 1987 or section 52 of the Criminal Justice (Scotland) Act 1987 (fraud investigations), or
(d) any information obtained under section 83 of the Companies Act 1989 (powers exercisable for purpose of assisting overseas regulatory authorities),

that it is expedient in the public interest that a company should be wound up, he may present a petition for it to be wound up if the court thinks it just and equitable for it to be so.

(2) This section does not apply if the company is already being wound up by the court.]

NOTES

Inserted by the Companies Act 1989, s 60(3).
Sub-s (1): paras (b), (bb) substituted, for para (b) as originally enacted, by SI 2001/3649, art 305.
Date in force: 1 December 2001: see SI 2001/3649, art 1.

125 Powers of court on hearing of petition

(1) On hearing a winding-up petition the court may dismiss it, or adjourn the hearing conditionally or unconditionally, or make an interim order, or any other order that it thinks fit; but the court shall not refuse to make a winding-up order on the ground only that the company's assets have been mortgaged to an amount equal to or in excess of those assets, or that the company has no assets.

(2) If the petition is presented by members of the company as contributories on the ground that it is just and equitable that the company should be wound up, the court, if it is of opinion—
(a) that the petitioners are entitled to relief either by winding up the company or by some other means, and
(b) that in the absence of any other remedy it would be just and equitable that the company should be wound up,

shall make a winding-up order; but this does not apply if the court is also of the opinion both that some other remedy is available to the petitioners and that they are acting unreasonably in seeking to have the company wound up instead of pursuing that other remedy.

126 Power to stay or restrain proceedings against company

(1)   At any time after the presentation of a winding-up petition, and before a winding-up order has been made, the company, or any creditor or contributory, may—

(a)   where any action or proceeding against the company is pending in the High Court or Court of Appeal in England and Wales or Northern Ireland, apply to the court in which the action or proceeding is pending for a stay of proceedings therein, and

(b)   where any other action or proceeding is pending against the company, apply to the court having jurisdiction to wind up the company to restrain further proceedings in the action or proceeding;

and the court to which application is so made may (as the case may be) stay, sist or restrain the proceedings accordingly on such terms as it thinks fit.

(2)   In the case of a company registered under section 680 of the Companies Act (pre-1862 companies; companies formed under legislation other than the Companies Acts) or the previous corresponding legislation, where the application to stay, sist or restrain is by a creditor, this section extends to actions and proceedings against any contributory of the company.

127 Avoidance of property dispositions, etc

In a winding up by the court, any disposition of the company's property, and any transfer of shares, or alteration in the status of the company's members, made after the commencement of the winding up is, unless the court otherwise orders, void.

128 Avoidance of attachments, etc

(1)   Where a company registered in England and Wales is being wound up by the court, any attachment, sequestration, distress or execution put in force against the estate or effects of the company after the commencement of the winding up is void.

(2)   This section, so far as relates to any estate or effects of the company situated in England and Wales, applies in the case of a company registered in Scotland as it applies in the case of a company registered in England and Wales.

Commencement of winding up

129 Commencement of winding up by the court

(1)   If, before the presentation of a petition for the winding up of a company by the court, a resolution has been passed by the company for voluntary winding up, the winding up of the company is deemed to have commenced at the time of the passing of the resolution; and unless the court, on proof of fraud or mistake, directs otherwise, all proceedings taken in the voluntary winding up are deemed to have been validly taken.

(2)   In any other case, the winding up of a company by the court is deemed to commence at the time of the presentation of the petition for winding up.

130 Consequences of winding-up order

(1)   On the making of a winding-up order, a copy of the order must forthwith be forwarded by the company (or otherwise as may be prescribed) to the registrar of companies, who shall enter it in his records relating to the company.

(2)   When a winding-up order has been made or a provisional liquidator has been appointed, no action or proceeding shall be proceeded with or commenced against the company or its property, except by leave of the court and subject to such terms as the court may impose.

(3)   When an order has been made for winding up a company registered under section 680 of the Companies Act, no action or proceeding shall be commenced or proceeded with against the company or its property or any contributory of the company, in respect of any debt of the company, except by leave of the court, and subject to such terms as the court may impose.

(4)   An order for winding up a company operates in favour of all the creditors and of all contributories of the company as if made on the joint petition of a creditor and of a contributory.

Investigation procedures

131 Company's statement of affairs

(1)   Where the court has made a winding-up order or appointed a provisional liquidator, the official receiver may require some or all of the persons mentioned in subsection (3) below to make out and submit to him a statement in the prescribed form as to the affairs of the company.

(2)   The statement shall be verified by affidavit by the persons required to submit it and shall show—
   (a)   particulars of the company's assets, debts and liabilities;
   (b)   the names and addresses of the company's creditors;
   (c)   the securities held by them respectively;
   (d)   the dates when the securities were respectively given; and
   (e)   such further or other information as may be prescribed or as the official receiver may require.

(3)   The persons referred to in subsection (1) are—
   (a)   those who are or have been officers of the company;
   (b)   those who have taken part in the formation of the company at any time within one year before the relevant date;
   (c)   those who are in the company's employment, or have been in its employment within that year, and are in the official receiver's opinion capable of giving the information required;

(d) those who are or have been within that year officers of, or in the employment of, a company which is, or within that year was, an officer of the company.

(4) Where any persons are required under this section to submit a statement of affairs to the official receiver, they shall do so (subject to the next subsection) before the end of the period of 21 days beginning with the day after that on which the prescribed notice of the requirement is given to them by the official receiver.

(5) The official receiver, if he thinks fit, may—
(a) at any time release a person from an obligation imposed on him under subsection (1) or (2) above; or
(b) either when giving the notice mentioned in subsection (4) or subsequently, extend the period so mentioned;

and where the official receiver has refused to exercise a power conferred by this subsection, the court, if it thinks fit, may exercise it.

(6) In this section—
"employment" includes employment under a contract for services; and
"the relevant date" means—
(a) in a case where a provisional liquidator is appointed, the date of his appointment; and
(b) in a case where no such appointment is made, the date of the winding-up order.

(7) If a person without reasonable excuse fails to comply with any obligation imposed under this section, he is liable to a fine and, for continued contravention, to a daily default fine.

(8) In the application of this section to Scotland references to the official receiver are to the liquidator or, in a case where a provisional liquidator is appointed, the provisional liquidator.

132 Investigation by official receiver

(1) Where a winding-up order is made by the court in England and Wales, it is the duty of the official receiver to investigate—
(a) if the company has failed, the causes of the failure; and
(b) generally, the promotion, formation, business, dealings and affairs of the company,

and to make such report (if any) to the court as he thinks fit.

(2) The report is, in any proceedings, prima facie evidence of the facts stated in it.

133 Public examination of officers

(1) Where a company is being wound up by the court, the official receiver or, in Scotland, the liquidator may at any time before the dissolution of the company apply to the court for the public examination of any person who—
(a) is or has been an officer of the company; or

(b) has acted as liquidator or administrator of the company or as receiver or manager or, in Scotland, receiver of its property; or

(c) not being a person falling within paragraph (a) or (b), is or has been concerned, or has taken part, in the promotion, formation or management of the company.

(2) Unless the court otherwise orders, the official receiver or, in Scotland, the liquidator shall make an application under subsection (1) if he is requested in accordance with the rules to do so by—

(a) one-half, in value, of the company's creditors; or

(b) three-quarters, in value, of the company's contributories.

(3) On an application under subsection (1), the court shall direct that a public examination of the person to whom the application relates shall be held on a day appointed by the court; and that person shall attend on that day and be publicly examined as to the promotion, formation or management of the company or as to the conduct of its business and affairs, or his conduct or dealings in relation to the company.

(4) The following may take part in the public examination of a person under this section and may question that person concerning the matters mentioned in subsection (3), namely—

(a) the official receiver;

(b) the liquidator of the company;

(c) any person who has been appointed as special manager of the company's property or business;

(d) any creditor of the company who has tendered a proof or, in Scotland, submitted a claim in the winding up;

(e) any contributory of the company.

134 Enforcement of s 133

(1) If a person without reasonable excuse fails at any time to attend his public examination under section 133, he is guilty of a contempt of court and liable to be punished accordingly.

(2) In a case where a person without reasonable excuse fails at any time to attend his examination under section 133 or there are reasonable grounds for believing that a person has absconded, or is about to abscond, with a view to avoiding or delaying his examination under that section, the court may cause a warrant to be issued to a constable or prescribed officer of the court—

(a) for the arrest of that person; and

(b) for the seizure of any books, papers, records, money or goods in that person's possession.

(3) In such a case the court may authorise the person arrested under the warrant to be kept in custody, and anything seized under such a warrant to be held, in accordance with the rules, until such time as the court may order.

Appointment of liquidator

135 Appointment and powers of provisional liquidator

(1) Subject to the provisions of this section, the court may, at any time after the presentation of a winding-up petition, appoint a liquidator provisionally.

(2) In England and Wales, the appointment of a provisional liquidator may be made at any time before the making of a winding-up order; and either the official receiver or any other fit person may be appointed.

(3) In Scotland, such an appointment may be made at any time before the first appointment of liquidators.

(4) The provisional liquidator shall carry out such functions as the court may confer on him.

(5) When a liquidator is provisionally appointed by the court, his powers may be limited by the order appointing him.

136 Functions of official receiver in relation to office of liquidator

(1) The following provisions of this section have effect, subject to section 140 below, on a winding-up order being made by the court in England and Wales.

(2) The official receiver, by virtue of his office, becomes the liquidator of the company and continues in office until another person becomes liquidator under the provisions of this Part.

(3) The official receiver is, by virtue of his office, the liquidator during any vacancy.

(4) At any time when he is the liquidator of the company, the official receiver may summon separate meetings of the company's creditors and contributories for the purpose of choosing a person to be liquidator of the company in place of the official receiver.

(5) It is the duty of the official receiver—
  (a) as soon as practicable in the period of 12 weeks beginning with the day on which the winding-up order was made, to decide whether to exercise his power under subsection (4) to summon meetings, and
  (b) if in pursuance of paragraph (a) he decides not to exercise that power, to give notice of his decision, before the end of that period, to the court and to the company's creditors and contributories, and
  (c) (whether or not he has decided to exercise that power) to exercise his power to summon meetings under subsection (4) if he is at any time requested, in accordance with the rules, to do so by one-quarter, in value, of the company's creditors;

and accordingly, where the duty imposed by paragraph (c) arises before the official receiver has performed a duty imposed by paragraph (a) or (b), he is not required to perform the latter duty.

(6) A notice given under subsection (5)(b) to the company's creditors shall contain an explanation of the creditors' power under subsection (5)(c) to require the official receiver to summon meetings of the company's creditors and contributories.

139 Choice of liquidator at meetings of creditors and contributories

(1) This section applies where a company is being wound up by the court and separate meetings of the company's creditors and contributories are summoned for the purpose of choosing a person to be liquidator of the company.

(2) The creditors and the contributories at their respective meetings may nominate a person to be liquidator.

(3) The liquidator shall be the person nominated by the creditors or, where no person has been so nominated, the person (if any) nominated by the contributories.

(4) In the case of different persons being nominated, any contributory or creditor may, within 7 days after the date on which the nomination was made by the creditors, apply to the court for an order either—

(a) appointing the person nominated as liquidator by the contributories to be a liquidator instead of, or jointly with, the person nominated by the creditors; or

(b) appointing some other person to be liquidator instead of the person nominated by the creditors.

140 Appointment by the court following administration or voluntary arrangement

(1) Where a winding-up order is made immediately upon the discharge of an administration order, the court may appoint as liquidator of the company the person who has ceased on the discharge of the administration order to be the administrator of the company.

(2) Where a winding-up order is made at a time when there is a supervisor of a voluntary arrangement approved in relation to the company under Part I, the court may appoint as liquidator of the company the person who is the supervisor at the time when the winding-up order is made.

(3) Where the court makes an appointment under this section, the official receiver does not become the liquidator as otherwise provided by section 136(2), and he has no duty under section 136(5)(a) or (b) in respect of the summoning of creditors' or contributories' meetings.

Liquidation committees

141 Liquidation committee (England and Wales)

(1) Where a winding-up order has been made by the court in England and Wales and separate meetings of creditors and contributories have been summoned for the purpose of choosing a person to be liquidator, those meetings may establish a committee ("the liquidation committee") to exercise the functions conferred on it by or under this Act.

(2)   The liquidator (not being the official receiver) may at any time, if he thinks fit, summon separate general meetings of the company's creditors and contributories for the purpose of determining whether such a committee should be established and, if it is so determined, of establishing it.

The liquidator (not being the official receiver) shall summon such a meeting if he is requested, in accordance with the rules, to do so by one-tenth, in value, of the company's creditors.

(3)   Where meetings are summoned under this section, or for the purpose of choosing a person to be liquidator, and either the meeting of creditors or the meeting of contributories decides that a liquidation committee should be established, but the other meeting does not so decide or decides that a committee should not be established, the committee shall be established in accordance with the rules, unless the court otherwise orders.

(4)   The liquidation committee is not to be able or required to carry out its functions at any time when the official receiver is liquidator; but at any such time its functions are vested in the Secretary of State except to the extent that the rules otherwise provide.

(5)   Where there is for the time being no liquidation committee, and the liquidator is a person other than the official receiver, the functions of such a committee are vested in the Secretary of State except to the extent that the rules otherwise provide.

The liquidator's functions

143 General functions in winding up by the court

(1)   The functions of the liquidator of a company which is being wound up by the court are to secure that the assets of the company are got in, realised and distributed to the company's creditors and, if there is a surplus, to the persons entitled to it.

(2)   It is the duty of the liquidator of a company which is being wound up by the court in England and Wales, if he is not the official receiver—
  (a)   to furnish the official receiver with such information,
  (b)   to produce to the official receiver, and permit inspection by the official receiver of, such books, papers and other records, and
  (c)   to give the official receiver such other assistance,

as the official receiver may reasonably require for the purposes of carrying out his functions in relation to the winding up.

144 Custody of company's property

(1)   When a winding-up order has been made, or where a provisional liquidator has been appointed, the liquidator or the provisional liquidator (as the case may be) shall take into his custody or under his control all the property and things in action to which the company is or appears to be entitled.

(2) In a winding up by the court in Scotland, if and so long as there is no liquidator, all the property of the company is deemed to be in the custody of the court.

145 Vesting of company property in liquidator

(1) When a company is being wound up by the court, the court may on the application of the liquidator by order direct that all or any part of the property of whatsoever description belonging to the company or held by trustees on its behalf shall vest in the liquidator by his official name; and thereupon the property to which the order relates vests accordingly.

(2) The liquidator may, after giving such indemnity (if any) as the court may direct, bring or defend in his official name any action or other legal proceeding which relates to that property or which it is necessary to bring or defend for the purpose of effectually winding up the company and recovering its property.

146 Duty to summon final meeting

(1) Subject to the next subsection, if it appears to the liquidator of a company which is being wound by the court that the winding up of the company is for practical purposes complete and the liquidator is not the official receiver, the liquidator shall summon a final general meeting of the company's creditors which—
  (a)   shall receive the liquidator's report of the winding up, and
  (b)   shall determine whether the liquidator should have his release under section 174 in Chapter VII of this Part.

(2) The liquidator may, if he thinks fit, give the notice summoning the final general meeting at the same time as giving notice of any final distribution of the company's property but, if summoned for an earlier date, that meeting shall be adjourned (and, if necessary, further adjourned) until a date on which the liquidator is able to report to the meeting that the winding up of the company is for practical purposes complete.

(3) In the carrying out of his functions in the winding up it is the duty of the liquidator to retain sufficient sums from the company's property to cover the expenses of summoning and holding the meeting required by this section.

General powers of court

148 Settlement of list of contributories and application of assets

(1) As soon as may be after making a winding-up order, the court shall settle a list of contributories, with power to rectify the register of members in all cases where rectification is required in pursuance of the Companies Act or this Act, and shall cause the company's assets to be collected, and applied in discharge of its liabilities.

(2) If it appears to the court that it will not be necessary to make calls on or adjust the rights of contributories, the court may dispense with the settlement of a list of contributories.

(3) In settling the list, the court shall distinguish between persons who are contributories in their own right and persons who are contributories as being representatives of or liable for the debts of others.

149 Debts due from contributory to company

(1) The court may, at any time after making a winding-up order, make an order on any contributory for the time being on the list of contributories to pay, in manner directed by the order, any money due from him (or from the estate of the person who he represents) to the company, exclusive of any money payable by him or the estate by virtue of any call in pursuance of the Companies Act or this Act.

(2) The court in making such an order may—
  (a) in the case of an unlimited company, allow to the contributory by way of set-off any money due to him or the estate which he represents from the company on any independent dealing or contract with the company, but not any money due to him as a member of the company in respect of any dividend or profit, and
  (b) in the case of a limited company, make to any director or manager whose liability is unlimited or to his estate the like allowance.

(3) In the case of any company, whether limited or unlimited, when all the creditors are paid in full (together with interest at the official rate), any money due on any account whatever to a contributory from the company may be allowed to him by way of set-off against any subsequent call.

150 Power to make calls

(1) The court may, at any time after making a winding-up order, and either before or after it has ascertained the sufficiency of the company's assets, make calls on all or any of the contributories for the time being settled on the list of the contributories to the extent of their liability, for payment of any money which the court considers necessary to satisfy the company's debts and liabilities, and the expenses of winding up, and for the adjustment of the rights of the contributories among themselves, and make an order for payment of any calls so made.

(2) In making a call the court may take into consideration the probability that some of the contributories may partly or wholly fail to pay it.

153 Power to exclude creditors not proving in time

The court may fix a time or times within which creditors are to prove their debts or claims or to be excluded from the benefit of any distribution made before those debts are proved.

155 Inspection of books by creditors, etc

(1) The court may, at any time after making a winding-up order, make such order for inspection of the company's books and papers by creditors and contributories as the court thinks just; and any books and papers in the company's possession may be inspected by creditors and contributories accordingly, but not further or otherwise.

(2) Nothing in this section excludes or restricts any statutory rights of a government department or person acting under the authority of a government department.

[(3) For the purposes of subsection (2) above, references to a government department shall be construed as including references to any part of the Scottish Administration.]

NOTES

Sub-s (3): inserted by SI 1999/1820, art 4, Sch 2, Pt I, para 85.
Date in force: 1 July 1999: see SI 1999/1820, art 1(2).

156 Payment of expenses of winding up

The court may, in the event of the assets being insufficient to satisfy the liabilities, make an order as to the payment out of the assets of the expenses incurred in the winding up in such order of priority as the court thinks just.

160 Delegation of powers to liquidator (England and Wales)

(1) Provision may be made by rules for enabling or requiring all or any of the powers and duties conferred and imposed on the court in England and Wales by the Companies Act and this Act in respect of the following matters—
- (a) the holding and conducting of meetings to ascertain the wishes of creditors and contributories,
- (b) the settling of lists of contributories and the rectifying of the register of members where required, and the collection and application of the assets,
- (c) the payment, delivery, conveyance, surrender or transfer of money, property, books or papers to the liquidator,
- (d) the making of calls,
- (e) the fixing of a time within which debts and claims must be proved,

to be exercised or performed by the liquidator as an officer of the court, and subject to the court's control.

(2) But the liquidator shall not, without the special leave of the court, rectify the register of members, and shall not make any call without either that special leave or the sanction of the liquidation committee.

CHAPTER VII
LIQUIDATORS

Liquidator's powers and duties

165 Voluntary winding up

(1) This section has effect where a company is being wound up voluntarily, but subject to section 166 below in the case of a creditors' voluntary winding up.

(2) The liquidator may—

(a) in the case of a member's voluntary winding up, with the sanction of an extraordinary resolution of the company, and

(b) in the case of a creditors' voluntary winding up, with the sanction of the court or the liquidation committee (or, if there is no such committee, a meeting of the company's creditors),

exercise any of the powers specified in Part I of Schedule 4 to this Act (payment of debts, compromise of claims, etc.).

(3) The liquidator may, without sanction, exercise either of the powers specified in Part II of that Schedule (institution and defence of proceedings; carrying on the business of the company) and any of the general powers specified in Part III of that Schedule.

(4) The liquidator may—

(a) exercise the court's power of settling a list of contributories (which list is prima facie evidence of the liability of the persons named in it to be contributories),

(b) exercise the court's power of making calls,

(c) summon general meetings of the company for the purpose of obtaining its sanction by special or extraordinary resolution or for any other purpose he may think fit.

(5) The liquidator shall pay the company's debts and adjust the rights of the contributories among themselves.

(6) Where the liquidator in exercise of the powers conferred on him by this Act disposes of any property of the company to a person who is connected with the company (within the meaning of section 249 in Part VII), he shall, if there is for the time being a liquidation committee, give notice to the committee of that exercise of his powers.

166 Creditors' voluntary winding up

(1) This section applies where, in the case of a creditors' voluntary winding up, a liquidator has been nominated by the company.

(2) The powers conferred on the liquidator by section 165 shall not be exercised, except with the sanction of the court, during the period before the holding of the creditors' meeting under section 98 in Chapter IV.

(3) Subsection (2) does not apply in relation to the power of the liquidator—

(a) to take into his custody or under his control all the property to which the company is or appears to be entitled;

(b) to dispose of perishable goods and other goods the value of which is likely to diminish if they are not immediately disposed of; and

(c) to do all such other things as may be necessary for the protection of the company's assets.

(4) The liquidator shall attend the creditors' meeting held under section 98 and shall report to the meeting on any exercise by him of his powers (whether or not under this section or under section 112 or 165).

(5) If default is made—
   (a) by the company in complying with subsection (1) or (2) of section 98, or
   (b) by the directors in complying with subsection (1) or (2) of section 99,

the liquidator shall, within 7 days of the relevant day, apply to the court for directions as to the manner in which that default is to be remedied.

(6) "The relevant day" means the day on which the liquidator was nominated by the company or the day on which he first became aware of the default, whichever is the later.

(7) If the liquidator without reasonable excuse fails to comply with this section, he is liable to a fine.

167 Winding up by the court

(1) Where a company is being wound up by the court, the liquidator may—
   (a) with the sanction of the court or the liquidation committee, exercise any of the powers specified in Parts I and II of Schedule 4 to this Act (payment of debts; compromise of claims, etc; institution and defence of proceedings; carrying on of the business of the company), and
   (b) with or without that sanction, exercise any of the general powers specified in Part III of that Schedule.

(2) Where the liquidator (not being the official receiver), in exercise of the powers conferred on him by this Act—
   (a) disposes of any property of the company to a person who is connected with the company (within the meaning of section 249 in Part VII), or
   (b) employs a solicitor to assist him in the carrying out of his functions,

he shall, if there is for the time being a liquidation committee, give notice to the committee of that exercise of his powers.

(3) The exercise by the liquidator in a winding up by the court of the powers conferred by this section is subject to the control of the court, and any creditor or contributory may apply to the court with respect to any exercise or proposed exercise of any of those powers.

168 Supplementary powers (England and Wales)

(1) This section applies in the case of a company which is being wound up by the court in England and Wales.

(2) The liquidator may summon general meetings of the creditors or contributories for the purpose of ascertaining their wishes; and it is his duty to summon meetings at such times as the creditors or contributories by resolution (either at the meeting appointing the liquidator or otherwise) may direct, or whenever requested in writing to do so by one-tenth in value of the creditors or contributories (as the case may be).

(3) The liquidator may apply to the court (in the prescribed manner) for directions in relation to any particular matter arising in the winding up.

(4) Subject to the provisions of this Act, the liquidator shall use his own discretion in the management of the assets and their distribution among the creditors.

(5)   If any person is aggrieved by an act or decision of the liquidator, that person may apply to the court; and the court may confirm, reverse or modify the act or decision complained of, and make such order in the case as it thinks just.

[(5A)   Where at any time after a winding-up petition has been presented to the court against any person (including an insolvent partnership or other body which may be wound up under Part V of the Act as an unregistered company), whether by virtue of the provisions of the Insolvent Partnerships Order 1994 or not, the attention of the court is drawn to the fact that the person in question is a member of an insolvent partnership, the court may make an order as to the future conduct of the insolvency proceedings and any such order may apply any provisions of that Order with any necessary modifications.

(5B)   Any order or directions under subsection (5A) may be made or given on the application of the official receiver, any responsible insolvency practitioner, the trustee of the partnership or any other interested person and may include provisions as to the administration of the joint estate of the partnership, and in particular how it and the separate estate of any member are to be administered.

(5C)   . . .]

NOTES

Sub-ss (5A)–(5C): inserted by SI 1994/2421, art 14(1).
Sub-s (5C): repealed by SI 2001/3649, art 306.
Date in force: 1 December 2001: see SI 2001/3649, art 1.

Removal; vacation of office

171 Removal, etc (voluntary winding up)

(1)   This section applies with respect to the removal from office and vacation of office of the liquidator of a company which is being wound up voluntarily.

(2)   Subject to the next subsection, the liquidator may be removed from office only by an order of the court or—
- (a)   in the case of a members' voluntary winding up, by a general meeting of the company summoned specially for that purpose, or
- (b)   in the case of a creditors' voluntary winding up, by a general meeting of the company's creditors summoned specially for that purpose in accordance with the rules.

(3)   Where the liquidator was appointed by the court under section 108 in Chapter V, a meeting such as is mentioned in subsection (2) above shall be summoned for the purpose of replacing him only if he thinks fit or the court so directs or the meeting is requested, in accordance with the rules—
- (a)   in the case of a members' voluntary winding up, by members representing not less than one-half of the total voting rights of all the members having at the date of the request a right to vote at the meeting, or
- (b)   in the case of a creditors' voluntary winding up, by not less than one-half, in value, of the company's creditors.

(4)   A liquidator shall vacate office if he ceases to be a person who is qualified to act as an insolvency practitioner in relation to the company.

(5)   A liquidator may, in the prescribed circumstances, resign his office by giving notice of his resignation to the registrar of companies.

(6)   Where—
  (a)   in the case of a members' voluntary winding up, a final meeting of the company has been held under section 94 in Chapter III, or
  (b)   in the case of a creditors' voluntary winding up, final meetings of the company and of the creditors have been held under section 106 in Chapter IV,

the liquidator whose report was considered at the meeting or meetings shall vacate office as soon as he has complied with subsection (3) of that section and has given notice to the registrar of companies that the meeting or meetings have been held and of the decisions (if any) of the meeting or meetings.

172 Removal, etc (winding up by the court)

(1)   This section applies with respect to the removal from office and vacation of office of the liquidator of a company which is being wound up by the court, or of a provisional liquidator.

(2)   Subject as follows, the liquidator may be removed from office only by an order of the court or by a general meeting of the company's creditors summoned specially for that purpose in accordance with the rules; and a provisional liquidator may be removed from office only by an order of the court.

(3)   Where—
  (a)   the official receiver is liquidator otherwise than in succession under section 136(3) to a person who held office as a result of a nomination by a meeting of the company's creditors or contributories, or
  (b)   the liquidator was appointed by the court otherwise than under section 139(4)(a) or 140(1), or was appointed by the Secretary of State,

a general meeting of the company's creditors shall be summoned for the purpose of replacing him only if he thinks fit, or the court so directs, or the meeting is requested, in accordance with the rules, by not less that one-quarter, in value, of the creditors.

(4)   If appointed by the Secretary of State, the liquidator may be removed from office by a direction of the Secretary of State.

(5)   A liquidator or provisional liquidator, not being the official receiver, shall vacate office if he ceases to be a person who is qualified to act as an insolvency practitioner in relation to the company.

(6)   A liquidator may, in the prescribed circumstances, resign his office by giving notice of his resignation to the court.

(7)   Where an order is made under section 204 (early dissolution in Scotland) for the dissolution of the company, the liquidator shall vacate office when the dissolution of the company takes effect in accordance with that section.

(8)   Where a final meeting has been held under section 146 (liquidator's report on completion of winding up), the liquidator who$\cdot$e report was considered at the meeting shall vacate office as soon as he has given notice to the court and the registrar of companies that the meeting has been held and of the decisions (if any) of the meeting.

Release of liquidator

173 Release (voluntary winding up)

(1)   This section applies with respect to the release of the liquidator of a company which is being wound up voluntarily.

(2)   A person who has ceased to be a liquidator shall have his release with effect from the following time, that is to say—

(a)   in the case of a person who has been removed from office by a general meeting of the company or by a general meeting of the company's creditors that has not resolved against his release or who has died, the time at which notice is given to the registrar of companies in accordance with the rules that that person has ceased to hold office;

(b)   in the case of a person who has been removed from office by a general meeting of the company's creditors that has resolved against his release, or by the court, or who has vacated office under section 171(4) above, such time as the Secretary of State may, on the application of that person, determine;

(c)   in the case of a person who has resigned, such time as may be prescribed;

(d)   in the case of a person who has vacated office under subsection (6)(a) of section 171, the time at which he vacated office;

(e)   in the case of a person who has vacated office under subsection (6)(b) of that section—

(i)   if the final meeting of the creditors referred to in that subsection has resolved against that person's release, such time as the Secretary of State may, on an application by that person, determine, and

(ii)   if that meeting has not resolved against that person's release, the time at which he vacated office.

(3)   In the application of subsection (2) to the winding up of a company registered in Scotland, the references to a determination by the Secretary of State as to the time from which a person who has ceased to be liquidator shall have his release are to be read as references to such a determination by the Accountant of Court.

(4)   Where a liquidator has his release under subsection (2), he is, with effect from the time specified in that subsection, discharged from all liability both in respect of acts or omissions of his in the winding up and otherwise in relation to his conduct as liquidator.

But nothing in this section prevents the exercise, in relation to a person who has had his release under subsection (2), of the court's powers under section 212 of this Act (summary remedy against delinquent directors, liquidators, etc.).

174 Release (winding up by the court)

(1)   This section applies with respect to the release of the liquidator of a company which is being wound up by the court, or of a provisional liquidator.

(2)   Where the official receiver has ceased to be liquidator and a person becomes liquidator in his stead, the official receiver has his release with effect from the following time, that is to say—

    (a)   in a case where that person was nominated by a general meeting of creditors or contributories, or was appointed by the Secretary of State, the time at which the official receiver gives notice to the court that he has been replaced;

    (b)   in a case where that person is appointed by the court, such time as the court may determine.

(3)   If the official receiver while he is a liquidator gives notice to the Secretary of State that the winding up is for practical purposes complete, he has his release with effect from such time as the Secretary of State may determine.

(4)   A person other than the official receiver who has ceased to be a liquidator has his release with effect from the following time, that is to say—

    (a)   in the case of a person who has been removed from office by a general meeting of creditors that has not resolved against his release or who has died, the time at which notice is given to the court in accordance with the rules that that person has ceased to hold office;

    (b)   in the case of a person who has been removed from office by a general meeting of creditors that has resolved against his release, or by the court or the Secretary of State, or who has vacated office under section 172(5) or (7), such time as the Secretary of State may, on an application by that person, determine;

    (c)   in the case of a person who has resigned, such time as may be prescribed;

    (d)   in the case of a person who has vacated office under section 172(8)—

        (i)   if the final meeting referred to in that subsection has resolved against that person's release, such time as the Secretary of State may, on an application by that person, determine, and

        (ii)   if that meeting has not so resolved, the time at which that person vacated office.

(5)   A person who has ceased to hold office as a provisional liquidator has his release with effect from such time as the court may, on an application by him, determine.

(6)   Where the official receiver or a liquidator or provisional liquidator has his release under this section, he is, with effect from the time specified in the preceding provisions of this section, discharged from all liability both in respect of acts or omissions of his in the winding up and otherwise in relation to his conduct as liquidator or provisional liquidator.

But nothing in this section prevents the exercise, in relation to a person who has had his release under this section, of the court's powers under section 212 (summary remedy against delinquent directors, liquidators, etc.).

(7) In the application of this section to a case where the order for winding up has been made by the court in Scotland, the references to a determination by the Secretary of State as to the time from which a person who has ceased to be liquidator has his release are to such a determination by the Accountant of Court.

CHAPTER VIII
PROVISIONS OF GENERAL APPLICATION IN WINDING UP

Preferential debts

175 Preferential debts (general provision)

(1) In a winding up the company's preferential debts (within the meaning given by section 386 in Part XII) shall be paid in priority to all other debts.

(2) Preferential debts—
    (a) rank equally among themselves after the expenses of the winding up and shall be paid in full, unless the assets are insufficient to meet them, in which case they abate in equal proportions; and
    (b) so far as the assets of the company available for payment of general creditors are insufficient to meet them, have priority over the claims of holders of debentures secured by, or holders of, any floating charge created by the company, and shall be paid accordingly out of any property comprised in or subject to that charge.

176 Preferential charge on goods distrained

(1) This section applies where a company is being wound up by the court in England and Wales, and is without prejudice to section 128 (avoidance of attachments, etc.).

(2) Where any person (whether or not a landlord or person entitled to rent) has distrained upon the goods or effects of the company in the period of 3 months ending with the date of the winding-up order, those goods or effects, or the proceeds of their sale, shall be charged for the benefit of the company with the preferential debts of the company to the extent that the company's property is for the time being insufficient for meeting them.

(3) Where by virtue of a charge under subsection (2) any person surrenders any goods or effects to a company or makes a payment to a company, that person ranks, in respect of the amount of the proceeds of sale of those goods or effects by the liquidator or (as the case may be) the amount of the payment, as a preferential creditor of the company, except as against so much of the company's property as is available for the payment of preferential creditors by virtue of the surrender or payment.

Disclaimer (England and Wales only)

178 Power to disclaim onerous property

(1)   This and the next two sections apply to a company that is being wound up in England and Wales.

(2)   Subject as follows, the liquidator may, by the giving of the prescribed notice, disclaim any onerous property and may do so notwithstanding that he has taken possession of it, endeavoured to sell it, or otherwise exercised rights of ownership in relation to it.

(3)   The following is onerous property for the purposes of this section—
   (a)   any unprofitable contract, and
   (b)   any other property of the company which is unsaleable or not readily saleable or is such that it may give rise to a liability to pay money or perform any other onerous act.

(4)   A disclaimer under this section—
   (a)   operates so as to determine, as from the date of the disclaimer, the rights, interests and liabilities of the company in or in respect of the property disclaimed; but
   (b)   does not, except so far as is necessary for the purpose of releasing the company from any liability, affect the rights or liabilities of any other person.

(5)   A notice of disclaimer shall not be given under this section in respect of any property if—
   (a)   a person interested in the property has applied in writing to the liquidator or one of his predecessors as liquidator requiring the liquidator or that predecessor to decide whether he will disclaim or not, and
   (b)   the period of 28 days beginning with the day on which that application was made, or such longer period as the court may allow, has expired without a notice of disclaimer having been given under this section in respect of that property.

(6)   Any person sustaining loss or damage in consequence of the operation of a disclaimer under this section is deemed a creditor of the company to the extent of the loss or damage and accordingly may prove for the loss or damage in the winding up.

179 Disclaimer of leaseholds

(1)   The disclaimer under section 178 of any property of a leasehold nature does not take effect unless a copy of the disclaimer has been served (so far as the liquidator is aware of their addresses) on every person claiming under the company as underlessee or mortgagee and either—
   (a)   no application under section 181 below is made with respect to that property before the end of the period of 14 days beginning with the day on which the last notice served under this subsection was served; or
   (b)   where such an application has been made, the court directs that the disclaimer shall take effect.

(2)   Where the court gives a direction under subsection (1)(b it may also, instead of or in addition to any order it makes under section 181, make such orders with respect to fixtures, tenant's improvements and other matters arising out of the lease as it thinks fit.

181 Powers of court (general)

(1)   This section and the next apply where the liquidator has disclaimed property under section 178.

(2)   An application under this section may be made to the court by—
   (a)   any person who claims an interest in the disclaimed property, or
   (b)   any person who is under any liability in respect of the disclaimed property, not being a liability discharged by the disclaimer.

(3)   Subject as follows, the court may on the application make an order, on such terms as it thinks fit, for the vesting of the disclaimed property in, or for its delivery to—
   (a)   a person entitled to it or a trustee for such a person, or
   (b)   a person subject to such a liability as is mentioned in subsection (2)(b) or a trustee for such a person.

(4)   The court shall not make an order under subsection (3)(b) except where it appears to the court that it would be just to do so for the purpose of compensating the person subject to the liability in respect of the disclaimer.

(5)   The effect of any order under this section shall be taken into account in assessing for the purpose of section 178(6) the extent of any loss or damage sustained by any person in consequence of the disclaimer.

(6)   An order under this section vesting property in any person need not be completed by conveyance, assignment or transfer.

182 Powers of court (leaseholds)

(1)   The court shall not make an order under section 181 vesting property of a leasehold nature in any person claiming under the company as underlessee or mortgagee except on terms making that person—
   (a)   subject to the same liabilities and obligations as the company was subject to under the lease at the commencement of the winding up, or
   (b)   if the court thinks fit, subject to the same liabilities and obligations as that person would be subject to if the lease had been assigned to him at the commencement of the winding up.

(2)   For the purposes of an order under section 181 relating to only part of any property comprised in a lease, the requirements of subsection (1) apply as if the lease comprised only the property to which the order relates.

(3)   Where subsection (1) applies and no person claiming under the company as underlessee or mortgagee is willing to accept an order under section 181 on the terms required by virtue of that subsection, the court may, by order under that section, vest the company's estate or interest in the property in any person who is

liable (whether personally or in a representative capacity, and whether alone or jointly with the company) to perform the lessee's covenants in the lease.

The court may vest that estate and interest in such a person freed and discharged from all estates, incumbrances and interests created by the company.

(4)   Where subsection (1) applies and a person claiming under the company as underlessee or mortgagee declines to accept an order under section 181, that person is excluded from all interest in the property.

Execution, attachment and the Scottish equivalents

183 Effect of execution or attachment (England and Wales)

(1)   Where a creditor has issued execution against the goods or land of a company or has attached any debt due to it, and the company is subsequently wound up, he is not entitled to retain the benefit of the execution or attachment against the liquidator unless he has completed the execution or attachment before the commencement of the winding up.

(2)   However—
   (a)   if a creditor has had notice of a meeting having been called at which a resolution for voluntary winding up is to be proposed, the date on which he had notice is substituted, for the purpose of subsection (1), for the date of commencement of the winding up;
   (b)   a person who purchases in good faith under a sale by the sheriff any goods of a company on which execution has been levied in all cases acquires a good title to them against the liquidator; and
   (c)   the rights conferred by subsection (1) on the liquidator may be set aside by the court in favour of the creditor to such extent and subject to such terms as the court thinks fit.

(3)   For the purposes of this Act—
   (a)   an execution against goods is completed by seizure and sale, or by the making of a charging order under section 1 of the Charging Orders Act 1979;
   (b)   an attachment of a debt is completed by receipt of the debt; and
   (c)   an execution against land is completed by seizure, by the appointment of a receiver, or by the making of a charging order under section 1 of the Act above-mentioned.

(4)   In this section "goods" includes all chattels personal; and "the sheriff" includes any officer charged with the execution of a writ or other process.

(5)   This section does not apply in the case of a winding up in Scotland.

Miscellaneous matters

188 Notification that company is in liquidation

(1)   When a company is being wound up, whether by the court or voluntarily, every invoice, order for goods or business letter issued by or on behalf of the

company, or a liquidator of the company, or a receiver or manager of the company's property, being a document on or in which the name of the company appears, shall contain a statement that the company is being wound up.

(2) If default is made in complying with this section, the company and any of the following persons who knowingly and wilfully authorises or permits the default, namely, any officer of the company, any liquidator of the company and any receiver or manager, is liable to a fine.

189 Interest on debts

(1) In a winding up interest is payable in accordance with this section on any debt proved in the winding up, including so much of any such debt as represents interest on the remainder.

(2) Any surplus remaining after the payment of the debts proved in a winding up shall, before being applied for any other purpose, be applied in paying interest on those debts in respect of the periods during which they have been outstanding since the company went into liquidation.

(3) All interest under this section ranks equally, whether or not the debts on which it is payable rank equally.

(4) The rate of interest payable under this section in respect of any debt ("the official rate" for the purposes of any provision of this Act in which that expression is used) is whichever is the greater of—

    (a) the rate specified in section 17 of the Judgments Act 1838 on the day on which the company went into liquidation, and

    (b) the rate applicable to that debt apart from the winding up.

(5) In the application of this section to Scotland—

    (a) references to a debt proved in a winding up have effect as references to a claim accepted in a winding up, and

    (b) the reference to section 17 of the Judgments Act 1838 has effect as a reference to the rules.

192 Information as to pending liquidations

(1) If the winding up of a company is not concluded within one year after its commencement, the liquidator shall, at such intervals as may be prescribed, until the winding up is concluded, send to the registrar of companies a statement in the prescribed form and containing the prescribed particulars with respect to the proceedings in, and position of, the liquidation.

(2) If a liquidator fails to comply with this section, he is liable to a fine and, for continued contravention, to a daily default fine.

195 Meetings to ascertain wishes of creditors or contributories

(1)   The court may—
   (a)   as to all matters relating to the winding up of a company, have regard to the wishes of the creditors or contributories (as proved to it by any sufficient evidence), and
   (b)   if it thinks fit, for the purpose of ascertaining those wishes, direct meetings of the creditors or contributories to be called, held and conducted in such manner as the court directs, and appoint a person to act as chairman of any such meeting and report the result of it to the court.

(2)   In the case of creditors, regard shall be had to the value of each creditor's debt.

(3)   In the case of contributories, regard shall be had to the number of votes conferred on each contributory by the Companies Act or the articles.

CHAPTER IX
DISSOLUTION OF COMPANIES AFTER WINDING UP

201 Dissolution (voluntary winding up)

(1)   This section applies, in the case of a company wound up voluntarily, where the liquidator has sent to the registrar of companies his final account and return under section 94 (members' voluntary) or section 106 (creditors' voluntary).

(2)   The registrar on receiving the account and return shall forthwith register them; and on the expiration of 3 months from the registration of the return the company is deemed to be dissolved.

(3)   However, the court may, on the application of the liquidator or any other person who appears to the court to be interested, make an order deferring the date at which the dissolution of the company is to take effect for such time as the court thinks fit.

(4)   It is the duty of the person on whose application an order of the court under this section is made within 7 days after the making of the order to deliver to the registrar an office copy of the order for registration; and if that person fails to do so he is liable to a fine and, for continued contravention, to a daily default fine.

202 Early dissolution (England and Wales)

(1)   This section applies where an order for the winding up of a company has been made by the court in England and Wales.

(2)   The official receiver, if—
   (a)   he is the liquidator of the company, and
   (b)   it appears to him—
      (i)   that the realisable assets of the company are insufficient to cover the expenses of the winding up, and
      (ii)   that the affairs of the company do not require any further investigation,

may at any time apply to the registrar of companies for the early dissolution of the company.

(3)   Before making that application, the official receiver shall give not less than 28 days' notice of his intention to do so to the company's creditors and contributories and, if there is an administrative receiver of the company, to that receiver.

(4)   With the giving of that notice the official receiver ceases (subject to any directions under the next section) to be required to perform any duties imposed on him in relation to the company, its creditors or contributories by virtue of any provision of this Act, apart from a duty to make an application under subsection (2) of this section.

(5)   On the receipt of the official receiver's application under subsection (2) the registrar shall forthwith register it and, at the end of the period of 3 months beginning with the day of the registration of the application, the company shall be dissolved.

However, the Secretary of State may, on the application of the official receiver or any other person who appears to the Secretary of State to be interested, give directions under section 203 at any time before the end of that period.

203 Consequence of notice under s 202

(1)   Where a notice has been given under section 202(3), the official receiver or any creditor or contributory of the company, or the administrative receiver of the company (if there is one) may apply to the Secretary of State for directions under this section.

(2)   The grounds on which that application may be made are—
 (a)   that the realisable assets of the company are sufficient to cover the expenses of the winding up;
 (b)   that the affairs of the company do require further investigation; or
 (c)   that for any other reason the early dissolution of the company is inappropriate.

(3)   Directions under this section—
 (a)   are directions making such provision as the Secretary of State thinks fit for enabling the winding up of the company to proceed as if no notice had been given under section 202(3), and
 (b)   may, in the case of an application under section 202(5), include a direction deferring the date at which the dissolution of the company is to take effect for such period as the Secretary of State thinks fit.

(4)   An appeal to the court lies from any decision of the Secretary of State on an application for directions under this section.

(5)   It is the duty of the person on whose application any directions are given under this section, or in whose favour an appeal with respect to an application for such directions is determined, within 7 days after the giving of the directions or the determination of the appeal, to deliver to the registrar of companies for registration such a copy of the directions or determination as is prescribed.

(6)   If a person without reasonable excuse fails to deliver a copy as required by subsection (5), he is liable to a fine and, for continued contravention, to a daily default fine.

205 Dissolution otherwise than under ss 202–204

(1)   This section applies where the registrar of companies receives—

   (a)   a notice served for the purposes of section 172(8) (final meeting of creditors and vacation of office by liquidator), or

   (b)   a notice from the official receiver that the winding up of a company by the court is complete.

(2)   The registrar shall, on receipt of the notice, forthwith register it; and, subject as follows, at the end of the period of 3 months beginning with the day of the registration of the notice, the company shall be dissolved.

(3)   The Secretary of State may, on the application of the official receiver or any other person who appears to the Secretary of State to be interested, give a direction deferring the date at which the dissolution of the company is to take effect for such period as the Secretary of State thinks fit.

(4)   An appeal to the court lies from any decision of the Secretary of State on an application for a direction under subsection (3).

(5)   Subsection (3) does not apply in a case where the winding-up order was made by the court in Scotland, but in such a case the court may, on an application by any person appearing to the court to have an interest, order that the date at which the dissolution of the company is to take effect shall be deferred for such period as the court thinks fit.

(6)   It is the duty of the person—

   (a)   on whose application a direction is given under subsection (3);

   (b)   in whose favour an appeal with respect to an application for such a direction is determined; or

   (c)   on whose application an order is made under subsection (5),

within 7 days after the giving of the direction, the determination of the appeal or the making of the order, to deliver to the registrar for registration such a copy of the direction, determination or order as is prescribed.

(7)   If a person without reasonable excuse fails to deliver a copy as required by subsection (6), he is liable to a fine and, for continued contravention to a daily default fine.

CHAPTER X
MALPRACTICE BEFORE AND DURING LIQUIDATION; PENALISATION OF COMPANIES AND COMPANY OFFICERS; INVESTIGATIONS AND PROSECUTIONS

Offences of fraud, deception, etc

206 Fraud, etc in anticipation of winding up

(1)   When a company is ordered to be wound up by the court, or passes a resolution for voluntary winding up, any person, being a past or present officer of

the company, is deemed to have committed an offence if, within the 12 months immediately preceding the commencement of the winding up, he has—

    (a) concealed any part of the company's property to the value of [£500] or more, or concealed any debt due to or from the company, or

    (b) fraudulently removed any part of the company's property to the value of [£500] or more, or

    (c) concealed, destroyed, mutilated or falsified any book or paper affecting or relating to the company's property or affairs, or

    (d) made any false entry in any book or paper affecting or relating to the company's property or affairs, or

    (e) fraudulently parted with, altered or made any omission in any document affecting or relating to the company's property or affairs, or

    (f) pawned, pledged or disposed of any property of the company which has been obtained on credit and has not been paid for (unless the pawning, pledging or disposal was in the ordinary way of the company's business).

(2)   Such a person is deemed to have committed an offence if within the period above mentioned he has been privy to the doing by others of any of the things mentioned in paragraphs (c), (d) and (e) of subsection (1); and he commits an offence if, at any time after the commencement of the winding up, he does any of the things mentioned in paragraphs (a) to (f) of that subsection, or is privy to the doing by others of any of the things mentioned in paragraphs (c) to (e) of it.

(3)   For purposes of this section, "officer" includes a shadow director.

(4)   It is a defence—

    (a) for a person charged under paragraph (a) or (f) of subsection (1) (or under subsection (2) in respect of the things mentioned in either of those two paragraphs) to prove that he had no intent to defraud, and

    (b) for a person charged under paragraph (c) or (d) of subsection (1) (or under subsection (2) in respect of the things mentioned in either of those two paragraphs) to prove that he had no intent to conceal the state of affairs of the company or to defeat the law.

(5)   Where a person pawns, pledges or disposes of any property in circumstances which amount to an offence under subsection (1)(f), every person who takes in pawn or pledge, or otherwise receives, the property knowing it to be pawned, pledged or disposed of in such circumstances, is guilty of an offence.

(6)   A person guilty of an offence under this section is liable to imprisonment or a fine, or both.

(7)   The money sums specified in paragraphs (a) and (b) of subsection (1) are subject to increase or reduction by order under section 416 in Part XV.

NOTES

Sub-s (1): in paras (a), (b) figures in square brackets substituted by SI 1986/1996, art 2, Schedule, Part I.

207 Transactions in fraud of creditors

(1)   When a company is ordered to be wound up by the court or passes a resolution for voluntary winding up, a person is deemed to have committed an offence if he, being at the time an officer of the company—
   (a)   has made or caused to be made any gift or transfer of, or charge on, or has caused or connived at the levying of any execution against, the company's property, or
   (b)   has concealed or removed any part of the company's property since, or within 2 months before, the date of any unsatisfied judgment or order for the payment of money obtained against the company.

(2)   A person is not guilty of an offence under this section—
   (a)   by reason of conduct constituting an offence under subsection (1)(a) which occurred more than 5 years before the commencement of the winding up, or
   (b)   if he proves that, at the time of the conduct constituting the offence, he had no intent to defraud the company's creditors.

(3)   A person guilty of an offence under this section is liable to imprisonment or a fine, or both.

208 Misconduct in course of winding up

(1)   When a company is being wound up, whether by the court or voluntarily, any person, being a past or present officer of the company, commits an offence if he—
   (a)   does not to the best of his knowledge and belief fully and truly discover to the liquidator all the company's property, and how and to whom and for what consideration and when the company disposed of any part of that property (except such part as has been disposed of in the ordinary way of the company's business), or
   (b)   does not deliver up to the liquidator (or as he directs) all such part of the company's property as is in his custody or under his control, and which he is required by law to deliver up, or
   (c)   does not deliver up to the liquidator (or as he directs) all books and papers in his custody or under his control belonging to the company and which he is required by law to deliver up, or
   (d)   knowing or believing that a false debt has been proved by any person in the winding up, fails to inform the liquidator as soon as practicable, or
   (e)   after the commencement of the winding up, prevents the production of any book or paper affecting or relating to the company's property or affairs.

(2)   Such a person commits an offence if after the commencement of the winding up he attempts to account for any part of the company's property by fictitious losses or expenses; and he is deemed to have committed that offence if he has so attempted at any meeting of the company's creditors within the 12 months immediately preceding the commencement of the winding up.

(3)   For purposes of this section, "officer" includes a shadow director.

(4)   It is a defence—

(a) for a person charged under paragraph (a), (b) or (c) of subsection (1) to prove that he had no intent to defraud, and

(b) for a person charged under paragraph (e) of that subsection to prove that he had no intent to conceal the state of affairs of the company or to defeat the law.

(5) A person guilty of an offence under this section is liable to imprisonment or a fine, or both.

209 Falsification of company's books

(1) When a company is being wound up, an officer or contributory of the company commits an offence if he destroys, mutilates, alters or falsifies any books, papers or securities, or makes or is privy to the making of any false or fraudulent entry in any register, book of account or document belonging to the company with intent to defraud or deceive any person.

(2) A person guilty of an offence under this section is liable to imprisonment or a fine, or both.

210 Material omissions from statement relating to company's affairs

(1) When a company is being wound up, whether by the court or voluntarily, any person, being a past or present officer of the company, commits an offence if he makes any material omission in any statement relating to the company's affairs.

(2) When a company has been ordered to be wound up by the court, or has passed a resolution for voluntary winding up, any such person is deemed to have committed that offence if, prior to the winding up, he has made any material omission in any such statement.

(3) For purposes of this section, "officer" includes a shadow director.

(4) It is a defence for a person charged under this section to prove that he had no intent to defraud.

(5) A person guilty of an offence under this section is liable to imprisonment or a fine, or both.

211 False representations to creditors

(1) When a company is being wound up, whether by the court or voluntarily, any person, being a past or present officer of the company—

(a) commits an offence if he makes any false representation or commits any other fraud for the purpose of obtaining the consent of the company's creditors or any of them to an agreement with reference to the company's affairs or to the winding up, and

(b) is deemed to have committed that offence if, prior to the winding up, he has made any false representation, or committed any other fraud, for that purpose.

(2) For purposes of this section, "officer" includes a shadow director.

(3)   A person guilty of an offence under this section is liable to imprisonment or a fine, or both.

Penalisation of directors and officers

212 Summary remedy against delinquent directors, liquidators, etc

(1)   This section applies if in the course of the winding up of a company it appears that a person who—

(a)   is or has been an officer of the company,

(b)   has acted as liquidator, administrator or administrative receiver of the company, or

(c)   not being a person falling within paragraph (a) or (b), is or has been concerned, or has taken part, in the promotion, formation or management of the company,

has misapplied or retained, or become accountable for, any money or other property of the company, or been guilty of any misfeasance or breach of any fiduciary or other duty in relation to the company.

(2)   The reference in subsection (1) to any misfeasance or breach of any fiduciary or other duty in relation to the company includes, in the case of a person who has acted as liquidator or administrator of the company, any misfeasance or breach of any fiduciary or other duty in connection with the carrying out of his functions as liquidator or administrator of the company.

(3)   The court may, on the application of the official receiver or the liquidator, or of any creditor or contributory, examine into the conduct of the person falling within subsection (1) and compel him—

(a)   to repay, restore or account for the money or property or any part of it, with interest at such rate as the court thinks just, or

(b)   to contribute such sum to the company's assets by way of compensation in respect of the misfeasance or breach of fiduciary or other duty as the court thinks just.

(4)   The power to make an application under subsection (3) in relation to a person who has acted as liquidator or administrator of the company is not exercisable, except with the leave of the court, after that person has had his release.

(5)   The power of a contributory to make an application under subsection (3) is not exercisable except with the leave of the court, but is exercisable notwithstanding that he will not benefit from any order the court may make on the application.

213 Fraudulent trading

(1)   If in the course of the winding up of a company it appears that any business of the company has been carried on with intent to defraud creditors of the company or creditors of any other person, or for any fraudulent purpose, the following has effect.

(2)   The court, on the application of the liquidator may declare that any persons who were knowingly parties to the carrying on of the business in the manner

above-mentioned are to be liable to make such contributions (if any) to the company's assets as the court thinks proper.

214 Wrongful trading

(1) Subject to subsection (3) below, if in the course of the winding up of a company it appears that subsection (2) of this section applies in relation to a person who is or has been a director of the company, the court, on the application of the liquidator, may declare that that person is to be liable to make such contribution (if any) to the company's assets as the court thinks proper.

(2) This subsection applies in relation to a person if—
  (a) the company has gone into insolvent liquidation,
  (b) at some time before the commencement of the winding up of the company, that person knew or ought to have concluded that there was no reasonable prospect that the company would avoid going into insolvent liquidation, and
  (c) that person was a director of the company at that time;

but the court shall not make a declaration under this section in any case where the time mentioned in paragraph (b) above was before 28th April 1986.

(3) The court shall not make a declaration under this section with respect to any person if it is satisfied that after the condition specified in subsection (2)(b) was first satisfied in relation to him that person took every step with a view to minimising the potential loss to the company's creditors as (assuming him to have known that there was no reasonable prospect that the company would avoid going into insolvent liquidation) he ought to have taken.

(4) For the purposes of subsections (2) and (3), the facts which a director of a company ought to know or ascertain, the conclusions which he ought to reach and the steps which he ought to take are those which would be known or ascertained, or reached or taken, by a reasonably diligent person having both—
  (a) the general knowledge, skill and experience that may reasonably be expected of a person carrying out the same functions as are carried out by that director in relation to the company, and
  (b) the general knowledge, skill and experience that that director has.

(5) The reference in subsection (4) to the functions carried out in relation to a company by a director of the company includes any functions which he does not carry out but which have been entrusted to him.

(6) For the purposes of this section a company goes into insolvent liquidation if it goes into liquidation at a time when its assets are insufficient for the payment of its debts and other liabilities and the expenses of the winding up.

(7) In this section "director" includes a shadow director.

(8) This section is without prejudice to section 213.

215 Proceedings under ss 213, 214

(1) On the hearing of an application under section 213 or 214, the liquidator may himself give evidence or call witnesses.

(2)   Where under either section the court makes a declaration, it may give such further directions as it thinks proper for giving effect to the declaration; and in particular, the court may—

    (a) provide for the liability of any person under the declaration to be a charge on any debt or obligation due from the company to him, or on any mortgage or charge or any interest in a mortgage or charge on assets of the company held by or vested in him, or any person on his behalf, or any person claiming as assignee from or through the person liable or any person acting on his behalf, and

    (b) from time to time make such further order as may be necessary for enforcing any charge imposed under this subsection.

(3)   For the purposes of subsection (2), "assignee"—

    (a) includes a person to whom or in whose favour, by the directions of the person made liable, the debt, obligation, mortgage or charge was created, issued or transferred or the interest created, but

    (b) does not include an assignee for valuable consideration (not including consideration by way of marriage) given in good faith and without notice of any of the matters on the ground of which the declaration is made.

(4)   Where the court makes a declaration under either section in relation to a person who is a creditor of the company, it may direct that the whole or any part of any debt owed by the company to that person and any interest thereon shall rank in priority after all other debts owed by the company and after any interest on those debts.

(5)   Sections 213 and 214 have effect notwithstanding that the person concerned may be criminally liable in respect of matters on the ground of which the declaration under the section is to be made.

216 Restriction on re-use of company names

(1)   This section applies to a person where a company ("the liquidating company") has gone into insolvent liquidation on or after the appointed day and he was a director or shadow director of the company at any time in the period of 12 months ending with the day before it went into liquidation.

(2)   For the purposes of this section, a name is a prohibited name in relation to such a person if—

    (a) it is a name by which the liquidating company was known at any time in that period of 12 months, or

    (b) it is a name which is so similar to a name falling within paragraph (a) as to suggest an association with that company.

(3)   Except with leave of the court or in such circumstances as may be prescribed, a person to whom this section applies shall not at any time in the period of 5 years beginning with the day on which the liquidating company went into liquidation—

    (a) be a director of any other company that is known by a prohibited name, or

    (b) in any way, whether directly or indirectly, be concerned or take part in the promotion, formation or management of any such company, or

(c) in any way, whether directly or indirectly, be concerned or take part in the carrying on of a business carried on (otherwise than by a company) under a prohibited name.

(4) If a person acts in contravention of this section, he is liable to imprisonment or a fine, or both.

(5) In subsection (3) "the court" means any court having jurisdiction to wind up companies; and on an application for leave under that subsection, the Secretary of State or the official receiver may appear and call the attention of the court to any matters which seem to him to be relevant.

(6) References in this section, in relation to any time, to a name by which a company is known are to the name of the company at that time or to any name under which the company carries on business at that time.

(7) For the purposes of this section a company goes into insolvent liquidation if it goes into liquidation at a time when its assets are insufficient for the payment of its debts and other liabilities and the expenses of the winding up.

(8) In this section "company" includes a company which may be wound up under Part V of this Act.

217 Personal liability for debts, following contravention of s 216

(1) A person is personally responsible for all the relevant debts of a company if at any time—
  (a) in contravention of section 216, he is involved in the management of the company, or
  (b) as a person who is involved in the management of the company, he acts or is willing to act on instructions given (without the leave of the court) by a person whom he knows at that time to be in contravention in relation to the company of section 216.

(2) Where a person is personally responsible under this section for the relevant debts of a company, he is jointly and severally liable in respect of those debts with the company and any other person who, whether under this section or otherwise, is so liable.

(3) For the purposes of this section the relevant debts of a company are—
  (a) in relation to a person who is personally responsible under paragraph (a) of subsection (1), such debts and other liabilities of the company as are incurred at a time when that person was involved in the management of the company, and
  (b) in relation to a person who is personally responsible under paragraph (b) of that subsection, such debts and other liabilities of the company as are incurred at a time when that person was acting or was willing to act on instructions given as mentioned in that paragraph.

(4) For the purposes of this section, a person is involved in the management of a company if he is a director of the company or if he is concerned, whether directly or indirectly, or takes part, in the management of the company.

(5)   For the purposes of this section a person who, as a person involved in the management of a company, has at any time acted on instructions given (without the leave of the court) by a person whom he knew at that time to be in contravention in relation to the company of section 216 is presumed, unless the contrary is shown, to have been willing at any time thereafter to act on any instructions given by that person.

(6)   In this section "company" includes a company which may be wound up under Part V.

Investigation and prosecution of malpractice

218   Prosecution of delinquent officers and members of company

(1)   If it appears to the court in the course of a winding up by the court that any past or present officer, or any member, of the company has been guilty of any offence in relation to the company for which he is criminally liable, the court may (either on the application of a person interested in the winding up or of its own motion) direct the liquidator to refer the matter
  [(a)   in the case of a winding up in England and Wales, to the Secretary of State, and
  (b)   in the case of a winding up in Scotland, to the Lord Advocate].

(2)   . . .

(3)   If in the case of a winding up by the court in England and Wales it appears to the liquidator, not being the official receiver, that any past or present officer of the company, or any member of it, has been guilty of an offence in relation to the company for which he is criminally liable, the liquidator shall report the matter to the official receiver.

(4)   If it appears to the liquidator in the course of a voluntary winding up that any past or present officer of the company, or any member of it, has been guilty of an offence in relation to the company for which he is criminally liable, he shall [forthwith report the matter—
  (a)   in the case of a winding up in England and Wales, to the Secretary of State, and
  (b)   in the case of a winding up in Scotland, to the Lord Advocate,

and shall furnish to the Secretary of State or (as the case may be) the Lord Advocate] such information and give to him such access to and facilities for inspecting and taking copies of documents (being information or documents in the possession or under the control of the liquidator and relating to the matter in question) as [the Secretary of State or (as the case may be) the Lord Advocate] requires.

[(5)   Where a report is made to the Secretary of State under subsection (4) he may, for the purpose of investigating the matter reported to him and such other matters relating to the affairs of the company as appear to him to require investigation, exercise any of the powers which are exercisable by inspectors appointed under section 431 or 432 of the Companies Act to investigate a company's affairs.]

(6) If it appears to the court in the course of a voluntary winding up that—

    (a) any past or present officer of the company, or any member of it, has been guilty as above-mentioned, and

    (b) no report with respect to the matter has been made by the liquidator . . . under subsection (4),

the court may (on the application of any person interested in the winding up or of its own motion) direct the liquidator to make such a report.

On a report being made accordingly, this section has effect as though the report had been made in pursuance of subsection (4).

NOTES

Sub-s (1): paras (a), (b) substituted by the Insolvency Act 2000, s 10(1), (2).

Date in force: 2 April 2001 (except where a court has directed a liquidator to refer a matter under sub-s (1) hereof before that date): see SI 2001/766, arts 2(1)(b), 3(4)(a).

Sub-s (2): repealed by the Insolvency Act 2000, ss 10(1), (3), 15(1), Sch 5.

Date in force: 2 April 2001 (except where a court has directed a liquidator to refer a matter, a liquidator has reported a matter or a court has directed a liquidator to make a report under sub-ss (1), (4), (6) hereof before that date): see SI 2001/766, arts 2(1)(b), (c)(i), 3(4).

Sub-s (4): words from "forthwith report the" to "the Lord Advocate" in square brackets substituted by the Insolvency Act 2000, s 10(1), (4)(a).

Date in force: 2 April 2001 (except where a liquidator has reported a matter under sub-s (4) hereof before that date): see SI 2001/766, arts 2(1)(b), 3(4)(b).

Sub-s (4): words "the Secretary of State or (as the case may be) the Lord Advocate" in square brackets substituted by the Insolvency Act 2000, s 10(1), (4)(b).

Date in force: 2 April 2001 (except where a liquidator has reported a matter under sub-s (4) hereof before that date): see SI 2001/766, arts 2(1)(b), 3(4)(b).

Sub-s (5): substituted by the Insolvency Act 2000, s 10(1), (5).

Date in force: 2 April 2001 (except where a liquidator has reported a matter under sub-s (4) hereof before that date): see SI 2001/766, arts 2(1)(b), 3(4)(b).

Sub-s (6): in para (b) words omitted repealed by the Insolvency Act 2000, ss 10(1), (6), 15(1), Sch 5.

Date in force: 2 April 2001 (except where a court has directed a liquidator to make a report under sub-s (6) hereof before that date): see SI 2001/766, arts 2(1)(b), (c)(i), 3(4)(c).

219 Obligations arising under s 218

(1) For the purpose of an investigation by the Secretary of State [in consequence of a report made to him under section 218(4)], any obligation imposed on a person by any provision of the Companies Act to produce documents or give information to, or otherwise to assist, inspectors appointed as mentioned in [section 218(5)] is to be regarded as an obligation similarly to assist the Secretary of State in his investigation.

(2) An answer given by a person to a question put to him in exercise of the powers conferred by section 218(5) may be used in evidence against him.

[(2A) However, in criminal proceedings in which that person is charged with an offence to which this subsection applies—

    (a) no evidence relating to the answer may be adduced, and

    (b) no question relating to it may be asked,

by or on behalf of the prosecution, unless evidence relating to it is adduced, or a question relating to it is asked, in the proceedings by or on behalf of that person.

(2B)   Subsection (2A) applies to any offence other than—

    (a)   an offence under section 2 or 5 of the Perjury Act 1911 (false statements made on oath otherwise than in judicial proceedings or made otherwise than on oath), or

    (b)   an offence under section 44(1) or (2) of the Criminal Law (Consolidation) (Scotland) Act 1995 (false statements made on oath or otherwise than on oath).]

(3)   Where criminal proceedings are instituted by [the Director of Public Prosecutions, the Lord Advocate] or the Secretary of State following any report or reference under section 218, it is the duty of the liquidator and every officer and agent of the company past and present (other than the defendant or defender) to give to [the Director of Public Prosecutions, the Lord Advocate] or the Secretary of State (as the case may be) all assistance in connection with the prosecution which he is reasonably able to give.

For this purpose "agent" includes any banker or solicitor of the company and any person employed by the company as auditor, whether that person is or is not an officer of the company.

(4)   If a person fails or neglects to give assistance in the manner required by subsection (3), the court may, on the application of the [Director of Public Prosecutions, the Lord Advocate] or the Secretary of State (as the case may be) direct the person to comply with that subsection; and if the application is made with respect to a liquidator, the court may (unless it appears that the failure or neglect to comply was due to the liquidator not having in his hands sufficient assets of the company to enable him to do so) direct that the costs shall be borne by the liquidator personally.

NOTES

Sub-s (1): words "in consequence of a report made to him under section 218(4)" in square brackets substituted by the Insolvency Act 2000, s 10(1), (7)(a).

Date in force: 2 April 2001: see SI 2001/766, art 2(1)(b).

Sub-s (1): words "section 218(5)" in square brackets substituted by the Insolvency Act 2000, s 10(1), (7)(a).

Date in force: 2 April 2001: see SI 2001/766, art 2(1)(b).

Sub-ss (2A), (2B): inserted by the Insolvency Act 2000, s 11.

Date in force: 2 April 2001: see SI 2001/766, art 2(1)(b).

Sub-s (3): words "the Director of Public Prosecutions, the Lord Advocate" in square brackets substituted by the Insolvency Act 2000, s 10(1), (7)(b).

Date in force: 2 April 2001: see SI 2001/766, art 2(1)(b).

Sub-s (3): words "the Director of Public Prosecutions, the Lord Advocate" in square brackets substituted by the Insolvency Act 2000, s 10(1), (7)(b).

Date in force: 2 April 2001: see SI 2001/766, art 2(1)(b).

Sub-s (4): words "Director of Public Prosecutions, the Lord Advocate" in square brackets substituted by the Insolvency Act 2000, s 10(1), (7)(c).

Date in force: 2 April 2001: see SI 2001/766, art 2(1)(b).

PART VI

MISCELLANEOUS PROVISIONS APPLYING TO COMPANIES WHICH ARE INSOLVENT OR IN LIQUIDATION

Office-holders

230 Holders of office to be qualified insolvency practitioners

(1) Where an administration order is made in relation to a company, the administrator must be a person who is qualified to act as an insolvency practitioner in relation to the company.

(2) Where an administrative receiver of a company is appointed, he must be a person who is so qualified.

(3) Where a company goes into liquidation, the liquidator must be a person who is so qualified.

(4) Where a provisional liquidator is appointed, he must be a person who is so qualified.

(5) Subsections (3) and (4) are without prejudice to any enactment under which the official receiver is to be, or may be, liquidator or provisional liquidator.

232 Validity of office-holder's acts

The acts of an individual as administrator, administrative receiver, liquidator or provisional liquidator of a company are valid notwithstanding any defect in his appointment, nomination or qualifications.

Management by administrators, liquidators, etc

233 Supplies of gas, water, electricity, etc

(1) This section applies in the case of a company where—
   (a) an administration order is made in relation to the company, or
   (b) an administrative receiver is appointed, or
   [(ba) a moratorium under section 1A is in force, or]
   (c) a voluntary arrangement *under Part I, approved by meetings summoned under section 3* [approved under Part I], has taken effect, or
   (d) the company goes into liquidation, or
   (e) a provisional liquidator is appointed;

and "the office-holder" means the administrator, the administrative receiver, [the nominee,] the supervisor of the voluntary arrangement, the liquidator or the provisional liquidator, as the case may be.

(2) If a request is made by or with the concurrence of the office-holder for the giving, after the effective date, of any of the supplies mentioned in the next subsection, the supplier—

(a)   may make it a condition of the giving of the supply that the office-holder personally guarantees the payment of any charges in respect of the supply, but

(b)   shall not make it a condition of the giving of the supply, or do anything which has the effect of making it a condition of the giving of the supply, that any outstanding charges in respect of a supply given to the company before the effective date are paid.

(3)   The supplies referred to in subsection (2) are—

[(a) a supply of gas by a gas supplier within the meaning of Part I of the Gas Act 1986;]

[(b) a supply of electricity by an electricity supplier within the meaning of Part I of the Electricity Act 1989;]

(c)   a supply of water by [a water undertaker] or, in Scotland, a water authority,

(d)   a supply of telecommunication services by a public telecommunications operator.

(4)   "The effective date" for the purposes of this section is whichever is applicable of the following dates—

(a)   the date on which the administration order was made,

(b)   the date on which the administrative receiver was appointed (or, if he was appointed in succession to another administrative receiver, the date on which the first of his predecessors was appointed),

[(ba) the date on which the moratorium came into force]

(c)   the date on which the voluntary arrangement *was approved by the meetings summoned under section 3* [took effect],

(d)   the date on which the company went into liquidation,

(e)   the date on which the provisional liquidator was appointed.

(5)   The following applies to expressions used in subsection (3)—

(a)   . . .

(b)   . . .

(c)   "water authority" means the same as in the Water (Scotland) Act 1980, and

(d)   "telecommunication services" and "public telecommunications operator" mean the same as in the Telecommunications Act 1984, except that the former does not include [local delivery services within the meaning of Part II of the Broadcasting Act 1990.]

NOTES

Sub-s (1): para (ba) inserted by the Insolvency Act 2000, s 1, Sch 1, paras 1, 8(1), (2)(a).
Date in force: to be appointed: see the Insolvency Act 2000, s 16(1).
Sub-s (1): in para (c) words "under Part I, approved by meetings summoned under section 3" in italics repealed and subsequent words in square brackets substituted by the Insolvency Act 2000, s 1, Sch 1, paras 1, 8(1), (2)(b).
Date in force: to be appointed: see the Insolvency Act 2000, s 16(1).
Sub-s (1): words "the nominee," in square brackets inserted by the Insolvency Act 2000, s 1, Sch 1, paras 1, 8(1), (2)(c).
Date in force: to be appointed: see the Insolvency Act 2000, s 16(1).
Sub-s (3): para (a) substituted by the Gas Act 1995, s 16(1), Sch 4, para 14(1).
Sub-s (3): para (b) substituted by the Utilities Act 2000, s 108, Sch 6, Pt III, para 47(1), (2)(a).

Date in force: 1 October 2001: see SI 2001/3266, art 2, Schedule.

Sub-s (3): in para (c) words "a water undertaker" in square brackets substituted by the Water Act 1989, s 190, Sch 25, para 78.

Sub-s (4): para (ba) inserted by the Insolvency Act 2000, s 1, Sch 1, paras 1, 8(1), (3)(a).

Date in force: to be appointed: see the Insolvency Act 2000, s 16(1).

Sub-s (4): in para (c) words "was approved by the meetings summoned under section 3" in italics repealed and subsequent words in square brackets substituted by the Insolvency Act 2000, s 1, Sch 1, paras 1, 8(1), (3)(b).

Date in force: to be appointed: see the Insolvency Act 2000, s 16(1).

Sub-s (5): para (a) repealed by the Gas Act 1995, ss 16(1), 17(5), Sch 4, para 14(2), Sch 6.

Sub-s (5): para (b) repealed by the Utilities Act 2000, s 108, Sch 6, Pt III, para 47(1), (2)(b), Sch 8.

Date in force: 1 October 2001: see SI 2001/3266, art 2, Schedule.

Sub-s (5): in para (d) words "local delivery services within the meaning of Part II of the Broadcasting Act 1990." in square brackets substituted by the Broadcasting Act 1990, s 203(1), Sch 20, para 43.

234 Getting in the company's property

(1)   This section applies in the case of a company where—
  (a)   an administration order is made in relation to the company, or
  (b)   an administrative receiver is appointed, or
  (c)   the company goes into liquidation, or
  (d)   a provisional liquidator is appointed;

and "the office-holder" means the administrator, the administrative receiver, the liquidator or the provisional liquidator, as the case may be.

(2)   Where any person has in his possession or control any property, books, papers or records to which the company appears to be entitled, the court may require that person forthwith (or within such period as the court may direct) to pay, deliver, convey, surrender or transfer the property, books, papers or records to the office-holder.

(3)   Where the office-holder—
  (a)   seizes or disposes of any property which is not property of the company, and
  (b)   at the time of seizure or disposal believes, and has reasonable grounds for believing, that he is entitled (whether in pursuance of an order of the court or otherwise) to seize or dispose of that property,

the next subsection has effect.

(4)   In that case the office-holder—
  (a)   is not liable to any person in respect of any loss or damage resulting from the seizure or disposal except in so far as that loss or damage is caused by the office-holder's own negligence, and
  (b)   has a lien on the property, or the proceeds of its sale, for such expenses as were incurred in connection with the seizure or disposal.

235 Duty to co-operate with office-holder

(1)   This section applies as does section 234; and it also applies, in the case of a company in respect of which a winding-up order has been made by the court in

England and Wales, as if references to the office-holder included the official receiver, whether or not he is the liquidator.

(2)   Each of the persons mentioned in the next subsection shall—

  (a)   give to the office-holder such information concerning the company and its promotion, formation, business, dealings, affairs or property as the office-holder may at any time after the effective date reasonably require, and

  (b)   attend on the office-holder at such times as the latter may reasonably require.

(3)   The persons referred to above are—

  (a)   those who are or have at any time been officers of the company,

  (b)   those who have taken part in the formation of the company at any time within one year before the effective date,

  (c)   those who are in the employment of the company, or have been in its employment (including employment under a contract for services) within that year, and are in the office-holder's opinion capable of giving information which he requires,

  (d)   those who are, or have within that year been, officers of, or in the employment (including employment under a contract for services) of, another company which is, or within that year was, an officer of the company in question, and

  (e)   in the case of a company being wound up by the court, any person who has acted as administrator, administrative receiver or liquidator of the company.

(4)   For the purposes of subsections (2) and (3), "the effective date" is whichever is applicable of the following dates—

  (a)   the date on which the administration order was made,

  (b)   the date on which the administrative receiver was appointed or, if he was appointed in succession to another administrative receiver, the date on which the first of his predecessors was appointed,

  (c)   the date on which the provisional liquidator was appointed, and

  (d)   the date on which the company went into liquidation.

(5)   If a person without reasonable excuse fails to comply with any obligation imposed by this section, he is liable to a fine and, for contravention, to a daily default fine.

236   Inquiry into company's dealings, etc

(1)   This section applies as does section 234; and it also applies in the case of a company in respect of which a winding-up order has been made by the court in England and Wales as if references to the office-holder included the official receiver, whether or not he is the liquidator.

(2)   The court may, on the application of the office-holder, summon to appear before it—

  (a)   any officer of the company,

  (b)   any person known or suspected to have in his possession any property of the company or supposed to be indebted to the company, or

(c) any person whom the court thinks capable of giving information concerning the promotion, formation, business, dealings, affairs or property of the company.

(3) The court may require any such person as is mentioned in subsection (2)(a) to (c) to submit an affidavit to the court containing an account of his dealings with the company or to produce any books, papers or other records in his possession or under his control relating to the company or the matters mentioned in paragraph (c) of the subsection.

(4) The following applies in a case where—
  (a) a person without reasonable excuse fails to appear before the court when he is summoned to do so under this section, or
  (b) there are reasonable grounds for believing that a person has absconded, or is about to abscond, with a view to avoiding his appearance before the court under this section.

(5) The court may, for the purpose of bringing that person and anything in his possession before the court, cause a warrant to be issued to a constable or prescribed officer of the court—
  (a) for the arrest of that person, and
  (b) for the seizure of any books, papers, records, money or goods in that person's possession.

(6) The court may authorise a person arrested under such a warrant to be kept in custody, and anything seized under such a warrant to be held, in accordance with the rules, until that person is brought before the court under the warrant or until such other time as the court may order.

237 Court's enforcement powers under s 236

(1) If it appears to the court, on consideration of any evidence obtained under section 236 or this section, that any person has in his possession any property of the company, the court may, on the application of the office-holder, order that person to deliver the whole or any part of the property to the office-holder at such time, in such manner and on such terms as the court thinks fit.

(2) If it appears to the court, on consideration of any evidence so obtained, that any person is indebted to the company, the court may, on the application of the office-holder, order that person to pay to the office-holder, at such time and in such manner as the court may direct, the whole or any part of the amount due, whether in full discharge of the debt or otherwise, as the court thinks fit.

(3) The court may, if it thinks fit, order that any person who if within the jurisdiction of the court would be liable to be summoned to appear before it under section 236 or this section shall be examined in any part of the United Kingdom where he may for the time being be, or in a place outside the United Kingdom.

(4) Any person who appears or is brought before the court under section 236 or this section may be examined on oath, either orally or (except in Scotland) by interrogatories, concerning the company or the matters mentioned in section 236(2)(c).

Adjustment of prior transactions (administration and liquidation)

238 Transactions at an undervalue (England and Wales)

(1)   This section applies in the case of a company where—

  (a)   an administration order is made in relation to the company, or

  (b)   the company goes into liquidation;

and "the office-holder" means the administrator or the liquidator, as the case may be.

(2)   Where the company has at a relevant time (defined in section 240) entered into a transaction with any person at an undervalue, the office-holder may apply to the court for an order under this section.

(3)   Subject as follows, the court shall, on such an application, make such order as it thinks fit for restoring the position to what it would have been if the company had not entered into that transaction.

(4)   For the purposes of this section and section 241, a company enters into a transaction with a person at an undervalue if—

  (a)   the company makes a gift to that person or otherwise enters into a transaction with that person on terms that provide for the company to receive no consideration, or

  (b)   the company enters into a transaction with that person for a consideration the value of which, in money or money's worth, is significantly less than the value, in money or money's worth, of the consideration provided by the company.

(5)   The court shall not make an order under this section in respect of a transaction at an undervalue if it is satisfied—

  (a)   that the company which entered into the transaction did so in good faith and for the purpose of carrying on its business, and

  (b)   that at the time it did so there were reasonable grounds for believing that the transaction would benefit the company.

239 Preferences (England and Wales)

(1)   This section applies as does section 238.

(2)   Where the company has at a relevant time (defined in the next section) given a preference to any person, the office-holder may apply to the court for an order under this section.

(3)   Subject as follows, the court shall, on such an application, make such order as it thinks fit for restoring the position to what it would have been if the company had not given that preference.

(4)   For the purposes of this section and section 241, a company gives a preference to a person if—

  (a)   that person is one of the company's creditors or a surety or guarantor for any of the company's debts or other liabilities, and

(b) the company does anything or suffers anything to be done which (in either case) has the effect of putting that person into a position which, in the event of the company going into insolvent liquidation, will be better than the position he would have been in if that thing had not been done.

(5)   The court shall not make an order under this section in respect of a preference given to any person unless the company which gave the preference was influenced in deciding to give it by a desire to produce in relation to that person the effect mentioned in subsection (4)(b).

(6)   A company which has given a preference to a person connected with the company (otherwise than by reason only of being its employee) at the time the preference was given is presumed, unless the contrary is shown, to have been influenced in deciding to give it by such a desire as is mentioned in subsection (5).

(7)   The fact that something has been done in pursuance of the order of a court does not, without more, prevent the doing or suffering of that thing from constituting the giving of a preference.

240 "Relevant time" under ss 238, 239

(1)   Subject to the next subsection, the time at which a company enters into a transaction at an undervalue or gives a preference is a relevant time if the transaction is entered into, or the preference given—
(a)   in the case of a transaction at an undervalue or of a preference which is given to a person who is connected with the company (otherwise than by reason only of being its employee), at a time in the period of 2 years ending with the onset of insolvency (which expression is defined below),
(b)   in the case of a preference which is not such a transaction and is not so given, at a time in the period of 6 months ending with the onset of insolvency, and
(c)   in either case, at a time between the presentation of a petition for the making of an administration order in relation to the company and the making of such an order on that petition.

(2)   Where a company enters into a transaction at an undervalue or gives a preference at a time mentioned in subsection (1)(a) or (b), that time is not a relevant time for the purposes of section 238 or 239 unless the company—
(a)   is at that time unable to pay its debts within the meaning of section 123 in Chapter VI of Part IV, or
(b)   becomes unable to pay its debts within the meaning of that section in consequence of the transaction or preference;

but the requirements of this subsection are presumed to be satisfied, unless the contrary is shown, in relation to any transaction at an undervalue which is entered into by a company with a person who is connected with the company.

(3)   For the purposes of subsection (1), the onset of insolvency is—
(a)   in a case where section 238 or 239 applies by reason of the making of an administration order or of a company going into liquidation immediately upon the discharge of an administration order, the date of the presentation of the petition on which the administration order was made,

[(aa) in a case where section 238 or 239 applies by reason of a company going into liquidation following conversion of administration into winding up by virtue of Article 37 of the EC Regulation, the date of the presentation of the petition on which the administration order was made,] and

(b) in a case where the section applies by reason of a company going into liquidation at any other time, the date of the commencement of the winding up.

NOTES

Sub-s (3): para (aa) inserted by SI 2002/1240, regs 3, 11.
Date in force: 31 May 2002: see SI 2002/1240, reg 1.

241 Orders under ss 238, 239

(1) Without prejudice to the generality of sections 238(3) and 239(3), an order under either of those sections with respect to a transaction or preference entered into or given by a company may (subject to the next subsection)—

(a) require any property transferred as part of the transaction, or in connection with the giving of the preference, to be vested in the company,

(b) require any property to be so vested if it represents in any person's hands the application either of the proceeds of sale of property so transferred or of money so transferred,

(c) release or discharge (in whole or in part) any security given by the company,

(d) require any person to pay, in respect of benefits received by him from the company, such sums to the office-holder as the court may direct,

(e) provide for any surety or guarantor whose obligations to any person were released or discharged (in whole or in part) under the transaction, or by the giving of the preference, to be under such new or revived obligations to that person as the court thinks appropriate,

(f) provide for security to be provided for the discharge of any obligation imposed by or arising under the order, for such an obligation to be charged on any property and for the security or charge to have the same priority as a security or charge released or discharged (in whole or in part) under the transaction or by the giving of the preference, and

(g) provide for the extent to which any person whose property is vested by the order in the company, or on whom obligations are imposed by the order, is to be able to prove in the winding up of the company for debts or other liabilities which arose from, or were released or discharged (in whole or in part) under or by, the transaction or the giving of the preference.

(2) An order under section 238 or 239 may affect the property of, or impose any obligation on, any person whether or not he is the person with whom the company in question entered into the transaction or (as the case may be) the person to whom the preference was given; but such an order—

(a) shall not prejudice any interest in property which was acquired from a person other than the company and was acquired [in good faith and for value], or prejudice any interest deriving from such an interest, and

(b) shall not require a person who received a benefit from the transaction or preference [in good faith and for value] to pay a sum to the office-holder, except where that person was a party to the transaction or the payment is to be in respect of a preference given to that person at a time when he was a creditor of the company.

[(2A)   Where a person has acquired an interest in property from a person other than the company in question, or has received a benefit from the transaction or preference, and at the time of that acquisition or receipt—
- (a)   he had notice of the relevant surrounding circumstances and of the relevant proceedings, or
- (b)   he was connected with, or was an associate of, either the company in question or the person with whom that company entered into the transaction or to whom that company gave the preference,

then, unless the contrary is shown, it shall be presumed for the purposes of paragraph (a) or (as the case may be) paragraph (b) of subsection (2) that the interest was acquired or the benefit was received otherwise than in good faith.]

[(3)   For the purposes of subsection (2A)(a), the relevant surrounding circumstances are (as the case may require)—
- (a)   the fact that the company in question entered into the transaction at an undervalue; or
- (b)   the circumstances which amounted to the giving of the preference by the company in question;

and subsections (3A) to (3C) have effect to determine whether, for those purposes, a person has notice of the relevant proceedings.

(3A)   In a case where section 238 or 239 applies by reason of the making of an administration order, a person has notice of the relevant proceedings if he has notice—
- (a)   of the fact that the petition on which the administration order is made has been presented; or
- (b)   of the fact that the administration order has been made.

(3B)   In a case where section 238 or 239 applies by reason of the company in question going into liquidation immediately upon the discharge of an administration order, a person has notice of the relevant proceedings if he has notice—
- (a)   of the fact that the petition on which the administration order is made has been presented;
- (b)   of the fact that the administration order has been made; or
- (c)   of the fact that the company has gone into liquidation.

(3C)   In a case where section 238 or 239 applies by reason of the company in question going into liquidation at any other time, a person has notice of the relevant proceedings if he has notice—
- (a)   where the company goes into liquidation on the making of a winding-up order, of the fact that the petition on which the winding-up order is made has been presented or of the fact that the company has gone into liquidation;
- (b)   in any other case, of the fact that the company has gone into liquidation.]

(4)   The provisions of sections 238 to 241 apply without prejudice to the availability of any other remedy, even in relation to a transaction or preference which the company had no power to enter into or give.

NOTES

Sub-s (2): words in square brackets substituted by the Insolvency (No 2) Act 1994, s 1(1).
Sub-s (2A): inserted by the Insolvency (No 2) Act 1994, s 1(2).
Sub-ss (3)–(3C): substituted for sub-s (3) as originally enacted, by the Insolvency (No 2) Act 1994, s 1(3).

244 Extortionate credit transactions

(1)   This section applies as does section 238, and where the company is, or has been, a party to a transaction for, or involving, the provision of credit to the company.

(2)   The court may, on the application of the office-holder, make an order with respect to the transaction if the transaction is or was extortionate and was entered into in the period of 3 years ending with the day on which the administration order was made or (as the case may be) the company went into liquidation.

(3)   For the purposes of this section a transaction is extortionate if, having regard to the risk accepted by the person providing the credit—

  (a)   the terms of it are or were such as to require grossly exorbitant payments to be made (whether unconditionally or in certain contingencies) in respect of the provision of the credit, or

  (b)   it otherwise grossly contravened ordinary principles of fair dealing;

and it shall be presumed, unless the contrary is proved, that a transaction with respect to which an application is made under this section is or, as the case may be, was extortionate.

(4)   An order under this section with respect to any transaction may contain such one or more of the following as the court thinks fit, that is to say—

  (a)   provision setting aside the whole or part of any obligation created by the transaction,

  (b)   provision otherwise varying the terms of the transaction or varying the terms on which any security for the purposes of the transaction is held,

  (c)   provision requiring any person who is or was a party to the transaction to pay to the office-holder any sums paid to that person, by virtue of the transaction, by the company,

  (d)   provision requiring any person to surrender to the office-holder any property held by him as security for the purposes of the transaction,

  (e)   provision directing accounts to be taken between any persons.

(5)   The powers conferred by this section are exercisable in relation to any transaction concurrently with any powers exercisable in relation to that transaction as a transaction at an undervalue or under section 242 (gratuitous alienations in Scotland).

PART VI

MISCELLANEOUS PROVISIONS APPLYING TO COMPANIES WHICH ARE
INSOLVENT OR IN LIQUIDATION

Adjustment of prior transactions (administration and liquidation)

245 Avoidance of certain floating charges

(1)   This section applies as does section 238, but applies to Scotland as well as to England and Wales.

(2)   Subject as follows, a floating charge on the company's undertaking or property created at a relevant time is invalid except to the extent of the aggregate of—

(a)   the value of so much of the consideration for the creation of the charge as consists of money paid, or goods or services supplied, to the company at the same time as, or after, the creation of the charge,

(b)   the value of so much of that consideration as consists of the discharge or reduction, at the same time as, or after the creation of the charge, of any debt of the company, and

(c)   the amount of such interest (if any) as is payable on the amount falling within paragraph (a) or (b) in pursuance of any agreement under which the money was so paid, the goods or services were so supplied or the debt was so discharged or reduced.

(3)   Subject to the next subsection, the time at which a floating charge is created by a company is a relevant time for the purposes of this section if the charge is created—

(a)   in the case of a charge which is created in favour of a person who is connected with the company, at a time in the period of 2 years ending with the onset of insolvency,

(b)   in the case of a charge which is created in favour of any other person, at a time in the period of 12 months ending with the onset of insolvency, or

(c)   in either case, at a time between the presentation of a petition for the making of an administration order in relation to the company and the making of such an order on that petition.

(4)   Where a company creates a floating charge at a time mentioned in subsection (3)(b) and the person in favour of whom the charge is created is not connected with the company, that time is not a relevant time for the purposes of this section unless the company—

(a)   is at that time unable to pay its debts within the meaning of section 123 in Chapter VI of Part IV, or

(b)   becomes unable to pay its debts within the meaning of that section in consequence of the transaction under which the charge is created.

(5)   For the purposes of subsection (3), the onset of insolvency is—

(a)   in a case where this section applies by reason of the making of an administration order, the date of the presentation of the petition on which the order was made, and

(b)   in a case where this section applies by reason of a company going into liquidation, the date of the commencement of the winding up.

(6)   For the purposes of subsection (2)(a) the value of any goods or services supplied by way of consideration for a floating charge is the amount in money which at the time they were supplied could reasonably have been expected to be obtained for supplying the goods or services in the ordinary course of business and on the same terms (apart from the consideration) as those on which they were supplied to the company.

246 Unenforceability of liens on books, etc

(1)   This section applies in the case of a company where—
(a)   an administration order is made in relation to the company, or
(b)   the company goes into liquidation, or
(c)   a provisional liquidator is appointed;

and "the office-holder" means the administrator, the liquidator or the provisional liquidator, as the case may be.

(2)   Subject as follows, a lien or other right to retain possession of any of the books, papers or other records of the company is unenforceable to the extent that its enforcement would deny possession of any books, papers or other records to the office-holder.

(3)   This does not apply to a lien on documents which give a title to property and are held as such.

PART VII

INTERPRETATION FOR FIRST GROUP OF PARTS

247 "Insolvency" and "go into liquidation"

(1)   In this Group of Parts, except in so far as the context otherwise requires, "insolvency", in relation to a company, includes the approval of a voluntary arrangement under Part I, the making of an administration order or the appointment of an administrative receiver.

(2)   For the purposes of any provision in this Group of Parts, a company goes into liquidation if it passes a resolution for voluntary winding up or an order for its winding up is made by the court at a time when it has not already gone into liquidation by passing such a resolution.

[(3)   The reference to a resolution for voluntary winding up in subsection (2) includes a resolution deemed to occur by virtue of an order made following conversion of a voluntary arrangement or administration into winding up under Article 37 of the EC Regulation.]

NOTES

Sub-s (3): inserted by SI 2002/1240, regs 3, 12.
Date in force: 31 May 2002: see SI 2002/1240, reg 1.

248 "Secured creditor", etc

In this Group of Parts, except in so far as the context otherwise requires—

    (a) "secured creditor", in relation to a company, means a creditor of the company who holds in respect of his debt a security over property of the company, and "unsecured creditor" is to be read accordingly; and

    (b) "security" means—

        (i) in relation to England and Wales, any mortgage, charge, lien or other security, and

        (ii) in relation to Scotland, any security (whether heritable or moveable), any floating charge and any right of lien or preference and any right of retention (other than a right of compensation or set off).

249 "Connected" with a company

For the purposes of any provision in this Group of Parts, a person is connected with a company if—

    (a) he is a director or shadow director of the company or an associate of such a director or shadow director, or

    (b) he is an associate of the company;

and "associate" has the meaning given by section 435 in Part XVIII of this Act.

250 "Member" of a company

For the purposes of any provision in this Group of Parts, a person who is not a member of a company but to whom shares in the company have been transferred, or transmitted by operation of law, is to be regarded as a member of the company, and references to a member or members are to be read accordingly.

251 Expressions used generally

In this Group of Parts, except in so far as the context otherwise requires—

"administrative receiver" means—

    (a) an administrative receiver as defined by section 29(2) in Chapter I of Part III, or

    (b) a receiver appointed under section 51 in Chapter II of that Part in a case where the whole (or substantially the whole) of the company's property is attached by the floating charge;

"business day" means any day other than a Saturday, a Sunday, Christmas Day, Good Friday or a day which is a bank holiday in any part of Great Britain;

"chattel leasing agreement" means an agreement for the bailment or, in Scotland, the hiring of goods which is capable of subsisting for more than 3 months;

"contributory" has the meaning given by section 79;

"director" includes any person occupying the position of director, by whatever name called;

"floating charge" means a charge which, as created, was a floating charge and includes a floating charge within section 462 of the Companies Act (Scottish floating charges);

"office copy", in relation to Scotland, means a copy certified by the clerk of court;

"the official rate", in relation to interest, means the rate payable under section 189(4);

"prescribed" means prescribed by the rules;

"receiver", in the expression "receiver or manager", does not include a receiver appointed under section 51 in Chapter II of Part III;

"retention of title agreement" means an agreement for the sale of goods to a company, being an agreement—

(a) which does not constitute a charge on the goods, but

(b) under which, if the seller is not paid and the company is wound up, the seller will have priority over all other creditors of the company as respects the goods or any property representing the goods;

"the rules" means rules under section 411 in Part XV; and

"shadow director", in relation to a company, means a person in accordance with whose directions or instructions the directors of the company are accustomed to act (but so that a person is not deemed a shadow director by reason only that the directors act on advice given by him in a professional capacity);

and any expression for whose interpretation provision is made by Part XXVI of the Companies Act, other than an expression defined above in this section, is to be construed in accordance with that provision.

THE THIRD GROUP OF PARTS
MISCELLANEOUS MATTERS BEARING ON BOTH COMPANY AND INDIVIDUAL INSOLVENCY; GENERAL INTERPRETATION; FINAL PROVISIONS

PART XII
PREFERENTIAL DEBTS IN COMPANY AND INDIVIDUAL INSOLVENCY

386 Categories of preferential debts

(1) A reference in this Act to the preferential debts of a company or an individual is to the debts listed in Schedule 6 to this Act (money owed to the Inland Revenue for income tax deducted at source; VAT, [insurance premium tax,] [landfill tax,] [climate change levy,] [aggregates levy,] car tax, betting and gaming duties[, beer duty][, lottery duty][, air passenger duty]; social security and pension scheme contributions; remuneration etc of employees[; levies on coal and steel production]); and references to preferential creditors are to be read accordingly.

(2) In that Schedule "the debtor" means the company or the individual concerned.

(3) Schedule 6 is to be read with [Schedule 4 to the Pension Schemes Act 1993] (occupational pension scheme contributions).

NOTES

Sub-s (1): words "insurance premium tax," in square brackets inserted by the Finance Act 1994, s 64, Sch 7, para 7(2).

Sub-s (1): words "landfill tax," in square brackets inserted by the Finance Act 1996, s 60, Sch 5, para 12(1).

Sub-s (1): words "climate change levy," in square brackets inserted by the Finance Act 2000, s 30, Sch 7, para 3(1)(a).

Date in force: this amendment came into force on 28 July 2000 (date of Royal Assent of the Finance Act 2000) in the absence of any specific commencement provision.

Sub-s (1): words "aggregates levy," in square brackets inserted by the Finance Act 2001, s 27, Sch 5, para 17(1)(a).

Date in force: this amendment came into force on 11 May 2001 (date of Royal Assent of the Finance Act 2001) in the absence of any specific commencement provision.

Sub-s (1): words ", beer duty" in square brackets inserted by the Finance Act 1991, s 7, Sch 2 (as amended by the Finance (No 2) Act 1992, s 9).

Sub-s (1): words ", lottery duty" in square brackets inserted by the Finance Act 1993, s 36(1).

Sub-s (1): words ", air passenger duty" in square brackets inserted by the Finance Act 1995, s 17.

Sub-s (1): words "; levies on coal and steel production" in square brackets inserted by SI 1987/2093, reg 2.

Sub-s (3): words in square brackets substituted by the Pension Schemes Act 1993, s 190, Sch 8, para 18.

387 "The relevant date"

(1)   This section explains references in Schedule 6 to the relevant date (being the date which determines the existence and amount of a preferential debt).

(2)   For the purposes of section 4 in Part I (meetings to consider company voluntary arrangement), the relevant date in relation to a company which is not being wound up is—

- (a)   where an administration order is in force in relation to the company, the date of the making of that order, and
- (b)   where no such order has been made, the date *of the approval of the voluntary arrangement* [on which the voluntary arrangement takes effect].

[(2A)   For the purposes of paragraph 31 of Schedule A1 (meetings to consider company voluntary arrangement where a moratorium under section 1A is in force), the relevant date in relation to a company is the date of filing.]

(3)   In relation to a company which is being wound up, the following applies—

- (a)   if the winding up is by the court, and the winding-up order was made immediately upon the discharge of an administration order, the relevant date is the date of the making of the administration order;
- [(aa) if the winding up is by the court and the winding-up order was made following conversion of administration into winding up by virtue of Article 37 of the EC Regulation, the relevant date is the date of the making of the administration order;
- (ab) if the company is deemed to have passed a resolution for voluntary winding up by virtue of an order following conversion of administration into winding up under Article 37 of the EC Regulation, the relevant date is the date of the making of the administration order;]
- (b)   if the case does not fall within paragraph (a)[, (aa) or (ab)] and the company—
  - (i)   is being wound up by the court, and

(ii) had not commenced to be wound up voluntarily before the date of the making of the winding-up order,

the relevant date is the date of the appointment (or first appointment) of a provisional liquidator or, if no such appointment has been made, the date of the winding-up order;

(c) if the case does not fall within [paragraph (a), (aa), (ab) or (b)], the relevant date is the date of the passing of the resolution for the winding up of the company.

(4) In relation to a company in receivership (where section 40 or, as the case may be, section 59 applies), the relevant date is—

(a) in England and Wales, the date of the appointment of the receiver by debenture-holders, and

(b) in Scotland, the date of the appointment of the receiver under section 53(6) or (as the case may be) 54(5).

(5) For the purposes of section 258 in Part VIII (individual voluntary arrangements), the relevant date is, in relation to a debtor who is not an undischarged bankrupt, *the date of the interim order made under section 252 with respect to his proposal*

[(a) where an interim order has been made under section 252 with respect to his proposal, the date of that order, and

(b) in any other case, the date on which the voluntary arrangement takes effect].

(6) In relation to a bankrupt, the following applies—

(a) where at the time the bankruptcy order was made there was an interim receiver appointed under section 286, the relevant date is the date on which the interim receiver was first appointed after the presentation of the bankruptcy petition;

(b) otherwise, the relevant date is the date of the making of the bankruptcy order.

NOTES

Sub-s (2): in para (b) words "of the approval of the voluntary arrangement" in italics repealed and subsequent words in square brackets substituted by the Insolvency Act 2000, s 2(a), Sch 2, Pt I, paras 1, 11.

Date in force: to be appointed: see the Insolvency Act 2000, s 16(1).

Sub-s (2A): inserted by the Insolvency Act 2000, s 1, Sch 1, paras 1, 9.

Date in force: to be appointed: see the Insolvency Act 2000, s 16(1).

Sub-s (3): paras (aa), (ab) inserted by SI 2002/1240, regs 3, 16(a).

Date in force: 31 May 2002: see SI 2002/1240, reg 1.

Sub-s (3): in para (b) words ", (aa) or (ab)" in square brackets inserted by SI 2002/1240, regs 3, 16(b).

Date in force: 31 May 2002: see SI 2002/1240, reg 1.

Sub-s (3): in para (c) words "paragraph (a), (aa), (ab) or (b)" in square brackets substituted by SI 2002/1240, regs 3, 16(c).

Date in force: 31 May 2002: see SI 2002/1240, reg 1.

Sub-s (5): words ", the date of the interim order made under section 252 with respect to his proposal" in italics repealed and subsequent paras (a), (b) substituted by the Insolvency Act 2000, s 3, Sch 3, paras 1, 15.

Date in force: to be appointed: see the Insolvency Act 2000, s 16(1).

PART XIII

INSOLVENCY PRACTITIONERS AND THEIR QUALIFICATION

Restrictions on unqualified persons acting as liquidator, trustee in bankruptcy, etc

388 Meaning of "act as insolvency practitioner"

(1)   A person acts as an insolvency practitioner in relation to a company by acting—

(a)   as its liquidator, provisional liquidator, administrator or administrative receiver, or

(b)   as supervisor of a voluntary arrangement approved by it under Part I

[(b)   where a voluntary arrangement in relation to the company is proposed or approved under Part I, as nominee or supervisor].

(2)   A person acts as an insolvency practitioner in relation to an individual by acting—

(a)   as his trustee in bankruptcy or interim receiver of his property or as permanent or interim trustee in the sequestration of his estate; or

(b)   as trustee under a deed which is a deed of arrangement made for the benefit of his creditors or, in Scotland, a trust deed for his creditors; or

(c)   as supervisor of a voluntary arrangement proposed by him and approved under Part VIII; or

[(c)   where a voluntary arrangement in relation to the individual is proposed or approved under Part VIII, as nominee or supervisor]

(d)   in the case of a deceased individual to the administration of whose estate this section applies by virtue of an order under section 421 (application of provisions of this Act to insolvent estates of deceased persons), as administrator of that estate.

[(2A)   A person acts as an insolvency practitioner in relation to an insolvent partnership by acting—

(a)   as its liquidator, provisional liquidator or administrator, or

(b)   as trustee of the partnership under article 11 of the Insolvent Partnerships Order 1994, or

(c)   as supervisor of a voluntary arrangement approved in relation to it under Part I of this Act.]

[(2B)   In relation to a voluntary arrangement proposed under Part I or VIII, a person acts as nominee if he performs any of the functions conferred on nominees under the Part in question.]

(3)   References in this section to an individual include, except in so far as the context otherwise requires, references < . . . > to any debtor within the meaning of the Bankruptcy (Scotland) Act 1985.

(4)   In this section—

"administrative receiver" has the meaning given by section 251 in Part VII;

"company" means a company within the meaning given by section 735(1) of the Companies Act or a company which may be wound up under Part V of this Act (unregistered companies); and "interim trustee" and "permanent trustee" mean the same as in the Bankruptcy (Scotland) Act 1985.

[(5) Nothing in this section applies to anything done by—
- (a) the official receiver; or
- (b) the Accountant in Bankruptcy (within the meaning of the Bankruptcy (Scotland) Act 1985).]

[(6) Nothing in this section applies to anything done (whether in the United Kingdom or elsewhere) in relation to insolvency proceedings under the EC Regulation in a member State other than the United Kingdom.]

NOTES

Sub-s (1): para (b) substituted by the Insolvency Act 2000, s 4(1), (2)(a).
Date in force: to be appointed: see the Insolvency Act 2000, s 16(1).
Sub-s (2): para (c) substituted by the Insolvency Act 2000, s 4(1), (2)(b).
Date in force: to be appointed: see the Insolvency Act 2000, s 16(1).
Sub-s (2A): inserted by SI 1994/2421, art 15(1).
Sub-s (2B): inserted by the Insolvency Act 2000, s 4(1), (2)(c).
Date in force: to be appointed: see the Insolvency Act 2000, s 16(1).
Sub-s (3): words omitted repealed by SI 1994/2421, art 15(2).
Sub-s (5): substituted by the Bankruptcy (Scotland) Act 1993, s 11(1).
Sub-s (6): inserted by SI 2002/1240, regs 3, 17.
Date in force: 31 May 2002: see SI 2002/1240, reg 1.

The requisite qualification, and the means of obtaining it

390 Persons not qualified to act as insolvency practitioners

(1) A person who is not an individual is not qualified to act as an insolvency practitioner.

(2) A person is not qualified to act as an insolvency practitioner at any time unless at that time—
- (a) he is authorised so to act by virtue of membership of a professional body recognised under section 391 below, being permitted so to act by or under the rules of that body, or
- (b) he holds an authorisation granted by a competent authority under section 393.

(3) A person is not qualified to act as an insolvency practitioner in relation to another person at any time unless—
- (a) there is in force at that time security or, in Scotland, caution for the proper performance of his functions, and
- (b) that security or caution meets the prescribed requirements with respect to his so acting in relation to that other person.

(4) A person is not qualified to act as an insolvency practitioner at any time if at that time—
- (a) he has been adjudged bankrupt or sequestration of his estate has been awarded and (in either case) he has not been discharged,

   (b)   he is subject to a disqualification order made [or a disqualification undertaking accepted] under the Company Directors Disqualification Act 1986 [or to a disqualification order made under Part II of the Companies (Northern Ireland) Order 1989], or

   (c)   he is a patient within the meaning of Part VII of the Mental Health Act 1983 or section 125(1) of the Mental Health (Scotland) Act 1984 [or has had a guardian appointed to him under the Adults with Incapacity (Scotland) Act 2000 (asp 4)].

NOTES

Sub-s (4): in para (b) words "or a disqualification undertaking accepted" in square brackets inserted by the Insolvency Act 2000, s 8, Sch 4, Pt II, para 16(1), (2)(a).

Date in force: 2 April 2001: see SI 2001/766, art 2(1)(a).

Sub-s (4): in para (b) words "or to a disqualification order made under Part II of the Companies (Northern Ireland) Order 1989" in square brackets inserted by the Insolvency Act 2000, s 8, Sch 4, Pt II, para 16(1), (2)(b).

Date in force: 2 April 2001: see SI 2001/766, art 2(1)(a).

Sub-s (4): in para (c) words "or has had a guardian appointed to him under the Adults with Incapacity (Scotland) Act 2000 (asp 4)" in square brackets inserted by the Adults with Incapacity (Scotland) Act 2000, s 88(2), Sch 5, para 18.

Date in force: 1 April 2002: see SSI 2001/81, art 3, Sch 2.

391 Recognised professional bodies

(1)   The Secretary of State may by order declare a body which appears to him to fall within subsection (2) below to be a recognised professional body for the purposes of this section.

(2)   A body may be recognised if it regulates the practice of a profession and maintains and enforces rules for securing that such of its members as are permitted by or under the rules to act as insolvency practitioners—

   (a)   are fit and proper persons so to act, and

   (b)   meet acceptable requirements as to education and practical training and experience.

(3)   References to members of a recognised professional body are to persons who, whether members of that body or not, are subject to its rules in the practice of the profession in question.

The reference in section 390(2) above to membership of a professional body recognised under this section is to be read accordingly.

(4)   An order made under subsection (1) in relation to a professional body may be revoked by a further order if it appears to the Secretary of State that the body no longer falls within subsection (2).

(5)   An order of the Secretary of State under this section has effect from such date as is specified in the order; and any such order revoking a previous order may make provision whereby members of the body in question continue to be treated as authorised to act as insolvency practitioners for a specified period after the revocation takes effect.

392 Authorisation by competent authority

(1)   Application may be made to a competent authority for authorisation to act as an insolvency practitioner.

(2)   The competent authorities for this purpose are—
   (a)   in relation to a case of any description specified in directions given by the Secretary of State, the body or person so specified in relation to cases of that description, and
   (b)   in relation to a case not falling within paragraph (a), the Secretary of State.

(3)   The application—
   (a)   shall be made in such manner as the competent authority may direct,
   (b)   shall contain or be accompanied by such information as that authority may reasonably require for the purpose of determining the application, and
   (c)   shall be accompanied by the prescribed fee;

and the authority may direct that notice of the making of the application shall be published in such manner as may be specified in the direction.

(4)   At any time after receiving the application and before determining it the authority may require the applicant to furnish additional information.

(5)   Directions and requirements given or imposed under subsection (3) or (4) may differ as between different applications.

(6)   Any information to be furnished to the competent authority under this section shall, if it so requires, be in such form or verified in such manner as it may specify.

(7)   An application may be withdrawn before it is granted or refused.

(8)   Any sums received under this section by a competent authority other than the Secretary of State may be retained by the authority; and any sums so received by the Secretary of State shall be paid into the Consolidated Fund.

PART XIV
PUBLIC ADMINISTRATION (ENGLAND AND WALES)

Official receivers

399 Appointment, etc of official receivers

(1)   For the purposes of this Act the official receiver, in relation to any bankruptcy or winding up, is any person who by virtue of the following provisions of this section or section 401 below is authorised to act as the official receiver in relation to that bankruptcy or winding up.

(2)   The Secretary of State may (subject to the approval of the Treasury as to numbers) appoint persons to the office of official receiver, and a person appointed to that office (whether under this section or section 70 of the Bankruptcy Act 1914)—
   (a)   shall be paid out of money provided by Parliament such salary as the Secretary of State may with the concurrence of the Treasury direct,

(b) shall hold office on such other terms and conditions as the Secretary of State may with the concurrence of the Treasury direct, and

(c) may be removed from office by a direction of the Secretary of State.

(3) Where a person holds the office of official receiver, the Secretary of State shall from time to time attach him either to the High Court or to a county court having jurisdiction for the purposes of the second Group of Parts of this Act.

(4) Subject to any directions under subsection (6) below, an official receiver attached to a particular court is the person authorised to act as the official receiver in relation to every bankruptcy or winding up falling within the jurisdiction of that court.

(5) The Secretary of State shall ensure that there is, at all times, at least one official receiver attached to the High Court and at least one attached to each county court having jurisdiction for the purposes of the second Group of Parts; but he may attach the same official receiver to two or more different courts.

(6) The Secretary of State may give directions with respect to the disposal of the business of official receivers, and such directions may, in particular—

(a) authorise an official receiver attached to one court to act as the official receiver in relation to any case or description of cases falling within the jurisdiction of another court;

(b) provide, where there is more than one official receiver authorised to act as the official receiver in relation to cases falling within the jurisdiction of any court, for the distribution of their business between or among themselves.

(7) A person who at the coming into force of section 222 of the Insolvency Act 1985 (replaced by this section) is an official receiver attached to a court shall continue in office after the coming into force of that section as an official receiver attached to that court under this section.

400 Functions and status of official receivers

(1) In addition to any functions conferred on him by this Act, a person holding the office of official receiver shall carry out such other functions as may from time to time be conferred on him by the Secretary of State.

(2) In the exercise of the functions of his office a person holding the office of official receiver shall act under the general directions of the Secretary of State and shall also be an officer of the court in relation to which he exercises those functions.

(3) Any property vested in his official capacity in a person holding the office of official receiver shall, on his dying, ceasing to hold office or being otherwise succeeded in relation to the bankruptcy or winding up in question by another official receiver, vest in his successor without any conveyance, assignment or transfer.

PART XVI
PROVISIONS AGAINST DEBT AVOIDANCE (ENGLAND AND WALES ONLY)

423 Transactions defrauding creditors

(1)   This section relates to transactions entered into at an undervalue; and a person enters into such a transaction with another person if—

   (a)   he makes a gift to the other person or he otherwise enters into a transaction with the other on terms that provide for him to receive no consideration;

   (b)   he enters into a transaction with the other in consideration of marriage; or

   (c)   he enters into a transaction with the other for a consideration the value of which, in money or money's worth, is significantly less than the value, in money or money's worth, of the consideration provided by himself.

(2)   Where a person has entered into such a transaction, the court may, if satisfied under the next subsection, make such order as it thinks fit for—

   (a)   restoring the position to what it would have been if the transaction had not been entered into, and

   (b)   protecting the interests of persons who are victims of the transaction.

(3)   In the case of a person entering into such a transaction, an order shall only be made if the court is satisfied that it was entered into by him for the purpose—

   (a)   of putting assets beyond the reach of a person who is making, or may at some time make, a claim against him, or

   (b)   of otherwise prejudicing the interests of such a person in relation to the claim which he is making or may make.

(4)   In this section "the court" means the High Court or—

   (a)   if the person entering into the transaction is an individual, any other court which would have jurisdiction in relation to a bankruptcy petition relating to him;

   (b)   if that person is a body capable of being wound up under Part IV or V of this Act, any other court having jurisdiction to wind it up.

(5)   In relation to a transaction at an undervalue, references here and below to a victim of the transaction are to a person who is, or is capable of being, prejudiced by it; and in the following two sections the person entering into the transaction is referred to as "the debtor".

424 Those who may apply for an order under s 423

(1)   An application for an order under section 423 shall not be made in relation to a transaction except—

   (a)   in a case where the debtor has been adjudged bankrupt or is a body corporate which is being wound up or in relation to which an administration order is in force, by the official receiver, by the trustee of the bankrupt's estate or the liquidator or administrator of the body corporate or (with the leave of the court) by a victim of the transaction;

   (b)   in a case where a victim of the transaction is bound by a voluntary arrangement approved under Part I or Part VIII of this Act, by the supervisor of the voluntary arrangement or by any person who (whether or not so bound) is such a victim; or

(c) in any other case, by a victim of the transaction.

(2) An application made under any of the paragraphs of subsection (1) is to be treated as made on behalf of every victim of the transaction.

425 Provision which may be made by order under s 423

(1) Without prejudice to the generality of section 423, an order made under that section with respect to a transaction may (subject as follows)—

(a) require any property transferred as part of the transaction to be vested in any person, either absolutely or for the benefit of all the persons on whose behalf the application for the order is treated as made;

(b) require any property to be so vested if it represents, in any person's hands, the application either of the proceeds of sale of property so transferred or of money so transferred;

(c) release or discharge (in whole or in part) any security given by the debtor;

(d) require any person to pay to any other person in respect of benefits received from the debtor such sums as the court may direct;

(e) provide for any surety or guarantor whose obligations to any person were released or discharged (in whole or in part) under the transaction to be under such new or revived obligations as the court thinks appropriate;

(f) provide for security to be provided for the discharge of any obligation imposed by or arising under the order, for such an obligation to be charged on any property and for such security or charge to have the same priority as a security or charge released or discharged (in whole or in part) under the transaction.

(2) An order under section 423 may affect the property of, or impose any obligation on, any person whether or not he is the person with whom the debtor entered into the transaction; but such an order—

(a) shall not prejudice any interest in property which was acquired from a person other than the debtor and was acquired in good faith, for value and without notice of the relevant circumstances, or prejudice any interest deriving from such an interest, and

(b) shall not require a person who received a benefit from the transaction in good faith, for value and without notice of the relevant circumstances to pay any sum unless he was a party to the transaction.

(3) For the purposes of this section the relevant circumstances in relation to a transaction are the circumstances by virtue of which an order under section 423 may be made in respect of the transaction.

(4) In this section "security" means any mortgage, charge, lien or other security.

PART XVIII
INTERPRETATION

435 Meaning of "associate"

(1) For the purposes of this Act any question whether a person is an associate of another person is to be determined in accordance with the following provisions of this section (any provision that a person is an associate of another person being taken to mean that they are associates of each other).

(2) A person is an associate of an individual if that person is the individual's husband or wife, or is a relative, or the husband or wife of a relative, of the individual or of the individual's husband or wife.

(3) A person is an associate of any person with whom he is in partnership, and of the husband or wife or a relative of any individual with whom he is in partnership; and a Scottish firm is an associate of any person who is a member of the firm.

(4) A person is an associate of any person whom he employs or by whom he is employed.

(5) A person in his capacity as trustee of a trust other than—
    (a) a trust arising under any of the second Group of Parts or the Bankruptcy (Scotland) Act 1985, or
    (b) a pension scheme or an employees' share scheme (within the meaning of the Companies Act),

is an associate of another person if the beneficiaries of the trust include, or the terms of the trust confer a power that may be exercised for the benefit of, that other person or an associate of that other person.

(6) A company is an associate of another company—
    (a) if the same person has control of both, or a person has control of one and persons who are his associates, or he and persons who are his associates, have control of the other, or
    (b) if a group of two or more persons has control of each company, and the groups either consist of the same persons or could be regarded as consisting of the same persons by treating (in one or more cases) a member of either group as replaced by a person of whom he is an associate.

(7) A company is an associate of another person if that person has control of it or if that person and persons who are his associates together have control of it.

(8) For the purposes of this section a person is a relative of an individual if he is that individual's brother, sister, uncle, aunt, nephew, niece, lineal ancestor or lineal descendant, treating—
    (a) any relationship of the half blood as a relationship of the whole blood and the stepchild or adopted child of any person as his child, and
    (b) an illegitimate child as the legitimate child of his mother and reputed father;

and references in this section to a husband or wife include a former husband or wife and a reputed husband or wife.

(9)   For the purposes of this section any director or other officer of a company is to be treated as employed by that company.

(10)   For the purposes of this section a person is to be taken as having control of a company if—
  (a)   the directors of the company or of another company which has control of it (or any of them) are accustomed to act in accordance with his directions or instructions, or
  (b)   he is entitled to exercise, or control the exercise of, one third or more of the voting power at any general meeting of the company or of another company which has control of it;

and where two or more persons together satisfy either of the above conditions, they are to be taken as having control of the company.

(11)   In this section "company" includes any body corporate (whether incorporated in Great Britain or elsewhere); and references to directors and other officers of a company and to voting power at any general meeting of a company have effect with any necessary modifications.

436 Expressions used generally

In this Act, except in so far as the context otherwise requires (and subject to Parts VII and XI)—
  "the appointed day" means the day on which this Act comes into force under section 443;
  "associate" has the meaning given by section 435;
  "business" includes a trade or profession;
  "the Companies Act" means the Companies Act 1985;
  "conditional sale agreement" and "hire-purchase agreement" have the same meanings as in the Consumer Credit Act 1974;
  ["the EC Regulation" means Council Regulation (EC) No 1346/2000;]
  "modifications" includes additions, alterations and omissions and cognate expressions shall be construed accordingly;
  "property" includes money, goods, things in action, land and every description of property wherever situated and also obligations and every description of interest, whether present or future or vested or contingent, arising out of, or incidental to, property;
  "records" includes computer records and other non-documentary records;
  "subordinate legislation" has the same meaning as in the Interpretation Act 1978; and
  "transaction" includes a gift, agreement or arrangement, and references to entering into a transaction shall be construed accordingly.

NOTES
Definition "the EC Regulation" inserted by SI 2002/1037, regs 2, 4.
Date in force: 3 May 2002: see SI 2002/1037, reg 1(1).

SCHEDULE 1
POWERS OF ADMINISTRATOR OR ADMINISTRATIVE RECEIVER

Sections 14, 42

1 Power to take possession of, collect and get in the property of the company and, for that purpose, to take such proceedings as may seem to him expedient.

2 Power to sell or otherwise dispose of the property of the company by public auction or private contract or, in Scotland, to sell, *feu,* hire out or otherwise dispose of the property of the company by public roup or private bargain.

3 Power to raise or borrow money and grant security therefor over the property of the company.

4 Power to appoint a solicitor or accountant or other professionally qualified person to assist him in the performance of his functions.

5 Power to bring or defend any action or other legal proceedings in the name and on behalf of the company.

6 Power to refer to arbitration any question affecting the company.

7 Power to effect and maintain insurances in respect of the business and property of the company.

8 Power to use the company's seal.

9 Power to do all acts and to execute in the name and on behalf of the company any deed, receipt or other document.

10 Power to draw, accept, make and endorse any bill of exchange or promissory note in the name and on behalf of the company.

11 Power to appoint any agent to do any business which he is unable to do himself or which can more conveniently be done by an agent and power to employ and dismiss employees.

12 Power to do all such things (including the carrying out of works) as may be necessary for the realisation of the property of the company.

13 Power to make any payment which is necessary or incidental to the performance of his functions.

14 Power to carry on the business of the company.

15 Power to establish subsidiaries of the company.

16 Power to transfer to subsidiaries of the company the whole or any part of the business and property of the company.

17 Power to grant or accept a surrender of a lease or tenancy of any of the property of the company, and to take a lease or tenancy of any property required or convenient for the business of the company.

18 Power to make any arrangement or compromise on behalf of the company.

19 Power to call up any uncalled capital of the company.

20 Power to rank and claim in the bankruptcy, insolvency, sequestration or liquidation of any person indebted to the company and to receive dividends, and to accede to trust deeds for the creditors of any such person.

21 Power to present or defend a petition for the winding up of the company.

22   Power to change the situation of the company's registered office.

23   Power to do all other things incidental to the exercise of the foregoing powers.

NOTES

Para 2: word "feu," in italics repealed by the Abolition of Feudal Tenure etc (Scotland) Act 2000, s 76(2), Sch 13, Pt 1.

Date in force: to be appointed: see the Abolition of Feudal Tenure etc (Scotland) Act 2000, ss 71, 77(2).

SCHEDULE 4
POWERS OF LIQUIDATOR IN A WINDING UP

Sections 165, 167

PART I
POWERS EXERCISABLE WITH SANCTION

1   Power to pay any class of creditors in full.

2   Power to make any compromise or arrangement with creditors or persons claiming to be creditors, or having or alleging themselves to have any claim (present or future, certain or contingent, ascertained or sounding only in damages) against the company, or whereby the company may be rendered liable.

3   Power to compromise, on such terms as may be agreed—
   (a)   all calls and liabilities to calls, all debts and liabilities capable of resulting in debts, and all claims (present or future, certain or contingent, ascertained or sounding only in damages) subsisting or supposed to subsist between the company and a contributory or alleged contributory or other debtor or person apprehending liability to the company, and
   (b)   all questions in any way relating to or affecting the assets or the winding up of the company,

and take any security for the discharge of any such call, debt, liability or claim and give a complete discharge in respect of it.

PART II
POWERS EXERCISABLE WITHOUT SANCTION IN VOLUNTARY WINDING UP, WITH SANCTION IN WINDING UP BY THE COURT

4   Power to bring or defend any action or other legal proceeding in the name and on behalf of the company.

5   Power to carry on the business of the company so far as may be necessary for its beneficial winding up.

PART III
POWERS EXERCISABLE WITHOUT SANCTION IN ANY WINDING UP

6   Power to sell any of the company's property by public auction or private contract with power to transfer the whole of it to any person or to sell the same in parcels.

7   Power to do all acts and execute, in the name and on behalf of the company, all deeds, receipts and other documents and for that purpose to use, when necessary, the company's seal.

8 Power to prove, rank and claim in the bankruptcy, insolvency or sequestration of any contributory for any balance against his estate, and to receive dividends in the bankruptcy, insolvency or sequestration in respect of that balance, as a separate debt due from the bankrupt or insolvent, and rateably with the other separate creditors.

9 Power to draw, accept, make and indorse any bill of exchange or promissory note in the name and on behalf of the company, with the same effect with respect to the company's liability as if the bill or note had been drawn, accepted, made or indorsed by or on behalf of the company in the course of its business.

10 Power to raise on the security of the assets of the company any money requisite.

11 Power to take out in his official name letters of administration to any deceased contributory, and to do in his official name any other act necessary for obtaining payment of any money due from a contributory or his estate which cannot conveniently be done in the name of the company.

In all such cases the money due is deemed, for the purpose of enabling the liquidator to take out the letters of administration or recover the money, to be due to the liquidator himself.

12 Power to appoint an agent to do any business which the liquidator is unable to do himself.

13 Power to do all such other things as may be necessary for winding up the company's affairs and distributing its assets.

SCHEDULE 6
THE CATEGORIES OF PREFERENTIAL DEBTS

Section 386

Category 1: Debts due to Inland Revenue

1 Sums due at the relevant date from the debtor on account of deductions of income tax from emoluments paid during the period of 12 months next before that date.

The deductions here referred to are those which the debtor was liable to make under section [203 of the Income and Corporation Taxes Act 1988] (pay as you earn), less the amount of the repayments of income tax which the debtor was liable to make during that period.

2 Sums due at the relevant date from the debtor in respect of such deductions as are required to be made by the debtor for that period under section [559 of the Income and Corporation Taxes Act 1988] (sub-contractors in the construction industry).

Category 2: Debts due to Customs and Excise

3 Any value added tax which is referable to the period of 6 months next before the relevant date (which period is referred to below as "the 6-month period").

For the purposes of this paragraph—
(a) where the whole of the prescribed accounting period to which any value added tax is attributable falls within the 6-month period, the whole amount of that tax is referable to that period; and
(b) in any other case the amount of any value added tax which is referable to the 6-month period is the proportion of the tax which is equal to such proportion (if any) of the accounting reference period in question as falls within the 6-month period;

and in sub-paragraph (a) "prescribed" means prescribed by regulations under the Value Added Tax Act [1994].

[3A Any insurance premium tax which is referable to the period of 6 months next before the relevant date (which period is referred to below as "the 6-month period").

For the purposes of this paragraph—
(a)   where the whole of the accounting period to which any insurance premium tax is attributable falls within the 6-month period, the whole amount of that tax is referable to that period; and
(b)   in any other case the amount of any insurance premium tax which is referable to the 6-month period is the proportion of the tax which is equal to such proportion (if any) of the accounting period in question as falls within the 6-month period;

and references here to accounting periods shall be construed in accordance with Part III of the Finance Act 1994.]

[3B Any landfill tax which is referable to the period of 6 months next before the relevant date (which period is referred to below as "the 6-month period").

For the purposes of this paragraph—
(a)   where the whole of the accounting period to which any landfill tax is attributable falls within the 6-month period, the whole amount of that tax is referable to that period; and
(b)   in any other case the amount of any landfill tax which is referable to the 6-month period is the proportion of the tax which is equal to such proportion (if any) of the accounting period in question as falls within the 6-month period;

and references here to accounting periods shall be construed in accordance with Part III of the Finance Act 1996.]

[3C Any climate change levy which is referable to the period of 6 months next before the relevant date (which period is referred to below as "the 6-month period").

For the purposes of this paragraph—
(a)   where the whole of the accounting period to which any climate change levy is attributable falls within the 6-month period, the whole amount of that levy is referable to that period; and
(b)   in any other case the amount of any climate change levy which is referable to the 6-month period is the proportion of the levy which is equal to such proportion (if any) of the accounting period in question as falls within the 6-month period;

and references here to accounting periods shall be construed in accordance with Schedule 6 to the Finance Act 2000.]

[3D Any aggregates levy which is referable to the period of 6 months next before the relevant date (which period is referred to below as 'the 6-month period').

For the purposes of this paragraph—
(a)   where the whole of the accounting period to which any aggregates levy is attributable falls within the 6-month period, the whole amount of that levy is referable to that period; and
(b)   in any other case the amount of any aggregates levy which is referable to the 6-month period is the proportion of the levy which is equal to such proportion (if any) of the accounting period in question as falls within the 6-month period;

and references here to accounting periods shall be construed in accordance with Part II of the Finance Act 2001.]

4   The amount of any car tax which is due at the relevant date from the debtor and which became due within a period of 12 months next before that date.

5   Any amount which is due—

(a)   by way of general betting duty[, bingo duty or gaming duty], or

(b)   under section 12(1) of the Betting and Gaming Duties Act 1981 (general betting duty and pool betting duty recoverable from agent collecting stakes), . . .

(c)   . . .,

from the debtor at the relevant date and which became due within the period of 12 months next before that date.

[**5A**   The amount of any excise duty on beer which is due at the relevant date from the debtor and which became due within a period of 6 months next before that date.]

[**5B**   Any amount which is due by way of lottery duty from the debtor at the relevant date and which became due within the period of 12 months next before that date.]

[**5C**   Any amount which is due by way of air passenger duty from the debtor at the relevant date and which became due within the period of six months next before that date.]

Category 3: Social security contributions

6   All sums which on the relevant date are due from the debtor on account of Class 1 or Class 2 contributions under the [Social Security Contributions and Benefits Act 1992] or the Social Security (Northern Ireland) Act 1975 and which became due from the debtor in the 12 months next before the relevant date.

7   All sums which on the relevant date have been assessed on and are due from the debtor on account of Class 4 contributions under either of those Acts of 1975, being sums which—

(a)   are due to the Commissioners of Inland Revenue (rather than to the Secretary of State or a Northern Ireland department), and

(b)   are assessed on the debtor up to 5th April next before the relevant date,

but not exceeding, in the whole, any one year's assessment.

Category 4: Contributions to occupational pension schemes, etc

8   Any sum which is owed by the debtor and is a sum to which [Schedule 4 to the Pension Schemes Act 1993] applies (contributions to occupational pension schemes and state scheme premiums).

Category 5: Remuneration, etc, of employees

9   So much of any amount which—

(a)   is owed by the debtor to a person who is or has been an employee of the debtor, and

(b)   is payable by way of remuneration in respect of the whole or any part of the period of 4 months next before the relevant date,

as does not exceed so much as may be prescribed by order made by the Secretary of State.

10   An amount owed by way of accrued holiday remuneration, in respect of any period of employment before the relevant date, to a person whose employment by the debtor has been terminated, whether before, on or after that date.

11   So much of any sum owed in respect of money advanced for the purpose as has been applied for the payment of a debt which, if it had not been paid, would have been a debt falling within paragraph 9 or 10.

12   So much of any amount which—

(a)   is ordered (whether before or after the relevant date) to be paid by the debtor under the Reserve Forces (Safeguard of Employment) Act 1985, and

(b)   is so ordered in respect of a default made by the debtor before that date in the discharge of his obligations under that Act,

as does no exceed such amount as may be prescribed by order made by the Secretary of State.

Interpretation for Category 5

13   (1)   For the purposes of paragraphs 9 to 12, a sum is payable by the debtor to a person by way of remuneration in respect of any period if—
    (a)   it is paid as wages or salary (whether payable for time or for piece work or earned wholly or partly by way of commission) in respect of services rendered to the debtor in that period, or
    (b)   it is an amount falling within the following sub-paragraph and is payable by the debtor in respect of that period.

[(2)   An amount falls within this sub-paragraph if it is—
    (a)   a guarantee payment under Part III of the Employment Rights Act 1996 (employee without work to do);
    (b)   any payment for time off under section 53 (time off to look for work or arrange training) or section 56 (time off for ante-natal care) of that Act or under section 169 of the Trade Union and Labour Relations (Consolidation) Act 1992 (time off for carrying out trade union duties etc);
    (c)   remuneration on suspension on medical grounds, or on maternity grounds, under Part VII of the Employment Rights Act 1996; or
    (d)   remuneration under a protective award under section 189 of the Trade Union and Labour Relations (Consolidation) Act 1992 (redundancy dismissal with compensation).]

14   (1)   This paragraph relates to a case in which a person's employment has been terminated by or in consequence of his employer going into liquidation or being adjudged bankrupt or (his employer being a company not in liquidation) by or in consequence of—
    (a)   a receiver being appointed as mentioned in section 40 of this Act (debenture-holders secured by floating charge), or
    (b)   the appointment of a receiver under section 53(6) or 54(5) of this Act (Scottish company with property subject to floating charge), or
    (c)   the taking of possession by debenture-holders (so secured), as mentioned in section 196 of the Companies Act.

(2)   For the purposes of paragraphs 9 to 12, holiday remuneration is deemed to have accrued to that person in respect of any period of employment if, by virtue of his contract of employment or of any enactment that remuneration would have accrued in respect of that period if his employment had continued until he became entitled to be allowed the holiday.

(3)   The reference in sub-paragraph (2) to any enactment includes an order or direction made under an enactment.

15   Without prejudice to paragraphs 13 and 14—
    (a)   any remuneration payable by the debtor to a person in respect of a period of holiday or of absence from work through sickness or other good cause is deemed to be wages or (as the case may be) salary in respect of services rendered to the debtor in that period, and
    (b)   references here and in those paragraphs to remuneration in respect of a period of holiday include any sums which, if they had been paid, would have been treated for the purposes of the enactments to social security as earnings in respect of that period.

[Category 6: Levies on coal and steel production

15A   Any sums due at the relevant date from the debtor in respect of—
  (a)   the levies on the production of coal and steel referred to in Articles 49 and 50 of the E.C.S.C. Treaty, or
  (b)   any surcharge for delay provided for in Article 50(3) of that Treaty and Article 6 of Decision 3/52 of the High Authority of the Coal and Steel Community.]

Orders

16   An order under paragraph 9 or 12—
  (a)   may contain such transitional provisions as may appear to the Secretary of State necessary or expedient;
  (b)   shall be made by statutory instrument subject to annulment in pursuance of a resolution of either House of Parliament.

NOTES

Paras 1, 2: words in square brackets substituted by the Income and Corporation Taxes Act 1988, s 844, Sch 29, para 32.

Para 3: year in square brackets substituted by the Value Added Tax Act 1994, s 100(1), Sch 14, para 8.

Para 3A: inserted by the Finance Act 1994, s 64, Sch 7, para 7(2).

Para 3B: inserted by the Finance Act 1996, s 60, Sch 5, para 12(1).

Para 3C: inserted by the Finance Act 2000, s 30, Sch 7, paras 3(1)(b), (2).

Date in force: this amendment came into force on 28 July 2000 (date of Royal Assent of the Finance Act 2000) in the absence of any specific commencement provision.

Para 3D: inserted by the Finance Act 2001, s 27, Sch 5, para 17(1)(b), (2).

Date in force: this amendment came into force on 11 May 2001 (date of Royal Assent of the Finance Act 2001) in the absence of any specific commencement provision.

Para 5: in sub-para (a) words in square brackets substituted by the Finance Act 1997, s 13, Sch 2, para 6, and by virtue of s 10(1) thereof gaming duty is chargeable for any gaming on or after 1 October 1997; sub-para (c) and the word "or" immediately preceding it repealed, in relation to amounts due in respect of duty chargeable for periods beginning on or after 1 October 1997, by the Finance Act 1997, s 113, Sch 18, Part II.

Para 5A: inserted by the Finance Act 1991, s 7, Sch 2, para 22.

Para 5B: inserted by the Finance Act 1993, s 36(2).

Para 5C: inserted, in relation to any carriage of a passenger on an aircraft which begins after 31 October 1994, by the Finance Act 1994, s 40, Sch 6, para 13(1), in accordance with s 44 thereof.

Para 6: words in square brackets substituted by the Social Security (Consequential Provisions) Act 1992, s 4, Sch 2, para 73.

Para 8: words in square brackets substituted by the Pension Schemes Act 1993, s 190, Sch 8, para 18.

Para 13: sub-para (2) substituted by the Employment Rights Act 1996, s 240, Sch 1, para 29.

Para 15A: inserted by SI 1987/2093, reg 2.

Company Directors Disqualification Act 1986

1986 CHAPTER 46

ARRANGEMENT OF SECTIONS

Preliminary

Part I—Matters applicable in all cases
Part II—Matters applicable where company has become insolvent

An Act to consolidate certain enactments relating to the disqualification of persons from being directors of companies, and from being otherwise concerned with a company's affairs

[25th July 1986]

Preliminary

1 Disqualification orders: general

(1)   In the circumstances specified below in this Act a court may, and under section 6 shall, make against a person a disqualification order, that is to say an order that [for a period specified in the order—

(a)   he shall not be a director of a company, act as receiver of a company's property or in any way, whether directly or indirectly, be concerned or take part in the promotion, formation or management of a company unless (in each case) he has the leave of the court, and

(b)   he shall not act as an insolvency practitioner].

(2)   In each section of this Act which gives to a court power or, as the case may be, imposes on it the duty to make a disqualification order there is specified the maximum (and, in section 6, the minimum) period of disqualification which may or (as the case may be) must be imposed by means of the order [and, unless the court otherwise orders, the period of disqualification so imposed shall begin at the end of the period of 21 days beginning with the date of the order].

(3)   Where a disqualification order is made against a person who is already subject to such an order [or to a disqualification undertaking], the periods specified in those orders [or, as the case may be, in the order and the undertaking] shall run concurrently.

(4)   A disqualification order may be made on grounds which are or include matters other than criminal convictions, notwithstanding that the person in respect of whom it is to be made may be criminally liable in respect of those matters.

NOTES

Sub-s (1): words from "for a period specified in the order—" in square brackets and paras (a), (b) substituted by the Insolvency Act 2000, s 5(1).
   Date in force: 2 April 2001: see SI 2001/766, art 2(1)(a).
   Sub-s (2) words from "and, unless the" to "of the order" in square brackets inserted by the Insolvency Act 2000, s 5(2).
   Date in force: 2 April 2001: see SI 2001/766, art 2(1)(a).
   Sub-s (3): words "or to a disqualification undertaking" in square brackets inserted by the Insolvency Act 2000, s 8, Sch 4, Pt I, paras 1, 2.
   Date in force: 2 April 2001: see SI 2001/766, art 2(1)(a).
   Sub-s (3): words "or, as the case may be, in the order and the undertaking" in square brackets inserted by the Insolvency Act 2000, s 8, Sch 4, Pt I, paras 1, 2.
   Date in force: 2 April 2001: see SI 2001/766, art 2(1)(a).

[1A Disqualification undertakings: general]

[(1)   In the circumstances specified in sections 7 and 8 the Secretary of State may accept a disqualification undertaking, that is to say an undertaking by any person that, for a period specified in the undertaking, the person—

   (a)   will not be a director of a company, act as receiver of a company's property or in any way, whether directly or indirectly, be concerned or take part in the promotion, formation or management of a company unless (in each case) he has the leave of a court, and

   (b)   will not act as an insolvency practitioner.

(2)   The maximum period which may be specified in a disqualification undertaking is 15 years; and the minimum period which may be specified in a disqualification undertaking under section 7 is two years.

(3)   Where a disqualification undertaking by a person who is already subject to such an undertaking or to a disqualification order is accepted, the periods specified in those undertakings or (as the case may be) the undertaking and the order shall run concurrently.

(4)   In determining whether to accept a disqualification undertaking by any person, the Secretary of State may take account of matters other than criminal convictions, notwithstanding that the person may be criminally liable in respect of those matters.]

NOTES

Inserted by the Insolvency Act 2000, s 6(1), (2).
Date in force: 2 April 2001: see SI 2001/766, art 2(1)(a).

Disqualification for general misconduct in connection with companies

2 Disqualification on conviction of indictable offence

(1)   The court may make a disqualification order against a person where he is convicted of an indictable offence (whether on indictment or summarily) in connection with the promotion, formation, management[, liquidation or striking off] of a company, [with the receivership of a company's property or with his being an administrative receiver of a company].

(2)   "The court" for this purpose means—

   (a)   any court having jurisdiction to wind up the company in relation to which the offence was committed, or

   (b)   the court by or before which the person is convicted of the offence, or

   (c)   in the case of a summary conviction in England and Wales, any other magistrates' court acting for the same petty sessions area;

and for the purposes of this section the definition of "indictable offence" in Schedule 1 to the Interpretation Act 1978 applies for Scotland as it does for England and Wales.

(3)   The maximum period of disqualification under this section is—

   (a)   where the disqualification order is made by a court of summary jurisdiction, 5 years, and

(b)   in any other case, 15 years.

NOTES

Sub-s (1): words ", liquidation or striking off" in square brackets substituted by the Deregulation and Contracting Out Act 1994, s 39, Sch 11, para 6.

Sub-s (1): words "with the receivership of a company's property or with his being an administrative receiver of a company" in square brackets substituted by the Insolvency Act 2000, s 8, Sch 4, Pt I, paras 1, 3.

Date in force: 2 April 2001: see SI 2001/766, art 2(1)(a).

3 Disqualification for persistent breaches of companies legislation

(1)   The court may make a disqualification order against a person where it appears to it that he has been persistently in default in relation to provisions of the companies legislation requiring any return, account or other document to be filed with, delivered or sent, or notice of any matter to be given, to the registrar of companies.

(2)   On an application to the court for an order to be made under this section, the fact that a person has been persistently in default in relation to such provisions as are mentioned above may (without prejudice to its proof in any other manner) be conclusively proved by showing that in the 5 years ending with the date of the application he has been adjudged guilty (whether or not on the same occasion) of three or more defaults in relation to those provisions.

(3)   A person is to be treated under subsection (2) as being adjudged guilty of a default in relation to any provision of that legislation if—

(a)   he is convicted (whether on indictment or summarily) of an offence consisting in a contravention of or failure to comply with that provision (whether on his own part or on the part of any company), or

(b)   a default order is made against him, that is to say an order under any of the following provisions—

(i)   [section 242(4)] of the Companies Act (order requiring delivery of company accounts),

[(ia) section 245B of that Act (order requiring preparation of revised accounts),]

(ii)   section 713 of that Act (enforcement of company's duty to make returns),

(iii)   section 41 of the Insolvency Act (enforcement of receiver's or manager's duty to make returns), or

(iv)   section 170 of that Act (corresponding provision for liquidator in winding up),

in respect of any such contravention of or failure to comply with that provision (whether on his own part or on the part of any company).

(4)   In this section "the court" means any court having jurisdiction to wind up any of the companies in relation to which the offence or other default has been or is alleged to have been committed.

(5)   The maximum period of disqualification under this section is 5 years.

Sub-s (3): words in square brackets in para (b)(i) substituted, and para (b)(ia) inserted, by the Companies Act 1989, s 23, Sch 10, Part II, para 35.

4 Disqualification for fraud, etc, in winding up

(1)   The court may make a disqualification order against a person if, in the course of the winding up of a company, it appears that he—
  (a)   has been guilty of an offence for which he is liable (whether he has been convicted or not) under section 458 of the Companies Act (fraudulent trading), or
  (b)   has otherwise been guilty, while an officer or liquidator of the company [receiver of the company's property or administrative receiver of the company], of any fraud in relation to the company or of any breach of his duty as such officer, liquidator, [receiver or administrative receiver].

(2)   In this section "the court" means any court having jurisdiction to wind up any of the companies in relation to which the offence or other default has been or is alleged to have been committed; and "officer" includes a shadow director.

(3)   The maximum period of disqualification under this section is 15 years.

Sub-s (1): in para (b) words "receiver of the company's property or administrative receiver of the company" in square brackets substituted by the Insolvency Act 2000, s 8, Sch 4, Pt I, paras 1, 4.
Date in force: 2 April 2001: see SI 2001/766, art 2(1)(a).
Sub-s (1): in para (b) words "receiver or administrative receiver" in square brackets substituted by the Insolvency Act 2000, s 8, Sch 4, Pt I, paras 1, 4.
Date in force: 2 April 2001: see SI 2001/766, art 2(1)(a).

5 Disqualification on summary conviction

(1)   An offence counting for the purposes of this section is one of which a person is convicted (either on indictment or summarily) in consequence of a contravention of, or failure to comply with, any provision of the companies legislation requiring a return, account or other document to be filed with, delivered or sent, or notice of any matter to be given, to the registrar of companies (whether the contravention or failure is on the person's own part or on the part of any company).

(2)   Where a person is convicted of a summary offence counting for those purposes, the court by which he is convicted (or, in England and Wales, any other magistrates' court acting for the same petty sessions area) may make a disqualification order against him if the circumstances specified in the next subsection are present.

(3)   Those circumstances are that, during the 5 years ending with the date of the conviction, the person has had made against him, or has been convicted of, in total not less than 3 default orders and offences counting for the purposes of this section; and those offences may include that of which he is convicted as mentioned in subsection (2) and any other offence of which he is convicted on the same occasion.

(4) For the purposes of this section—
  (a) the definition of "summary offence" in Schedule 1 to the Interpretation Act 1978 applies for Scotland as for England and Wales, and
  (b) "default order" means the same as in section 3(3)(b).

(5) The maximum period of disqualification under this section is 5 years.

Disqualification for unfitness

6 Duty of court to disqualify unfit directors of insolvent companies

(1) The court shall make a disqualification order against a person in any case where, on an application under this section, it is satisfied—
  (a) that he is or has been a director of a company which has at any time become insolvent (whether while he was a director or subsequently), and
  (b) that his conduct as a director of that company (either taken alone or taken together with his conduct as a director of any other company or companies) makes him unfit to be concerned in the management of a company.

(2) For the purposes of this section and the next, a company becomes insolvent if—
  (a) the company goes into liquidation at a time when its assets are insufficient for the payment of its debts and other liabilities and the expenses of the winding up,
  (b) an administration order is made in relation to the company, or
  (c) an administrative receiver of the company is appointed;

and references to a person's conduct as a director of any company or companies include, where that company or any of those companies has become insolvent, that person's conduct in relation to any matter connected with or arising out of the insolvency of that company.

[(3) In this section and section 7(2), "the court" means—
  (a) where the company in question is being or has been wound up by the court, that court,
  (b) where the company in question is being or has been wound up voluntarily, any court which has or (as the case may be) had jurisdiction to wind it up,
  (c) where neither of the preceding paragraphs applies but an administration order has at any time been made, or an administrative receiver has at any time been appointed, in relation to the company in question, any court which has jurisdiction to wind it up.

(3A) Sections 117 and 120 of the Insolvency Act 1986 (jurisdiction) shall apply for the purposes of subsection (3) as if the references in the definitions of "registered office" to the presentation of the petition for winding up were references—
  (a) in a case within paragraph (b) of that subsection, to the passing of the resolution for voluntary winding up,
  (b) in a case within paragraph (c) of that subsection, to the making of the administration order or (as the case may be) the appointment of the administrative receiver.

(3B)   Nothing in subsection (3) invalidates any proceedings by reason of their being taken in the wrong court; and proceedings—

(a)   for or in connection with a disqualification order under this section, or

(b)   in connection with a disqualification undertaking accepted under section 7,

may be retained in the court in which the proceedings were commenced, although it may not be the court in which they ought to have been commenced.

(3C)   In this section and section 7, "director" includes a shadow director.]

(4)   Under this section the minimum period of disqualification is 2 years, and the maximum period is 15 years.

NOTES

Sub-ss (3)–(3C): substituted, for sub-s (3) as originally enacted, by the Insolvency Act 2000, s 8, Sch 4, Pt I, paras 1, 5(1).

Date in force: 2 April 2001: see SI 2001/766, art 2(1)(a).

7 [Disqualification order or undertaking; and reporting provisions]

(1)   If it appears to the Secretary of State that it is expedient in the public interest that a disqualification order under section 6 should be made against any person, an application for the making of such an order against that person may be made—

(a)   by the Secretary of State, or

(b)   if the Secretary of State so directs in the case of a person who is or has been a director of a company which is being [or has been] wound up by the court in England and Wales, by the official receiver.

(2)   Except with the leave of the court, an application for the making under that section of a disqualification order against any person shall not be made after the end of the period of 2 years beginning with the day on which the company of which that person is or has been a director became insolvent.

[(2A)   If it appears to the Secretary of State that the conditions mentioned in section 6(1) are satisfied as respects any person who has offered to give him a disqualification undertaking, he may accept the undertaking if it appears to him that it is expedient in the public interest that he should do so (instead of applying, or proceeding with an application, for a disqualification order).]

(3)   If it appears to the office-holder responsible under this section, that is to say—

(a)   in the case of a company which is being wound up by the court in England and Wales, the official receiver,

(b)   in the case of a company which is being wound up otherwise, the liquidator,

(c)   in the case of a company in relation to which an administration order is in force, the administrator, or

(d)   in the case of a company of which there is an administrative receiver, that receiver,

that the conditions mentioned in section 6(1) are satisfied as respects a person who is or has been a director of that company, the office-holder shall forthwith report the matter to the Secretary of State.

(4)   The Secretary of State or the official receiver may require the liquidator, administrator or administrative receiver of a company, or the former liquidator, administrator or administrative receiver of a company—

(a)   to furnish him with such information with respect to any person's conduct as a director of the company, and

(b)   to produce and permit inspection of such books, papers and other records relevant to that person's conduct as such a director,

as the Secretary of State or the official receiver may reasonably require for the purpose of determining whether to exercise, or of exercising, any function of his under this section.

8 Disqualification after investigation of company

[(1)   If it appears to the Secretary of State from investigative material that it is expedient in the public interest that a disqualification order should be made against a person who is, or has been, a director or shadow director of a company, he may apply to the court for such an order.

(1A)   "Investigative material" means—

(a)   a report made by inspectors under—

(i)   section 437 of the Companies Act 1985;

(ii)   section 167, 168, 169 or 284 of the Financial Services and Markets Act 2000; or

(iii) where the company is an open-ended investment company (within the meaning of that Act) regulations made as a result of section 262(2)(k) of that Act; and

(b)   information or documents obtained under—

(i)   section 447 or 448 of the Companies Act 1985;

(ii)   section 2 of the Criminal Justice Act 1987;

(iii) section 28 of the Criminal Law (Consolidation) (Scotland) Act 1995;

(iv)   section 83 of the Companies Act 1989; or

(v)   section 165, 171, 172, 173 or 175 of the Financial Services and Markets Act 2000.]

(2)   The court may make a disqualification order against a person where, on an application under this section, it is satisfied that his conduct in relation to the company makes him unfit to be concerned in the management of a company.

[(2A)   Where it appears to the Secretary of State from such report, information or documents that, in the case of a person who has offered to give him a disqualification undertaking—

  (a)   the conduct of the person in relation to a company of which the person is or has been a director or shadow director makes him unfit to be concerned in the management of a company, and

  (b)   it is expedient in the public interest that he should accept the undertaking (instead of applying, or proceeding with an application, for a disqualification order),

he may accept the undertaking.]

(3)   In this section "the court" means the High Court or, in Scotland, the Court of Session.

(4)   The maximum period of disqualification under this section is 15 years.

NOTES

Sub-ss (1), (1A): substituted, for sub-s (1) as originally enacted, by SI 2001/3649, art 39.
Date in force: 1 December 2001: see SI 2001/3649, art 1.
Sub-s (2A): inserted by the Insolvency Act 2000, s 6(1), (4).
Date in force: 2 April 2001: see SI 2001/766, art 2(1)(a).

[8A Variation etc of disqualification undertaking]

[(1)   The court may, on the application of a person who is subject to a disqualification undertaking—

  (a)   reduce the period for which the undertaking is to be in force, or

  (b)   provide for it to cease to be in force.

(2)   On the hearing of an application under subsection (1), the Secretary of State shall appear and call the attention of the court to any matters which seem to him to be relevant, and may himself give evidence or call witnesses.

(3)   In this section "the court" has the same meaning as in section 7(2) or (as the case may be) 8.]

NOTES

Inserted by the Insolvency Act 2000, s 6(1), (5).
Date in force: 2 April 2001: see SI 2001/766, art 2(1)(a).

9 Matters for determining unfitness of directors

(1)   Where it falls to a court to determine whether a person's conduct as a director . . . of any particular company or companies makes him unfit to be concerned in the management of a company, the court shall, as respects his conduct as a director of that company or, as the case may be, each of those companies, have regard in particular—

  (a)   to the matters mentioned in Part I of Schedule 1 to this Act, and

  (b)   where the company has become insolvent, to the matters mentioned in Part II of that Schedule;

and references in that Schedule to the director and the company are to be read accordingly.

[(1A)   In determining whether he may accept a disqualification undertaking from any person the Secretary of State shall, as respects the person's conduct as a director of any company concerned, have regard in particular—

(a)   to the matters mentioned in Part I of Schedule 1 to this Act, and

(b)   where the company has become insolvent, to the matters mentioned in Part II of that Schedule;

and references in that Schedule to the director and the company are to be read accordingly.]

(2)   Section 6(2) applies for the purposes of this section and Schedule 1 as it applies for the purposes of sections 6 and 7 [and in this section and that Schedule "director" includes a shadow director].

(3)   Subject to the next subsection, any reference in Schedule 1 to an enactment contained in the Companies Act or the Insolvency Act includes, in relation to any time before the coming into force of that enactment, the corresponding enactment in force at that time.

(4)   The Secretary of State may by order modify any of the provisions of Schedule 1; and such an order may contain such transitional provisions as may appear to the Secretary of State necessary or expedient.

(5)   The power to make orders under this section is exercisable by statutory instrument subject to annulment in pursuance of a resolution of either House of Parliament.

NOTES

Sub-s (1): words omitted repealed by the Insolvency Act 2000, ss 8, 15(1) Sch 4, Pt I, paras 1, 7(a), Sch 5.

Date in force: 2 April 2001: see SI 2001/766, art 2(1)(a), (c)(ii).

Sub-s (1A): inserted by the Insolvency Act 2000, s 6(1), (6).

Date in force: 2 April 2001: see SI 2001/766, art 2(1)(a).

Sub-s (2): words "and in this section and that Schedule "director" includes a shadow director" in square brackets inserted by the Insolvency Act 2000, s 8, Sch 4, Pt I, paras 1, 7(b).

Date in force: 2 April 2001: see SI 2001/766, art 2(1)(a).

Other cases of disqualification

10 Participation in wrongful trading

(1)   Where the court makes a declaration under section 213 or 214 of the Insolvency Act that a person is liable to make a contribution to a company's assets, then, whether or not an application for such an order is made by any person, the court may, if it thinks fit, also make a disqualification order against the person to whom the declaration relates.

(2)   The maximum period of disqualification under this section is 15 years.

11 Undischarged bankrupts

(1)   It is an offence for a person who is an undischarged bankrupt to act as director of, or directly or indirectly to take part in or be concerned in the promotion, formation or management of, a company, except with the leave of the court.

(2)   "The court" for this purpose is the court by which the person was adjudged bankrupt or, in Scotland, sequestration of his estates was awarded.

(3)   In England and Wales, the leave of the court shall not be given unless notice of intention to apply for it has been served on the official receiver; and it is the latter's duty, if he is of opinion that it is contrary to the public interest that the application should be granted, to attend on the hearing of the application and oppose it.

Consequences of contravention

13 Criminal penalties

(1)   If a person acts in contravention of a disqualification order or [disqualification undertaking or in contravention] of section 12(2) [or 12A], or is guilty of an offence under section 11, he is liable—
-   (a)   on conviction on indictment, to imprisonment for not more than 2 years or a fine, or both; and
-   (b)   on summary conviction, to imprisonment for not more than 6 months or a fine not exceeding the statutory maximum, or both.

NOTES

Sub-s (1): words "disqualification undertaking or in contravention" in square brackets inserted by the Insolvency Act 2000, s 8, Sch 4, Pt I, paras 1, 8(a).

Date in force: 2 April 2001: see SI 2001/766, art 2(1)(a).

Sub-s (1): words "or 12A" in square brackets inserted by the Insolvency Act 2000, s 8, Sch 4, Pt I, paras 1, 8(b).

Date in force: 2 April 2001 (except in relation to a person subject to a disqualification order under the Companies (Northern Ireland) Order 1989, Pt II, SI 1989/2404 made before that date): see SI 2001/766, arts 2(1)(a), 3(3)(b).

15 Personal liability for company's debts where person acts while disqualified

(1)   A person is personally responsible for all the relevant debts of a company if at any time—
-   (a)   in contravention of a disqualification order or [disqualification undertaking or in contravention] of section 11 [or 12A] of this Act he is involved in the management of the company, or
-   (b)   as a person who is involved in the management of the company, he acts or is willing to act on instructions given without the leave of the court by a person whom he knows at that time to be the subject of a disqualification order [or disqualification undertaking or a disqualification order under Part II of the Companies (Northern Ireland) Order 1989] or to be an undischarged bankrupt.

(2)   Where a person is personally responsible under this section for the relevant debts of a company, he is jointly and severally liable in respect of those debts with the company and any other person who, whether under this section or otherwise, is so liable.

(3)   For the purposes of this section the relevant debts of a company are—

(a)   in relation to a person who is personally responsible under paragraph (a) of subsection (1), such debts and other liabilities of the company as are incurred at a time when that person was involved in the management of the company, and

(b)   in relation to a person who is personally responsible under paragraph (b) of that subsection, such debts and other liabilities of the company as are incurred at a time when that person was acting or was willing to act on instructions given as mentioned in that paragraph.

(4)   For the purposes of this section, a person is involved in the management of a company if he is a director of the company or if he is concerned, whether directly or indirectly, or takes part, in the management of the company.

(5)   For the purposes of this section a person who, as a person involved in the management of a company, has at any time acted on instructions given without the leave of the court by a person whom he knew at that time to be the subject of a disqualification order [or disqualification undertaking or a disqualification order under Part II of the Companies (Northern Ireland) Order 1989] or to be an undischarged bankrupt is presumed, unless the contrary is shown, to have been willing at any time thereafter to act on any instructions given by that person.

NOTES

Sub-s (1): in para (a) words "disqualification undertaking or in contravention" in square brackets inserted by the Insolvency Act 2000, s 8, Sch 4, Pt I, paras 1, 10(1), (2)(a).

Date in force: 2 April 2001: see SI 2001/766, art 2(1)(a).

Sub-s (1): in para (a) words "or 12A" in square brackets inserted by the Insolvency Act 2000, s 8, Sch 4, Pt I, paras 1, 10(1), (2)(a).

Date in force: 2 April 2001 (except in relation to a person subject to a disqualification order under the Companies (Northern Ireland) Order 1989, Pt II, SI 1989/2404 made before that date): see SI 2001/766, arts 2(1)(a), 3(3)(d).

Sub-s (1): in para (b) words from "or disqualification undertaking" to "the Companies (Northern Ireland) Order 1989" in square brackets inserted by the Insolvency Act 2000, s 8, Sch 4, Pt I, paras 1, 10(1), (2)(b).

Date in force: 2 April 2001 (except in relation to a person subject to a disqualification order under the Companies (Northern Ireland) Order 1989, Pt II, SI 1989/2404 made before that date): see SI 2001/766, arts 2(1)(a), 3(3)(e).

Sub-s (5): words from "or disqualification undertaking" to "the Companies (Northern Ireland) Order 1989" in square brackets inserted by the Insolvency Act 2000, s 8, Sch 4, Pt I, paras 1, 10(1), (3).

Date in force: 2 April 2001 (except in relation to a person subject to a disqualification order under the Companies (Northern Ireland) Order 1989, Pt II, SI 1989/2404 made before that date): see SI 2001/766, arts 2(1)(a), 3(3)(f).

Supplementary provisions

18 [Register of disqualification orders and undertakings]

(1)   The Secretary of State may make regulations requiring officers of courts to furnish him with such particulars as the regulations may specify of cases in which—

    (a)   a disqualification order is made, or

    (b)   any action is taken by a court in consequence of which such an order [or a disqualification undertaking] is varied or ceases to be in force, or

    (c)   leave is granted by a court for a person subject to such an order to do any thing which otherwise the order prohibits him from doing[, or

    (d)   leave is granted by a court for a person subject to such an undertaking to do anything which otherwise the undertaking prohibits him from doing];

and the regulations may specify the time within which, and the form and manner in which, such particulars are to be furnished.

(2)   The Secretary of State shall, from the particulars so furnished, continue to maintain the register of orders, and of cases in which leave has been granted as mentioned in subsection (1)(c), which was set up by him under section 29 of the Companies Act 1976 and continued under section 301 of the Companies Act 1985.

[(2A)   The Secretary of State shall include in the register such particulars as he considers appropriate of disqualification undertakings accepted by him under section 7 or 8 and of cases in which leave has been granted as mentioned in subsection (1)(d).]

(3)   When an order [or undertaking] of which entry is made in the register ceases to be in force, the Secretary of State shall delete the entry from the register and all particulars relating to it which have been furnished to him under this section or any previous corresponding provision [and, in the case of a disqualification undertaking, any other particulars he has included in the register].

(4)   The register shall be open to inspection on payment of such fee as may be specified by the Secretary of State in regulations.

[(4A)   Regulations under this section may extend the preceding provisions of this section, to such extent and with such modifications as may be specified in the regulations, to disqualification orders made under Part II of the Companies (Northern Ireland) Order 1989.]

(5)   Regulations under this section shall be made by statutory instrument subject to annulment in pursuance of a resolution of either House of Parliament.

NOTES

   Provision heading: words "Register of disqualification orders and undertakings" in square brackets substituted by the Insolvency Act 2000, s 8, Sch 4, Pt I, paras 1, 13(1), (6).

   Date in force: 2 April 2001: see SI 2001/766, art 2(1)(a).

   Sub-s (1): in para (b) words "or a disqualification undertaking" in square brackets inserted by the Insolvency Act 2000, s 8, Sch 4, Pt I, paras 1, 13(1), (2)(a).

   Date in force: 2 April 2001: see SI 2001/766, art 2(1)(a).

   Sub-s (1): para (d) and word ", or" immediately preceding it inserted by the Insolvency Act 2000, s 8, Sch 4, Pt I, paras 1, 13(1), (2)(b).

Date in force: 2 April 2001: see SI 2001/766, art 2(1)(a).

Sub-s (2A): inserted by the Insolvency Act 2000, s 8, Sch 4, Pt I, paras 1, 13(1), (3).

Date in force: 2 April 2001: see SI 2001/766, art 2(1)(a).

Sub-s (3): words "or undertaking" in square brackets inserted by the Insolvency Act 2000, s 8, Sch 4, Pt I, paras 1, 13(1), (4)(a).

Date in force: 2 April 2001: see SI 2001/766, art 2(1)(a).

Sub-s (3): words from "and, in the" to "in the register" in square brackets inserted by the Insolvency Act 2000, s 8, Sch 4, Pt I, paras 1, 13(1), (4)(b).

Date in force: 2 April 2001: see SI 2001/766, art 2(1)(a).

Sub-s (4A): inserted by the Insolvency Act 2000, s 8, Sch 4, Pt I, paras 1, 13(1), (5).

Date in force: 2 April 2001: see SI 2001/766, art 2(1)(a).

SCHEDULE 1
MATTERS FOR DETERMINING UNFITNESS OF DIRECTORS

Section 9

PART I
MATTERS APPLICABLE IN ALL CASES

1   Any misfeasance or breach of any fiduciary or other duty by the director in relation to the company.

2   Any misapplication or retention by the director of, or any conduct by the director giving rise to an obligation to account for, any money or other property of the company.

3   The extent of the director's responsibility for the company entering into any transaction liable to be set aside under Part XVI of the Insolvency Act (provisions against debt avoidance).

4   The extent of the director's responsibility for any failure by the company to comply with any of the following provisions of the Companies Act, namely—
   (a)   section 221 (companies to keep accounting records);
   (b)   section 222 (where and for how long records to be kept);
   (c)   section 288 (register of directors and secretaries);
   (d)   section 352 (obligation to keep and enter up register of members);
   (e)   section 353 (location of register of members);
   [(f)   section 363 (duty of company to make annual returns);]
   (h)   sections 399 and 415 (company's duty to register charges it creates).
   [(h)   sections 398 and 703D (duty of company to deliver particulars of charges on its property)].

[5   The extent of the director's responsibility for any failure by the directors of the company to comply with—
   (a)   section 226 or 227 of the Companies Act (duty to prepare annual accounts), or
   (b)   section 233 of that Act (approval and signature of accounts).]

[5A   In the application of this Part of this Schedule in relation to any person who is a director of an open-ended investment company, any reference to a provision of the Companies Act is to be taken to be a reference to the corresponding provision of the Open-Ended Investment Companies Regulations 2001 or of any rules made under regulation 6 of those Regulations (Financial Services Authority rules).]

NOTES

Para 4: sub-para (f) substituted, for sub-paras (f), (g) as originally enacted, by the Companies Act 1989, s 139(4); sub-para (h) prospectively substituted by the Companies Act

1989, s 107, Sch 16, para 4, as from a day to be appointed.

Para 5: substituted by the Companies Act 1989, s 23, Sch 10, Part II, para 35.

Para 5A: inserted by SI 1996/2827, reg 75, Sch 8, para 10.

Para 5A: substituted by SI 2001/1228, reg 84, Sch 7, Pt I, para 9.

Date in force: 1 December 2001 (being the date on which the Financial Services and Markets Act 2000, s 19, came into force): see SI 2001/3538, art 2(1) and SI 2001/1228, reg 1(2)(c).

PART II
MATTERS APPLICABLE WHERE COMPANY HAS BECOME INSOLVENT

6 The extent of the director's responsibility for the causes of the company becoming insolvent.

7 The extent of the director's responsibility for any failure by the company to supply any goods or services which have been paid for (in whole or in part).

8 The extent of the director's responsibility for the company entering into any transaction or giving any preference, being a transaction or preference—

    (a)   liable to be set aside under section 127 or sections 238 to 240 of the Insolvency Act, or

    (b)   challengeable under section 242 or 243 of that Act or under any rule of law in Scotland.

9 The extent of the director's responsibility for any failure by the directors of the company to comply with section 98 of the Insolvency Act (duty to call creditors' meeting in creditors' voluntary winding up).

10 Any failure by the director to comply with any obligation imposed on him by or under any of the following provisions of the Insolvency Act—

    (a)   section 22 (company's statement of affairs in administration);

    (b)   section 47 (statement of affairs to administrative receiver);

    (c)   section 66 (statement of affairs in Scottish receivership);

    (d)   section 99 (directors' duty to attend meeting; statement of affairs in creditors' voluntary winding up);

    (e)   section 131 (statement of affairs in winding up by the court);

    (f)   section 234 (duty of any one with company property to deliver it up);

    (g)   section 235 (duty to co-operate with liquidator, etc).

Companies Act 1989

1989 CHAPTER 40

ARRANGEMENT OF SECTIONS

PART II
ELIGIBILITY FOR APPOINTMENT AS COMPANY AUDITOR

PART IV
REGISTRATION OF COMPANY CHARGES

PART V
OTHER AMENDMENTS OF COMPANY LAW

An Act to amend the law relating to company accounts; to make new provision with respect to the persons eligible for appointment as company auditors; to amend the Companies Act 1985 and certain other enactments with respect to investigations and powers to obtain information and to confer new powers exercisable to assist overseas regulatory authorities; to make new provision with respect to the registration of company charges and otherwise to amend the law relating to companies; to amend the Fair Trading Act 1973; to enable provision to be made for the payment of fees in connection with the exercise by the Secretary of State, the Director General of Fair Trading and the Monopolies and Mergers Commission of their functions under Part V of that Act; to make provision for safeguarding the operation of certain financial markets; to amend the Financial Services Act 1986; to enable provision to be made for the recording and transfer of title to securities without a written instrument; the Company Directors Disqualification Act 1986, the Company Securities (Insider Dealing) Act 1985, the Policyholders Protection Act 1975 and the law relating to building societies; and for connected purposes

[16th November 1989]

PART II
ELIGIBILITY FOR APPOINTMENT AS COMPANY AUDITOR

Introduction

24 Introduction

(1)   The main purposes of this Part are to secure that only persons who are properly supervised and appropriately qualified are appointed company auditors, and that audits by persons so appointed are carried out properly and with integrity and with a proper degree of independence.

(2)   A "company auditor" means a person appointed as auditor under Chapter V of Part XI of the Companies Act 1985; and the expressions "company audit" and "company audit work" shall be construed accordingly.

Eligibility for appointment

25 Eligibility for appointment

(1)   A person is eligible for appointment as a company auditor only if he—
   (a)   is a member of a recognised supervisory body, and
   (b)   is eligible for the appointment under the rules of that body.

(2)   An individual or a firm may be appointed a company auditor.

(3)   In the cases to which section 34 applies (individuals retaining only 1967 Act authorisation) a person's eligibility for appointment as a company auditor is restricted as mentioned in that section.

27 Ineligibility on ground of lack of independence

(1)   A person is ineligible for appointment as company auditor of a company if he is—

   (a)   an officer or employee of the company, or
   (b)   a partner or employee of such a person, or a partnership of which such a person is a partner,

or if he is ineligible by virtue of paragraph (a) or (b) for appointment as company auditor of any associated undertaking of the company.

   For this purpose an auditor of a company shall not be regarded as an officer or employee of the company.

(2)   A person is also ineligible for appointment as company auditor of a company if there exists between him or any associate of his and the company or any associated undertaking a connection of any such description as may be specified by regulations made by the Secretary of State.

   The regulations may make different provisions for different cases.

(3)   In this section "associated undertaking", in relation to a company, means—

   (a)   a parent undertaking or subsidiary undertaking of the company, or
   (b)   a subsidiary undertaking of any parent undertaking of the company.

(4)   Regulations under this section shall be made by statutory instrument which shall be subject to annulment in pursuance of a resolution of either House of Parliament.

Recognition of supervisory bodies and professional qualifications

30 Supervisory bodies

(1)   In this Part a "supervisory body" means a body established in the United Kingdom (whether a body corporate or an unincorporated association) which maintains and enforces rules as to—

   (a)   the eligibility of persons to seek appointment as company auditors, and
   (b)   the conduct of company audit work,

which are binding on persons seeking appointment or acting as company auditors either because they are members of that body or because they are otherwise subject to its control.

(2)   In this Part references to the members of a supervisory body are to the persons who, whether or not members of the body, are subject to its rules in seeking appointment or acting as company auditors.

(3)   In this Part references to the rules of a supervisory body are to the rules (whether or not laid down by the body itself) which the body has power to enforce and which are relevant for the purposes of this Part.

   This includes rules relating to the admission and expulsion of members of the body, so far as relevant for the purposes of this Part.

(4) In this Part references to guidance issued by a supervisory body are to guidance issued or any recommendation made by it to all or any class of its members or persons seeking to become members which would, if it were a rule, fall within subsection (3).

(5) The provisions of Parts I and II of Schedule 11 have effect with respect to the recognition of supervisory bodies for the purposes of this Part.

31 Meaning of "appropriate qualification"

(1) A person holds an appropriate qualification for the purposes of this Part if—
  (a) he was, by virtue of membership of a body recognised for the purposes of section 389(1)(a) of the Companies Act 1985, qualified for appointment as auditor of a company under that section immediately before 1st January 1990 and immediately before the commencement of section 25 above,
  (b) he holds a recognised professional qualification obtained in the United Kingdom, or
  (c) he holds an approved overseas qualification and satisfies any additional educational requirements applicable in accordance with section 33(4).

(2) A person who, immediately before 1st January 1990 and immediately before the commencement of section 25 above, was qualified for appointment as auditor of a company under section 389 of the Companies Act 1985 otherwise than by virtue of membership of a body recognised for the purposes of section 389(1)(a)—
  (a) shall be treated as holding an appropriate qualification for twelve months from the day on which section 25 comes into force, and
  (b) shall continue to be so treated if within that period he notifies the Secretary of State that he wishes to retain the benefit of his qualification.

The notice shall be in writing and shall contain such information as the Secretary of State may require.

(3) If a person fails to give such notice within the time allowed he may apply to the Secretary of State, giving such information as would have been required in connection with a notice, and the Secretary of State may, if he is satisfied—
  (a) that there was good reason why the applicant did not give notice in time, and
  (b) that the applicant genuinely intends to practise as an auditor in Great Britain,

direct that he shall be treated as holding an appropriate qualification for the purposes of this Part.

(4) A person who—
  (a) began before 1st January 1990 a course of study or practical training leading to a professional qualification in accountancy offered by a body established in the United Kingdom, and
  (b) obtained that qualification on or after that date and before 1st January 1996,

shall be treated as holding an appropriate qualification if the qualification is approved by the Secretary of State for the purposes of this subsection.

(5) Approval shall not be given unless the Secretary of State is satisfied that the body concerned has or, as the case may be, had at the relevant time adequate arrangements to ensure that the qualification is, or was, awarded only to persons

educated and trained to a standard equivalent to that required in the case of a recognised professional qualification.

(6)   A person shall not be regarded as holding an appropriate qualification for the purposes of this Part except in the above cases.

32 Qualifying bodies and recognised professional qualifications

(1)   In this Part a "qualifying body" means a body established in the United Kingdom (whether a body corporate or an unincorporated association) which offers a professional qualification in accountancy.

(2)   In this Part references to the rules of a qualifying body are to the rules (whether or not laid down by the body itself) which the body has power to enforce and which are relevant for the purposes of this Part.

This includes rules relating to—
   (a)   admission to or expulsion from a course of study leading to a qualification,
   (b)   the award or deprivation of a qualification, or
   (c)   the approval of a person for the purposes of giving practical training or the withdrawal of such approval,

so far as relevant for the purposes of this Part.

(3)   In this Part references to guidance issued by any such body are to any guidance which the body issues, or any recommendation it makes to all or any class of persons holding or seeking to hold a qualification, or approved or seeking to be approved by the body for the purpose of giving practical training, which would, if it were a rule, fall within subsection (2).

(4)   The provisions of Parts I and II of Schedule 12 have effect with respect to the recognition for the purposes of this Part of a professional qualification offered by a qualifying body.

Duties of recognised bodies

35 The register of auditors

(1)   The Secretary of State shall make regulations requiring the keeping of a register of—
   (a)   the individuals and firms eligible for appointment as company auditor, and
   (b)   the individuals holding an appropriate qualification who are responsible for company audit work on behalf of such firms.

(2)   The regulations shall provide that each person's entry in the register shall give—
   (a)   his name and address, and
   (b)   in the case of a person eligible as mentioned in subsection (1)(a), the name of the relevant supervisory body,

together with such other information as may be specified by the regulations.

(3)   The regulations may impose such obligations as the Secretary of State thinks fit—
   (a)   on recognised supervisory bodies,
   (b)   on persons eligible for appointment as company auditor, and
   (c)   on any person with whom arrangements are made by one or more recognised supervisory bodies with respect to the keeping of the register.

(4)   The regulations may include provision—
   (a)   requiring the register to be open to inspection at such times and places as may be specified in the regulations or determined in accordance with them,
   (b)   enabling a person to require a certified copy of an entry in the register, and
   (c)   authorising the charging of fees for inspection, or the provision of copies, of such reasonable amount as may be specified in the regulations or determined in accordance with them;

and may contain such other supplementary and incidental provisions as the Secretary of State thinks fit.

(5)   Regulations under this section shall be made by statutory instrument which shall be subject to annulment in pursuance of a resolution of either House of Parliament.

(6)   The obligations imposed by regulations under this section on such persons as are mentioned in subsection (3)(a) or (c) are enforceable on the application of the Secretary of State by injunction or, in Scotland, by an order under section 45 of the Court of Session Act 1988.

36 Information about firms to be available to public

(1)   The Secretary of State shall make regulations requiring recognised supervisory bodies to keep and make available to the public the following information with respect to the firms eligible under their rules for appointment as a company auditor—
   (a)   in relation to a body corporate, the name and address of each person who is a director of the body or holds any shares in it,
   (b)   in relation to a partnership, the name and address of each partner,

and such other information as may be specified in the regulations.

(2)   The regulations may impose such obligations as the Secretary of State thinks fit—
   (a)   on recognised supervisory bodies,
   (b)   on persons eligible for appointment as company auditor, and
   (c)   on any person with whom arrangements are made by one or more recognised supervisory bodies with respect to the keeping of the information.

(3)   The regulations may include provision—
   (a)   requiring that the information be open to inspection at such times and places as may be specified in the regulations or determined in accordance with them,
   (b)   enabling a person to require a certified copy of the information or any part of it, and

(c)   authorising the charging of fees for inspection, or the provision of copies, of such reasonable amount as may be specified in the regulations or determined in accordance with them;

and may contain such other supplementary and incidental provisions as the Secretary of State thinks fit.

(4)   The regulations may make different provision in relation to different descriptions of information and may contain such other supplementary and incidental provisions as the Secretary of State thinks fit.

(5)   Regulations under this section shall be made by statutory instrument which shall be subject to annulment in pursuance of a resolution of either House of Parliament.

(6)   The obligations imposed by regulations under this section on such persons as are mentioned in subsection (2)(a) or (c) are enforceable on the application of the Secretary of State by injunction or, in Scotland, by an order under section 45 of the Court of Session Act 1988.

PART IV

REGISTRATION OF COMPANY CHARGES

Introduction

92 Introduction

The provisions of this Part amend the provisions of the Companies Act 1985 relating to the registration of company charges—
  (a)   by inserting in Part XII of that Act (in place of sections 395 to 408 and 410 to 423) new provisions with respect to companies registered in Great Britain, and
  (b)   by inserting as Chapter III of Part XXIII of that Act (in place of sections 409 and 424) new provisions with respect to oversea companies.

PART V

OTHER AMENDMENTS OF COMPANY LAW

De-regulation of private companies

117 Power to make further provision by regulations

(1)   The Secretary of State may by regulations make provision enabling private companies to elect, by elective resolution in accordance with section 379A of the Companies Act 1985, to dispense with compliance with such requirements of that Act as may be specified in the regulations, being requirements which appear to the Secretary of State to relate primarily to the internal administration and procedure of companies.

(2)   The regulations may add to, amend or repeal provisions of that Act; and may provide for any such provision to have effect, where an election is made, subject to such adaptations and modifications as appear to the Secretary of State to be appropriate.

(3)   The regulations may make different provision for different cases and may contain such supplementary, incidental and transitional provisions as appear to the Secretary of State to be appropriate.

(4)   Regulations under this section shall be made by statutory instrument.

(5)   No regulations under this section shall be made unless a draft of the instrument containing the regulations has been laid before Parliament and approved by a resolution of each House.

Miscellaneous

135 Orders imposing restrictions on shares

(1)   The Secretary of State may by regulations made by statutory instrument make such amendments of the provisions of the Companies Act 1985 relating to orders imposing restrictions on shares as appear to him necessary or expedient—

  (a)   for enabling orders to be made in a form protecting the rights of third parties;
  (b)   with respect to the circumstances in which restrictions may be relaxed or removed;
  (c)   with respect to the making of interim orders by a court.

(2)   The provisions referred to in subsection (1) are section 210(5), section 216(1) and (2), section 445 and Part XV of the Companies Act 1985.

(3)   The regulations may make different provision for different cases and may contain such transitional and other supplementary and incidental provisions as appear to the Secretary of State to be appropriate.

(4)   Regulations under this section shall not be made unless a draft of the regulations has been laid before Parliament and approved by resolution of each House of Parliament.

141 Application to declare dissolution of company void

(1)–(3)   . . .

(4)   An application may be made under section 651(5) of the Companies Act 1985 as inserted by subsection (3) above (proceedings for damages for personal injury, &c.) in relation to a company dissolved before the commencement of this section notwithstanding that the time within which the dissolution might formerly have been declared void under that section had expired before commencement.

But no such application shall be made in relation to a company dissolved more than twenty years before the commencement of this section.

(5)   Except as provided by subsection (4), the amendments made by this section do not apply in relation to a company which was dissolved more than two years before the commencement of this section.

NOTES

Sub-ss (1)–(3): amend the Companies Act 1985, s 651.

Criminal Justice Act 1993

1993 CHAPTER 36

ARRANGEMENT OF SECTIONS

PART V
INSIDER DEALING

The offence of insider dealing

An Act to make provision about the jurisdiction of courts in England and Wales in relation to certain offences of dishonesty and blackmail; to amend the law about drug trafficking offences and to implement provisions of the Community Council Directive No 91/308/EEC; to amend Part VI of the Criminal Justice Act 1988; to make provision with respect to the financing of terrorism, the proceeds of terrorist-related activities and the investigation of terrorist activities; to amend Part I of the Criminal Justice Act 1991; to implement provisions of the Community Council Directive No 89/592/EEC and to amend and restate the law about insider dealing in securities; to provide for certain offences created by the Banking Coordination (Second Council Directive) Regulations 1992 to be punishable in the same way as offences under sections 39, 40 and 41 of the Banking Act 1987 and to enable regulations implementing Article 15 of the Community Council Directive No 89/646/EEC and Articles 3, 6 and 7 of the Community Council Directive No 92/30/EEC to create offences punishable in that way; to make provision with respect to the penalty for causing death by dangerous driving or causing death by careless driving while under the influence of drink or drugs; to make it an offence to assist in or induce certain conduct which for the purposes of, or in connection with, the provisions of Community law is unlawful in another member State; to provide for the introduction of safeguards in connection with the return of persons under backing of warrants arrangements; to amend the Criminal Procedure (Scotland) Act 1975 and Part I of the Prisoners and Criminal Proceedings (Scotland) Act 1993; and for connected purposes

[27th July 1993]

PART V
INSIDER DEALING

The offence of insider dealing

52 The offence

(1)   An individual who has information as an insider is guilty of insider dealing if, in the circumstances mentioned in subsection (3), he deals in securities that are price-affected securities in relation to the information.

(2)   An individual who has information as an insider is also guilty of insider dealing if—

    (a)   he encourages another person to deal in securities that are (whether or not that other knows it) price-affected securities in relation to the information, knowing or having reasonable cause to believe that the dealing would take place in the circumstances mentioned in subsection (3); or

    (b)   he discloses the information, otherwise than in the proper performance of the functions of his employment, office or profession, to another person.

(3)   The circumstances referred to above are that the acquisition or disposal in question occurs on a regulated market, or that the person dealing relies on a professional intermediary or is himself acting as a professional intermediary.

(4)   This section has effect subject to section 53.

53 Defences

(1)   An individual is not guilty of insider dealing by virtue of dealing in securities if he shows—
- (a)   that he did not at the time expect the dealing to result in a profit attributable to the fact that the information in question was price-sensitive information in relation to the securities, or
- (b)   that at the time he believed on reasonable grounds that the information had been disclosed widely enough to ensure that none of those taking part in the dealing would be prejudiced by not having the information, or
- (c)   that he would have done what he did even if he had not had the information.

(2)   An individual is not guilty of insider dealing by virtue of encouraging another person to deal in securities if he shows—
- (a)   that he did not at the time expect the dealing to result in a profit attributable to the fact that the information in question was price-sensitive information in relation to the securities, or
- (b)   that at the time he believed on reasonable grounds that the information had been or would be disclosed widely enough to ensure that none of those taking part in the dealing would be prejudiced by not having the information, or
- (c)   that he would have done what he did even if he had not had the information.

(3)   An individual is not guilty of insider dealing by virtue of a disclosure of information if he shows—
- (a)   that he did not at the time expect any person, because of the disclosure, to deal in securities in the circumstances mentioned in subsection (3) of section 52; or
- (b)   that, although he had such an expectation at the time, he did not expect the dealing to result in a profit attributable to the fact that the information was price-sensitive information in relation to the securities.

(4)   Schedule 1 (special defences) shall have effect.

(5)   The Treasury may by order amend Schedule 1.

(6)   In this section references to a profit include references to the avoidance of a loss.

Interpretation

54 Securities to which Part V applies

(1)   This Part applies to any security which—
- (a)   falls within any paragraph of Schedule 2; and
- (b)   satisfies any conditions applying to it under an order made by the Treasury for the purposes of this subsection;

and in the provisions of this Part (other than that Schedule) any reference to a security is a reference to a security to which this Part applies.

(2)   The Treasury may by order amend Schedule 2.

55 "Dealing" in securities

(1) For the purposes of this Part, a person deals in securities if—
  (a) he acquires or disposes of the securities (whether as principal or agent); or
  (b) he procures, directly or indirectly, an acquisition or disposal of the securities by any other person.

(2) For the purposes of this Part, "acquire", in relation to a security, includes—
  (a) agreeing to acquire the security; and
  (b) entering into a contract which creates the security.

(3) For the purposes of this Part, "dispose", in relation to a security, includes—
  (a) agreeing to dispose of the security; and
  (b) bringing to an end a contract which created the security.

(4) For the purposes of subsection (1), a person procures an acquisition or disposal of a security if the security is acquired or disposed of by a person who is—
  (a) his agent,
  (b) his nominee, or
  (c) a person who is acting at his direction,

in relation to the acquisition or disposal.

(5) Subsection (4) is not exhaustive as to the circumstances in which one person may be regarded as procuring an acquisition or disposal of securities by another.

56 "Inside information", etc

(1) For the purposes of this section and section 57, "inside information" means information which—
  (a) relates to particular securities or to a particular issuer of securities or to particular issuers of securities and not to securities generally or to issuers of securities generally;
  (b) is specific or precise;
  (c) has not been made public; and
  (d) if it were made public would be likely to have a significant effect on the price of any securities.

(2) For the purposes of this Part, securities are "price-affected securities" in relation to inside information, and inside information is "price-sensitive information" in relation to securities, if and only if the information would, if made public, be likely to have a significant effect on the price of the securities.

(3) For the purposes of this section "price" includes value.

57 "Insiders"

(1) For the purposes of this Part, a person has information as an insider if and only if—
  (a) it is, and he knows that it is, inside information, and
  (b) he has it, and knows that he has it, from an inside source.

(2) For the purposes of subsection (1), a person has information from an inside source if and only if—

   (a) he has it through—

      (i) being a director, employee or shareholder of an issuer of securities; or

      (ii) having access to the information by virtue of his employment, office or profession; or

   (b) the direct or indirect source of his information is a person within paragraph (a).

58 Information "made public"

(1) For the purposes of section 56, "made public", in relation to information, shall be construed in accordance with the following provisions of this section; but those provisions are not exhaustive as to the meaning of that expression.

(2) Information is made public if—

   (a) it is published in accordance with the rules of a regulated market for the purpose of informing investors and their professional advisers;

   (b) it is contained in records which by virtue of any enactment are open to inspection by the public;

   (c) it can be readily acquired by those likely to deal in any securities—

      (i) to which the information relates, or

      (ii) of an issuer to which the information relates; or

   (d) it is derived from information which has been made public.

(3) Information may be treated as made public even though—

   (a) it can be acquired only by persons exercising diligence or expertise;

   (b) it is communicated to a section of the public and not to the public at large;

   (c) it can be acquired only by observation;

   (d) it is communicated only on payment of a fee; or

   (e) it is published only outside the United Kingdom.

59 "Professional intermediary"

(1) For the purposes of this Part, a "professional intermediary" is a person—

   (a) who carries on a business consisting of an activity mentioned in subsection (2) and who holds himself out to the public or any section of the public (including a section of the public constituted by persons such as himself) as willing to engage in any such business; or

   (b) who is employed by a person falling within paragraph (a) to carry out any such activity.

(2) The activities referred to in subsection (1) are—

   (a) acquiring or disposing of securities (whether as principal or agent); or

   (b) acting as an intermediary between persons taking part in any dealing in securities.

(3) A person is not to be treated as carrying on a business consisting of an activity mentioned in subsection (2)—

   (a) if the activity in question is merely incidental to some other activity not falling within subsection (2); or

(b) merely because he occasionally conducts one of those activities.

(4) For the purposes of section 52, a person dealing in securities relies on a professional intermediary if and only if a person who is acting as a professional intermediary carries out an activity mentioned in subsection (2) in relation to that dealing.

60 Other interpretation provisions

(1) For the purposes of this Part, "regulated market" means any market, however operated, which, by an order made by the Treasury, is identified (whether by name or by reference to criteria prescribed by the order) as a regulated market for the purposes of this Part.

(2) For the purposes of this Part an "issuer", in relation to any securities, means any company, public sector body or individual by which or by whom the securities have been or are to be issued.

(3) For the purposes of this Part—
   (a) "company" means any body (whether or not incorporated and wherever incorporated or constituted) which is not a public sector body; and
   (b) "public sector body" means—
      (i) the government of the United Kingdom, of Northern Ireland or of any country or territory outside the United Kingdom;
      (ii) a local authority in the United Kingdom or elsewhere;
      (iii) any international organisation the members of which include the United Kingdom or another member State;
      (iv) the Bank of England; or
      (v) the central bank of any sovereign State.

(4) For the purposes of this Part, information shall be treated as relating to an issuer of securities which is a company not only where it is about the company but also where it may affect the company's business prospects.

Miscellaneous

61 Penalties and prosecution

(1) An individual guilty of insider dealing shall be liable—
   (a) on summary conviction, to a fine not exceeding the statutory maximum or imprisonment for a term not exceeding six months or to both; or
   (b) on conviction on indictment, to a fine or imprisonment for a term not exceeding seven years or to both.

(2) Proceedings for offences under this Part shall not be instituted in England and Wales except by or with the consent of—
   (a) the Secretary of State; or
   (b) the Director of Public Prosecutions.

(3) In relation to proceedings in Northern Ireland for offences under this Part, subsection (2) shall have effect as if the reference to the Director of Public Prosecutions were a reference to the Director of Public Prosecutions for Northern Ireland.

62 Territorial scope of offence of insider dealing

(1) An individual is not guilty of an offence falling within subsection (1) of section 52 unless—

   (a) he was within the United Kingdom at the time when he is alleged to have done any act constituting or forming part of the alleged dealing;

   (b) the regulated market on which the dealing is alleged to have occurred is one which, by an order made by the Treasury, is identified (whether by name or by reference to criteria prescribed by the order) as being, for the purposes of this Part, regulated in the United Kingdom; or

   (c) the professional intermediary was within the United Kingdom at the time when he is alleged to have done anything by means of which the offence is alleged to have been committed.

(2) An individual is not guilty of an offence falling within subsection (2) of section 52 unless—

   (a) he was within the United Kingdom at the time when he is alleged to have disclosed the information or encouraged the dealing; or

   (b) the alleged recipient of the information or encouragement was within the United Kingdom at the time when he is alleged to have received the information or encouragement.

63 Limits on section 52

(1) Section 52 does not apply to anything done by an individual acting on behalf of a public sector body in pursuit of monetary policies or policies with respect to exchange rates or the management of public debt or foreign exchange reserves.

(2) No contract shall be void or unenforceable by reason only of section 52.

64 Orders

(1) Any power under this Part to make an order shall be exercisable by statutory instrument.

(2) No order shall be made under this Part unless a draft of it has been laid before and approved by a resolution of each House of Parliament.

(3) An order under this Part—

   (a) may make different provision for different cases; and

   (b) may contain such incidental, supplemental and transitional provisions as the Treasury consider expedient.

PART VII
SUPPLEMENTARY

SCHEDULE I
SPECIAL DEFENCES

Section 53(4)

Market makers

1   (1)   An individual is not guilty of insider dealing by virtue of dealing in securities or encouraging another person to deal if he shows that he acted in good faith in the course of—
   (a)   his business as a market maker, or
   (b)   his employment in the business of a market maker.

(2)   A market maker is a person who—
   (a)   holds himself out at all normal times in compliance with the rules of a regulated market or an approved organisation as willing to acquire or dispose of securities; and
   (b)   is recognised as doing so under those rules.

(3)   In this paragraph "approved organisation" means an international securities self-regulating organisation approved [by the Treasury under any relevant order under section 22 of the Financial Services and Markets Act 2000].

Market information

2   (1)   An individual is not guilty of insider dealing by virtue of dealing in securities or encouraging another person to deal if he shows that—
   (a)   the information which he had as an insider was market information; and
   (b)   it was reasonable for an individual in his position to have acted as he did despite having that information as an insider at the time.

(2)   In determining whether it is reasonable for an individual to do any act despite having market information at the time, there shall, in particular, be taken into account—
   (a)   the content of the information;
   (b)   the circumstances in which he first had the information and in what capacity; and
   (c)   the capacity in which he now acts.

3   An individual is not guilty of insider dealing by virtue of dealing in securities or encouraging another person to deal if he shows—
   (a)   that he acted—
      (i)   in connection with an acquisition or disposal which was under consideration or the subject of negotiation, or in the course of a series of such acquisitions or disposals; and
      (ii)   with a view to facilitating the accomplishment of the acquisition or disposal or the series of acquisitions or disposals; and
   (b)   that the information which he had as an insider was market information arising directly out of his involvement in the acquisition or disposal or series of acquisitions or disposals.

4   For the purposes of paragraphs 2 and 3 market information is information consisting of one or more of the following facts—
   (a)   that securities of a particular kind have been or are to be acquired or disposed of, or that their acquisition or disposal is under consideration or the subject of negotiation;
   (b)   that securities of a particular kind have not been or are not to be acquired or disposed of;

(c)   the number of securities acquired or disposed of or to be acquired or disposed of or whose acquisition or disposal is under consideration or the subject of negotiation;

(d)   the price (or range of prices) at which securities have been or are to be acquired or disposed of or the price (or range of prices) at which securities whose acquisition or disposal is under consideration or the subject of negotiation may be acquired or disposed of;

(e)   the identity of the persons involved or likely to be involved in any capacity in an acquisition or disposal.

Price stabilisation

5   (1)   An individual is not guilty of insider dealing by virtue of dealing in securities or encouraging another person to deal if he shows that he acted in conformity with the price stabilisation rules.

[(2)   "Price stabilisation rules" means rules made under section 144(1) of the Financial Services and Markets Act 2000.]

NOTES

Para 1: in sub-para (3) words "by the Treasury under any relevant order under section 22 of the Financial Services and Markets Act 2000" in square brackets substituted by SI 2001/3649, art 341(1), (2).

Date in force: 1 December 2001: see SI 2001/3649, art 1.

Para 5: sub-para (2) substituted by SI 2001/3649, art 341(1), (3).

Date in force: 1 December 2001: see SI 2001/3649, art 1.

SCHEDULE 2
SECURITIES

Section 54

Shares

1   Shares and stock in the share capital of a company ("shares").

Debt securities

2   Any instrument creating or acknowledging indebtedness which is issued by a company or public sector body, including, in particular, debentures, debenture stock, loan stock, bonds and certificates of deposit ("debt securities").

Warrants

3   Any right (whether conferred by warrant or otherwise) to subscribe for shares or debt securities ("warrants").

Depositary receipts

4   (1)   The rights under any depositary receipt.

(2)   For the purposes of sub-paragraph (1) a "depositary receipt" means a certificate or other record (whether or not in the form of a document)—

(a)   which is issued by or on behalf of a person who holds any relevant securities of a particular issuer; and

(b)   which acknowledges that another person is entitled to rights in relation to the relevant securities or relevant securities of the same kind.

(3)   In sub-paragraph (2) "relevant securities" means shares, debt securities and warrants.

Options

5   Any option to acquire or dispose of any security falling within any other paragraph of this Schedule.

Futures

6   (1)   Rights under a contract for the acquisition or disposal of relevant securities under which delivery is to be made at a future date and at a price agreed when the contract is made.

(2)   In sub-paragraph (1)—
    (a)   the references to a future date and to a price agreed when the contract is made include references to a date and a price determined in accordance with terms of the contract; and
    (b)   "relevant securities" means any security falling within any other paragraph of this Schedule.

Contracts for differences

7   (1)   Rights under a contract which does not provide for the delivery of securities but whose purpose or pretended purpose is to secure a profit or avoid a loss by reference to fluctuations in—
    (a)   a share index or other similar factor connected with relevant securities;
    (b)   the price of particular relevant securities; or
    (c)   the interest rate offered on money placed on deposit.

(2)   In sub-paragraph (1) "relevant securities" means any security falling within any other paragraph of this Schedule.

Financial Services and Markets Act 2000

2000 CHAPTER 8

ARRANGEMENT OF SECTIONS

PART VI
OFFICIAL LISTING

The competent authority

The official list

PART XXIV
INSOLVENCY

PART XXVII
OFFENCES

PART XXIX
INTERPRETATION

An Act to make provision about the regulation of financial services and markets; to provide for the transfer of certain statutory functions relating to building societies, friendly societies, industrial and provident societies and certain other mutual societies; and for connected purposes.

[14th June 2000]

PART VI
OFFICIAL LISTING

The competent authority

72 The competent authority

(1) On the coming into force of this section, the functions conferred on the competent authority by this Part are to be exercised by the Authority.

(2) Schedule 7 modifies this Act in its application to the Authority when it acts as the competent authority.

(3) But provision is made by Schedule 8 allowing some or all of those functions to be transferred by the Treasury so as to be exercisable by another person.

73 General duty of the competent authority

(1) In discharging its general functions the competent authority must have regard to—
  (a) the need to use its resources in the most efficient and economic way;
  (b) the principle that a burden or restriction which is imposed on a person should be proportionate to the benefits, considered in general terms, which are expected to arise from the imposition of that burden or restriction;
  (c) the desirability of facilitating innovation in respect of listed securities;
  (d) the international character of capital markets and the desirability of maintaining the competitive position of the United Kingdom;
  (e) the need to minimise the adverse effects on competition of anything done in the discharge of those functions;
  (f) the desirability of facilitating competition in relation to listed securities.

(2) The competent authority's general functions are—
  (a) its function of making rules under this Part (considered as a whole);
  (b) its functions in relation to the giving of general guidance in relation to this Part (considered as a whole);
  (c) its function of determining the general policy and principles by reference to which it performs particular functions under this Part.

The official list

74 The official list

(1) The competent authority must maintain the official list.

(2) The competent authority may admit to the official list such securities and other things as it considers appropriate.

(3) But—
  (a) nothing may be admitted to the official list except in accordance with this Part; and
  (b) the Treasury may by order provide that anything which falls within a description or category specified in the order may not be admitted to the official list.

(4) The competent authority may make rules ("listing rules") for the purposes of this Part.

(5) In the following provisions of this Part—
  "security" means anything which has been, or may be, admitted to the official list; and
  "listing" means being included in the official list in accordance with this Part.

Listing

75 Applications for listing

(1)   Admission to the official list may be granted only on an application made to the competent authority in such manner as may be required by listing rules.

(2)   No application for listing may be entertained by the competent authority unless it is made by, or with the consent of, the issuer of the securities concerned.

(3)   No application for listing may be entertained by the competent authority in respect of securities which are to be issued by a body of a prescribed kind.

(4)   The competent authority may not grant an application for listing unless it is satisfied that—
   (a)   the requirements of listing rules (so far as they apply to the application), and
   (b)   any other requirements imposed by the authority in relation to the application,

are complied with.

(5)   An application for listing may be refused if, for a reason relating to the issuer, the competent authority considers that granting it would be detrimental to the interests of investors.

(6)   An application for listing securities which are already officially listed in another EEA State may be refused if the issuer has failed to comply with any obligations to which he is subject as a result of that listing.

76 Decision on application

(1)   The competent authority must notify the applicant of its decision on an application for listing—
   (a)   before the end of the period of six months beginning with the date on which the application is received; or
   (b)   if within that period the authority has required the applicant to provide further information in connection with the application, before the end of the period of six months beginning with the date on which that information is provided.

(2)   If the competent authority fails to comply with subsection (1), it is to be taken to have decided to refuse the application.

(3)   If the competent authority decides to grant an application for listing, it must give the applicant written notice.

(4)   If the competent authority proposes to refuse an application for listing, it must give the applicant a warning notice.

(5)   If the competent authority decides to refuse an application for listing, it must give the applicant a decision notice.

(6)   If the competent authority decides to refuse an application for listing, the applicant may refer the matter to the Tribunal.

(7)   If securities are admitted to the official list, their admission may not be called in question on the ground that any requirement or condition for their admission has not been complied with.

77 Discontinuance and suspension of listing

(1)   The competent authority may, in accordance with listing rules, discontinue the listing of any securities if satisfied that there are special circumstances which preclude normal regular dealings in them.

(2)   The competent authority may, in accordance with listing rules, suspend the listing of any securities.

(3)   If securities are suspended under subsection (2) they are to be treated, for the purposes of sections 96 and 99, as still being listed.

(4)   This section applies to securities whenever they were admitted to the official list.

(5)   If the competent authority discontinues or suspends the listing of any securities, the issuer may refer the matter to the Tribunal.

78 Discontinuance or suspension: procedure

(1)   A discontinuance or suspension takes effect—
(a)   immediately, if the notice under subsection (2) states that that is the case;
(b)   in any other case, on such date as may be specified in that notice.

(2)   If the competent authority—
(a)   proposes to discontinue or suspend the listing of securities, or
(b)   discontinues or suspends the listing of securities with immediate effect,

it must give the issuer of the securities written notice.

(3)   The notice must—
(a)   give details of the discontinuance or suspension;
(b)   state the competent authority's reasons for the discontinuance or suspension and for choosing the date on which it took effect or takes effect;
(c)   inform the issuer of the securities that he may make representations to the competent authority within such period as may be specified in the notice (whether or not he has referred the matter to the Tribunal);
(d)   inform him of the date on which the discontinuance or suspension took effect or will take effect; and
(e)   inform him of his right to refer the matter to the Tribunal.

(4)   The competent authority may extend the period within which representations may be made to it.

(5)   If, having considered any representations made by the issuer of the securities, the competent authority decides—
(a)   to discontinue or suspend the listing of the securities, or
(b)   if the discontinuance or suspension has taken effect, not to cancel it,

the competent authority must give the issuer of the securities written notice.

(6)   A notice given under subsection (5) must inform the issuer of the securities of his right to refer the matter to the Tribunal.

(7)   If a notice informs a person of his right to refer a matter to the Tribunal, it must give an indication of the procedure on such a reference.

(8)   If the competent authority decides—
(a)   not to discontinue or suspend the listing of the securities, or
(b)   if the discontinuance or suspension has taken effect, to cancel it,

the competent authority must give the issuer of the securities written notice.

(9)   The effect of cancelling a discontinuance is that the securities concerned are to be readmitted, without more, to the official list.

(10)   If the competent authority has suspended the listing of securities and proposes to refuse an application by the issuer of the securities for the cancellation of the suspension, it must give him a warning notice.

(11)   The competent authority must, having considered any representations made in response to the warning notice—
(a)   if it decides to refuse the application, give the issuer of the securities a decision notice;
(b)   if it grants the application, give him written notice of its decision.

(12)   If the competent authority decides to refuse an application for the cancellation of the suspension of listed securities, the applicant may refer the matter to the Tribunal.

(13)   "Discontinuance" means a discontinuance of listing under section 77(1).

(14)   "Suspension" means a suspension of listing under section 77(2).

Listing particulars

79 Listing particulars and other documents

(1)   Listing rules may provide that securities (other than new securities) of a kind specified in the rules may not be admitted to the official list unless—
(a)   listing particulars have been submitted to, and approved by, the competent authority and published; or
(b)   in such cases as may be specified by listing rules, such document (other than listing particulars or a prospectus of a kind required by listing rules) as may be so specified has been published.

(2)   "Listing particulars" means a document in such form and containing such information as may be specified in listing rules.

(3)   For the purposes of this Part, the persons responsible for listing particulars are to be determined in accordance with regulations made by the Treasury.

(4)   Nothing in this section affects the competent authority's general power to make listing rules.

80 General duty of disclosure in listing particulars

(1)   Listing particulars submitted to the competent authority under section 79 must contain all such information as investors and their professional advisers would reasonably require, and reasonably expect to find there, for the purpose of making an informed assessment of—
  (a)   the assets and liabilities, financial position, profits and losses, and prospects of the issuer of the securities; and
  (b)   the rights attaching to the securities.

(2)   That information is required in addition to any information required by—
  (a)   listing rules, or
  (b)   the competent authority,
as a condition of the admission of the securities to the official list.

(3)   Subsection (1) applies only to information—
  (a)   within the knowledge of any person responsible for the listing particulars; or
  (b)   which it would be reasonable for him to obtain by making enquiries.

(4)   In determining what information subsection (1) requires to be included in listing particulars, regard must be had (in particular) to—
  (a)   the nature of the securities and their issuer;
  (b)   the nature of the persons likely to consider acquiring them;
  (c)   the fact that certain matters may reasonably be expected to be within the knowledge of professional advisers of a kind which persons likely to acquire the securities may reasonably be expected to consult; and
  (d)   any information available to investors or their professional advisers as a result of requirements imposed on the issuer of the securities by a recognised investment exchange, by listing rules or by or under any other enactment.

81 Supplementary listing particulars

(1)   If at any time after the preparation of listing particulars which have been submitted to the competent authority under section 79 and before the commencement of dealings in the securities concerned following their admission to the official list—
  (a)   there is a significant change affecting any matter contained in those particulars the inclusion of which was required by—
    (i)   section 80,
    (ii)   listing rules, or
    (iii) the competent authority, or
  (b)   a significant new matter arises, the inclusion of information in respect of which would have been so required if it had arisen when the particulars were prepared,
the issuer must, in accordance with listing rules, submit supplementary listing particulars of the change or new matter to the competent authority, for its approval and, if they are approved, publish them.

(2)   "Significant" means significant for the purpose of making an informed assessment of the kind mentioned in section 80(1).

(3)   If the issuer of the securities is not aware of the change or new matter in question, he is not under a duty to comply with subsection (1) unless he is notified of the change or new matter by a person responsible for the listing particulars.

(4)   But it is the duty of any person responsible for those particulars who is aware of such a change or new matter to give notice of it to the issuer.

(5)   Subsection (1) applies also as respects matters contained in any supplementary listing particulars previously published under this section in respect of the securities in question.

82 Exemptions from disclosure

(1)   The competent authority may authorise the omission from listing particulars of any information, the inclusion of which would otherwise be required by section 80 or 81, on the ground—
- (a)   that its disclosure would be contrary to the public interest;
- (b)   that its disclosure would be seriously detrimental to the issuer; or
- (c)   in the case of securities of a kind specified in listing rules, that its disclosure is unnecessary for persons of the kind who may be expected normally to buy or deal in securities of that kind.

(2)   But—
- (a)   no authority may be granted under subsection (1)(b) in respect of essential information; and
- (b)   no authority granted under subsection (1)(b) extends to any such information.

(3)   The Secretary of State or the Treasury may issue a certificate to the effect that the disclosure of any information (including information that would otherwise have to be included in listing particulars for which they are themselves responsible) would be contrary to the public interest.

(4)   The competent authority is entitled to act on any such certificate in exercising its powers under subsection (1)(a).

(5)   This section does not affect any powers of the competent authority under listing rules made as a result of section 101(2).

(6)   "Essential information" means information which a person considering acquiring securities of the kind in question would be likely to need in order not to be misled about any facts which it is essential for him to know in order to make an informed assessment.

(7)   "Listing particulars" includes supplementary listing particulars.

83 Registration of listing particulars

(1)   On or before the date on which listing particulars are published as required by listing rules, a copy of the particulars must be delivered for registration to the registrar of companies.

(2)   A statement that a copy has been delivered to the registrar must be included in the listing particulars when they are published.

(3)   If there has been a failure to comply with subsection (1) in relation to listing particulars which have been published—
  (a)   the issuer of the securities in question, and
  (b)   any person who is a party to the publication and aware of the failure,

is guilty of an offence.

(4)   A person guilty of an offence under subsection (3) is liable—
  (a)   on summary conviction, to a fine not exceeding the statutory maximum;
  (b)   on conviction on indictment, to a fine.

(5)   "Listing particulars" includes supplementary listing particulars.

(6)   "The registrar of companies" means—
  (a)   if the securities are, or are to be, issued by a company incorporated in Great Britain whose registered office is in England and Wales, the registrar of companies in England and Wales;
  (b)   if the securities are, or are to be, issued by a company incorporated in Great Britain whose registered office is in Scotland, the registrar of companies in Scotland;
  (c)   if the securities are, or are to be, issued by a company incorporated in Northern Ireland, the registrar of companies for Northern Ireland; and
  (d)   in any other case, any of those registrars.

Prospectuses

84 Prospectuses

(1)   Listing rules must provide that no new securities for which an application for listing has been made may be admitted to the official list unless a prospectus has been submitted to, and approved by, the competent authority and published.

(2)   "New securities" means securities which are to be offered to the public in the United Kingdom for the first time before admission to the official list.

(3)   "Prospectus" means a prospectus in such form and containing such information as may be specified in listing rules.

(4)   Nothing in this section affects the competent authority's general power to make listing rules.

85 Publication of prospectus

(1)   If listing rules made under section 84 require a prospectus to be published before particular new securities are admitted to the official list, it is unlawful for any of those securities to be offered to the public in the United Kingdom before the required prospectus is published.

(2)   A person who contravenes subsection (1) is guilty of an offence and liable—
  (a)   on summary conviction, to imprisonment for a term not exceeding three months or a fine not exceeding level 5 on the standard scale;
  (b)   on conviction on indictment, to imprisonment for a term not exceeding two years or a fine, or both.

(3)   A person is not to be regarded as contravening subsection (1) merely because a prospectus does not fully comply with the requirements of listing rules as to its form or content.

(4)   But subsection (3) does not affect the question whether any person is liable to pay compensation under section 90.

(5)   Any contravention of subsection (1) is actionable, at the suit of a person who suffers loss as a result of the contravention, subject to the defences and other incidents applying to actions for breach of statutory duty.

86 Application of this Part to prospectuses

(1)   The provisions of this Part apply in relation to a prospectus required by listing rules as they apply in relation to listing particulars.

(2)   In this Part—
  (a)   any reference to listing particulars is to be read as including a reference to a prospectus; and
  (b)   any reference to supplementary listing particulars is to be read as including a reference to a supplementary prospectus.

87 Approval of prospectus where no application for listing

(1)   Listing rules may provide for a prospectus to be submitted to and approved by the competent authority if—
  (a)   securities are to be offered to the public in the United Kingdom for the first time;
  (b)   no application for listing of the securities has been made under this Part; and
  (c)   the prospectus is submitted by, or with the consent of, the issuer of the securities.

(2)   "Non-listing prospectus" means a prospectus submitted to the competent authority as a result of any listing rules made under subsection (1).

(3)   Listing rules made under subsection (1) may make provision—
  (a)   as to the information to be contained in, and the form of, a non-listing prospectus; and
  (b)   as to the timing and manner of publication of a non-listing prospectus.

(4)   The power conferred by subsection (3)(b) is subject to such provision made by or under any other enactment as the Treasury may by order specify.

(5)   Schedule 9 modifies provisions of this Part as they apply in relation to non-listing prospectuses.

Sponsors

88 Sponsors

(1)   Listing rules may require a person to make arrangements with a sponsor for the performance by the sponsor of such services in relation to him as may be specified in the rules.

(2) "Sponsor" means a person approved by the competent authority for the purposes of the rules.

(3) Listing rules made by virtue of subsection (1) may—
- (a) provide for the competent authority to maintain a list of sponsors;
- (b) specify services which must be performed by a sponsor;
- (c) impose requirements on a sponsor in relation to the provision of services or specified services;
- (d) specify the circumstances in which a person is qualified for being approved as a sponsor.

(4) If the competent authority proposes—
- (a) to refuse a person's application for approval as a sponsor, or
- (b) to cancel a person's approval as a sponsor,

it must give him a warning notice.

(5) If, after considering any representations made in response to the warning notice, the competent authority decides—
- (a) to grant the application for approval, or
- (b) not to cancel the approval,

it must give the person concerned, and any person to whom a copy of the warning notice was given, written notice of its decision.

(6) If, after considering any representations made in response to the warning notice, the competent authority decides—
- (a) to refuse to grant the application for approval, or
- (b) to cancel the approval,

it must give the person concerned a decision notice.

(7) A person to whom a decision notice is given under this section may refer the matter to the Tribunal.

89 Public censure of sponsor

(1) Listing rules may make provision for the competent authority, if it considers that a sponsor has contravened a requirement imposed on him by rules made as a result of section 88(3)(c), to publish a statement to that effect.

(2) If the competent authority proposes to publish a statement it must give the sponsor a warning notice setting out the terms of the proposed statement.

(3) If, after considering any representations made in response to the warning notice, the competent authority decides to make the proposed statement, it must give the sponsor a decision notice setting out the terms of the statement.

(4) A sponsor to whom a decision notice is given under this section may refer the matter to the Tribunal.

Compensation

90 Compensation for false or misleading particulars

(1)   Any person responsible for listing particulars is liable to pay compensation to a person who has—
- (a)   acquired securities to which the particulars apply; and
- (b)   suffered loss in respect of them as a result of—
  - (i)   any untrue or misleading statement in the particulars; or
  - (ii)   the omission from the particulars of any matter required to be included by section 80 or 81.

(2)   Subsection (1) is subject to exemptions provided by Schedule 10.

(3)   If listing particulars are required to include information about the absence of a particular matter, the omission from the particulars of that information is to be treated as a statement in the listing particulars that there is no such matter.

(4)   Any person who fails to comply with section 81 is liable to pay compensation to any person who has—
- (a)   acquired securities of the kind in question; and
- (b)   suffered loss in respect of them as a result of the failure.

(5)   Subsection (4) is subject to exemptions provided by Schedule 10.

(6)   This section does not affect any liability which may be incurred apart from this section.

(7)   References in this section to the acquisition by a person of securities include references to his contracting to acquire them or any interest in them.

(8)   No person shall, by reason of being a promoter of a company or otherwise, incur any liability for failing to disclose information which he would not be required to disclose in listing particulars in respect of a company's securities—
- (a)   if he were responsible for those particulars; or
- (b)   if he is responsible for them, which he is entitled to omit by virtue of section 82.

(9)   The reference in subsection (8) to a person incurring liability includes a reference to any other person being entitled as against that person to be granted any civil remedy or to rescind or repudiate an agreement.

(10)   "Listing particulars", in subsection (1) and Schedule 10, includes supplementary listing particulars.

Penalties

91 Penalties for breach of listing rules

(1)   If the competent authority considers that—
- (a)   an issuer of listed securities, or
- (b)   an applicant for listing,

has contravened any provision of listing rules, it may impose on him a penalty of such amount as it considers appropriate.

(2)   If, in such a case, the competent authority considers that a person who was at the material time a director of the issuer or applicant was knowingly concerned in the contravention, it may impose on him a penalty of such amount as it considers appropriate.

(3)   If the competent authority is entitled to impose a penalty on a person under this section in respect of a particular matter it may, instead of imposing a penalty on him in respect of that matter, publish a statement censuring him.

(4)   Nothing in this section prevents the competent authority from taking any other steps which it has power to take under this Part.

(5)   A penalty under this section is payable to the competent authority.

(6)   The competent authority may not take action against a person under this section after the end of the period of two years beginning with the first day on which it knew of the contravention unless proceedings against that person, in respect of the contravention, were begun before the end of that period.

(7)   For the purposes of subsection (6)—
  (a)   the competent authority is to be treated as knowing of a contravention if it has information from which the contravention can reasonably be inferred; and
  (b)   proceedings against a person in respect of a contravention are to be treated as begun when a warning notice is given to him under section 92.

92 Procedure

(1)   If the competent authority proposes to take action against a person under section 91, it must give him a warning notice.

(2)   A warning notice about a proposal to impose a penalty must state the amount of the proposed penalty.

(3)   A warning notice about a proposal to publish a statement must set out the terms of the proposed statement.

(4)   If the competent authority decides to take action against a person under section 91, it must give him a decision notice.

(5)   A decision notice about the imposition of a penalty must state the amount of the penalty.

(6)   A decision notice about the publication of a statement must set out the terms of the statement.

(7)   If the competent authority decides to take action against a person under section 91, he may refer the matter to the Tribunal.

93 Statement of policy

(1)   The competent authority must prepare and issue a statement ("its policy statement") of its policy with respect to—
   (a)   the imposition of penalties under section 91; and
   (b)   the amount of penalties under that section.

(2)   The competent authority's policy in determining what the amount of a penalty should be must include having regard to—
   (a)   the seriousness of the contravention in question in relation to the nature of the requirement contravened;
   (b)   the extent to which that contravention was deliberate or reckless; and
   (c)   whether the person on whom the penalty is to be imposed is an individual.

(3)   The competent authority may at any time alter or replace its policy statement.

(4)   If its policy statement is altered or replaced, the competent authority must issue the altered or replacement statement.

(5)   In exercising, or deciding whether to exercise, its power under section 91 in the case of any particular contravention, the competent authority must have regard to any policy statement published under this section and in force at the time when the contravention in question occurred.

(6)   The competent authority must publish a statement issued under this section in the way appearing to the competent authority to be best calculated to bring it to the attention of the public.

(7)   The competent authority may charge a reasonable fee for providing a person with a copy of the statement.

(8)   The competent authority must, without delay, give the Treasury a copy of any policy statement which it publishes under this section.

94 Statements of policy: procedure

(1)   Before issuing a statement under section 93, the competent authority must publish a draft of the proposed statement in the way appearing to the competent authority to be best calculated to bring it to the attention of the public.

(2)   The draft must be accompanied by notice that representations about the proposal may be made to the competent authority within a specified time.

(3)   Before issuing the proposed statement, the competent authority must have regard to any representations made to it in accordance with subsection (2).

(4)   If the competent authority issues the proposed statement it must publish an account, in general terms, of—
   (a)   the representations made to it in accordance with subsection (2); and
   (b)   its response to them.

(5)   If the statement differs from the draft published under subsection (1) in a way which is, in the opinion of the competent authority, significant, the competent authority must (in addition to complying with subsection (4)) publish details of the difference.

(6)   The competent authority may charge a reasonable fee for providing a person with a copy of a draft published under subsection (1).

(7)   This section also applies to a proposal to alter or replace a statement.

Competition

95 Competition scrutiny

(1)   The Treasury may by order provide for—
  (a)   regulating provisions, and
  (b)   the practices of the competent authority in exercising its functions under this Part ("practices"),

to be kept under review.

(2)   Provision made as a result of subsection (1) must require the person responsible for keeping regulating provisions and practices under review to consider—
  (a)   whether any regulating provision or practice has a significantly adverse effect on competition; or
  (b)   whether two or more regulating provisions or practices taken together have, or a particular combination of regulating provisions and practices has, such an effect.

(3)   An order under this section may include provision corresponding to that made by any provision of Chapter III of Part X.

(4)   Subsection (3) is not to be read as in any way restricting the power conferred by subsection (1).

(5)   Subsections (6) to (8) apply for the purposes of provision made by or under this section.

(6)   Regulating provisions or practices have a significantly adverse effect on competition if—
  (a)   they have, or are intended or likely to have, that effect; or
  (b)   the effect that they have, or are intended or likely to have, is to require or encourage behaviour which has, or is intended or likely to have, a significantly adverse effect on competition.

(7)   If regulating provisions or practices have, or are intended or likely to have, the effect of requiring or encouraging exploitation of the strength of a market position they are to be taken to have, or be intended or be likely to have, an adverse effect on competition.

(8)   In determining whether any of the regulating provisions or practices have, or are intended or likely to have, a particular effect, it may be assumed that the persons to whom the provisions concerned are addressed will act in accordance with them.

(9)   "Regulating provisions" means—
  (a)   listing rules,
  (b)   general guidance given by the competent authority in connection with its functions under this Part.

Miscellaneous

96 Obligations of issuers of listed securities

(1)   Listing rules may—
  (a)   specify requirements to be complied with by issuers of listed securities; and
  (b)   make provision with respect to the action that may be taken by the competent authority in the event of non-compliance.

(2)   If the rules require an issuer to publish information, they may include provision authorising the competent authority to publish it in the event of his failure to do so.

(3)   This section applies whenever the listed securities were admitted to the official list.

97 Appointment by competent authority of persons to carry out investigations

(1)   Subsection (2) applies if it appears to the competent authority that there are circumstances suggesting that—
  (a)   there may have been a breach of listing rules;
  (b)   a person who was at the material time a director of an issuer of listed securities has been knowingly concerned in a breach of listing rules by that issuer;
  (c)   a person who was at the material time a director of a person applying for the admission of securities to the official list has been knowingly concerned in a breach of listing rules by that applicant;
  (d)   there may have been a contravention of section 83, 85 or 98.

(2)   The competent authority may appoint one or more competent persons to conduct an investigation on its behalf.

(3)   Part XI applies to an investigation under subsection (2) as if—
  (a)   the investigator were appointed under section 167(1);
  (b)   references to the investigating authority in relation to him were to the competent authority;
  (c)   references to the offences mentioned in section 168 were to those mentioned in subsection (1)(d);
  (d)   references to an authorised person were references to the person under investigation.

98 Advertisements etc in connection with listing applications

(1)   If listing particulars are, or are to be, published in connection with an application for listing, no advertisement or other information of a kind specified by listing rules may be issued in the United Kingdom unless the contents of the advertisement or other information have been submitted to the competent authority and that authority has—
  (a)   approved those contents; or
  (b)   authorised the issue of the advertisement or information without such approval.

(2)   A person who contravenes subsection (1) is guilty of an offence and liable—
    (a)   on summary conviction, to a fine not exceeding the statutory maximum;
    (b)   on conviction on indictment, to imprisonment for a term not exceeding two years or a fine, or both.

(3)   A person who issues an advertisement or other information to the order of another person is not guilty of an offence under subsection (2) if he shows that he believed on reasonable grounds that the advertisement or information had been approved, or its issue authorised, by the competent authority.

(4)   If information has been approved, or its issue has been authorised, under this section, neither the person issuing it nor any person responsible for, or for any part of, the listing particulars incurs any civil liability by reason of any statement in or omission from the information if that information and the listing particulars, taken together, would not be likely to mislead persons of the kind likely to consider acquiring the securities in question.

(5)   The reference in subsection (4) to a person incurring civil liability includes a reference to any other person being entitled as against that person to be granted any civil remedy or to rescind or repudiate an agreement.

99 Fees

(1)   Listing rules may require the payment of fees to the competent authority in respect of—
    (a)   applications for listing;
    (b)   the continued inclusion of securities in the official list;
    (c)   applications under section 88 for approval as a sponsor; and
    (d)   continued inclusion of sponsors in the list of sponsors.

(2)   In exercising its powers under subsection (1), the competent authority may set such fees as it considers will (taking account of the income it expects as the competent authority) enable it—
    (a)   to meet expenses incurred in carrying out its functions under this Part or for any incidental purpose;
    (b)   to maintain adequate reserves; and
    (c)   in the case of the Authority, to repay the principal of, and pay any interest on, any money which it has borrowed and which has been used for the purpose of meeting expenses incurred in relation to—
        (i)   its assumption of functions from the London Stock Exchange Limited in relation to the official list; and
        (ii)   its assumption of functions under this Part.

(3)   In fixing the amount of any fee which is to be payable to the competent authority, no account is to be taken of any sums which it receives, or expects to receive, by way of penalties imposed by it under this Part.

(4)   Subsection (2)(c) applies whether expenses were incurred before or after the coming into force of this Part.

(5)   Any fee which is owed to the competent authority under any provision made by or under this Part may be recovered as a debt due to it.

100 Penalties

(1)   In determining its policy with respect to the amount of penalties to be imposed by it under this Part, the competent authority must take no account of the expenses which it incurs, or expects to incur, in discharging its functions under this Part.

(2)   The competent authority must prepare and operate a scheme for ensuring that the amounts paid to it by way of penalties imposed under this Part are applied for the benefit of issuers of securities admitted to the official list.

(3)   The scheme may, in particular, make different provision with respect to different classes of issuer.

(4)   Up to date details of the scheme must be set out in a document ("the scheme details").

(5)   The scheme details must be published by the competent authority in the way appearing to it to be best calculated to bring them to the attention of the public.

(6)   Before making the scheme, the competent authority must publish a draft of the proposed scheme in the way appearing to it to be best calculated to bring it to the attention of the public.

(7)   The draft must be accompanied by notice that representations about the proposals may be made to the competent authority within a specified time.

(8)   Before making the scheme, the competent authority must have regard to any representations made to it under subsection (7).

(9)   If the competent authority makes the proposed scheme, it must publish an account, in general terms, of—
    (a)   the representations made to it in accordance with subsection (7); and
    (b)   its response to them.

(10)   If the scheme differs from the draft published under subsection (6) in a way which is, in the opinion of the competent authority, significant the competent authority must (in addition to complying with subsection (9)) publish details of the difference.

(11)   The competent authority must, without delay, give the Treasury a copy of any scheme details published by it.

(12)   The competent authority may charge a reasonable fee for providing a person with a copy of—
    (a)   a draft published under subsection (6);
    (b)   scheme details.

(13)   Subsections (6) to (10) and (12) apply also to a proposal to alter or replace the scheme.

101 Listing rules: general provisions

(1)   Listing rules may make different provision for different cases.

(2)   Listing rules may authorise the competent authority to dispense with or modify the application of the rules in particular cases and by reference to any circumstances.

(3)   Listing rules must be made by an instrument in writing.

(4)   Immediately after an instrument containing listing rules is made, it must be printed and made available to the public with or without payment.

(5)   A person is not to be taken to have contravened any listing rule if he shows that at the time of the alleged contravention the instrument containing the rule had not been made available as required by subsection (4).

(6)   The production of a printed copy of an instrument purporting to be made by the competent authority on which is endorsed a certificate signed by an officer of the authority authorised by it for that purpose and stating—
  (a)   that the instrument was made by the authority,
  (b)   that the copy is a true copy of the instrument, and
  (c)   that on a specified date the instrument was made available to the public as required by subsection (4),

is evidence (or in Scotland sufficient evidence) of the facts stated in the certificate.

(7)   A certificate purporting to be signed as mentioned in subsection (6) is to be treated as having been properly signed unless the contrary is shown.

(8)   A person who wishes in any legal proceedings to rely on a rule-making instrument may require the Authority to endorse a copy of the instrument with a certificate of the kind mentioned in subsection (6).

102 Exemption from liability in damages

(1)   Neither the competent authority nor any person who is, or is acting as, a member, officer or member of staff of the competent authority is to be liable in damages for anything done or omitted in the discharge, or purported discharge, of the authority's functions.

(2)   Subsection (1) does not apply—
  (a)   if the act or omission is shown to have been in bad faith; or
  (b)   so as to prevent an award of damages made in respect of an act or omission on the ground that the act or omission was unlawful as a result of section 6(1) of the Human Rights Act 1998.

103 Interpretation of this Part

(1)   In this Part—
    "application" means an application made under section 75;
    "issuer", in relation to anything which is or may be admitted to the official list, has such meaning as may be prescribed by the Treasury;
    "listing" has the meaning given in section 74(5);
    "listing particulars" has the meaning given in section 79(2);
    "listing rules" has the meaning given in section 74(4);
    "new securities" has the meaning given in section 84(2);
    "the official list" means the list maintained as the official list by the Authority immediately before the coming into force of section 74, as that list has effect for the time being;

"security" (except in section 74(2)) has the meaning given in section 74(5).

(2) In relation to any function conferred on the competent authority by this Part, any reference in this Part to the competent authority is to be read as a reference to the person by whom that function is for the time being exercisable.

(3) If, as a result of an order under Schedule 8, different functions conferred on the competent authority by this Part are exercisable by different persons, the powers conferred by section 91 are exercisable by such person as may be determined in accordance with the provisions of the order.

(4) For the purposes of this Part, a person offers securities if, and only if, as principal—

    (a) he makes an offer which, if accepted, would give rise to a contract for their issue or sale by him or by another person with whom he has made arrangements for their issue or sale; or

    (b) he invites a person to make such an offer.

(5) "Offer" and "offeror" are to be read accordingly.

(6) For the purposes of this Part, the question whether a person offers securities to the public in the United Kingdom is to be determined in accordance with Schedule 11.

(7) For the purposes of subsection (4) "sale" includes any disposal for valuable consideration.

PART VIII
PENALTIES FOR MARKET ABUSE

Market abuse

118 Market abuse

(1) For the purposes of this Act, market abuse is behaviour (whether by one person alone or by two or more persons jointly or in concert)—

    (a) which occurs in relation to qualifying investments traded on a market to which this section applies;

    (b) which satisfies any one or more of the conditions set out in subsection (2); and

    (c) which is likely to be regarded by a regular user of that market who is aware of the behaviour as a failure on the part of the person or persons concerned to observe the standard of behaviour reasonably expected of a person in his or their position in relation to the market.

(2) The conditions are that—

    (a) the behaviour is based on information which is not generally available to those using the market but which, if available to a regular user of the market, would or would be likely to be regarded by him as relevant when deciding the terms on which transactions in investments of the kind in question should be effected;

(b) the behaviour is likely to give a regular user of the market a false or misleading impression as to the supply of, or demand for, or as to the price or value of, investments of the kind in question;

(c) a regular user of the market would, or would be likely to, regard the behaviour as behaviour which would, or would be likely to, distort the market in investments of the kind in question.

(3) The Treasury may by order prescribe (whether by name or by description)—
(a) the markets to which this section applies; and
(b) the investments which are qualifying investments in relation to those markets.

(4) The order may prescribe different investments or descriptions of investment in relation to different markets or descriptions of market.

(5) Behaviour is to be disregarded for the purposes of subsection (1) unless it occurs—
(a) in the United Kingdom; or
(b) in relation to qualifying investments traded on a market to which this section applies which is situated in the United Kingdom or which is accessible electronically in the United Kingdom.

(6) For the purposes of this section, the behaviour which is to be regarded as occurring in relation to qualifying investments includes behaviour which—
(a) occurs in relation to anything which is the subject matter, or whose price or value is expressed by reference to the price or value, of those qualifying investments; or
(b) occurs in relation to investments (whether qualifying or not) whose subject matter is those qualifying investments.

(7) Information which can be obtained by research or analysis conducted by, or on behalf of, users of a market is to be regarded for the purposes of this section as being generally available to them.

(8) Behaviour does not amount to market abuse if it conforms with a rule which includes a provision to the effect that behaviour conforming with the rule does not amount to market abuse.

(9) Any reference in this Act to a person engaged in market abuse is a reference to a person engaged in market abuse whether alone or with one or more other persons.

(10) In this section—
"behaviour" includes action or inaction;
"investment" is to be read with section 22 and Schedule 2;
"regular user", in relation to a particular market, means a reasonable person who regularly deals on that market in investments of the kind in question.

The code

119 The code

(1)   The Authority must prepare and issue a code containing such provisions as the Authority considers will give appropriate guidance to those determining whether or not behaviour amounts to market abuse.

(2)   The code may among other things specify—
  (a)   descriptions of behaviour that, in the opinion of the Authority, amount to market abuse;
  (b)   descriptions of behaviour that, in the opinion of the Authority, do not amount to market abuse;
  (c)   factors that, in the opinion of the Authority, are to be taken into account in determining whether or not behaviour amounts to market abuse.

(3)   The code may make different provision in relation to persons, cases or circumstances of different descriptions.

(4)   The Authority may at any time alter or replace the code.

(5)   If the code is altered or replaced, the altered or replacement code must be issued by the Authority.

(6)   A code issued under this section must be published by the Authority in the way appearing to the Authority to be best calculated to bring it to the attention of the public.

(7)   The Authority must, without delay, give the Treasury a copy of any code published under this section.

(8)   The Authority may charge a reasonable fee for providing a person with a copy of the code.

120 Provisions included in the Authority's code by reference to the City Code

(1)   The Authority may include in a code issued by it under section 119 ("the Authority's code") provision to the effect that in its opinion behaviour conforming with the City Code—
  (a)   does not amount to market abuse;
  (b)   does not amount to market abuse in specified circumstances; or
  (c)   does not amount to market abuse if engaged in by a specified description of person.

(2)   But the Treasury's approval is required before any such provision may be included in the Authority's code.

(3)   If the Authority's code includes provision of a kind authorised by subsection (1), the Authority must keep itself informed of the way in which the Panel on Takeovers and Mergers interprets and administers the relevant provisions of the City Code.

(4)   "City Code" means the City Code on Takeovers and Mergers issued by the Panel as it has effect at the time when the behaviour occurs.

(5)   "Specified" means specified in the Authority's code.

121 Codes: procedure

(1)   Before issuing a code under section 119, the Authority must publish a draft of the proposed code in the way appearing to the Authority to be best calculated to bring it to the attention of the public.

(2)   The draft must be accompanied by—
  (a)   a cost benefit analysis; and
  (b)   notice that representations about the proposal may be made to the Authority within a specified time.

(3)   Before issuing the proposed code, the Authority must have regard to any representations made to it in accordance with subsection (2)(b).

(4)   If the Authority issues the proposed code it must publish an account, in general terms, of—
  (a)   the representations made to it in accordance with subsection (2)(b); and
  (b)   its response to them.

(5)   If the code differs from the draft published under subsection (1) in a way which is, in the opinion of the Authority, significant—
  (a)   the Authority must (in addition to complying with subsection (4)) publish details of the difference; and
  (b)   those details must be accompanied by a cost benefit analysis.

(6)   Subsections (1) to (5) do not apply if the Authority considers that there is an urgent need to publish the code.

(7)   Neither subsection (2)(a) nor subsection (5)(b) applies if the Authority considers—
  (a)   that, making the appropriate comparison, there will be no increase in costs; or
  (b)   that, making that comparison, there will be an increase in costs but the increase will be of minimal significance.

(8)   The Authority may charge a reasonable fee for providing a person with a copy of a draft published under subsection (1).

(9)   This section also applies to a proposal to alter or replace a code.

(10)   "Cost benefit analysis" means an estimate of the costs together with an analysis of the benefits that will arise—
  (a)   if the proposed code is issued; or
  (b)   if subsection (5)(b) applies, from the code that has been issued.

(11)   "The appropriate comparison" means—
  (a)   in relation to subsection (2)(a), a comparison between the overall position if the code is issued and the overall position if it is not issued;

    (b)   in relation to subsection (5)(b), a comparison between the overall position after the issuing of the code and the overall position before it was issued.

122 Effect of the code

(1)   If a person behaves in a way which is described (in the code in force under section 119 at the time of the behaviour) as behaviour that, in the Authority's opinion, does not amount to market abuse that behaviour of his is to be taken, for the purposes of this Act, as not amounting to market abuse.

(2)   Otherwise, the code in force under section 119 at the time when particular behaviour occurs may be relied on so far as it indicates whether or not that behaviour should be taken to amount to market abuse.

Power to impose penalties

123 Power to impose penalties in cases of market abuse

(1)   If the Authority is satisfied that a person ("A")—
    (a)   is or has engaged in market abuse, or
    (b)   by taking or refraining from taking any action has required or encouraged another person or persons to engage in behaviour which, if engaged in by A, would amount to market abuse,

it may impose on him a penalty of such amount as it considers appropriate.

(2)   But the Authority may not impose a penalty on a person if, having considered any representations made to it in response to a warning notice, there are reasonable grounds for it to be satisfied that—
    (a)   he believed, on reasonable grounds, that his behaviour did not fall within paragraph (a) or (b) of subsection (1), or
    (b)   he took all reasonable precautions and exercised all due diligence to avoid behaving in a way which fell within paragraph (a) or (b) of that subsection.

(3)   If the Authority is entitled to impose a penalty on a person under this section it may, instead of imposing a penalty on him, publish a statement to the effect that he has engaged in market abuse.

Statement of policy

124 Statement of policy

(1)   The Authority must prepare and issue a statement of its policy with respect to—
    (a)   the imposition of penalties under section 123; and
    (b)   the amount of penalties under that section.

(2)   The Authority's policy in determining what the amount of a penalty should be must include having regard to—
    (a)   whether the behaviour in respect of which the penalty is to be imposed had an adverse effect on the market in question and, if it did, how serious that effect was;

(b)   the extent to which that behaviour was deliberate or reckless; and

(c)   whether the person on whom the penalty is to be imposed is an individual.

(3)   A statement issued under this section must include an indication of the circumstances in which the Authority is to be expected to regard a person as—

(a)   having a reasonable belief that his behaviour did not amount to market abuse; or

(b)   having taken reasonable precautions and exercised due diligence to avoid engaging in market abuse.

(4)   The Authority may at any time alter or replace a statement issued under this section.

(5)   If a statement issued under this section is altered or replaced, the Authority must issue the altered or replacement statement.

(6)   In exercising, or deciding whether to exercise, its power under section 123 in the case of any particular behaviour, the Authority must have regard to any statement published under this section and in force at the time when the behaviour concerned occurred.

(7)   A statement issued under this section must be published by the Authority in the way appearing to the Authority to be best calculated to bring it to the attention of the public.

(8)   The Authority may charge a reasonable fee for providing a person with a copy of a statement published under this section.

(9)   The Authority must, without delay, give the Treasury a copy of any statement which it publishes under this section.

125 Statement of policy: procedure

(1)   Before issuing a statement of policy under section 124, the Authority must publish a draft of the proposed statement in the way appearing to the Authority to be best calculated to bring it to the attention of the public.

(2)   The draft must be accompanied by notice that representations about the proposal may be made to the Authority within a specified time.

(3)   Before issuing the proposed statement, the Authority must have regard to any representations made to it in accordance with subsection (2).

(4)   If the Authority issues the proposed statement it must publish an account, in general terms, of—

(a)   the representations made to it in accordance with subsection (2); and

(b)   its response to them.

(5)   If the statement differs from the draft published under subsection (1) in a way which is, in the opinion of the Authority, significant, the Authority must (in addition to complying with subsection (4)) publish details of the difference.

(6)   The Authority may charge a reasonable fee for providing a person with a copy of a draft published under subsection (1).

(7)   This section also applies to a proposal to alter or replace a statement.

Procedure

126 Warning notices

(1)   If the Authority proposes to take action against a person under section 123, it must give him a warning notice.

(2)   A warning notice about a proposal to impose a penalty must state the amount of the proposed penalty.

(3)   A warning notice about a proposal to publish a statement must set out the terms of the proposed statement.

127 Decision notices and right to refer to Tribunal

(1)   If the Authority decides to take action against a person under section 123, it must give him a decision notice.

(2)   A decision notice about the imposition of a penalty must state the amount of the penalty.

(3)   A decision notice about the publication of a statement must set out the terms of the statement.

(4)   If the Authority decides to take action against a person under section 123, that person may refer the matter to the Tribunal.

Miscellaneous

128 Suspension of investigations

(1)   If the Authority considers it desirable or expedient because of the exercise or possible exercise of a power relating to market abuse, it may direct a recognised investment exchange or recognised clearing house—
  (a)   to terminate, suspend or limit the scope of any inquiry which the exchange or clearing house is conducting under its rules; or
  (b)   not to conduct an inquiry which the exchange or clearing house proposes to conduct under its rules.

(2)   A direction under this section—
  (a)   must be given to the exchange or clearing house concerned by notice in writing; and
  (b)   is enforceable, on the application of the Authority, by injunction or, in Scotland, by an order under section 45 of the Court of Session Act 1988.

(3)   The Authority's powers relating to market abuse are its powers—
  (a)   to impose penalties under section 123; or
  (b)   to appoint a person to conduct an investigation under section 168 in a case falling within subsection (2)(d) of that section.

129 Power of court to impose penalty in cases of market abuse

(1) The Authority may on an application to the court under section 381 or 383 request the court to consider whether the circumstances are such that a penalty should be imposed on the person to whom the application relates.

(2) The court may, if it considers it appropriate, make an order requiring the person concerned to pay to the Authority a penalty of such amount as it considers appropriate.

130 Guidance

(1) The Treasury may from time to time issue written guidance for the purpose of helping relevant authorities to determine the action to be taken in cases where behaviour occurs which is behaviour—
  (a) with respect to which the power in section 123 appears to be exercisable; and
  (b) which appears to involve the commission of an offence under section 397 of this Act or Part V of the Criminal Justice Act 1993 (insider dealing).

(2) The Treasury must obtain the consent of the Attorney General and the Secretary of State before issuing any guidance under this section.

(3) In this section "relevant authorities"—
  (a) in relation to England and Wales, means the Secretary of State, the Authority, the Director of the Serious Fraud Office and the Director of Public Prosecutions;
  (b) in relation to Northern Ireland, means the Secretary of State, the Authority, the Director of the Serious Fraud Office and the Director of Public Prosecutions for Northern Ireland.

(4) Subsections (1) to (3) do not apply to Scotland.

(5) In relation to Scotland, the Lord Advocate may from time to time, after consultation with the Treasury, issue written guidance for the purpose of helping the Authority to determine the action to be taken in cases where behaviour mentioned in subsection (1) occurs.

131 Effect on transactions

The imposition of a penalty under this Part does not make any transaction void or unenforceable.

PART IX
HEARINGS AND APPEALS

132 The Financial Services and Markets Tribunal

(1) For the purposes of this Act, there is to be a tribunal known as the Financial Services and Markets Tribunal (but referred to in this Act as "the Tribunal").

(2) The Tribunal is to have the functions conferred on it by or under this Act.

(3)   The Lord Chancellor may by rules make such provision as appears to him to be necessary or expedient in respect of the conduct of proceedings before the Tribunal.

(4)   Schedule 13 is to have effect as respects the Tribunal and its proceedings (but does not limit the Lord Chancellor's powers under this section).

PART XVII
COLLECTIVE INVESTMENT SCHEMES

Chapter I
Interpretation

236 Open-ended investment companies

(1)   In this Part "an open-ended investment company" means a collective investment scheme which satisfies both the property condition and the investment condition.

(2)   The property condition is that the property belongs beneficially to, and is managed by or on behalf of, a body corporate ("BC") having as its purpose the investment of its funds with the aim of—
   (a)   spreading investment risk; and
   (b)   giving its members the benefit of the results of the management of those funds by or on behalf of that body.

(3)   The investment condition is that, in relation to BC, a reasonable investor would, if he were to participate in the scheme—
   (a)   expect that he would be able to realize, within a period appearing to him to be reasonable, his investment in the scheme (represented, at any given time, by the value of shares in, or securities of, BC held by him as a participant in the scheme); and
   (b)   be satisfied that his investment would be realized on a basis calculated wholly or mainly by reference to the value of property in respect of which the scheme makes arrangements.

(4)   In determining whether the investment condition is satisfied, no account is to be taken of any actual or potential redemption or repurchase of shares or securities under—
   (a)   Chapter VII of Part V of the Companies Act 1985;
   (b)   Chapter VII of Part VI of the Companies (Northern Ireland) Order 1986;
   (c)   corresponding provisions in force in another EEA State; or
   (d)   provisions in force in a country or territory other than an EEA state which the Treasury have, by order, designated as corresponding provisions.

(5)   The Treasury may by order amend the definition of "an open-ended investment company" for the purposes of this Part.

PART XVIII
RECOGNISED INVESTMENT EXCHANGES AND CLEARING HOUSES

Chapter I
Exemption

285 Exemption for recognised investment exchanges and clearing houses

(1) In this Act—
  (a) "recognised investment exchange" means an investment exchange in relation to which a recognition order is in force; and
  (b) "recognised clearing house" means a clearing house in relation to which a recognition order is in force.

(2) A recognised investment exchange is exempt from the general prohibition as respects any regulated activity—
  (a) which is carried on as a part of the exchange's business as an investment exchange; or
  (b) which is carried on for the purposes of, or in connection with, the provision of clearing services by the exchange.

(3) A recognised clearing house is exempt from the general prohibition as respects any regulated activity which is carried on for the purposes of, or in connection with, the provision of clearing services by the clearing house.

PART XXIV
INSOLVENCY

Voluntary arrangements

356 Authority's powers to participate in proceedings: company voluntary arrangements

(1) This section applies if a voluntary arrangement has been approved under Part I of the 1986 Act (or Part II of the 1989 Order) in respect of a company or insolvent partnership which is an authorised person.

[(1) Where a voluntary arrangement has effect under Part I of the 1986 Act in respect of a company or insolvent partnership which is an authorised person, the Authority may apply to the court under section 6 or 7 of that Act.]

(2) The Authority may make an application to the court in relation to the company or insolvent partnership under section 6 of the 1986 Act (or Article 19 of the 1989 Order).

[(2) Where a voluntary arrangement has been approved under Part II of the 1989 Order in respect of a company or insolvent partnership which is an authorised person, the Authority may apply to the court under Article 19 or 20 of that Order.]

(3)   If a person other than the Authority makes an application to the court in relation to the company or insolvent partnership under *either* [any] of those provisions, the Authority is entitled to be heard at any hearing relating to the application.

NOTES

Sub-s (1): substituted by the Insolvency Act 2000, s 15(3)(a).
Date in force: to be appointed: see the Insolvency Act 2000, s 16(1).
Sub-s (2): substituted by the Insolvency Act 2000, s 15(3)(b).
Date in force: to be appointed: see the Insolvency Act 2000, s 16(1).
Sub-s (3): word "either" in italics repealed and subsequent word in square brackets substituted by the Insolvency Act 2000, s 15(3)(c).
Date in force: to be appointed: see the Insolvency Act 2000, s 16(1).

357 Authority's powers to participate in proceedings: individual voluntary arrangements

(1)   The Authority is entitled to be heard on an application by an individual who is an authorised person under section 253 of the 1986 Act (or Article 227 of the 1989 Order).

(2)   Subsections (3) to (6) apply if such an order is made on the application of such a person.

(3)   A person appointed for the purpose by the Authority is entitled to attend any meeting of creditors of the debtor summoned under section 257 of the 1986 Act (or Article 231 of the 1989 Order).

(4)   Notice of the result of a meeting so summoned is to be given to the Authority by the chairman of the meeting.

(5)   The Authority may apply to the court—
   (a)   under section 262 of the 1986 Act (or Article 236 of the 1989 Order); or
   (b)   under section 263 of the 1986 Act (or Article 237 of the 1989 Order).

(6)   If a person other than the Authority makes an application to the court under any provision mentioned in subsection (5), the Authority is entitled to be heard at any hearing relating to the application.

Administration orders

359 Petitions

(1)   The Authority may present a petition to the court under section 9 of the 1986 Act (or Article 22 of the 1989 Order) in relation to a company or insolvent partnership which—
   (a)   is, or has been, an authorised person;
   (b)   is, or has been, an appointed representative; or
   (c)   is carrying on, or has carried on, a regulated activity in contravention of the general prohibition.

(2) Subsection (3) applies in relation to a petition presented by the Authority by virtue of this section.

(3) If the company or partnership is in default on an obligation to pay a sum due and payable under an agreement, it is to be treated for the purpose of section 8(1)(a) of the 1986 Act (or Article 21(1)(a) of the 1989 Order) as unable to pay its debts.

(4) "Agreement" means an agreement the making or performance of which constitutes or is part of a regulated activity carried on by the company or partnership.

(5) "Company" means—
   (a) a company to which section 8 of the 1986 Act applies; or
   (b) in relation to Northern Ireland, a company to which Article 21 of the 1989 Order applies.

361 Administrator's duty to report to Authority

(1) If—
   (a) an administration order is in force in relation to a company or partnership by virtue of a petition presented by a person other than the Authority, and
   (b) it appears to the administrator that the company or partnership is carrying on, or has carried on, a regulated activity in contravention of the general prohibition,

the administrator must report the matter to the Authority without delay.

(2) "An administration order" means an administration order under Part II of the 1986 Act (or Part III of the 1989 Order).

Provisions against debt avoidance

375 Authority's right to apply for an order

(1) The Authority may apply for an order under section 423 of the 1986 Act (or Article 367 of the 1989 Order) in relation to a debtor if—
   (a) at the time the transaction at an undervalue was entered into, the debtor was carrying on a regulated activity (whether or not in contravention of the general prohibition); and
   (b) a victim of the transaction is or was party to an agreement entered into with the debtor, the making or performance of which constituted or was part of a regulated activity carried on by the debtor.

(2) An application made under this section is to be treated as made on behalf of every victim of the transaction to whom subsection (1)(b) applies.

(3) Expressions which are given a meaning in Part XVI of the 1986 Act (or Article 367, 368 or 369 of the 1989 Order) have the same meaning when used in this section.

PART XXVII
OFFENCES

Miscellaneous offences

397 Misleading statements and practices

(1) This subsection applies to a person who—
   (a) makes a statement, promise or forecast which he knows to be misleading, false or deceptive in a material particular;
   (b) dishonestly conceals any material facts whether in connection with a statement, promise or forecast made by him or otherwise; or
   (c) recklessly makes (dishonestly or otherwise) a statement, promise or forecast which is misleading, false or deceptive in a material particular.

(2) A person to whom subsection (1) applies is guilty of an offence if he makes the statement, promise or forecast or conceals the facts for the purpose of inducing, or is reckless as to whether it may induce, another person (whether or not the person to whom the statement, promise or forecast is made)—
   (a) to enter or offer to enter into, or to refrain from entering or offering to enter into, a relevant agreement; or
   (b) to exercise, or refrain from exercising, any rights conferred by a relevant investment.

(3) Any person who does any act or engages in any course of conduct which creates a false or misleading impression as to the market in or the price or value of any relevant investments is guilty of an offence if he does so for the purpose of creating that impression and of thereby inducing another person to acquire, dispose of, subscribe for or underwrite those investments or to refrain from doing so or to exercise, or refrain from exercising, any rights conferred by those investments.

(4) In proceedings for an offence under subsection (2) brought against a person to whom subsection (1) applies as a result of paragraph (a) of that subsection, it is a defence for him to show that the statement, promise or forecast was made in conformity with price stabilising rules or control of information rules.

(5) In proceedings brought against any person for an offence under subsection (3) it is a defence for him to show—
   (a) that he reasonably believed that his act or conduct would not create an impression that was false or misleading as to the matters mentioned in that subsection;
   (b) that he acted or engaged in the conduct—
      (i) for the purpose of stabilising the price of investments; and
      (ii) in conformity with price stabilising rules; or
   (c) that he acted or engaged in the conduct in conformity with control of information rules.

(6) Subsections (1) and (2) do not apply unless—
   (a) the statement, promise or forecast is made in or from, or the facts are concealed in or from, the United Kingdom or arrangements are made in or

from the United Kingdom for the statement, promise or forecast to be made or the facts to be concealed;

(b) the person on whom the inducement is intended to or may have effect is in the United Kingdom; or

(c) the agreement is or would be entered into or the rights are or would be exercised in the United Kingdom.

(7) Subsection (3) does not apply unless—

(a) the act is done, or the course of conduct is engaged in, in the United Kingdom; or

(b) the false or misleading impression is created there.

(8) A person guilty of an offence under this section is liable—

(a) on summary conviction, to imprisonment for a term not exceeding six months or a fine not exceeding the statutory maximum, or both;

(b) on conviction on indictment, to imprisonment for a term not exceeding seven years or a fine, or both.

(9) "Relevant agreement" means an agreement—

(a) the entering into or performance of which by either party constitutes an activity of a specified kind or one which falls within a specified class of activity; and

(b) which relates to a relevant investment.

(10) "Relevant investment" means an investment of a specified kind or one which falls within a prescribed class of investment.

(11) Schedule 2 (except paragraphs 25 and 26) applies for the purposes of subsections (9) and (10) with references to section 22 being read as references to each of those subsections.

(12) Nothing in Schedule 2, as applied by subsection (11), limits the power conferred by subsection (9) or (10).

(13) "Investment" includes any asset, right or interest.

(14) "Specified" means specified in an order made by the Treasury.

PART XXIX
INTERPRETATION

417 Definitions

(1) In this Act—

"appointed representative" has the meaning given in section 39(2);

"auditors and actuaries rules" means rules made under section 340;

"authorisation offence" has the meaning given in section 23(2);

"authorised open-ended investment company" has the meaning given in section 237(3);

"authorised person" has the meaning given in section 31(2);

"the Authority" means the Financial Services Authority;

"body corporate" includes a body corporate constituted under the law of a country or territory outside the United Kingdom;

"chief executive"—

(a) in relation to a body corporate whose principal place of business is within the United Kingdom, means an employee of that body who, alone or jointly with one or more others, is responsible under the immediate authority of the directors, for the conduct of the whole of the business of that body; and

(b) in relation to a body corporate whose principal place of business is outside the United Kingdom, means the person who, alone or jointly with one or more others, is responsible for the conduct of its business within the United Kingdom;

"collective investment scheme" has the meaning given in section 235;

"the Commission" means the European Commission (except in provisions relating to the Competition Commission);

"the compensation scheme" has the meaning given in section 213(2);

"control of information rules" has the meaning given in section 147(1);

"director", in relation to a body corporate, includes—

(a) a person occupying in relation to it the position of a director (by whatever name called); and

(b) a person in accordance with whose directions or instructions (not being advice given in a professional capacity) the directors of that body are accustomed to act;

"documents" includes information recorded in any form and, in relation to information recorded otherwise than in legible form, references to its production include references to producing a copy of the information in legible form[, or in a form from which it can readily be produced in visible and legible form];

"exempt person", in relation to a regulated activity, means a person who is exempt from the general prohibition in relation to that activity as a result of an exemption order made under section 38(1) or as a result of section 39(1) or 285(2) or (3);

"financial promotion rules" means rules made under section 145;

"friendly society" means an incorporated or registered friendly society;

"general prohibition" has the meaning given in section 19(2);

"general rules" has the meaning given in section 138(2);

"incorporated friendly society" means a society incorporated under the Friendly Societies Act 1992;

"industrial and provident society" means a society registered or deemed to be registered under the Industrial and Provident Societies Act 1965 or the Industrial and Provident Societies Act (Northern Ireland) 1969;

"market abuse" has the meaning given in section 118;

"Minister of the Crown" has the same meaning as in the Ministers of the Crown Act 1975;

"money laundering rules" means rules made under section 146;

"notice of control" has the meaning given in section 178(5);

"the ombudsman scheme" has the meaning given in section 225(3);

"open-ended investment company" has the meaning given in section 236;

"Part IV permission" has the meaning given in section 40(4);

"partnership" includes a partnership constituted under the law of a country or territory outside the United Kingdom;

"prescribed" (where not otherwise defined) means prescribed in regulations made by the Treasury;

"price stabilising rules" means rules made under section 144;

"private company" has the meaning given in section 1(3) of the Companies Act 1985 or in Article 12(3) of the Companies (Northern Ireland) Order 1986;

"prohibition order" has the meaning given in section 56(2);

"recognised clearing house" and "recognised investment exchange" have the meaning given in section 285;

"registered friendly society" means a society which is—

    (a) a friendly society within the meaning of section 7(1)(a) of the Friendly Societies Act 1974; and

    (b) registered within the meaning of that Act;

"regulated activity" has the meaning given in section 22;

"regulating provisions" has the meaning given in section 159(1);

"regulatory objectives" means the objectives mentioned in section 2;

"regulatory provisions" has the meaning given in section 302;

"rule" means a rule made by the Authority under this Act;

"rule-making instrument" has the meaning given in section 153;

"the scheme manager" has the meaning given in section 212(1);

"the scheme operator" has the meaning given in section 225(2);

"scheme particulars rules" has the meaning given in section 248(1);

"Seventh Company Law Directive" means the European Council Seventh Company Law Directive of 13 June 1983 on consolidated accounts (No 83/349/EEC);

"threshold conditions", in relation to a regulated activity, has the meaning given in section 41;

"the Treaty" means the treaty establishing the European Community;

"trust scheme rules" has the meaning given in section 247(1);

"UK authorised person" has the meaning given in section 178(4); and

"unit trust scheme" has the meaning given in section 237.

(2) In the application of this Act to Scotland, references to a matter being actionable at the suit of a person are to be read as references to the matter being actionable at the instance of that person.

(3) For the purposes of any provision of this Act authorising or requiring a person to do anything within a specified number of days no account is to be taken of any day which is a public holiday in any part of the United Kingdom.

NOTES

Sub-s (1): in definition "documents" words from ", or in a" to "and legible form" in square brackets inserted by the Criminal Justice and Police Act 2001, s 70, Sch 2, Pt 2, para 16(1), (2)(f).

Date in force: to be appointed: see the Criminal Justice and Police Act 2001, s 138(2).

SCHEDULE 8
TRANSFER OF FUNCTIONS UNDER PART VI

Section 72(3)

The power to transfer

1   (1)   The Treasury may by order provide for any function conferred on the competent authority which is exercisable for the time being by a particular person to be transferred so as to be exercisable by another person.

(2)   An order may be made under this paragraph only if—
- (a)   the person from whom the relevant functions are to be transferred has agreed in writing that the order should be made;
- (b)   the Treasury are satisfied that the manner in which, or efficiency with which, the functions are discharged would be significantly improved if they were transferred to the transferee; or
- (c)   the Treasury are satisfied that it is otherwise in the public interest that the order should be made.

Supplemental

2   (1)   An order under this Schedule does not affect anything previously done by any person ("the previous authority") in the exercise of functions which are transferred by the order to another person ("the new authority").

(2)   Such an order may, in particular, include provision—
- (a)   modifying or excluding any provision of Part VI, IX or XXVI in its application to any such functions;
- (b)   for reviews similar to that made, in relation to the Authority, by section 12;
- (c)   imposing on the new authority requirements similar to those imposed, in relation to the Authority, by sections 152, 155 and 354;
- (d)   as to the giving of guidance by the new authority;
- (e)   for the delegation by the new authority of the exercise of functions under Part VI and as to the consequences of delegation;
- (f)   for the transfer of any property, rights or liabilities relating to any such functions from the previous authority to the new authority;
- (g)   for the carrying on and completion by the new authority of anything in the process of being done by the previous authority when the order takes effect;
- (h)   for the substitution of the new authority for the previous authority in any instrument, contract or legal proceedings;
- (i)   for the transfer of persons employed by the previous authority to the new authority and as to the terms on which they are to transfer;
- (j)   making such amendments to any primary or subordinate legislation (including any provision of, or made under, this Act) as the Treasury consider appropriate in consequence of the transfer of functions effected by the order.

(3)   Nothing in this paragraph is to be taken as restricting the powers conferred by section 428.

3   If the Treasury have made an order under paragraph 1 ("the transfer order") they may, by a separate order made under this paragraph, make any provision of a kind that could have been included in the transfer order.

SCHEDULE 9
NON-LISTING PROSPECTUSES

Section 87(5)

General application of Part VI

1   The provisions of Part VI apply in relation to a non-listing prospectus as they apply in relation to listing particulars but with the modifications made by this Schedule.

References to listing particulars

2   (1)   Any reference to listing particulars is to be read as a reference to a prospectus.

(2)   Any reference to supplementary listing particulars is to be read as a reference to a supplementary prospectus.

General duty of disclosure

3   (1)   In section 80(1), for "section 79" substitute "section 87".

(2)   In section 80(2), omit "as a condition of the admission of the securities to the official list".

Supplementary prospectuses

4   In section 81(1), for "section 79 and before the commencement of dealings in the securities concerned following their admission to the official list" substitute "section 87 and before the end of the period during which the offer to which the prospectus relates remains open".

Exemption from liability for compensation

5   (1)   In paragraphs 1(3) and 2(3) of Schedule 10, for paragraph (d) substitute—
[IPSB
   "(d)   the securities were acquired after such a lapse of time that he ought in the circumstances to be reasonably excused and, if the securities are dealt in on an approved exchange, he continued in that belief until after the commencement of dealings in the securities on that exchange."
   [IPSE

(2)   After paragraph 8 of that Schedule, insert—
[IPSB

"Meaning of "approved exchange"

9   "Approved exchange" has such meaning as may be prescribed."
[IPSE

Advertisements

6   In section 98(1), for "If listing particulars are, or are to be, published in connection with an application for listing," substitute "If a prospectus is, or is to be, published in connection with an application for approval, then, until the end of the period during which the offer to which the prospectus relates remains open,".

Fees

7   Listing rules made under section 99 may require the payment of fees to the competent authority in respect of a prospectus submitted for approval under section 87.

SCHEDULE 10
COMPENSATION: EXEMPTIONS

Section 90(2) and (5)

Statements believed to be true

1   (1)   In this paragraph "statement" means—
- (a)   any untrue or misleading statement in listing particulars; or
- (b)   the omission from listing particulars of any matter required to be included by section 80 or 81.

(2)   A person does not incur any liability under section 90(1) for loss caused by a statement if he satisfies the court that, at the time when the listing particulars were submitted to the competent authority, he reasonably believed (having made such enquiries, if any, as were reasonable) that—
- (a)   the statement was true and not misleading, or
- (b)   the matter whose omission caused the loss was properly omitted,

and that one or more of the conditions set out in sub-paragraph (3) are satisfied.

(3)   The conditions are that—
- (a)   he continued in his belief until the time when the securities in question were acquired;
- (b)   they were acquired before it was reasonably practicable to bring a correction to the attention of persons likely to acquire them;
- (c)   before the securities were acquired, he had taken all such steps as it was reasonable for him to have taken to secure that a correction was brought to the attention of those persons;
- (d)   he continued in his belief until after the commencement of dealings in the securities following their admission to the official list and they were acquired after such a lapse of time that he ought in the circumstances to be reasonably excused.

Statements by experts

2   (1)   In this paragraph "statement" means a statement included in listing particulars which—
- (a)   purports to be made by, or on the authority of, another person as an expert; and
- (b)   is stated to be included in the listing particulars with that other person's consent.

(2)   A person does not incur any liability under section 90(1) for loss in respect of any securities caused by a statement if he satisfies the court that, at the time when the listing particulars were submitted to the competent authority, he reasonably believed that the other person—
- (a)   was competent to make or authorise the statement, and
- (b)   had consented to its inclusion in the form and context in which it was included,

and that one or more of the conditions set out in sub-paragraph (3) are satisfied.

(3)   The conditions are that—
- (a)   he continued in his belief until the time when the securities were acquired;

(b)   they were acquired before it was reasonably practicable to bring the fact that the expert was not competent, or had not consented, to the attention of persons likely to acquire the securities in question;

(c)   before the securities were acquired he had taken all such steps as it was reasonable for him to have taken to secure that that fact was brought to the attention of those persons;

(d)   he continued in his belief until after the commencement of dealings in the securities following their admission to the official list and they were acquired after such a lapse of time that he ought in the circumstances to be reasonably excused.

Corrections of statements

3   (1)   In this paragraph "statement" has the same meaning as in paragraph 1.

(2)   A person does not incur liability under section 90(1) for loss caused by a statement if he satisfies the court—

(a)   that before the securities in question were acquired, a correction had been published in a manner calculated to bring it to the attention of persons likely to acquire the securities; or

(b)   that he took all such steps as it was reasonable for him to take to secure such publication and reasonably believed that it had taken place before the securities were acquired.

(3)   Nothing in this paragraph is to be taken as affecting paragraph 1.

Corrections of statements by experts

4   (1)   In this paragraph "statement" has the same meaning as in paragraph 2.

(2)   A person does not incur liability under section 90(1) for loss caused by a statement if he satisfies the court—

(a)   that before the securities in question were acquired, the fact that the expert was not competent or had not consented had been published in a manner calculated to bring it to the attention of persons likely to acquire the securities; or

(b)   that he took all such steps as it was reasonable for him to take to secure such publication and reasonably believed that it had taken place before the securities were acquired.

(3)   Nothing in this paragraph is to be taken as affecting paragraph 2.

Official statements

5   A person does not incur any liability under section 90(1) for loss resulting from—

(a)   a statement made by an official person which is included in the listing particulars, or

(b)   a statement contained in a public official document which is included in the listing particulars,

if he satisfies the court that the statement is accurately and fairly reproduced.

False or misleading information known about

6   A person does not incur any liability under section 90(1) or (4) if he satisfies the court that the person suffering the loss acquired the securities in question with knowledge—

(a)   that the statement was false or misleading,

(b)   of the omitted matter, or

(c)   of the change or new matter,

as the case may be.

Belief that supplementary listing particulars not called for

7 A person does not incur any liability under section 90(4) if he satisfies the court that he reasonably believed that the change or new matter in question was not such as to call for supplementary listing particulars.

Meaning of "expert"

8 "Expert" includes any engineer, valuer, accountant or other person whose profession, qualifications or experience give authority to a statement made by him.

SCHEDULE 11
OFFERS OF SECURITIES

Section 103(6)

The general rule

1 (1) A person offers securities to the public in the United Kingdom if—
 (a) to the extent that the offer is made to persons in the United Kingdom, it is made to the public; and
 (b) the offer is not an exempt offer.

(2) For this purpose, an offer which is made to any section of the public, whether selected—
 (a) as members or debenture holders of a body corporate,
 (b) as clients of the person making the offer, or
 (c) in any other manner,

is to be regarded as made to the public.

Exempt offers

2 (1) For the purposes of this Schedule, an offer of securities is an "exempt offer" if, to the extent that the offer is made to persons in the United Kingdom—
 (a) the condition specified in any of paragraphs 3 to [24A] is satisfied in relation to the offer; or
 (b) the condition specified in one relevant paragraph is satisfied in relation to part, but not the whole, of the offer and, in relation to each other part of the offer, the condition specified in a different relevant paragraph is satisfied.

(2) The relevant paragraphs are 3 to 8, 12 to 18 and 21.

Offers for business purposes

3 The securities are offered to persons—
 (a) whose ordinary activities involve them in acquiring, holding, managing or disposing of investments (as principal or agent) for the purposes of their businesses, or
 (b) who it is reasonable to expect will acquire, hold, manage or dispose of investments (as principal or agent) for the purposes of their businesses,

or are otherwise offered to persons in the context of their trades, professions or occupations.

Offers to limited numbers

4 (1) The securities are offered to no more than fifty persons.

(2)   In determining whether this condition is satisfied, the offer is to be taken together with any other offer of the same securities which was—

(a)   made by the same person;

(b)   open at any time within the period of 12 months ending with the date on which the offer is first made; and

(c)   not an offer to the public in the United Kingdom by virtue of this condition being satisfied.

(3)   For the purposes of this paragraph—

(a)   the making of an offer of securities to trustees or members of a partnership in their capacity as such, or

(b)   the making of such an offer to any other two or more persons jointly,

is to be treated as the making of an offer to a single person.

Clubs and associations

5   The securities are offered to the members of a club or association (whether or not incorporated) and the members can reasonably be regarded as having a common interest with each other and with the club or association in the affairs of the club or association and in what is to be done with the proceeds of the offer.

Restricted circles

6   (1)   The securities are offered to a restricted circle of persons whom the offeror reasonably believes to be sufficiently knowledgeable to understand the risks involved in accepting the offer.

(2)   In determining whether a person is sufficiently knowledgeable to understand the risks involved in accepting an offer of securities, any information supplied by the person making the offer is to be disregarded, apart from information about—

(a)   the issuer of the securities; or

(b)   if the securities confer the right to acquire other securities, the issuer of those other securities.

Underwriting agreements

7   The securities are offered in connection with a genuine invitation to enter into an underwriting agreement with respect to them.

Offers to public authorities

8   (1)   The securities are offered to a public authority.

(2)   "Public authority" means—

(a)   the government of the United Kingdom;

(b)   the government of any country or territory outside the United Kingdom;

(c)   a local authority in the United Kingdom or elsewhere;

(d)   any international organisation the members of which include the United Kingdom or another EEA State; and

(e)   such other bodies, if any, as may be specified.

Maximum consideration

9   (1)   The total consideration payable for the securities cannot exceed 40,000 euros (or an equivalent amount).

(2)   In determining whether this condition is satisfied, the offer is to be taken together with any other offer of the same securities which was—
   (a)   made by the same person;
   (b)   open at any time within the period of 12 months ending with the date on which the offer is first made; and
   (c)   not an offer to the public in the United Kingdom by virtue of this condition being satisfied.

(3)   An amount (in relation to an amount denominated in euros) is an "equivalent amount" if it is an amount of equal value, calculated at the latest practicable date before (but in any event not more than 3 days before) the date on which the offer is first made, denominated wholly or partly in another currency or unit of account.

Minimum consideration

10   (1)   The minimum consideration which may be paid by any person for securities acquired by him pursuant to the offer is at least 40,000 euros (or an equivalent amount).

(2)   Paragraph 9(3) also applies for the purposes of this paragraph.

Securities denominated in euros

11   (1)   The securities are denominated in amounts of at least 40,000 euros (or an equivalent amount).

(2)   Paragraph 9(3) also applies for the purposes of this paragraph.

Takeovers

12   (1)   The securities are offered in connection with a takeover offer.

(2)   "Takeover offer" means—
   (a)   an offer to acquire shares in a body incorporated in the United Kingdom which is a takeover offer within the meaning of the takeover provisions (or would be such an offer if those provisions applied in relation to any body corporate);
   (b)   an offer to acquire all or substantially all of the shares, or of the shares of a particular class, in a body incorporated outside the United Kingdom; or
   (c)   an offer made to all the holders of shares, or of shares of a particular class, in a body corporate to acquire a specified proportion of those shares.

(3)   "The takeover provisions" means—
   (a)   Part XIIIA of the Companies Act 1985; or
   (b)   in relation to Northern Ireland, Part XIVA of the Companies (Northern Ireland) Order 1986.

(4)   For the purposes of sub-paragraph (2)(b), any shares which the offeror or any associate of his holds or has contracted to acquire are to be disregarded.

(5)   For the purposes of sub-paragraph (2)(c), the following are not to be regarded as holders of the shares in question—
   (a)   the offeror;
   (b)   any associate of the offeror; and
   (c)   any person whose shares the offeror or any associate of the offeror has contracted to acquire.

(6)   "Associate" has the same meaning as in—
   (a)   section 430E of the Companies Act 1985; or

    (b)   in relation to Northern Ireland, Article 423E of the Companies (Northern Ireland) Order 1986.

Mergers

13   The securities are offered in connection with a merger (within the meaning of Council Directive No 78/855/EEC).

Free shares

14   (1)   The securities are shares and are offered free of charge to any or all of the holders of shares in the issuer.

(2)   "Holders of shares" means the persons who at the close of business on a date—
    (a)   specified in the offer, and
    (b)   falling within the period of 60 days ending with the date on which the offer is first made,

were holders of such shares.

Exchange of shares

15   The securities—
    (a)   are shares, or investments of a specified kind relating to shares, in a body corporate, and
    (b)   are offered in exchange for shares in the same body corporate,

and the offer cannot result in any increase in the issued share capital of the body corporate.

Qualifying persons

16   (1)   The securities are issued by a body corporate and are offered—
    (a)   by the issuer, by a body corporate connected with the issuer or by a relevant trustee;
    (b)   only to qualifying persons; and
    (c)   on terms that a contract to acquire any such securities may be entered into only by the qualifying person to whom they were offered or, if the terms of the offer so permit, any qualifying person.

(2)   A person is a "qualifying person", in relation to an issuer, if he is a genuine employee or former employee of the issuer or of another body corporate in the same group or the wife, husband, widow, widower or child or stepchild under the age of eighteen of such an employee or former employee.

(3)   In relation to an issuer of securities, "connected with" has such meaning as may be prescribed.

(4)   "Group" and "relevant trustee" have such meaning as may be prescribed.

Convertible securities

17   (1)   The securities result from the conversion of convertible securities and listing particulars (or a prospectus) relating to the convertible securities were (or was) published in the United Kingdom under or by virtue of Part VI or such other provisions applying in the United Kingdom as may be specified.

(2)   "Convertible securities" means securities of a specified kind which can be converted into, or exchanged for, or which confer rights to acquire, other securities.

(3) "Conversion" means conversion into or exchange for, or the exercise of rights conferred by the securities to acquire, other securities.

Charities

18 The securities are issued by—
- (a) a charity within the meaning of—
  - (i) section 96(1) of the Charities Act 1993, or
  - (ii) section 35 of the Charities Act (Northern Ireland) 1964,
- (b) a recognised body within the meaning of section 1(7) of the Law Reform (Miscellaneous Provisions) (Scotland) Act 1990,
- (c) a housing association within the meaning of—
  - (i) section 5(1) of the Housing Act 1985,
  - (ii) section 1 of the Housing Associations Act 1985, or
  - (iii) Article 3 of the Housing (Northern Ireland) Order 1992,
- (d) an industrial or provident society registered in accordance with—
  - (i) section 1(2)(b) of the Industrial and Provident Societies Act 1965, or
  - (ii) section 1(2)(b) of the Industrial and Provident Societies Act 1969, or
- (e) a non-profit making association or body, recognised by the country or territory in which it is established, with objectives similar to those of a body falling within any of paragraphs (a) to (c),

and the proceeds of the offer will be used for the purposes of the issuer's objectives.

Building societies etc

19 The securities offered are shares which are issued by, or ownership of which entitles the holder to membership of or to obtain the benefit of services provided by—
- (a) a building society incorporated under the law of, or of any part of, the United Kingdom;
- (b) any body incorporated under the law of, or of any part of, the United Kingdom relating to industrial and provident societies or credit unions; or
- (c) a body of a similar nature established in another EEA State.

Euro-securities

20 (1) The securities offered are Euro-securities and no advertisement relating to the offer is issued in the United Kingdom, or is caused to be so issued—
- (a) by the issuer of the Euro-securities;
- (b) by any credit institution or other financial institution through which the Euro-securities may be acquired pursuant to the offer; or
- (c) by any body corporate which is a member of the same group as the issuer or any of those institutions.

(2) But sub-paragraph (1) does not apply to an advertisement of a prescribed kind.

(3) "Euro-securities" means investments which—
- (a) are to be underwritten and distributed by a syndicate at least two of the members of which have their registered offices in different countries or territories;
- (b) are to be offered on a significant scale in one or more countries or territories, other than the country or territory in which the issuer has its registered office; and
- (c) may be acquired pursuant to the offer only through a credit institution or other financial institution.

(4) "Credit institution" means a credit institution as defined in [Article 1(1)(a)] of [the banking consolidation directive].

(5)   "Financial institution" means a financial institution as defined in Article 1 of [the banking consolidation directive].

(6)   "Underwritten" means underwritten by whatever means, including by acquisition or subscription, with a view to resale.

Same class securities

21   The securities are of the same class, and were issued at the same time, as securities in respect of which a prospectus has been published under or by virtue of—
(a)   Part VI;
(b)   Part III of the Companies Act 1985; or
(c)   such other provisions applying in the United Kingdom as may be specified.

Short date securities

22   The securities are investments of a specified kind with a maturity of less than one year from their date of issue.

Government and public securities

23   (1)   The securities are investments of a specified kind creating or acknowledging indebtedness issued by or on behalf of a public authority.

(2)   "Public authority" means—
(a)   the government of the United Kingdom;
(b)   the government of any country or territory outside the United Kingdom;
(c)   a local authority in the United Kingdom or elsewhere;
(d)   any international organisation the members of which include the United Kingdom or another EEA State; and
(e)   such other bodies, if any, as may be specified.

Non-transferable securities

24   The securities are not transferable.

[Units in a collective investment scheme

24A   The securities are units (as defined by section 237(2)) in a collective investment scheme.]

General definitions

25   For the purposes of this Schedule—
   "shares" has such meaning as may be specified; and
   "specified" means specified in an order made by the Treasury.

NOTES

Para 2: in sub-para (1)(a) reference to "24A" in square brackets substituted by SI 2001/2955, reg 2(a).
   Date in force: 14 September 2001: see SI 2001/2955, reg 1.
   Para 20: in sub-para (4) words "Article 1(1)(a)" in square brackets substituted by SI 2002/765, reg 4.
   Date in force: 27 April 2002: see SI 2002/765, reg 1.

Para 20: in sub-para (4) words "the banking consolidation directive" in square brackets substituted by SI 2000/2952, reg 8(1), (6)(a).

Date in force: 22 November 2000: see SI 2000/2952, reg 1.

Para 20: in sub-para (5) words "the banking consolidation directive" in square brackets substituted by SI 2000/2952, reg 8(1), (6)(b).

Date in force: 22 November 2000: see SI 2000/2952, reg 1.

Para 24A: inserted by SI 2001/2955, reg 2(b).

Date in force: 14 September 2001: see SI 2001/2955, reg 1.

PART II

COMPANIES REGULATIONS

Company and Business Names Regulations 1981

1981 No 1685

NOTES
Made - - - 24th November 1981

1

These Regulations may be cited as the Company and Business Names Regulations 1981 and shall come into operation on 26th February 1982.

2

In these Regulations, unless the context otherwise requires, "the Act" means the Companies Act 1981.

3

The words and expressions stated in column (1) of the Schedule hereto [(together with the plural and the possessive forms of those words and expressions)] are hereby specified as words and expressions for the registration of which as or as part of a company's corporate name the approval of the Secretary of State is required by section 22(2)(b) of the Act or for the use of which as or as part of a business name his approval is required by section 28(2)(b) of the Act.

NOTES
Words in square brackets inserted by SI 1992/1196, reg 2(2).

4

Subject to Regulation 5, each Government department or other body stated in column (2) of the Schedule hereto is hereby specified as the relevant body for the purposes of section 31(2) and (3) of the Act in relation to the word or expression [(and the plural and the possessive forms of that word or expression)] opposite to it in column (1).

NOTES
Words in square brackets inserted by SI 1992/1196, reg 2(3).

5

Where two Government departments or other bodies are specified in the alternative in Column (2) of the Schedule hereto the second alternative is to be treated as specified,
   (a)   in the case of the corporate name of a company,

    (i)   if the company has not yet been registered and its principal or only place of business in Great Britain is to be in Scotland or, if it will have no place of business in Great Britain, its proposed registered office is in Scotland, and

    (ii)   if the company is already registered and its principal or only place of business in Great Britain is in Scotland or, if it has no place of business in Great Britain, its registered office is in Scotland, and

  (b)   in the case of a business name, if the principal or only place of the business carried on or to be carried on in Great Britain is or is to be in Scotland,

and the first alternative is to be treated as specified in any other case.

SCHEDULE
SPECIFICATION OF WORDS, EXPRESSIONS AND RELEVANT BODIES

Regulations 3, 5

Column (1) Word or expression	Column (2) Relevant body
Abortion	Department of Health and Social Security
Apothecary	[Worshipful Society of Apothecaries of London] or Pharmaceutical Society of Great Britain
Association	
Assurance	
Assurer	
Authority	
Benevolent	
Board	
. . .	. . .
. . .	. . .
. . .	. . .
British	
. . .	
[Chamber (or Chambers) of Business (or their Welsh equivalents, Siambr Fusnes; Siambrau Busnes)	
Chamber (or Chambers) of Commerce (or their Welsh equivalents, Siambr Fasnach; Siambrau Masnach)	
Chamber (or Chambers) of Commerce and Industry (or their Welsh equivalents, Siambr Masnach a Diwydiant; Siambrau Masnach a Diwydiant)	
Chamber (or Chambers) of Commerce, Training and Enterprise (or their Welsh equivalents, Siambr Masnach, Hyfforddiant a Menter; Siambrau Masnach, Hyfforddiant a Menter)	

Chamber (or Chambers) of Enterprise (or their Welsh equivalents, Siambr Fenter; Siambrau Menter)
Chamber (or Chambers) of Industry (or their Welsh equivalents, Siambr Ddiwydiant; Siambrau Diwydiant)
Chamber (or Chambers) of Trade (or their Welsh equivalents, Siambr Fasnach; Siambrau Masnach)
Chamber (or Chambers) of Trade and Industry (or their Welsh equivalents, Siambr Masnach a Diwydiant; Siambrau Masnach a Diwydiant)
Chamber (or Chambers) of Training (or their Welsh equivalents, Siambr Hyfforddiant; Siambrau Hyfforddiant)
Chamber (or Chambers) of Training and Enterprise (or their Welsh equivalents, Siambr Hyfforddiant a Menter; Siambrau Hyfforddiant a Menter)]

Charitable	Charity Commission or [the Scottish Ministers]
Charity	Charity Commission or [the Scottish Ministers]
Charter	
Chartered	
[Chemist]	
[Chemistry]	
Contact Lens	General Optical Council
Co-operative	
Council	
Dental	General Dental Council
Dentistry	General Dental Council
District Nurse	Panel of Assessors in District Nurse Training
Duke	Home Office or [the Scottish Ministers]
England	
English	
European	
Federation	
Friendly Society	
Foundation	
Fund	
Giro	
Great Britain	
Group	
Health Centre	Department of Health and Social Security
Health Service	Department of Health and Social Security
Health Visitor	Council for the Education and Training of Health Visitors
Her Majesty	Home Office or [the Scottish Ministers]
His Majesty	Home Office or [the Scottish Ministers]
Holding	

Industrial and Provident Society	
Institute	
Institution	
Insurance	
Insurer	
International	
Ireland	
Irish	
King	Home Office or [the Scottish Ministers]
Midwife	Central Midwives Board or Central Midwives Board for Scotland
Midwifery	Central Midwives Board or Central Midwives Board for Scotland
National	
Nurse	General Nursing Council for England and Wales or General Nursing Council for Scotland
Nursing	General Nursing Council for England and Wales or General Nursing Council for Scotland
. . .	. . .
Patent	
Patentee	
Police	Home Office or [the Scottish Ministers]
[Polytechnic	[Department for Education and Skills]]
Post Office	
Pregnancy Termination	Department of Health and Social Security
Prince	Home Office or [the Scottish Ministers]
Princess	Home Office or [the Scottish Ministers]
Queen	Home Office or [the Scottish Ministers]
Reassurance	
Reassurer	
Register	
Registered	
Reinsurance	
Reinsurer	
Royal	Home Office or [the Scottish Ministers]
Royale	Home Office or [the Scottish Ministers]
Royalty	Home Office or [the Scottish Ministers]
Scotland	
Scottish	
Sheffield	
Society	
Special School	[Department for Education and Skills]
Stock Exchange	
Trade Union	
Trust	
United Kingdom	
[University]	[The Privy Council]
Wales	
Welsh	
Windsor	Home Office or [the Scottish Ministers]

[**Note:** The reference in Column (2) to the Home Office shall be treated as a reference to the Lord Chancellor's Department in relation to the following entries in Column (1)—

(a) Duke,
(b) Her Majesty,
(c) His Majesty,
(d) King,
(e) Prince,
(f) Princess,
(g) Queen,
(h) Royal,
(i) Royale,
(j) Royalty, and
(k) Windsor.]

NOTES

In entry "Apothecary" in column (2) words "Worshipful Society of Apothecaries of London" in square brackets substituted by SI 1982/1653, reg 2(a).

Entries "Breed", "Breeder", "Breeding" and "Nursing Home" (omitted) revoked by SI 1995/3022, reg 3(b).

Entry "Building Society" (omitted) revoked by SI 1992/1196, reg 2(1), (4)

Entries from "Chamber (or Chambers) of Business (or their Welsh equivalents, Siambr Fusnes; Siambrau Busnes)" to "Chamber (or Chambers) of Training and Enterprise (or their Welsh equivalents, Siambr Hyfforddiant a Menter; Siambrau Hyfforddiant a Menter)" substituted, for entries "Chamber of Commerce", "Chamber of Industry", "Chamber of Commerce, Training and Enterprise" (originally inserted by SI 1995/3022, reg 3(a)) and "Chamber of Trade" as originally enacted, by SI 2001/259, reg 3.

Date in force: 10 May 2001 (except in relation to a business name lawfully used until 12 months after any transfer of the business concerned before that date): see SI 2001/259, regs 1, 4.

In column (2) words "the Scottish Ministers" in square brackets in each place they occur substituted by SI 1999/1820, art 4, Sch 2, Pt II, para 139.

Date in force: 1 July 1999: see SI 1999/1820, art 1(2).

Entries "Chemist" and "Chemistry" inserted by SI 1982/1653, reg 2(b).

Entries "Polytechnic" and "University" inserted by SI 1982/1653, reg 2(c).

In column (2) words "Department for Education and Skills" in square brackets in both places they occur substituted by SI 2002/1397, art 12, Schedule, Pt II, para 17.

Date in force: 27 June 2002: see SI 2002/1397, art 1(2).

In entry "University" words "The Privy Council" in column (2) substituted by SI 1992/1196, reg 2(1), (5).

Note: inserted by SI 2001/3500, art 8, Sch 2, Pt II, para 14.

Date in force: 26 November 2001: see SI 2001/3500, art 1(2).

Companies (Disclosure of Directors' Interests) (Exceptions) Regulations 1985

1985 No 802

NOTES

Made - - - 21st May 1985

Authority: Companies Act 1985, s 324(3)

1

These Regulations may be cited as the Companies (Disclosure of Directors' Interests) (Exceptions) Regulations 1985 and shall come into operation on 1st July 1985.

2

Section 324(1) and (2) of the Companies Act 1985 shall not require notification of—

(a) interests in shares or debentures of any person in his capacity as trustee or personal representative of any trust or estate of which the Public Trustee is also a trustee (otherwise than as custodian trustee) or, as the case may be, a personal representative;

(b) interests in shares in, or debentures of, a society registered under the Industrial and Provident Societies Act 1965 or deemed to be so registered by virtue of section 4 of that Act;

(c) interests in shares or debentures of a person in his capacity as trustee of, or as beneficiary under, a trust relating exclusively to—

(i) any retirement benefits scheme which is an approved scheme or a statutory scheme as defined in section 26(1) of the Finance Act 1970, and any retirement benefit scheme which is treated as being two or more separate retirement benefit schemes under section 25(3) of that Act where any of those separate schemes is an approved scheme or a statutory scheme, or

(ii) a superannuation fund to which section 36 of the Finance Act 1980 applies;

(d) any event occurring in relation to any person in any such capacity as is mentioned in paragraph (a) or (c) of this Regulation or in relation to any such shares or debentures as are mentioned in paragraph (b);

(e) interests in shares or debentures which a person is taken to have under paragraph 4 of Part 1 of Schedule 13 to the Companies Act 1985 where the body corporate referred to in that paragraph is interested in those shares or debentures in its capacity as trustee of any such trust as is mentioned in paragraph (c) of this Regulation;

(f) any event occurring in relation to any person as a result of which he is taken to have any such interest as is mentioned in paragraph (e) of this Regulation;

(g)   interests in shares in a body corporate which arise solely on account of any limitation imposed by the memorandum or articles of association of the body corporate on a person's right to dispose of a share.

3

(1)   The said section 324(1) and (2) shall not require notification—

(a)   to a company which is the wholly owned subsidiary of a body corporate incorporated outside Great Britain of interests in shares in, or debentures of, that body corporate or any other body corporate so incorporated, or of any event occurring in relation to any such shares or debentures;

(b)   to a company by a director of the company who is also the director of a body corporate of which the company is the wholly owned subsidiary and which is itself required to keep a register under section 325(1) of the Companies Act 1985, of interests in any shares or debentures or of any event occurring in relation to any shares or debentures.

(2)   For the purposes of paragraph (1) of this Regulation, a company shall be deemed to be the wholly owned subsidiary of another body corporate if it has no members but that other and that other's wholly owned subsidiaries and its or their nominees.

Companies (Tables A to F) Regulations 1985

1985 No 805

NOTES

Made ....22nd May 1985

1

These Regulations may be cited as the Companies (Tables A to F) Regulations 1985 and shall come into operation on 1st July 1985.

2

The regulations in Table A and the forms in Tables B, C, D, E and F in the Schedule to these Regulations shall be the regulations and forms of memorandum and articles of association for the purposes of sections 3 and 8 of the Companies Act 1985.

3

. . .

This regulation revokes SI 1984/1717.

SCHEDULE

Regulation 2

TABLE A
REGULATIONS FOR MANAGEMENT OF A COMPANY LIMITED BY SHARES

1 In these regulations—

"the Act" means the Companies Act 1985 including any statutory modification or re-enactment thereof for the time being in force.

"the articles" means the articles of the company.

"clear days" in relation to the period of a notice means that period excluding the day when the notice is given or deemed to be given and the day for which it is given or on which it is to take effect.

["communication" means the same as in the Electronic Communications Act 2000.]

["electronic communication" means the same as in the Electronic Communications Act 2000.]

"executed" includes any mode of execution.

"office" means the registered office of the company.

"the holder" in relation to shares means the member whose name is entered in the register of members as the holder of the shares.

"the seal" means the common seal of the company.

"secretary" means the secretary of the company or any other person appointed to perform the duties of the secretary of the company, including a joint, assistant or deputy secretary.

"the United Kingdom" means Great Britain and Northern Ireland.

Unless the context otherwise requires, words or expressions contained in these regulations bear the same meaning as in the Act but excluding any statutory modification thereof not in force when these regulations become binding on the company.

SHARE CAPITAL

2 Subject to the provisions of the Act and without prejudice to any rights attached to any existing shares, any share may be issued with such rights or restrictions as the company may by ordinary resolution determine.

3 Subject to the provisions of the Act, shares may be issued which are to be redeemed or are to be liable to be redeemed at the option of the company or the holder on such terms and in such manner as may be provided by the articles.

4 The company may exercise the powers of paying commissions conferred by the Act. Subject to the [provisions] of the Act, any such commission may be satisfied by the payment of cash or by the allotment of fully or partly paid shares or partly in one way and partly in the other.

5 Except as required by law, no person shall be recognised by the company as holding any share upon any trust and (except as otherwise provided by the articles or by law) the company shall not be bound by or recognise any interest in any share except an absolute right to the entirety thereof in the holder.

SHARE CERTIFICATES

6 Every member, upon becoming the holder of any shares, shall be entitled without payment to one certificate for all the shares of each class held by him (and, upon transferring a part of his holding of shares of any class, to a certificate for the balance of such holding) or several certificates each for one or more of his shares of any class, to a certificate for the balance of such holding) or several certificates each for one or more of his shares upon payment for every certificate after the first of such reasonable sum as the directors may determine. Every certificate shall be sealed with the seal and shall specify the number, class and distinguishing numbers (if any) of the shares to which it relates and the amount or respective amounts paid up thereon. The company shall not be bound to issue more than one certificate for shares held jointly by several persons and delivery of a certificate to one joint holder shall be a sufficient delivery to all of them.

7 If a share certificate is defaced, worn-out, lost or destroyed, it may be renewed on such terms (if any) as to evidence and indemnity and payment of the expenses reasonably incurred by the company in investigating evidence as the directors may determine but otherwise free of charge, and (in the case of defacement or wearing-out) on delivery up of the old certificate.

LIEN

8 The company shall have a first and paramount lien on every share (not being a fully paid share) for all moneys (whether presently payable or not) payable at a fixed time or called in respect of that share. The directors may at any time declare any share to be wholly or in part exempt from the provisions of this regulation. The company's lien on a share shall extend to any amount payable in respect of it.

9 The company may sell in such manner as the directors determine any shares on which the company has a lien if a sum in respect of which the lien exists is presently payable and is not paid within fourteen clear days after notice has been given to the holder of the share or to the person entitled to it in consequence of the death or bankruptcy of the holder, demanding payment and stating that if the notice is not complied with the shares may be sold.

10 To give effect to a sale the directors may authorise some person to execute an instrument of transfer of the shares sold to, or in accordance with the directions of, the purchaser. The title of the transferee to the shares shall not be affected by any irregularity in or invalidity of the proceedings in reference to the sale.

11 The net proceeds of the sale, after payment of the costs, shall be applied in payment of so much of the sum for which the lien exists as is presently payable, and any residue shall (upon surrender to the company for cancellation of the certificate for the shares sold and subject to a like lien for any moneys not presently payable as existed upon the shares before the sale) be paid to the person entitled to the shares at the date of the sale.

CALLS ON SHARES AND FORFEITURE

12 Subject to the terms of allotment, the directors may make calls upon the members in respect of any moneys unpaid on their shares (whether in respect of nominal value or premium) and each member shall (subject to receiving at least fourteen clear days' notice specifying when and where payment is to be made) pay to the company as required by the notice the amount called on his shares. A call may, before receipt by the company of any sum due thereunder, be revoked in whole or part and payment of a call may be postponed in whole or part. A person upon whom a call is made shall remain liable for calls made upon him notwithstanding the subsequent transfer of the shares in respect whereof the call was made.

13   A call shall be deemed to have been made at the time when the resolution of the directors authorising the call was passed.

14   The joint holders of a share shall be jointly and severally liable to pay all calls in respect thereof.

15   If a call remains unpaid after it has become due and payable the person from whom it is due and payable shall pay interest on the amount unpaid from the day it became due and payable until it is paid at the rate fixed by the terms of allotment of the share or in the notice of the call or, if no rate is fixed, at the appropriate rate (as defined by the Act) but the directors may waive payment of the interest wholly or in part.

16   An amount payable in respect of a share on allotment or at any fixed date, whether in respect of nominal value or premium or as an instalment of a call, shall be deemed to be a call and if it is not paid the provisions of the articles shall apply as if that amount had become due and payable by virtue of a call.

17   Subject to the terms of allotment, the directors may make arrangements on the issue of shares for a difference between the holders in the amounts and times of payment of calls on their shares.

18   If a call remains unpaid after it has become due and payable the directors may give to the person from whom it is due not less than fourteen clear days' notice requiring payment of the amount unpaid together with any interest which may have accrued. The notice shall name the place where payment is to be made and shall state that if the notice is not complied with the shares in respect of which the call was made will be liable to be forfeited.

19   If the notice is not complied with any share in respect of which it was given may, before the payment required by the notice has been made, be forfeited by a resolution of the directors and the forfeiture shall include all dividends or other moneys payable in respect of the forfeited shares and not paid before the forfeiture.

20   Subject to the provisions of the Act, a forfeited share may be sold, re-alloted or otherwise disposed of on such terms and in such manner as the directors determine either to the person who was before the forfeiture the holder or to any other person and at any time before sale, re-allotment or other disposition, the forfeiture may be cancelled on such terms as the directors think fit. Where for the purposes of its disposal a forfeited share is to be transferred to any person the directors may authorise some person to execute an instrument of transfer of the share to that person.

21   A person any of whose shares have been forfeited shall cease to be a member in respect of them and shall surrender to the company for cancellation the certificate for the shares forfeited but shall remain liable to the company for all moneys which at the date of forfeiture were presently payable by him to the company in respect of those shares with interest at the rate at which interest was payable on those moneys before the forfeiture or, if no interest was so payable, at the appropriate rate (as defined in the Act) from the date of forfeiture until payment but the directors may waive payment wholly or in part or enforce payment without any allowance for the value of the shares at the time of forfeiture or for any consideration received on their disposal.

22   A statutory declaration by a director or the secretary that a share has been forfeited on a specified date shall be conclusive evidence of the facts stated in it as against all persons claiming to be entitled to the share and the declaration shall (subject to the execution of an instrument of transfer if necessary) constitute a good title to the share and the person to whom the share is disposed of shall not be bound to see to the application of the consideration, if any, nor shall his title to the share be affected by any irregularity in or invalidity of the proceedings in reference to the forfeiture or disposal of the share.

TRANSFER OF SHARES

23   The instrument of transfer of a share may be in any usual form or in any other form which the directors may approve and shall be executed by or on behalf of the transferor and, unless the share is fully paid, by or on behalf of the transferee.

24   The directors may refuse to register the transfer of a share which is not fully paid to a person of whom they do not approve and they may refuse to register the transfer of a share on which the company has a lien. They may also refuse to register a transfer unless—

   (a)   it is lodged at the office or at such other place as the directors may appoint and is accompanied by the certificate for the shares to which it relates and such other evidence as the directors may reasonably require to show the right of the transferor to make the transfer;

   (b)   it is in respect of only one class of shares; and

   (c)   it is in favour of not more than four transferees.

25   If the directors refuse to register a transfer of a share, they shall within two months after the date on which the transfer was lodged with the company send to the transferee notice of the refusal.

26   The registration of transfers of shares or of transfers of any class of shares may be suspended at such times and for such periods (not exceeding thirty days in any year) as the directors may determine.

27   No fee shall be charged for the registration of any instrument of transfer or other document relating to or affecting the title to any share.

28   The company shall be entitled to retain any instrument of transfer which is registered, but any instrument of transfer which the directors refuse to register shall be returned to the person lodging it when notice of the refusal is given.

TRANSMISSION OF SHARES

29   If a member dies the survivor or survivors where he was a joint holder, and his personal representatives where he was a sole holder or the only survivor of joint holders, shall be the only persons recognised by the company as having any title to his interest; but nothing herein contained shall release the estate of a deceased member from any liability in respect of any share which had been jointly held by him.

30   A person becoming entitled to a share in consequence of the death or bankruptcy of a member may, upon such evidence being produced as the directors may properly require, elect either to become the holder of the share or to have some person nominated by him registered as the transferee. If he elects to become the holder he shall give notice to the company to that effect. If he elects to have another person registered he shall execute an instrument of transfer of the share to that person. All the articles relating to the transfer of shares shall apply to the notice or instrument of transfer as if it were an instrument of transfer executed by the member and the death or bankruptcy of the member had not occurred.

31   A person becoming entitled to a share in consequence of the death or bankruptcy of a member shall have the rights to which he would be entitled if he were the holder of the share, except that he shall not, before being registered as the holder of the share, be entitled in respect of it to attend or vote at any meeting of the company or at any separate meeting of the holders of any class of shares in the company.

ALTERATION OF SHARE CAPITAL

32   The company may by ordinary resolution—

(a)   increase its share capital by new shares of such amount as the resolution prescribes;

(b)   consolidate and divide all or any of its share capital into shares of larger amount than its existing shares;

(c)   subject to the provisions of the Act, sub-divide its shares, or any of them, into shares of smaller amount and the resolution may determine that, as between the shares resulting from the sub-division, any of them may have any preference or advantage as compared with the others; and

(d)   cancel shares which, at the date of the passing of the resolution, have not been taken or agreed to be taken by any person and diminish the amount of its share capital by the amount of the shares so cancelled.

33   Whenever as a result of a consolidation of shares any members would become entitled to fractions of a share, the directors may, on behalf of those members, sell the shares representing the fractions for the best price reasonably obtainable to any person (including, subject to the provisions of the Act, the company) and distribute the net proceeds of sale in due proportion among those members, and the directors may authorise some person to execute an instrument of transfer of the shares to, or in accordance with the directions of, the purchaser. The transferee shall not be bound to see to the application of the purchase money nor shall his title to the shares be affected by any irregularity in or invalidity of the proceedings in reference to the sale.

34   Subject to the provisions of the Act, the company may by special resolution reduce its share capital, any capital redemption reserve and any share premium account in any way.

PURCHASE OF OWN SHARES

35   Subject to the provisions of the Act, the company may purchase its own shares (including any redeemable shares) and, if it is a private company, make a payment in respect of the redemption or purchase of its own shares otherwise than out of distributable profits of the company or the proceeds of a fresh issue of shares.

GENERAL MEETING

36   All general meetings other than annual general meetings shall be called extraordinary general meetings.

37   The directors may call general meetings and, on the requisition of members pursuant to the provisions of the Act, shall forthwith proceed to convene an extraordinary general meeting for a date not later than eight weeks after receipt of the requisition. If there are not within the United Kingdom sufficient directors to call a general meeting, any director or any member of the company may call a general meeting.

NOTICE OF GENERAL MEETINGS

38   An annual general meeting and an extraordinary general meeting called for the passing of a special resolution or a resolution appointing a person as a director shall be called by at least twenty-one clear days' notice. All other extraordinary general meetings shall be called by at least fourteen clear days' notice but a general meeting may be called by shorter notice if is so agreed—

(a)   in the case of an annual general meeting, by all the members entitled to attend and vote thereat; and

(b)   in the case of any other meeting by a majority in number of the members having a right to attend and vote being a majority together holding not less than ninety-five per cent. in nominal value of the shares giving that right.

The notice shall specify the time and place of the meeting and the general nature of the business to be transacted and, in the case of an annual general meeting, shall specify the meeting as such.

Subject to the provisions of the articles and to any restrictions imposed on any shares, the notice shall be given to all the members, to all persons entitled to a share in consequence of the death or bankruptcy of a member and to the directors and auditors.

39   The accidental omission to give notice of a meeting to, or the non-receipt of notice of a meeting by, any person entitled to receive notice shall not invalidate the proceedings at that meeting.

PROCEEDINGS AT GENERAL MEETINGS

40   No business shall be transacted at any meeting unless a quorum is present. Two persons entitled to vote upon the business to be transacted, each being a member or a proxy for a member or a duly authorised representative of a corporation, shall be a quorum.

41   If such a quorum is not present within half an hour from the time appointed for the meeting, or if during a meeting such a quorum ceases to be present, the meeting shall stand adjourned to the same day in the next week at the same time and place or [to] such time and place as the directors may determine.

42   The chairman, if any, of the board of directors or in his absence some other director nominated by the directors shall preside as chairman of the meeting, but if neither the chairman nor such other director (if any) be present within fifteen minutes after the time appointed for holding the meeting and willing to act, the directors present shall elect one of their number to be chairman and, if there is only one director present and willing to act, he shall be chairman.

43   If no director is willing to act as chairman, or if no director is present within fifteen minutes after the time appointed for holding the meeting, the members present and entitled to vote shall choose one of their number to be chairman.

44   A director shall, notwithstanding that he is not a member, be entitled to attend and speak at any general meeting and at any separate meeting of the holders of any class of shares in the company.

45   The chairman may, with the consent of a meeting at which a quorum is present (and shall if so directed by the meeting), adjourn the meeting from time to time and from place to place, but no business shall be transacted at an adjourned meeting other than business which might properly have been transacted at the meeting had the adjournment not taken place. When a meeting is adjourned for fourteen days or more, at least seven clear days' notice shall be given specifying the time and place of the adjourned meeting and the general nature of the business to be transacted. Otherwise it shall not be necessary to give any such notice.

46   A resolution put to the vote of a meeting shall be decided on a show of hands unless before or on the declaration of the result of, the show of hands a poll is duly demanded. Subject to the provisions of the Act, a poll may be demanded—

(a)   by the chairman; or

(b)   by at least two members having the right to vote at the meeting; or

(c)   by a member or members representing not less than one-tenth of the total voting rights of all the members having the right to vote at the meeting; or

(d)   by a member or members holding shares conferring a right to vote at the meeting being shares on which an aggregate sum has been paid up equal to not less than one-tenth of the total sum paid up on all the shares conferring that right;

and a demand by a person as proxy for a member shall be the same as a demand by the member.

47   Unless a poll is duly demanded a declaration by the chairman that a resolution has been carried or carried unanimously, or by a particular majority, or lost, or not carried by a particular majority and an entry to that effect in the minutes of the meeting shall be conclusive evidence of the fact without proof of the number or proportion of the votes recorded in favour of or against the resolution.

48   The demand for a poll may, before the poll is taken, be withdrawn but only with the consent of the chairman and a demand so withdrawn shall not be taken to have invalidated the result of a show of hands declared before the demand was made.

49   A poll shall be taken as the chairman directs and he may appoint scrutineers (who need not be members) and fix a time and place for declaring the result of the poll. The result of the poll shall be deemed to be the resolution of the meeting at which the poll was demanded.

50   In the case of an equality of votes, whether on a show of hands or on a poll, the chairman shall be entitled to a casting vote in addition to any other vote he may have.

51   A poll demanded on the election of a chairman or on a question of adjournment shall be taken forthwith. A poll demanded on any other question shall be taken either forthwith or at such time and place as the chairman directs not being more than thirty days after the poll is demanded. The demand for a poll shall not prevent the continuance of a meeting for the transaction of any business other than the question on which the poll was demanded. If a poll is demanded before the declaration of the result of a show of hands and the demand is duly withdrawn, the meeting shall continue as if the demand had not been made.

52   No notice need be given of a poll not taken forthwith if the time and place at which it is to be taken are announced at the meeting at which it is demanded. In any other case at least seven clear days' notice shall be given specifying the time and place at which the poll is to be taken.

53   A resolution in writing executed by or on behalf of each member who would have been entitled to vote upon it if it had been proposed at a general meeting at which he was present shall be as effectual as if it had been passed at a general meeting duly convened and held and may consist of several instruments in the like form each executed by or on behalf of one or more members.

VOTES OF MEMBERS

54   Subject to any rights or restrictions attached to any shares, on a show of hands every member who (being an individual) is present in person or (being a corporation) is present by a duly authorised representative, not being himself a member entitled to vote, shall have one vote and on a poll every member shall have one vote for every share of which he is the holder.

55   In the case of joint holders the vote of the senior who tenders a vote, whether in person or by proxy, shall be accepted to the exclusion of the votes of the other joint holders' and seniority shall be determined by the order in which the names of the holders stand in the register of members.

56   A member in respect of whom an order has been made by any court having jurisdiction (whether in the United Kingdom or elsewhere) in matters concerning mental disorder may vote, whether on a show of hands or on a poll, by his receiver, curator bonis or other person authorised in that behalf appointed by that court, and any such receiver, curator bonis or other person may, on a poll, vote by proxy. Evidence to the satisfaction of the directors of the authority of the person claiming to exercise the right to vote shall be deposited at the office, or at such other place as is specified in accordance with the articles for the deposit of instruments of proxy, not less than 48 hours before the time appointed for holding the meeting or adjourned meeting at which the right to vote is to be exercised and in default the right to vote shall not be exercisable.

57   No member shall vote at any general meeting or at any separate meeting of the holders of any class of shares in the company, either in person or by proxy, in respect of any share held by him unless all moneys presently payable by him in respect of that share have been paid.

58   No objection shall be raised to the qualification of any voter except at the meeting or adjourned meeting at which the vote objected to is tendered, and every vote not disallowed at the meeting shall be valid. Any objection made in due time shall be referred to the chairman whose decision shall be final and conclusive.

59   On a poll votes may be given either personally or by proxy. A member may appoint more than one proxy to attend on the same occasion.

60   [The appointment of] a proxy shall be . . ., executed by or on behalf of the appointor and shall be in the following form (or in a form as near thereto as circumstances allow or in any other form which is usual or which the directors may approve)—

"................. PLC/Limited................. I/We,................., of................., being a member/members of the above-named company, hereby appoint................. of................., or failing him,................. of................., as my/our proxy to vote in my/our name[s] and on my/our behalf at the annual/extraordinary general meeting of the company to be held on...... .... 19................., and at any adjournment thereof.

Signed on................. 19..................."

61   Where it is desired to afford members an opportunity of instructing the proxy how he shall act the [appointment of] a proxy shall be in the following form (or in a form as near thereto as circumstances allow or in any other form which is usual or which the directors may approve)—

"................. PLC/Limited................. I/We,................., of................., being a member/members of the above-named company, hereby appoint................. of................., or failing him................. of................., as my/our proxy to vote in my/our name[s] and on my/our behalf at the annual/extraordinary general meeting of the company, to be held on...... .... 19 ,................., and at any adjournment thereof.

This form is to be used in respect of the resolutions mentioned below as follows:
  Resolution No. 1 *for *against
  Resolution No. 2 *for *against.

*Strike out whichever is not desired.

Unless otherwise instructed, the proxy may vote as he thinks fit or abstain from voting.

Signed this................. day of................. 19................. ."

62   [The appointment of] a proxy and any authority under which it is executed or a copy of such authority certified notarially or in some other way approved by the directors may—
  (a)   [in the case of an instrument in writing] be deposited at the office or at such other places within the United kingdom as is specified in the notice convening the meeting or in any instrument of proxy sent out by the company in relation to the meeting not

less than 48 hours before the time for holding the meeting or adjourned meeting at which the person named in the instrument proposes to vote; or

[(aa) in the case of an appointment contained in an electronic communication, where an address has been specified for the purpose of receiving electronic communications—
    (i)   in the notice convening the meeting, or
    (ii) in any instrument of proxy sent out by the company in relation to the meeting, or
    (iii) in any invitation contained in an electronic communication to appoint a proxy issued by the company in relation to the meeting,
    be received at such address not less than 48 hours before the time for holding the meeting or adjourned meeting at which the person named in the appointment proposes to vote;]
(b)   in the case of a poll taken more than 48 hours after it is demanded, be deposited [or received] as aforesaid after the poll has been demanded and not less than 24 hours before the time appointed for the taking of the poll; or
(c)   where the poll is not taken forthwith but is taken not more than 48 hours after it was demanded, be delivered at the meeting at which the poll was demanded to the chairman or to the secretary or to any director;

[and an appointment of proxy which is not deposited, delivered or received] in a manner so permitted shall be invalid.

[In this regulation and the next, "address", in relation to electronic communications, includes any number or address used for the purposes of such communications.]

63   A vote given or poll demanded by proxy or by the duly authorised representative of a corporation shall be valid notwithstanding the previous determination of the authority of the person voting or demanding a poll unless notice of the determination was received by the company at the office or at such other place at which the instrument of proxy was duly deposited [or, where the appointment of the proxy was contained in an electronic communication, at the address at which such appointment was duly received] before the commencement of the meeting or adjourned meeting at which the vote is given or the poll demanded or (in the case of a poll taken otherwise than on the same day as the meeting or adjourned meeting) the time appointed for taking the poll.

NUMBER OF DIRECTORS

64   Unless otherwise determined by ordinary resolution, the number of directors (other than alternate directors) shall not be subject to any maximum but shall be not less than two.

ALTERNATE DIRECTORS

65   Any director (other than an alternate director) may appoint any other director, or any other person approved by resolution of the directors and willing to act, to be an alternate director and may remove from office an alternate director so appointed by him.

66   An alternate director shall be entitled to receive notice of all meetings of directors and of all meetings of committees of directors of which his appointor is a member, to attend and vote at any such meeting at which the director appointing him is not personally present and generally to perform all the functions of his appointor as a director in his absence but shall not be entitled to receive any remuneration from the company for his services as an alternate director. But it shall not be necessary to give notice of such a meeting to an alternate director who is absent from the United Kingdom.

67   An alternate director shall cease to be an alternate director if his appointor ceases to be a director; but, if a director retires by rotation or otherwise but is reappointed or deemed to have been reappointed at the meeting at which he retires, any appointment of an alternate director made by him which was in force immediately prior to his retirement shall continue after his reappointment.

68 Any appointment or removal of an alternate director shall be by notice to the company signed by the director making or revoking the appointment or in any other manner approved by the directors.

69 Save as otherwise provided in the articles, an alternate director shall be deemed for all purposes to be a director and shall alone be responsible for his own acts and defaults and he shall not be deemed to be the agent of the director appointing him.

POWERS OF DIRECTORS

70 Subject to the provisions of the Act, the memorandum and the articles and to any directions given by special resolution, the business of the company shall be managed by the directors who may exercise all the powers of the company.

71 The directors may, by power of attorney or otherwise, appoint any person to be the agent of the company for such purposes and on such conditions as they determine, including authority for the agent to delegate all or any of his powers.

DELEGATION OF DIRECTORS' POWERS

72 The directors may delegate any of their powers to any committee consisting of one or more directors. They may also delegate to any managing director or any director holding any other executive office such of their powers as they consider desirable to be exercised by him. Any such delegation may be made subject to any conditions the directors may impose, and either collaterally with or to the exclusion of their own powers and may be revoked or altered. Subject to any such conditions, the proceedings of a committee with two or more members shall be governed by the articles regulating the proceedings of directors so far as they are capable of applying.

APPOINTMENT AND RETIREMENT OF DIRECTORS

73 At the first annual general meeting all the directors shall retire from office, and at every subsequent annual general meeting one-third of the directors who are subject to retirement by rotation or, if their number is not three or a multiple of three, the number nearest to one-third shall retire from office; but, if there is only one director who is subject to retirement by rotation, he shall retire.

74 Subject to the provisions of the Act, the directors to retire by rotation shall be those who have been longest in office since their last appointment or reappointment, but as between persons who became or were last reappointed directors on the same day those to retire shall (unless they otherwise agree among themselves) be determined by lot.

75 If the company, at the meeting at which a director retires by rotation, does not fill the vacancy the retiring director shall, if willing to act, be deemed to have been reappointed unless at the meeting it is resolved not to fill the vacancy or unless a resolution for the reappointment of the director is put to the meeting and lost.

76 No person other than a director retiring by rotation shall be appointed or reappointed a director at any general meeting unless—
(a) he is recommended by the directors; or
(b) not less than fourteen nor more than thirty-five clear days before the date appointed for the meeting, notice executed by a member qualified to vote at the meeting has been given to the company of the intention to propose that person for appointment or

reappointment stating the particulars which would, if he were so appointed or reappointed, be required to be included in the company's register of directors together with notice executed by that person of his willingness to be appointed or reappointed.

77 Not less than seven nor more than twenty-eight clear days before the date appointed for holding a general meeting notice shall be given to all who are entitled to receive notice of the meeting of any person (other than a director retiring by rotation at the meeting) who is recommended by the directors for appointment or reappointment as a director at the meeting or in respect of whom notice has been duly given to the company of the intention to propose him at the meeting for appointment or reappointment as a director. The notice shall give the particulars of that person which would, if he were so appointed or reappointed, be required to be included in the company's register of directors.

78 Subject as aforesaid, the company may by ordinary resolution appoint a person who is willing to act to be a director either to fill a vacancy or as an additional director and may also determine the rotation in which any additional directors are to retire.

79 The directors may appoint a person who is willing to act to be a director, either to fill a vacancy or as an additional director, provided that the appointment does not cause the number of directors to exceed any number fixed by or in accordance with the articles as the maximum number of directors. A director so appointed shall hold office only until the next following annual general meeting and shall not be taken into account in determining the directors who are to retire by rotation at the meeting. If not reappointed at such annual general meeting, he shall vacate office at the conclusion thereof.

80 Subject as aforesaid, a director who retires at an annual general meeting may, if willing to act, be reappointed. If he is not reappointed, he shall retain office until the meeting appoints someone in his place, or if it does not do so, until the end of the meeting.

DISQUALIFICATION AND REMOVAL OF DIRECTORS

81 The office of a director shall be vacated if—
  (a) he ceases to be a director by virtue of any provision of the Act or he becomes prohibited by law from being a director; or
  (b) he becomes bankrupt or makes any arrangement or composition with his creditors generally; or
  (c) he is, or may be, suffering from mental disorder and either—
      (i) he is admitted to hospital in pursuance of an application for admission for treatment under the Mental Health Act 1983 or, in Scotland, an application for admission under the Mental Health (Scotland) Act 1960, or
      (ii) an order is made by a court having jurisdiction (whether in the United Kingdom or elsewhere) in matters concerning mental disorder for his detention or for the appointment of a receiver, curator bonis or other person to exercise powers with respect to his property or affairs; or
  (d) he resigns his office by notice to the company; or
  (e) he shall for more than six consecutive months have been absent without permission of the directors from meetings of directors held during that period and the directors resolve that his office be vacated.

REMUNERATION OF DIRECTORS

82 The directors shall be entitled to such remuneration as the company may by ordinary resolution determine and, unless the resolution provides otherwise, the remuneration shall be deemed to accrue from day to day.

DIRECTORS' EXPENSES

83 The directors may be paid all travelling, hotel, and other expenses properly incurred by them in connection with their attendance at meetings of directors or committees of directors or general meetings or separate meetings of the holders of any class of shares or of debentures of the company or otherwise in connection with the discharge of their duties.

DIRECTORS' APPOINTMENTS AND INTERESTS

84 Subject to the provisions of the Act, the directors may appoint one or more of their number to the office of managing director or to any other executive office under the company and may enter into an agreement or arrangement with any director for his employment by the company or for the provision by him of any services outside the scope of the ordinary duties of a director. Any such appointment, agreement or arrangement may be made upon such terms as the directors determine and they may remunerate any such director for his services as they think fit. Any appointment of a director to an executive office shall terminate if he ceases to be a director but without prejudice to any claim to damages for breach of the contract of service between the director and the company. A managing director and a director holding any other executive office shall not be subject to retirement by rotation.

85 Subject to the provisions of the Act, and provided that he has disclosed to the directors the nature and extent of any material interest of his, a director notwithstanding his office—
- (a) may be a party to, or otherwise interested in, any transaction or arrangement with the company or in which the company or in which the company is otherwise interested; and
- (b) may be a director or other officer of, or employed by, or a party to any transaction or arrangement with, or otherwise interested in, any body corporate promoted by the company or in which the company is otherwise interested; and
- (c) shall not, by reason of his office, be accountable to the company for any benefit which he derives from any such office or employment or from any such transaction or arrangement or from any interest in any such body corporate and no such transaction or arrangement shall be liable to be avoided on the ground of any such interest or benefit.

86 For the purposes of regulation 85—
- (a) a general notice given to the directors that a director is to be regarded as having an interest of the nature and extent specified in the notice in any transaction or arrangement in which a specified person or class of persons is interested shall be deemed to be a disclosure that the director has an interest in any such transaction of the nature and extent so specified; and
- (b) an interest of which a director has no knowledge and of which it is unreasonable to expect him to have knowledge shall not be treated as an interest of his.

DIRECTORS' GRATUITIES AND PENSIONS

87 The directors may provide benefits, whether by the payment of gratuities or pensions or by insurance or otherwise, for any director who has held but no longer holds any executive office or employment with the company or with any body corporate which is or has been a subsidiary of the company or a predecessor in business of the company or of any such subsidiary, and for any member of his family (including a spouse and a former spouse) or any person who is or was dependent on him, and may (as well before as after he ceases to hold such office or employment) contribute to any fund and pay premiums for the purchase or provision of any such benefit.

PROCEEDINGS OF DIRECTORS

88 Subject to the provisions of the articles, the directors may regulate their proceedings as they think fit. A director may, and the secretary at the request of a director shall, call a meeting of the directors. It shall not be necessary to give notice of a meeting to a director who is absent from the United Kingdom. Questions arising at a meeting shall be decided by a majority of votes. In the case of an equality of votes, the chairman shall have a second or casting vote. A director who is also an alternate director shall be entitled in the absence of his appointor to a separate vote on behalf of his appointor in addition to his own vote.

89 The quorum for the transaction of the business of the directors may be fixed by the directors and unless so fixed at any other number shall be two. A person who holds office only as an alternate director shall, if his appointor is not present, be counted in the quorum.

90 The continuing directors or a sole continuing director may act notwithstanding any vacancies in their number, but, if the number of directors is less than the number fixed as the quorum, the continuing director may act only for the purpose of filling vacancies or of calling a general meeting.

91 The directors may appoint one of their number to be the chairman of the board of directors and may at any time remove him from that office. Unless he is unwilling to do so, the director so appointed shall preside at every meeting of directors at which he is present. But if there is no director holding that office, or if the director holding it is unwilling to preside or is not present within five minutes after the time appointed for the meeting, the directors present may appoint one of their number to be chairman of the meeting.

92 All acts done by a meeting of directors, or of a committee of directors, or by a person acting as a director shall, notwithstanding that it be afterwards discovered that there was a defect in the appointment of any director or that any of them were disqualified from holding office, or had vacated office, or were not entitled to vote, be as valid as if every such person had been duly appointed and was qualified and had continued to be a director and had been entitled to vote.

93 A resolution in writing signed by all the directors entitled to receive notice of a meeting of directors or of a committee of directors shall be as valid and effectual as it if had been passed at a meeting of directors or (as the case may be) a committee of directors duly convened and held and may consist of several documents in the like form each signed by one or more directors; but a resolution signed by an alternate director need not also be signed by his appointor and, if it is signed by a director who has appointed an alternate director, it need not be signed by the alternate director in that capacity.

94 Save as otherwise provided by the articles, a director shall not vote at a meeting of directors or of a committee of directors on any resolution concerning a matter in which he has, directly or indirectly, an interest or duty which is material and which conflicts or may conflict with the interests of the company unless his interest or duty arises only because the case falls within one or more of the following paragraphs—

    (a)   the resolution relates to the giving to him of a guarantee, security, or indemnity in respect of money lent to, or an obligation incurred by him for the benefit of, the company or any of its subsidiaries;

    (b)   the resolution relates to the giving to a third party of a guarantee, security, or indemnity in respect of an obligation of the company or any of its subsidiaries for which the director has assumed responsibility in whole or part and whether alone or jointly with others under a guarantee or indemnity or by the giving of security;

    (c)   his interest arises by virtue of his subscribing or agreeing to subscribe for any shares, debentures, or other securities of the company or any of its subsidiaries, or by virtue of his being, or intending to become, a participant in the underwriting or sub-underwriting of an offer of any such shares, debentures, or other securities by the company or any of its subsidiaries for subscription, purchase or exchange;

(d)   the resolution relates in any way to a retirement benefits scheme which has been approved, or is conditional upon approval, by the Board of Inland Revenue for taxation purposes.

For the purposes of this regulation, an interest of a person who is, for any purpose of the Act (excluding any statutory modification thereof not in force when this regulation becomes binding on the company), connected with a director shall be treated as an interest of the director and, in relation to an alternate director, an interest of his appointor shall be treated as an interest of the alternate director without prejudice to any interest which the alternate director has otherwise.

95   A director shall not be counted in the quorum present at a meeting in relation to a resolution on which he is not entitled to vote.

96   The company may by ordinary resolution suspend or relax to any extent, either generally or in respect of any particular matter, any provision of the articles prohibiting a director from voting at a meeting of directors or of a committee of directors.

97   Where proposals are under consideration concerning the appointment of two or more directors to offices or employments with the company or any body corporate in which the company is interested the proposals may be divided and considered in relation to each director separately and (provided he is not for another reason precluded from voting) each of the directors concerned shall be entitled to vote and be counted in the quorum in respect of each resolution except that concerning his own appointment.

98   If a question arises at a meeting of directors or of a committee of directors as to the right of a director to vote, the question may, before the conclusion of the meeting, be referred to the chairman of the meeting and his ruling in relation to any director other than himself shall be final and conclusive.

SECRETARY

99   Subject to the provisions of the Act, the secretary shall be appointed by the directors for such term, at such remuneration and upon such conditions as they may think fit; and any secretary so appointed may be removed by them.

MINUTES

100   The directors shall cause minutes to be made in books kept for the purpose—

(a)   of all appointments of officers made by the directors; and

(b)   of all proceedings at meetings of the company, of the holders of any class of shares in the company, and of the directors, and of committees of directors, including the names of the directors present at each such meeting.

THE SEAL

101   The seal shall only be used by the authority of the directors or of a committee of directors authorised by the directors. The directors may determine who shall sign any instrument to which the seal is affixed and unless otherwise so determined it shall be signed by a director and by the secretary or by a second director.

DIVIDENDS

102   Subject to the provisions of the Act, the company may by ordinary resolution declare dividends in accordance with the respective rights of the members, but no dividend shall exceed the amount recommended by the directors.

103   Subject to the provisions of the Act, the directors may pay interim dividends if it appears to them that they are justified by the profits of the company available for distribution. If the share capital is divided into difference classes, the directors may pay interim dividends on shares which confer deferred or non-preferred rights with regard to dividend as well as on shares which confer preferential rights with regard to dividend, but no interim dividend shall be paid on shares carrying deferred or non-preferred rights if, at the time of payment, any preferential dividend is in arrear. The directors may also pay at intervals settled by them any dividend payable at a fixed rate if it appears to them that the profits available for distribution justify the payment. Provided the directors act in good faith they shall not incur any liability to the holders of shares conferring preferred rights for any loss they may suffer by the lawful payment of an interim dividend on any shares having deferred or non-preferred rights.

104   Except as otherwise provided by the rights attached to shares, all dividends shall be declared and paid according to the amounts paid up on the shares on which the dividend is paid. All dividends shall be apportioned and paid proportionately to the amounts paid up on the shares during any portion or portions of the period in respect of which the dividend is paid; but, if any share is issued on terms providing that it shall rank for dividend as from a particular date, that share shall rank for dividend accordingly.

105   A general meeting declaring a dividend may, upon the recommendation of the directors, direct that it shall be satisfied wholly or partly by the distribution of assets and, where any difficulty arises in regard to the distribution, the directors may settle the same and in particular may issue fractional certificates and fix the value for distribution of any assets and may determine that cash shall be paid to any member upon the footing of the value so fixed in order to adjust the rights of members and may vest any assets in trustees.

106   Any dividend or other moneys payable in respect of a share may be paid by cheque sent by post to the registered address of the person entitled or, if two or more persons are the holders of the share or are jointly entitled to it by reason of the death or bankruptcy of the holder, to the registered address of that one of those persons who is first named in the register of members or to such person and to such address as the person or persons entitled may in writing direct. Every cheque shall be made payable to the order of the person or persons entitled or to such other person as the person or persons entitled may in writing direct and payment of the cheque shall be a good discharge to the company. Any joint holder or other person jointly entitled to a share as aforesaid may give receipts for any dividend or other moneys payable in respect of the share.

107   No dividend or other moneys payable in respect of a share shall bear interest against the company unless otherwise provided by the rights attached to the share.

108   Any dividend which has remained unclaimed for twelve years from the date when it became due for payment shall, if the directors so resolve, be forfeited and cease to remain owing by the company.

ACCOUNTS

109   No member shall (as such) have any right of inspecting any accounting records or other book or document of the company except as conferred by statute or authorised by the directors or by ordinary resolution of the company.

CAPITALISATION OF PROFITS

110 The directors may with the authority of an ordinary resolution of the company—

(a) subject as hereinafter provided, resolve to capitalise any undivided profits of the company not required for paying any preferential dividend (whether or not they are available for distribution) or any sum standing to the credit of the company's share premium account or capital redemption reserve;

(b) appropriate the sum resolved to be capitalised to the members who would have been entitled to it if it were distributed by way of dividend and in the same proportions and apply such sum on their behalf either in or towards paying up the amounts, if any, for the time being unpaid on any shares held by them respectively, or in paying up in full unissued shares or debentures of the company of a nominal amount equal to that sum, and allot the shares or debentures credited as fully paid to those members, or as they may direct, in those proportions, or partly in one way and partly in the other: but the share premium account, the capital redemption reserve, and any profits which are not available for distribution may, for the purposes of this regulation, only be applied in paying up unissued to be allotted to members credited as fully paid;

(c) make such provision by the issue of fractional certificates or by payment in cash or otherwise as they determine in the case of shares or debentures becoming distributable under this regulation in fractions; and

(d) authorise any person to enter on behalf of all the members concerned into an agreement with the company providing for the allotment to them respectively, credited as fully paid, of any shares or debentures to which they are entitled upon such capitalisation, any agreement made under such authority being binding on all such members.

NOTICES

[**111** Any notice to be given to or by any person pursuant to the articles (other than a notice calling a meeting of the directors) shall be in writing or shall be given using electronic communications to an address for the time being notified for that purpose to the person giving the notice.

In this regulation, "address", in relation to electronic communications, includes any number or address used for the purposes of such communications.]

112 The company may give any notice to a member either personally or by sending it by post in a prepaid envelope addressed to the member at his registered address or by leaving it at that address [or by giving it using electronic communications to an address for the time being notified to the company by the member]. In the case of joint holders of a share, all notices shall be given to the joint holder whose name stands first in the register of members in respect of the joint holding and notice so given shall be sufficient notice to all the joint holders. A member whose registered address is not within the United Kingdom and who gives to the company an address within the United Kingdom at which notices may be given to him[, or an address to which notices may be sent using electronic communications,] shall be entitled to have notices given to him at that address, but otherwise no such member shall be entitled to receive any notice from the company.

[In this regulation and the next, "address", in relation to electronic communications, includes any number or address used for the purposes of such communications.]

113 A member present, either in person or by proxy, at any meeting of the company or of the holders of any class of shares in the company shall be deemed to have received notice of the meeting and, where requisite, of the purposes for which it was called.

114 Every person who becomes entitled to a share shall be bound by any notice in respect of that share which, before his name is entered in the register of members, has been duly given to a person from whom he derives his title.

115 Proof that an envelope containing a notice was properly addressed, prepaid and posted shall be conclusive evidence that that the notice was given. [Proof that a notice contained in an electronic communication was sent in accordance with guidance issued by the Institute of Chartered Secretaries and Administrators shall be conclusive evidence that the notice was given.] A notice shall, . . . be deemed to be given at the expiration of 48 hours after the envelope containing it was posted [or, in the case of a notice contained in an electronic communication, at the expiration of 48 hours after the time it was sent].

116 A notice may be given by the company to the persons entitled to a share in consequence of the death or bankruptcy of a member by sending or delivering it, in any manner authorised by the articles for the giving of notice to a member, addressed to them by name, or by the title of representatives of the deceased, or trustee of the bankrupt or by any like description at the address, if any, within the United Kingdom supplied for that purpose by the persons claiming to be so entitled. Until such an address has been supplied, a notice may be given in any manner in which it might have been given if the death or bankruptcy had not occurred.

WINDING UP

117 If the company is wound up, the liquidator may, with the sanction of an extraordinary resolution of the company and any other sanction required by the Act, divide among the members in specie the whole or any part of the assets of the company and may, for that purpose, value any assets and determine how the division shall be carried out as between the members or different classes of members. The liquidator may, with the like sanction, vest the whole or any part of the assets in trustees upon such trusts for the benefit of the members as he with the like sanction determines, but no member shall be compelled to accept any assets upon which there is a liability.

INDEMNITY

118 Subject to the provisions of the Act but without prejudice to any indemnity to which a director may otherwise be entitled, every director or other officer or auditor of the company shall be indemnified out of the assets of the company against any liability incurred by him in defending any proceedings, whether civil or criminal, in which judgment is given in his favour or in which he is acquitted or in connection with any application in which relief is granted to him by the court from liability for negligence, default, breach of duty or breach of trust in relation to the affairs of the company.

NOTES

Reg 1: definition "communication" inserted by SI 2000/3373, art 32(1), Sch 1, para 1.
Date in force: 22 December 2000: see SI 2000/3373, art 1(1).
Reg 1: definition "electronic communication" inserted by SI 2000/3373, art 32(1), Sch 1, para 1.
Date in force: 22 December 2000: see SI 2000/3373, art 1(1).
Reg 4: word "provisions" in square brackets substituted by SI 1985/1052.
Reg 41: word "to" in square brackets substituted by SI 1985/1052.
Reg 60: words "The appointment of" in square brackets substituted by SI 2000/3373, art 32(1), Sch 1, para 2.
Date in force: 22 December 2000: see SI 2000/3373, art 1(1).
Reg 60: words omitted revoked by SI 2000/3373, art 32(1), Sch 1, para 2.

Date in force: 22 December 2000: see SI 2000/3373, art 1(1).

Reg 61: words "appointment of" in square brackets substituted by SI 2000/3373, art 32(1), Sch 1, para 3.

Date in force: 22 December 2000: see SI 2000/3373, art 1(1).

Reg 62: words "The appointment of" in square brackets substituted by SI 2000/3373, art 32(1), Sch 1, para 4(1), (2).

Date in force: 22 December 2000: see SI 2000/3373, art 1(1).

Reg 62: in para (a) words "in the case of an instrument in writing" in square brackets inserted by SI 2000/3373, art 32(1), Sch 1, para 4(1), (3).

Date in force: 22 December 2000: see SI 2000/3373, art 1(1).

Reg 62: para (aa) inserted by SI 2000/3373, art 32(1), Sch 1, para 4(1), (4).

Date in force: 22 December 2000: see SI 2000/3373, art 1(1).

Reg 62: in para (b) words "or received" in square brackets inserted by SI 2000/3373, art 32(1), Sch 1, para 4(1), (5).

Date in force: 22 December 2000: see SI 2000/3373, art 1(1).

Reg 62: words "and an appointment of proxy which is not deposited, delivered or received" in square brackets substituted by SI 2000/3373, art 32(1), Sch 1, para 4(1), (6).

Date in force: 22 December 2000: see SI 2000/3373, art 1(1).

Reg 62: words from "In this regulation" to "of such communications." in square brackets inserted by SI 2000/3373, art 32(1), Sch 1, para 4(1), (7).

Date in force: 22 December 2000: see SI 2000/3373, art 1(1).

Reg 63: words from "or, where the appointment" to "was duly received" in square brackets inserted by SI 2000/3373, art 32(1), Sch 1, para 5.

Date in force: 22 December 2000: see SI 2000/3373, art 1(1).

Reg 111: substituted by SI 2000/3373, art 32(1), Sch 1, para 6.

Date in force: 22 December 2000: see SI 2000/3373, art 1(1).

Reg 112: words from "or by giving it" to "company by the member" in square brackets inserted by SI 2000/3373, art 32(1), Sch 1, para 7(a).

Date in force: 22 December 2000: see SI 2000/3373, art 1(1).

Reg 112: words ", or an address to which notices may be sent using electronic communications," in square brackets inserted by SI 2000/3373, art 32(1), Sch 1, para 7(b).

Date in force: 22 December 2000: see SI 2000/3373, art 1(1).

Reg 112: words from "In this regulation" to "of such communications." in square brackets inserted by SI 2000/3373, art 32(1), Sch 1, para 7(c).

Date in force: 22 December 2000: see SI 2000/3373, art 1(1).

Reg 115: words from "Proof that a notice" to "notice was given." in square brackets inserted by SI 2000/3373, art 32(1), Sch 1, para 8(1), (2).

Date in force: 22 December 2000: see SI 2000/3373, art 1(1).

Reg 115: words omitted revoked by SI 1985/1052.

Reg 115: words from "or, in the case" to "time it was sent" in square brackets inserted by SI 2000/3373, art 32(1), Sch 1, para 8(1), (3).

Date in force: 22 December 2000: see SI 2000/3373, art 1(1).

TABLE B
A PRIVATE COMPANY LIMITED BY SHARES

MEMORANDUM OF ASSOCIATION . . .

1 The company's name is "The South Wales Motor Transport Company cyfyngedig".

2 The company's registered office is to be situated in Wales.

3   The company's objects are the carriage of passengers and goods in motor vehicles between such places as the company may from time to time determine and the doing of all such other things as are incidental or conducive to the attainment of that object.

4   The liability of the members is limited.

5   The company's share capital is £50,000 divided into 50,000 shares of £1 each.

We, the subscribers to this memorandum of association, wish to be formed into a company pursuant to this memorandum; and we agree to take the number of shares shown opposite our respective names.

Names and Addresses of................. Names and Addresses of Subscribers

Number of shares taken by each Subscriber

.... *Subscriber*

1. Thomas Jones, 138 Mountfield................. Street, Tredegar.................. 1

2. Mary Evans, 19 Merthyr Road,................. Aberystwyth.................. 1
         Total shares taken.................. 2

Dated................. 19...................

Witness to the above signatures,

Anne Brown, "Woodlands", Fieldside Road, Bryn Mawr.

TABLE C
A COMPANY LIMITED BY GUARANTEE AND NOT HAVING A SHARE CAPITAL

MEMORANDUM OF ASSOCIATION

1   The company's name is "The Dundee School Association Limited".

2   The company's registered office is to be situated in Scotland.

3   The company's objects are the carrying on of a school for boys and girls in Dundee and the doing of all such other things as are incidental or conducive to the attainment of that object.

4   The liability of the members is limited.

5   Every member of the company undertakes to contribute such amount as may be required (not exceeding £100) to the company's assets if it should be wound up while he is member or within one year after he ceases to be a member, for payment of the company's debts and liabilities contracted before he ceases to be a member, and of the costs, charges and expenses of winding up, and for the adjustment of the rights of the contributories among themselves.

We, the subscribers to this memorandum of association, wish to be formed into a company pursuant to this memorandum.

Names and Addresses of Subscribers.

1   Kenneth Brodie, 14 Bute Street, Dundee.

2   Ian Davis, 2 Burns Avenue, Dundee.

Dated................. 19...................

Witness to the above signatures.

Anne Brown, 149 Princes Street, Edinburgh.

ARTICLES OF ASSOCIATION

PRELIMINARY

1 Regulations 2 to 35 inclusive, 54, 55, 57, 59, 102 to 108 inclusive, 110, 114, 116 and 117 of Table A, shall not apply to the company but the articles hereinafter contained and, subject to the modifications hereinafter expressed, the remaining regulations of Table A shall constitute the articles of association of the company.

INTERPRETATION

2 In regulation 1 of Table A, the definition of "the holder" shall be omitted.

MEMBERS

3 The subscribers to the memorandum of association of the company and such other persons as are admitted to membership in accordance with the articles shall be members of the company. No person shall be admitted a member of the company unless he is approved by the directors. Every person who wishes to become a member shall deliver to the company an application for membership in such form as the directors require executed by him.

4 A member may at any time withdraw from the company by giving at least seven clear days' notice to the company. Membership shall not be transferable and shall cease on death.

NOTICE OF GENERAL MEETINGS

5 In regulation 38 of Table A—
   (a)   in paragraph (b) the words "of the total voting rights at the meeting of all the members' shall be substituted for "in nominal value of the shares giving that right" and
   (b)   the words "The notice shall be given to all the members and to the directors and auditors" shall be substituted for the last sentence.

PROCEEDINGS AT GENERAL MEETINGS

6 The words "and at any separate meeting of the holders of any class of shares in the company" shall be omitted from regulation 44 of Table A.

7 Paragraph (d) of regulation 46 of Table A shall be omitted.

VOTES OF MEMBERS

8 On a show of hands every member present in person shall have one vote. On a poll every member present in person or by proxy shall have one vote.

DIRECTORS' EXPENSES

9 The words "of any class of shares or" shall be omitted from regulation 83 of Table A.

PROCEEDINGS OF DIRECTORS

10 In paragraph (c) of regulation 94 of Table A the word "debentures" shall be substituted for the words "shares, debentures or other securities" in both places where they occur.

MINUTES

11   The words "of the holders of any class of shares in the company" shall be omitted from regulation 100 of Table A.

NOTICES

12   The second sentence of regulation 112 of Table A shall be omitted.

13   The words "or of the holders of any class of shares in the company" shall be omitted from regulation 113 of Table A.

TABLE D

Part I
A Public Company Limited by Guarantee and having a Share Capital

MEMORANDUM OF ASSOCIATION

1   The company's name is "Gwestai Glyndwr, cwmni cyfyngedig cyhoeddus".

2   The company is to be a public company.

3   The company's registered office is to be situated in Wales.

4   The company's objects are facilitating travelling in Wales by providing hotels and conveyances by sea and by land for the accommodation of travellers and the doing of all such other things as are incidental or conducive to the attainment of those objects.

5   The liability of the members is limited.

6   Every member of the company undertakes to contribute such amount as may be required (not exceeding £100) to the company's assets if it should be wound up while he is a member or within one year after he ceases to be a member, for payment of the company's debts and liabilities contracted before he ceases to be a member, and of the costs, charges and expenses of winding up, and for the adjustment of the rights of the contributories among themselves.

7   The company's share capital is £50,000 divided into 50,000 shares of £1 each.

We, the subscribers to this memorandum of association, wish to be formed into a company pursuant to this memorandum; and we agree to take the number of shares shown opposite our respective names.

Names and Addresses of Subscribers	Number of shares taken by each Subscriber	
1	Thomas Jones, 138 Mountfield Street, Tredegar	1
2	Andrew Smith, 19 Merthyr Road, Aberystwyth	1
	Total shares taken	2

Dated.................. 19....................

Witness to the above signatures,

Anne Brown, "Woodlands", Fieldside Road, Bryn Mawr.

Part II

A Private Company Limited by Guarantee and having a Share Capital

MEMORANDUM OF ASSOCIATION

1   The company's name is "The Highland Hotel Company Limited".

2   The company's registered office is to be situated in Scotland.

3   The company's objects are facilitating travelling in the Highlands of Scotland by providing hotels and conveyances by sea and by land for the accommodation of travellers and the doing of all such other things as are incidental or conducive to the attainment of those objects.

4   The liability of the members is limited.

5   Every member of the company undertakes to contribute such amount as may be required (not exceeding £100) to the company's assets if it should be wound up while he is a member or within one year after he ceases to be a member, for payment of the company's debts and liabilities contracted before he ceases to be a member, and of the costs, charges and expenses of winding up, and for the adjustment of the rights of the contributories among themselves.

6   The company's share capital is £50,000 divided into 50,000 shares of £1 each.

We, the subscribers to this memorandum of association, wish to be formed into a company pursuant to this memorandum; and we agree to take the number of shares shown opposite our respective names.

Names and Addresses of Subscribers	Number of shares taken by each Subscriber
Kenneth Brodie, 14 Bute Street, Dundee	1
Ian Davis, 2 Burns Avenue, Dundee	1
Total shares taken	2

Dated................. 19...................

Witness to the above signatures.

Anne Brown, 149 Princes Street, Edinburgh.

Part III

A Company (Public or Private) Limited by Guarantee and having a Share Capital

ARTICLES OF ASSOCIATION

The regulations of Table A shall constitute the articles of association of the company.

TABLE E
AN UNLIMITED COMPANY HAVING A SHARE CAPITAL

MEMORANDUM OF ASSOCIATION

1   The company's name is "The Woodford Engineering Company".

2   The company's registered office is to be situated in England and Wales.

3   The company's objects are the working of certain patented inventions relating to the application of microchip technology to the improvement of food processing, and the doing of all such other things as are incidental or conducive to the attainment of that object.

We, the subscribers to this memorandum of association, wish to be formed into a company pursuant to this memorandum; and we agree to take the number of shares shown opposite our respective names.

Names and Addresses of Sub-scribers	Numbers of shares taken by each subscriber	
1	Brian Smith, 24 Nibley Road, Wotton-under-Edge, Gloucester	3
2	William Green, 278 High Street, Chipping Sodbury, Avon	5
	Total shares taken	8

Dated.................. 19....................

Witness to the above signatures,

Anne Brown, 108 Park Way, Bristol 8.

ARTICLES OF ASSOCIATION

1   Regulations 3, 32, 34 and 35 of Table A shall not apply to the company, but the articles hereinafter contained and, subject to the modification hereinafter expressed, the remaining regulations of Table A shall constitute the articles of association of the company.

2   The words "at least seven clear days' notice" shall be substituted for the words "at least fourteen days' notice" in regulation 38 of Table A.

3   The share capital of the company is £20,000 divided into 20,000 shares of £1 each.

4   The company may by special resolution—
  (a)   increase the share capital by such sum to be divided into shares of such amount as the resolution may prescribe;
  (b)   consolidate and divide all or any of its share capital into shares of a larger amount than its existing shares;
  (c)   subdivide its shares, or any of them, into shares of a smaller amount than its existing shares;
  (d)   cancel any shares which at the date of the passing of the resolution have not been taken or agreed to be taken by any person;
  (e)   reduce its share capital and any share premium account in any way.

TABLE F
A PUBLIC COMPANY LIMITED BY SHARES

MEMORANDUM OF ASSOCIATION

1   The company's name is "Western Electronics Public Limited Company".

2   The company is to be a public company.

3   The company's registered office is to be situated in England and Wales.

4   The company's objects are the manufacture and development of such descriptions of electronic equipment, instruments and appliances as the company may from time to time determine, and the doing of all such other things as are incidental or conducive to the attainment of that object.

5   The liability of the members is limited.

6   The company's share capital is £5,000,000 divided into 5,000,000 shares of £1 each.

We, the subscribers to this memorandum of association, wish to be formed into a company pursuant to this memorandum; and we agree to take the number of shares shown opposite our respective names.

Names and Addresses of Sub-scribers	*Names of shares taken by each Subscriber*	
1	James White, 12 Broadmead, Birmingham	1
2	Patrick Smith, 145A Huntley House, London Wall, London, EC2	1
	Total shares taken	2

Dated.................. 19.................. .

Witness to the above signatures,

Anne Brown, 13 Hute Street, London WC2.

Companies (Single Member Private Limited Companies) Regulations 1992

1992 No 1699

NOTES

Made - - - 14th July 1992

ARRANGEMENT OF REGULATIONS

1 Citation and commencement
2 Single member private companies limited by shares or by guarantee
3 Transitional provision
SCHEDULE-Amendments to the Companies Act 1985 and the Insolvency Act 1986

1 Citation and commencement

These Regulations may be cited as the Companies (Single Member Private Limited Companies) Regulations 1992 and shall come into force on the day after the day on which they were made.

2 Single member private companies limited by shares or by guarantee

(1) Notwithstanding any enactment or rule of law to the contrary, a private company limited by shares or by guarantee within the meaning of section 1 of the Companies Act 1985 may be formed by one person (in so far as permitted by that section as amended by these Regulations) and may have one member; and accordingly—

    (a) any enactment or rule of law which applies in relation to a private company limited by shares or by guarantee shall, in the absence of any express provision to the contrary, apply with such modification as may be necessary in relation to such a company which is formed by one person or which has only one person as a member as it does in relation to such a company which is formed by two or more persons or which has two or more persons as members; and

    (b) without prejudice to the generality of the foregoing, the Companies Act 1985 and the Insolvency Act 1986 shall have effect with the amendments specified in the Schedule to these Regulations.

(2) In this regulation "enactment" shall include an enactment comprised in subordinate legislation and "subordinate legislation" shall have the same meaning as in section 21(1) of the Interpretation Act 1978.

3 Transitional provision

A person who, before the coming into force of these Regulations, is liable by virtue of section 24 of the Companies Act 1985 for the payment of the debts of a private company limited by shares or by guarantee, shall not be so liable for the payment of the company's debts contracted on or after the day on which these Regulations come into force.

SCHEDULE
AMENDMENTS TO THE COMPANIES ACT 1985 AND THE INSOLVENCY ACT 1986

Regulation 2

. . .

NOTES

This Schedule amends the Companies Act 1985, ss 1, 24, 680, 741 and the Insolvency Act 1986, s 122, inserts Companies Act 1985, ss 322B, 352A, 370A, 382B.

Insider Dealing (Securities and Regulated Markets) Order 1994

1994 No 187

NOTES

Made - - - 1st February 1994

ARRANGEMENT OF REGULATIONS

Title, commencement and interpretation

Securities

Regulated markets

United Kingdom regulated markets

SCHEDULE-REGULATED MARKETS

Title, commencement and interpretation

1

This Order may be cited as the Insider Dealing (Securities and Regulated Markets) Order 1994 and shall come into force on the twenty eighth day after the day on which it is made.

2

In this Order a "State within the European Economic Area" means a State which is a member of the European Communities and the Republics of Austria, Finland and Iceland, the Kingdoms of Norway and Sweden and the Principality of Liechtenstein.

Securities

3

Articles 4 to 8 set out conditions for the purposes of section 54(1) of the Criminal Justice Act 1993 (securities to which Part V of the Act of 1993 applies).

4

The following condition applies in relation to any security which falls within any paragraph of Schedule 2 to the Act of 1993, that is, that it is officially listed in a

State within the European Economic Area or that it is admitted to dealing on, or has its price quoted on or under the rules of, a regulated market.

5

The following alternative condition applies in relation to a warrant, that is, that the right under it is a right to subscribe for any share or debt security of the same class as a share or debt security which satisfies the condition in article 4.

6

The following alternative condition applies in relation to a depositary receipt, that is, that the rights under it are in respect of any share or debt security which satisfies the condition in article 4.

7

The following alternative conditions apply in relation to an option or a future, that is, that the option or rights under the future are in respect of—
(a) any share or debt security which satisfies the condition in article 4, or
(b) any depositary receipt which satisfies the condition in article 4 or article 6.

8

The following alternative condition applies in relation to a contract for differences, that is, that the purpose or pretended purpose of the contract is to secure a profit or avoid a loss by reference to fluctuations in—
(a) the price of any shares or debt securities which satisfy the condition in article 4, or
(b) an index of the price of such shares or debt securities.

Regulated markets

9

The following markets are regulated markets for the purposes of Part V of the Act of 1993—
[(a)] any market which is established under the rules of an investment exchange specified in the Schedule to this Order;
[(b) the market known as OFEX, operated by J P Jenkins Limited].

NOTES

Reference to "(a)" in square brackets inserted by SI 2000/1923, art 2(1), (2).
Date in force: 20 July 2000: see SI 2000/1923, art 1.
Para (b) inserted by SI 2000/1923, art 2(1), (2).
Date in force: 20 July 2000: see SI 2000/1923, art 1.

United Kingdom regulated markets

10

The regulated markets which are regulated in the United Kingdom for the purposes of Part V of the Act of 1993 are any market which is established under the rules of—

[(a) the London Stock Exchange Limited;]
(b) LIFFE Administration & Management; . . .
(c) OMLX, the London Securities and Derivatives Exchange Limited [. . .
(d) Tradepoint Financial Networks plc;]
[(e) COREDEAL Limited;

together with the market known as OFEX, operated by J P Jenkins Limited].

NOTES

Para (a) substituted by SI 1996/1561, art 3(1).
Para (b) word omitted revoked by SI 1996/1561, art 3(2).
Para (d) and word omitted immediately preceding it inserted by SI 1996/1561, art 3(2).
Para (c) word omitted revoked by SI 2000/1923, art 2(1), (3).
Date in force: 20 July 2000: see SI 2000/1923, art 1.
Para (e) and words from "together with the" to "J P Jenkins Limited" inserted by SI 2000/1923, art 2(1), (3).
Date in force: 20 July 2000: see SI 2000/1923, art 1.

SCHEDULE
REGULATED MARKETS

Article 9

Any market which is established under the rules of one of the following investment exchanges:

Amsterdam Stock Exchange.

Antwerp Stock Exchange.

Athens Stock Exchange.

Barcelona Stock Exchange.

Bavarian Stock Exchange.

Berlin Stock Exchange.

Bilbao Stock Exchange.

Bologna Stock Exchange.

. . .

Bremen Stock Exchange.

Brussels Stock Exchange.

Copenhagen Stock Exchange.

[COREDEAL Limited.]

Dusseldorf Stock Exchange.

[The exchange known as EASDAQ.]

Florence Stock Exchange.

Frankfurt Stock Exchange.

Genoa Stock Exchange.

. . .

Hamburg Stock Exchange.

Hanover Stock Exchange.

Helsinki Stock Exchange.

[Iceland Stock Exchange.

The Irish Stock Exchange Limited.]

. . .

. . .

Lisbon Stock Exchange.

LIFFE Administration & Management.

[The London Stock Exchange Limited.]

Luxembourg Stock Exchange.

Lyon Stock Exchange.

Madrid Stock Exchange.

. . .

Milan Stock Exchange.

. . .

. . .

Naples Stock Exchange.

The exchange known as NASDAQ.

[The exchange known as the Nouveau Marche.]

OMLX, the London Securities and Derivatives Exchange Limited.

Oporto Stock Exchange.

Oslo Stock Exchange.

Palermo Stock Exchange.

Paris Stock Exchange.

Rome Stock Exchange.

. . .

Stockholm Stock Exchange.

Stuttgart Stock Exchange.

[Tradepoint Financial Networks plc.]

Trieste Stock Exchange.

Turin Stock Exchange.

Valencia Stock Exchange.

Venice Stock Exchange.

Vienna Stock Exchange.

NOTES

Entry "Bordeaux Stock Exchange" (omitted) revoked by SI 1996/1561, art 4(a).

Entry "COREDEAL Limited" inserted by SI 2000/1923, art 2(1), (4)(a).

Date in force: 20 July 2000: see SI 2000/1923, art 1.

Entry "The exchange known as EASDAQ" inserted by SI 2000/1923, art 2(1), (4)(b).

Date in force: 20 July 2000: see SI 2000/1923, art 1.

Entry "Ghent Stock Exchange" (omitted) revoked by SI 1996/1561, art 4(a).

Entries "Iceland Stock Exchange" and "The Irish Stock Exchange Limited" substituted, for entry "The International Stock Exchange of the United Kingdom and the Republic of Ireland Limited" as originally enacted, by SI 1996/1561, art 4(b).

Entries "Liege Stock Exchange" and "Lille Stock Exchange" (omitted) revoked by SI 1996/1561, art 4(a).

Entry "The London Stock Exchange Limited" inserted by SI 1996/1561, art 4(c).

Entry "Marseille Stock Exchange" (omitted) revoked by SI 1996/1561, art 4(a).

Entries "Nancy Stock Exchange" and "Nantes Stock Exchange" (omitted) revoked by SI 1996/1561, art 4(a).

Entry "The exchange known as the Nouveau Marche" inserted by SI 1996/1561, art 4(e).

Entry "Securities Exchange of Iceland" (omitted) revoked by SI 2000/1923, art 2(1), (4)(c).

Date in force: 20 July 2000: see SI 2000/1923, art 1.

Entry "Tradepoint Financial Networks plc" inserted by SI 1996/1561, art 4(d).

Traded Securities (Disclosure) Regulations 1994

1994 No 188

NOTES

Made - - - 1st February 1994

ARRANGEMENT OF REGULATIONS

Citation and commencement

Interpretation

Obligation to disclose information

SCHEDULE

Citation and commencement

1

(1) These Regulations may be cited as the Traded Securities (Disclosure) Regulations 1994.

(2) These Regulations shall come into force on 1st March 1994.

Interpretation

2

In these Regulations:—

["the Official List" means the list maintained by the competent authority in accordance with section 74 of the Financial Services and Markets Act 2000;]

["overseas investment exchange" means a recognised investment exchange in the case of which a recognition order was made by virtue of section 292(2) of the Financial Services and Markets Act 2000;]

["recognised investment exchange" has the same meaning as in section 285 of the Financial Services and Markets Act 2000;]

"regulated market" means any market in the United Kingdom on which securities are admitted to trading being a market which is regulated and supervised by a recognised investment exchange and which operates regularly and is accessible directly or indirectly to the public; and

"security" means any security which falls within any paragraph of the Schedule to these Regulations but does not include an investment which is admitted to the Official List in accordance with [Part VI of the Financial Services and Markets Act 2000];

and the expressions "admitting to trading" and "company" and "undertaking" have the same meaning as in the Council Directive of 13th November 1989 co-ordinating regulations on insider dealing (89/592/EEC).

NOTES

Definition "the Official List" substituted by SI 2001/3649, art 453(a).

Date in force: 1 December 2001: see SI 2001/3649, art 1.

Definition "overseas investment exchange" substituted, for definition ""overseas investment exchange" and "recognised investment exchange"" as originally enacted, by SI 2001/3649, art 453(b).

Date in force: 1 December 2001: see SI 2001/3649, art 1.

Definition "recognised investment exchange" inserted by SI 2001/3649, art 453(c).

Date in force: 1 December 2001: see SI 2001/3649, art 1.

In definition "security" words "Part VI of the Financial Services and Markets Act 2000" in square brackets substituted by SI 2001/3649, art 453(d).

Date in force: 1 December 2001: see SI 2001/3649, art 1.

Obligation to disclose information

3

(1) Subject to paragraph (2) below, a company or undertaking which is an issuer of a security admitted to trading on a regulated market (an "issuer") shall inform the public as soon as possible of any major new developments in the issuer's sphere of activity which are not public knowledge and which may, by virtue of their effect on the issuer's assets and liabilities or financial position or on the general course of its business, lead to substantial movements in the price of that security.

(2) A recognised investment exchange which regulates and supervises a regulated market on which an issuer's securities are admitted to trading may exempt the issuer from the obligation imposed by paragraph (1) above if satisfied that the disclosure of the particular information would prejudice the legitimate interests of that issuer.

(3) The rules of a recognised investment exchange must, at least, enable the exchange, in the event of a failure by an issuer whose securities are admitted to trading on a regulated market which the exchange regulates and supervises to comply with the obligation imposed by paragraph (1) above, to do any of the following, that is to say—
  (a) discontinue the admission of the securities to trading;
  (b) suspend trading in the securities;
  (c) publish the fact that the issuer has failed to comply with the obligation; and
  (d) itself make public any information which the issuer has failed to publish.

4

[The Financial Services and Markets Act 2000 shall have effect as if the requirement set out in paragraph (3) of regulation 3 above were, in the case of an overseas investment exchange, among those specified in section 292(3) of that Act (requirements for recognition of overseas investment exchange) and mentioned in section 297(2)(a) of that Act (revocation of recognition order).]

NOTES
Substituted by SI 2001/3649, art 454.
Date in force: 1 December 2001: see SI 2001/3649, art 1.

SCHEDULE

Regulation 2

1   Shares and stock in the share capital of a company ("shares").

2   Any instrument creating or acknowledging indebtedness which is issued by a company or undertaking, including, in particular, debentures, debenture stock, loan stock, bonds and certificates of deposit ("debt securities").

3   Any right (whether conferred by warrant or otherwise) to subscribe for shares or debt securities ("warrants").

4   (1)   The rights under any depositary receipt.

(2)   For the purposes of sub-paragraph (1) above a "depositary receipt" means a certificate or other record (whether or not in the form of a document)—
    (a)   which is issued by or on behalf of a person who holds any relevant securities of a particular issuer; and
    (b)   which acknowledges that another person is entitled to rights in relation to the relevant securities or relevant securities of the same kind.

(3)   In sub-paragraph (2) above "relevant securities" means shares, debt securities and warrants.

5   Any option to acquire or dispose of any security falling within any other paragraph of this Schedule.

6   (1)   Rights under a contract for the acquisition or disposal of relevant securities under which delivery is to be made at a future date and at a price agreed when the contract is made.

(2)   In sub-paragraph (1) above—
    (a)   the references to a future date and to a price agreed when the contract is made include references to a date and a price determined in accordance with the terms of the contract; and
    (b)   "relevant securities" means any security falling within any other paragraph of this Schedule.

7   (1)   Rights under a contract which does not provide for the delivery of securities but whose purpose or pretended purpose is to secure a profit or avoid a loss by reference to fluctuations in—
    (a)   a share index or other similar factor connected with relevant securities; or
    (b)   the price of particular relevant securities.

(2)   In sub-paragraph (1) above "relevant securities" means any security falling within any other paragraph of this Schedule.

Public Offers of Securities Regulations 1995

1995 No 1537

NOTES

Made - - - 14th June 1995

ARRANGEMENT OF REGULATIONS

PART I

GENERAL

1 Citation, commencement and extent

(1)   These Regulations may be cited as the Public Offers of Securities Regulations 1995 and shall come into force on 19th June 1995.

(2)   These Regulations extend to Northern Ireland.

2 Interpretation

(1)   In these Regulations, except where the context otherwise requires—
    "the Act" means the [Financial Services and Markets Act 2000];
    "approved exchange" means, in relation to dealings in securities, a recognised investment exchange approved by the Treasury for the purposes of these Regulations either generally or in relation to such dealings, and the Treasury shall give notice in such manner as they think appropriate of the exchanges which are for the time being approved;
    "body corporate" shall be construed in accordance with [section 417(1)] of the Act;
    "convertible securities" means—
        [(i) instruments creating or acknowledging indebtedness of a kind which can be converted into or exchanged for, or which confer rights to acquire, securities;
        (ii) instruments giving entitlements to securities; or
        (iii) certificates representing securities;]
        and "conversion" in relation to convertible securities means their conversion into or exchange for, or the exercise of rights conferred by them to acquire,

other securities ("underlying securities");

["credit institution" means a credit institution as defined in [Article 1(1)(a)] of Directive 2000/12/EC of the European Parliament and of the Council;]

"director" shall be construed in accordance with [section 417(1)] of the Act;

. . .

. . .

["Euro-securities" means securities which—

    (a) are to be underwritten (by whatever means, including acquisition or subscription, with a view to resale) and distributed by a syndicate at least two of the members of which have their registered offices in different countries or territories;

    (b) are to be offered on a significant scale in one or more countries or territories other than the country or territory in which the issuer has its registered office; and

    (c) may be acquired pursuant to the offer only through a credit institution or other financial institution;]

["financial institution" means a financial institution as defined in Article 1 of the Directive 2000/12/EC of the European Parliament and of the Council;]

["group", in relation to a body corporate ("A") means A and any other body corporate which is—

    (i) a subsidiary of A,

    (ii) a holding company of A, or

    (iii) a subsidiary of such a holding company;]

. . .

"issuer", in relation to any securities, means the person by whom they have been or are to be issued;

"member State" means a State which is a Contracting Party to the Agreement on the European Economic Area signed at Oporto on 2nd May 1992 as adjusted by the Protocol signed at Brussels on 17th March 1993;

"private company" has the meaning given in section 1(3) of the Companies Act 1985;

"the registrar of companies", in relation to a prospectus relating to any securities, means—

    (a) if the securities are or are to be issued by a company incorporated in Great Britain, the registrar of companies in England and Wales or the registrar of companies in Scotland according to whether the company's registered office is in England and Wales or in Scotland;

    (b) if the securities are or are to be issued by a company incorporated in Northern Ireland, the registrar of companies for Northern Ireland;

    (c) in any other case, any of those registrars;

"recognised investment exchange" has the meaning given in [section 285] of the Act;

"securities" means investments to which Part II of these Regulations applies; and

"sale" includes any disposal for valuable consideration.

[(1A) Paragraphs (i), (ii) and (iii) of the definition of "convertible securities" in paragraph (1) above, together with regulations 3(2) and (5), 7(2)(f),(n), 8(4) and (5), and 9(4) must be read with—

(a)   section 22 of the Financial Services and Markets Act 2000;

(b)   any relevant order under that section; and

(c)   Schedule 2 to that Act.]

(2)   In the application of these Regulations to Scotland, references to a matter being actionable at the suit of a person shall be construed as references to the matter being actionable at the instance of that person.

(3)   References to the Companies Act 1985 include references to the corresponding Northern Ireland provision.

NOTES

Para (1): in definition "the Act" words "Financial Services and Markets Act 2000" in square brackets substituted by SI 2001/3649, art 501(1), (2)(a).

Date in force: 1 December 2001: see SI 2001/3649, art 1.

Para (1): in definition "body corporate" words "section 417(1)" in square brackets substituted by SI 2001/3649, art 501(1), (2)(b).

Date in force: 1 December 2001: see SI 2001/3649, art 1.

Para (1): in definition "convertible securities" paras (i)–(iii) substituted, for paras (i), (ii) as originally enacted, by SI 2001/3649, art 501(1), (2)(c).

Date in force: 1 December 2001: see SI 2001/3649, art 1.

Para (1): definition "credit institution" substituted by SI 2001/3649, art 501(1), (2)(d).

Date in force: 1 December 2001: see SI 2001/3649, art 1.

Para (1): in definition "credit institution" words "Article 1(1)(a)" in square brackets substituted by SI 2002/765, reg 5.

Date in force: 27 April 2002: see SI 2002/765, reg 1.

Para (1): in definition "director" words "section 417(1)" in italics revoked and subsequent words in square brackets substituted by SI 2001/3649, art 501(1), (2)(e).

Date in force: 1 December 2001: see SI 2001/3649, art 1.

Para (1): definition "ecu" (omitted) revoked by SI 2001/3649, art 501(1), (2)(f).

Date in force: 1 December 2001: see SI 2001/3649, art 1.

Para (1): definition "European institution" (omitted) revoked by SI 2001/3649, art 501(1), (2)(g).

Date in force: 1 December 2001: see SI 2001/3649, art 1.

Para (1): definition "Euro-securities" substituted by SI 1999/734, reg 2(a).

Date in force: 10 May 1999: see SI 1999/734, reg 1.

Para (1): definition "financial institution" substituted by SI 2001/3649, art 501(1), (2)(h).

Date in force: 1 December 2001: see SI 2001/3649, art 1.

Para (1): definition "group" substituted by SI 2001/3649, art 501(1), (2)(i).

Date in force: 1 December 2001: see SI 2001/3649, art 1.

Para (1): definition "home-regulated investment business" (omitted) revoked by SI 2001/3649, art 501(1), (2)(j).

Date in force: 1 December 2001: see SI 2001/3649, art 1.

Para (1): in definition "recognised investment exchange" words "section 285" in square brackets substituted by SI 2001/3649, art 501(1), (2)(k).

Date in force: 1 December 2001: see SI 2001/3649, art 1.

Para (1A): inserted by SI 2001/3649, art 501(1), (3).

Date in force: 1 December 2001: see SI 2001/3649, art 1.

PART II
PUBLIC OFFERS OF UNLISTED SECURITIES

[3 Investments to which this Part applies]

[(1)   This Part of these Regulations applies to any investment which—
  (a)   is not admitted to official listing, nor is the subject of an application for listing, in accordance with Part VI of the Act; and
  (b)   is of a kind specified in paragraph (2).

(2)   Subject to paragraphs (3) to (5) below, the kinds of investments specified for the purposes of paragraph (1)(b) are—
  (a)   shares, including for those purposes deferred shares of a building society, within the meaning of section 119 of the Building Societies Act 1986;
  (b)   instruments creating or acknowledging indebtedness;
  (c)   instruments giving entitlements to securities, including warrants and other instruments entitling the holder to acquire any share or instrument creating or acknowledging indebtedness; and
  (d)   certificates representing securities.

(3)   For the purposes of paragraph (1)(b), investments of the kind specified in paragraph (2)(a) (shares) do not include transferable shares in a body incorporated under the law relating to industrial and provident societies.

(4)   For the purposes of paragraph (1)(b), investments of the kind specified in paragraph (2)(b) (instruments creating or acknowledging indebtedness) do not include—
  (a)   debentures having a maturity of less than one year from their date of issue, and
  (b)   bills of exchange accepted by a banker.

(5)   For the purposes of paragraph (1)(b)—
  (a)   investments of the kind specified in sub-paragraph (c) of paragraph (2) do not include instruments giving entitlements in connection with government and public securities; and
  (b)   investments of the kind specified in sub-paragraph (d) of paragraph (2) do not include investments and certificates representing government or public securities.]

NOTES
Substituted by SI 2001/3649, art 502.
Date in force: 1 December 2001: see SI 2001/3649, art 1.

4 Registration and publication of prospectus

(1)   When securities are offered to the public in the United Kingdom for the first time the offeror shall publish a prospectus by making it available to the public, free of charge, at an address in the United Kingdom, from the time he first offers the securities until the end of the period during which the offer remains open.

(2)   The offeror shall, before the time of publication of the prospectus, deliver a copy of it to the registrar of companies for registration.

(3)   Paragraph (2) and regulations 5, 6 and 8 to 15 shall not apply to a prospectus submitted for approval in accordance with listing rules made under [section 87] of the Act.

NOTES

Para (3): words "section 87" in square brackets substituted by SI 2001/3649, art 503.
Date in force: 1 December 2001: see SI 2001/3649, art 1.

5 Offers of securities

A person is to be regarded as offering securities if, as principal—
  (a)   he makes an offer which, if accepted, would give rise to a contract for the issue or sale of the securities by him or by another person with whom he has made arrangements for the issue or sale of the securities; or
  (b)   he invites a person to make such an offer;

but not otherwise; and, except where the context otherwise requires, in this Part of these Regulations "offer" and "offeror" shall be construed accordingly.

6 Offers to the public in the United Kingdom

A person offers securities to the public in the United Kingdom if, to the extent that the offer is made to persons in the United Kingdom, it is made to the public; and, for this purpose, an offer which is made to any section of the public, whether selected as members or debenture holders of a body corporate, or as clients of the person making the offer, or in any other manner, is to be regarded as made to the public.

7 Exemptions

(1)   For the purposes of these Regulations, an offer of securities shall be deemed not to be an offer to the public in the United Kingdom if, to the extent that the offer is made to persons in the United Kingdom—
  (a)   the condition specified in any one of the sub-paragraphs of paragraph (2) is satisfied in relation to the offer; or
  (b)   paragraph (3) applies in relation to the offer.

(2)   The following are the conditions specified in this paragraph—
  (a)   the securities are offered to persons—
      (i)   whose ordinary activities involve them in acquiring, holding, managing or disposing of investments (as principal or agent) for the purposes of their businesses; or
      (ii)   who it is reasonable to expect will acquire, hold, manage or dispose of investments (as principal or agent) for the purposes of their businesses; or are otherwise offered to persons in the context of their trades, professions or occupations;
  (b)   the securities are offered to no more than fifty persons;

(c) the securities are offered to the members of a club or association (whether or not incorporated) and the members can reasonably be regarded as having a common interest with each other and with the club or association in the affairs of the club or association and in what is to be done with the proceeds of the offer;

(d) the securities are offered to a restricted circle of persons whom the offeror reasonably believes to be sufficiently knowledgeable to understand the risks involved in accepting the offer;

(e) the securities are offered in connection with a bona fide invitation to enter into an underwriting agreement with respect to them;

(f) the securities are the securities of a private company and are offered by that company to—
  (i) members or employees of the company;
  (ii) members of the families of any such members or employees; or
  [(iii)persons holding instruments creating or acknowledging indebtedness issued by the company;]

[(ff) the securities are the securities of a private company and are offered to holders of other securities in that company (whether or not of the same class) in pursuance of a requirement imposed by a provision in its articles of association or in an agreement between all the holders of securities, or all the holders of one or more classes of security, of that company;]

(g) the securities are offered to a government, local authority or public authority, . . .;

(h) the total consideration payable for the securities cannot exceed ecu 40,000 (or an equivalent amount);

(i) the minimum consideration which may be [paid by any person for securities acquired by him] pursuant to the offer is at least ecu 40,000 (or an equivalent amount);

(j) the securities are denominated in amounts of at least ecu 40,000 (or an equivalent amount);

(k) the securities are offered in connection with a takeover offer;

(l) the securities are offered in connection with a merger within the meaning of Council Directive No 78/855/EEC;

(m) the securities are shares and are offered free of charge to any or all of the holders of shares in the issuer;

(n) [the securities are—
  (i) shares,
  (ii) instruments giving entitlements to subscribe for shares, or
  (iii) certificates representing shares,]
  in a body corporate and are offered in exchange for shares in the same body corporate, and the offer cannot result in any increase in the issued share capital of the body corporate;

(o) the securities are issued by a body corporate and offered—
  (i) by the issuer[, by [a member of the same group as the issuer] or by a relevant trustee];
  (ii) only to qualifying persons; and

(iii) on terms that a contract to acquire any such securities may be entered into only by the qualifying person to whom they were offered or, if the terms of the offer so permit, any qualifying person;

(p) the securities result from the conversion of convertible securities and listing particulars or a prospectus relating to the convertible securities were or was published in the United Kingdom under or by virtue of [Part VI] of the Act, Part III of the Companies Act 1985 or these Regulations;

(q) the securities are issued by—

(i) a charity within the meaning of section 96(1) of the Charities Act 1993;

(ii) a housing association within the meaning of section 5(1) of the Housing Act 1985;

(iii) an industrial or provident society registered in accordance with section 1(2)(b) of the Industrial and Provident Societies Act 1965; or

(iv) a non-profit making association or body, recognised by the country or territory in which it is established, with objectives similar to those of a body falling within any of paragraphs (i) to (iii);

and the proceeds of the offer will be used for the purposes of the issuer's objectives;

(r) the securities offered are shares and ownership of the securities entitles the holder—

(i) to obtain the benefit of services provided by a building society within the meaning of section 119(1) of the Building Societies Act, an industrial or provident society registered in accordance with section 1(2) of the Industrial and Provident Societies Act 1965 or a body of a like nature established in a member State; or

(ii) to membership of such a body;

[(s) the securities offered are Euro-securities, and no advertisement relating to the offer is [issued in, or directed at persons in, the United Kingdom (or is caused to be so issued or so directed),] by the issuer of the Euro-securities or by any credit institution or other financial institution through which the Euro-securities may be acquired pursuant to the offer, or by any body corporate which is a member of the same group as that issuer or any of those institutions, other than—

[(i) an advertisement which is an exempt communication falling within article 19 of the Financial Services and Markets Act 2000 (Financial Promotion) Order 2001 (Investment professionals); or

(ii) an advertisement which would be an exempt communication falling within article 19 of that Order if the meaning of "investment professionals" in paragraph (5) of that article included a person with or for whom any credit institution or other financial institution through which the Euro-securities may be acquired pursuant to the offer has effected or arranged for the effecting of a transaction within the period of twelve months ending with the date on which the offer is first made;]]

(t) the securities are of the same class, and were issued at the same time, as securities in respect of which a prospectus has been published under or by virtue of [Part VI] of the Act, Part III of the Companies Act 1985 or these Regulations;

(u) the securities are not transferable.

(3) This paragraph applies in relation to an offer where the condition specified in one relevant sub-paragraph is satisfied in relation to part, but not the whole, of the offer and, in relation to each other part of the offer, the condition specified in a different relevant sub-paragraph is satisfied.

(4) For the purposes of paragraph (3), "relevant sub-paragraph" means any of [sub-paragraphs (a) to (f), (g), (k) to (q) and (t)] of paragraph (2).

(5) For the purposes of this regulation, "shares", except in relation to a takeover offer, [must be read with—
  (a) section 22 to the Financial Services and Markets Act 2000,
  (b) any relevant order under that section; and
  (c) Schedule 2 to that Act].

(6) For the purposes of determining whether the condition specified in sub-paragraph (b) or (h) of paragraph (2) is satisfied in relation to an offer, the offer shall be taken together with any other offer of securities of the same class which was—
  (a) made by the same person;
  (b) open at any time within the period of 12 months ending with the date on which the offer is first made; and
  (c) deemed not to be an offer to the public in the United Kingdom by virtue of that condition being satisfied.

[(6A) For the purposes of paragraph (2)(b), the making of an offer of securities to trustees of a trust or members of a partnership in their capacity as such, or the making of such an offer to any other two or more persons jointly, shall be treated as the making of an offer to a single person.]

(7) In determining for the purposes of paragraph (2)(d) whether a person is sufficiently knowledgeable to understand the risks involved in accepting an offer of securities, any information supplied by the offeror shall be disregarded, apart from information about—
  (a) the issuer of the securities, or
  (b) if the securities confer the right to acquire other securities, the issuer of those other securities.

(8) For the purposes of paragraph (2)(f)—
  (a) the members of a person's family are the person's husband or wife, widow or widower and children (including stepchildren) and their descendants, and any trustee (acting in his capacity as such) of a trust the principal beneficiary of which is the person himself or herself, or any of those relatives; and
  (b) regulation 3(2)(a) shall not apply.

[(8A) For the purposes of paragraph (2)(g), a government, local authority or public authority means—
  (a) the government of the United Kingdom;
  (b) the Scottish Administration;
  (c) the Executive Committee of the Northern Ireland Assembly;
  (d) the National Assembly for Wales;
  (e) the government of any country or territory outside the United Kingdom;
  (f) a local authority in the United Kingdom or elsewhere; or
  (g) a body the members of which comprise—

    (i)   states including the United Kingdom or another EEA State, or

    (ii) bodies whose members comprise states including the United Kingdom or another EEA State.]

(9) For the purposes of determining whether the condition mentioned in sub-paragraph (h), (i) or (j) of paragraph (2) is satisfied in relation to an offer, an amount, in relation to an amount denominated in ecu, is an "equivalent amount" if it is an amount of equal value, calculated at the latest practicable date before (but in any event not more than 3 days before) the date on which the offer is first made, denominated wholly or partly in another currency or unit of account.

[(10) For the purposes of paragraph (2)(k), "takeover offer" means—

  (a) an offer to acquire shares in a body corporate incorporated in the United Kingdom which is a takeover offer within the meaning of Part XIIIA of the Companies Act 1985 (or would be such an offer if that Part of that Act applied in relation to any body corporate);

  (b) an offer to acquire all or substantially all the shares, or the shares of a particular class, in a body corporate incorporated outside the United Kingdom; or

  (c) an offer made to all the holders of shares, or of shares of a particular class, in a body corporate to acquire a specified proportion of those shares;

but in determining whether an offer falls within sub-paragraph (b) there shall be disregarded any shares which the offeror or any associate of his holds or has contracted to acquire; and in determining whether an offer falls within sub-paragraph (c) the offeror, any associate of his and any person whose shares the offeror or any such associate has contracted to acquire shall not be regarded as holders of the shares.

(10A) In paragraph (10)—

"associate" has the same meaning as in section 430E of the Companies Act 1985; and

"share" has the same meaning as in section 428(1) of that Act.]

(11) For the purposes of paragraph (2)(m), "holders of shares" means the persons who, at the close of business on a date specified in the offer and falling within the period of [60 days] ending with the date on which the offer is first made, were holders of such shares.

(12) For the purposes of paragraph (2)(o), a person is a "qualifying person", in relation to an issuer, if he is a bona fide employee or former employee of the issuer or of another body corporate in the same group [(within the meaning of section 421 of the Act)] or the wife, husband, widow, widower or child or stepchild under the age of eighteen of such an employee or former employee.

[(13) In paragraph (2)(o)—

"group" has the same meaning as in section 421 of the Act, and

"a relevant trustee" has the same meaning as in article 71(6)(b) of the Financial Services and Markets Act 2000 (Regulated Activities) Order 2001 (Activities carried on in connection with employee share schemes).]

NOTES

Para (2): sub-para (f)(iii) substituted by SI 2001/3649, art 504(1), (2).

Date in force: 1 December 2001: see SI 2001/3649, art 1.

Para (2): sub-para (ff) inserted by SI 1999/734, reg 2(b).

Date in force: 10 May 1999: see SI 1999/734, reg 1.

Para (2): in sub-para (g) words omitted revoked by SI 2001/3649, art 504(1), (3).

Date in force: 1 December 2001: see SI 2001/3649, art 1.

Para (2): in sub-para (i) words "paid by any person for securities acquired by him" in square brackets substituted by SI 1999/734, reg 2(c).

Date in force: 10 May 1999: see SI 1999/734, reg 1.

Para (2): in sub-para (n) words from "the securities are—" to "certificates representing shares," in square brackets substituted by SI 2001/3649, art 504(1), (4).

Date in force: 1 December 2001: see SI 2001/3649, art 1.

Para (2): in sub-para (o)(i) words in square brackets ending with the words "or by a relevant trustee" inserted by SI 1999/734, reg 2(d).

Date in force: 10 May 1999: see SI 1999/734, reg 1.

Para (2): in sub-para (o)(i) words "a member of the same group as the issuer" in square brackets substituted by SI 2001/3649, art 504(1), (5).

Date in force: 1 December 2001: see SI 2001/3649, art 1.

Para (2): in sub-para (p) words "Part VI" in square brackets substituted by SI 2001/3649, art 504(1), (6).

Date in force: 1 December 2001: see SI 2001/3649, art 1.

Para (2): sub-para (s) substituted by SI 1999/1146, reg 2.

Date in force: 10 May 1999: see SI 1999/1146, reg 1.

Para (2): in sub-para (s) words from "issued in, or" to "or so directed)," in square brackets substituted by SI 2001/3649, art 504(1), (7)(a).

Date in force: 1 December 2001: see SI 2001/3649, art 1.

Para (2): sub-para (s)(i), (ii) substituted by SI 2001/3649, art 504(1), (7)(b).

Date in force: 1 December 2001: see SI 2001/3649, art 1.

Para (2): in sub-para (t) words "Part VI" in square brackets substituted by SI 2001/3649, art 504(1), (6).

Date in force: 1 December 2001: see SI 2001/3649, art 1.

Para (4): words "sub-paragraphs (a) to (f), (g), (k) to (q) and (t)" in square brackets substituted by SI 1999/734, reg 2(f).

Date in force: 10 May 1999: see SI 1999/734, reg 1.

Para (5): words from "must be read" to "to that Act" in square brackets substituted by SI 2001/3649, art 504(1), (8).

Date in force: 1 December 2001: see SI 2001/3649, art 1.

Para (6A): inserted by SI 1999/734, reg 2(g).

Date in force: 10 May 1999: see SI 1999/734, reg 1.

Para (8A): inserted by SI 2001/3649, art 504(1), (9).

Date in force: 1 December 2001: see SI 2001/3649, art 1.

Paras (10), (10A): substituted, for original para (10), by SI 1999/734, reg 2(h).

Date in force: 10 May 1999: see SI 1999/734, reg 1.

Para (11): words "60 days" in square brackets substituted by SI 1999/734, reg 2(i).

Date in force: 10 May 1999: see SI 1999/734, reg 1.

Para (12): words "(within the meaning of section 421 of the Act)" in square brackets (inserted by SI 1999/734, reg 2(j)) substituted by SI 2001/3649, art 504(1), (10).

Date in force: 1 December 2001: see SI 2001/3649, art 1.

Para (13): substituted by SI 2001/3649, art 504(1), (11).

Date in force: 1 December 2001: see SI 2001/3649, art 1.

8 Form and content of prospectus

(1)   Subject to regulation 11 and to paragraphs (2), (4), (5) and (6), a prospectus shall contain the information specified in Parts II to X of Schedule 1 to these Regulations (which shall be construed in accordance with Part I of that Schedule).

(2)   Where the requirement to include in a prospectus any information (the "required information") is inappropriate to the issuer's sphere of activity or to [the legal form of the issuer or the offeror] or to the securities to which the prospectus relates, the requirement—

   (a)   shall have effect as a requirement that the prospectus contain information equivalent to the required information; but

   (b)   if there is no such equivalent information, shall not apply.

(3)   The information in a prospectus shall be presented in as easily analysable and comprehensible a form as possible.

(4)   Where, on the occasion of their admission to dealings on an approved exchange, [shares] are offered on a pre-emptive basis to some or all of the existing holders of such [shares], a body or person designated for the purposes of this paragraph by the Treasury shall have power to authorise the omission from a prospectus subject to this regulation of specified information provided that up-to-date information equivalent to that which would otherwise be required by this regulation is available as a result of the requirements of that approved exchange.

   In this paragraph, "specified information" means information specified in paragraphs 41 to 47 of Schedule 1 to these Regulations.

[(4A)   In determining for the purposes of paragraph (4) whether information is equivalent to that specified in paragraph 45 of Schedule 1, there shall be disregarded—

   (a)   the requirements of sub-paragraphs (1)(a)(i), (1)(a)(iv), (1)(b)(iii), (2)(a)(ii), (2)(a)(iv) and (8)(b) of that paragraph; and

   (b)   any requirement of sub-paragraph (10)(a), (10)(b) or (11)(c) to include a statement by the person responsible for the interim accounts or report.]

(5)   Where a class of [shares] has been admitted to dealings on an approved exchange, a body or person designated for the purposes of this paragraph by the Treasury shall have power to authorise the making of an offer without a prospectus, provided that—

   (a)   the number or estimated market value or the nominal value or, in the absence of a nominal value, the accounting par value of the [shares] offered amounts to less than ten per cent of the number or of the corresponding value of [shares] of the same class already admitted to dealings; and

   (b)   up-to-date information equivalent to that required by this regulation is available as a result of the requirements of that approved exchange.

(6)   Where a person—

   (a)   makes an offer to the public in the United Kingdom of securities which he proposes to issue; and

(b) has, within the 12 months preceding the date on which the offer is first made, published a full prospectus relating to a different class of securities which he has issued, or to an earlier issue of the same class of securities,

he may publish, instead of a full prospectus, a prospectus which contains only the differences which have arisen since the publication of the full prospectus mentioned in sub-paragraph (b) and any supplementary prospectus and which are likely to influence the value of the securities, provided that the prospectus is accompanied by that full prospectus and any supplementary prospectus or contains a reference to it or them; and, for this purpose, a full prospectus is one which contains the information specified in Parts II to X of Schedule 1 (other than any information whose omission is authorised by or under paragraph (2) or (4) or regulation 11).

NOTES

Para (2): words "the legal form of the issuer or the offeror" in square brackets substituted by SI 1999/734, reg 2(l).

Date in force: 10 May 1999: see SI 1999/734, reg 1.

Paras (4), (5): word "shares" in square brackets in each place it occurs substituted by SI 2001/3649, art 505(1).

Date in force: 1 December 2001: see SI 2001/3649, art 1.

Para (4A): inserted by SI 1999/734, reg 2(m).

Date in force: 10 May 1999: see SI 1999/734, reg 1.

9 General duty of disclosure in prospectus

(1) In addition to the information required to be included in a prospectus by virtue of regulation 8 a prospectus shall (subject to these Regulations) contain all such information as investors would reasonably require, and reasonably expect to find there, for the purpose of making an informed assessment of—

(a) the assets and liabilities, financial position, profits and losses, and prospects of the issuer of the securities; and

(b) the rights attaching to those securities.

(2) The information to be included by virtue of this regulation shall be such information as is mentioned in paragraph (1) which is within the knowledge of any person responsible for the prospectus or which it would be reasonable for him to obtain by making enquiries.

(3) In determining what information is required to be included in a prospectus by virtue of this regulation regard shall be had to the nature of the securities and of the issuer of the securities.

(4) For the purposes of this regulation "issuer", in relation to [a certificate or other instrument representing securities], means the person who issued or is to issue the securities to which the certificate or instrument relates.

NOTES

Para (4): words "a certificate or other instrument representing securities" in square brackets substituted by SI 2001/3649, art 505(2).

Date in force: 1 December 2001: see SI 2001/3649, art 1.

10 Supplementary prospectus

(1)   Where a prospectus has been registered under this Part of these Regulations in respect of an offer of securities and at any time while an agreement in respect of those securities can be entered into in pursuance of that offer—

- (a)   there is a significant change affecting any matter contained in the prospectus whose inclusion was required by regulation 8 or 9; or
- (b)   a significant new matter arises the inclusion of information in respect of which would have been so required if it had arisen when the prospectus was prepared; or
- (c)   there is a significant inaccuracy in the prospectus,

the offeror shall deliver to the registrar of companies for registration, and publish in accordance with paragraph (3), a supplementary prospectus containing particulars of the change or new matter or, in the case of an inaccuracy, correcting it.

(2)   In paragraph (1) "significant" means significant for the purpose of making an informed assessment of the matters mentioned in regulation 9(1)(a) and (b).

(3)   Regulation 4(1) shall apply to a supplementary prospectus delivered for registration to the registrar of companies in the same way as it applies to a prospectus except that the obligation to publish the supplementary prospectus shall begin with the time it is delivered for registration to the registrar of companies.

(4)   Where the offeror is not aware of the change, new matter or inaccuracy in question he shall not be under any duty to comply with paragraphs (1) and (3) unless he is notified of it by a person responsible for the prospectus; but any person responsible for the prospectus who is aware of such a matter shall be under a duty to give him notice of it.

(5)   Where a supplementary prospectus has been registered under this regulation in respect of an offer, the preceding paragraphs of this regulation have effect as if any reference to a prospectus were a reference to the prospectus originally registered and that supplementary prospectus, taken together.

11 Exceptions

(1)   The Treasury or the Secretary of State may authorise the omission from a prospectus or supplementary prospectus of information whose inclusion would otherwise be required by these Regulations if they or he consider that disclosure of that information would be contrary to the public interest.

(2)   An offeror may omit from a prospectus or supplementary prospectus information with respect to an issuer whose inclusion would otherwise be required by these Regulations if—

- (a)   he is not that issuer, nor acting in pursuance of an agreement with that issuer;
- (b)   the information is not available to him because he is not that issuer; and
- (c)   he has been unable, despite making such efforts (if any) as are reasonable, to obtain the information.

(3)   The competent authority for the purposes of [Part VI] of the Act ("the competent authority") may authorise the omission from a prospectus or supplemen-

tary prospectus of information whose inclusion would otherwise be required by these Regulations, if—

(a) the information is of minor importance only, and is not likely to influence assessment of the issuer's assets and liabilities, financial position, profits and losses and prospects; or

(b) disclosure of that information would be seriously detrimental to the issuer and its omission would not be likely to mislead investors with regard to facts and circumstances necessary for an informed assessment of the securities.

(4) Paragraph (4) of regulation 9 applies for the purposes of paragraph (3) as it applies for the purposes of that regulation.

(5) The competent authority may make rules providing for the payment of fees to it for the discharge of its functions under paragraph (3).

(6) [Section 101] of the Act shall apply to rules made under paragraph (5) as it applies to listing rules.

NOTES

Para (3): words "Part VI" in square brackets substituted by SI 2001/3649, art 506(a).
Date in force: 1 December 2001: see SI 2001/3649, art 1.
Para (6): words "Section 101" in square brackets substituted by SI 2001/3649, art 506(b).
Date in force: 1 December 2001: see SI 2001/3649, art 1.

12 Advertisements etc in connection with offer of securities

An advertisement, notice, poster or document (other than a prospectus) announcing a public offer of securities for which a prospectus is or will be required under this Part of these Regulations shall not be issued to or caused to be issued to the public in the United Kingdom by the person proposing to make the offer unless it states that a prospectus is or will be published, as the case may be, and gives an address in the United Kingdom from which it can be obtained or will be obtainable.

13 Persons responsible for prospectus

(1) For the purpose of this Part of these Regulations the persons responsible for a prospectus or supplementary prospectus are—

(a) the issuer of the securities to which the prospectus or supplementary prospectus relates;

(b) where the issuer is a body corporate, each person who is a director of that body corporate at the time when the prospectus or supplementary prospectus is published;

(c) where the issuer is a body corporate, each person who has authorised himself to be named, and is named, in the prospectus or supplementary prospectus as a director or as having agreed to become a director of that body either immediately or at a future time;

(d) each person who accepts, and is stated in the prospectus or supplementary prospectus as accepting, responsibility for, or for any part of, the prospectus or supplementary prospectus;

(e) the offeror of the securities, where he is not the issuer;

(f)   where the offeror is a body corporate, but is not the issuer and is not making the offer in association with the issuer, each person who is a director of that body corporate at the time when the prospectus or supplementary prospectus is published; and

(g)   each person not falling within any of the foregoing paragraphs who has authorised the contents of, or of any part of, the prospectus or supplementary prospectus.

(2)   A person is not responsible under paragraph (1)(a), (b) or (c) unless the issuer has made or authorised the offer in relation to which the prospectus or supplementary prospectus was published; and a person is not responsible for a prospectus or supplementary prospectus by virtue of paragraph (1)(b) if it is published without his knowledge or consent and on becoming aware of its publication he forthwith gives reasonable public notice that it was published without his knowledge or consent.

[(2A)   A person is not responsible under paragraph (1)(e) as the offeror of the securities if—

(a)   the issuer is responsible for the prospectus or supplementary prospectus in accordance with this regulation;

(b)   the prospectus or supplementary prospectus was drawn up primarily by the issuer, or by one or more persons acting on behalf of the issuer; and

(c)   the offeror is making the offer in association with the issuer.]

(3)   Where a person has accepted responsibility for, or authorised, only part of the contents of any prospectus or supplementary prospectus, he is responsible under paragraph (1)(d) or (g) only for that part and only if it is included in (or substantially in) the form and context to which he has agreed.

(4)   Nothing in this regulation shall be construed as making a person responsible for any prospectus or supplementary prospectus by reason only of giving advice as to its contents in a professional capacity.

(5)   Where by virtue of this regulation the issuer of any shares pays or is liable to pay compensation under regulation 14 for loss suffered in respect of shares for which a person has subscribed no account shall be taken of that liability or payment in determining any question as to the amount paid on subscription for those shares or as to the amount paid up or deemed to be paid up on them.

NOTES

Para (2A): inserted by SI 1999/734, reg 2(n).
Date in force: 10 May 1999: see SI 1999/734, reg 1.

14 Compensation for false or misleading prospectus

(1)   Subject to regulation 15 the person or persons responsible for a prospectus or supplementary prospectus shall be liable to pay compensation to any person who has acquired the securities to which the prospectus relates and suffered loss in respect of them as a result of any untrue or misleading statement in the prospectus or supplementary prospectus or the omission from it of any matter required to be included by regulation 9 or 10.

(2)   Where regulation 8 requires a prospectus to include information as to any particular matter on the basis that the prospectus must include a statement either as to that matter or, if such is the case, that there is no such matter, the omission from the prospectus of the information shall be treated for the purposes of paragraph (1) as a statement that there is no such matter.

(3)   Subject to regulation 15, a person who fails to comply with regulation 10 shall be liable to pay compensation to any person who has acquired any of the securities in question and suffered loss in respect of them as a result of the failure.

(4)   This regulation does not affect any liability which any person may incur apart from this regulation.

(5)   References in this regulation to the acquisition by any person of securities include references to his contracting to acquire them or an interest in them.

15 Exemption from liability to pay compensation

(1)   A person shall not incur any liability under regulation 14(1) for any loss in respect of securities caused by any such statement or omission as is there mentioned if he satisfies the court that at the time when the prospectus or supplementary prospectus was delivered for registration he reasonably believed, having made such enquiries (if any) as were reasonable, that the statement was true and not misleading or that the matter whose omission caused the loss was properly omitted and—
- (a)   that he continued in that belief until the time when the securities were acquired; or
- (b)   that they were acquired before it was reasonably practicable to bring a correction to the attention of persons likely to acquire the securities in question; or
- (c)   that before the securities were acquired he had taken all such steps as it was reasonable for him to have taken to secure that a correction was forthwith brought to the attention of those persons; or
- (d)   that the securities were acquired after such a lapse of time that he ought in the circumstances to be reasonably excused, and, if the securities are dealt in on an approved exchange, that he continued in that belief until after the commencement of dealings in the securities on that exchange.

(2)   A person shall not incur any liability under regulation 14(1) for any loss in respect of securities caused by a statement purporting to be made by or on the authority of another person as an expert which is, and is stated to be, included in the prospectus or supplementary prospectus with that other person's consent if he satisfies the court that at the time when the prospectus or supplementary prospectus was delivered for registration he believed on reasonable grounds that the other person was competent to make or authorise the statement and had consented to its inclusion in the form and context in which it was included and—
- (a)   that he continued in that belief until the time when the securities were acquired; or
- (b)   that they were acquired before it was reasonably practicable to bring the fact that the expert was not competent or had not consented to the attention of persons likely to acquire the securities in question; or

(c) that before the securities were acquired he had taken all such steps as it was reasonable for him to have taken to secure that that fact was forthwith brought to the attention of those persons; or

(d) that the securities were acquired after such a lapse of time that he ought in the circumstances to be reasonably excused and, if the securities are dealt in on an approved exchange, that he continued in that belief until after the commencement of dealings in the securities on that exchange.

(3) Without prejudice to paragraphs (1) and (2), a person shall not incur any liability under regulation 14(1) for any loss in respect of any securities caused by any such statement or omission as is there mentioned if he satisfies the court—

(a) that before the securities were acquired a correction or, where the statement was such as is mentioned in paragraph (2), the fact that the expert was not competent or had not consented had been published in a manner calculated to bring it to the attention of persons likely to acquire the securities in question; or

(b) that he took all such steps as it was reasonable for him to take to secure such publication and reasonably believed that it had taken place before the securities were acquired.

(4) A person shall not incur any liability under regulation 14(1) for any loss resulting from a statement made by an official person or contained in a public official document which is included in the prospectus or supplementary prospectus if he satisfies the court that the statement is accurately and fairly reproduced.

(5) A person shall not incur any liability under regulation 14(1) or (3) if he satisfies the court that the person suffering the loss acquired the securities in question with knowledge that the statement was false or misleading, of the omitted matter or of the change, new matter or inaccuracy, as the case may be.

(6) A person shall not incur any liability under regulation 14(3) if he satisfies the court that he reasonably believed that the change, new matter or inaccuracy in question was not such as to call for a supplementary prospectus.

(7) In this regulation "expert" includes any engineer, valuer, accountant or other person whose profession, qualifications or experience give authority to a statement made by him; and references to the acquisition of securities include references to contracting to acquire them or an interest in them.

16 Contraventions

[(1) An authorised person who contravenes regulation 4(1) or, where it applies, regulation 4(2), or who contravenes regulation 12, or who assists another person to contravene any of those provisions, shall be treated as having contravened rules under Part X of the Act.]

(2) A person other than an authorised person who contravenes regulation 4(1) or, where it applies, regulation 4(2), or who contravenes regulation 12, or who assists another person to contravene any of those provisions, shall be guilty of an offence and liable—

(a) on conviction on indictment, to imprisonment for a term not exceeding two years or to a fine or to both;

(b) on summary conviction, to imprisonment for a term not exceeding three months or to a fine not exceeding level 5 on the standard scale.

(3) Without prejudice to any liability under regulation 14, a person shall not be regarded as having contravened regulation 4 by reason only of a prospectus not having fully complied with the requirements of these Regulations as to its form or content.

(4) Any contravention to which this regulation applies shall be actionable at the suit of a person who suffers loss as a result of the contravention subject to the defences and other incidents applying to actions for breach of statutory duty.

[(5) In this regulation—
"authorised person" means a person who is authorised for the purposes of the Act; and
"exempt regulated activity" has the same meaning as in section 325(2) of the Act.]

(6) . . .

NOTES
Para (1): substituted by SI 2001/3649, art 507(a).
Date in force: 1 December 2001: see SI 2001/3649, art 1.
Para (5): substituted by SI 2001/3649, art 507(b).
Date in force: 1 December 2001: see SI 2001/3649, art 1.
Para (6): revoked by SI 2001/3649, art 507(c).
Date in force: 1 December 2001: see SI 2001/3649, art 1.

PART III
AMENDMENTS TO PART IV OF THE ACT ETC

17 . . .

. . .

NOTES
Revoked by SI 2001/3649, art 512(a).
Date in force: 1 December 2001: see SI 2001/3649, art 1.

18 Penalties

Where these Regulations amend, extend the application of, or modify the effect of, a provision contained in [Part VI] of the Act and thereby create a new criminal offence which, but for this regulation, would be punishable to a greater extent than is permitted under paragraph 1(1)(d) of Schedule 2 to the European Communities Act 1972, the maximum punishment for the offence shall be the maximum permitted under that paragraph at the time the offence was committed, on conviction on indictment or on summary conviction, as the case may be.

NOTES
Words "Part VI" in square brackets substituted by SI 2001/3649, art 508.
Date in force: 1 December 2001: see SI 2001/3649, art 1.

PART IV
MISCELLANEOUS

19 Designations

For the purposes of Articles 11, 12, 13, 14, 18, 19, 20, 21 and 22 of Council Directive No 89/298/EEC the Treasury may designate such bodies as they think fit and they shall give notice in such manner as they think appropriate of the designations they have made.

20 Mutual recognition

Schedule 4 to these Regulations shall have effect to make provision for the recognition of prospectuses and listing particulars approved in other member States.

22 Registration of documents by the registrar of companies

For the purposes of the provisions mentioned in section 735B of the Companies Act 1985, regulations 4(2) and 10(1) shall be regarded as provisions of the Companies Acts.

23 [Miscellaneous and Supplementary]

(1) [Paragraph 19(1) of Schedule 1 to the Act] shall apply to the competent authority in the discharge or purported discharge of its functions under these Regulations as it applies to it in the discharge or purported discharge of its functions under [Part VI] of the Act.

(2) [Section 415] of the Act shall apply to proceedings arising out of any act or omission (or proposed act or omission) of the competent authority in the discharge or purported discharge of any function under regulation 11 as it applies to the proceedings mentioned in that section.

(3) [Section 410] of the Act shall apply to a person designated under regulation 19 in respect of any action which he proposes to take or has power to take by virtue of being so designated.

[(4) Section 176 of the Act shall have effect, in relation to these Regulations, as if for the purposes of subsection (4) of section 176 the offences mentioned in section 168 of the Act included an offence under these Regulations.]

[(5) Subsections (1) and (3) of section 398 of the Act shall apply in relation to information given to the competent authority—
  (a) for the purposes of or in connection with an application under these Regulations, or
  (b) in purported compliance with requirements imposed by or under these Regulations,

as they apply in relation to information given in purported compliance with any requirement imposed by or under the Act.]

(6) [Sections 400, 401 and 403] of the Act shall apply to offences under these Regulations as they apply to offences under the Act.

NOTES

Provision heading: words "Miscellaneous and Supplementary" in square brackets substituted by SI 2001/3649, art 509(a).

Date in force: 1 December 2001: see SI 2001/3649, art 1.

Para (1): words "Paragraph 19(1) of Schedule 1 to the Act" in square brackets substituted by SI 2001/3649, art 509(b)(i).

Date in force: 1 December 2001: see SI 2001/3649, art 1.

Para (1): words "Part VI" in square brackets substituted by SI 2001/3649, art 509(b)(ii).

Date in force: 1 December 2001: see SI 2001/3649, art 1.

Para (2): words "Section 415" in square brackets substituted by SI 2001/3649, art 509(c).

Date in force: 1 December 2001: see SI 2001/3649, art 1.

Para (3): words "Section 410" in square brackets substituted by SI 2001/3649, art 509(d).

Date in force: 1 December 2001: see SI 2001/3649, art 1.

Para (4): substituted by SI 2001/3649, art 509(e).

Date in force: 1 December 2001: see SI 2001/3649, art 1.

Para (5): substituted by SI 2001/3649, art 509(f).

Date in force: 1 December 2001: see SI 2001/3649, art 1.

Para (6): words "Sections 400, 401 and 403" in square brackets substituted by SI 2001/3649, art 509(g).

Date in force: 1 December 2001: see SI 2001/3649, art 1.

SCHEDULE 1
FORM AND CONTENT OF PROSPECTUS

Regulation 8

PART I
INTERPRETATION

1 In this Schedule, except where the context otherwise requires—

"annual accounts" has the same meaning as in Part VII of the Companies Act 1985;

"control" means the ability, in practice, to determine the actions of the issuer; and "joint control" means control exercised by two or more persons who have an agreement or understanding (whether formal or informal) which may lead to their adopting a common policy in respect of the issuer;

"debentures" means [instruments creating or acknowledging indebtedness];

"financial year" has the same meaning as in Part VII of the Companies Act 1985;

"group accounts" has the same meaning as in Part VII of the Companies Act 1985;

"the last three years", in relation to an undertaking whose accounts are required to be dealt with in a prospectus, means three completed financial years which immediately precede the date on which the offer is first made and which cover a continuous period of at least 35 months, disregarding a financial year which ends less than three months before the date on which the offer is first made and for which accounts have not been prepared by that date;

"parent undertaking" and "subsidiary undertaking" have the same meaning as in Part VII of the Companies Act 1985;

"state of affairs" means the state of affairs of an undertaking, in relation to its balance sheet, at the end of a financial year;

"subsidiary" and "holding company" have the same meanings as in sections 736 and 736A of the Companies Act 1985; and

"undertaking" has the same meaning as in Part VII of the Companies Act 1985.

[1A The definition of "debentures" in paragraph 1 must be read with—

(a) section 22 of the Financial Services and Markets Act 2000;

(b) any relevant order under that section; and

(c) Schedule 2 to that Act.]

NOTES

Para 1: in definition "debentures" words "instruments creating or acknowledging indebtedness" in square brackets substituted by SI 2001/3649, art 510(a).

Date in force: 1 December 2001: see SI 2001/3649, art 1.

Para 1A: inserted by SI 2001/3649, art 510(b).

Date in force: 1 December 2001: see SI 2001/3649, art 1.

PART II
GENERAL REQUIREMENTS

2 The name of the issuer and the address of its registered office.

3 If different, the name and address of the person offering the securities.

4 The names and functions of the directors of the issuer.

5 The date of publication of the prospectus.

6 A statement that a copy of the prospectus has been delivered for registration to the registrar of companies in accordance with regulation 4(2), indicating to which registrar of companies it has been delivered.

7 A statement that the prospectus has been drawn up in accordance with these Regulations.

8 The following words, "If you are in any doubt about the contents of this document you should consult a person [authorised for the purposes of the Financial Services and Markets Act 2000] who specialises in advising on the acquisition of shares and other securities", or words to the like effect.

NOTES

Para 8: words "authorised for the purposes of the Financial Services and Markets Act 2000" in square brackets substituted by SI 2001/3649, art 510(c).

Date in force: 1 December 2001: see SI 2001/3649, art 1.

PART III
THE PERSONS RESPONSIBLE FOR THE PROSPECTUS AND ADVISERS

9 The names, addresses (home or business) and functions of those persons responsible (which in this Part of this Schedule has the same meaning as in regulation 13) for the prospectus or any part of the prospectus, specifying such part.

10 [(1) A declaration by the directors of the issuer (where it is responsible for the prospectus) or (in any other case) by the directors of the offeror, that to the best of their knowledge the information contained in the prospectus is in accordance with the facts and that the prospectus makes no omission likely to affect the import of such information.]

(2) Without prejudice to paragraph 45 of this Schedule, a statement by any person who accepts responsibility for the prospectus, or any part of it, that he does so.

NOTES

Para 10: sub-para (1) substituted by SI 1999/734, reg 2(o).

Date in force: 10 May 1999: see SI 1999/734, reg 1.

PART IV
THE SECURITIES TO WHICH THE PROSPECTUS RELATES AND THE OFFER

11   A description of the securities being offered, including the class to which they belong and a description of the rights attaching to them including (where applicable)—
  (a) if the securities are shares, rights as regards—
    (i) voting;
    (ii) dividends;
    (iii) return of capital on the winding up of the issuer;
    (iv) redemption;
    and a summary of the consents necessary for the variation of any of those rights;
  (b) if the securities are debentures, rights as regards—
    (i) interest payable;
    (ii) repayment of principal;
  (c) if the securities are convertible securities—
    (i) the terms and dates on which the holder of the convertible securities is entitled to acquire the related underlying securities;
    (ii) the procedures for exercising the entitlement to the underlying securities; and
    (iii) such information relating to the underlying securities as would have been required under paragraphs (a) or (b) if the securities being offered had been the underlying securities.

12   The date(s) (if any) on which entitlement to dividends or interest arises.

13   Particulars of tax on income from the securities withheld at source, including tax credits.

14   The procedure for the exercise of any right of preemption attaching to the securities.

15   Any restrictions on the free transferability of the securities being offered.

16   (1) A statement as to whether—
  (a) the securities being offered have been admitted to dealings on a recognised investment exchange; or
  (b) an application for such admission has been made.

(2)   Where no such application for dealings has been made, or such an application has been made and refused, a statement as to whether or not there are, or are intended to be, any other arrangements for there to be dealings in the securities and, if there are, a brief description of such arrangements.

17   The purpose for which the securities are being issued.

18   The number of securities being issued.

19   The number of securities being offered.

20   The total proceeds which it is expected will be raised by the offer and the expected net proceeds, after deduction of the expenses, of the offer.

21   Where the prospectus relates to shares which are offered for subscription, particulars as to—
  (a) the minimum amount which, in the opinion of the directors of the issuer, must be raised by the issue of those shares in order to provide the sums (or, if any part of them is to be defrayed in any other manner, the balance of the sums) required to be provided in respect of each of the following—
    (i) the purchase price of any property purchased, or to be purchased, which is to be defrayed in whole or in part out of the proceeds of the issue;

      (ii) any preliminary expenses payable by the issuer and any commission so payable to any person in consideration of his agreeing to subscribe for, or of his procuring or agreeing to procure subscriptions for, any shares in the issuer;

      (iii) the repayment of any money borrowed by the issuer in respect of any of the foregoing matters;

      (iv) working capital; and

    (b)   the amounts to be provided in respect of the matters mentioned otherwise than out of the proceeds of the issue and the sources out of which those amounts are to be provided.

22   The names of any persons underwriting or guaranteeing the offer.

23   The amount or the estimated amount of the expenses of the offer and by whom they are payable, including (except in so far as information is required to be included in the prospectus by section 97(3) of the Companies Act 1985) a statement as to any commission payable by the issuer to any person in consideration of his agreeing to subscribe for securities to which the prospectus relates or of his procuring or agreeing to procure subscriptions for such securities.

24   The names and addresses of the paying agents (if any).

25   The period during which the offer of the securities is open.

26   The price at which the securities are offered or, if appropriate, the procedure, method and timetable for fixing the price.

27   The arrangements for payment for the securities being offered and the arrangements and timetable for their delivery.

28   The arrangements during the period prior to the delivery of the securities being offered relating to the moneys received from applicants including the arrangements for the return of moneys to applicants where their applications are not accepted in whole or in part and the timetable for the return of such moneys.

PART V
GENERAL INFORMATION ABOUT THE ISSUER AND ITS CAPITAL

29   The date and place of incorporation of the issuer. In the case of an issuer not incorporated in the United Kingdom, the address of its principal place of business in the United Kingdom (if any).

30   The place of registration of the issuer and the number with which it is registered.

31   The legal form of the issuer, the legislation under which it was formed and (if different) the legislation now applicable to it.

32   A summary of the provisions in the issuer's memorandum of association determining its objects.

33   If the liability of the members of the issuer is limited, a statement of that fact.

34   The amount of the issuer's authorised share capital and any limit on the duration of the authorisation to issue such share capital.

35   The amount of the issuer's issued share capital.

36   The number and particulars of any listed and unlisted securities issued by the issuer not representing share capital.

37   The number of shares of each class making up each of the authorised and issued share capital, the nominal value of such shares and, in the case of the issued share capital, the amount paid up on the shares.

38   The amount of any outstanding listed and unlisted convertible securities issued by the issuer, the conditions and procedures for their conversion and the number of shares which would be issued as a result of their conversion.

39   If the issuer is a member of a group, a brief description of the group and of the issuer's position in it, stating, where the issuer is a subsidiary, the name of its holding company.

40   Insofar the offeror has the information, an indication of the persons, who, directly or indirectly, jointly or severally, exercise or could exercise control over the issuer and particulars of the proportion of the issuer's voting capital held by such persons.

PART VI
THE ISSUER'S PRINCIPAL ACTIVITIES

41   A description of the issuer's principal activities and of any exceptional factors which have influenced its activities.

42   A statement of any dependence of the issuer on patents or other intellectual property rights, licences or particular contracts, where any of these are of fundamental importance to the issuer's business.

43   Information regarding investments in progress where they are significant.

44   Information on any legal or arbitration proceedings, active, pending or threatened against, or being brought by, the issuer or any member of its group which are having or may have a significant effect on the issuer's financial position.

PART VII
THE ISSUER'S ASSETS AND LIABILITIES, FINANCIAL POSITION AND PROFITS AND LOSSES

45   (1)   If the issuer is a company to which Part VII of the Companies Act 1985 applies otherwise than by virtue of section 700 of that Act—
- (a)   the issuer's annual accounts for the last three years together with—
  - (i)   a statement by the directors of the issuer that the accounts have been prepared in accordance with the law, and that they accept responsibility for them, or a statement why they are unable to make such a statement;
  - (ii)   the names and addresses of the auditors of the accounts;
  - (iii)   a copy of the auditors' reports on the accounts, within the meaning of section 235 of the Companies Act 1985; and
  - (iv)   a statement by the auditors that they consent to the inclusion of their reports in the prospectus and accept responsibility for them, and have not become aware, since the date of any report, of any matter affecting the validity of that report at that date; or a statement why they are unable to make such a statement; or
- (b)   a report by a person qualified to act as an auditor with respect to the state of affairs and profit or loss shown by the issuer's annual accounts for the last three years together with—
  - (i)   the name and address of the person responsible for the report;
  - (ii)   if different, the name and address of the person who audited the accounts on which the report is based; and
  - (iii)   a statement by the person responsible for the report that in his opinion the report gives a true and fair view of the state of affairs and profit or loss of the issuer

and its subsidiary undertakings, and that he consents to the inclusion of his report in the prospectus and accepts responsibility for it; or a statement why he is unable to make such a statement.

(2)   If the issuer is not a company to which Part VII of the Companies Act 1985 applies (or is a company to which that Part of that Act applies by virtue of section 700 of that Act)—

    (a)   the issuer's accounts (and, if it is a parent undertaking, its subsidiary undertakings' accounts) for the last three years, prepared in accordance with the applicable law, together with—

        (i)   the name and address of the person responsible for the accounts;

        (ii) a statement by the person responsible for the accounts that they have been properly prepared in accordance with the applicable law, and that he accepts responsibility for them, or statement why he is unable to make such a statement;

        (iii) the names and addresses of the auditors of the accounts and their reports; and

        (iv) a statement by the auditors that they consent to the inclusion of their reports in the prospectus and accept responsibility for them, and have not become aware, since the date of any report, of any matter affecting the validity of that report at that date; or a statement why they are unable to make such a statement; or

    (b)   a report by a person qualified to act as an auditor with respect to the state of affairs and profit or loss shown by the issuer's accounts (and, if the issuer is a parent undertaking, by its subsidiary undertakings' accounts) for the last three years, such report to be drawn up in accordance with the applicable law, or as if the provisions of the Companies Act 1985 relating to annual accounts applied to the issuer, together with—

        (i)   the name and address of the person responsible for the report;

        (ii) if different, the name and address of the person who audited the accounts on which the report is based; and

        (iii) a statement by the person responsible for the report that in his opinion the report gives a true and fair view of the state of affairs and profit or loss of the issuer and its subsidiary undertakings and that he consents to the inclusion of his report in the prospectus and accepts responsibility for it; or a statement why he is unable to make such a statement.

(3)   If, in accordance with the law applicable to it, the accounts of an issuer falling within sub-paragraph (2) consist only of consolidated accounts with respect to itself and its subsidiary undertakings, the prospectus is not required by virtue of sub-paragraph (2) to include separate accounts for each undertaking, or to include a report which deals with the accounts of each undertaking separately.

(4)   If, in the case of an issuer falling within sub-paragraph (1) or (2), the prospectus would, but for this sub-paragraph, include both separate accounts for the issuer and its subsidiary undertakings and consolidated accounts, either the separate accounts or the consolidated accounts may be omitted from the prospectus if their inclusion would not provide any significant additional information.

(5)   If an issuer falling within sub-paragraph (2) is not required by the law applicable to it to have its accounts audited—

    (a)   if the accounts have not been audited—

        (i)   the prospectus shall contain a statement to that effect; and

        (ii) paragraph (a)(iii) and (iv) or, as the case may be, paragraph (b)(ii) of sub-paragraph (2) shall not apply to the issuer; and

    (b)   if the accounts have nonetheless been audited, the prospectus shall contain a statement to that effect.

(6) Sub-paragraphs (7) and (8) shall apply in so far as the issuer has not been in existence for the whole of the last three years.

(7) Subject to sub-paragraph (8)—

(a) the requirement in sub-paragraphs (1)(a) and (2)(a) that the prospectus contain accounts for the last three years shall be construed as a requirement that the prospectus contain the accounts which the undertaking concerned was required (by its constitution or by the law under which it is established) to prepare for financial years during its existence, disregarding a financial year which ends less than three months before the date on which the offer is first made and for which accounts have not been prepared by that date; and

(b) the requirement in sub-paragraphs (1)(b) and (2)(b) that the prospectus contain a report with respect to the state of affairs and profit or loss for the last three years shall be construed as a requirement that the prospectus contain a report with respect to the accounts which the undertaking concerned was required (by its constitution or by the law under which it is established) to prepare for financial years during its existence, disregarding a financial year which ends less than three months before the date on which the offer is first made and for which accounts have not been prepared by that date.

(8) If an undertaking has not been required (by its constitution or by the law under which it is established) to prepare any accounts for financial years, the requirement in sub-paragraphs (1) and (2) that the prospectus contain accounts for, or a report with respect to, the last three years shall be construed as a requirement that the prospectus contain a report by a person qualified to act as an auditor which includes—

(a) details of the profit or loss of the undertaking in respect of the period beginning with the date of its formation and ending on the latest practicable date before (but not in any event more than three months before) the date on which the offer is first made, and of its state of affairs at that latest practicable date; and

(b) a statement by the person responsible for the report that in his opinion it gives a true and fair view of the state of affairs and profit or loss of the undertaking and that he consents to the inclusion of his report in the prospectus and accepts responsibility for it; or a statement why he is unable to make such a statement.

(9) If the issuer is a parent undertaking, the requirements of sub-paragraph (1) or, as the case may be, sub-paragraph (2), shall apply to each subsidiary undertaking in respect of any part of the last three years for which information is not otherwise required by those sub-paragraphs[, and for this purpose any reference in sub-paragraphs (3) to (8) to the issuer shall have effect as a reference to the subsidiary undertaking].

[(9A) Neither sub-paragraph (2) nor sub-paragraph (9) requires the inclusion in the prospectus of the accounts of a subsidiary undertaking, a report dealing with those accounts, or any other information relating to a subsidiary undertaking, if the accounts are not, or the report or the information is not, reasonably necessary for the purpose of making an informed assessment of the issuer's assets and liabilities, financial position, profits and losses and prospects, or of the securities being offered.]

(10) Where more than nine months have elapsed at the date on which the offer is first made since the end of the last financial year in respect of which accounts or a report are required to be included in the prospectus by this paragraph, there shall also be included in the prospectus—

(a) interim accounts of the undertaking concerned (which need not be audited but which must otherwise be prepared to the standard applicable to accounts required for each financial year) covering the period beginning at the end of the last financial year in respect of which accounts or a report are required to be included in the prospectus by this paragraph, [and ending not less than six months after the end of that financial year], together with the name and address of the person responsible for the interim accounts and a statement by him that the interim accounts have been properly prepared in accordance with the law applicable to the undertaking, and that he consents to the inclusion of the accounts and statement in the prospectus and accepts responsibility for them; or a statement why he is unable to make such a statement; or

(b)   a report by a person qualified to act as an auditor covering the same period with respect to the state of affairs and profit or loss of the undertaking concerned, prepared in accordance with the law applicable to the undertaking, together with the name and address of the person responsible for preparing the report, and a statement by him that he consents to the inclusion of the report in the prospectus and accepts responsibility for it; or a statement why he is unable to make such a statement.

(11)   If any interim accounts of the issuer have been published since the end of the last financial year of the issuer in respect of which accounts or a report are required to be included in the prospectus by this paragraph, other than interim accounts included in a prospectus in accordance with sub-paragraph (10), they shall be included in the prospectus, together with—

(a)   an explanation of the purpose for which the accounts were prepared;

(b)   a reference to the legislation in accordance with which they were prepared; and

(c)   the name and address of the person responsible for them, and a statement from him that he consents to the inclusion of the accounts in the prospectus and accepts responsibility for them.

NOTES

Para 45: in sub-para (9) words ", and for this purpose any reference in sub-paragraphs (3) to (8) to the issuer shall have effect as a reference to the subsidiary undertaking" in square brackets inserted by SI 1999/734, reg 2(p)(i).

Date in force: 10 May 1999: see SI 1999/734, reg 1.

Para 45: sub-para (9A) inserted by SI 1999/734, reg 2(p)(ii).

Date in force: 10 May 1999: see SI 1999/734, reg 1.

Para 45: in sub-para (10)(a) words "and ending not less than six months after the end of that financial year" in square brackets substituted by SI 1999/734, reg 2(p)(iii).

Date in force: 10 May 1999: see SI 1999/734, reg 1.

PART VIII
THE ISSUER'S ADMINISTRATION, MANAGEMENT AND SUPERVISION

46   A concise description of the directors' existing or proposed service contracts with the issuer or any subsidiary of the issuer, excluding contracts expiring, or determinable by the employing company without payment of compensation within one year, or an appropriate negative statement.

47   (1)   The aggregate remuneration paid and benefits in kind granted to the directors of the issuer during the last completed financial year of the issuer, together with an estimate of the aggregate amount payable and benefits in kind to be granted to the directors, and proposed directors, for the current financial year under the arrangements in force at the date on which the offer is first made.

(2)   The interests of each director of the issuer in the share capital of the issuer, distinguishing between beneficial and non-beneficial interests, or an appropriate negative statement.

PART IX
RECENT DEVELOPMENTS IN THE ISSUER'S BUSINESS AND PROSPECTS

48   The significant recent trends concerning the development of the issuer's business since the end of the last completed financial year of the issuer.

49   Information on the issuer's prospects for at least the current financial year of the issuer.

PART X
CONVERTIBLE SECURITIES AND GUARANTEED DEBENTURES

50   Where the prospectus relates to convertible securities, and the issuer of the related underlying securities is not the same as the issuer of the convertible securities, the information specified in this Schedule must be given in respect of the issuer of the convertible securities, and the information specified in paragraph 2 and Parts V, VI, VII, VIII and IX of this Schedule must be given in respect of the issuer of the underlying securities.

51   Where the prospectus relates to debentures which are guaranteed by one or more persons, the name and address and the information specified in Parts V, VI, VII, VIII and IX of this Schedule must also be given in respect of any guarantor who is not an individual.

SCHEDULE 2
. . .

NOTES
Revoked by SI 2001/3649, art 512(a).
Date in force: 1 December 2001: see SI 2001/3649, art 1.

. . .

NOTES
Revoked by SI 2001/3649, art 512(a).
Date in force: 1 December 2001: see SI 2001/3649, art 1.

PART I
. . .

NOTES
Revoked by SI 2001/3649, art 512(a).
Date in force: 1 December 2001: see SI 2001/3649, art 1.

. . .

PART II
. . .

NOTES
Revoked by SI 2001/3649, art 512(a).
Date in force: 1 December 2001: see SI 2001/3649, art 1.

. . .

NOTES
Revoked by SI 2001/3649, art 512(a).
Date in force: 1 December 2001: see SI 2001/3649, art 1.

SCHEDULE 4
MUTUAL RECOGNITION OF PROSPECTUSES AND LISTING PARTICULARS

Regulation 20

PART I
RECOGNITION FOR THE PURPOSES OF [PART VI OF THE FINANCIAL SERVICES AND MARKETS ACT 2000] OF PROSPECTUSES AND LISTING PARTICULARS APPROVED IN OTHER MEMBER STATES

NOTES
Part heading: words "Part VI of the Financial Services and Markets Act 2000" in square brackets substituted by SI 2001/3649, art 511(a).
Date in force: 1 December 2001: see SI 2001/3649, art 1.

1 In this Part of this Schedule—
  (a) the term "competent authority" includes a body designated by a member State pursuant to Article 12 of Council Directive No 89/298/EEC;
  (b) "the UK authority" means the competent authority for the purposes of Part IV of the Act;
  (c) "European document" means—
    (i) listing particulars which have been approved by the competent authority in another member State and which Article 24a of Council Directive No 80/390/EEC requires or paragraph 5 of that article permits to be recognised as listing particulars;
    (ii) a prospectus which has been approved by the competent authority in another member State and which Article 24b of Council Directive No 80/390/EEC requires or which paragraph 2 of that article, in referring to paragraph 5 of article 24a of that Directive, permits to be recognised as listing particulars; or
    (iii) a prospectus which has been approved by the competent authority in another member State, which Article 21 of Council Directive No 89/298/EEC requires or which paragraph 4 of that article permits to be recognised and which relates to securities which are the subject of an application for listing in the United Kingdom and which are to be offered in the United Kingdom prior to admission to listing in the United Kingdom by means of the prospectus;
    including in each case any supplement to listing particulars or a prospectus which, before the completion of the preparation of the recognised document for submission to the UK authority pursuant to an application for listing, has been approved pursuant to Article 23 of Council Directive No 80/390/EEC or Article 18 of Council Directive No 89/298/EEC by the competent authorities which approved the listing particulars or prospectus.

Where the European document submitted to the UK authority is a translation into English of the document approved by the competent authorities in another member State then, unless the context otherwise requires, the document as translated shall be regarded as the European document rather than the document as approved.

2 In this Part of this Schedule, "recognised European document" means a document consisting of a European document submitted to the UK authority pursuant to an application for listing under [section 75] of the Act and, if information is required to be added to it in accordance with listing rules, including that information.

3 Subject to paragraph 4, [Part VI] of the Act shall apply to a recognised European document as it applies—

(a) in relation to listing particulars, within the meaning of [section 79(2)] of the Act (in a case where the securities to which it relates will not be offered in the United Kingdom prior to admission to listing in the United Kingdom); or

(b) in relation to a prospectus [required by listing rules made under section 84 of the Act] (in a case where the recognised European document is a prospectus and the securities to which it relates are to be offered in the United Kingdom prior to admission to listing in the United Kingdom).

4 [Part VI] of the Act shall apply to a recognised European document subject to the following modifications—

(a) nothing in [Part VI] shall require the approval by the UK authority of a recognised European document which has been approved as described in paragraph 1(c);

(b) in [sections 80, 81(1)(a) and 90(3)] of the Act, any reference to information specified or required by listing rules or required by the competent authority or to matter whose inclusion was required by listing rules or by the competent authority shall apply as if it were a reference to information required by or to matter whose inclusion was required by the legislation relating to the contents of prospectuses and listing particulars, or by the competent authorities, of the member State where the European document forming part of that recognised European document was approved;

(c) nothing in [section 81] of the Act shall require the approval by the UK authority of supplementary listing particulars or a supplementary prospectus which is, or is a translation into English of, a supplement which has been approved pursuant to Article 23 of Council Directive No 80/390/EEC or Article 18 of Council Directive No 89/298/EEC by the competent authority which approved the listing particulars or prospectus to which the supplement relates.

5 Subject to paragraphs 1 and 3, references in [Part VI] of the Act to supplementary listing particulars shall be taken to include references to supplementary prospectuses.

6 This Part of this Schedule shall not apply to listing particulars or a prospectus approved in another member State prior to the coming into force of these Regulations.

NOTES

Para 2: words "section 75" in square brackets substituted by SI 2001/3649, art 511(b).
Date in force: 1 December 2001: see SI 2001/3649, art 1.
Para 3: words "Part VI" in square brackets substituted by SI 2001/3649, art 511(c)(i).
Date in force: 1 December 2001: see SI 2001/3649, art 1.
Para 3: in sub-para (a) words "section 79(2)" in square brackets substituted by SI 2001/3649, art 511(c)(ii).
Date in force: 1 December 2001: see SI 2001/3649, art 1.
Para 3: in sub-para (b) words "required by listing rules made under section 84 of the Act" in square brackets substituted by SI 2001/3649, art 511(c)(iii).
Date in force: 1 December 2001: see SI 2001/3649, art 1.
Para 4: words "Part VI" in square brackets in both places they occur substituted by SI 2001/3649, art 511(d)(i).
Date in force: 1 December 2001: see SI 2001/3649, art 1.
Para 4: in sub-para (b) words "sections 80, 81(1)(a) and 90(3)" in square brackets substituted by SI 2001/3649, art 511(d)(ii).

Date in force: 1 December 2001: see SI 2001/3649, art 1.

Para 4: in sub-para (c) words "section 81" in square brackets substituted by SI 2001/3649, art 511(d)(iii).

Date in force: 1 December 2001: see SI 2001/3649, art 1.

Para 5: words "Part VI" in square brackets substituted by SI 2001/3649, art 511(e).

Date in force: 1 December 2001: see SI 2001/3649, art 1.

PART II

RECOGNITION FOR THE PURPOSES OF PART II OF THESE REGULATIONS OF PRO-
SPECTUSES APPROVED IN OTHER MEMBER STATES

7 In this Part of this Schedule "recognised prospectus" means a prospectus which has been approved in accordance with Article 20 of Council Directive No 89/298/EEC in another member State and satisfies the requirements of paragraphs (a) to (c) of paragraph 8(1); and where the prospectus has been translated into English, the English version shall be the recognised prospectus.

8 (1) Where a prospectus has been approved in accordance with Article 20 of Council Directive No 89/298/EEC in another member State it shall, subject to sub-paragraph (2), be deemed for the purposes of regulation 4(1) to comply with regulations 8 and 9 of these Regulations provided that—

    (a) . . .

    (b) the offer of securities to which the prospectus relates is made in the United Kingdom simultaneously with the making of the offer in the member State where the prospectus was approved or within 3 months after the making of that offer;

    (c) there is added to the information contained in the prospectus as approved in the other member State such of the following information as is not included in the prospectus as so approved—

        (i) . . .

        (ii) the names and addresses of the paying agents for the securities in the United Kingdom (if any);

        (iii) a statement of how notice of meetings and other notices from the issuer of the securities will be given to United Kingdom resident holders of the securities; and

    (d) where a partial exemption or partial derogation has been granted in the other member State pursuant to Council Directive No 89/298/EEC—

        (i) the partial exemption or partial derogation in question is of a type for which a corresponding partial exemption or partial derogation is made in these Regulations; and

        (ii) the circumstances that justify the partial exemption or partial derogation also exist in the United Kingdom.

(2) Where, prior to the delivery for registration to the registrar of companies of a prospectus which has been approved in another member State, a supplement to the prospectus has been approved pursuant to Article 23 of Council Directive No 80/390/EEC or Article 18 of Council Directive No 89/298/EEC in the member State where the prospectus was approved, the references in sub-paragraph (1) and in paragraph 7 to a prospectus shall be taken to be references to the prospectus taken together with the supplement.

9 Subject to paragraph 8(2), Part II of these Regulations shall apply in relation to a recognised prospectus as it applies in relation to a prospectus to which the said Part II would apply apart from this paragraph except that in regulations 9(1), 10(1)(a) and 14(2) of these Regulations the references to information or any matter required to be included in a prospectus by these Regulations shall be taken to be references to information or any matter required to be included by virtue of the legislation relating to the contents of prospectuses of the member State where the recognised prospectus was approved and by virtue of paragraph 8(1)(c).

Para 8: sub-paras (1)(a), (c)(i) revoked by SI 1999/734, reg 2(q).
Date in force: 10 May 1999: see SI 1999/734, reg 1.

PART III
RECOGNITION FOR THE PURPOSES OF THE COMPANIES ACT 1985 OF PROSPEC-TUSES APPROVED IN OTHER MEMBER STATES

10   In this Part of this Schedule, "recognised prospectus" has the same meaning as in Part II of this Schedule.

11   . . .

12   A recognised prospectus shall be deemed to comply with sections 97(3) and 693(1)(a) and (d) of the Companies Act 1985.

Para 11: revoked by SI 1999/734, reg 2(r).
Date in force: 10 May 1999: see SI 1999/734, reg 1.

PART III

PARTNERSHIP STATUTES AND REGULATIONS

Partnership Act 1890

1890 CHAPTER 39

An Act to declare and amend the Law of Partnership

[14th August 1890]

Nature of Partnership

1 Definition of Partnership

(1) Partnership is the relation which subsists between persons carrying on a business in common with a view of profit.

(2) But the relation between members of any company or association which is—
  (a) Registered as a Company under the Companies Act 1862 or any other Act of Parliament for the time being in force and relating to the registration of joint stock companies; or
  (b) Formed or incorporated by or in pursuance of any other Act of Parliament or letters patent, or Royal Charter. . .
  (c) . . .:

is not a partnership within the meaning of this Act.

NOTES

Sub-s (2): para (c) and word preceding it repealed by the Statute Law (Repeals) Act 1998. Date in force: 19 November 1998: (no specific commencement provision).

2 Rules for determining existence of partnership

In determining whether a partnership does or does not exist, regard shall be had to the following rules:
  (1) Joint tenancy, tenancy in common, joint property, common property, or part ownership does not of itself create a partnership as to anything so held or owned, whether the tenants or owners do or do not share any profits made by the use thereof.
  (2) The sharing of gross returns does not of itself create a partnership, whether the persons sharing such returns have or have not a joint or common right or interest in any property from which or from the use of which the returns are derived.
  (3) The receipt by a person of a share of the profits of a business is *prima facie* evidence that he is a partner in the business, but receipt of such a share, or of a payment contingent on or varying with the profits of a business, does not of itself make him a partner in the business; and in particular—
    (a) The receipt by a person of a debt or other liquidated amount by instalments or otherwise out of the accruing profits of a business does not of itself make him a partner in the business or liable as such:

(b) A contract for the remuneration of a servant or agent of a person engaged in a business by a share of the profits of the business does not of itself make the servant or agent a partner in the business or liable as such:

(c) A person being the widow or child of a deceased partner, and receiving by way of annuity a portion of the profits made in the business in which the deceased person was a partner, is not by reason only of such receipt a partner in the business or liable as such:

(d) The advance of money by way of loan to a person engaged or about to engage in any business on a contract with that person that the lender shall receive a rate of interest varying with the profits, or shall receive a share of the profits arising from carrying on the business, does not of itself make the lender a partner with the person or persons carrying on the business or liable as such. Provided that the contract is in writing, and signed by or on behalf of all the parties thereto:

(e) A person receiving by way of annuity or otherwise a portion of the profits of a business in consideration of the sale by him of the goodwill of the business is not by reason only of such receipt a partner in the business or liable as such.

3 Postponement of rights of person lending or selling in consideration of share of profits in case of insolvency

In the event of any person to whom money has been advanced by way of loan upon such a contract as is mentioned in the last foregoing section, or of any buyer of a goodwill in consideration of a share of the profits of the business, being adjudged a bankrupt, entering into an arrangement to pay his creditors less than [100p] in the pound, or dying in insolvent circumstances, the lender of the loan shall not be entitled to recover anything in respect of his loan, and the seller of the goodwill shall not be entitled to recover anything in respect of the share of profits contracted for, until the claims of the other creditors of the borrower or buyer for valuable consideration in money or money's worth have been satisfied.

NOTES

Sum "100p" in square brackets substituted by virtue of the Decimal Currency Act 1969, s 10(1).

4 Meaning of firm

(1) Persons who have entered into partnership with one another are for the purposes of this Act called collectively a firm, and the name under which their business is carried on is called the firm-name.

(2) In Scotland a firm is a legal person distinct from the partners of whom it is composed, but an individual partner may be charged on a decree or diligence directed against the firm, and on payment of the debts is entitled to relief pro rata from the firm and its other members.

Relations of Partners to persons dealing with them

5 Power of partner to bind the firm

Every partner is an agent of the firm and his other partners for the purpose of the business of the partnership; and the acts of every partner who does any act for carrying on in the usual way business of the kind carried on by the firm of which he is a member bind the firm and his partners, unless the partner so acting has in fact no authority to act for the firm in the particular matter, and the person with whom he is dealing either knows that he has no authority, or does not know or believe him to be a partner.

6 Partners bound by acts on behalf of firm

An act or instrument relating to the business of the firm done or executed in the firm-name, or in any other manner showing an intention to bind the firm, by any person thereto authorised, whether a partner or not, is binding on the firm and all the partners.

Provided that this section shall not affect any general rule of law relating to the execution of deeds or negotiable instruments.

7 Partner using credit of firm for private purposes

Where one partner pledges the credit of the firm for a purpose apparently not connected with the firm's ordinary course of business, the firm is not bound, unless he is in fact specially authorised by the other partners; but this section does not affect any personal liability incurred by an individual partner.

8 Effect of notice that firm will not be bound by acts of partner

If it has been agreed between the partners that any restriction shall be placed on the power of any one or more of them to bind the firm, no act done in contravention of the agreement is binding on the firm with respect to persons having notice of the agreement.

9 Liability of partners

Every partner in a firm is liable jointly with the other partners, and in Scotland severally also, for all debts and obligations of the firm incurred while he is a partner; and after his death his estate is also severally liable in a due course of administration for such debts and obligations, so far as they remain unsatisfied, but subject in England or Ireland to the prior payment of his separate debts.

10 Liability of the firm for wrongs

Where, by any wrongful act or omission of any partner acting in the ordinary course of the business of the firm, or with the authority of his co-partners, loss or injury is caused to any person not being a partner in the firm, or any penalty is incurred, the firm is liable therefor to the same extent as the partner so acting or omitting to act.

11 Misapplication of money or property received for or in custody of the firm

In the following cases; namely—

(a) Where one partner acting within the scope of his apparent authority receives the money or property of a third person and misapplies it; and

(b) Where a firm in the course of its business receives money or property of a third person, and the money or property so received is misapplied by one or more of the partners while it is in the custody of the firm;

the firm is liable to make good the loss.

12 Liability for wrongs joint and several

Every partner is liable jointly with his co-partners and also severally for everything for which the firm while he is a partner therein becomes liable under either of the two last preceding sections.

13 Improper employment of trust-property for partnership purposes

If a partner, being a trustee, improperly employs trust-property in the business or on the account of the partnership, no other partner is liable for the trust property to the persons beneficially interested therein:

Provided as follows:—

(1) This section shall not affect any liability incurred by any partner by reason of his having notice of a breach of trust; and

(2) Nothing in this section shall prevent trust money from being followed and recovered from the firm if still in its possession or under its control.

14 Persons liable by "holding out"

(1) Every one who by words spoken or written or by conduct represents himself, or who knowingly suffers himself to be represented, as a partner in a particular firm, is liable as a partner to any one who has on the faith of any such representation given credit to the firm, whether the representation has or has not been made or communicated to the person so giving credit by or with the knowledge of the apparent partner making the representation or suffering it to be made.

(2) Provided that where after a partner's death the partnership business is continued in the old firm's name, the continued use of that name or of the deceased partner's name as part thereof shall not of itself make his executors or administrators estate or effects liable for any partnership debts contracted after his death.

15 Admissions and representation of partners

An admission or representation made by any partner concerning the partnership affairs, and in the ordinary course of its business, is evidence against the firm.

16 Notice to acting partner to be notice to the firm

Notice to any partner who habitually acts in the partnership business of any matter relating to partnership affairs operates as notice to the firm, except in the case of a fraud on the firm committed by or with the consent of that partner.

17 Liabilities of incoming and outgoing partners

(1) A person who is admitted as a partner into an existing firm does not thereby become liable to the creditors of the firm for anything done before he became a partner.

(2) A partner who retires from a firm does not thereby cease to be liable for partnership debts or obligations incurred before his retirement.

(3) A retiring partner may be discharged from any existing liabilities, by an agreement to that effect between himself and the members of the firm as newly constituted and the creditors, and this agreement may be either expressed or inferred as a fact from the course of dealing between the creditors and the firm as newly constituted.

18 Revocation of continuing guaranty by change in firm

A continuing guaranty or cautionary obligation given either to a firm or to a third person in respect of the transactions of a firm is, in the absence of agreement to the contrary, revoked as to future transactions by any change in the constitution of the firm to which, or of the firm in respect of the transactions of which, the guaranty or obligation was given.

Relations of Partners to one another

19 Variation by consent of terms of partnership

The mutual rights and duties of partners, whether ascertained by agreement or defined by this Act, may be varied by the consent of all the partners, and such consent may be either express or inferred from a course of dealing.

20 Partnership property

(1) All property and rights and interests in property originally brought into the partnership stock or acquired, whether by purchase or otherwise, on account of the firm, or for the purposes and in the course of the partnership business, are called in this Act partnership property, and must be held and applied by the partners exclusively for the purposes of the partnership and in accordance with the partnership agreement.

(2) Provided that the legal estate or interest in any land, or in Scotland the title to and interest in any heritable estate, which belongs to the partnership shall devolve according to the nature and tenure thereof, and the general rules of law thereto applicable, but in trust, so far as necessary, for the persons beneficially interested in the land under this section.

(3)   Where co-owners of an estate or interest in any land, or in Scotland of any heritable estate, not being itself partnership property, are partners as to profits made by the use of that land or estate, and purchase other land or estate out of the profits to be used in like manner, the land or estate so purchased belongs to them, in the absence of an agreement to the contrary, not as partners, but as co-owners for the same respective estates and interests as are held by them in the land or estate first mentioned at the date of the purchase.

21 Property bought with partnership money

Unless the contrary intention appears, property bought with money belonging to the firm is deemed to have been bought on account of the firm.

23 Procedure against partnership property for a partner's separate judgement debt

(1)   . . . A writ of execution shall not issue against any partnership property except on a judgment against the firm.

(2)   The High Court, or a judge thereof, . . ., or a county court, may, on the application by summons of any judgment creditor of a partner, make an order charging that partner's interest in the partnership property and profits with payment of the amount of the judgment debt and interest thereon, and may by the same or a subsequent order appoint a receiver of that partner's share of profits (whether already declared or accruing), and of any other money which may be coming to him in respect of the partnership, and direct all accounts and inquiries, and give all other orders and directions which might have been directed or given if the charge had been made in favour of the judgment creditor by the partner, or which the circumstances of the case may require.

(3)   The other partner or partners shall be at liberty at any time to redeem the interest charged, or in case of a sale being directed, to purchase the same.

(4)   . . .

(5)   This section shall not apply to Scotland.

NOTES

Sub-s (1): words omitted repealed by the Statute Law Revision Act 1908.
Sub-s (2): words omitted repealed by the Courts Act 1971, s 56(4), Sch 11, Part II.
Sub-s (4): repealed by the Statute Law (Repeals) Act 1998.
Date in force: 19 November 1998: (no specific commencement provision).

24 Rules as to interests and duties of partners subject to special agreement

The interests of partners in the partnership property and their rights and duties in relation to the partnership shall be determined, subject to any agreement express or implied between the partners, by the following rules:—

(1) All the partners are entitled to share equally in the capital and profits of the business, and must contribute equally towards the losses whether of capital or otherwise sustained by the firm.

(2) The firm must indemnify every partner in respect of payments made and personal liabilities incurred by him—

    (a) In the ordinary and proper conduct of the business of the firm; or,

    (b) In or about anything necessarily done for the preservation of the business or property of the firm.

(3) A partner making, for the purpose of the partnership, any actual payment or advance beyond the amount of capital which he has agreed to subscribe, is entitled to interest at the rate of five per cent. per annum from the date of the payment or advance.

(4) A partner is not entitled, before the ascertainment of profits, to interest on the capital subscribed by him.

(5) Every partner may take part in the management of the partnership business.

(6) No partner shall be entitled to remuneration for acting in the partnership business.

(7) No person may be introduced as a partner without the consent of all existing partners.

(8) Any difference arising as to ordinary matters connected with the partnership business may be decided by a majority of the partners, but no change may be made in the nature of the partnership business without the consent of all existing partners.

(9) The partnership books are to be kept at the place of business of the partnership (or the principal place, if there is more than one), and every partner may, when he thinks fit, have access to and inspect and copy any of them.

25 Expulsion of partner

No majority of the partners can expel any partner unless a power to do so has been conferred by express agreement between the partners.

26 Retirement from partnership at will

(1) Where no fixed term has been agreed upon for the duration of the partnership, any partner may determine the partnership at any time on giving notice of his intention so to do to all the other partners.

(2) Where the partnership has originally been constituted by deed, a notice in writing, signed by the partner giving it, shall be sufficient for this purpose.

27 Where partnership for term is continued over, continuance on old terms presumed

(1) Where a partnership entered into for a fixed term is continued after the term has expired, and without any express new agreement, the rights and duties of the partners remain the same as they were at the expiration of the term, so far as is consistent with the incidents of a partnership at will.

(2)   A continuance of the business by the partners or such of them as habitually acted therein during the term, without any settlement or liquidation of the partnership affairs, is presumed to be a continuance of the partnership.

28 Duty of partners to render accounts, etc

Partners are bound to render true accounts and full information of all things affecting the partnership to any partner or his legal representatives.

29 Accountability of partners for private profits

(1)   Every partner must account to the firm for any benefit derived by him without the consent of the other partners from any transaction concerning the partnership, or from any use by him of the partnership property name or business connexion.

(2)   This section applies also to transactions undertaken after a partnership has been dissolved by the death of a partner, and before the affairs thereof have been completely wound up, either by any surviving partner or by the representatives of the deceased partner.

30 Duty of partner not to compete with firm

If a partner, without the consent of the other partners, carries on any business of the same nature as and competing with that of the firm, he must account for and pay over to the firm all profits made by him in that business.

31 Rights of assignee of share in partnership

(1)   An assignment by any partner of his share in the partnership, either absolute or by way of mortgage or redeemable charge, does not, as against the other partners, entitle the assignee, during the continuance of the partnership, to interfere in the management or administration of the partnership business or affairs, or to require any accounts of the partnership transactions, or to inspect the partnership books, but entitles the assignee only to receive the share of profits to which the assigning partner would otherwise be entitled, and the assignee must accept the account of profits agreed to by the partners.

(2)   In case of a dissolution of the partnership, whether as respects all the partners or as respects the assigning partner, the assignee is entitled to receive the share of the partnership assets to which the assigning partner is entitled as between himself and the other partners, and, for the purpose of ascertaining that share, to an account as from the date of the dissolution.

Dissolution of Partnership, and its consequences

32 Dissolution by expiration or notice

Subject to any agreement between the partners, a partnership is dissolved—
  (a) If entered into for a fixed term, by the expiration of that term:
  (b) If entered into for a single adventure or undertaking, by the termination of that adventure or undertaking:

(c) If entered into for an undefined time, by any partner giving notice to the other or others of his intention to dissolve the partnership.

In the last-mentioned case the partnership is dissolved as from the date mentioned in the notice as the date of dissolution, or, if no date is so mentioned, as from the date of the communication of the notice.

33 Dissolution by bankruptcy, death or charge

(1)   Subject to any agreement between the partners, every partnership is dissolved as regards all the partners by the death or bankruptcy of any partner.

(2)   A partnership may, at the option of the other partners, be dissolved if any partner suffers his share of the partnership property to be charged under this Act for his separate debt.

34 Dissolution by illegality of partnership

A partnership is in every case dissolved by the happening of any event which makes it unlawful for the business of the firm to be carried on or for the members of the firm to carry it on in partnership.

35 Dissolution by the Court

On application by a partner the Court may decree a dissolution of the partnership in any of the following cases:
(a) . . .
(b) When a partner, other than the partner suing, becomes in any other way permanently incapable of performing his part of the partnership contract:
(c) When a partner, other than the partner suing, has been guilty of such conduct as, in the opinion of the Court, regard being had to the nature of the business, is calculated to prejudicially affect the carrying on of the business:
(d) When a partner, other than the partner suing, wilfully or persistently commits a breach of the partnership agreement, or otherwise so conducts himself in matters relating to the partnership business that it is not reasonably practicable for the other partner or partners to carry on the business in partnership with him:
(e) When the business of the partnership can only be carried on at a loss:
(f) Whenever in any case circumstances have arisen which, in the opinion of the Court, render it just and equitable that the partnership be dissolved.

NOTES

Para (a): repealed by the Mental Health Act 1959, s 149(2), Sch 8.

36 Rights of persons dealing with firm against apparent members of firm

(1)   Where a person deals with a firm after a change in its constitution he is entitled to treat all apparent members of the old firm as still being members of the firm until he has notice of the change.

(2)   An advertisement in the London Gazette as to a firm whose principal place of business is in England or Wales, in the Edinburgh Gazette as to a firm whose principal place of business is in Scotland, and in the Dublin Gazette as to a firm whose principal place of business is in Ireland, shall be notice as to persons who had not dealings with the firm before the date of the dissolution or change so advertised.

(3)   The estate of a partner who dies, or who becomes bankrupt, or of a partner who, not having been known to the person dealing with the firm to be a partner, retires from the firm, is not liable for partnership debts contracted after the date of the death, bankruptcy, or retirement respectively.

37 Right of partners to notify dissolution

On the dissolution of a partnership or retirement of a partner any partner may publicly notify the same, and may require the other partner or partners to concur for that purpose in all necessary or proper acts, if any, which cannot be done without his or their concurrence.

38 Continuing authority of partners for purposes of winding up

After the dissolution of a partnership the authority of each partner to bind the firm, and the other rights and obligations of the partners, continue notwithstanding the dissolution so far as may be necessary to wind up the affairs of the partnership, and to complete transactions begun but unfinished at the time of the dissolution, but not otherwise.

Provided that the firm is in no case bound by the acts of a partner who has become bankrupt; but this proviso does not affect the liability of any person who has after the bankruptcy represented himself or knowingly suffered himself to be represented as a partner of the bankrupt.

39 Rights of partners as to application of partnership property

On the dissolution of a partnership every partner is entitled, as against the other partners in the firm, and all persons claiming through them in respect of their interests as partners, to have the property of the partnership applied in payment of the debts and liabilities of the firm, and to have the surplus assets after such payment applied in payment of what may be due to the partners respectively after deducting what may be due from them as partners to the firm; and for that purpose any partner or his representatives may on the termination of the partnership apply to the Court to wind up the business and affairs of the firm.

40 Apportionment of premium where partnership prematurely dissolved

Where one partner has paid a premium to another on entering into a partnership for a fixed term, and the partnership is dissolved before the expiration of that term otherwise than by the death of a partner, the Court may order the repayment of the premium, or of such part thereof as it thinks just, having regard to the terms of the partnership contract and to the length of time during which the partnership has continued; unless

(a) the dissolution is, in the judgment of the Court, wholly or chiefly due to the misconduct of the partner who paid the premium; or

(b) the partnership has been dissolved by an agreement containing no provision for a return of any part of the premium.

41 Rights where partnership dissolved for fraud or misrepresentation

Where a partnership contract is rescinded on the ground of the fraud or misrepresentation of one of the parties thereto, the party entitled to rescind is, without prejudice to any other right, entitled—

(a) to a lien on, or right of retention of, the surplus of the partnership assets, after satisfying the partnership liabilities, for any sum of money paid by him for the purchase of a share in the partnership and for any capital contributed by him, and is

(b) to stand in the place of the creditors of the firm for any payments made by him in respect of the partnership liabilities, and

(c) to be indemnified by the person guilty of the fraud or making the representation against all the debts and liabilities of the firm.

42 Right of outgoing partner in certain cases to share profits made after dissolution

(1)   Where any member of a firm has died or otherwise ceased to be a partner, and the surviving or continuing partners carry on the business of the firm with its capital or assets without any final settlement of accounts as between the firm and the outgoing partner or his estate, then, in the absence of any agreement to the contrary, the outgoing partner or his estate is entitled at the option of himself or his representatives to such share of the profits made since the dissolution as the Court may find to be attributable to the use of his share of the partnership assets, or to interest at the rate of five per cent. per annum on the amount of his share of the partnership assets.

(2)   Provided that where by the partnership contract an option is given to surviving or continuing partners to purchase the interest of a deceased or outgoing partner, and that option is duly exercised, the estate of the deceased partner, or the outgoing partner or his estate, as the case may be, is not entitled to any further or other share of profits; but if any partner assuming to act in exercise of the option does not in all material respects comply with the terms thereof, he is liable to account under the foregoing provisions of this section.

43 Retiring or deceased partner's share to be a debt

Subject to any agreement between the partners, the amount due from surviving or continuing partners to an outgoing partner or the representatives of a deceased partner in respect of the outgoing or deceased partner's share is a debt accruing at the date of the dissolution or death.

44 Rule for distribution of assets on final settlement of accounts

In settling accounts between the partners after a dissolution of partnership, the following rules shall, subject to any agreement, be observed:

(a) Losses, including losses and deficiencies of capital, shall be paid first out of profits, next out of capital, and lastly, if necessary, by the partners individually in the proportion in which they were entitled to share profits:

(b) The assets of the firm including the sums, if any, contributed by the partners to make up losses or deficiencies of capital, shall be applied in the following manner and order:

    1 In paying the debts and liabilities of the firm to persons who are not partners therein:

    2 In paying to each partner rateably what is due from the firm to him for advances as distinguished from capital:

    3 In paying to each partner rateably what is due from the firm to him in respect of capital:

    4 The ultimate residue, if any, shall be divided among the partners in the proportion in which profits are divisible.

Supplemental

45 Definitions of "court" and "business"

In this Act, unless the contrary intention appears,—

The expression "court" includes every court and judge having jurisdiction in the case:

The expression "business" includes every trade, occupation, or profession.

46 Saving for rules of equity and common law

The rules of equity and of common law applicable to partnership shall continue in force except so far as they are inconsistent with the express provisions of this Act.

50 Short title

This Act may be cited as the Partnership Act 1890.

Limited Partnerships Act 1907

1907 CHAPTER 24

An Act to establish Limited Partnership

[28th August 1907]

1 Short title

This Act may be cited for all purposes as the Limited Partnerships Act 1907.

3 Interpretation of terms

In the construction of this Act the following words and expressions shall have the meanings respectively assigned to them in this section, unless there be something in the subject or context repugnant to such construction:—

"Firm," "firm name," and "business" have the same meanings as in the Partnership Act 1890:

"General partner" shall mean any partner who is not a limited partner as defined by this Act.

4 Definition and constitution of limited partnership

(1) . . . Limited partnerships may be formed in the manner and subject to the conditions by this Act provided.

(2) A limited partnership shall not consist . . . of more than twenty persons, and must consist of one or more persons called general partners, who shall be liable for all debts and obligations of the firm, and one or more persons to be called limited partners, who shall at the time of entering into such partnership contribute thereto a sum or sums as capital or property valued at a stated amount, and who shall not be liable for the debts or obligations of the firm beyond the amount so contributed.

(3) A limited partner shall not during the continuance of the partnership, either directly or indirectly, draw out or receive back any part of his contribution, and if he does so draw out or receive back any such part shall be liable for the debts and obligations of the firm up to the amount so drawn out or received back.

(4) A body corporate may be a limited partner.

NOTES

Sub-s (1): words omitted repealed by the Statute Law Revision Act 1927.
Sub-s (2): words omitted repealed by the Banking Act 1979, s 51(2), Sch 7.

5 Registration of limited partnership required

Every limited partnership must be registered as such in accordance with the provisions of this Act, or in default thereof it shall be deemed to be a general partnership, and every limited partner shall be deemed to be a general partner.

6 Modifications of general law in case of limited partnerships

(1) A limited partner shall not take part in the management of the partnership business, and shall not have power to bind the firm:

Provided that a limited partner may by himself or his agent at any time inspect the books of the firm and examine into the state and prospects of the partnership business, and may advise with the partners thereon.

If a limited partner takes part in the management of the partnership business he shall be liable for all debts and obligations of the firm incurred while he so takes part in the management as though he were a general partner.

(2)   A limited partnership shall not be dissolved by the death or bankruptcy of a limited partner, and the lunacy of a limited partner shall not be a ground for dissolution of the partnership by the court unless the lunatic's share cannot be otherwise ascertained and realised.

(3)   In the event of the dissolution of a limited partnership its affairs shall be wound up by the general partners unless the court otherwise orders.

(4)   . . .

(5)   Subject to any agreement expressed or implied between the partners—
    (a)   Any difference arising as to ordinary matters connected with the partnership business may be decided by a majority of the general partners;
    (b)   A limited partner may, with the consent of the general partners, assign his share in the partnership, and upon such an assignment the assignee shall become a limited partner with all the rights of the assignor;
    (c)   The other partners shall not be entitled to dissolve the partnership by reason of any limited partner suffering his share to be charged for his separate debt;
    (d)   A person may be introduced as a partner without the consent of the existing limited partners;
    (e)   A limited partner shall not be entitled to dissolve the partnership by notice.

NOTES

Sub-s (4): repealed by the Companies (Consolidation) Act 1908, s 286, Sch 6, Part I.

7 Law as to private partnerships to apply where not excluded by this Act

Subject to the provisions of this Act, the Partnership Act 1890 and the rules of equity and of common law applicable to partnerships, except so far as they are inconsistent with the express provisions of the last-mentioned Act, shall apply to limited partnerships.

8 Manner and particulars of registration

The registration of a limited partnership shall be effected by sending by post or delivering to the registrar at the register office in that part of the United Kingdom in which the principal place of business of the limited partnership is situated or proposed to be situated a statement signed by the partners containing the following particulars:—
    (a)   The firm name;
    (b)   The general nature of the business;
    (c)   The principal place of business;
    (d)   The full name of each of the partners;
    (e)   The term, if any, for which the partnership is entered into, and the date of its commencement;
    (f)   A statement that the partnership is limited, and the description of every limited partner as such;

(g) The sum contributed by each limited partner, and whether paid in cash or how otherwise.

9 Registration of changes in partnerships

(1) If during the continuance of a limited partnership any change is made or occurs in—

(a) the firm name,
(b) the general nature of the business,
(c) the principal place of business,
(d) the partners or the name of any partner,
(e) the term or character of the partnership,
(f) the sum contributed by any limited partner,
(g) the liability of any partner by reason of his becoming a limited instead of a general partner or a general instead of a limited partner,

a statement, signed by the firm, specifying the nature of the change shall within seven days be sent by post or delivered to the registrar at the register office in that part of the United Kingdom in which the partnership is registered.

(2) If default is made in compliance with the requirements of this section each of the general partners shall, on conviction under the Summary Jurisdiction Acts, be liable to a fine not exceeding one pound for each day during which the default continues.

10 Advertisement in Gazette of statement of general partner becoming a limited partner and of assignment of share of limited partner

(1) Notice of any arrangement or transaction under which any person will cease to be a general partner in any firm, and will become a limited partner in that firm, or under which the share of a limited partner in a firm will be assigned to any person, shall be forthwith advertised in the Gazette, and until notice of the arrangement or transaction is so advertised the arrangement or transaction shall, for the purposes of this Act, be deemed to be of no effect.

(2) For the purposes of this section, the expression "the Gazette" means—
In the case of a limited partnership registered in England, the London Gazette.
In the case of a limited partnership registered in Scotland, the Edinburgh Gazette.
In the case of a limited partnership registered in Ireland, the Dublin Gazette.

13 Registrar to file statement and issue certificate of registration

On receiving any statement made in pursuance of this Act the registrar shall cause the same to be filed, and he shall send by post to the firm from whom such statement shall have been received a certificate of the registration thereof.

14 Register and index to be kept

At each of the register offices herein-after referred to the registrar shall keep, in proper books to be provided for the purpose, a register and an index of all the limited partnerships registered as aforesaid, and of all the statements registered in relation to such partnerships.

15 Registrar of joint stock companies to be registrar under Act

The registrar of joint stock companies shall be the registrar of limited partnerships, and the several offices for the registration of joint stock companies in London, Edinburgh, and Dublin shall be the offices for the registration of limited partnerships carrying on business within those parts of the United Kingdom in which they are respectively situated.

16 Inspection of statements registered

(1) Any person may inspect the statements filed by the registrar in the register offices aforesaid, and there shall be paid for such inspection such fees as may be appointed by the Board of Trade, not exceeding [5p] for each inspection; and any person may require a certificate of the registration of any limited partnership, or a copy of or extract from any registered statement, to be certified by the registrar, and there shall be paid for such certificate of registration, certified copy, or extract such fees as the Board of Trade may appoint, not exceeding [10p] for the certificate of registration, and not exceeding [2 p] for each folio of seventy-two words, or in Scotland for each sheet of two hundred words.

(2) A certificate of registration or a copy of or extract from any statement registered under this Act, if duly certified to be a true copy under the hand of the registrar or one of the assistant registrars (whom it shall not be necessary to prove to be the registrar or assistant registrar) shall, in all legal proceedings, civil or criminal, and in all cases whatsoever be received in evidence.

NOTES

Sub-s (1): amended by the Decimal Currency Act 1969, s 10(1).

17 Power to Board of Trade to make rules

The Board of Trade may make rules (but as to fees with the concurrence of the Treasury) concerning any of the following matters:—
- (a) The fees to be paid to the registrar under this Act, so that they do not exceed in the case of the original registration of a limited partnership the sum of two pounds, and in any other case the sum of [25p];
- (b) The duties or additional duties to be performed by the registrar for the purposes of this Act;
- (c) The performance by assistant registrars and other officers of acts by this Act required to be done by the registrar;
- (d) The forms to be used for the purposes of this Act;
- (e) Generally, the conduct and regulation of registration under this Act and any matters incidental thereto.

NOTES

Sub-para (a): sum in square brackets substituted by the Decimal Currency Act 1969, s 10(1).

Limited Liability Partnerships Act 2000

2000 CHAPTER 12

An Act to make provision for limited liability partnerships.

[20th July 2000]

Introductory

1 Limited liability partnerships

(1)   There shall be a new form of legal entity to be known as a limited liability partnership.

(2)   A limited liability partnership is a body corporate (with legal personality separate from that of its members) which is formed by being incorporated under this Act; and—

   (a)   in the following provisions of this Act (except in the phrase "oversea limited liability partnership"), and
   (b)   in any other enactment (except where provision is made to the contrary or the context otherwise requires),

references to a limited liability partnership are to such a body corporate.

(3)   A limited liability partnership has unlimited capacity.

(4)   The members of a limited liability partnership have such liability to contribute to its assets in the event of its being wound up as is provided for by virtue of this Act.

(5)   Accordingly, except as far as otherwise provided by this Act or any other enactment, the law relating to partnerships does not apply to a limited liability partnership.

(6)   The Schedule (which makes provision about the names and registered offices of limited liability partnerships) has effect.

Incorporation

2 Incorporation document etc

(1)   For a limited liability partnership to be incorporated—

   (a)   two or more persons associated for carrying on a lawful business with a view to profit must have subscribed their names to an incorporation document,
   (b)   there must have been delivered to the registrar either the incorporation document or a copy authenticated in a manner approved by him, and
   (c)   there must have been so delivered a statement in a form approved by the registrar, made by either a solicitor engaged in the formation of the limited

liability partnership or anyone who subscribed his name to the incorporation document, that the requirement imposed by paragraph (a) has been complied with.

(2) The incorporation document must—
  (a) be in a form approved by the registrar (or as near to such a form as circumstances allow),
  (b) state the name of the limited liability partnership,
  (c) state whether the registered office of the limited liability partnership is to be situated in England and Wales, in Wales or in Scotland,
  (d) state the address of that registered office,
  (e) state the name and address of each of the persons who are to be members of the limited liability partnership on incorporation, and
  (f) either specify which of those persons are to be designated members or state that every person who from time to time is a member of the limited liability partnership is a designated member.

[(2A) Where a confidentiality order, made under section 723B of the Companies Act 1985 as applied to a limited liability partnerships, is in force in respect of any individual named as a member of a limited liability partnership under subsection (2) that subsection shall have effect as if the reference to the address of the individual were a reference to the address for the time being notified by him under the Limited Liability Partnerships (Particulars of Usual Residential Address) (Confidentiality Orders) Regulations 2002 to any limited liability partnership of which he is a member or if he is not such a member either the address specified in his application for a confidentiality order or the address last notified by him under such a confidentiality order as the case may be.

(2B) Where the incorporation document or a copy of such delivered under this section includes an address specified in reliance on subsection (2A) there shall be delivered with it or the copy of it a statement in a form approved by the registrar containing particulars of the usual residential address of the member whose address is so specified.]

(3) If a person makes a false statement under subsection (1)(c) which he—
  (a) knows to be false, or
  (b) does not believe to be true,

he commits an offence.

(4) A person guilty of an offence under subsection (3) is liable—
  (a) on summary conviction, to imprisonment for a period not exceeding six months or a fine not exceeding the statutory maximum, or to both, or
  (b) on conviction on indictment, to imprisonment for a period not exceeding two years or a fine, or to both.

NOTES

Sub-ss (2A), (2B): inserted by SI 2002/915, reg 16, Sch 2, para 1.
Date in force: 2 April 2002: see SI 2002/915, reg 1(2).

3 Incorporation by registration

(1)   When the requirements imposed by paragraphs (b) and (c) of subsection (1) of section 2 have been complied with, the registrar shall retain the incorporation document or copy delivered to him and, unless the requirement imposed by paragraph (a) of that subsection has not been complied with, he shall—
(a)   register the incorporation document or copy, and
(b)   give a certificate that the limited liability partnership is incorporated by the name specified in the incorporation document.

(2)   The registrar may accept the statement delivered under paragraph (c) of subsection (1) of section 2 as sufficient evidence that the requirement imposed by paragraph (a) of that subsection has been complied with.

(3)   The certificate shall either be signed by the registrar or be authenticated by his official seal.

(4)   The certificate is conclusive evidence that the requirements of section 2 are complied with and that the limited liability partnership is incorporated by the name specified in the incorporation document.

Membership

4 Members

(1)   On the incorporation of a limited liability partnership its members are the persons who subscribed their names to the incorporation document (other than any who have died or been dissolved).

(2)   Any other person may become a member of a limited liability partnership by and in accordance with an agreement with the existing members.

(3)   A person may cease to be a member of a limited liability partnership (as well as by death or dissolution) in accordance with an agreement with the other members or, in the absence of agreement with the other members as to cessation of membership, by giving reasonable notice to the other members.

(4)   A member of a limited liability partnership shall not be regarded for any purpose as employed by the limited liability partnership unless, if he and the other members were partners in a partnership, he would be regarded for that purpose as employed by the partnership.

5 Relationship of members etc

(1)   Except as far as otherwise provided by this Act or any other enactment, the mutual rights and duties of the members of a limited liability partnership, and the mutual rights and duties of a limited liability partnership and its members, shall be governed—
(a)   by agreement between the members, or between the limited liability partnership and its members, or
(b)   in the absence of agreement as to any matter, by any provision made in relation to that matter by regulations under section 15(c).

(2)   An agreement made before the incorporation of a limited liability partnership between the persons who subscribe their names to the incorporation document may impose obligations on the limited liability partnership (to take effect at any time after its incorporation).

6 Members as agents

(1)   Every member of a limited liability partnership is the agent of the limited liability partnership.

(2)   But a limited liability partnership is not bound by anything done by a member in dealing with a person if—
- (a)   the member in fact has no authority to act for the limited liability partnership by doing that thing, and
- (b)   the person knows that he has no authority or does not know or believe him to be a member of the limited liability partnership.

(3)   Where a person has ceased to be a member of a limited liability partnership, the former member is to be regarded (in relation to any person dealing with the limited liability partnership) as still being a member of the limited liability partnership unless—
- (a)   the person has notice that the former member has ceased to be a member of the limited liability partnership, or
- (b)   notice that the former member has ceased to be a member of the limited liability partnership has been delivered to the registrar.

(4)   Where a member of a limited liability partnership is liable to any person (other than another member of the limited liability partnership) as a result of a wrongful act or omission of his in the course of the business of the limited liability partnership or with its authority, the limited liability partnership is liable to the same extent as the member.

7 Ex-members

(1)   This section applies where a member of a limited liability partnership has either ceased to be a member or—
- (a)   has died,
- (b)   has become bankrupt or had his estate sequestrated or has been wound up,
- (c)   has granted a trust deed for the benefit of his creditors, or
- (d)   has assigned the whole or any part of his share in the limited liability partnership (absolutely or by way of charge or security).

(2)   In such an event the former member or—
- (a)   his personal representative,
- (b)   his trustee in bankruptcy or permanent or interim trustee (within the meaning of the Bankruptcy (Scotland) Act 1985) or liquidator,
- (c)   his trustee under the trust deed for the benefit of his creditors, or
- (d)   his assignee,

may not interfere in the management or administration of any business or affairs of the limited liability partnership.

(3)   But subsection (2) does not affect any right to receive an amount from the limited liability partnership in that event.

8 Designated members

(1)   If the incorporation document specifies who are to be designated members—
  (a)   they are designated members on incorporation, and
  (b)   any member may become a designated member by and in accordance with an agreement with the other members,

and a member may cease to be a designated member in accordance with an agreement with the other members.

(2)   But if there would otherwise be no designated members, or only one, every member is a designated member.

(3)   If the incorporation document states that every person who from time to time is a member of the limited liability partnership is a designated member, every member is a designated member.

(4)   A limited liability partnership may at any time deliver to the registrar—
  (a)   notice that specified members are to be designated members, or
  (b)   notice that every person who from time to time is a member of the limited liability partnership is a designated member,

and, once it is delivered, subsection (1) (apart from paragraph (a)) and subsection (2), or subsection (3), shall have effect as if that were stated in the incorporation document.

(5)   A notice delivered under subsection (4)—
  (a)   shall be in a form approved by the registrar, and
  (b)   shall be signed by a designated member of the limited liability partnership or authenticated in a manner approved by the registrar.

(6)   A person ceases to be a designated member if he ceases to be a member.

9 Registration of membership changes

(1)   A limited liability partnership must ensure that—
  (a)   where a person becomes or ceases to be a member or designated member, notice is delivered to the registrar within fourteen days, and
  (b)   where there is any change in the name or address of a member, notice is delivered to the registrar within 28 days.

(2)   Where all the members from time to time of a limited liability partnership are designated members, subsection (1)(a) does not require notice that a person has become or ceased to be a designated member as well as a member.

(3)   A notice delivered under subsection (1)—
  (a)   shall be in a form approved by the registrar, and
  (b)   shall be signed by a designated member of the limited liability partnership or authenticated in a manner approved by the registrar,

and, if it relates to a person becoming a member or designated member, shall contain a statement that he consents to becoming a member or designated member signed by him or authenticated in a manner approved by the registrar.

[(3A)   Where a confidentiality order under section 723B of the Companies Act 1985 as applied to limited liability partnerships is made in respect of an existing member, the limited liability partnership must ensure that there is delivered within 28 days to the registrar notice in a form approved by the registrar containing the address for the time being notified to it by the member under the Limited Liability Partnerships (Particulars of Usual Residential Address) (Confidentiality Orders) Regulations 2002.

(3B)   Where such a confidentiality order is in force in respect of a member the requirement in subsection (1)(b) to notify a change in the address of a member shall be read in relation to that member as a requirement to deliver to the registrar, within 28 days, notice of—

(a)   any change in the usual residential address of that member; and

(b)   any change in the address for the time being notified to the limited liability partnership by the member under the Limited Liability Partnerships (Particulars of Usual Residential Address) (Confidentiality Orders) Regulations 2002,

and the registrar may approve different forms for the notification of each kind of address.]

(4)   If a limited liability partnership fails to comply with subsection (1), the partnership and every designated member commits an offence.

(5)   But it is a defence for a designated member charged with an offence under subsection (4) to prove that he took all reasonable steps for securing that subsection (1) was complied with.

(6)   A person guilty of an offence under subsection (4) is liable on summary conviction to a fine not exceeding level 5 on the standard scale.

NOTES

Sub-ss (3A), (3B): inserted by SI 2002/915, reg 16, Sch 2, para 3.
Date in force: 2 April 2002: see SI 2002/915, reg 1(2).

Regulations

14 Insolvency and winding up

(1)   Regulations shall make provision about the insolvency and winding up of limited liability partnerships by applying or incorporating, with such modifications as appear appropriate, Parts I to IV, VI and VII of the Insolvency Act 1986.

(2)   Regulations may make other provision about the insolvency and winding up of limited liability partnerships, and provision about the insolvency and winding up of oversea limited liability partnerships, by—

(a)   applying or incorporating, with such modifications as appear appropriate, any law relating to the insolvency or winding up of companies or other corporations which would not otherwise have effect in relation to them, or

(b) providing for any law relating to the insolvency or winding up of companies or other corporations which would otherwise have effect in relation to them not to apply to them or to apply to them with such modifications as appear appropriate.

(3) In this Act "oversea limited liability partnership" means a body incorporated or otherwise established outside Great Britain and having such connection with Great Britain, and such other features, as regulations may prescribe.

15 Application of company law etc

Regulations may make provision about limited liability partnerships and oversea limited liability partnerships (not being provision about insolvency or winding up) by—

(a) applying or incorporating, with such modifications as appear appropriate, any law relating to companies or other corporations which would not otherwise have effect in relation to them,

(b) providing for any law relating to companies or other corporations which would otherwise have effect in relation to them not to apply to them or to apply to them with such modifications as appear appropriate, or

(c) applying or incorporating, with such modifications as appear appropriate, any law relating to partnerships.

16 Consequential amendments

(1) Regulations may make in any enactment such amendments or repeals as appear appropriate in consequence of this Act or regulations made under it.

(2) The regulations may, in particular, make amendments and repeals affecting companies or other corporations or partnerships.

17 General

(1) In this Act "regulations" means regulations made by the Secretary of State by statutory instrument.

(2) Regulations under this Act may in particular—

(a) make provisions for dealing with non-compliance with any of the regulations (including the creation of criminal offences),

(b) impose fees (which shall be paid into the Consolidated Fund), and

(c) provide for the exercise of functions by persons prescribed by the regulations.

(3) Regulations under this Act may—

(a) contain any appropriate consequential, incidental, supplementary or transitional provisions or savings, and

(b) make different provision for different purposes.

(4) No regulations to which this subsection applies shall be made unless a draft of the statutory instrument containing the regulations (whether or not together with other provisions) has been laid before, and approved by a resolution of, each House of Parliament.

(5)   Subsection (4) applies to—
  (a) regulations under section 14(2) not consisting entirely of the application or incorporation (with or without modifications) of provisions contained in or made under the Insolvency Act 1986,
  (b) regulations under section 15 not consisting entirely of the application or incorporation (with or without modifications) of provisions contained in or made under Part I, Chapter VIII of Part V, Part VII, Parts XI to XIII, Parts XVI to XVIII, Part XX or Parts XXIV to XXVI of the Companies Act 1985,
  (c) regulations under section 14 or 15 making provision about oversea limited liability partnerships, and
  (d) regulations under section 16.

(6)   A statutory instrument containing regulations under this Act shall (unless a draft of it has been approved by a resolution of each House of Parliament) be subject to annulment in pursuance of a resolution of either House of Parliament.

Supplementary

18 Interpretation

In this Act—
    "address", in relation to a member of a limited liability partnership, means—
        (a) if an individual, his usual residential address, and
        (b) if a corporation or Scottish firm, its registered or principal office,
    "business" includes every trade, profession and occupation,
    "designated member" shall be construed in accordance with section 8,
    "enactment" includes subordinate legislation (within the meaning of the Interpretation Act 1978),
    "incorporation document" shall be construed in accordance with section 2,
    "limited liability partnership" has the meaning given by section 1(2),
    "member" shall be construed in accordance with section 4,
    "modifications" includes additions and omissions,
    "name", in relation to a member of a limited liability partnership, means—
        (a) if an individual, his forename and surname (or, in the case of a peer or other person usually known by a title, his title instead of or in addition to either or both his forename and surname), and
        (b) if a corporation or Scottish firm, its corporate or firm name,
    "oversea limited liability partnership" has the meaning given by section 14(3),
    "the registrar" means—
        (a) if the registered office of the limited liability partnership is, or is to be, situated in England and Wales or in Wales, the registrar or other officer performing under the Companies Act 1985 the duty of registration of companies in England and Wales, and
        (b) if its registered office is, or is to be, situated in Scotland, the registrar or other officer performing under that Act the duty of registration of companies in Scotland, and
    "regulations" has the meaning given by section 17(1).

19 Commencement, extent and short title

(1)   The preceding provisions of this Act shall come into force on such day as the Secretary of State may by order made by statutory instrument appoint; and different days may be appointed for different purposes.

(2)   The Secretary of State may by order made by statutory instrument make any transitional provisions and savings which appear appropriate in connection with the coming into force of any provision of this Act.

(3)   For the purposes of the Scotland Act 1998 this Act shall be taken to be a pre-commencement enactment within the meaning of that Act.

(4)   Apart from sections 10 to 13 (and this section), this Act does not extend to Northern Ireland.

(5)   This Act may be cited as the Limited Liability Partnerships Act 2000.

SCHEDULE
NAMES AND REGISTERED OFFICES

Section 1

PART I
NAMES

Index of names

1   In section 714(1) of the Companies Act 1985 (index of names), after paragraph (d) insert—

"(da) limited liability partnerships incorporated under the Limited Liability Partnerships Act 2000,".

Name to indicate status

2   (1)   The name of a limited liability partnership must end with—
(a)   the expression "limited liability partnership", or
(b)   the abbreviation "llp" or "LLP".

(2)   But if the incorporation document for a limited liability partnership states that the registered office is to be situated in Wales, its name must end with—
(a)   one of the expressions "limited liability partnership" and "partneriaeth atebolrwydd cyfyngedig", or
(b)   one of the abbreviations "llp", "LLP", "pac" and "PAC".

Registration of names

3   (1)   A limited liability partnership shall not be registered by a name—
(a)   which includes, otherwise than at the end of the name, either of the expressions "limited liability partnership" and "partneriaeth atebolrwydd cyfyngedig" or any of the abbreviations "llp", "LLP", "pac" and "PAC",
(b)   which is the same as a name appearing in the index kept under section 714(1) of the Companies Act 1985,
(c)   the use of which by the limited liability partnership would in the opinion of the Secretary of State constitute a criminal offence, or

(d) which in the opinion of the Secretary of State is offensive.

(2) Except with the approval of the Secretary of State, a limited liability partnership shall not be registered by a name which—

(a) in the opinion of the Secretary of State would be likely to give the impression that it is connected in any way with Her Majesty's Government or with any local authority, or

(b) includes any word or expression for the time being specified in regulations under section 29 of the Companies Act 1985 (names needing approval),

and in paragraph (a) "local authority" means any local authority within the meaning of the Local Government Act 1972 or the Local Government etc (Scotland) Act 1994, the Common Council of the City of London or the Council of the Isles of Scilly.

Change of name

4 (1) A limited liability partnership may change its name at any time.

(2) Where a limited liability partnership has been registered by a name which—

(a) is the same as or, in the opinion of the Secretary of State, too like a name appearing at the time of registration in the index kept under section 714(1) of the Companies Act 1985, or

(b) is the same as or, in the opinion of the Secretary of State, too like a name which should have appeared in the index at that time,

the Secretary of State may within twelve months of that time in writing direct the limited liability partnership to change its name within such period as he may specify.

(3) If it appears to the Secretary of State—

(a) that misleading information has been given for the purpose of the registration of a limited liability partnership by a particular name, or

(b) that undertakings or assurances have been given for that purpose and have not been fulfilled,

he may, within five years of the date of its registration by that name, in writing direct the limited liability partnership to change its name within such period as he may specify.

(4) If in the Secretary of State's opinion the name by which a limited liability partnership is registered gives so misleading an indication of the nature of its activities as to be likely to cause harm to the public, he may in writing direct the limited liability partnership to change its name within such period as he may specify.

(5) But the limited liability partnership may, within three weeks from the date of the direction apply to the court to set it aside and the court may set the direction aside or confirm it and, if it confirms it, shall specify the period within which it must be complied with.

(6) In sub-paragraph (5) "the court" means—

(a) if the registered office of the limited liability partnership is situated in England and Wales or in Wales, the High Court, and

(b) if it is situated in Scotland, the Court of Session.

(7) Where a direction has been given under sub-paragraph (2), (3) or (4) specifying a period within which a limited liability partnership is to change its name, the Secretary of State may at any time before that period ends extend it by a further direction in writing.

(8) If a limited liability partnership fails to comply with a direction under this paragraph—

(a) the limited liability partnership, and

(b) any designated member in default,

commits an offence.

(9)   A person guilty of an offence under sub-paragraph (8) is liable on summary conviction to a fine not exceeding level 3 on the standard scale.

Notification of change of name

5   (1)   Where a limited liability partnership changes its name it shall deliver notice of the change to the registrar.

(2)   A notice delivered under sub-paragraph (1)—
- (a)   shall be in a form approved by the registrar, and
- (b)   shall be signed by a designated member of the limited liability partnership or authenticated in a manner approved by the registrar.

(3)   Where the registrar receives a notice under sub-paragraph (2) he shall (unless the new name is one by which a limited liability partnership may not be registered)—
- (a)   enter the new name in the index kept under section 714(1) of the Companies Act 1985, and
- (b)   issue a certificate of the change of name.

(4)   The change of name has effect from the date on which the certificate is issued.

Effect of change of name

6   A change of name by a limited liability partnership does not—
- (a)   affect any of its rights or duties,
- (b)   render defective any legal proceedings by or against it,

and any legal proceedings that might have been commenced or continued against it by its former name may be commenced or continued against it by its new name.

Improper use of "limited liability partnership" etc

7   (1)   If any person carries on a business under a name or title which includes as the last words—
- (a)   the expression "limited liability partnership" or "partneriaeth atebolrwydd cyfynge-dig", or
- (b)   any contraction or imitation of either of those expressions,

that person, unless a limited liability partnership or oversea limited liability partnership, commits an offence.

(2)   A person guilty of an offence under sub-paragraph (1) is liable on summary conviction to a fine not exceeding level 3 on the standard scale.

Similarity of names

8   In determining for the purposes of this Part whether one name is the same as another there are to be disregarded—
- (1)   the definite article as the first word of the name,
- (2)   any of the following (or their Welsh equivalents or abbreviations of them or their Welsh equivalents) at the end of the name—
  "limited liability partnership",
  "company",
  "and company",
  "company limited",

"and company limited",
"limited",
"unlimited",
"public limited company", . . .
"investment company with variable capital", and
["open-ended investment company", and]
  (3)   type and case of letters, accents, spaces between letters and punctuation marks,

and "and" and "&" are to be taken as the same.

NOTES
Para 8: in sub-para (2) word omitted following entry "public limited company" repealed by SI 2001/1228, reg 84, Sch 7, Pt I, para 11.
Date in force: 1 December 2001 (being the date on which the Financial Services and Markets Act 2000, s 19, came into force): see SI 2001/3538, art 2(1) and SI 2001/1228, reg 1(2)(c).
Para 8: in sub-para (2) entry relating to "open-ended investment company" inserted by SI 2001/1228, reg 84, Sch 7, Pt I, para 11.
Date in force: 1 December 2001 (being the date on which the Financial Services and Markets Act 2000, s 19, came into force): see SI 2001/3538, art 2(1) and SI 2001/1228, reg 1(2)(c).

PART II
REGISTERED OFFICES

Situation of registered office

9   (1)   A limited liability partnership shall—
  (a)   at all times have a registered office situated in England and Wales or in Wales, or
  (b)   at all times have a registered office situated in Scotland,

to which communications and notices may be addressed.

(2)   On the incorporation of a limited liability partnership the situation of its registered office shall be that stated in the incorporation document.

(3)   Where the registered office of a limited liability partnership is situated in Wales, but the incorporation document does not state that it is to be situated in Wales (as opposed to England and Wales), the limited liability partnership may deliver notice to the registrar stating that its registered office is to be situated in Wales.

(4)   A notice delivered under sub-paragraph (3)—
  (a)   shall be in a form approved by the registrar, and
  (b)   shall be signed by a designated member of the limited liability partnership or authenticated in a manner approved by the registrar.

Limited Liability Partnerships Regulations 2001

2001 No 1090

NOTES

Made ....19th March 2001

Coming into force ....6th April 2001

PART I
CITATION, COMMENCEMENT AND INTERPRETATION

1 Citation and commencement

These Regulations may be cited as the Limited Liability Partnerships Regulations 2001 and shall come into force on 6th April 2001.

2 Interpretation

In these Regulations—

"the 1985 Act" means the Companies Act 1985;

"the 1986 Act" means the Insolvency Act 1986;

"the 2000 Act" means the Financial Services and Markets Act 2000;

"devolved", in relation to the provisions of the 1986 Act, means the provisions of the 1986 Act which are listed in Schedule 4 and, in their application to Scotland, concern wholly or partly, matters which are set out in Section C 2 of Schedule 5 to the Scotland Act 1998 as being exceptions to the reservations made in that Act in the field of insolvency;

"limited liability partnership agreement", in relation to a limited liability partnership, means any agreement express or implied between the members of the limited liability partnership or between the limited liability partnership and the members of the limited liability partnership which determines the mutual rights and duties of the members, and their rights and duties in relation to the limited liability partnership;

"the principal Act" means the Limited Liability Partnerships Act 2000; and

"shadow member", in relation to limited liability partnerships, means a person in accordance with whose directions or instructions the members of the limited liability partnership are accustomed to act (but so that a person is not deemed a shadow member by reason only that the members of the limited partnership act on advice given by him in a professional capacity).

PART II
ACCOUNTS AND AUDIT

3 Application of the accounts and audit provisions of the 1985 Act to limited liability partnerships

(1)   Subject to paragraph (2), the provisions of Part VII of the 1985 Act (Accounts and Audit) shall apply to limited liability partnerships.

(2)   The enactments referred to in paragraph (1) shall apply to limited liability partnerships, except where the context otherwise requires, with the following modifications—

   (a)   references to a company shall include references to a limited liability partnership;
   (b)   references to a director or to an officer of a company shall include references to a member of a limited liability partnership;
   (c)   references to other provisions of the 1985 Act and to provisions of the Insolvency Act 1986 shall include references to those provisions as they apply to limited liability partnerships in accordance with Parts III and IV of these Regulations;
   (d)   the modifications set out in Schedule 1 to these Regulations; and
   (e)   such further modifications as the context requires for the purpose of giving effect to those provisions as applied by this Part of these Regulations.

PART III
COMPANIES ACT 1985 AND COMPANY DIRECTORS DISQUALIFICATION ACT 1986

4 Application of the remainder of the provisions of the 1985 Act and of the provisions of the Company Directors Disqualification Act 1986 to limited liability partnerships

(1)   The provisions of the 1985 Act specified in the first column of Part I of Schedule 2 to these Regulations shall apply to limited liability partnerships, except where the context otherwise requires, with the following modifications—

   (a)   references to a company shall include references to a limited liability partnership;
   (b)   references to the Companies Acts shall include references to the principal Act and regulations made thereunder;
   (c)   references to the Insolvency Act 1986 shall include references to that Act as it applies to limited liability partnerships by virtue of Part IV of these Regulations;
   (d)   references in a provision of the 1985 Act to other provisions of that Act shall include references to those other provisions as they apply to limited liability partnerships by virtue of these Regulations;
   (e)   references to the memorandum of association of a company shall include references to the incorporation document of a limited liability partnership;

(f) references to a shadow director shall include references to a shadow member;

(g) references to a director of a company or to an officer of a company shall include references to a member of a limited liability partnership;

(h) the modifications, if any, specified in the second column of Part I of Schedule 2 opposite the provision specified in the first column; and

(i) such further modifications as the context requires for the purpose of giving effect to that legislation as applied by these Regulations.

(2) The provisions of the Company Director Disqualification Act 1986 shall apply to limited liability partnerships, except where the context otherwise requires, with the following modifications—

(a) references to a company shall include references to a limited liability partnership;

(b) references to the Companies Acts shall include references to the principal Act and regulations made thereunder and references to the companies legislation shall include references to the principal Act, regulations made thereunder and to any enactment applied by regulations to limited liability partnerships;

(d) references to the Insolvency Act 1986 shall include references to that Act as it applies to limited liability partnerships by virtue of Part IV of these Regulations;

(e) references to the memorandum of association of a company shall include references to the incorporation document of a limited liability partnership;

(f) references to a shadow director shall include references to a shadow member;

(g) references to a director of a company or to an officer of a company shall include references to a member of a limited liability partnership;

(h) the modifications, if any, specified in the second column of Part II of Schedule 2 opposite the provision specified in the first column; and

(i) such further modifications as the context requires for the purpose of giving effect to that legislation as applied by these Regulations.

PART IV
WINDING UP AND INSOLVENCY

5 Application of the 1986 Act to limited liability partnerships

(1) Subject to paragraphs (2) and (3), the following provisions of the 1986 Act, shall apply to limited liability partnerships—

(a) Parts I, II, III, IV, VI and VII of the First Group of Parts (company insolvency; companies winding up),

(b) the Third Group of Parts (miscellaneous matters bearing on both company and individual insolvency; general interpretation; final provisions).

(2) The provisions of the 1986 Act referred to in paragraph (1) shall apply to limited liability partnerships, except where the context otherwise requires, with the following modifications—

(a) references to a company shall include references to a limited liability partnership;

(b) references to a director or to an officer of a company shall include references to a member of a limited liability partnership;

(c) references to a shadow director shall include references to a shadow member;

(d) references to the 1985 Act, the Company Directors Disqualification Act 1986, the Companies Act 1989 or to any provisions of those Acts or to any provisions of the 1986 Act shall include references to those Acts or provisions as they apply to limited liability partnerships by virtue of the principal Act;

(e) references to the memorandum of association of a company and to the articles of association of a company shall include references to the limited liability partnership agreement of a limited liability partnership;

(f) the modifications set out in Schedule 3 to these Regulations; and

(g) such further modifications as the context requires for the purpose of giving effect to that legislation as applied by these Regulations.

(3) In the application of this regulation to Scotland, the provisions of the 1986 Act referred to in paragraph (1) shall not include the provisions listed in Schedule 4 to the extent specified in that Schedule.

PART V
FINANCIAL SERVICES AND MARKETS

6 Application of provisions contained in Parts XV and XXIV of the 2000 Act to limited liability partnerships

(1) Subject to paragraph (2), sections 215(3),(4) and (6), 356, 359(1) to (4), 361 to 365, 367, 370 and 371 of the 2000 Act shall apply to limited liability partnerships.

(2) The provisions of the 2000 Act referred to in paragraph (1) shall apply to limited liability partnerships, except where the context otherwise requires, with the following modifications—

(a) references to a company shall include references to a limited liability partnership;

(b) references to body shall include references to a limited liability partnership; and

(c) references to the 1985 Act, the 1986 Act or to any of the provisions of those Acts shall include references to those Acts or provisions as they apply to limited liability partnerships by virtue of the principal Act.

PART VI
DEFAULT PROVISION

7 Default provision for limited liability partnerships

The mutual rights and duties of the members and the mutual rights and duties of the limited liability partnership and the members shall be determined, subject to the provisions of the general law and to the terms of any limited liability partnership agreement, by the following rules:

(1)   All the members of a limited liability partnership are entitled to share equally in the capital and profits of the limited liability partnership.

(2)   The limited liability partnership must indemnify each member in respect of payments made and personal liabilities incurred by him—

    (a)   in the ordinary and proper conduct of the business of the limited liability partnership; or

    (b)   in or about anything necessarily done for the preservation of the business or property of the limited liability partnership.

(3)   Every member may take part in the management of the limited liability partnership.

(4)   No member shall be entitled to remuneration for acting in the business or management of the limited liability partnership.

(5)   No person may be introduced as a member or voluntarily assign an interest in a limited liability partnership without the consent of all existing members.

(6)   Any difference arising as to ordinary matters connected with the business of the limited liability partnership may be decided by a majority of the members, but no change may be made in the nature of the business of the limited liability partnership without the consent of all the members.

(7)   The books and records of the limited liability partnership are to be made available for inspection at the registered office of the limited liability partnership or at such other place as the members think fit and every member of the limited liability partnership may when he thinks fit have access to and inspect and copy any of them.

(8)   Each member shall render true accounts and full information of all things affecting the limited liability partnership to any member or his legal representatives.

(9)   If a member, without the consent of the limited liability partnership, carries on any business of the same nature as and competing with the limited liability partnership, he must account for and pay over to the limited liability partnership all profits made by him in that business.

(10)   Every member must account to the limited liability partnership for any benefit derived by him without the consent of the limited liability partnership from any transaction concerning the limited liability partnership, or from any use by him of the property of the limited liability partnership, name or business connection.

8 Expulsion

No majority of the members can expel any member unless a power to do so has been conferred by express agreement between the members.

PART VII
MISCELLANEOUS

9 General and consequential amendments

(1)   Subject to paragraph (2), the enactments mentioned in Schedule 5 shall have effect subject to the amendments specified in that Schedule.

(2)   In the application of this regulation to Scotland—
  (a)   paragraph 15 of Schedule 5 which amends section 110 of the 1986 Act shall not extend to Scotland; and
  (b)   paragraph 22 of Schedule 5 which applies to limited liability partnerships the culpable officer provisions in existing primary legislation shall not extend to Scotland insofar as it relates to matters which have not been reserved by Schedule 5 to the Scotland Act 1998.

10 Application of subordinate legislation

(1)   The subordinate legislation specified in Schedule 6 shall apply as from time to time in force to limited liability partnerships and—
  (a)   in the case of the subordinate legislation listed in Part I of that Schedule with such modifications as the context requires for the purpose of giving effect to the provisions of the Companies Act 1985 which are applied by these Regulations;
  (b)   in the case of the subordinate legislation listed in Part II of that Schedule with such modifications as the context requires for the purpose of giving effect to the provisions of the Insolvency Act 1986 which are applied by these Regulations; and
  (c)   in the case of the subordinate legislation listed in Part III of that Schedule with such modifications as the context requires for the purpose of giving effect to the provisions of the Business Names Act 1985 and the Company Directors Disqualification Act 1986 which are applied by these Regulations.

(2)   In the case of any conflict between any provision of the subordinate legislation applied by paragraph (1) and any provision of these Regulations, the latter shall prevail.